797,885 Books

are available to read at

www.ForgottenBooks.com

Forgotten Books' App
Available for mobile, tablet & eReader

ISBN 978-1-330-88752-3
PIBN 10117305

This book is a reproduction of an important historical work. Forgotten Books uses state-of-the-art technology to digitally reconstruct the work, preserving the original format whilst repairing imperfections present in the aged copy. In rare cases, an imperfection in the original, such as a blemish or missing page, may be replicated in our edition. We do, however, repair the vast majority of imperfections successfully; any imperfections that remain are intentionally left to preserve the state of such historical works.

Forgotten Books is a registered trademark of FB &c Ltd.
Copyright © 2015 FB &c Ltd.
FB &c Ltd, Dalton House, 60 Windsor Avenue, London, SW19 2RR.
Company number 08720141. Registered in England and Wales.

For support please visit www.forgottenbooks.com

1 MONTH OF FREE READING

at

www.ForgottenBooks.com

By purchasing this book you are eligible for one month membership to ForgottenBooks.com, giving you unlimited access to our entire collection of over 700,000 titles via our web site and mobile apps.

To claim your free month visit:
www.forgottenbooks.com/free117305

* Offer is valid for 45 days from date of purchase. Terms and conditions apply.

Similar Books Are Available from
www.forgottenbooks.com

The Christian Mythology
by Brigham Leatherbee

Jesus and What He Said
by Arthur Salter Burrows

Reincarnation in the New Testament
by James Morgan Pryse

Dictionary of the Holy Bible
by William Wilberforce Rand

Being a Christian
by Jas A. Duncan

Heaven
by Dwight Lyman Moody

How to Pray
by R. A. Torrey

The Bible and Evolution
by W. H. Sparshott

The Aquarian Gospel of Jesus the Christ
by Levi

Christ and His Church in the Book of Psalms
by Andrew A. Bonar

Christian Healing
A Sermon Delivered at Boston, by Mary Baker Eddy

Church History Through All Ages
by Thomas Timpson

The Life of Jesus, Vol. 1 of 2
For the People, by David Friedrich Strauss

The Serpent, Satan and False Prophet
Or the Trinity of Evil, by Unknown Author

The Christian Faith and the Old Testament
by John M. Thomas

Christianity and Sex Problems
by Hugh Northcote

The Evolution of Spiritual Man
by William McIntire Lisle

The Beacon of Truth
Or Testimony of the Coran to the Truth of the Christian Religion, by William Muir

A Biblical View of the Church
by Josiah Goodman Bishop

Muhammad and Christ
by Moulvi Muhammad Ali

THE
KEY OF TRUTH

A MANUAL OF THE

PAULICIAN CHURCH OF ARMENIA

𝕿𝖍𝖊 𝕬𝖗𝖒𝖊𝖓𝖎𝖆𝖓 𝕿𝖊𝖝𝖙

EDITED AND TRANSLATED WITH ILLUSTRATIVE
DOCUMENTS AND INTRODUCTION

BY

FRED. C. CONYBEARE, M.A.
FORMERLY FELLOW OF UNIVERSITY COLLEGE
OXFORD

Oxford
AT THE CLARENDON PRESS
1898

Oxford
PRINTED AT THE CLARENDON PRESS
BY HORACE HART, M.A.
PRINTER TO THE UNIVERSITY

In the autumn of the year 1891, I went to Armenia for a second time, in the hope of finding an ancient version of the Book of Enoch, and of recovering documents illustrative of the ancient heretics of that land, particularly of the Paulicians. For Gibbon's picture of their puritanism, fresh and vigorous in an age when Greek Christianity had degenerated into the court superstition of Constantinople, had fascinated my imagination; and I could not believe that some fuller records of their inner teaching did not survive in the Armenian tongue. In this quest, though my other failed, I was rewarded. I learned during my stay at Edjmiatzin, that in the library of the Holy Synod there was preserved a manuscript of *The Key of Truth*, the book of the Thonraketzi or Paulicians of Thonrak, with whom I was familiar from reading the letters of Gregory Magistros, Duke of Mesopotamià in the eleventh century.

I was permitted to see the book, of which a perfunctory examination convinced me that it was a genuine monument, though, as I then thought it, a late one of the Paulicians. For I found in it the same rejection of image-worship, of mariolatry, and of the cult of saints and holy crosses, which was characteristic of the Paulicians. I could not copy it then without leaving unfinished a mass of other work which I had begun in the conventual library; and I was anxious to get to Dathev, or at least back to Tiflis, before the snow fell on the passes of the anti-Caucasus. However, I arranged that a copy of the book should be made and sent to me; and this I received late in the year 1893 from the deacon Galoust Têr Mkherttschian.

My first impression on looking into it afresh was one of disappointment. I had expected to find in it a Marcionite, or at least a Manichean book; but, beyond the extremely sparse use made in it of the Old Testament, I found nothing that savoured of these ancient heresies. Accordingly I laid it aside, in the press of other work which I had undertaken. It was not until the summer of 1896 that, at the urgent request of Mr. Darwin Swift, who had come to me for information about the history of Manicheism in Armenia, I returned to it, and translated it into English in the hope that it might advance his researches.

And now I at last understood who the Paulicians really were. All who had written about them had been misled by the calumnies of Photius, Petrus Siculus, and the other Greek writers, who describe them as Manicheans. I now realized that I had stumbled on the monument of a phase of the Christian Church so old and so outworn, that the very memory of it was well-nigh lost. For *The Key of Truth* contains the baptismal service and ordinal of the Adoptionist Church, almost in the form in which Theodotus of Rome may have celebrated those rites. These form the oldest part of the book, which, however, also contains much controversial matter of a later date, directed against what the compiler regarded as the abuses of the Latin and Greek Churches. The date at which the book was written in its present form cannot be put later than the ninth century, nor earlier than the seventh. But we can no more argue thence that the prayers and teaching and rites preserved in it are not older, than we could contend, because our present English Prayer Book was only compiled in the sixteenth century, that its contents do not go back beyond that date. The problem therefore of determining the age of the doctrine and rites detailed in *The Key of Truth* is like any other problem of Christian palaeontology. It resembles the questions which arise in connexion with the *Didaché* or *The Shepherd* of Hermas; and can only be resolved by a careful consideration of the stage which it represents in the development of the opinions and rites of the church. In my prolegomena I have attempted to solve this problem. I may here briefly indicate the results arrived at.

The characteristic note of the Adoptionist phase of Christian opinion was the absence of the recognized doctrine of the Incarnation. Jesus was mere man until he reached his thirtieth year, when he came to John on the bank of the Jordan to receive baptism. Then his sinless nature received the guerdon. The heavens opened and the Spirit of God came down and abode with him. The voice from above proclaimed him the chosen Son of God; a glory rested on him, and thenceforth he was the New Adam, the Messiah; was the power and wisdom of God, Lord of all creation, the first-born in the kingdom of grace. Of divine Incarnation other than this possession of the man Jesus by the divine Spirit, other than this acquiescence of it in him, who had as no other man kept the commands of God, the Adoptionists knew nothing. And as he was chosen out to be the elect Son of God in baptism, so it is the end and vocation of all men, by gradual self-conquest, to prepare themselves for the fruition of God's grace. They must believe and repent, and then at a mature age ask for the baptism, which alone admits them into the Church or invisible union of the faithful; the spirit electing and adopting them to be sons of the living God, filled like Jesus, though not in the same degree, with the Holy Spirit. 'Et ille Christus, et nos Christi[1].'

For those who held this faith, the Baptism of Jesus was necessarily the chief of all Christian feasts; and the Fish the favourite symbol of Jesus Christ, because he, like it, was born in the waters. Hence it is that when we first, about the end of the third century, obtain a clear knowledge of the feasts of the church, we find that the Baptism stands at the head of them. It is not until the close of the fourth century that the modern Christmas, the Birth of Jesus from the Virgin, emerges among the orthodox festivals, and displaces in the minds of the faithful his spiritual birth in the Jordan. First in Rome, and soon in Antioch and the nearer East, this new festival was kept on Dec. 25. In the farther East, however, in Egypt,

---

[1] The phrase is that of the Spanish Adoptionists. But the thought was fully expressed five centuries earlier by Methodius, *Conviv.* viii. 8: ἡ ἐκκλησία σπαργᾷ καὶ ὠδίνει, μέχριπερ ὁ Χριστὸς ἐν ἡμῖν μορφωθῇ γεννηθείς, ὅπως ἕκαστος τῶν ἁγίων τῷ μετέχειν Χριστοῦ Χριστὸς γεννηθῇ. 'The Church is big with child, and is in travail, until the Christ in us is fully formed into birth, in order that each of the saints by sharing in Christ may be born a Christ,' that is, through baptism. And just below he continues thus: 'This is why in a certain scripture we read, "Touch not my Christs..."; which means that those who have been baptized by participation of the Spirit into Christ, have become Christs.' Harnack well sums up the teaching of Methodius as follows (*Dogmengesch.* bd. i. 746 (701): 'For Methodius the history of the Logos-Christ, as Faith holds it, is but the general background for an inner history, which must repeat itself in every believer: the Logos must in his behalf once more come down from heaven, must suffer and die and rise again in the faithful.' So Augustine, *in Ioh. tr.* 21, n. 8: 'Gratias agamus non solum nos Christianos factos esse, sed Christum.' Such then was also the Paulician conviction.

in Armenia, and in Mesopotamia, the new date for the chief festival was not accepted, and the commemoration of the earthly or human birth of Jesus was merely added alongside of the older feast of his Baptism, both being kept on the old day, Jan. 6.

We are only acquainted with the early Christianity of the Jewish Church through the reports of those who were hostile to it, and who gave to it the name of Ebionite, signifying probably such an outward poverty in its adherents, and such a rigid simplicity in its liturgy and rites, as characterized the Paulician Church, and provoked the ridicule of the orthodox Armenian writers.

It is certain, however, that the christology of this church was Adoptionist. Through Antioch and Palmyra this faith must have spread into Mesopotamia and Persia; and in those regions became the basis of that Nestorian Christianity which spread over Turkestan, invaded China, and still has a foothold in Urmiah and in Southern India. From centres like Edessa, Nisibis, and Amida it was diffused along the entire range of the Taurus, from Cilicia as far as Ararat, and beyond the Araxes into Albania, on the southern slopes of the Eastern Caucasus. Its proximate centre of diffusion in the latter region seems to have been the upper valley of the great Zab, where was the traditional site of the martyrdom of St. Bartholomew, to whom the Armenians traced back the succession of the bishops of the canton of Siuniq, north of the Araxes. In Albania, Atropatene, and Vaspurakan to the east of Lake Van, and in Moxoëne, Arzanene, and Taraunitis to its south and west, as most of the early Armenian historians admit, Christianity was not planted by the efforts of Gregory the Illuminator, but was long anterior to him and had an apostolic origin. That it was a faith of strictly Adoptionist or Ebionite type we know from the Disputation of Archelaus with Mani. For Archelaus, though he wrote and spoke in Syriac, was the bishop of an Armenian see which lay not far from Lake Van [1]

---

[1] The identification (see pp. cii, ciii) of the See of Archelaus is somewhat confirmed by the fact (communicated to me by Father Basil Sarkisean) that Karkhar is the name of a hilly region (not of a town) in the vilayet of Bitlis, about one hour south of Van. But De Morgan's map (*Mission Scientifique en Perse*, 1896) of the country east of Lake Urmiah inclines one to identify the Karkhar of Archelaus with that of Wardan, which certainly lay in the canton of Golthn, on the Araxes. For this map marks a town called Arablou (i.e. Arabion castellum) on the north bank of the river Karanghou (which

The Taurus range thus formed a huge recess or circular dam into which flowed the early current of the Adoptionist faith, to be therein caught and detained for centuries, as it were a backwater from the main stream of Christian development. Here in the eighth and ninth centuries, even after the destruction of the Montanist Church, it still lingered in glen and on mountain crest, in secular opposition to the Nicene faith, which, backed by the armies of Byzantium, pressed eastward and southward from Caesarea of Cappadocia. The historical Church of Armenia was a compromise between these opposed forces; and on the whole, especially in the monasteries, the Nicene or grecizing party won the upper hand; dictating the creed and rites, and creating the surviving literature of that Church. But the older Adoptionist Christianity of south-east Armenia was not extinct. In the eighth century there was that great revival of it, known in history as the Paulician movement. A Paulician emperor sat on the throne of Byzantium; and away in Taron, about 800 A.D., the old believers seem to have organized themselves outwardly as a separate church; and a great leader stereotyped their chief rites by committing them to writing in an authoritative book. That book survives, and is *The Key of Truth*.

In the West the Adoptionist faith was anathematized at Rome in the person of Theodotus as early as 190 A.D., but not before it had left a lasting monument of itself, namely, *The Shepherd* of Hermas. It still survived in Moorish Spain, and was there vigorous as late as the ninth century; and it lived on in other parts of Europe, in Burgundy, in Bavaria, and in the Balkan Peninsula, where it was probably the basis of Bogomilism. It is even not improbable that

may be the modern form of Stranga), halfway from its source in the Sahend hills (due south of Tabreez) towards Sefid, near Resht, where it flows into the Caspian. This Arablou is about 100 miles, or three days' ride, south of Urdubad on the Araxes, the traditional site of the evangelizing activity of St. Bartholomew. Cedrenus (xi. 575) indicates that the Stranga was the boundary between Persia and Roman Vaspurakan in the eleventh century just as it had been in the third. This view would still locate the See of Archelaus in Pers-Armenia, on the borders of Albania and Siuniq, and in the very region where King Arshak (see p. cxiii), the enemy of St. Basil, found heretically minded bishops ready to consecrate as catholicos his own nominee. In the absence of surveys and better maps it is difficult to decide between these alternative views; but one or other of them must be correct, and they both prove that Archelaus was an Armenian bishop.

it was the heresy of the early British Church. But it has left few landmarks, for the rival christology which figured Jesus Christ not as a man, who by the descent of the Spirit on him was filled with the Godhead, but as God incarnate from his virgin mother's womb, advanced steadily, and, like a rising tide, soon swept over the whole face of Christendom; everywhere effacing literary and other traces of the Adoptionist faith, which seems thenceforward to have only lived on in Languedoc and along the Rhine as the submerged Christianity of the Cathars, and perhaps also among the Waldenses. In the Reformation this Catharism comes once more to the surface, particularly among the so-called Anabaptist and Unitarian Christians, between whom and the most primitive church *The Key of Truth* and the Cathar Ritual of Lyon supply us with two great connecting links.

How, it may be asked, could such a revolution of religious opinion as the above sketch implies take place and leave so little trace behind? But it has left some traces. The *Liber Sententiarum* is the record of the Inquisition of Toulouse from 1307–1323, and for that short period its 400 closely printed folio pages[1] barely suffice to chronicle the cruelties perpetrated in the name of the God of mercy by the clergy of the orthodox or persecuting Church of Rome. A hundred such volumes would be needed to record the whole tale of the suppression of the European Cathars. And if we ask what has become of the literature of these old believers of Europe, an examination of the lately found eleventh-century MS. of the *Peregrinatio* of St. Sylvia suggests an answer. This precious codex contained a description of the Feast of the Baptism, the old Christmas day, as it was celebrated on Jan. 6 in Jerusalem towards the close of the fourth century. It was the one tell-tale feast, the one relic of the Adoptionist phase of Christianity which the book contained; and the details of its celebration would have had an exceptional interest for the Christian archaeologist of to-day. But the particular folio which contained this information, at some remote period, and probably in the monastery of Monte Casino where it was written, has been carefully cut out. If such precautions were necessary as late as the twelfth century, what must not have been destroyed in the fourth and fifth centuries, when the struggle between the rival christologies raged all over the East

---

[1] I refer to Limborch's edition.

and West? Then it was that the bulk of the Christian literature of the second and early third centuries perished, and was irrevocably lost.

Because I have sometimes referred to the Adoptionists as heretics, I trust I may not be supposed to have prejudged the case against them. In doing so I have merely availed myself of a conventional phrase, because it was convenient and clear. For it has been no part of my task to appraise the truth or falsehood of various forms of Christian opinion, but merely to exhibit them in their mutual relations; and, treating my subject as a scientific botanist treats his *flora*, to show how an original genus is evolved, in the process of adaptation to different circumstances, into various species. It rests with the authoritative teacher of any sect to determine, like a good gardener, which species he will sow in his particular plot. The aim of the scientific historian of opinion is only to be accurate and impartial; and this I have tried to be, moving among warring opinions, 'sine ira et studio, quorum causas procul habeo.' If I have occasionally waxed warm, it has been before the spectacle of the cruel persecution of innocent people. And of a truth a pathetic interest attaches to such a book as this *Key of Truth*, in which, in tardy fulfilment of Gibbon's hope, the Paulicians are at last able to plead for themselves. It was no empty vow of their elect ones, 'to be baptized with the baptism of Christ, to take on themselves scourgings, imprisonments, tortures, reproaches, crosses, blows, tribulation, and all temptations of the world.' Theirs the tears, theirs the blood shed during more than 'ten centuries of fierce persecution in the East; and if we reckon of their number, as well we may, the early puritans of Europe, then the tale of wicked deeds wrought by the persecuting churches reaches dimensions which appal the mind. And as it was all done, nominally out of reverence for, but really in mockery of, the Prince of Peace, it is hard to say of the Inquisitors that they knew not what they did.

Even while we reprobate the tone of certain chapters of *The Key*, in which the orthodox churches are represented as merely Satanic agencies, we must not forget the extenuating fact that for over five centuries the Adoptionists had in Rome and elsewhere been under the heel of the dominant faction. If we hunt down innocent men like wild animals, they are more than mortal, if they do not requite many evil deeds with some few bitter words. And one point in their favour must be noticed, and it is this. Their system was, like that of the European Cathars, in its basal idea and conception alien to persecution; for membership in it depended upon baptism, voluntarily sought for, even with tears and supplications, by the faithful and penitent adult. Into such a church there could be no dragooning of the unwilling. On the contrary, the whole purpose of the scrutiny, to which the candidate for baptism was subjected, was to ensure that his heart and intelligence were won, and to guard against that merely outward conformity, which is all that a persecutor can hope to impose. It was one of the worst results of infant baptism, that by making membership in the Christian Church mechanical and outward, it made it cheap; and so paved the way for the persecutor. Under this aspect, as under some others, the Adoptionist believers, and the Montanists, and certain other sects, passed with the triumph and secularization of Christianity under Theodosius into the same relative position which the early Christians had themselves occupied under the persecuting Roman government; whose place in turn the dominant or orthodox church now took in all respects save one,—namely, that it was better able to hunt down dissenters, because the Inquisitors knew just enough of the Christian religion to detect with ease the comings in and goings forth of their victims.

Built into the walls and foundations of a modern church we can often trace the fragments of an earlier and ruined edifice, but are seldom privileged to come upon a complete specimen of the older structure. Now into the fabric of many of our beliefs to-day are built not a few stones taken from the Adoptionists; often retrimmed to suit their new environment. In *The Key of Truth* we for the first time recover a long-past phase of Christian life, and that, not in the garbled account of an Epiphanius, or in the jejune pages of an Irenaeus or Hippolytus; but in the very words of those who lived it. A lost church rises before our eyes; not a dead anatomy, but a living organism. We can, as it were, enter the humble congregation, be present at the simple rites, and find ourselves at home among the worshippers. And it is remarkable how this long-lost church recalls to us the *Teaching of the Apostles*. There is the same Pauline conception of the Eucharist indicated by the stress laid on the use of a single loaf, the same baptism in living water, the same absence of a hierarchy, the same description of the President as an Apostle, the same implied Christhood of the elect who teach the word, the same claim to possess the Apostolical tradition. It is no far-fetched hypothesis that the *Didachê* is itself the handbook of an Adoptionist Church.

My Introduction contains many hints towards a history of the feast of Christmas; but I have mostly confined myself to Armenian sources inaccessible to many scholars. The Greek evidence is well gathered together in Prof. Hermann Usener's suggestive study on the subject; and I have hardly noticed it, lest my book should assume unwieldy dimensions. Another work to the author of which I am under obligations is the *Dogmengeschichte* of Prof. Harnack. In my discussion of the origins of the Armenian Church I have been largely guided by the luminous tract of Prof. Gelzer on the subject. Of other works consulted by me I have added a list at the end of my book.

I feel that many of the views advanced in my Introduction will be sharply criticized, but I do not think that my main conclusions in regard to the character of the Paulician Church can be touched. The intimate connexion between adult baptism and the school of Christian thought represented by Paul of Samosata is evidenced in a passage of Cyril of Alexandria's commentary on Luke, first published by Mai[1]. In it Cyril assails Paul of Samosata's interpretation of the word ἀρχόμενος in Luke iii. 23, namely, that the man Jesus then *began* to be the Son of God, though he was, in the eye of the law (ὡς ἐνομίζετο), only son of Joseph. There follows a lacuna[2] in which Cyril coupled with this interpretation a form of teaching which he equally censured, namely, that all persons should be baptized on the model of Jesus at thirty years of age. This teaching was plainly that of the Pauliani, and we find it again among the Paulicians.

---

[1] *Noua Biblioth. Patrum*, tom. ix; reprinted in Migne, *Patr. Gr.* vol. 72, col. 524. The Syriac version (edited by R. Payne Smith) has not this passage, which however seems to me to be Cyril's.

[2] Cyril continues: 'Thus much harm and unexpected results from such a delaying of the grace through baptism to a late and over-ripe age. For firstly, one's hope is not secure (i. e. a man may die prematurely), that one will attain one's own particular wishes; and even if in the end one does so gain them, one is indeed made holy; but gains no more than remission of sins, having hidden away the talent, so that it is infructuous for the Lord, because one has added no works thereunto.' Mai's note on the above is just : ' Uidetur in praecedentibus (nunc deperditis) Cyrillus uerba eorum retulisse, qui ut baptismum differrent, Christi exemplum obiiciebant anno aetatis trigesimo baptizati.'

Where my conclusions are at best inferential, I have qualified them as such. To this class belongs the view that Gregory the Illuminator was himself an Adoptionist. I agree with Gelzer that his Teaching as preserved in the Armenian Agathangelus or in the independent volume of his *Stromata* cannot be regarded as altogether authentic. It would be interesting to know in what relation the fragments of his Teaching preserved in Ethiopic stand to the Armenian documents. An *Anaphora* ascribed to him is also found in the Ethiopic tongue, but is so common in collections of Ethiopic liturgies that it is probably worthless. It is, however, remarkable that no trace of it remains in Armenian.

My suggestion that the European Cathars were of Adoptionist origin also rests on mere inference. But they had so much in common with the Paulicians, that it is highly probable. My kindred surmise that the early British Church was Adoptionist seems to be confirmed by two inscriptions recently communicated to me by Prof. J. Rhys. These were found in North Wales and belong to the sixth to eighth centuries. They both begin with the words: 'In nomine Dei patris et filii Spiritus Sancti[1].' This formula takes us straight back to *The Shepherd* of Hermas[2], in which the Son of God is equated with the Holy Spirit; and it

---

[1] These inscriptions occur on archaic crosses and are figured in Prof. Westwood's work. He agrees with Prof. Rhys about their date. *Filii* in one of them is represented only by an *F*, detected by Prof. Rhys alone. In the other the word *Sancti* is barely legible. The same formula, 'Sanctus Spiritus, Dei filius,' occurs in the Adoptionist tract, *De Montibus Sina et Sion, c.* 13, quoted in my Introduction, p. ci. The formula 'In nomine Dei summi' also occurs four times in these early Christian inscriptions of Wales, and seems to be both anti-Trinitarian and connected with the series of inscriptions in honour of θεὸς ὕψιστος, found in Asia Minor and referred by Schurer (*Sitzungsber. der Akad. d. Wiss. zu Berlin*, March 4, 1897, t. xiii. p. 200) and Franz Cumont (*Supplém. à la Revue de l'instruction publique*, Bruxelles, 1897) to Jewish influence. The occurrence of the same formula on early crosses in Wales shows that it may have been used in Asia Minor by Christians; and Gregory of Nyssa (*c. Eunom.* xi, sub fin.) accuses the 'Arians,' i. e. the Adoptionists of Asia Minor, of baptizing not in the name of Father, Son, and Holy Ghost; but of the Creator and Maker only, whom they, like the author of the *Key* (p. 115), 'regarded as not only the Father, but as the God of the only-born Son.' The survival of such formulae on these old Welsh crosses explains why Bede rejected the baptism of the British Christians, and why Aldhelm (A. D. 705) denied that they had the 'Catholicae fidei regula' at all.

[2] See *Hermae Pastor* (edit. Oscar de Gebhardt and Ad. Harnack, Lipsiae, 1877), Sim. v. 5, with the editors' notes.

also exactly embodies the heresy of which Basil deplored the prevalence in the eastern regions of Asia Minor[1]. These inscriptions therefore rudely disturb the ordinary assumption that the early Celtic Church was 'catholic in doctrine and practice[2],' as if Bede had meant nothing when he studiously ignored St. Patrick and denied that the British bishops even preached the Word.

In the Appendices which follow the text of the *Key*, I have translated from old Armenian authors such connected notices of the Paulicians as they preserve. I have also added the letter of Macarius to the Armenians, because of the light which it sheds on their early Church. The Provençal Cathar ritual of Lyon, which I also include, has never been translated into English; though it is an unique monument of the forerunners of the European reformation.

It remains for me to thank those who have helped me with their advice and encouragement. Mr. Rendel Harris read the translation of the text and made many valuable suggestions. Most of all my thanks are due to the Clarendon Press for their liberality in publishing my book, and to the deacon Galoust Têr Mkherttschian, who both copied for me the Edjmiatzin MS. of *The Key of Truth* and collated my text with it after it was in print. I earnestly hope that there may be found a second MS. of the book, which, by filling up the large lacunae of this, may clear up the many points which because of them remain obscure.

---

[1] See below, p. cxiv.
[2] I quote Warren's *Liturgy and Ritual of the Celtic Church*, p. 45.

CONTENTS

	PAGE
PREFACE	v
SUMMARY OF THE INTRODUCTION	xvii
INTRODUCTION	xxiii–cxcvi
ARMENIAN TEXT	1–66
TRANSLATION OF THE ARMENIAN TEXT	67–124
APPENDIX I. THE LETTER OF GREGORY OF NAREK	125
,, II. EXCERPTS FROM ARISTACES OF LASTIVERT	131
,, III. EXCERPTS FROM GREGORY MAGISTROS	141
,, IV. EXCERPTS FROM JOHN OF OTZUN	152
,, V. EXCERPTS FROM NERSES SHNORHALI	155
,, VI. THE PROVENÇAL RITUAL OF THE ALBIGEOIS	160
,, VII. EXCERPTS FROM ISAAC CATHOLICOS	171
,, VIII. EXCERPTS FROM PAUL OF TARON	174
,, IX. MACARIUS' EPISTLE TO THE ARMENIANS	178
EXCURSUS ON THE ARMENIAN STYLE OF *The Key of Truth*	187
NOTE ON THE TRANSLITERATION OF ARMENIAN NAMES	190
INDEX	191
LIST OF WORKS CONSULTED	202

SUMMARY OF THE INTRODUCTION

(P. xxiii) Armenian Paulicians, called Thonraki, emigrate from Khnus in Turkey, and settle in Akhaltzik in Russian Armenia, A.D. 1828.—(xxiv) The Synod of Edjmiatzin appeals to the Russian Government to suppress them. An Inquisition opened, 1837.—(xxv–xxvi) Four confessions made of Paulician tenets.—(xxvii) *The Key of Truth* admitted to be their authoritative book.—(xxviii) The Russian Court at Tiflis fines the Paulicians, 1843.—(xxix) *The Key of Truth* is seized during this Inquisition. Description of it. Its age attested both by the colophon, and—(xxx) by the style.—(xxxi) The liturgical parts of the book are older than the rest, and belong perhaps to fourth century. The exordium the work of a great Paulician leader,—(xxxii) probably of Smbat, A.D. 800–850. Evidence on this point of Gregory Magistros.—(xxxiii-xl) The teaching of the *Key* is summarized under thirty-seven heads and shown to conform with the notices of Paulicians given in Armenian writers of the eighth to the twelfth centuries;—(xli) and equally with the Greek sources in respect of the following points, viz.: their claim to be the Catholic Church, their rejection of similar claims on the part of the orthodox, their Adoptionist Christology, and belief that Jesus Christ was a creature only,—(xlii) their rejection of Mariolatry and of intercession of saints and of cult of the cross,—(xliii) their canon of Scripture, their view of the Eucharist, their hatred of monks, and—(xliv) their appeal to Scripture. The Escurial MS. of Georgius Monachus is the oldest Greek source and best agrees with the *Key*. The Paulicians not Manicheans.—(xlv) Loose use of 'Manichean' by orthodox writers in dealing with opponents.—(xlvi) Did Paulicians hold that Jesus took flesh of the virgin?—(xlvii) Their Eucharist not merely figurative. They only rejected orthodox rites because the orthodox had lost true baptism.—(xlviii) The Paulicians were 'old believers.' The report of the Inquisition of Arkhwêli in 1837 fills up lacunae in the *Key*,—(xlix) as to Paulician baptism and Eucharist. Baptism at thirty years of age.—(l) Nocturnal Eucharistic celebrations. Baptism in rivers.—(li) Nature of Paulician elect ones. Evidence on this point of letters of Sergius, and—(lii) of exordium of *Key*.—(lii) Were the elect ones adored as

Christs, because Christ was immanent in them?—(liii) The Eucharistic elements in becoming the body of the elect became the body of Christ, and vice versa.—(liv) But the Paulicians admitted a metabolism of the blessed elements. St. Paul on immanence of Christ.—(lv) Resemblance with the Paulician of the view of the Eucharist taken by Eckbert's Rhenish Cathars in 1160.—(lvi) Proof from the *Liber Sententiarum* (1307) that the Cathars adored their elect ones.—(lvii) Relation of Greek to Armenian sources about Paulicians. Analysis of John of Otzun's account, A.D. 719.—(lviii) He seems to refer the heresy back to fourth century, and notices the solidarity of Albanian with Armenian Paulicians.—(lix) He evidences that they already sought the protection of the Arabs. Paulicians called Thonraki from Thonrak.—(lx) Description of Thonrak, their centre.—(lxi) Reasons for identifying Smbat of Thonrak with Smbat Bagratuni, adduced from Mekhitar, 1300, from Gregory of Narek, *c.* 975.—(lxii) But Gregory Magistros does not favour this identification—(lxiii) Evidence of Constantine Porphyrogenitus, *c.* 958; of Thomas Artsruni, *c.* 940, and—(lxiv) of other Armenian chroniclers is favourable. History of Smbat Bagratuni. He was martyred by the Arabs, *c.* 854, and—(lxv) avenged by the men of Sasoun. The charge of apostasy made against him points to his having been a Paulician.—(lxvi) Smbat must have belonged to the Bagratuni clan.—(lxvii) Evidence that he was an earlier Smbat, and minister of Chosrow, *c.* 648. List of heresiarchs who succeeded Smbat.—(lxviii) The Sergius of the Greek sources unknown to the Armenians.—(lxix) Aristaces' narrative, where laid. Topography of Harq and Mananali. Photius' error as to Mananali. —(lxx) Topography of Tdjaurm. Paulicianism rife in entire upper valleys of Euphrates and Tigris.—(lxxi) Policy of Byzantine emperors to drive the Paulicians out of the empire. Magistros' campaign did not get rid of them. Their recrudescence in Taron in eighteenth century,—(lxxii) under the abbot John, the copyist of the *Key*.— (lxxiii) Geographical diffusion in Asia Minor of the Paulicians.— (lxxiv) The Greek writers familiar with those of the Western Taurus, the Armenians with those of the Eastern only. Solidarity of Paulicians in West with those in East of the range.—(lxxv) Their destruction by the Greek emperors paved the way for the Mohammedan conquest. —(lxxvi) A Greek summary of Paulician tenets preserved in Isaac Catholicos, twelfth century.—(lxxvii-lxxx) Translation with comments of Isaac's summary.—(lxxxi) The evidence of John of Otzun (*c.* 700) agrees point for point with the above summary, especially in respect of the Paulician rejection,—(lxxxii) of stone altars and fonts,—(lxxxiii) of adult baptism. The union of Agapê and Eucharist. Agreements of Isaac's summary with the *Didachê*.—(lxxxiv) Evidence of the Canons of Sahak (*c.* 425) as to union of Agapê and Eucharist.—(lxxxv) Early Armenian fasts. Isaac's summary borne out by Nerses of Lambron's picture of Armenian Christianity in Cilicia in twelfth century.— (lxxxvi) The place of Paulicianism in the general history of Christian opinion. Its antiquity evidenced by John of Otzun, and by—(lxxxvii) Lazar of Pharp (*c.* 480). The organic unity of beliefs with rites seen in the *Key* is a proof of age and primitiveness.—(lxxxviii) Coherence of Paulician Christology with baptismal usages and with rite of election. —(lxxxix) The *Key* a monument of the Adoptionist Church, of which *The Shepherd* of Hermas is also a monument.—(xc) The Christology of latter book examined and shown to agree with that of Theodotus. —(xci) Traces of Adoptionism in Justin Martyr.—(xcii) Its identity with Ebionite Christology. Hippolytus' account of Theodotus.—(xciii) Probability that Theodotus, like the Paulicians, accepted John's Gospel; though the Alogi, his predecessors, rejected it.—(xciv) Adoptionism in Melito. Condemnation of Paul of Samosata.—(cxv) The latter's teaching.—(xcvi) Traces of Adoptionism in Lactantius. Evolution of Christian dogmas in the great centres of culture.—(xcvii) The Disputation of Archelaus with Mani is an Adoptionist monument, for it teaches that Jesus was merely man before his baptism—(xcviii) and that he was not God incarnate. It excludes the ordinary interpretation of the miraculous birth.—(xcix) Jesus was *filius per profectum*. Parallel descent of Holy Spirit on the faithful.—(c) Jesus became Christ and Son of God at his baptism.—(ci) Karkhar the see of Archelaus was near Arabion Castellum on the Stranga, or—(cii) upper Zab ;—(ciii) and was therefore an Armenian see. Antiquity of Christianity in south-east Armenia.—(civ) The early Christianity of the Taurus range was Adoptionist, and—(cv) the name Paulician originally meant a follower of Paul of Samosata.—(cvi) The Paulicians, therefore, the same as the Pauliani of the Nicene fathers and of Ephrem. The Paulianist heresy reappeared in the empire in eighth century as a characteristically Armenian heresy.—(cvii) Early conflict in Armenia of the Adoptionist Christology with the Nicene, which came in from Cappadocia.— (cviii) The Adoptionists under name of Messalians condemned in Armenian council of Shahapivan (A. D. 447). Lazar of Pharp's description (A. D. 480) of Armenian heresy.—(cix) The heresy condemned at Shahapivan was the primitive Syriac Christianity of south-east Armenia, which—(cx) the grecizing Armenian fathers ignored, though it provided them with their earliest version of New Testament.— (cxi) Gregory the Illuminator was probably an Adoptionist believer, but his 'Teaching' has been falsified.—(cxii) Evidence of St. Basil's letters as to the conflict in Armenia in fourth century of the rival schools of Christology. St. Nerses (died *c.* 374), Basil's lieutenant, deposed by King Pap, who—(cxiii) effected the final rupture with Caesarea. —(cxiv) Basil's description of the popular heresy of Armenia proves that it was Adoptionist.—(cxv) It affirmed, like Eunomius' creed, that Jesus Christ was a created being.—(cxvi) The orthodox Armenians shifted their ecclesiastical centre to Valarshapat from Taron, because of the prevalence of Adoptionists in latter region. Constantine V a Paulician.—(cxvii) The rôle of Smbat. He did not create the heresy of the Thonraki, but only organized the old believers of Taron,—

(cxviii) under a primate of their own. Till then the old belief had lurked among isolated clans.—(cxix) As their first primate he wrote down their rites in an authoritative book.—(cxx) The Thonraki claim to be the catholic church of St. Gregory, and to have the apostolical tradition. They repudiated the sacraments and orders of the grecizing Armenians as false.—(cxxi) The archaic nature of their baptismal views proved by their agreement with Tertullian, who—(cxxii) like them denounced infant-baptism. — (cxxiii) Macarius of Jerusalem (*c*. 330) on 'Arian' heresy in Armenia. Paulicians hostile to a real hierarchy and to monks.—(cxxiv) The Paulician 'elect' one the *synecdemos* of the Greek sources. Were the 'rulers' in the Paulician Church Elect ones?—(cxxv) Use of the phrase 'original sin' in the *Key*.—(cxxvi) The Paulicians borrowed it from the West, where it was already used in fifth century,—(cxxvii) and where the Latin Adoptionists may have originated it.—(cxxviii) Paulician system was opposed to hereditary priesthood and to blood-offerings in expiation of the sins of the dead.—(cxxix) Why the Western Paulicians renamed their congregations. No trace of this *Schwärmerei* among the Thonraki.— (cxxx) Their hostility to papal usurpation mistaken by their enemies for hostility to St. Peter.—(cxxxi) Differences between the Elect of the Manicheans and the Elect of the Paulicians. — (cxxxii) Both Churches held that Christ is immanent in the Elect. The real Manicheans of Armenia.—(cxxxiii) The immanence of Christ in the Elect exampled from the New Testament, and—(cxxxiv) from early Christian writers; especially Tertullian,—(cxxxv) whose views of the Virgin Mary and of the Eucharist were also shared by the Paulicians. —(cxxxvi) Tertullian, like them, held that the elements are typically and yet in some sense really the body and blood of Christ.—(cxxxvii) Deportation to Thrace of Paulicians of the Taurus,—(cxxxviii) where they created the Bogomile Church and survived into the last century.— (cxxxix) Crusaders met with Paulicians in Syria. First mention of them in Europe.—(cxl) Eckbert's description of Rhenish Cathars indicates a sect akin to the Paulicians.—(cxli) The Cathar ritual of Lyon is an Albigeois book and has affinities with the Paulician ordinal, —(cxlii) though in some respects it is more primitive. Did the Albigeois baptize with water?—(cxliii) The common ritual use of the name Peter in the Albigeois *Consolamentum* and Paulician election service proves their common origin.—(cxliv) Both sects had the same conception of the Church as the communion of saints.—(cxlv) The Albigeois were not Manicheans, nor did they advocate the suicide of persons consoled. —(cxlvi) Differences in respect of baptism between the Lyon ritual and the *Key*.—(cxlvii) A knowledge of the Paulicians was brought to Europe by the Crusaders,—(cxlviii) and there is no affiliation of the Cathars to the Bogomiles before Reinerius Saccho in 1254.—(cxlix) The *Consolamentum* was a general form of laying on of hands in order to the reception of all gifts alike of the Spirit.—(cl) Possibility that Armenian refugees and colonists in Europe contributed to the Anabaptist movement.—(cli) Wiszowaty on the origin of the Anabaptists and Unitarians. (clii) The Pauliani were quartodecumans. Adoptionist festival of the Baptism of Jesus on sixth of January.—(cliii) The Bezan reading of Luke iii. 22. The Fish an Adoptionist emblem of Christ. The Gospel of the Baptism read on sixth of January.—(cliv) *Testimonia* concerning the feast on sixth of January from canons of Clemens, Macarius,— (clv) from Nectarius and Hippolytus.—(clvi) Artemon, the reputed founder of the Christmas feast on December 25.—(clvii) Testimony of Melito, Cyprian, Marutha.—(clviii) The Syrian doctors on origin in Sun-worship of the Roman Christmas.—(clix) Isaac Catholicos on heretical character of Armenian feasts.—(clx) List of Armenian feasts in canons of Sahak.—(clxi) Was the Sabbath observed in the early Armenian Church?—(clxii) Was the later Lenten fast evolved out of the forty days' fast of the Adoptionists?—(clxiii) The Paulician Eucharist a sacred meal symbolic of Christian unity.—(clxiv) The *mataḷ* or eating of the flesh of a victim. St. Sahak's conception of 'Church' the same as that of the Paulicians.—(clxv) Use of the terms synagogue and *proseucha* in early Armenian Church.—(clxvi) The *wanq* or shelter-houses. Dislike of Paulicians for churches of wood and stone evidenced by—(clxvii) Nerses of Lambron, *c.* 1170. Dislike of vestments and ceremonies, universal among—(clxviii) Armenians of Western Taurus. —(clxix) Faustus the Manichean witnesses to the changed Christology of the Catholics of fourth century.—(clxx) Survival of Adoptionism in Spain, *c.* 800. Elipandus and the Pope.—(clxxi) Elipandus appeals to use of *adoptiuus* in Muzarabic liturgy.—(clxxii) Felix of Urgel explicitly Adoptionist in his views.—(clxxiii) He was controverted by Heterius and Alcuin.—(clxxiv) The heresy was not devised by Felix by way of converting Arabs.—(clxxv) Elipandus' formula *Christus inter Christos.* — (clxxvi) Resemblance with Archelaus of Elipandus and Felix.—(clxxvii) Elipandus overlaid his Adoptionism with Nicene faith.— (clxxviii) But Heterius and Alcuin detected his heresy.— (clxxix) The early British Church was probably Adoptionist.— (clxxx) This implied by Bede's persistent attacks on Adoptionism. —(clxxxi) Early faith of Gascony and Bavaria Adoptionist. The immanence of Christ in the preacher taught in the *Didachê* and in *The Shepherd* of Hermas.—(clxxxii) Origen's view of the Incarnation agrees with that of the Adoptionists.—(clxxxiii) Montanists held the same view of the immanence of Christ, and extended it to women.— (clxxxiv) Traces of a similar view in Mani and the heretic Marcus. (clxxxv) Were the Paulicians in communion with the remnant of the Montanists?—(clxxxvi) Two ways of eliminating original sin in Jesus: to deny, like Marcion, that he took flesh from his mother; or— (clxxxvii) to affirm with the Latin Church the immaculate conception of his mother. The former view may have been taken by the author of the Paulician Catechism.—(clxxxviii) Traces of an older Adoptionism in the existing rites of orthodox Armenians, e.g. in their Baptismal Service, which—(clxxxix) is meaningless, except in relation to adults;—

(cxc) and in their ordinal. The two rival Christologies foreshadowed in Philo.—(cxci) Recapitulation of Adoptionist conceptions of priesthood, of baptism, and of Eucharist.—(cxcii) Probability that the Adoptionists used and disseminated the Western Text of New Testament. Traces of the same in the *Key*.—(cxciii) The Adoptionist Christian year compared with that of the orthodox Churches. Philo on Epiphanies of the Logos.—(cxciv) Docetic tendencies inherent in the Incarnation-Christology ;—(cxcv) both in respect of the body and of the mind of Jesus. Reasons why this Christology allied itself with infant-baptism.—(cxcvi) Retrospect of the history of the Adoptionist Church.

INTRODUCTION

At[1] the end of the Russo-Turkish war in 1828-1829, a number of Turkish Armenians settled in the newly-acquired Russian territory between Akhaltzik and Erivan, under the leadership of their bishop Karapet. In February, 1837, this bishop warned the Synod of the Orthodox Armenians in Edjmiatzin that in the village Arkhwêli in the province of Shirak there were twenty-five families of refugees from the village of Djêwiurm in the canton of Khnus, who were Thondraketzi[2] or Paulicians of Thondrak or Thonrak.

He complained that these heretics were carrying on a propaganda among their simple-minded neighbours, although in the presence of civil or ecclesiastical functionaries they feigned adhesion to the orthodox Armenian Church. 'Some of our villagers,' he wrote, 'inform us how they openly, in the presence of the simple-minded, deny that the saints help us, deny the value of fasting, the benefit of prayer, and the like. . . . And, although they have a priest, whom I saw in Khnus, and who is wholly without a knowledge of letters, he cannot lead them straight. Perhaps he does not care, for until now he keeps his peace.' The bishop then prays the Synod to send to Arkhwêli a learned priest, to combat the spread of heresy.

Two priests armed with authority were, in consequence of these representations, sent to the neighbourhood, but they could get no other answer from the persons suspected than: 'We are children of the Illuminator[3].' However, others, who had listened

---

[1] For most of the historical matter in pp. xxiii-xxviii I am indebted to an article published by M. A. Eritzean, of Tiflis, in the journal called *Phords*, Tiflis, 1880, under the title 'The Armenian Thonraketzi.'

[2] In general I shall drop the general termination *-tzi*, and speak of the Thonraki or Thondraki, though of course Thonraketzi is the only Armenian equivalent for a dweller in Thonrak.

[3] See p. 132 for the testimony of Aristaces to the fact that the Paulician Church was one with the church founded by Gregory the Illuminator; and compare Gregory Mag., p. 147, 'We are of the tribe of Aram, and agree with them in faith.'

to their attacks on religion, admitted that a false elder, preaching the heresy, had appeared in Khnus, and had wished to enter their houses; but they averred that they had repelled him with anathemas. Five men pleaded that they had received the false teaching not knowing that it was opposed to that of the Armenian Church, and sued for forgiveness. This was on April 13, 1837.

Not content with repressing the movement in Arkhwêli, the Holy Synod, through the Catholicos, made representations to the Bishop of Erzeroum in Turkey, requesting him to send agents to Khnus, which was in his diocese, and where a priest since dead had spread the heresy. These agents were to root out the heresy, if it still survived there. The aid of the Russian Government was also invoked in the person of Baron Posên, Governor of the Caucasus, to put down the sectaries of Arkhwêli. The Governor in reply asked in what consisted the heresy of these villagers, and was informed that 'they rejected the intercession of the saints and spurned their images, denied the value of fasts and the benefit of prayer, disbelieved in the immaculateness of the holy Virgin, Mother of God, repudiated the sacrament of baptism, and the rest.'

About the same time an inhabitant of Giumri (now Alexandrapol) named Karapet Mkrttchean, in a death-bed confession, revealed to an orthodox priest that he, with six others, some with their households, and some apart, had joined the Thonraki sect, being converted by persons from Arkhwêli, which is in the neighbourhood. His written confession was sent to the consistory of Erivan. He could read and write, and it runs as follows:—

'In 1837, at the feast of the Transfiguration in the month of June, Kirakos of Giumri Qôsababayean, after hearing George the elder of Arkhwêli preach, renounced the holy faith, and also preached to me, Karapet, that Christ is not God. Through the preaching of Kirakos, Tharzi Sarkis with his family, Dilband Manuk, Grigor of Kalzwan with his household, Jacob Ergar, Avon of Kalzwan, and I, met in the room of Grigor of Kalzwan; and we took oath one with another not to disclose our secret to any. They in particular told me to inform no man of it. They

'1. convinced me that Christ is not God;

'2. made me blaspheme the cross, as being nothing;

'3. told me that the baptism and holy oil of the Armenians is false; and that

'4. we must rebaptize all of us on whose foreheads the sacred oil of the wild beast is laid.

'5. The mother of God[1] is not believed to be a virgin, but to have lost her virginity.

'6. We reject her intercession; and also

'7. whatever saints there be, they reject their intercession.

'8. They reject the mass and the communion and the confession, but say instead (i.e. to the orthodox): "Confess to your stocks and stones, and leave God alone."

'9. Moreover, those who choose to communicate eat the morsel and drink down the wine upon it, but do not admit the communion of the mass.

'10. They say that we are the only true Christians on earth, whereas Armenians, Russians, Georgians, and others, are false Christians and idolators.

'11. On our faces we make no sign of the cross.

'12. Genuflexions are false, if made superstitiously.

'13. During fasts they eat.

'14. The canon-lore of the holy patriarchs they reject, and say that the councils of the patriarchs were false, and that their canons were written by the devil.'

After making this confession, Karapet affirmed his penitence and sought forgiveness. Three other confessions were obtained about the same time, which we give in the order in which M. Eritzean has printed them. The following is the deposition of Manuk Davthean of Giumri, who could not write:—

'In 1837, in February, during Shrovetide, on the first of the week, in the chamber of Grigor Kalzwan, 'I saw Tharzi Sargis reading the Gospel. First he read it, and then explained it.

'1. He told us not to worship things made with hands; that is to say, images (*or* pictures) of saints and the cross, because these are made of silver, and are the same as idols.

'2. Christ is the Son of God, but was born a man of Mary, she losing her virginity, as it were by the earthly[2] annunciation of Gabriel.

'3. After suffering, being buried, and rising again, he ascended into heaven, and sat on the right hand of the Father, and is our Intercessor.

---

[1] The word answers to *Theotokos*, and was conventionally used by these late Paulicians to denote the mother of Jesus. They of course reject the idea conveyed in it.

[2] The text has *holelên* = earthly, or made of dust; but *hogelên* = 'spiritual,' should perhaps be read. On the heresy involved, see below, p. clxxxvii.

'4. Except Christ we have no other intercessor; for

'5. the mother of God they do not believe to be virgin; nor

'6. do they admit the intercession of saints.

'7. Neither are fasts ordained of God, but prelates have ingeniously devised them to suit themselves; wherefore it is right to break the fasts as we will. When you go into church, pray only to God, and do not adore pictures.

'8. In the time of baptism it is unnecessary to anoint with oil, for this is an ordinance of men, and not of God.

'9. Ye shall not commit sin: but when ye have committed sin, whether or no ye confess to priests, there is no remission. It only avails you, if you pour out your sins to God.

'10. Genuflexion is unnecessary.

'11. To say "Lord, Lord," to priests is not necessary, but it is meet to say regularly that God and not man is Lord.

'12. Nor is it necessary to go to places on vows.

'13. Last of all he told me that Christ is not God, and then I understood the falsity of their faith.'

The third recantation written down was that of Avôs Marturosean of Giumri, who could not himself write. He deposed that in 1837 in February, in the chamber of Grigor of Kalzwan, he not only heard the teaching already detailed in the second recantation, but the following as well:

'1. Ye shall keep the ten commandments which God gave to Moses.

'2. Christ is not God, but the Son of God and our Intercessor, sitting on the right hand of God.

'3. Ye shall know Christ alone, and the Father. All other saints which are or have been on the earth are false.

'4. There is no need to go on vows to Edjmiatzin or Jerusalem.

'5. Ye shall confess your sins in church before God alone.

'6. The holy oil of Edjmiatzin is false, nor is it necessary unto baptism; but whenever ye pour one handful of water over the catechumen, he is baptized. For Christ commanded us to baptize with water.

'7. Ye shall always go to church; and to the priest at the time of confession ye shall not tell your sins, for they do not understand. But talk to them in a general sort of way.

'8. Always go to church, not that our kind considers it real; but externally ye shall perform everything, and keep yourselves concealed, until we find an opportunity; and then, if we can, we will all return to this faith of ours. And we swear, even if they cut us to pieces, that we will not reveal it.'

'Gregory of Kalzwan said as follows: "Behold, I am the Cross; light your tapers on my two hands, and give worship. I am able to give you salvation, just as much as the cross and the saints."'

The fourth confession referred to four of the persons whose names are given in the first. Two of them could read. Kirakos Khôsay Babayean, already mentioned, deposes in his own writing to the truth of the previous recantations, and attests that he learned of Tharzi Sarkis Haruthiunean; and the latter, also in writing, admitted all, and added that he had learned everything in 1835 from George the church-singer (or elder) of Arkhwêli, who had in his possession a MS. called *The Key of Truth*[1], in which 'everything was written.' It was this George who taught that all are false Christians, except the Nemetzni[2] who are true Christians.

These revelations led to increased activity on the part of the synod of Edjmiatzin. Fresh representations were made to the Russian Governor of the Caucasus to put down the sectaries of Arkhwêli, and also to suppress the newly-arrived German Protestant missionaries, with whose activity the recrudescence of ancient heresy was alleged to be connected[3]. There were thirty families of Paulicians in Arkhwêli, who pretended that they had given up the heresy; and they had even built an orthodox church in their midst in order to avoid suspicion. Also five of the inhabitants had drawn up a document, entitled, 'About the causes of the heresy of the new Manicheans and their followers.' This they sent to the Government. In it was stated that 'in the province of Khnus in the village of Djaurm (or Tschaurm) fifty-five years previously, a certain Armenian priest Ohannes (i.e. John) had joined the sect, and composed a book called *The Key of Truth*. This Ohannes, under pressure from the Osmanli Government, had afterwards, along with his companions, accepted the Mohammedan

---

[1] Cp. p. lxxii below.

[2] That is, the German Millennarists from Wurtemburg who were settled in the Caucasus in 1817. They chose the Caucasus because they believed that at the end of the world Christians would find a place of refuge near the Caspian. See *Missionary Researches in Armenia*, by Eli Smith and H. G. O. Dwight. London, 1834.

[3] These missionaries came from Basle, and, with the approbation of the Czar Alexander, settled at Shusha, a little south of the present city of Elizabetpol, in 1827. There they set up an Armenian and Tartar printing-press, which before long was forbidden.

faith.' Of this Ohannes we shall give further details later on from another source [1]. It is enough here to remark that he was only the copyist, and not the composer of *The Key of Truth*, as his own colophon therein sufficiently proves.

In June, 1838, in consequence of fresh representations on the part of the Holy Synod of Edjmiatzin, the governor of Tiflis ordered an inquiry to be opened in Arkhwêli, to which the Erivan consistory was invited to send a deputy who could speak Russian, and should be versed in the doctrines of the orthodox Armenian Church. What came of this inquiry we do not know. In 1841, in consequence of fresh reports of the activity of the Paulicians of Arkhwêli in baptizing and communicating the peasants, the Erivan consistory once more petitioned the Holy Synod to set the civil power in motion. It is to the credit of the latter synod that, before taking so extreme a step, they advised the consistory to replace the incompetent orthodox priest of the village with one who could preach and had zeal and intelligence. The consistory replied that there was no priest in the diocese possessing such qualifications. It appears notwithstanding that the civil power was once more invoked; for in 1841 the military governor of Tiflis, General Praigon, ordered the local judge of Alexandrapol to decide the matter; and the latter had actually drawn up a voluminous report, when a general letter of amnesty was issued by the new Czar, April 16, 1841. In this amnesty the sectaries were included along with other offenders, and so gained a brief respite from the malice of their own countrymen.

The Holy Synod, however, did not rest until in February, 1843, it procured that the sectaries should be excluded from the benefits of the amnesty, and the judicial inquiry into their doings, after all, carried out. The result was that in 1845 the criminal court of Tiflis fined the sectaries accused forty roubles, ordered them to conform to the orthodox Armenian Church, and forbad their ministrant to call himself a deacon. The synod represented that this punishment was quite incommensurable with the heinous character of the offenders; but their representations had no effect, and they do not seem to have since resumed these petty persecutions of their own compatriots. Perhaps one should be grateful to them for having, in the course of the struggle in 1837, seized and kept safe until now the Paulician manual of which I now proceed to speak in detail.

[1] See below, pp. lxxi, lxxii.

The copy of *The Key of Truth*, now preserved in the Archives of the Holy Synod of Edjmiatzin, is a small octavo MS. on paper, written neatly in what is called *notergir* or minuscule in Taron in 1782. Many leaves are missing, about 38 out of the 150 which the book originally contained. According to the 'Acts of the Holy Synod' they were torn out by George of Arkhwêli, the owner of the book, when he found that he was detected and feared that it would be seized. The pages torn out were certainly those of which the contents were likely to give most offence. For the context shows that the lost leaves contained attacks on the abuses of the orthodox churches and doctrinal expositions, especially of the Christology of the sect. It is unfortunate that so much is lost, along with the liturgy of the mass which the copyist of 1782 also transcribed; the first half of the colophon is also lost. These lost portions, if we only had them, would have furnished decisive evidence in regard to a point which must be raised at the offset, namely this · Can this *Key of Truth* be regarded as a monument of the Paulicians of the eighth to the twelfth centuries?

That it was composed long before 1782 is evident from the colophon, in which the copyist deplores the shortcomings, the faults of spelling, composition, and grammar in the book; and declares that they have all been introduced into it by unpractised copyists. He was conscious therefore that the work, before it reached his hands in 1782, had been handed down through at least several generations. The many omissions in scripture citations plainly due to similar endings point to the same conclusion. The marginal notes in the book are written by a hand later than that which wrote the text. The citations of scripture are in nearly all cases taken from the Armenian Vulgate as it was completed soon after A.D. 400. What differences there are may be due to inaccurate copyists. The references' to the chapters and verses of Stephanus—which are added after citations, sometimes in the text, sometimes in the margin, sometimes in both at once—were already given by the scribe of 1782, at which date printed copies of the Armenian New Testament containing the chapters and verses of Stephanus had long been in circulation in Armenia. Some copyist of the *Key* between 1680 and 1780 inserted these references; perhaps by way of shortening the work of transcription, for the text is often merely referred to and not copied out in full.

Thus the colophon of 1782 at once disarms the criticism which would deny the book to be as old as the ninth century, because of the many vulgarisms of the text. These chiefly consist in a loose use of prepositions, such as would be most likely to creep in. Of the leading characteristics, however, which distinguish the modern dialects of Armenian from the old classical language there is barely any trace, as any one acquainted with them will be able to judge. Some of these characteristics, e.g. the lengthened form of verbs like *karenam* for *karem* already confront us in more popularly written books (like the Armenian version of the *Geoponica*) of the thirteenth and fourteenth centuries. *The Key of Truth* must long precede that age. The use of the accusative of the relative pronoun *zor* at the beginning of a new sentence, to connect it with what precedes, is very common in the *Key*, and is at first sight modern; yet it is frequent in Zenob, who wrote about A.D. 800 a history of Taron, the region in which Thondrak or Thonrak, a centre of the Armenian Paulicians, lay. This fact of the near geographical origin of both books also explains the considerable resemblance of style between Zenob's history and the *Key*. There are not a great many words in the *Key* foreign to classical Armenian of the fifth century; but what there are we find, with three or four exceptions, in writers of the eighth to the thirteenth centuries, particularly in Gregory of Narek in the tenth. This statement is based on a study of nearly thirty such words[1].

It has to be borne in mind that, whereas all the works of the orthodox Armenian Church of an earlier time were composed in the learned language, *The Key of Truth* is not likely to have been written in any tongue except that which was spoken among the poorer country people to whom the great Paulician leaders addressed themselves. Certainly the use of the Armenian New Testament might impart a slight classical tinge to their writings; but there was no other influence at work to produce such a result. Like the great heretical writers who founded the vernacular literatures of modern Europe, Huss, Wycliffe, Luther, the unknown translators of the Provençal Testament of Lyon, so the founders of the Paulician Church must have addressed themselves not to monks and learned men but to the common people. But if this be so, we cannot suppose *The Key of Truth* to have been written later than 850.

The prayers in it remain pure and limpid examples of the

---

[1] See the excursus at the end of the appendices, in which I enter into a more technical discussion of the style of the book.

classical speech; and it is natural that they should have most successfully resisted the vulgarizing influence of centuries of rude and untaught copyists. They seem to me to be older than the controversial chapters which accompany them, and to belong to the fourth or fifth century. He who considers in what form an English book, written in the tongue of the ninth century and transmitted almost ever since entirely by copyists who were ignorant and persecuted peasants, would have come down to the present age, has a right to pass judgement on *The Key of Truth*. The history of the sect as we read it fills us with just wonder that their book is not tenfold more corrupt and vulgarized than it is. There is constantly visible in it the hand of some eloquent and earnest writer, who knew how to pen clear, bold, nervous, freely flowing and unembarrassed paragraphs in an age when, to judge by the works of Gregory of Narek and Gregory Magistros, the Armenian Church writers were about to reach the lowest level of obscurity and affectation, of turgid pomposity and involution of phrase.

On the whole, therefore, the evidence of the style is in favour of, and not against an early date. But when we consider the contents we are obliged to refer the book to the ninth century at latest. The exordium is unmistakably from the pen of some great leader and missionary of the Paulician Church. Mark the words: 'I have not spared to give unto you, my new-born children of the universal apostolic Church of our Lord Jesus Christ, the holy milk, whereby ye may grow in the faith.' He has been inspired by the Holy Spirit to reveal 'the way, the truth, and the life' to those from whom till now the truth had been hidden by pedantry and deceit. He will with *The Key of Truth* open 'the door of truth,' long since shut upon his flock by Satan. This exordium, almost Pauline in its mixture of tenderness and authority, bespeaks some great missionary and restorer of religion in Armenia. We have also hints of the cruel persecutions and vicissitudes which had too long delayed the appearance of a manual, to the composition of which 'love of the truth of our Lord and zeal for the Holy Ghost, and the urgent entreaties of many believers had long since impelled him.' At last, in response to the entreaties of many believers, and urged by supreme necessity, he has thrown aside all other interests of this transitory life in order to compose this humble and unpretentious book, which they are nevertheless to read and ponder unto the glory of Jesus Christ their mediator.

All this presupposes a numerous body of believers looking up to one great teacher who has spent his life in ministering to them. The 'supreme necessity' must surely have been the approach of fierce persecution and perhaps of death. The reference in the context to the transitoriness of our life implies as much.

Who can this teacher have been? Gregory Magistros records[1] that the ordinances of the Paulicians, whom A.D. 1042–1054 he drove out of the district of Thonrak and Khnus, had been drawn up for them 170[2] to 200 years before by Smbat, whom Gregory of Narek[3], c. 960, also accuses of being the founder of the sect. This Smbat seems from their accounts to have made Thondrak or Thonrak the focus from which his missionary efforts radiated. That he also died in this region, or that anyhow his tomb was there, may perhaps be inferred from the words of Gregory Magistros[4].

It is at least certain that the district of Thonrak continued to be after his death the religious centre of the Paulicians, who on that account were called Thonraki or Thonraketzi by the Armenians, just as the *boni homines* of the south of France were called Albigenses, from their association with Albi. If we may take the words of Magistros to imply that Smbat left writings regulating the faith and rites of his church, what more natural than to see in *The Key of Truth* one of these writings? It is even not rash to suppose that our *Key of Truth* was actually in the hands of Gregory Magistros; since this writer ascribes to the 'accursed Smbat' the teaching that dogs and wolves appear in the form of priests, a tenet which is thoroughly in keeping with Chapter viii of the *Key*. We do not, it is true, find the exact words, but they may well have stood in the lost chapters. But after all we here are moving in a realm of surmise only, and we cannot assume as a fact, but only suggest as a hypothesis, that this Smbat was the author of *The Key of Truth*. Apart from the notices of Gregory of Narek and Gregory Magistros, we should be inclined to refer the work to Sergius, the great Paulician apostle of the ninth century, concerning whom we have many notices in the Greek writers of that and the two following centuries.

Even if Smbat's authorship be questioned, there can be no doubt that the *Key* accurately reflects the opinions and rites of the Paulicians of the four centuries, 800–1200. We may discount the falsehood and ferocity of the orthodox or persecuting writers in

---

[1] See below, p. 148: 'Smbat giving them their laws.'
[2] See pp. 142, 145.   [3] See pp. 126, 127, 129: 'their *founder* Smbat.'
[4] Cp. p. 146: 'where the leaven of the Sadducees was buried.'

their portraiture of those with whom they differed, and yet are struck by the agreement of the contents of the *Key* with the rites and beliefs of the Paulician Church as we can glean them from the writings of John of Otzun in the eighth, of Narekatzi in the tenth, of Aristaces and Paul of Taron and Magistros in the eleventh, of Nerses in the twelfth centuries. In the following summary of Paulician tenets, as they may be gathered from the pages of the *Key*, we add continual references to the works of these contemporary Armenian writers. Thus the reader can himself make a comparison, and judge how closely *The Key of Truth* corresponds with their statements.

1. The writer and the reader of the *Key* did not call themselves Paulicians, still less Thonraketzi. They were the 'holy, universal, and apostolic Church,' founded by Jesus Christ and his apostles. In describing themselves the words catholic and orthodox are sometimes, but less often, added; perhaps because they shrank from the use of titles so closely identified with their persecutors.

See the *Key*, pp. 73, 76, 80, 86, 87, and *passim*; and cp. Greg. Mag. p. 147, where we read that the Paulicians, after anathematizing the ancient sects, would say: 'We do not belong to these, for they have long ago broken connexion with the *church*,' &c. Also it is clear from pp. 141, 142 that the Paulicians of Thulail had, in their letter to the Syrian catholicos, represented themselves as belonging to the true Church. For this is the contention which Gregory so vehemently traverses. So also Greg. Mag. p. 148: 'They say, We are Christians.'

2. The Church consists of all baptized persons, and preserves the apostolical tradition which Christ revealed to the apostles and they to the Church, which has handed it on by unbroken transmission from the first.

See the *Key*, pp. 73, 74, 76, 80, 86, 87, 91, and *passim*; and cp. Greg. Narek, p. 126: 'They are not alien to the *apostolical* tradition'; and p. 127: 'Such then are your *apostolic* men.' Also the words on p. 126 hint at the Paulician claim: 'There is much that is divine and everything that is *apostolical* that is yet denied by them. Of divine ordinances, the laying on of hands, as the *apostles* received it from Christ.'

3. The sacraments are three which are requisite to salvation, to wit, Repentance, Baptism, and the Body and Blood of Christ. Marriage, ordination, confirmation, extreme unction, are not necessary to salvation.

See the *Key*, chap. iii. pp. 76, 77, and chap. xvi. pp. 86, 87; and in the Catechism, p. 119; and cp. John of Otzun, p. 154.

4. All true baptism in accordance with the precepts of Christ, especially Mark xvi. 16, must be preceded by repentance and faith.

See the *Key*, chaps. i-iii. pp. 72-77; and Catechism, p. 117.

5. Consequently infant baptism is invalid; and, in admitting it, the Latins, Greeks, and Armenians have lost their Christianity, lost the sacraments, forfeited their orders and have become a mere Satanic mimicry of the true faith. If any of them, even their patriarchs, would rejoin the true Church, they must be baptized.

See in the *Key*, *passim*, but especially pp. 73, 74, 86; chap. xviii. p. 92; and the Catechism, p. 118. And cp. Greg. Nar. pp. 126, 127: 'We know that the Font is denied by them'; and Arist. p. 140: 'They reject the Church's baptism'; and Greg. Mag. p. 146: 'Our holy bishops,' &c., and p. 147 he describes how in Thonrak alone he baptized over a thousand. 'We ask, Why do you not allow yourselves to be baptized . 'We are in no hurry to be baptized.' ... So p. 148. On p. 144 he records that Smbat reckoned as in vain 'all priestly functions,' i. e. in the orthodox churches. So also Aristaces, p. 140: 'Church and church ordinances they utterly reject.' Greg. Mag. p. 144: 'Their graceless baptism.'

5. The catechumen or candidate for baptism must be of mature age, as was Jesus of Nazareth, in order that he may be able to understand, recognize, and repent of his sin, which is twofold, viz.: original, and operative or effective.

See the *Key*, chap. ii. p. 74; chap. iii. p. 76; and particularly on p. 88, the words: 'So must we also perform baptism when they are of full age like our Lord'; and in the Catechism, p. 118. And cp. the passage of Greg. Mag. p. 146, just referred to, from which we may infer that the 'young men' of Thonrak were still unbaptized. Of similar import are the words addressed by Greg. Mag. p. 142, to the Thulaili: 'Hold yourselves far aloof from these innocent children, ... and let them come and receive baptism.'

6. Baptism is only to be performed by an elect or ordained member of the Church, and in answer to the personal demand of the person who seeks to be admitted into the Church.

See the *Key*, pp. 77, 91, 92, 96.

7. On the eighth day from birth the elect one shall solemnly confer a name on the new-born child, using a prescribed form of prayer. But he shall not allow any mythical or superstitious names.

See the *Key*, chap. xvi; and cp. the passage in John of Otzun, p. 153, beginning: Similiter et primum parientis feminae ..., in which the writer seems to glance at the ceremony of name-giving.

8. In doctrine the Paulicians were Adoptionist, and held that Jesus the Messiah was born a man, though a new man, of the Virgin Mary; and that, having fulfilled all righteousness and having come to John for baptism, he received in reward for his struggles the Lordship of all things in heaven and earth, the grace of the divine spirit, whereby he was anointed and became the Messiah, and was elected or chosen to be the eternal only-born Son, mediator of God and man, and intercessor.

See the *Key*, chap. ii. pp. 74, 75; chap. v. p. 80; the prayer to the Holy Spirit on p. 100; p. 108, the whole prayer beginning, 'King of Kings'; p. 114, and *passim*.

9. They may also be called Unitarians, in so far as they believed that Jesus Christ was not creator but created, man, made and not maker. He was never God at all, but only the new-created Adam.

See the *Key*, p. 79, and especially the Confession of Faith in chap. xx. p. 94; pp. 108, 119, and *passim*. Greg. Mag. attests this, p. 148: 'At heart they do not own him (i.e. Jesus Christ) God, whether circumcised or not.' The context implies that the Paulicians of Khnus had objected as against those who deified Jesus that a circumcised man could not be God. And it was this tenet, that Jesus was God, which the Thulaili rejected when they denied that they confessed any circumcised God. Perhaps the text of Gregory means that it was Jesus Christ, and not the position of the Paulicians of Khnus, that was rejected. I have not seen his text here.

10. Jesus was born without original sin.

See the Catechism, p. 119.

11. The Holy Ghost enters the catechumen immediately after baptism (to exclude evil spirits), when a third handful of water is, in his honour, poured out over the catechumen's head. He is also breathed into the elect one by the bishop at the close of the ordination service.

See the *Key*, pp. 100, 109, 111, 112. [The beginning words of the prayer before the Holy Spirit, 'Forasmuch as thou wast *made* by the Father,' are heretical. The MS. has եղեալ, which means 'made' or 'created.' A slightly different reading, ելեալ, would make the sense to be, 'Thou didst proceed (*or* issue) from the Father.' But եղեալ is the right reading. It is meant to contrast the Spirit with God the Father, who alone is աճեղ, or 'increate.']

12. The word Trinity is nowhere used, and was almost certainly rejected as being unscriptural. In baptism, however, three separate handfuls of water were poured over the head in the name of the Father, in the name of the Son, and in the name of the Holy Spirit. Two or three words are erased in the baptismal formula,

which would have explained more clearly the significance they attached to this proceeding, but it was clearly heretical or they would not have been erased. A 'figure' follows in the text, p. 98, shadowing forth the meaning. The king, we learn, releases certain rulers (? ἄρχοντας) from the prison of sin; the Son calls them to himself and comforts and gives them hope; and then the Holy Spirit at once crowns them and dwells in them for ever and ever. This figure is also meant to exhibit the significance of genuine baptism.

13. The Virgin Mary lost her virginity at the birth of Jesus, and is not ἀειπάρθενος, ever virgin. She was a virgin, however, till the new Adam was born. She cannot intercede for us, for Christ, our only intercessor, expressly denied blessedness to her because of her unbelief.

See the *Key*, pp. 113, 114; and cp. Greg. Mag. p. 146 : 'They indulge in many other blasphemies against the holy virgin.'

14. There is no intercession of saints, for the dead rather need the prayers of the living than the living of the dead.

See the Catechism, p. 120.

15. The idea of Purgatory is false and vain. There is but one last judgement for all, for which the quick and the dead (including saints) wait.

See the Catechism, pp. 121, 122 ; and cp. Paul of Taron, pp. 175, 176.

16. Images, pictures, holy crosses, springs, incense, candles are all to be condemned as idolatrous and unnecessary, and alien to the teaching of Christ.

See the *Key*, pp. 86, 115; and cp. Greg. Mag. p. 145 : 'We are no worshippers of matter,' &c. Also p. 149 : 'They represent our worship of God as a worship of idols ... we who honour the sign of the cross and the holy pictures.' And cp. Greg. Nar. p. 127 : 'They deny the adored sign' (i.e. the cross). Compare especially Arist. p. 137.

17. The Paulicians are not dualists in any other sense than the New Testament is itself dualistic. Satan is simply the adversary of man and God, and owing to the fall of Adam held all, even patriarchs and prophets, in his bonds before the advent of Christ.

See the *Key*, pp. 79, 114 (where it is specially declared that God created heaven and earth by a single word, and by implication is denied that Christ had any creative functions).

18. Sins must be publicly confessed before God and the Church, which consists of the faithful.

See the *Key*, p. 96 : 'What fruit of absolution hast thou? Tell it us before the congregation'; and cp. Arist. p. 134: James the Thonraki 'refused to hear auricular confessions.'

19. The elect ones alone have the power of binding and loosing given by Christ to the Apostles and by them transmitted to their universal and apostolic Church.

See the *Key*, pp. 105, 108; and cp. Arist. p. 133, on James the Paulician: 'he began by establishing *election* among priests.' And cp. also the references under No. 37 below. Greg. Mag. says, p. 149: 'Many of them spare not to lay hands on the Church, on all priestly functions.'

20. Their canon included the whole of the New Testament except perhaps the Apocalypse, which is not mentioned or cited. The newly-elected one has given to him the Gospel and Apostolicon. The Old Testament is not rejected; and although rarely cited, is nevertheless, when it is, called the God-inspired book, *Astouadsashountch*, which in Armenian answers to our phrase 'Holy Scripture' or 'Bible.'

See the *Key, passim*; and cp. Greg. Mag. p. 148 : 'They are for ever ... quoting the Gospel and the apostolon.' None of the Armenian sources accuse the Paulicians of rejecting the Old Testament in a manner in which they did not reject the New Testament.

21. In the Eucharist the bread and wine are changed into the body and blood of Jesus Christ through the blessing invoked. Yet when he said to his followers : ' My body is the true food and my blood the true drink,' and again, 'I am the bread of life which came down from heaven,' he spoke in figures. However, in the last supper, when he blessed the elements, i.e. prayed the Lord that the bread might be truly changed into his body, it was verily so changed by the Holy Spirit, and Jesus *saw* that it was so and thanked the Almighty Father for the change of it into his body and blood.

See the Catechism, p. 123.

21. The false priests (of the orthodox Churches) either deceive the simple-minded with mere bread, or—what is worse—they change the elements into their own sinful bodies when they say 'This is *my* body,' instead of changing them into Christ's.

See the Catechism, pp. 123, 124; and cp. Greg. Nar. p. 126: 'This communion bread Smbat taught to be ordinary bread.' From this we cannot infer what exactly was Smbat's error, but the words testify to the Paulician sacrament of the body and blood, however they celebrated it. Cp. also Greg. Mag. p. 148: 'Jesus in the evening meal spoke not of the offering of the Mass, but of every table.'

22. One unleavened loaf and wine are to be offered in the eucharistic sacrifice.

See the *Key*, p. 123.

23. In baptism the catechumens pass naked into the middle of the water on their knees; but beside this immersion it was necessary to pour three handfuls of water over the head.

See the *Key*, p. 97.

24. Exorcism of the catechumen is performed by the elect one before baptism.

See the *Key*, pp. 92, 97.

25. The sponsors in the infant baptism of the heretics (i.e. the orthodox) churches are at best mere false witnesses.

See the *Key*, p. 88.

26. There is but a single grade of ecclesiastical authority, and this is that of the elect one. He bears the authority to bind and loose given by the Father to Jesus in the descent of the Holy Spirit in Jordan, handed on by Jesus to the apostles and by them to their successors.

See p. 105 of the *Key*. The historian Kirakos relates (p. 114) that 'a bishop, Khosrov by name, during the catholicate of Anania Mokatzi (c. 950), taught that it is not right to submit to the archbishop, that is to the catholicos; for that he is in no wise superior (to other priests) except in his bare name and title.' The Paulician tenet of a single grade of spiritual authority underlay such teaching. Cp. Paul of Taron, p. 176.

27. But although all authority is one and the same, the elect depositary of it may have various titles; and according to the particular function he is fulfilling he is called in the *Key*, priest, elder, bishop, doctor or *vardapet*, president or *hegumenos*, apostle, and chief.

See the *Key*, p. 105. Arist. p. 138, testifies to the order of Vardapet among the Paulicians; Greg. Mag. pp. 143, 155, to their priesthood and hegumenate. Cp. especially p. 149: 'They have appropriated to themselves the language and false signs of priesthood.'

27. The word used to denote authority is *ishkhan-uthiun*. Hence it is probable that the *ishkhanq*, or rulers who choose out and present to the bishop a candidate for election, and in conjunction with the bishop lay hands on him in ordination, were themselves elect ones.

See the *Key*, chap. xxii.

27. The presbyters and arch-presbyter mentioned in the ordinal or Service of Election seem to be identical with these *ishkhanq*, or

rulers. They seem to have the same duty of testing, choosing, and presenting before the bishop the candidate for election. On p. 108 the parties present at that service are summed up thus: 'The bishop, the newly-elected one, the rulers, archrulers, and congregation.' A little before we read that the presbyters and arch-presbyters bring up the candidate to the bishop and pray him to ordain. It would seem then that the rulers and presbyters are the same people.

See the *Key*, chap. xxii. Greg. Mag. p. 149, mentions their presbyters.

28. There is no trace of Docetism in the *Key*, nor any denial of the real character of the Passion. Christ's sufferings indeed are declared to have been insupportable.

See the *Key*, p. 108. The Armenian writers do not accuse the Paulicians of Docetism.

29. The office of Reader is mentioned. In the Ordination Service he is the candidate for election.

See the *Key*, p. 106.

30. There is no rejection of the Epistles of Peter, nor is any disrespect shown to that apostle. It is merely affirmed, p. 93, that the Church does not rest on him alone, but on all the apostles, including Paul. In the Election Service, p. 107, the bishop formally confers upon the candidate the ritual name of Peter, in token of the authority to loose and bind now bestowed on him. There was a similar ritual among the Cathars of France.

See the *Key*, chap. [xxii].

31. Sacrifices of animals (to expiate the sins of the dead) are condemned as contrary to Christ's teaching.

See the *Key*, p. 115; cp. Greg. Nar. p. 127: 'I know too of their railing and cavilling at the first fruits,' &c. Also Arist. p. 134, and note.

32. New-born children have neither original nor operative sin, and do not therefore need to be baptized.

See the Catechism, p. 118.

33. A strong prejudice against monks animates the *Key*. The devil's favourite disguise is that of a monk.

See the *Key*, chaps. viii, ix; and the Catechism, p. 122; and cp. Arist· pp. 136, 137. This writer's account confirms the enmity of the orthodox monks to the Paulicians.

34. The scriptures and a knowledge of divine truth are not to remain the exclusive possession of the orthodox priests.

See the *Key*, pp. 71-73.

35. Rejection of the Logos doctrine as developed in the other Churches. There is indeed no explicit rejection of it in the *Key*, but it is ignored, and the doctrine that Jesus Christ is a κτίσμα, a man and not God, leaves no room for it in the Paulician theology.

See the *Key*, p. 114; and cp. Greg. Mag. p. 147 : 'They make no confession at all except of what is repugnant to all Christian ordinances and beliefs.'

36. For the same reason they must have rejected the term θεοτόκος.

See the Key, p. 114.

37. The elect one was an anointed one, a Christ, and the ordinal is a ritual for the election and anointing of a presbyter in the same way as Jesus was elected and anointed, namely by the Holy Spirit.

See the *Key*, p. 95, the words beginning : 'Now therefore it is necessary,' &c. Also p. 40, the passage beginning : 'And then the elect one,' &c. ; and p. 102, beginning : 'Behold them,' &c. Compare Greg. Nar. p. 127 : 'of their self-conferred contemptible priesthood, which is a likening of themselves to Satan.' We may note that in the *Key* itself the elect one is not declared to be a Christ in the same trenchant terms which Gregory of Narek uses in levelling his accusations. Greg. Mag. also testifies to their ordinations, as in the phrases on p. 144 : 'their outlandish choice (*or* election) by consent '... 'their strange and horrible and loathsome assumption of sufferings ; of their priest-making without high priest'... 'their worthless ordinations with nothing at all.'

In addition to the Armenian writers, whose testimony we have adduced, there are the Greek writers who enumerate the Paulician tenets. They all used in turn an older document, namely, the description of the Paulicians inserted in the *Codex Scorialensis*, I. Φ. 1. of the *Chronicle of Georgius Monachus*[1] by some later editor of that chronicle[2]. This document is the nucleus of the accounts of them given by Photius (c. 820–c. 891), *Contra Manicheos*, liber i. §§ 1–10, and by Petrus Siculus, a contemporary of Photius. It was then used by Petrus Hegumenos, by Zigabenus (c. 1081–1118), by Pseudo-Photius, liber i. 10–iv. Each of these writers, no matter what his pretensions to originality, embodies this document in his account of the Paulicians, and adds to it details from other sources. Among these additions the citations of the Epistles of Sergius interest us most for our present

---

[1] To this source I allude as *Scor*.

[2] This document has been edited with commentary by J. Friedrich in the *Sitzungsberichte der Philos.-Philol. Classe der k. b. Akademie der Wissenschaften zu München*, 1896, Heft i, under the title : 'Der ursprungliche bei Georgios Monachos nur theilweise erhaltene Bericht über die Paulikianer.' I cannot exaggerate my indebtedness to the editor of it.

purpose, which is to adduce from them *testimonia* to these thirty-seven tenets or principles of practice of the Paulician Church. I shall also add some testimonies from Genesios' chronicle, and from Gregory of Asbesta in Sicily in his life of the Patriarch Methodius. For both these writers describe a sect of Selikiani in Constantinople, under the Empress Theodora, which was clearly Paulician. John of Damascus also contributes a few particulars to our knowledge of the Paulician Church.

1. *Scor.* xi : καὶ καθολικὴν ἐκκλησίαν τὰ ἑαυτῶν συνέδρια.

4. *Scor.* xiv : ὁμοίως μὲν καὶ τοὺς πρεσβυτέρους καὶ λοιποὺς ἱερεῖς τοὺς παρ' ἡμῖν ἀποβάλλονται. Because they were not really baptized. So also *Scor.* vi : καλοῦσι δὲ ἑαυτοὺς μὲν Χριστιανούς, ἡμᾶς δὲ Ῥωμαίους. So Phot. 24 B. The reason is hinted at by Photius, 29 A: οὐ μὴν ἀλλὰ καὶ τὸ σωτήριον διαπτύοντες βάπτισμα, ὑποπλάττονται παραδέχεσθαι αὐτό, τὰ τοῦ εὐαγγελίου ῥήματα τῇ τοῦ βαπτίσματος φωνῇ ὑποβάλλοντες. Καὶ γάρ φασιν· Ὁ κύριος ἔφη· Ἐγώ εἰμι τὸ ὕδωρ τὸ ζῶν. Anna Comn. Alexias, xiv. 8, 9 (ii. 299, ed. Bonn), relates that many of the Paulicians of Philippopolis were baptized (τοῦ θείου μετέσχον βαπτίσματος) in consequence of the joint crusade of arms and arguments directed against them by the emperor Alexius, c. 1116. The true significance also of the libellous anecdote told by orthodox writers, especially John of Damascus, of Constantine Copronymus, is revealed through the *Key*. The story was that, when as an infant he was baptized, he fouled with his excrement the water of the font. In other words, he was, as a Paulician, opposed to paedo-baptism.

8. *Scor.* xx. p. 76 : πρόσθες πάλιν· καὶ τίς ἦν ὁ κατελθὼν πρὸ τοῦ κατελθεῖν, ἄγγελος ἤ τι ἕτερον καὶ πῶς τὴν τοῦ υἱοῦ ἔλαβε κλῆσιν; καὶ τὰ λοιπά, ἅπερ ἀνωτέρω γέγραπται, ἤγουν τὸ προσκληθῆναι αὐτὸν παρὰ τοῦ θεοῦ, τῷ τὴν ἐντολὴν δέξασθαι καὶ τἆλλα. Καὶ ὁμολογήσει, ὡς ἄγγελος ἦν καὶ διηκόνησε τῇ ἐντολῇ τοῦ θεοῦ καὶ κατὰ χάριν τὴν τοῦ υἱοῦ κλῆσιν καὶ τὴν τοῦ Χριστοῦ εἴληφε. . . . . . Τί δέ, ὦ Μανιχαῖε. ἐπειδή σοι ἐξ ἀγγελῶν ὁ υἱὸς γεγένηται καὶ τῶν ἀνθρώπων αὐτῶν μεταγενέστερος ἐπὶ τοῦ Ὀκταβίου Καίσαρος εἰληφὼς ὡς φῂς τὴν υἱότητα.

9. *Scor.* xx. p. 76 : καὶ οὐ μόνον κτίσμα τοῦτον ἐπικαλεῖς κατὰ τὸν ματαιόφρονα Ἄρειον. So the Paulician Selix or Lizix, secretary of the empress Theodora, called Jesus Christ a creature : καὶ θεὸν ἡμῶν Ἰησοῦν Χριστὸν ὀνομάζων κτίσμα, according to Genesios[1]. So Pet. Sic. (sermo ii. adv. Manich. 71, 1338 D) : εἰ δὲ μὴ τὸν υἱὸν

---

[1] Migne, *Patr. Gr.* 140, 284, in Nicetas Chron., who cites a life of Methodius, patriarch of C. P., by Gregory, archbishop of Sicily.

αὐτῆς (Μαρίας) ἀληθῆ θεὸν ὁμολογεῖτε, πῶς τὴν τῆς σαρκώσεως αὐτοῦ μητέρα τιμήσοιτε;

12. *Scor.* vi: λέγουσι δὲ πρὸς τοὺς ἀγνοοῦντας αὐτοὺς προθύμως· πιστεύομεν εἰς πατέρα καὶ υἱὸν καὶ ἅγιον πνεῦμα, τὸν ἐπουράνιον πατέρα. So Phot. (24 B).

13. *Scor.* xxi: τὰς δὲ εἰς τὴν ἀεὶ παρθένον καὶ κυρίως καὶ ἀληθῶς θεοτόκον Μαρίαν βλασφημίας ὑμῶν ... οὐδὲ ἡ γλῶσσα ἡμῶν ἐκφῆναι δύναται ... ἐπιτιθέναι ἀπὸ τοῦ ἐν τῷ εὐαγγελίῳ[1] ῥητοῦ τοῦ φάσκοντος· ἀπηγγέλη τῷ Ἰησοῦ· ἡ μήτηρ σου καὶ οἱ ἀδελφοὶ [σου] ἑστήκασιν κ.τ.λ. ... λέγοντες, εἰ διὰ φροντίδος ταύτην ἐτίθει, προσυπήντησεν ἂν αὐτῇ ... καὶ ὅτι ἐφρόντιζε (sc. Jesus) ταύτης (sc. Mariam) δείκνυσι πάλιν τὸ εὐαγγέλιον. So Phot. (25 A), who adds the following tenet: τὴν ἄσπιλον καὶ καθαρὰν παρθένον μετὰ τὸν σωτήριον τόκον ἑτέρους υἱοὺς ἐκ τοῦ Ἰωσὴφ παιδοποιῆσαι. So Gregory of Sicily[2] says of Lizix: τὴν πάναγνον .. μητέρα θεοτόκον οὐκ ἔλεγε.

14. *Scor.* x: τοὺς προφήτας καὶ τοὺς λοιποὺς ἁγίους ἀποβάλλονται, ἐξ αὐτῶν μηδένα τινὰ ἐν μέρει τῶν σωζομένων εἶναι λέγοντες. So Photius (68 A) records that the Paulician woman who converted Sergius warned him that the 'sons of the kingdom to be cast out into outer darkness' (Matt. viii. 12) are no other than the saints: οὓς σύ τε καὶ οἱ κατά σε ἁγίους καλοῦσι καὶ νομίζουσι ... οἷς καὶ προσάγειν διεγνώκατε σέβας, τὸν μόνον ζῶντα καὶ ἀθάνατον καταλιπόντες θεόν. According to Joan. Damasc. *adv.* Constant. Cabalinum[3], Copronymus, who was almost openly a Paulician, denied that the Virgin can help us after death (μετὰ θάνατον αὐτὴν βοηθεῖν μὴ δυναμένην), or that the apostles and martyrs could intercede for us (πρεσβείαν μὴ κεκτημένους, μόνους ἑαυτοὺς ὠφελήσαντας διὰ τὰ πάθη, ἅπερ ὑπέστησαν, καὶ τὰς ἑαυτῶν ψυχὰς ἐκ τῆς κολάσεως διασώσαντας· ἐπεὶ τοὺς προσκαλουμένους αὐτοὺς ἢ προστρέχοντας, μηδὲν ὠφελοῦντας).

16. *Scor.* ix: βλασφημοῦσι δὲ καὶ εἰς τὸν τίμιον σταυρόν, λέγοντες, ὅτι σταυρὸς ὁ Χριστός ἐστιν· οὐ χρὴ δὲ προσκυνεῖσθαι τὸ ξύλον ὡς κατηραμένον ὄργανον. So Phot. (25 C) who adds, as the reason given by Paulicians why Christ is the Cross, the following: καὶ γὰρ αὐτός, φασίν, εἰς σταυροῦ σχῆμα τὰς χεῖρας ἐξήπλωσε. Photius also (32 A) remarks that the Paulicians were ready to kiss the Evangel, but avoided kissing that part of the cover, ἔνθα τοῦ τιμίου σταυροῦ ὁ τύπος διακεχάρακται, ἀλλ' ἐν τῷ λοιπῷ τοῦ βιβλίου μέρει, ἐν ᾧ τὸ ἀπεικόνισμα τοῦ σταυροῦ μὴ διασημαίνεται. Pet. Sic. bears similar testimony, ch. vii: οἱ τὴν δόξαν αὐτοῦ (τοῦ σταυροῦ) διαρνούμενοι καὶ μὴ προσ-

---

[1] Luke viii. 20, 21.   [2] See note on No. 9.
[3] Migne, *Patr. Gr.* 95, 337.

κυνοῦντες αὐτὸν ἀδιστάκτῳ πίστει. And Greg. of Sicily[1] of Lizix · τὸν προσκυνητὸν σταυρὸν μωρίαν ἡγεῖτο.

17. See on No. 14.

20. *Scor.* xv: ἔχουσι δὲ πάντα τὰ τοῦ εὐαγγελίου καὶ τοῦ ἀποστόλου ῥητὰ διάστροφα (? ἀδιάστροφα). So in xxi the writer appeals to the canonical New Testament as recognized by the Paulicians: ἀπὸ γὰρ τοῦ εὐαγγελίου καὶ τοῦ ἀποστόλου ὑμῖν προσδιαλέγομαι, τὰς ἄλλας μὴ παραδεχόμενος γραφάς, that is the four gospels and epistles. So in ii we have express testimony that Constantine Silvanus, though he did not embody his heresies in writing for his converts, yet gave them τὸ εὐαγγέλιον καὶ τὸν ἀπόστολον ἐγγράφως, ἀπαράλλακτα μὲν τῇ γραφῇ καὶ τοῖς λόγοις ὡς καὶ τὰ παρ' ἡμῖν ὄντα παραδούς ... νομοθετήσας αὐτοῖς καὶ τοῦτο· μὴ δεῖν ἑτέραν βίβλον τὴν οἱανοῦν ἀναγινώσκειν, εἰ μὴ τὸ εὐαγγέλιον καὶ τὸν ἀπόστολον.

Photius (28 C) alleges that they received all the New Testament except the Epistles of Peter: οἳ αὐτά τε τὰ κυριακὰ λόγια καὶ τὰ ἀποστολικὰ καὶ τὰς ἄλλας γραφάς, φημὶ δὴ τάς τε πράξεις τῶν ἀποστόλων καὶ τὰς καθολικὰς λεγομένας, πλὴν τῶν ἀναφερομένων εἰς τὸν κορυφαῖον· ἐκείνας γὰρ οὐδὲ τοῖς ῥήμασι παραδέχονται. Pet. Sic. (p. 14) and Photius (28 A) allege that they rejected the Old Testament and the Prophets. Pet. Sic. testifies to their reliance in argument on the New Testament: ξένα τινα καὶ ἀλλόκοτα ἐπιφημίζοντας προβλήματα, ὡς δῆθεν τοῖς τοῦ ἱεροῦ εὐαγγελίου καὶ τοῦ ἀποστόλου λόγοις ἐπερειδόμενοι.

21. Photius (29 B) admits that the Paulicians recognized the Eucharistic Sacrament, and received it, but only to deceive the simple-minded. Ναὶ δὴ καὶ τῆς κοινωνίας εἰσὶν αὐτῶν οὐκ ὀλίγοι τοῦ τιμίου σώματος καὶ αἵματος Χριστοῦ τοῦ Θεοῦ ἡμῶν. Ἀλλὰ τοῦτο πρὸς ἐξαπάτην τῶν ἁπλουστέρων μεταλαμβάνουσιν. Gregory of Sicily[1] indicates that they contemned the eucharist of the orthodox, for Lizix ἐγέλα ... τὴν τῶν φρικτῶν καὶ θείων μυστηρίων μετάληψιν.

30. *Scor.* x: ἔτι δὲ καὶ τὸν ἅγιον Πέτρον, τὸν μέγαν πρωταπόστολον, πλέον πάντων καὶ δυσφημοῦσι καὶ ἀποστρέφονται, ἀρνητὴν ἀποκαλοῦντες αὐτόν. Καὶ τὴν μετάνοιαν καὶ τὰ πικρὰ αὐτοῦ δάκρυα οὐ προσδέχονται οἱ Παμμίαροι. And see on No. 20 with regard to their rejection (alleged by Photius) of Peter's epistles.

33. *Scor.* x: καὶ διδάσκουσιν οἱ ὄντως ἐσκοτισμένοι παρὰ τοῦ διαβόλου ὑποδειχθῆναι τὸ παρὰ τοῦ θεοῦ δι' ἀγγέλου τοῖς ἀνθρώποις ὑποδειχθὲν καὶ δοθὲν ἅγιον σχῆμα, ὅπερ οἱ μοναχοὶ ἐνδεδύμεθα.

34. Photius (64 D) relates how Sergius was converted by a Paulician woman. She asked him: 'Why do you not read the divine

[1] See note on No. 9.

Gospels?' He replied that only the priests and not the laity might do so. Her answer was that God respects not persons, but desires that all be saved and brought to a knowledge of the truth; that it was a μηχανὴ καὶ σόφισμα τῶν λεγομένων ἱερέων, who desired to traffic in the word of God and deprive the people of their share in the mysteries contained in the Gospels. This is why they prevented the people from reading them. The teaching of the *Key* is, however, less explicit on this point than this passage of Photius would lead us to expect.

This detailed agreement of *The Key of Truth*, on the one hand with the Armenian writers of the tenth and eleventh centuries, and on the other hand with the Greek notices of an earlier date, is proof enough that in it we have recovered an early and authoritative exposition of Paulician tenets. And it is remarkable that the Escurial fragment which is the earliest form of the common document used by the Greek writers is also in the closest accord with the *Key*. For it alone records that the Paulicians regarded Jesus Christ not as God, but as a κτίσμα or mere creature of God; it alone, that they taught that Jesus was chosen Son of God and Christ κατὰ χάριν, in reward for his complete fulfilment of the divine command. On this point J. Friedrich, the editor of this fragment, has justly written as follows: '. . der Auszug des Petros Hegumenos und der gedruckten Chronik des Georgios Monachos sowie die Ueberarbeitung derselben, welcher unter dem Namen des Photius geht, diesen Punkt ganz unerwähnt lassen, so dass es scheinen konnte, die Paulikianer lehrten über Christus, seine irdische Geburt ausgenommen, ganz orthodox.'

Nevertheless, there are ascribed to the Paulicians in both sets of sources opinions of which we find little or no hint in the *Key*. First among these is a Manichean dualism according to which the visible universe was created by the devil.

Now firstly the *Key*, p. 48, asserts just the contrary. In it Satan is indeed frequently alluded to as the adversary of God himself, and the latter is usually characterized as the heavenly God or God in heaven. But there is no indication that the Paulicians went beyond the well-marked dualism of the New Testament itself, according to which (John xii. 31 and xiv. 30) Satan is the ruler of this world, or even, as Paul expressed it (2 Cor. iv. 4), the God of this world. The morbid anxiety of Augustine[1] and of the

---

[1] It was pretended that St. Paul's meaning was as follows: 'God has blinded the minds of the faithless of this age' by Origen, Eusebius, Athanasius, Augustine, Jerome, and in fact by nearly all the orthodox fathers.

fathers both before and after him to discount the force of these texts in their confutations of Marcion and of the Manicheans, raises the suspicion that the latter merely rested their dualism upon St. Paul and the fourth Gospel. In their confutations of heretics the orthodox fathers were not too scrupulous of the truth. They all carried in their bag two weights, a heavier and a lighter, and in their dealings with so-called heretics used the latter.

Secondly, Photius and other Greek writers, as well as Gregory Magistros, attest that the Paulicians rejected and anathematized Manes : Μάνεντα μὲν καὶ Παῦλον καὶ Ἰωάννην (two Armenian disciples of Manes), καὶ τοὺς ἄλλους προθύμως ἀναθεματίζουσιν. It is evident therefore that the name 'New Manicheans,' given by the orthodox Greek and Armenian writers to the Paulicians, was (as J. Friedrich charitably puts it) a bit of schematism. Manichean was in those ages a general term of abuse for all schismatics alike; and was applied by Photius and his contemporaries no less to the Latins (because they affirmed the double procession of the Holy Ghost) than to the Paulicians.

With like perfidy the theologians of the fifth century, Augustine (Epist. 165) and Pope Leo the Great (Epist. 15), had already striven to blacken the Priscillianists by identifying them with the Manicheans; and their identification was accepted almost till yesterday, when a lucky chance led to the discovery by G. Schepss of some authentic writings of Priscillian himself, in which we read as follows[1]: 'Anathema sit qui Manetem et opera eius doctrinas adque instituta non damnat; cuius peculiariter turpitudines persequentes gladio, si fieri posset, ad inferos mitteremus ac si quid est deterius gehennae tormentoque peruigili.' The tone of this fanatical Spaniard's reference to Manes forbids us indeed to lament the fate which befel him, yet in no way acquits Augustine and Leo of the charge of bearing false witness.

We should therefore attach no weight to the charge against the Paulicians, that they ascribed to Satan the creation of the visible world. It probably arose out of their rejection of the orthodox doctrine according to which Christ the eternal Word of God created all things. In the Escurial fragment published by J. Friedrich, § vi, this is almost implied, for we read in it of the Paulicians as follows : λέγουσι δὲ πρὸς τοὺς ἀγνοοῦντας αὐτοὺς προθύμως· πιστεύομεν εἰς πατέρα καὶ υἱὸν καὶ ἅγιον πνεῦμα, τὸν ἐπουράνιον πατέρα, καὶ ἀνάθεμα φησὶ τῷ μὴ οὕτως πιστεύοντι, μεμελετημένως λίαν τὴν ἑαυτῶν

---

[1] *Priscilliani* op. edit. Georg. Schepss, Vindob, 1889, p. 22. 13.

κακίαν μεθυδεύοντες· οὐ γὰρ προστιθέασι, ὅτε λέγουσι τὸν πατέρα τὸν ἐπουράνιον, ὅτι τὸν μόνον ἀληθινὸν θεὸν τὸν ποιήσαντα τὸν οὐρανὸν καὶ τὴν γῆν καὶ πάντα τὰ ἐν αὐτοῖς· χρὴ δὲ τὸν προσδιαλεγόμενον ὀρθόδοξον αἰτεῖν τὸν Μανιχαῖον τοῦ εἰπεῖν τὴν ἀρχὴν τοῦ συμβόλου τῆς ἀμωμήτου ἡμῶν πίστεως καὶ τὸ δι' οὗ τὰ πάντα, ὅπερ λέγειν ὅλως οὐ δύνανται· ἀνατιθέασι γὰρ οἱ ματαιόφρονες τὴν κτίσιν παντὸς τοῦ ὁρατοῦ κόσμου τούτου ἤγουν τῷ διαβόλῳ. τὸν δὲ θεόν φησιν ἐν τοῖς οὐρανοῖς εἶναι. Here the words in heavier type are from John i. 3, and suggest that the Paulician answer really was this, that God the Father, and not the Word of God, made heaven and earth and all things in them. Such an answer those who deified Jesus and substituted for the formula 'the Son of God' the formula 'God the Son,' would naturally pervert into this: that the devil made all things. At the same time the Paulicians, being averse to the falsification of scripture, must, like the church of an earlier age, have accepted in their plain and obvious sense such texts as John xii. 31 and xiv. 30, and 2 Cor. iv. 4. And the evil treatment they underwent fully justified them in their belief that Satan was responsible for the existing order of things, in particular for the administration of the Roman Empire.

It was also alleged that the Paulicians denied Christ to have taken flesh of the Virgin (ἐξ αὐτῆς σαρκωθῆναι τὸν κύριον); and Photius (25 B) adds that they held him to have passed through her body into the world as through a conduit-pipe (ὡς διὰ σωλῆνος διεληλυθέναι). It is possible that if we had in its entirety the chapter of the *Key* 'On the Creation of Adam and of our Lord,' we should find that it did teach this very ancient tenet; for it is one which in no way conflicts with the belief that Christ was κτίσμα θεοῦ and not θεός, and which coheres closely with the teaching that Jesus Christ was the new Adam. The survival of this tenet among the Anabaptists of a later age (who seem to have been the Paulician Church transferred to Western Europe) also makes it very probable that Paulicians may have held it. But here we are in the realm of mere surmise, for we do not find the idea in so much as survives to us of *The Key of Truth*. We recur to the point below (p. clxxxvii).

Another tenet ascribed to the Paulicians was this, that the Virgin Mary was an allegory of the 'heavenly Jerusalem, into which Christ has entered as our precursor and in our behalf[1].' Such teaching was not heretical; and that the Paulicians did not substitute this allegory for the actual belief that Jesus was born of the Virgin is

---

[1] *Scor.* vii : τὴν ἄνω Ἱερουσαλὴμ ἐν ᾗ πρόδρομος ὑπὲρ ἡμῶν εἰσῆλθε Χριστός.

certain. The *Key* attests that they held the belief, and Photius and Petrus Siculus allege as much. That they also indulged in this colourless bit of allegory is likely enough. For we find it among the orthodox Armenians of the region of Mananali, into whose hymn Aristaces[1], their eulogist, introduces it. We also meet with it in Adamantius (dial. C. Marc.) and other orthodox writings, as well as among the Manicheans and Albigenses.

In § viii of *Scor.* we read that the Paulicians blasphemed the divine mysteries of the holy communion of the body and blood, and declared that the Lord meaned not that they were to consume bread and wine when he said: 'Take ye, eat and drink,' to his apostles, but only gave them his words, ῥήματα. It accords with the closing words of the Catechism in the *Key* to suppose that they did attach such a figurative or mystical value as is here implied to the eucharistic meal; and that is all that *Scor.* § viii implies. It does not allege that they discarded the actual meal of bread and wine. The only sacraments against which they really blasphemed were those of the Greeks, Latins, and Armenians, for these were from their standpoint no sacraments at all, but only profane mummery.

And here we have the explanation of such statements as that of Aristaces[2], that the Paulicians utterly rejected church and church ordinances, baptism, the mass, the cross, and fasts. They necessarily rejected the ordinances of churches which, having wilfully corrupted the institution of baptism in its evangelical, primitive, and only genuine form, as they regarded it, had also lost their orders and sacraments and apostolical tradition. But they themselves, in repudiating the innovation of infant baptism, had kept all these things, and so formed the only true Church, and were the only real Christians left in the world. This is the significance of such utterances as this of Aristaces. Failure to comprehend it was natural enough in the absence of the fuller knowledge of Paulician tenets which the *Key* affords us. Such utterances, however, have led inquirers, e.g. the Archdeacon Karapet Ter Mkrttschian[3], to suppose that the Paulicians really discarded baptism, sacraments, and sacerdotal system; and that, 'following Marcion's example, they set up a purely spiritual church.' There is, as J. Friedrich rightly observes, no ground for saying that Marcion aimed at a spiritual church in this sense of detachment from outward ceremonies and observances.

---

[1] See p. 139.   [2] See p. 140.
[3] *Die Paulikianer*, Leipzig, 1893, p. 109.

But the Archdeacon Karapet is certainly right when, in the same context, he observes, a little inconsistently, that the Paulicians were not and did not claim to be reformers of the Greek church: 'Wahrlich, wundersam wäre es, wenn in einigen ein paar hundert Meilen von Byzantinien entfernten Gebirgsdörfern am Euphrat der Gedanke auftauchen sollte, die griechische Kirche zu reformieren.' The idea of a church without priests and sacraments, of a mysticism wherein the individual soul communes direct with God without such supports, was assuredly alien to the dark ages in which the Paulicians flourished, and was barely possible in any age before our own. Like most other heresies that in old times ramified far and wide, that of the Paulicians arose out of religious conservatism. They were 'old believers': not innovators, but enemies of Catholic innovations, of infant baptism, of the fourth century Christology, of all the circle of ideas summed up in the words ὁμοούσιος, θεοτόκος and ἀειπάρθενος, of images and pictures, of intercession of saints, of purgatory, of papal pretensions, of nearly everything later than Tertullian's age. They did not desire new things, but only to keep what they had got; and that, as we shall point out later on, was peculiarly primitive. They did not sit loose to priests and sacraments. If they erred at all, it was by making too much of them.

It is an irreparable loss that the sacramentary which the copyist of the *Key* of the year 1782 transcribed along with it has not been preserved; and we can only hope that the same tenacity of the Armenian race which has kept alive this ancient Church down into our own generation may yet be accountable for its being found. It might prove to be the most ancient in form of all the Christian liturgies. The catechism with which the *Key* concludes is later than the first twenty-two chapters[1], but the information it gives about the Paulician Eucharist doubtless represents the teaching of the Church. The acts of the inquisition of 1837-1845 also in some slight measure help to fill up the gap; for they contain the following description of their eucharist. It was sent on May 23, 1841, to the consistory of Erivan by the orthodox priest of Arkhwêli:—

'The villagers of Arkhwêli, before they were corrected, baptized and communicated one another according to the direction of

---

[1] Cp. p. l. From the statements of the Paulicians, from whom the book was seized, it is clear that the *Key* itself only comprises the first twenty-two chapters of the book.

The Key of Truth, their heretical book, after the erroneous manner of the Thonraki. These wicked practices were twice committed by them at that time under cover of darkness; once in the stable of the choir-singer (*or* church-assistant) Tônô Kirakosean, and on the other occasion in the inner chamber of Souwar Hovhannesean, in the following fashion. They meet and get ready water in a vessel, and upon a common table of wood they lay a single unleavened common loaf of small size, baked in an oven, and in a common vessel wine without water. Over the loaf they say: "Take ye, eat. This is the body of our Lord Jesus Christ." Over the wine they say: "This is the blood of our Lord Jesus Christ." The person to be baptized comes bare-headed before the baptist without stripping off of raiment[1]; then the baptist took and poured a handful of water over the head of the person to be baptized. At the first time of so pouring it he says, "In the name of the Father"; at the second, "and of the Son"; at the third, "and of the Holy Spirit. Amen." After that the person baptized first receives in his hands a portion of the bread, and eats it, and then drinks a little of the wine, and goes away.'

These depositions, which are signed by various of the persons concerned, also give the names and ages of four persons who were thus baptized or communicated in an heretical way. Souwar Hovhannesean was eighty years of age; his wife Mary was sixty; Aslan Hovhannesean was eighty; and Martoj Hovhannesean was eighty-five, since dead. These four persons had been baptized in the manner described thirty years before (therefore they were now only communicated) by the false priest (*lit.* 'lord) Hovhannes[2], a follower of the Thonraki cult, who subsequently became a Mohammedan.

The choir-singer Tônô Kirakosean, now fifty years of age, had been baptized in the time of the same priest (i. e. Hovhannes) by Meser Putalean, a disciple of the false priest.

Then follow the names of six persons, who were only baptized and not communicated, in Tônô Kirakosean's stable; their ages were respectively forty, forty-five, thirty-five, thirty, fifty, fifty. On the second occasion, in the chamber of Souwar Hovhannesean,

---

[1] This was a concession to the age and climate; for the *Key*, p. 97, prescribes that they shall be stripped after the primitive Christian manner.

[2] This person was the copyist of *The Key of Truth* in 1782. See below, p. lxxii. The book actually consists of twenty-two chapters, but the numeration only extends as far as chap. xxi. Hence the statement that it was written in twenty-one chapters. The Catechism was not regarded as part of the *Key*.

five persons were baptized in the manner described by Souwar, who had been baptized by the choir-singer, George Sargsean. I need not trouble the reader with their names, but their respective ages were forty-five, forty, thirty, thirty, thirty-five years. These depositions conclude with the notice that 'all these heretical proceedings were written in twenty-one chapters in the book called *The Key of Truth*,' which at first the offenders said they had torn up and burned, though, after repenting, they admitted they had not done so.

The copy of *The Key of Truth* here printed is the particular one here referred to, and we are therefore entitled to fill up its lacunae from these depositions, and from the confessions given above. As to the Eucharist we learn that it was celebrated after nightfall. This may have been only to protect themselves, but it is more probable that it was in strict following of the account preserved in the Gospels of the institution of the Eucharist, according to which it was a supper or evening meal, and not a morning celebration. The only communicants were four persons baptized thirty years before, and now averaging in age over seventy-six years each; and the youngest of them, a woman of sixty, was the wife of a man of eighty. Tônô Kirakosean, although a man of fifty, and baptized some twenty years before, did not communicate. We are tempted to infer that the participation in the eucharistic meal was, like the *hereticatio* of the Albigeois, deferred to extreme old age; but the indications are too slight to build so much upon, nor was the *hereticatio* the same thing as the Eucharist. We can, however, infer something about the age at which baptism was conferred. Its recipients ranged from thirty to fifty years. Making allowance for the fact that in Arkhwêli and Giumri (Alexandrapol) the new sect had only been disseminated since about the year 1828, and that these may have been for the most part new converts; still it would appear that baptism was deferred, as in the orthodox Church of the third and fourth century, until the catechumens were of a very mature age indeed; in no case less than thirty years.

The archives of the consistory of Erivan record two other cases of open-air baptism in a stream at mid-day in the neighbourhood of Alexandrapol. In the second of these cases a priest named Sahak was baptizing two men whose ages are not given, when a young man of twenty-three, named Sargis Harouthiun (who afterwards joined the sect), startled him by suddenly appearing on the scene. The priest instantly invited him also to be baptized in these words:

'Come and be justified by this baptism, that you may not die in your sins.'

We next must attempt to solve a difficult and delicate problem, this namely: What significance did the Paulicians really attach to their orders, and to election, as they termed their form of ordination? Gregory of Narek brings against them the charge of anthropolatry. Their founder Smbat, he says, claimed to be Christ; and he relates with zest the ribald story of the khalif who, in putting him to death, offered to believe that he was Christ if he would rise again, not after three, but after thirty days. Our earliest Greek document, *Scor.*, brings indeed no similar charge against the Paulicians, but we meet with it in Photius and Petrus Siculus. Photius, for example (*Contra Manichaeos*, i. § 21), alleges that Sergius, the great Paulician leader of the first half of the ninth century, taught that he himself, and such of his followers as were fully initiated in the mysteries, and were no longer merely *auditores* (ἀκροαταί), were themselves the Holy Spirit. This may, of course, be no more than the commentary of malice on the rite of election as given in the *Key*. But both Photius and Petrus Siculus preserve the following passage from an epistle of Sergius: 'Let no one deceive you in any way; but having these promises from God, be of good cheer. For we, being persuaded in our hearts, have written unto you, that I am the porter and the good shepherd and the leader of the body of Christ, and the light of the house of God, and I am with you always, even unto the end of the world. For even if I am away from you in the body, yet I am with you in spirit. For the rest fare ye well; perfect yourselves, and the God of peace shall be with you.' To the same congregation in Colonia in Armenia, to which the above words were addressed, he writes also as follows, according to Petrus Siculus (*Col.* 41, 1296 A): 'Knowing beforehand the tried quality (τὸ δοκίμιον) of your faith, we remind you how that, as the churches that were aforetime received shepherds and teachers (and he signifies Constantine and the others), so also ye have received a shining lamp and a beaming star and a guide to salvation, according to the Scripture: "that if thine eye be single, thy whole body shall be full of light [1]."'

These passages from the epistles of Sergius are strikingly similar to the exordium of *The Key of Truth*. A common *ethos* connects them; such as would, except for the absence of corroborative evidence, entitle us to suppose that the same hand wrote the one

---

[1] Matt. vi. 22.

and the other. The author of the *Key*, like the writer of these epistles, has caught the tone of St. Paul. There is the same assurance of being the vehicle of the Holy Spirit, of being a missionary inspired and sent by God to teach the way, the truth, and the life. It is to be regretted that our fragments of Sergius' epistles are so few and short; they contain, however, one magnificent utterance, worthy of a Paul or of a Wesley: 'I have run from east to west, and from north to south, preaching the gospel of Christ until my knees were weary[1].' And also the following, to Leo a Montanist, which likewise has about it the ring of St. Paul: 'But do thou beware of thyself. Cease to rend asunder the true faith. For what charge canst thou bring against us? Have I despoiled any one, or been overweening? Thou canst not allege it. But if thou dost, Thy witness is not true. Yet be it not mine to hate thee, but only to exhort thee, as thou hast received apostles and prophets, who are four in number, so receive (our) shepherds and teachers, lest thou become the prey of wild beasts.' Truly if this great teacher had faults, they were those of a St. Paul.

There is a certain self-exaltation in these citations of Sergius, of which we have not the setting and context; yet not such as to warrant the charge of anthropolatry brought by Greg. Nar. and by the Greek writers. In the third of the recantations however, made in 1837, there is a curious passage. Gregory (one of the elect of the Thonraki) said: 'Lo, I am the cross: on my two hands light tapers, and give me adoration. For I am able to give you salvation, as much as the cross and the saints[2].' This singular utterance must mean that in some ceremony the elect one or priest spread out his hands, like Jesus on the cross; and received the adoration of the faithful, who lit their tapers on either hand. Here we begin to see why the Paulicians repudiated crosses of lifeless stone, and even broke them up when they could. They had living crosses of their own, elect ones who were baptized with the baptism of Christ, crucified on his cross, dead, and buried with him, rising again with him, called with his calling, reasonable images of God into whom Christ's Spirit had been breathed, in whom he abode as they in him. It need not surprise us that they rejected the stocks and stones into which the Armenians of those ages (as of this) believed that the spirit and virtue of Christ could be magically introduced by the priest, just as a Brahman may be seen by any Indian roadside

---

[1] *Pet. Sic.* § 36, 1293 B. Also in Photius.   [2] See above, p. xxvii.

putting the god into little clay images brought to him by the faithful, and made hollow on purpose. Surely it was a noble idea to restrict possession by the Holy Spirit to living images, and not extend it to stocks and stones.

Such is the circle of ideas into which I believe we here enter, and perhaps we have a further trace of it at the end of the catechism which follows the *Key*. There we read that the false priests, when they took the elements and said, 'This is my body and blood,' turned them not into the body and blood of Christ, but into their own sinful body and blood.

How are we to interpret this enigmatical statement, twice repeated? Not otherwise, I think, than by supposing that the elect priest was himself, through community of suffering[1], and as possessed by the same Holy Spirit, in a mystical manner one with Christ; so that when he took the elements and said: 'These are *my* body and blood,' they were by the Spirit of the heavenly Father changed into Christ's body, because *his* body was also Christ's. On the other hand the false priest, not being of the body of Christ, by the use of the formula 'This is my body,' only converted the elements into his own sinful body, and not into Christ's. The underlying supposition must certainly be this, that every elect one was Christ; and it is quite in harmony with this that in the *Key* the apostles and evangelists are spoken of as *parts* or members of the Church. From Petrus Siculus[2] we learn that the Paulician Church was the body of Christ. The words in which Sergius warns his flock of the dreadful nature of apostasy are these: ὁ πορνεύων εἰς τὸ ἴδιον σῶμα ἁμαρτάνει. Ἡμεῖς ἐσμεν σῶμα Χριστοῦ· εἴ τις ἀφίσταται τῶν παραδόσεων τοῦ σώματος τοῦ Χριστοῦ, τουτέστι τῶν ἐμῶν, ἁμαρτάνει· ὅτι προστρέχει τοῖς ἑτεροδιδασκαλοῦσι, καὶ ἀπειθεῖ τοῖς ὑγιαίνουσι λόγοις. Here ἡμεῖς means '*we*, the elect.'

A difficulty remains. In the Catechism on p. 123, in the chapter on the 'Holy-making of the body and blood of our Lord,' we read that the Lord, desiring to distribute to disciples and believers his body and blood, began with *figures*, whereby he opened their minds, saying: ' My body is the true meat, and my blood the true drink'; and, 'I am the bread of life come down from heaven; whoever eateth this bread shall live for ever.'

---

[1] Perhaps the Marcionites had a similar idea of priesthood, and expressed it in their phrase: συνταλαίπωροι καὶ συμμισούμενοι (Tertul. *c. Marc.* iv. 9, 36), i.e. sharers with Jesus Christ (*not* with Marcion) of tribulations and of the world's hatred.

[2] *Hist. Man.* § 39, 1300 A.

Are we to infer that he only began with figures, but went on to really convert in the last supper the *substance* of the bread and wine into his true body and blood? And that the words of institution are to be taken literally, whereas the sayings with which he opened their minds were only figurative? If there be no real change of the elements, then what is meant by the saying that the false priests change the elements into their own bodies and not into Christ's?

The writer probably felt no difficulties, such as his statements raise in our minds. The ability to distinguish between an allegory and the facts allegorized, between a symbol and that which is symbolized, does not belong to every stage of culture. Philo sometimes lacked it; the early Christians barely had it at all. Nor can we expect it to be very developed in the ninth and tenth centuries. It is possible, therefore, that the Paulicians entertained several ideas at once, not all compatible with each other: firstly, the idea that the Lord in saying, 'take, eat and drink,' signified not real bread and wine, but his words, ῥήματα αὐτοῦ as *Scor.*[1] has it, λόγια κυριακά as Photius: secondly, the idea that the bread and wine really became the Lord's body and blood: thirdly, the idea that, the elect ones being Christ's body[2], the elements in becoming their body, became his; and in becoming his, became theirs. And lastly it must be borne in mind that we are not suitably placed for judging of the question, because the *Key* has been wilfully mutilated just in the pages which would have revealed to us how the writer of it conceived of Christ's flesh. He may have believed with Origen that Christ had an αἰθέριον σῶμα, and that he brought the same with him from heaven. Such a belief would have helped in his mind to obscure the issues so clear and hard to us; to veil the contradictions, to us so palpable. Or it may have been into the risen body of Jesus, which was only visible to the faithful, that the elements underwent a change.

However this be, it is certain that the Paulicians believed their elect ones to be, so to speak, reincarnations of Christ, and set such an interpretation on texts like John vi. 56: 'Whoever eats my body and drinks my blood, shall dwell in me and I in him.' Nor is it certain that this was not also a Pauline train of thought. It is difficult to attach any other meaning to such phrases as 'Not I, but Christ that dwelleth in me.' And in Gal. vi. 17, Paul writes: 'Henceforth let no man give me trouble; *he persecuteth Christ*

---

[1] *Scor.* viii.　　　　[2] Ἡμεῖς ἐσμεν σῶμα Χριστοῦ.

For I bear the *stigmata* of Jesus in my body.' The words italicized were read in Marcion's and probably in Tertullian's text, and are necessary to the sense; which is this, that Paul was a symbol or image of Christ, so that whoever harmed him harmed Christ[1]. Later on we shall return to this subject. It is enough now to remark that we here border on a field of primitive ideas and beliefs for which the modern psychologist has devised the title of sympathetic magic.

Later on I shall enumerate several points of contact between the European Cathars and the Paulicians. Here I must anticipate one of them. The Paulicians adored their elect ones as living representatives of Christ, shrines of his spirit which, in the sacred season of election, had chosen them as its vessels. Accordingly they adored them or prostrated themselves before them? and as their flesh was Christ's and they Christ's body, it was the same whether you declared the change of the eucharistic elements to be into their body and blood or into Christ's. The transubstantiation—if we may use a word which they did not—was not so much of the in themselves lifeless elements, as of the elect one who blessed and offered them; and their change of nature was but a corollary of his.

The heretics whom Eckbert found so widespread in the neighbourhood of Trèves and Cologne as early as A.D. 1160 held similar opinions. Of them Eckbert reports thus[2]:—

'They altogether despise, and consider as of no value, the masses which are celebrated in the churches; for if it happens that they go with the rest of their neighbours to hear masses, or even to receive the Eucharist, they do this in mere dissimulation, lest their infidelity should be discovered. For they say that the order of the priesthood is altogether lost in the Church of Rome, and in all the churches of the Catholic faith, and the true priests are not to be found except in their sect. They believe that the body and blood of Christ can be by no means made by our consecration, or received by us in our communion; but they say that they alone make the body of Christ at their tables. But in those words there

---

[1] It is a proof of the wide and early diffusion of the idea that in the *Clementine Homilies* (ed. Dressel, 1853, p. 11), an anti-Pauline work, we have it expressed almost in the same words: δήσει γὰρ (ὁ ἐπίσκοπος) ὃ δεῖ δεθῆναι, καὶ λύσει ὃ δεῖ λυθῆναι, ὡς τὸν τῆς ἐκκλησίας εἰδὼς κανόνα. αὐτοῦ οὖν ἀκούσατε, ὡς γνόντες ὅτι ὁ τὸν ἀληθείας προκαθεζόμενον λυπῶν, εἰς Χριστὸν ἁμαρτάνει καὶ τὸν πατέρα τῶν ὅλων παροργίζει· οὗ εἵνεκεν οὐ ζήσεται.

[2] See S. R. Maitland, *Albigenses and Waldenses*, 1832, p. 355.

is this deceit—for they do not mean that true body of Christ which we believe to have been born of the virgin and to have suffered on the cross, but *they call their own flesh the body of the Lord*; and forasmuch as they nourish their bodies by the food on their tables, they say that they make the body of the Lord.'

The same Eckbert also in another place apostrophizes these same heretics as follows [1]:—

'From one man who came out of your hiding-places, I heard this piece of your wisdom—your body is the Lord's; and therefore you make the body of the Lord, when you bless your bread, and support your body with it.'

We cannot doubt that these twelfth-century German heretics held the same theory of the Eucharist as the Paulicians. Among the Albigenses who seem to have been a kindred sect, the adoration of the elect or perfect one by the believers was an established custom. A single example from the *Liber Sententiarum*[2] (the record of the Inquisition of Toulouse between the years 1307–1323) will suffice:—

'And as he (the *credens*) was taught, he adored Peter Auterius and James his son (the two perfect ones), saying, "Good Christians, God's blessing and yours," bending his knees three times, with his hands on a certain bench, bowing before them and saying each time "Benedicite." And he saw them adored in the same way by others.'

In the same *culpa* we read that the two heretics, i.e. Peter Auterius and James, 'mutually adored each other.' The acts of inquisition plainly indicate that the inquisitors regarded this adoration as an act of anthropolatry, to be punished by sword and fire.

Nevertheless the same church which held the Inquisition of Toulouse has in our own generation, and in the face of an instructed Europe and America, formally decreed to the Bishop of Rome the miraculous and super-human attribute of infallibility. Surely the Paulician conception of the elect representatives of Christ on earth was a better way of apprehending the ὁμοίωσις θεῷ, which is man's vocation. Doubtless it was too exclusive a conception; and, if the church which held it had emerged triumphant, instead of being extinguished by ruthless massacres, it might have led to occasional displays of sacerdotal pride. Yet in the end a severalty of popes must be less hostile to the moral and intellec-

---

[1] Maitland, *Albigenses and Waldenses*, p. 361.
[2] *Petrus* 68, *Culpa* and Sentence. Maitland, p. 315.

tual progress of our race, than the grinding and levelling spiritual despotism of a single one.

It is difficult to bring the Greek and Armenian sources bearing on the history of the Paulician Church into line with each other. They nowhere overlap one another, and their lists of the names of Paulician leaders are different. It would appear that the Greeks were mainly interested in the Paulicians of Tephrik, whom the Armenian records do not notice. Assuming that my reader is familiar with the Greek sources, I will now proceed to summarize the scanty information supplied by the Armenian writers about the outward history of the Church.

John the Philosopher, who became Catholicos of Armenia A.D. 719, uses the name Paulician, but not Thonraki. Although he speaks of them as 'the dregs of the Messalianism of Paulicianism,' we need not suppose that they had anything in common with the Messalians or Euchitae of a previous age. All that we know of the latter, who are rightly described by Neander[1] as the first mendicant friars, contradicts not only the self-portraiture of the Armenian Paulicians in the *Key*, but in an equal degree conflicts with all we know of them from Greek sources. The Armenian word *mtslnêuthiun*, which I render Messalianism, was a mere term of abuse in the eighth century, and as such is again hurled, two centuries later, at the Paulicians by Gregory of Narek and Gregory Magistros. Of more value are four statements of · John the Philosopher which follow: (i) That the Paulicians had been rebuked and repressed by Nerses Catholicos, and had after his death fled into Armenia into hiding-places. (ii) That then certain Iconomachi expelled from Albania in the Eastern Caucasus had joined them. (iii) That as oppressed dissenters from the orthodox Church they had sought the protection of the Arab or Mohammedan powers. (iv) That they imagined themselves to have discovered something great and new in what was after all old and obsolete, and had left their hiding-places and ventured out into the populous centres of the land in order to preach it. Lastly (v) that their own centre was a region called Djrkay. In this region or from it (for the text is not clear) they flowed over the land like a flood of suffocating water.

Each of the above statements calls for some consideration. In regard to (i) there is a doubt as to which Nerses Catholicos is meant. A higher antiquity must at once be ascribed to the

---

[1] Vol. iii. p. 342, of English translation.

Paulician Church of Armenia than is usually supposed, if the Nerses intended was the Catholicos of that name, who is by the Armenian chroniclers said to have been patriarch for thirty-four years, and who died *c.* 374 A.D. He more than any one else was responsible for the introduction into Armenia of the peculiar Greek Christianity of the fourth century. As such he was the first great exponent there of the ideas and tendencies abhorred by the Paulicians; and would certainly have persecuted them, if they already existed in his day. There were, however, two later Catholici of the same name, one *c.* 524–533 A.D., the other *c.* 640–661, both of them anterior to John the Philosopher.

The next statement (ii) cannot be doubted, for later on in the tenth century we meet with the same connexion between Albania and the Paulicians of Taron. Albania, at the eastern end of the Caucasus, the modern Daghestan, seems from the very earliest times to have contained a population averse to the worship of images and imbued with the primitive Adoptionist faith. In the Armenian chroniclers, who were all orthodox, we only hear of the orthodox Church of the Albans which was a branch of the Gregorian Armenian, and went to Edjmiatzin for the consecration of their Catholicos. Gregory Magistros records that many of their Catholici in succession had anathematized the Paulicians of Albania. Aristaces, in the same age, bears witness to the frequent and close relations between the heretics of Albania and those of Taron. John of Otzun only alludes to the image-breakers of Albania,—this as early as 720. That they not only abhorred images, but held characteristically Paulician tenets at that date is certain from the testimony of Moses of Kaḷankatuk or his continuator in a passage written early in the eleventh century. Here we read that, in the time of John Mayrogomatzi, a contemporary of Ezr Catholicos (630–640), there was a party in Albania which rejected images, did not practise baptism, did not bless the salt (i.e. for animal sacrifices), did not conclude marriage with the blessing of the Church, raising the objection that the priesthood had been lost upon the earth. Here we recognize the Paulicians without difficulty. In the same passage great antiquity is ascribed to them. This sect, it says, arose in the time of the apostles and first appeared among the Romans, for which reason a great Synod was held in Caesarea, and people were instructed to paint pictures in the house of God. Here we have an echo of the claim raised by the Paulicians themselves to represent the true apostolic

Church. Whether we are to interpret the word 'Romans' of old or of new Rome, is not certain; probably of the old.

From (iii) it is clear that the Paulicians had already been driven by persecution to seek protection of the Arabs, who since the year 650 had successfully challenged the Roman or Greek political influence in Armenia. The same protection has probably enabled the Paulician Church to maintain its existence into the present century. At the same time it should be remarked that for a long time the Paulicians were equally opposed to Romans and Arabs. It was the government of Constantinople which, by its cruel persecutions of them, finally drove them into the camp of the Arabs, and so destroyed the only Christian outwork strong enough to ward off the Mohammedans.

The next statement (iv) is evidence that John recognized the primitive character of Paulician opinions.

It is to be regretted that John of Otzun does not more nearly locate the home and focus of Paulician activity in his day. Djrkay may be identified either with a canton of Perse-Armenia called by Indshidshian[1] Djrkhan or Djrgan, which lay on the Bitlis river, an arm of the Tigris, south-west of lake Van; or with Djrbashkh, a tract lying along the western slopes of Mount Masis or Ararat, in the neighbourhood of the modern Bayezid, close to Thonrak. Both districts at a later time were homes of the Paulicians; and, writing as late as 1800, Indshidshian (p. 113) notes that in the modern pashalik of Bayezid there was a tribe of Kurds called Manicheans, by which his informant no doubt meant Thonraki or Paulicians. And the names of both signify a region where water is plentiful; and neither of them is remote from the limits of Albania.

For the rest John the Philosopher, in the treatise in which he assails them *eo nomine*, tells us little of the Paulicians. He is content to retail nonsense about them, and was evidently subject to the same unwillingness or incapacity to communicate to his readers their real opinions, which we find in later Armenian writers.

Confining ourselves to Armenian sources we come next to the statements of Gregory of Narek and Gregory Magistros. According to these writers the founder of the Thonraki was one Smbat. Thonrak (or Thondrak or Thonrik, as it is variously spelt) is a lofty mountainous region running from about 39°–39·40 by south and

---

[1] *Geogr. of Armenia* (Mod. Arm.). Venice, 1806.

north, and 40·50–41·40 by west and east[1]. In Kiepert's map these mountains are called Niphates. Many streams, the easternmost sources of the Murad-Chai or South Euphrates, flow out of this *massive* on the north, the west, and the south-west sides of it. It is separated by the Bayezid branch of the Araxes from Mount Masis or Ararat, which towers with its lofty hump and peaked gendarme to the east, some fifty miles away. The Alashgerd plain watered by the upper Murad-Chai lies to the west, and stretches south-west to Melasgerd. The Turkish name of this mountain mass is Ala Dagh. Well away from it, beyond the rich plain of Melasgerd, rises the cone of Mount Sipan, 11,000 feet high, dominating the northern shore of Lake Van. Like Sipan, only more so, the Ala Dagh is volcanic; and the highest streams of the Murad-Chai, as they run down from its north side, are choked with sulphur and warm with the heat of hundreds of small geysers. These most eastern feeders of the Euphrates, as they run down to meet at Diadin, pierce their way through masses of volcanic basalt. The highest summit is a still smoking crater of 11,000 feet, called Thoonderlik, recently described by Texier and our own consul Taylor[2]. We recognize in the modern name the old Armenian 'Thondrik' or 'Thonrik,' derived from *Thonr*, an oven. And in the myriad sulphur-laden springs of this region we probably have an explanation of the language used by John the Philosopher, 'Suffocantium diluuii aquarum portio confluit.' The volcanic fire which in this region everywhere evidences itself, also explains the otherwise enigmatical language of Gregory Magistros (on pages 75 and 80). When he reached the sources of the Euphrates he found himself among mountains from whose hollows burst hot water springs and fumaroles. Some modern Armenians have absurdly misconstrued his language to mean that the Paulicians, whom he is describing, were fire-worshippers.

The village of Diadin or Diyadin, described on p. 223 of Murray's *Handbook to Asia Minor*, and Tozer's *Turkish Armenia*, p. 383, is called in the Armenian Tateôn, and probably occupies the site of the more ancient Zarehavan, the frontier town of the old Cantons of Tsalkotn and Kokowit of Bagrevandene. Built 6,000 above the sea, it is a poor and ruinous place to-day; but the

---

[1] Thonrak is by Aristaces (p. 135) located in Apahuni, a canton of Turubaran. It was on the extreme east of Apahuni probably. Alishian puts Thonrak in the canton of Tsalkotn. The limits of the old cantons cannot really be traced nowadays.

[2] *Proceedings of R. Geogr. Soc.* xiii.

ERRATUM

Page lxi, l. 9 from foot, *for* A.D. 721 *read* A.D. 821

The Key of Truth

remains of a massive fortress overhanging the basalt gorge, through which the feeders of the Euphrates now united into a single torrent run, prove that it was once an important place. It was probably the Zarouana of Ptolemy; and Faustus, the fourth century Armenian writer, records that here dwelt 5,000 Armenian families and 8,000 Jewish, numbers which we may safely halve. There still remained a circus or *stadion*, when in that century Shaphoy, the Persian tyrant, burned and sacked the city and massacred its inhabitants. In the next century the Armenian soldier Vardan defeated the Persians at this spot; and in 655, according to the historian Asolik, it still was a strong position. Here was born, late in the eighth century, one in whom we may perhaps recognize the founder, as Greg. Nar. and Greg. Mag. agree in calling him, of the Thonraki branch of the Paulician Church, Smbat the Bagratuni.

The prejudice of later Armenian historians has made it impossible to be sure of the identity of this great religious leader; but there are reasons for thinking that he was no other than Smbat Bagratuni, the founder of the petty Armenian dynasty of that name, which now under Persian, now under Byzantine suzerainty ruled over Taron or Taraunitis (in Kiepert's map), from A.D. 856 to 1062. Taron was properly but a single canton in the large province of Turuberan, which, roughly speaking, included the whole valley of the Murad-Chai or south-east Euphrates to the east of the modern Kharput. To-day Mush is the chief city and seat of government of this region. But the name Taron was extended by mediaeval Armenian historians and geographers to include the whole region.

The reasons for identifying the founder of the Thonraki with Smbat Bagratuni, the Confessor, as his countrymen owing to his martyr's death afterwards called him, are the following:—

1. The chronicler Mekhitar, of Airivanq, who, though he only wrote about 1300, compiled his work carefully from earlier sources, has the following entry under the year A. D. 721 : 'Sembat Ablabsay (i. e. Father of Abas). He was the leader (*or* 'the first') of the heresy of the Thonraki.'

2. Gregory of Narek implies that Smbat was murdered by a Mohammedan warrior. This warrior, he says, was himself nearly akin and allied to the madness of Smbat and his disciples, and had learned at first hand of Smbat's pretensions to be Christ.

3. On the other hand Gregory Magistros, like Gregory of Narek

had in his hands the book of Ananias Narekatzi against the Thonraki, a source which, if we had it, would outweigh in importance all the others. Whether it was also in the hands of Mekhitar we do not know; though it may well have been, as it was in those of Nerses Catholicos in 1165. Ananias, says Magistros, had let one know 'who and what Smbat was.' Now Gregory affirms not that Smbat was Smbat Bagratuni, but only that he flourished in his time and in that of a Lord (i.e. Catholicos) John, who if he preceded Gregory Magistros by as little as 200 years must be identified with John of Owaiq[1], who became Catholicos in 833. Gregory's term of 170 years is hardly long enough. Twice over he says that 170[2] years had elapsed and no less than thirteen patriarchs of Great Armenia had successively anathematized the sect between Smbat's day and his own. Now from John the Fifth to Sarkis the First inclusive, who died about 1019, immediately after issuing an anathema against the sect, there were, it is true, counted thirteen Catholici. And we must suppose that Gregory does not reckon among the thirteen Peter Getadards, who acceded in 1019 and died in 1058; because it was actually during his Catholicate that he (Gregory Magistros) was conducting against the Thonraki the persecutions which he relates. But for these thirteen Catholici 170 years is not enough, and we must rather adopt the term of 200 years which he gives in another letter (see p. 151) to the Vardapet Sargis or Sarkis.

4. Other sources, however, incline us to identify the Paulician

---

[1] Yet Greg. Mag. (p. 144) seems to identify the 'Lord John,' in whose day Smbat appeared, with John of Otzun, who wrote against the Paulicians. But John of Otzun became catholicos in 718, 330 years before Gregory Magistros was writing. He also implies that John of Otzun had assailed Smbat's heresy, which was hardly possible if Smbat lived a hundred years later. Gregory's account is impossible as it stands; and he apparently confuses John of Otzun, Catholicos in 719, with John of Owaiq, Catholicos in 833; and perhaps after all, as we shall suggest on p. lxvii, it was an earlier John Catholicos, soon after 600, whose contemporary Smbat the Paulician founder really was. Different Smbats of the house of Bagrat are also confused, it would seem; probably because they were all Paulicians together.

[2] So on pp. 142 and 145, but on p. 151 he assigns 200 years, which better agrees with the date of Smbat Bagratuni as attested by Arab sources. The discrepancy in the text of Greg. Mag. may be connected with a similar discrepancy among the Armenian historians of the ninth century, some of whom put Smbat thirty years later than others. Perhaps the text of Mag. has been altered to suit. Note that on p. 142 Mag. assigns fifteen patriarchs, and not thirteen, to the period which had elapsed since Smbat's appearance as heresiarch. See also p. lxviii.

WHO WAS SMBAT THE HERESIARCH? lxiii

leader with Smbat Bagratuni. Thus in Constantine Porphyrogenitus de Admin. Imp., cap. 44 (ed. Bekk. 1840, vol. iii. p. 191), we read this: ἰστέον ὅτι πρὸ τοῦ 'Ασωτίου τοῦ ἄρχοντος τῶν ἀρχόντων, τοῦ πατρὸς τοῦ Συμβατίου τοῦ ἄρχοντος τῶν ἀρχόντων, ὃν ἀπεκεφάλισεν ὁ ἀμηρᾶς Περσίδος ὁ 'Αποστάτας. Constantine wrote not later than 958. Unless two Smbats were murdered by the Arab invader, surely Smbat Bagratuni was the one intended by Gregory of Narek.

5. Thomas Artsruni, who died about 940, implies that Smbat Bagratuni was addicted to heresy. I quote him in Brosset's translation: John V. of Owaiq (says this authority) became Catholicos in 833, 'qui gouvernait la Sainte église, de la croyance orthodoxe apostolique, du Seigneur J. C., d'une manière tout-à-fait admirable, et imposait aux princes Arméniens l'obligation de marcher en dignes adhérents de la foi Chrétienne, afin que leurs œuvres témoignassent de la réalité de leur titre de Chrétiens. On accueillait ses avis, ou les écoutait volontiers; mais on ne renonçait pas aux actes impurs, aux dégoûtantes passions de Sodome; on imitait les vices de nos anciens rois, de la famille Arsacide. . . . Le Catholicos les exhortait à s'abstenir d'impuretés et des œuvres pernicieuses qu'ils commettaient . . . . nul ne levait les yeux vers les lois du Seigneur; les oreilles inattentives ne s'ouvraient que pour la vipère maudite et pour l'aspic aux morsures incurable.'

Here the charge of impurity assuredly means no more than it means from the lips of Gregory of Narek and Gregory Magistros and Aristaces[1], namely Paulicianism. As such it is opposed to the 'orthodox apostolic belief' of the Catholicos; the real antithesis to orthodoxy was not vice, but heresy, which was worse than vice. For the same reason the Armenian king, Smbat Bagratuni, is compared to the old Arsacide kings. These latter were not peculiarly addicted to nameless vice; but some of them were very conservative in matters of religion. Notably the king Arshak, who in the fourth century set up a rival Catholicos to the grecizing Catholicos Nerses; notably Arshak's successor Pap, who, after the death of Nerses, set himself to undo his so-called reforms of the Armenian Church, to send about their business the monks and nuns introduced by him and in other ways dispense with the orthodox Greek models imported from Caesarea.

If there were any doubt on this point, it is removed by other contemporary Armenian historians, such as Asoḷik, John Catholicos and Stephanus of Siuniq, who relate that Smbat Bagratuni had

[1] See pp. 125, 136, 144, 145.

a standing feud with John of Owaiq, and that, with the help of his nobles, he deprived him of his catholicate, and in 841 set up a rival in his place. They explain Smbat's subsequent defeat and capture by the Mohammedan Emir Abusa'ad as a punishment of God for his recalcitrancy towards the orthodox Catholicos, and for his heretical backslidings.

But before John the Fifth became catholicos Smbat had already been in conflict with his predecessor, David the Second, who acceded in 806 and died *c*. 833. Smbat had conspired with other chiefs of Armenia, named Sewaday and Sahak of Siuniq, to throw off the overlordship of the Khalifs of Bagdad. In these patriotic struggles the Catholicos David had taken part with Hôl or Haul, the Khalif's lieutenant. We can only explain David's somewhat unpatriotic policy by supposing that Smbat was already in religious antagonism with the orthodox patriarch; and the Mohammedans were quick to turn to account the religious feuds of a country which they coveted.

In the year 847 a new Khalif ascended the throne of Bagdad, Aboul-al Djafar, who took the title Motéwekkel-al' Allah. He commissioned Abousa'ad, an Arab chief who lived in the Armenian marches, to attack and reduce the Armenian princes—Ashot, who ruled in Vaspurakan, the province south and east of Van, and Bagarat, who ruled over Taron. Advancing through Atropatene, Abousa'ad (*or*, according to Thomas Artsruni, his son Joseph, the father having died on the way) routed Ashot; and, after making terms with him, went on to the fortress of Khlath[1], which lay under Mount Sipan at the north-west corner of Lake Van. There he halted and invited Smbat, who owed his title of king of kings and *Sparapet*, or governor of Armenia, to the Khalif's appointment, to come and see him. Smbat Bagarat, nothing suspecting, responded to the orders of the Khalif's representative and set out for Khelat, taking with him 'the holy Testaments, the divine books,' and attended by retainers and clergy. The Emir at once treacherously seized him and his relatives, and sent them in chains to Samara in Mesopotamia. Then he marched himself to Mush, where he fixed his winter quarters, after devastating the whole province and enslaving its inhabitants. The mountaineers of Sasoun, where Smbat had his castle of Sim, were alone unsubdued. They, at the approach of Spring (March, 852), rallied to avenge the treacherous capture of their loved chieftain, Smbat. They stormed Mush, and slew

---

[1] See Tozer's *Turkish Armenia*, chap. xii.

the *marzpan* Joseph, son of Abousa'ad, there where he had taken refuge, on the roof of the great church of Mush built by Smbat. Thomas Artsruni asserts that he had seen the very man who slew the Arab oppressor.

The same writer gives an interesting description of the *Khouth*, as the men of Sasoun were called. They lived in deep valleys and remote forests, or on the rough hill-tops. They had no towns, and went about in snow-shoes during winter. They all knew the Psalms by heart in the old Armenian translation. Indshidshian, the Armenian geographer, describing them about the year 1800, says that they still spoke in a dialect almost identical with the classical Armenian tongue; and this explains Thomas Artsruni's statement that they spoke in the ninth century a tongue hardly intelligible to their neighbours. There can be no doubt that these brave mountaineers were Armenian Puritans or Paulicians.

The prejudice of Armenian chroniclers, who were all drawn from the ranks of the orthodox Church, has obscured the subsequent fate of Smbat. Thomas Artsruni relates that he recanted his Christian faith and was circumcised as a Mussulman; and that the Artsruni princes, in submitting to the same fate, only followed his example. He allows, however, that Smbat really kept the true faith at heart; holding that outward apostasy through fear was no evil, if at heart the faith is retained. Herein, says Thomas, he followed the evil counsel of Elclésianos[1], the opponent of Novatian. The translator of the Armenian version of Nana's *Syriac Commentary on the Fourth Gospel*, a contemporary of Thomas, preserves in his colophon the same tale of Smbat's apostasy. He does not say indeed in so many words that he turned Mussulman, but only that ' he forsook the divine faith and fell never to rise again,—and this although he claimed to have for his own the whole and entire knowledge of the faith which is in Christ.'

But according to the chronicler, Vardan (d. *c.* 1270), Smbat *Sparapet*, having been removed about 855 by the Emir Bouba to Bagdad, died a martyr's death, refusing to abjure his faith. Bouha offered repeatedly to restore to him his kingdom of Armenia, but Smbat's answer was always the same: 'I cannot leave Christ. I cannot quit the Christian faith, which by the grace of the font I have received.' He was tortured and slain. Some of his fellow-prisoners who were Christians asked his body of the Khalif; and,

---

[1] i.e. Elkesaeus. See the original Greek of the 'counsel' in Euseb. *H. E.* vi. 38, whence Thomas probably derived his information.

according to John Catholicos (who heard it from an eye-witness), they took it to Babylon and laid it in the shrine erected on the site of the lion's den into which Daniel the prophet had been thrown. Smbat was known by Armenians after his death as the Confessor.

If this Smbat was not the founder of the Thonraki, then why did certain Armenian Church historians, among them Thomas Artsruni, conspire to blacken his memory with this charge of apostasy? Why the accusations of impurity merely because he was opposed to the orthodox prelates David and John? Why did these ecclesiastics make common cause against him with the infidel? Yet he built the great Church of Mush, and took with him the Scriptures wherever he went. It is not enough to suppose that he was an adherent of the Council of Chalcedon, then and later a bone of contention among Armenian churchmen. The assaults upon Smbat are too virulent to be so explained; nor does any writer give the least colour to the assertion that he was a Chalcedonist.

Thus Mekhitar's account is the one which best accords with most of the other sources. Nevertheless, we must accept it with all reserve in view of the positive statement in the letter of Gregory Magistros (see p. 144), that 'the accursed one appeared in the days of the Lord John and of the Smbat Bagratuni.' In any case it is certain that the heresiarch Smbat was a member of the royal house of Bagarat. His name Smbat, and Mekhitar's chronicle fully establish that: nor is it easy to escape the admission, painful to some Armenians, that the then head of the Bagratuni dynasty was also a heretic. Smbat the heresiarch may have been the same person whom Smbat Bagratuni elevated to the catholicate when he deposed the orthodox catholicos John of Owaiq. The Armenian sources, cited pell-mell and without any sense of their discrepancies or attempt to reconcile them, by Tchamtchean[1], in his great history of Armenia, imply that about A.D. 835 another Bagarat, a near relative of Smbat Sparapet, father of Abas, was made Patrik of Armenia. He, too, had his castle at Sim among the mountaineers of Sasoun. If this one was not a double of the former, he may have been the heresiarch.

My readers will, I am sure, appreciate the difficulty there is in obtaining a clear and unprejudiced account of events from Armenian chroniclers, and will not accuse me of vacillation if I now broach another and new hypothesis as to who Smbat was.

---

[1] In *Bodleian Catal.*, under 'Chamich.'

For the association in the pages of Gregory Magistros of Smbat the Paulician, leader and legislator, with a Persian physician Mdiusik, suggests quite another view of who he was. The historian Sebeos preserves a letter sent to the Emperor Constans by the Armenian clergy assembled in Dwin under the catholicos Nerses in A.D. 648, when the emperor was trying to force the decrees of the Council of Chalcedon on the Armenian Church. In this letter it is related that the Persian king, Aprouêz Chosrow, after his capture of Jerusalem in 614, convoked at his court an assembly of the eastern, especially of the Armenian and Syrian clergy, and appointed the Smbat Bagratuni, called Chosrow's Shoum (or Shnoum) to preside over it in conjunction with the 'chief physician of his court.' There was also present Zachariah, the captive patriarch of Jerusalem. 'There were many Nestorians present,' says the letter, 'and many other miscellaneous heretics. Moreover, the patriarch came forward and said: "Let not that man (? Jesus) be called God." The king, on being informed of this, had the patriarch beaten and turned out, and all the other heretics present were similarly treated.' The letter then records that King Chosrow, with the help of the orthodox Armenians, decided in favour of the Nicene and earlier councils, and against that of Chalcedon. Is it possible that here we have a garbled record of the results arrived at? May not Smbat Bagratuni, the minister of Chosrow, and joint president of this assembly with the Persian king's chief physician, be the Paulician founder? The conjunction of a Smbat Bagratuni with a Persian physician in connexion with Christian creeds is an odd one. Gregory Magistros records it, and here we meet with it exactly. Gregory also declares that a Lord John was catholicos at the time. John of Bagran was actually catholicos *c.* 595–620, when Chosrow's conference took place. Thus this Smbat fulfils all the requirements of the case save one, and that is this: Gregory Magistros implies that Smbat lived no more than 200 years before the date at which he was writing, i.e. about 850. But our present hypothesis would place him over 200 years further back, about 600. Perhaps Gregory confused the two Johns.

Gregory also gives us a list of the Paulician presidents or heads of the Church, who succeeded Smbat, the founder or organizer of the sect. Their names were Theodorus, Ananias, Sarkis, Cyrill, Joseph, Jesu, and in the days of Magistros himself, Lazar. The period covered by these seven leaders is reckoned by Magistros, sometimes at 170, sometimes at 200. In the former case he may be reckoning up to the year 1019, when Sarkis I issued his anathema; in the latter to the year 1050, when he was himself persecuting them. Now seven heresiarchs, succeeding each other, would fill up 170 or even 200 years, but hardly 400.

It is tempting to identify the third of these heresiarchs, Sarkis, with the Paulician leader Sergius, so well known from Photius, Peter of Sicily, and the other Greek writers; Sarkis being the Armenian form of Sergius. But since Petrus Siculus places the missionary activity of Sergius in the thirty-four years beginning from Irene's reign and extending to Theophilus, that is from *c.* 800–834, the identification is barely possible[1]. It is probable, however, that the Sergius of the Greek writers is the heresiarch mentioned, but not dated, by Matthew of Edessa (ch. 79), in the theological manifesto prepared by King Gagik of Ani for the Roman Emperor Dukas (1071–1078 A.D.). After anathematizing Valentinus, Marcion, Montanus, Manes, Nabateus, Sabellius, Arius, and Photinus, Gagik proceeds: 'We also anathematize Nestorius, and I anathematize Tychus, and by his Armenian name Sarkis, along with his dog and his ass, and may he in the last day partake of the lot of dogs and asses.'

I believe that for Tychus we should here read Tychicus[2], and that the great Paulician leader, who re-named himself Tychicus, is here meant. Even if Tychus is a mis-spelling of Eutyches, the identification of Sarkis with the Paulician leader is almost certain. But it would seem as if the Armenians only knew of their compatriot Sarkis through Greek sources. It was among Greeks that his missionary activity had lain; and all the fragments of him preserved in Petrus Siculus and Photius are Greek. The orthodox Greeks, for example Zigabenus, incessantly cast this famous heretic in the teeth even of orthodox Armenians, much to their annoyance.

---

[1] Several Armenian scholars have supposed that the Sergius of the Greek sources and the Smbat of the Armenian were the same person, because they agree so wonderfully both in the date and in the character of their activity. But the Greek sources fix the scene of the missionary labours of Sergius much further west than Thonrak, which is just behind Ararat. This is a greater objection to their identification than the difference of names; for the same person was often known to Greeks by one name and to Armenians by another.

[2] The converse error occurs in an early twelfth century copy of Zigabenus' redaction of *Scor.* preserved in a recently acquired British Museum codex. Here we read, in the list of Paulician heresiarchs: τὸν Σέργιον, τὸν καὶ Εὐτύχικον, where *Scor.* and the other texts have Τυχικόν. Here Εὐτύχικον must be a misplaced reminiscence of Eutyches, and so in Matthew of Edessa may be the reading Tychon for Tychicon.

TOPOGRAPHY OF HARQ AND MANANALI lxix

They on their part had no clear memory of who Sarkis was; and Nerses Clajensis (*c.* 1100-1170) in his sixth Epistle, § 8, identifies him with St. Sergius of Cappodocia, martyred by barbarians in the age of Constantine the Great. 'Sergius with his dog and ass,' brings vividly before us the great missionary who for thirty-four years wandered east and west, and north and south, evangelizing the people.

The events narrated by Aristaces are an isolated episode in the history of the Paulician Church, and must have occurred about the year 1000 A.D. Their scene was the country extending southwards from Erzeroum as far as the modern Mush. All the regions named are in the Turuberan province. The mountain Pakhr or hill of Emery must have been the range bordering the Euphrates to the south-west of Erzeroum or Karin. Harq is the Χάρκα of Constantine Porphyrogenitus (*De Adm. Imp.* cap. 44). It was a region south of Erzeroum, where numerous torrents take their rise among the north and east ridges of the Pinkeul or Bingeul range to flow away through deep ravines, ultimately to converge in the plain of Karachoban. After traversing that plain, they turn to the south, and run into the Murad Chai at Karaghil, almost doubling its volume. Khanus (Khynus in Stanford's royal atlas) is described by Consul Brandt in the proceedings of the Royal Geographical Society. It lies in a well-grassed valley, full of game, and the old castle built on a rock overhanging the river proves it to have been a stronghold in the past. It has always kept its name. It is situated on the dividing line between the old cantons of Pasen and Bagrevand, and about fifty miles in a direct line from Erzeroum, and fifty from Mush. It also gives its name to the confluent of the Murad Chai which flows under its walls.

Photius has misled every one by his location of Mananali close to Samosata. It was really a region round about the modern Karachoban; which must be the point at which, as Aristaces relates, it came down to the Eastern Euphrates, or rather to the Bingeul arm of that river, now called the Khanus or Khinis Chai, one mile from Karachoban, according to Murray's handbook of Asia Minor. This river is crossed by the *Kara Keupri* bridge, and near the Kuminji saltworks the same river can be forded. It was the presence of salt that gave this tract the name of Mananali, for *ali* means salt. The walled towns of Elia and Kother, where the Byzantine officer held his court[1], must have been close to this

[1] See p. 138.

ford on the north and south sides of the Khinis Chai. Such is the neighbourhood in which was born Constantine, the founder, according to the Greek sources, of the Paulician sect; and from this very same region came the Armenians who, early in this century, brought *The Key of Truth* to the village of Arkhwêli in Russian Armenia.

The village of Tdjaurm or Tschaurm where, according to these peasants, the book was actually copied by John in 1782, is easily identified with the modern Chevirme or Chaurma. This is, according to Murray's handbook, 'a hospitable Kurd village,' 6,645 feet above the sea, and one mile south of the ford over the Araxes, which, like the Khanus arm of the Eastern Euphrates, takes its rise in the Bingeul range due south of Erzeroum. Until the beginning of this century it was inhabited by the Armenian Paulicians. Aristaces spells it Djermay, and calls it a 'city-village.' Here also, according to him [1], met together the minions of the patriarch Samuel to anathematize the six Paulician doctors, and brand them on the forehead. The historian Sebeos mentions the same place in the seventh century, and relates that it was famous for its hot springs, to which the Roman governors of Theodosioupolis (Karin or Erzeroum) used to resort in search of health. The city called by Aristaces Muharkin on p. 136, where the Paulician James ended his days, must be the same with Mufarkin, another name for Nfrkert or Martyropolis on the upper Tigris, near Amid.

The letter of Gregory of Narek gives few details with regard to the geographical diffusion of the Paulician Church. The monastery of Kdshav, of which the inmates were affected, was situated in the province of Mok, north-west of the modern Bitlis, and not far east from the Sasun district. This province seems to have included the high ground in which rise the springs of the Bitlis branch of the Tigris and those of the Kara Su or Mush arm of the Murad Chai.

Gregory Magistros supplies a few more hints about the ramification of the Paulicians. Thulail, where they were so numerous that the sect was known as Thulaili, was a town-district in the district of Mananali, in the province of Turuberan or Taron. Yet another centre of them was Kaschê on the Araxes, near Joulfa.

We learn that the congregation of Thulail had entered into relations with the Syrian Patriarch, when the Armenian catholicos brusquely rejected their appeal to him to recognize them as orthodox Armenians. The congregation of Thonrak had done the same; and it is clear that the Paulicians looked to Syria for

---

[1] See p. 138.

sympathy, and found it there. It would appear that the persecution of the Paulicians was more vigorous in proportion as Byzantine influence in Taron and Vaspurakan was more felt. In the latter part of the tenth and the beginning of the eleventh century, the power of the Khalifs of Bagdad was almost annihilated in these provinces. Gregory Magistros drew his title of Duke of Vaspurakan and Taron from Constantinople, and held his commission to harry and destroy the Paulicians from Constantine IX Monomachus, who reigned from 1042–1054. This emperor's policy was but a continuation of the Byzantine policy of the ninth century; and Gregory takes much credit to himself for only harrying his Paulician compatriots, whereas the Byzantine generals of a former age had put out their eyes and turned them loose, in the few cases in which they had not murdered them outright. The favourite punishment devised by the orthodox catholici of Armenia was to brand their foreheads with the image of a fox. It is clear, from the campaign of Gregory Magistros, that the Armenian patriarchs, in spite of their quarrel with the Greeks over the Council of Chalcedon, were ever ready to co-operate with them, when there was a chance to outrage and murder their own Armenian heretics. Nor were things much otherwise in 1837. Then it was the Russian, and not the Byzantine authorities, whose aid was invoked; but there is not much difference.

From Nerses Clajensis we learn of another ramification of the Paulician Church in the province of Hamajch in Syrian Mesopotamia, and it is a devout prince Ariuz of the town of Thelkuran (north of Diarbekr) who solicits his advice about them.

This Nerses wrote in A.D. 1166, and after this date there follows a blank of six centuries, during which the published Armenian sources yield no notices of the Paulician Church; though it is probable that a careful scrutiny of unpublished chronicles written during this period would bring to light some particulars of its survival and vicissitudes all through the Middle Ages. That it had not been extinguished by the exertions of Gregory Magistros si certain; for in the narrative of an orthodox Armenian, Paul W. Mehêrean, written about the beginning of this century, we have proofs of the vitality which it still retained in the same tract of country between Erzeroum and Mush, in which it had always flourished. Paul Mehêrean's MS. is preserved in the library of San Lazaro, in Venice. On p. 120 of it he tells us that he met, when travelling to Karin or Erzeroum, with Armenians who had denied their faith, and were such heretics as are the Thonraki or *Késkés*. In the latter name we recognize the *Kaschetzi* of Gregory Magistros. He then relates that in the Wanq or monastery of Boṙdshimasur there was an abbot named Hovhannes, who, falsely assuming the style of bishop, had ordained fourteen priests, and had caused considerable stir in the neighbourhood of Karin. Attacked by the orthodox Armenians, he had fled to the neighbourhood of Manazkert, and there continued his propaganda. Next he tells us that under Zachariah, the Armenian Patriarch of Constantinople, between the years 1774 and 1781, an Armenian named Hovhannes, no doubt the abbot already mentioned—came to Constantinople, and spread his heresy there. In consequence, he was imprisoned for eight months by the Armenian Patriarch. Escaping from his bonds, he returned to the neighbourhood of Khanus, and began a systematic propaganda there and in the surrounding villages. Subsequently Hovhannes visited Venice, where Mekhitar had already planted his convent of San Lazaro, and thence returned to Erzeroum and Mush. To escape the persecutions of the orthodox Armenians he more than once proclaimed himself a Mohammedan; nevertheless he was imprisoned in Edjmiatzin, but escaping thence he returned to the village of Maroukh in the Khanus region, and began 'to diffuse his poison afresh.' The writer Paul pretends that in 1801 this missionary finally became a Turk or Mohammedan, 'a son of perdition,' as he puts it. We have seen that the same story was told eight centuries before of Smbat Bagratuni.

Truly the Armenians are a tenacious race, and neither their heresies nor the methods of combating them undergo much change. It is probable that in the present day many of the converts of the American Protestant missions in Erzeroum, Mush, Bitlis, Kharput, and other places, are Paulicians by heredity. As Protestant converts they have gained that protection from their countrymen's violence, which for centuries they must have sighed for.

The Hovhannes of whom we read in Paul W. Mehêrean was indubitably the Hovhannes who, in 1782, made the copy of *The Key of Truth* from which my text is printed. And he may very well have been the author of the appended catechism; though I am inclined to assign to this addition a more remote date, say the thirteenth or fourteenth century. As he began by being abbot of a monastery, he must have had some education such as the scribe of 1782, in his colophon, shows that he possessed. Whether he was a Paulician by birth or by conversion we do not know.

That he ordained twelve priests or elect ones proves that in the last decades of the last century the Paulician Church still had many adherents in Upper Armenia.

This exhausts the history of the Paulicians, so far as we can glean it from purely Armenian sources. Into their history as given by the Greek writers I have not entered and shall not enter in detail; for my readers will find excellent summaries in books easily procurable, for example in Gibbon's brilliant chapter, in Neander (vol. v), in Gieseler's *History of the Paulicians*, and in Smith's *Dictionary of Christian Biography*.

It is of interest, however, to notice the geographical distribution assigned to the Paulicians by the Greek writers. Constantine their founder was born in Mananali, a purely Armenian canton as we have seen, and close to Karin or Erzeroum, but remote from Samosata, where the Greek writers wrongly locate it. From Mananali he went to Cibossa, a town near Colonia, which lay east of Sebastia, on the Halys, the modern Sivas. One Colonia is identified with the modern Shabin Kara-hissar, 4,860 feet above the sea, fifty miles due south of Kerasund on the Black Sea. Perhaps, however, we should identify the Colonia of Paulician history with the ancient stronghold founded by Pompey on the west bank of the Euphrates and to the north of Melitene. The Armenians in the tenth century called it Aloons.

Constantine Copronymus, in the eleventh year of his reign, after reconquering the Armenian province of Melitene, transported numbers of the Paulicians, whom he found there and in Theodosioupolis or Karin, to Thrace to defend the line of the Danube. Under the Emperor Nikephorus, early in the ninth century, the Paulicians were numerous in Phrygia and Lycaonia. Under Leo the Armenian we read of them in Neo-Caesarea in Cappadocia, where an inquisition of them was opened in that reign.

Kunoskhora in Armenia, the place where, in consequence of the cruelties of this inquisition, the Paulicians rose in rebellion, I cannot locate. Magistros calls Thonrak 'a place of dogs,' which answers to οἱ κατοικοῦντες κυνὸς τὴν χώραν of Petrus Siculus, p. 66; but this cannot be the same place, for from 813–820, when Leo reigned, the Khalifs of Bagdad were paramount in Thonrak, and outside the Roman dominion the Paulicians were ever safe from Byzantine cruelty. Argaus, which, about the same time the Saracens assigned to the Paulicians, and where Sergius lived, was probably the modern Argovan, twenty-five miles north of Melitene. One of the chief Paulician congregations was at Mopsuestia, only five hours east of Adana. Lastly, Tephrike, where the Church made its famous stand, is a well-known site some seventy miles south-east of Sivas on the river Chalta, which, rising on the south side of Mount Argaeus, flows due east to join the northern Euphrates fifteen to twenty miles north of Egin.

The scanty historical notices which the Greek writers contain do not overlap the equally slender Armenian sources. The latter concern the Paulician movement to the east of the Euphrates; the former relate its struggles with Greek orthodoxy to the west of that great boundary. On this side of the Euphrates it was that the Greek populations were attracted by it. Here was a large bilingual Armenian population, speaking Greek, yet not forgetting their own tongue. They must have been the chief purveyors to the Greek world of a puritanism which essentially belonged to a race of vigorous mountaineers, and was alien to the debased Greek spirit of the eighth century. On this side of Asia Minor also, especially in Phrygia, they were in contact and, as I shall presently point out, probably in actual religious communion with the still surviving and ancient Montanist Church.

But although our two sets of sources have little in common beyond their sketch of Paulician tenets and character, there can be no doubt that the Puritan communities both east and west of the Euphrates were bound together in a common policy. If the early Bagratuni dynasty from 820–850 was hostile to the Arab Khalifs, it was because the latter hampered and curtailed the aspirations of Armenia after freedom, religious and political. For the same reason to the west of the Euphrates the Paulicians were enemies of the Byzantines who persecuted, and friends of the Arabs who protected, them. But the disasters which befell them in the west found their echo in Armenia Magna. And the persecution of the Empress Theodora, during whose regency (842–867) one hundred thousand of them were martyred, unquestionably weakened their influence further east. Smbat Bagratuni the *Sparapet* seems to have been the last of the petty Armenian dynasts who favoured them. Local heads of clans here and there, like the Wrwêr, and men of royal family like Mushel, continued here and there to take their part and share their sufferings. But they nowhere held the government in their hands; and from about the year 900 onwards they were outcasts, and their hand against every man's. And such have ever since continued to be their fortunes.

But it is against itself that a state or a church rejects the counsel of God; and Eastern Christianity, Greek and Armenian alike, is to this day bleeding from the wounds which, in its cruel persecutions of these early Puritans, it inflicted on itself. To us who are the heirs of the ages the truth of things is slowly unrobed; and there is an irony too painfully clear in the circumstance that in the chronicle of Aristaces the pages immediately following the two malignant chapters about the Paulicians, translated in my appendix, have for their topic the capture of the royal city of Ani and the massacre of its inhabitants by Alp Arslan. As we read these dreadful pages which tell us of the cruelties of the human wolf of the eleventh century, we seem to hear the shrieks and groans of the miserable victims of the human wolf of to-day, still ravening in the plains and valleys of Armenia. Fortune does not always smile on bigots and persecutors; and Gregory Magistros had scarcely ended his harryings of his Paulician countrymen, had hardly concluded his bombastic recital of his exploits as a persecutor, before the star of his country set in a mist of Tartar bloodshed and oppression out of which it was never again to emerge. Nor was retribution really less certain, if it was less swift, in the country west of the Euphrates. Paulicianism was the natural faith of the hardy mountaineers of the Taurus; and in destroying them the blind fanaticism of Byzantium destroyed its only bulwark against Saracen invasion.

'In the Greek borderlands, west of the Taurus and Euphrates, were encamped the Paulicians, opposing to the worldly orthodoxy of the empire a genuinely apostolical Christianity founded on the Bible. Persecuted under the emperors of the seventh century, they enjoyed (in the eighth) a thorough-going toleration, thanks to the wise policy of the Iconoclasts who followed. The brave bands of these Christian Maccabeans furnished a frontier-cordon against Islam as vigorous as it was indispensable. To strengthen this line of defence the extraordinary spiritual leadership of Sergius (about 800) had done not a little. Yet the persecutions under the Caesars Michael I and Leo V drove a portion of them into the Arab domain. But when Theodora began her extraordinarily bloody persecution, this brave population was seized with universal despair. The commissioners sent to inquire into their faith rivalled in bloodthirstiness the officers of the Spanish inquisition. They were murdered, and the robber-incursions into the empire began. The sect found in Karbeas, who had been a Roman officer, one who could lead them in the field as in the council-chamber; and from the frontier-fortress of Tephrike, like the later Waldensians against the Piedmontese, they waged a most successful guerilla-war against the Empire [1].'

Tephrike fell (873). But the backbone of Oriental Christianity was broken. What the Protestant Churches have achieved in Europe, that the Paulicians might have accomplished in the east. But from the ninth century onwards, wherever the Muslim met a Paulician, they met a friend; and the ultimate success of the most soldierly of the Mohammedan invading races was assured. It is the Osmanli Turks who have proved themselves to be that race.

There remains an important Greek source of information with respect to the Paulicians, which has not been noticed because the sect is not referred to in it *eo nomine*. It was first published in the learned *Historia Haeresiae Monothelitarum* of Franc. Combefisius, ed. Paris, 1648, col. 317 fol., and is entitled, λόγος στηλιτευτικὸς κατὰ 'Αρμενίων, and ascribed to 'our holy father Isaac, Catholicos of Great Armenia [2].' A reference to the baptism of Constantine as having occurred 800 years before the date of composition fixes its date in the twelfth century; and the author was clearly the contemporary and possibly the companion in the discussion with Theorian under Manuel Comnenus of Nerses the Graceful, from whom we print some excerpts in our fifth appendix. The tone of this 'oration' is throughout that of a renegade Armenian who had gone over to the Greeks, and who, in his anxiety to blacken his countrymen, ascribes to the orthodox Armenian Church not only the errors of Eutyches and Dioscurus, of Timotheus Aelurus and Petrus Fullo, of Julian of Halicarnassus, and of Aphthartodoketism, but also the characteristic errors of the Paulicians. These are summarized in chap. viii, and partly agree with and partly supplement our other sources of information.

(1) 'Christ was thirty years old when he was baptized. Therefore they baptize no one until he is thirty years of age.'

That this was and is still the custom of the Thonraki is implied in the *Key*, and may be inferred, as we have seen (p. l) from the Acts of the Inquisition of Arkhwêli. The same conclusion results

---

[1] Translated from the excellent 'Abriss der Byzantinischen Kaisergeschichte' in K. Krumbacher's *Geschichte der Byzantinischen Literatur*, 2nd Edition, p. 970.

[2] An *Abrégé* of the same is attributed to S. Nicon, and is printed among the notes in the *Patres Apostolici* of Cotelerius. The Greek text of Isaac, ch. viii, is printed in Appendix VII below.

from the so-called teaching of St. Gregory the Illuminator, to which we elsewhere refer (p. cxi). John of Otzun (for reference see below on No. 5) implies that infant baptism had become the rule rather than the exception in his church before 700 A.D., but he glances at the Paulician custom.

(2) 'Christ, after baptism, was not anointed with myrrh ($\mu\acute{v}\rho o\nu$) nor with holy oil, therefore let them not be anointed with myrrh or holy oil.'

In the baptismal service of the *Key* no allusion is made to the use of the holy oil, and the modern Paulicians reject it (see above, pp. xxvi and xlix).

(3) 'Christ was not baptized in a font, but in a river. Therefore let them not be baptized in a font.'

This seems to have been the practice of the Thonraki, judging from the same Acts of the Inquisition of Arkhwêli, wherein is described (see above, pp. l, li) a case of baptism in a river. The *Key* indicates that total immersion was the rule; but, during the best part of the year, immersion in a river was impossible in the highlands of Armenia, though feasible in the Mesopotamian districts. The *Didachê*, ch. vii, prescribes baptism $\dot{\epsilon}\nu$ $\ddot{v}\delta a\tau\iota$ $\zeta\hat{\omega}\nu\tau\iota$.

(4) 'Christ, when he was about to be baptized, did not recite the Creed of the 318 Fathers of Nice. Therefore shall they not make profession of it.'

It is clear from the *Key* that the Paulicians of Armenia rejected the entire theology of the great councils, and the Creed given on p. 94, to be imparted by the catechist to the catechumen, is a counterblast to the Nicene Creed. In the first Paulician confession of Arkhwêli (see above, p. xxv) we read that the great councils were inspired by Satan; and Isaac Catholicos indicates, towards the close of this eighth chapter, that the same people whose teaching is here summarized rejected the Nicene doctrine of the Incarnation.

(5) 'Christ. when he was about to be baptized, was not first made to turn to the west and renounce the Devil and blow upon him, nor again to turn to the east and make a compact with God. (For he was himself true God.) So let them not impose these things on those to be baptized.'

The baptismal service in chap. xxi of the *Key* implies that the above is correct; and John of Otzun, in his Synodal oration (*c.* 718 A.D.) chap. v, glances at the Paulician practice in the following passage (opera John Otzun. Venet. 1834, p. 25): 'Et istud quoque praeterea cernimus: quod ab iis, qui baptizandi sunt, *non exigunt quidam* interrogationis modo de abrenuntiando diabolo iuramentum, neque sanctissimae Trinitatis professionem ... sed tantummodo ad fontis baptismum illos temerarie admittunt.' The truth seems to be that John of Otzun was introducing these new practices into the ancient baptismal rite of the Armenians, and not that *some* were neglecting to observe them. In the same context he insists that, before baptism and before entering the baptistery, the priest should lay hands on the catechumen and anoint him—a practice which the orthodox Armenians have after all never adopted.

(6) 'Christ, after he had been baptized, did not partake of his own body. Nor let them so partake of it.'

In the Acts of the Inquisition of Arkhwêli (see above, p. xlix) the newly-baptized do not at once communicate. In the Greek and Roman and orthodox Armenian churches the host is put into the mouth of the child immediately it is baptized; and perhaps the delay interposed by the Paulicians was by way of protest against this superstitious custom. How long the interval was we know not, probably forty days.

(7) 'Christ, after he was baptized, fasted forty days, and only (that); and for 120 years such was the tradition which prevailed (in the Church). We, however, fast fifty days before (lit. near to) the Pascha.'

This means that the Paulicians kept a fast for forty days after the feast of the baptism of Jesus Christ, and that all Christians kept this fast during the first 120 years after Christ. The 'we' refers of course to Isaac and his party. To fast for fifty days before Easter was common in Syria at one time, and the Lenten fast was kept for various periods from forty hours to fifty days. The persistence of the name Quadragesima to denote it indicates that the Paulician fast was its original form. When the importance of the baptism was lost sight of in the Church, the earlier fast became a fast before Easter. The orthodox Armenians still identify Christmas with the Baptism.

(8) 'Christ did not hand down to us the teaching to celebrate the mystery of the offering of the bread in church, but in an ordinary house and sitting at a common table. So then let them not sacrifice the offering of bread in churches.'

The modern ·Paulicians (see above, p. xlix) celebrate their Eucharist in a cellar or stable, or wherever else they can.

(9) 'It was after supper, when his disciples were sated ($\chi o\rho\tau a$-

σθῆναι), that Christ gave them to eat of his own body. Therefore let them first eat meats and be sated, and then let them partake of the mysteries.'

This proves that the Paulicians kept up the primitive custom of an *agapé* preceding the Eucharist for centuries after the great Church abandoned it. So St. Paul (1 Cor. xi. 21) deprecates the practice of coming hungry to the Eucharist, no less than that of coming drunk. All were, by sharing, to have had enough to eat and drink, and no more.

(10) 'Christ, although he was crucified for us, yet did not enjoin us to adore the cross, as the Gospel testifies. Let them therefore not adore the cross.'

This is a point to which not only the *Key* but all the sources abundantly testify.

(11) 'The cross was of wood. Let them therefore not adore a cross of gold or silver or iron or bronze or stone.'

To this point also the *Key* testifies.

(12) 'Christ wore neither humeral nor amice nor maniple nor stole nor chasuble. Therefore let them not wear these garments.'

So the Greek source, *Scor.* xiv, asserts that the 'priests' of the Paulicians whom they called *synecdemi* and *notarii* dressed and looked and lived exactly like every one else. The only bit of ritual hinted at in the *Key* is the reservation for the bishop of a particular seat (p. 107). The orthodox Armenian Church has ever been almost barbaric in its wealth of ecclesiastical vestments. Yet any priest may assist in the service of the mass in his plain dress.

(13) 'Christ did not institute the prayers of the liturgy and of the holy epiphanies, and all the other prayers for every action and every hour. Let them therefore not repeat them or be hallowed by these holy prayers.'

So Nerses (see Appendix, p. 155), says: 'Liber Rituale et canones, qui in eo continentur, crucis et ecclesiae benedictio, et alia, non sunt admittenda.' This book of rituals for all occasions was called among the Armenians Mashtotz, from the name of the ninth-century compiler. The Paulicians, according to Nerses, rejected it as not being the work of the ancient fathers.

(14) 'Christ did not ordain (ἐχειροτόνησεν) patriarchs and metropolitans and bishops and presbyters and deacons and monks, nor their several prayers (i.e. services of ordination). Let them therefore not be ordained nor blessed with these prayers.'

So the *Key* deprecates the idea of any hierarchy in the Church (p. 105). And it is this that underlies the tirade of Gregory Magistros (p. 144). So, in the Albigensian Church, the lowest deacon could replace the highest bishop in every and any ecclesiastical function.

(15) 'Christ did not enjoin the building of churches and the furnishing of holy tables, and their anointing with myrrh and hallowing with ten thousand prayers. He did no such thing. Let them not do it either.'

So Nerses (see above on No. 12) states that they, the Paulicians, would not formally consecrate churches (ecclesiae benedictio). The Greek sources (*Scor.* xi) testify that they had *proseuchae* only. It must not be forgotten, however, that, from the reign of Constantine onwards, the cruellest edicts forbad the use of their churches to all heretical sects, and ordered their destruction. However, in this particular also the Paulicians preserved the primitive teaching of the Christian Church as expressed by Origen in the words (*C. Celsum*, viii. 20): φεύγομεν βωμοὺς καὶ ἀγάλματα καὶ νεὼς ἱδρύεσθαι. On this point there are many golden passages to be read in Origen, viz., *C. Celsum*, i. 5, viii. 17, 18, 19, 20. The Paulicians, as Nerses Shnorhali testified (p. 155), limited the church to the worshippers met together in Christ's name, and so did the Albigeois. The modern Paulicians (see above, p. xlix) celebrate the Eucharist in a stable on a common table of wood.

(16) 'Christ did not fast on the fourth day of the week and on the Paraskevê. Let them not fast either.'

So Aristaces testifies (p. 140) that the Paulicians rejected 'the ordinance of fasts.'

(17) 'Christ did not enjoin us to pray towards the east. Let them not either pray towards the east.'

The custom of turning to the east in prayer was so ancient in Christianity, being already attested by second-century fathers, that it is surprising, though not impossible, that the Paulicians had not adopted it[1]. It is hardly a charge that Isaac would invent. If it be true, it is another proof of the extremely primitive character of their Church. In ch. xiv, col. 384, Isaac condemns the Armenians for re-baptizing the Greeks ('Ρωμαίους); but the orthodox Armenians

---

[1] Or had they dropped it out of opposition to the Sun worship of the Manicheans?

probably did this no less than the Paulicians, so we need not suppose that he herein refers to them. In the summary, however, of Armenian errors which follows (col. 385) are some which must have been peculiar to the Paulicians, e. g. that they did not keep the Feast of the Annunciation; that they refused to adore the Images of Christ, and of the mother of God, and of the saints, and called them idols; that 'they denied the nativity of Christ,' which must mean that they regarded the Baptism as the real Nativity of Christ. The orthodox Armenians themselves retained so much of the original Adoptionist character of their Church as always to keep Christmas and the Baptism on one and the same day, Jan. 6[1]. The above summary is so terse, so instinct with the religious radicalism which must characterize every Christian system built on the Gospels alone, that we may fairly suppose that Isaac copied it[2] directly from some Paulician source, in which the principles of the sect were compendiously set out and defended. Being himself an Armenian, Isaac may well have had access to such a source.

John of Otzun (*c.* 680-725) wrote a separate 'discourse against the Paulicians' *eo nomine*; of it I print the relevant portions in my Fifth Appendix. But in his synodal oration there are many covert references to them, beside the one noticed in No. 5 of Isaac's list. And they are moreover introduced in such a way as to indicate that in his day the Armenian Church was still in transition from its older Adoptionist form to the later orthodox or Caesarean type; so that the traces of old belief and practice were still common among the clergy. Thus he begins his review of the newer system which he was seeking to impose with these words (ed. Venice, 1834, p. 15): 'I perceive numberless irregularities in many matters of deep moment, not only among the laity, but among the clergy as well, nay among the bishops (*lit.* primates or leaders) of our Church. With one language and by the help of one preacher (i. e. Gregory the Illuminator) we have started forth on the way of truth. Yet now we pursue many paths and tracks. Not only in our lives but in our forms of glorifying God (or ' in our doxologies ')

---

[1] See further on this point below, p. clii foll.

[2] The methodical manner in which the points are grouped in itself indicates that Isaac has embodied a Paulician document in his text. Their supreme tenet—the baptism of Jesus—comes first, and their teaching about baptism occupies the first seven sections. Then follow two concerning the Eucharist. The rest of the clauses convey their conceptions of priesthood, public worship, and of the Christian life in general.

we depart from what is correct in many and various ways.... And so it is that when we congregate before the God of peace to ask for peace, we are disturbed and confused; and, just as if we were aliens to one another in race and tongue, we fall into discord and faction, as though we were savages one to the other.'

The admission of Aristaces (see Appendix, p. 132) that the Thonraki, like the orthodox Armenians, were descendants of Gregory the Illuminator, well agrees with the above. There follows in John a passage, which, as it concerns not a few of the points enumerated by Isaac Catholicos, I transcribe from the faithful Latin version of the Mekhitarists (ed. Venice, p. 17):—

'Interea et istud nobis videre obtigit, quod quibusdam in locis Altaria et Baptisteria non extruuntur iuxta beatorum Patrum nostrorum praeceptum traditionemque, ambo lapidea et immobilia condendo; sed ligneum ac mobile altare quidam erigunt, et consuetum perficiunt lavacri ritum pro necessitate, ac pro tempore, et loco, per quodlibet vas prae manibus in promptu occurrens (cp. above, p. xlix), suorum excusationem errorum pueriliter quidem, et imperite adferentes, si quidquam priscis temporibus festinanter ab aliquo nostratum fuerit opus: a Christo, exempli gratia, qui ad communem mensam in caenaculo corporis et sanguinis sui Sacramentum confecit; et a Philippo, qui, ut ut accidit, Eunuchum in quavis aqua baptizavit. Similiter, aiunt, de aliis quoque Apostolis demonstrat historia, quod diversimode ab invicem, et quomodocumque tempus poscebat utrumque conficiebant Sacramentum. Sanctus quoque Illuminator noster ligneum, inquiunt, secum circumferebat altare (*or* table); atque in fluviis rivulisque ubicunque advenisset, baptismum peragebat.'

A more direct commentary on the charges of Isaac Catholicos, Nos. 3, 8, and 15, could not be than these remarks of John of Otzun afford; and it would almost seem as if Isaac had preserved to us a Paulician document, not of the twelfth, but of the seventh or eighth century. It is anyhow clear that in the seventh century the Adoptionists of Armenia made exactly the same appeal to the example of Christ and to the usages of the Illuminator which they made in the tenth to the twelfth centuries, and which meets us everywhere in *The Key of Truth*. John himself admits the antiquity of the usages he condemns in the words, ' si quidquam priscis temporibus festinanter ab aliquo nostratum fuerit opus,' where the word aliquo must refer to Gregory the Illuminator.

AGAPÊ AND EUCHARIST NOT SEPARATED lxxxiii

In further criticism of their constant appeal to Christ's example John continues thus :—

'Quibus dicendum est: O vos, si universa a Christo acta nobis ad exemplum adducenda essent, ergo oporteret, et triginta annorum unumquemque baptizari (cp. Isaac's document, No. 1), et octiduum circumcidi (cp. the name-giving of the Paulicians, p. 87 of the *Key*), et tertia die resurgere, et quadragesima die in caelum conscendere (cp. Narekatsi's ribaldry about Smbat, p. 128): hoc namque modo haec Christo peragere placuit. Item quoque post coenam hora vespertina mysterio communicari; quoniam Dominus, ubi vetus illud perficiens obsignavit, ibi per suum quoque novi testamenti fundamenta iecit. Nunc autem multas horas interponimus corpoream inter spiritualemque mensam, et octidui baptizamur.'

It is remarkable that some of these points were just those on which the persons denounced by Isaac Catholicos laid stress; namely the baptism in the thirtieth year, and the participation in the Eucharist immediately after an agapê. It would appear that the more thorough-going of the old Adoptionist believers had already been excluded in the days of John of Otzun from the church over which he presided; and now formed a distinct sect, being called Paulicians after Paul of Samosata. And John alludes to customs of the latter as a *reductio ad absurdum* of the arguments of the less rigorous Adoptionists who still lingered in the Church; half and half adherents of the older religion, who had perhaps abandoned the Adoptionist Christology, and had adopted infant baptism and separated the Eucharist from the agapê, yet in other respects clung to what was ancient.

It is certain from the teaching of Gregory the Illuminator (see p. cxi), that the original practice of the Armenians was to baptize at thirty years of age; and, from the teaching of the twelve apostles, we know that the union of Eucharist with agapê long continued in the Church. The language of the *Didachē*, ch. 10, is almost identical with that of Isaac Catholicos: μετὰ δὲ τὸ ἐμπλησθῆναι οὕτως εὐχαριστήσατε. St. Basil, *Ep.* xciii. (iii. 187 A) testifies that, in the fourth century, it was still usual in Alexandria and Egypt to celebrate the Communion in one's own house : ἕκαστος καὶ τῶν ἐν λαῷ τελούντων ὡς ἐπὶ τὸ πλεῖστον ἔχει κοινωνίαν ἐν τῷ οἴκῳ αὐτοῦ καὶ ὅτε βούλεται μεταλαμβάνει δι' ἑαυτοῦ. And Socrates, *H. E.* v. 22, testifies that the Egyptians in the neighbourhood of Alexandria and in the Thebaid kept up the agapê before the Eucharist and had not severed them: ἐν σαββάτῳ μὲν ποιοῦνται συνάξεις, οὐχ ὡς ἔθος δὲ

Χριστιανοῖς τῶν μυστηρίων μεταλαμβάνουσι, μετὰ γὰρ τὸ εὐωχηθῆναι καὶ παντοίων ἐδεσμάτων ἐμφορηθῆναι, περὶ ἑσπέραν προσφέροντες τῶν μυστηρίων μεταλαμβάνουσιν. I owe these references to Mr. Brightman's Liturgies, vol. i. p. 509. In the Armenian canons of St. Sahak (p. 96, ed. Venice, 1853) there is a trace of the same usage among the Armenians of the fourth and fifth centuries.

Canon 17. 'The priests shall in unanimity (*or* all together) perform the service (*or* ministration), and the offering (*or* mass) of the agapês. Without reading the Gospel let the priests not venture to present [the offering]. But if any one be found in a state of surfeit (i. e. having overeaten or overdrunk) before the offering (*or* mass) is made, in the offering let him not dare to take the bread, and let him be removed by his fellows.'

Canon 18. 'Likewise the laity (*lit.* cultivators) who have been invited to the agapê, shall share in the service and offering (*or* mass). Prior to the offering let them not venture to eat and drink in their own houses. And if any one has beforehand eaten and drunk in his own house, let him not dare to come to the offering of bread, that there be no condemnation of himself and insult to the spiritual feast; since such perversity is vain '

These two canons indicate the custom of an Agapê and Eucharist following such as we have before us in the New Testament. They are not directed against the eating of a supper in church before the Eucharist; but firstly against the priests overeating at the supper, and secondly against the laity eating that supper in their own houses and then coming into church to partake of the Eucharist separately. The reading of the Gospel is to intervene between the supper and the Eucharist, but nothing else is prescribed. The Paulician Eucharist was similar. In the time of John of Otzun the agapê still went on, but separated by an interval of time from the Eucharist.

That the orthodox Armenian Church in his day began the fast of forty days immediately from the Epiphany on Jan. 6th, cannot be inferred from John of Otzun, who, in his fifth and sixth canons (ed. Venice, 1834, p. 59), distinguishes indeed the 'holy forty days of Zatik' (Easter), which preceded Pentecost, from the 'holy quadragesimal fast' which followed the Epiphany, but does not explicitly say that the latter was an Epiphany fast. When in the Armenian canons of Sahak (p. 111) we have specific mention of the 'Festival of the Holy Epiphany and *its* forty days,' the feast of ὑπαπαντή called Quadragesimae de Epiphania in the

CANONS OF SAHAK, C. 425   lxxxv

Peregrinatio of St. Sylvia is referred to. It is possible that this feast originally marked the close of the Lord's fast of forty days and the beginning of his ministry, but we have no evidence on the point. The Armenians also kept, and still keep, a fast of five days or more called *Arhadjavor*, preliminary to the fast of our Lord. This originally commemorated the preaching of repentance by Jonah according to the Armenians themselves; but its real significance is very doubtful. Perhaps it at first commemorated the preaching of repentance by John the Baptist. The forty days' fast was so strictly kept by some in the days of John of Otzun that they passed the Sabbaths and Lord's Days during its continuance in sadness and penitence, without celebrating the Eucharist. John condemns this custom; and Gregory of Narek seems to glance at it when (see p. 126) he taxes the Thonraki with reckoning the Lord's day the same as any other. 'In tristitia et poenitentia transigunt, non secus ac reliquos quinque dies praeteritos . In hac die Christus mortem coercuit, secum ex morte humanam educens naturam,' says John of Otzun.

The strictures of Isaac Catholicos are largely borne out by the review of the ecclesiastical condition of Armenia with which Nerses of Lambron, his contemporary, concludes his commentary on the Armenian mass. Hierarchy, celebration of mass, ritual, observance of church feasts—all this was, he says, confined to the monasteries. The common people would not build churches, and if there were any they had been built by the Francs, or were derelict Armenian churches taken possession of by them. Even in the Armenian court the Armenian nobles could not go to the sacrament in church for fear of the populace, who rejected bishops in favour of elders, neglected the Lord's day and would permit no feasts in honour of saints, no church vestments, no ritual. Dulaurier has translated this striking chapter in his crusading documents. It entirely confirms the document given in Isaac Catholicos, and the two sources taken together prove that the Paulician heresy was as rife in the twelfth as it had been in the fifth when Lazar of Pharp was accused of it[1]. And, like Lazar, Isaac Catholicos seems to have known it not under the name Paulicianism, but simply as a heresy immemorial among his countrymen.

So far our chief aim has been to prove that the correspondence of *The Key of Truth* on the one hand with the old Armenian, and on the other with the Greek sources of information about the

[1] See below, p. cviii.

Paulicians, is so close that we cannot hesitate to recognize in it an authoritative manual of that Church. The Thonraki were the Armenian branch of that Church, since both Gregory of Narek[1] and Gregory Magistros identify them.

The problem which still confronts us is a more fundamental one, namely, what was the relation of this Paulician Church to the Great Church? Was it a paraphyadic outgrowth of the post-Nicene Church of Asia Minor and, as regards the Thonraki, of the orthodox Armenian Church? Or was it the survival of an early form of the Apostolic Church, so that its origin lay far back behind the Nicene Council? Was it Protestantism or opposition to what were regarded as the abuses of the Great Church, a return to lost evangelical standards consequent upon the diffusion of the Gospel texts; and in Armenia did this specially result from the diffusion of an excellent vernacular translation of the New Testament? Or was it rather the case that these early standards had never been lost? In the latter case Paulicianism was just the fruit of an inevitable antagonism felt by an older and simpler form of church towards the dogmatic and ritualistic developments which at once began when, under Constantine, the Great Church got the upper hand. The answer to this question has been in some measure forestalled in our discussion of the document preserved by Isaac the Catholicos. We shall now try to argue it on still wider and deeper grounds.

This question cannot be satisfactorily answered until we have examined and cleared up the relation of the Paulician system of belief and observance exhibited to us in the *Key* to ancient Christianity in general, and until we have determined to what stage of the Church's development and history it belongs. This is the more necessary because of the very conflicting accounts of the antiquity of the sect. For example, John of Otzun, the Catholicos, writing in 720, not only hints that their heresy was a rehabilitation of what was very old, but seems to connect them with heresies which were already ramifying in Armenia under Nerses in the middle of the fourth century. And we shall presently adduce

---

[1] Dr. Karapet Ter-Mkrttschian, p. 86, notices that Gregory of Narek, in his famous book of prayers, entitles one of his chapters 'Discourse about the Church against the Manicheans, that is the Paulicians.' In it Gregory enumerates the functions and elements of the Church as a visible edifice, and explains their significance. He is of course combating the Thonraki teaching—that the real Church was not of wood or stone, but the invisible communion of the faithful (see Appendix V, p. 155).

similar evidence from the writings of Lazar of Pharp in the fifth century. The Greek writer again, Zigabenus, declares that Sergius Tychicus flourished only 500 years after St. Paul, i.e. about 550; if so, Constantine Sylvanus, the founder of the Paulicians, must be put back at the least to 450. On the other hand, Pseudo-Photius dates the appearance of Sergius 700 years after St. Paul; while Peter of Sicily, who used the same sources, dates it 800 after.

An examination of the *Key* itself goes far to confirm the statements of John of Otzun and of Zigabenus; for note that in it belief and observance go hand in hand, and are so closely interdependent as to preclude the idea that the Church, whose book it was, was in any way an eclectic one. Everything grows organically out of their conception of Jesus, as a man, not divine, but created, and yet not like other men, since he was the new Adam, without sin. Purely human, though free from sin, Jesus came to John to be baptized in the Jordan, when he had reached his thirtieth year. Then his sinless nature, which had triumphed over all temptations and kept all the Father's commandments, received its reward. The Spirit of the Father descends on him, fills him with the Godhead, and invests him with authority; and a voice from heaven proclaims him to be the chosen Son in whom God is well pleased, and who, according to the older form of the text of Luke, is on that day begotten by the Father. Then it was that Jesus received all the high prerogatives which raised him above ordinary humanity, though always without making him God and Creator. For till then he had been, except in respect of his sinlessness, in no wise higher than Moses or Enoch. Filled with the spirit of adoption, the elect Christ is forthwith led up on to the mountain to enjoy, for forty days, the mystery of intercourse with the Father; and this feast of divine converse to which, after baptism, Christ was at once admitted, is the archetype of the sacramental meal for the reception of which baptism qualifies us [1]

---

[1] The antiquity of the idea worked out in ch. v of the *Key* is apparent, if we compare the similar account in Philo (*Vita Mosis*, iii. § 2) of the forty days' stay of Moses on the mountain, which for him, as for Jesus, was preliminary to the ministry. Ἔδει δὲ πρότερον, ὥσπερ τὴν ψυχήν, καὶ τὸ σῶμα καθαρεῦσαι, μηδενὸς πάθους προσαψάμενον, ἀλλ' ἁγνεῦσαι ἀπὸ πάντων ὅσα τῆς θνητῆς ἐστι φύσεως· σιτίων καὶ ποτῶν καὶ τῆς πρὸς γυναῖκας ὁμιλίας. ἀλλὰ ταύτης μὲν ἐκ πολλῶν χρόνων κατεφρόνησε, καὶ σχεδὸν ἀφ' οὗ τὸ πρῶτον ἤρξατο προφητεύειν καὶ θεοφορεῖσθαι, προσῆκον ἡγούμενος ἕτοιμον ἐμπαρέχειν ἀεὶ τοῖς χρησμοῖς ἑαυτόν· σιτίων τε καὶ ποτῶν ἐπὶ τεσσαράκοντα ἡμέρας ἑξῆς ἠλόγησε, δῆλον ὅτι τροφὰς ἔχων ἀμείνους τὰς διὰ θεωρίας, αἷς ἄνωθεν ἀπ' οὐρανοῦ καταπνεόμενος τὴν μὲν διάνοιαν τὸ

In such a scheme as this there is clearly no room for the view that Jesus was born the incarnate God. A man fore-ordained to be sent from God, to become the vehicle of the Holy Spirit, and by his example and teaching to save men from their sins, this Jesus might be, and in fact was, according to this scheme; but it absolutely excludes from the outset the Alexandrine theology, which has come to be the only teaching of the Catholic Church. From the standpoint of the *Key* there was no incarnation of Jesus other than his possession by the Holy Spirit, in his thirtieth year, on the occasion of his baptism by St. John.

Of this simple Adoptionist Christology the observances of the Paulicians, as detailed in the *Key*, are the organic outgrowth. At a mature age, that is, about thirty, the catechumen is baptized. By that time he has come to a knowledge of his sin, original and operative, and has repented of both. The age of reflection has been reached[1]; the first heats of youth are past, and his natural instincts are brought under control. Before a man reaches this age of discretion no remission of sins can be effective and real; nor is any baptism other than an empty and superstitious form, which precedes, instead of following upon the awakening of the individual conscience, upon repentance of sin and faith in Jesus Christ, the Son of God. Through baptism the man becomes a Christian, and is admitted to partake, as was Jesus, of the heavenly meal. In commemoration of the forty days' fast of Jesus he keeps holy forty days. Here we have outlined the two chief sacraments. The catechism mentions a third, namely penitence. This was probably ordained in view of sins committed after baptism. It was, like baptism and the Eucharist, only to be conferred by the elect one who had received through the Church, from Jesus Christ, the power of binding and loosing.

Whether the mass of the believers progressed further in their imitation of Christ than is implied in their baptism and participation of the eucharistic food, cannot be ascertained. Probably not, as the catechism mentions only the three sacraments as necessary to salvation. Election or ordination, of which the *Key* so fully details the rite, was not a sacrament at all. If we may venture on

πρῶτον, ἔπειτα δὲ καὶ τὸ σῶμα διὰ τῆς ψυχῆς ἐβελτιοῦτο. And, as Jesus regained on the mount the outward glory which Adam lost, so Moses ἡμέραις ὕστερον, ὡς ἐλέχθη, τετταράκοντα κατέβαινε πολὺ καλλίων τὴν ὄψιν ἢ ὅτε ἀνῄει.

[1] The whole scheme of the Adoptionist Church recalls the Ideal Polity of Plato, wherein the citizens were to be initiated in the study of dialectic in their thirtieth year and not before, because until then their characters were not fixed.

an inference, we may say that it was a solemn initiation through which the Christian not only completed his imitation of Christ, but became a Christ himself. It authorized him to preach the word as Christ preached it; to suffer for it as he suffered. It was the baptism with his baptism. As a Christ, the elect one could apparently dispense his body to the faithful, saying, 'This is *my* body.' And he alone could baptize, or even perform the less important rite of name-giving.

It is clear at a glance that *The Key of Truth* presents a picture to us of a Christian Church, rigorously Adoptionist in its doctrine and observances; and as such it is of first-rate importance to the student of Christian institutions. For though we have sources enough from which to glean a fairly detailed knowledge of Adoptionist tenets, we now for the first time learn what were the rites, the discipline, the ordinal, and the general organization of a Church holding these tenets. And as these tenets were unquestionably more ancient than any others, we get back through *The Key of Truth* to a more just and primitive representation of the earliest form of Christian community than the later Catholic Church provides us with. Let us now compare its teaching with the few memorials or records of Adoptionist teaching which the great Church has allowed to survive.

The Shepherd of Hermas, a document of the Roman Church, composed long before the New Testament canon was fixed, is similar in its teaching to the second chapter of the *Key*[1]. Therein in simil. 5. 5. we read as follows: 'God made his Holy Spirit, which pre-existed and created all creation, to enter[2] and dwell in the flesh (i.e. human body) which he approved. This flesh therefore, in which the Holy Spirit took up its dwelling, served the Spirit well in holiness and purity, having never in any way polluted the Spirit. Therefore, because it had lived well and purely, and had laboured with the Spirit and worked therewith in every matter, conversing bravely and manfully, God chose (εἵλατο) it to be participator along with the Holy Spirit. For this flesh walked as pleased God, because it was not polluted upon earth, having the

---

[1] Compare also the baptismal prayer on p. 100.
[2] Such is the force of κατῴκισεν εἰς σάρκα. The *Ebionite Gospel* (Epiphan. Haer. 30, 13) related that the Holy Spirit was seen in the form of a dove coming down *and entering* (κατελθούσης καὶ εἰσελθούσης) into Jesus. So the most ancient Arm. MSS. of the Gospels (e. g. Lord Crawford's) in Luke iii. 22, after καταβῆναι add ᴧ ⟨ⱳᵾᵫᵵᵬᴸ = καὶ ἀναπαύεσθαι. So the old Georgian text renders, in Matt. iii. 16, ἐρχόμενον, 'it came *and stayed* on him.'

Holy Spirit. God therefore took (ἔλαβε) into counsel the Son and the angels in their glory, to the end that this flesh, having blamelessly served the Spirit, might furnish[1], as it were, a place of tabernacling (for the Spirit), and might not seem to have lost the reward of its service. For all flesh shall receive the reward which shall be found without stain or spot, and in it the Holy Spirit shall make its home.'

We could hardly find a clearer expression than the above extract affords of the two cardinal doctrines of the *Key*, namely, that the man Jesus, being flesh, was, because of his progress in moral excellence, chosen by God and endowed with authority and lordship by the Holy Spirit, which in Jordan came down and dwelt in him: - and secondly that the faithful who acquit themselves, like Jesus, nobly, shall receive from God the same guerdon, the same grace of the Spirit as he. As Prof. Harnack[2] remarks: 'In the Adoptionist Christology the parallel between Jesus and all the faithful who possess the Spirit and are sons of God, is clearly and fully expressed.'

Bearing in mind the vogue which *The Shepherd* of Hermas enjoyed in the earliest Roman Church, we are not surprised to learn from Eusebius (*H. E.* v. 28) that the same teaching was still popular, though already condemned as heretical, in the third century, under the teachers Theodotus and Artemon. The followers of the latter asserted with some truth that theirs was the doctrine which all the ancients had inherited by tradition and taught; and that the truth of the preaching (*kerugma*) had been preserved until the times of Victor, by whose successor Zephyrinus (190 A.D.) the truth had for the first time been counterfeited. Their claim was no idle one, if, as competent teachers have acknowledged, the Adoptionist Christology is that of the Synoptic Gospels themselves[3]. This claim of the followers of Artemon, that

---

[1] The Greek text of Hermas has ἵνα καὶ ἡ σάρξ αὕτη ... σχῇ τόπον τινὰ κατασκηνώσεως. Of course the sense is 'that this flesh (i.e. the man Jesus) might furnish in itself a resting-place for the Spirit,' and so win the reward, not that he might have somewhere to lay his head, as Prof. Harnack and Dr. von Gebhardt suggest when, in their note *ad loc.*, they compare Matt. viii. 20. Probably παρασχῇ should be read instead of σχῇ. The real parallel is not Matt. viii. 20, but John i. 14 ὁ λόγος σὰρξ ἐγένετο καὶ ἐσκήνωσεν ἐν ἡμῖν. So Archelaus (see p. c, below) speaks of the '*habitaculum* illud, quod ex Maria fuerat effectum.'

[2] *Dogmen-Gesch.*, p. 183.

[3] See Harnack, *Dogmen-Gesch.*, ed. 3, Bd. i. p. 652. After distinguishing the Adoptionist view from the Pneumatic (i.e. that which saw in Jesus God

they were the representatives of the original apostolic tradition, agrees with the similar claim everywhere put forward in the pages of the *Key*. It was also a claim which, in the tenth century, was acknowledged to be just by erudite members of the orthodox Armenian Church, and also by the higher clergy of the Syrian catholicos [1]. We are certainly not in a position to-day to impugn its validity.

In Justin Martyr's Dialogue (ch. 48) with Tryphon the Adoptionist view is clearly expressed, and the Jew is exhorted at the least to accept it, in case the Christian interlocutor is unable to convince him that Jesus was the pre-existent Son of the Maker of all things, himself actually God, and only man as born of the Virgin. 'Even if I cannot demonstrate so much as that,' says Tryphon to the Jew, 'you will at least admit that Jesus is the Messiah of God, in case he can be shown to have been born as a man of men, and be proved to have been raised by election (κατ' ἐκλογήν) to the dignity of messiahship. For there are, my friends,' he continues, 'some of our (*or* your) persuasion who admit that he is the Messiah, but declare him to have been a man of men. I do not agree with them,' he adds, 'even though they speak from a basis of much opinion held in common by them with myself; because we have been commanded by Christ himself to acquiesce not in human teachings, but only in the messages of the blessed prophets and in his teachings.'

The Jewish interlocutor in Justin's Dialogue takes no objection to this admission on the part of the Christian that the divinity of Christ rested on a prophetic rather than on an historical basis. He merely answers that, in his opinion, it was much the more reasonable view that Jesus had been born simply human, and had been anointed by way of election [2], and so had become the Messiah. 'For we all,' he says, 'expect the Messiah to be born a man of men.'

incarnate in the Virgin's womb), Harnack proceeds thus: 'The holy Scriptures might be appealed to in favour of both views. But those (Scriptures) were distinctly at an advantage considering the circumstances of the time (150-250 A.D.) which recognized in Christ the incarnation of a separate divine being. Just as certainly those (Scriptures) were true, from the standpoint of the Synoptic Gospels, which saw in Jesus a man chosen out by God to be his Son, and filled with the Spirit.'

[1] See p. 126, n. 2, and p. 145, the words beginning, 'Thou hadst written ...'

[2] Κατ' ἐκλογὴν or κατὰ προκοπὴν κεχρίσθαι. The latter idea is a Stoic one expressed in Stoical phrase.

We see that this Jew took up the position which is ascribed by Hippolytus in his *Philosophumena*[1] to the Ebionites. I quote the Latin version of Duncker:—'Ebionaei autem consentiunt quidem mundum ab eo, qui re vera Deus est, factum esse; quae autem ad Christum pertinent, consimiliter Cerintho et Carpocrati fabulantur. Moribus Iudaicis utuntur, secundum legem dictitantes sese iustificari; et Iesum dicentes iustificatum esse, cum observaverit legem[2]. Quapropter et Christum (i.e. unctum) Dei vocatum esse Iesum, cum nemo ex reliquis observaverit legem; etenim si quis alius fecisset, quae in lege praescripta sunt, ille evasisset Christus. Posse autem et sese ipsos, similiter cum fecerint, Christos evadere; etenim et ipsum hominem aeque atque omnes esse dicunt.' Here the Christology is sufficiently like that of the *Key*, in spite of its Jewish tinge; and the idea that a man, by fulfilling all righteousness, actually becomes a Christ is the same elevated thought which inspired the Paulicians, and is more or less explicitly worked out in the *Key*.

In his very next chapter Hippolytus speaks of Theodotus, whom we have already mentioned. The description of his position tallies exactly with that of the *Key*, and we now quote it: 'Theodotus autem quidam natione Byzantius introduxit haeresim novam[3], docens ea quae sunt de origine universi, congrua ex parte doctrinae verae Ecclesiae; cum a Deo omnia profecta esse consentit. Christum autem, e Gnosticorum et Cerinthi Ebionisque schola avellens, ait tali quodam modo apparuisse: et Iesum quidem esse hominem ex virgine natum secundum voluntatem Patris. Cum vixisset autem eodem modo quo universi homines, et cum piissimus fuisset, postea in baptismo ad Iordanem cepisse Christum superne delapsum in specie columbae. Quapropter non prius potestates in eo viguisse, quam postquam is qui delapsus erat, emicuerit in illo Spiritus, quem esse Christum appellat. Deum autem nunquam hunc factum esse volunt per descensum Spiritus.' We shall see presently that the dogmatic position of Archelaus, the early fourth-century opponent of Manes, was absolutely the same as that here ascribed to Theodotus.

---

[1] Bk. vii. 34.

[2] Cp. the prayer on p. 108 of the *Key*, 'Christ Jesus kept thy ineffable commands,' &c.; and p. 14, 'Forasmuch as the created man, Jesus, was very faithful to his Father, for this reason the Father bestowed on him a name of praise which is above every name.'

[3] It is impossible to attach more than a controversial value to this statement of Hippolytus that Theodotus' faith was new.

The additional details about Theodotus which we glean from Epiphanius, *Haer.* 54, who followed the lost *Syntagma* of Hippolytus, render the sameness of his teaching with that of the *Key* still more apparent, for he shows that Theodotus accepted both the Gospel of John and the belief in the miraculous birth as related by Luke. He even made special use of the exordium of the fourth Gospel, in which, however, he interpreted the Logos as the Holy Spirit; and, here strictly in accord with *The Shepherd* of Hermas, explained the words 'The Word became flesh' to refer to the endowment of Jesus with the Holy Spirit in the Jordan.

In Luke i. 35 Theodotus eliminated or laid no stress on the words, '*Wherefore also*,' in order to guard against the supposition that the power of the Most High really entered into the womb of the Virgin. In other words, though the conception of Jesus was a special providence, and was as such announced by the angel, it was no Divine Incarnation. The Paulicians also accepted the Gospel of John along with the Synoptics, and must have used the same exegesis as Theodotus. Since the fourth Gospel was the sheet-anchor of the rival or Alexandrine school of Christology, its inclusion in the canon of Theodotus proves no less the depth and sincerity of his Adoptionist faith than the ineluctable religious value and literary merit of that Gospel, which could thus force its way into circles of the faithful, to whom it might by many be thought to be alien. And it may be that, after all, the fourth Gospel was susceptible of an Adoptionist interpretation. Equally with the Synoptics it makes the descent of the Spirit upon him in Jordan the central event in the life of Jesus, his ἀναγέννησις or spiritual birth. The language of *The Shepherd* of Hermas, in its most characteristically Adoptionist passages, strikingly recalls the prelude of the fourth Gospel.

Whether the Alogi were or were not right in their rejection of the fourth Gospel, it anyhow made its way into the canon. And this canon was accepted by the spiritual descendants of the Alogi, among whom Epiphanius reckons Theodotus. There is consequently no reason for surprise if the Paulicians, who continued the teaching of the Alogi, so far as this was Adoptionist, in a much later age felt no difficulty in accepting the fourth Gospel. There is no trace in the *Key* of the use of the Apocalypse, which the Alogi equally rejected. But if the Paulicians of Armenia rejected this— and it is not clear that they did—they were more probably actuated by the scruples long felt against it in the entire Catholic Church.

The orthodox Armenians themselves, though they had translated it, hardly accepted, and rarely used it, before the eleventh century.

In the fragments of Melito, Bishop of Sardis, who addressed an apology to Marcus Aurelius (161–180) we meet with a transitional Christology, Adoptionist in its basis, with a superstructure of Logos doctrine. For example, in the list of his works given by Eusebius (*H. E.* lib. iv. c. 26) is a book about the creation and birth of Christ (περὶ κτίσεως καὶ γενέσεως), from which it seems that he regarded Christ as a κτίσμα. Also in a fragment of his work on the Incarnation, adduced by Anastasius Sinaita (*in Hodego suo, contra Acephalos*, c. xiii. p. 260, ed. Gretseri), we find the baptism emphasized as the turning-point in the life of Jesus Christ, before which he was a mere man, after which he was God. 'The things done *after the baptism* by Christ, and especially the signs, manifested the Godhead of him hidden in flesh (τὴν αὐτοῦ κεκρυμμένην ἐν σαρκὶ θεότητα ἐδήλουν) and assured the world of it. For the same person being God at once and perfect man, he assured us of his two essences (τὰς δύο αὐτοῦ οὐσίας); namely, of his Godhead by means of the signs in the three years after the baptism, and of his humanity in the thirty years (χρόνοις) which preceded the baptism, in which, owing to the imperfection of the flesh (διὰ τὸ ἀτελὲς τὸ κατὰ σάρκα), the signs of his Godhead were concealed, *although being true God before the aeons.*' The last words, in italics, are out of all grammatical relation with what precedes, and must be set down to the excerptor. Melito's view then was that Jesus was merely human, or at most potentially divine, before the baptism. The divinity till then lay hidden in him. The baptism caused it to actualise and manifest itself in miracles. But it is not clear that Melito believed the Godhead to have entered Jesus at baptism. It was rather a latent potency then called out into play. Thus his view was an adaptation of the Adoptionist view to the Logos theory.

So far we have found the Adoptionist theology flourishing both in Rome, in Palestine, and in Asia Minor, from the very earliest age. In Antioch it reached its turning-point in the second half of the third century under the Bishop Paul of Samosata, who, in spite of the anathemas of his orthodox opponents, who to their own satisfaction deposed him in a synod in 269, retained his bishopric under the protection of Zenobia, Empress of Palmyra, until the year 272, when his patroness was vanquished by Aurelian. From motives of high policy, and not because he had any dogmatic predilections, the victorious emperor insisted that Antioch should conform in matters of doctrine to Rome, of which the then bishop was a violent antagonist of Paul. Thus the Adoptionist influence was paralyzed in Asia, and the Roman Church gained its first great dogmatic triumph through the favour of a pagan emperor.

The victorious faction in Antioch destroyed the books of Paul of Samosata; so that of all his many works there remain to us but a few lines, chiefly taken from his discourses to Sabinus. The following two extracts are worth quoting here as much because of their resemblance to *The Shepherd* of Hermas and to the second chapter of the *Key*, as for their lofty spiritual tone:—

1. 'Having been anointed by the Holy Spirit, he was given the title of Christ. He suffered according to his nature, he worked miracles according to grace. For by his unflinching, unblenched will and resolution he made himself like unto God; and, having kept himself free from sin, he was made one with him, and was empowered to take up as it were the power to work wonders. By means of these he was shown to have one and the same energy in addition to the will (i.e. of God), and so received the title of Redeemer and Saviour of our race.'

2. 'The Saviour having approved himself holy and just, and having overcome by conflict and labour the sins of our forefather (i.e. Adam)—having won these successes by his virtue—was joined with God, having by his progressive advances in goodness attained to one and the same will and energy with him. And having preserved the same undivided, he doth inherit the name which is above every name, the reward 'of love, that was vouchsafed to him.'

It is probable that Paul of Samosata went further than the writer of the *Key* in accommodating his language to the pneumatic or Logos Christology of his antagonists. For in the *Key* the Logos teaching is not alluded to, and the writer seems never to have heard of it. Whereas Paul identified the Logos and wisdom with the Spirit which descended on Jesus in the Jordan. 'The Word,' he taught, 'is greater than the Christ, for Christ became great through wisdom.' And 'Mary did not bring forth the Word, for Mary was not before the ages. But she brought forth a man on a level with ourselves. It is the man that is anointed, not the Word. It was the Nazarene, our Lord, that was anointed....' Paul therefore seems to have embraced the doctrine of a pre-existent Logos, identical with the Spirit, which was, in the baptism, united with Jesus. The *Key*, on the other hand, only speaks of the Holy Spirit as so united. At the same time we must not forget that the chapters in which the Paulician Christology may have been more fully worked out are lost. They might perhaps have brought the entire work more into line with Paul of Samosata.

But the Adoptionist doctrine did not quite receive its death-blow in the overthrow of Paul. It must have still worked on the minds even of the partisans of the higher Christology. We cannot otherwise explain the presence in the works of Lactantius[1] of such a remarkable passage as the following: 'Ille (i.e. Iesus) vero exhibuit Deo fidem; docuit enim quod Deus unus sit, eumque solum coli oportere. Neque unquam se ipse Deum dixit; quia non servasset fidem, si missus ut Deos tolleret et unum assereret, induceret alium praeter unum. Hoc erat non de uno Deo facere praeconium, nec eius qui miserat; sed suum proprium negotium gerere, ac se ab eo, quem illustratum venerat, separare. Propterea quia tam fidelis exstitit, quia sibi nihil prorsus assumpsit, (nisi) ut mandata mittentis impleret: et sacerdotis perpetui dignitatem, et regis summi honorem, et iudicis potestatem, et Dei nomen accepit.' In the above there is no item of teaching, except the words *Dei nomen accepit*, which does not come in the *Key*. In denying the title of God to Jesus the Paulicians undoubtedly adhered to the earliest form of the Adoptionist teaching. The same view of Jesus Christ is also met with in Tertullian, when he has no controversial exigencies to serve; and also presents itself from time to time in Origen, e.g. *C. Celsum*, lib. 2, c. 9.

It is an error to suppose that the evolution and acceptance of orthodox doctrine during the third and fourth century went on at the same rate in the outlying parts of the Roman Empire or among the Christian communities outside its pale, as in the great centres, such as Rome, and Antioch, and Alexandria, wherein there were, as it were, schools and academies of divines trained in Greek dialectic, and ready to elaborate the more primitive and inchoate teaching of the Gospel into the 'complicated and subtle developments' about which J. H. Newman[2] has written so eloquently Thus it is that the Adoptionist teaching of the East, owing to the wilful suppression of its monuments, has survived[3] to us in a single

---

[1] *De vera Sap.* iv. 14.

[2] See *Development of Christian Doctrine*, ch. ii. § 1.

[3] The writings of Photinus, like those of Paul of Samosata, are lost. He was condemned in the Synods of Milan (345, 347) for teaching the unity of the

exceptional writing, sufficiently remote from both Rome and Antioch in the place of its origin.

This writing is no other than the so-called *Acts of Archelaus*. These record a disputation held between Mani and Archelaus, Bishop of Karkhar, across the Tigris in Persia, before the beginning of the fourth century. It matters nothing whether the disputation was ever really held. Its importance lies in the doctrine it contains. For, apart from the light which it throws on the teaching of Mani, we learn from it exactly what was the type of Christology in vogue at that time in circles accounted outside the Empire to be quite orthodox[1], and vehemently opposed to Mani. The speeches of Archelaus show that his Christology was Adoptionist and in very close agreement with the *Key*. The classical passages are in chs. 49 and 50, wherein Archelaus combats the view of Mani that Jesus was a merely spiritual being, that he was the *Eternal* (i.e. pre-existent) Son of God, and was by nature (i.e. by birth) a perfect being[2]. 'Dic mihi,' says Archelaus, 'super quem Spiritus Sanctus sicut columba descendit. Quis est etiam qui baptizatur a Ioanne? Si perfectus erat, si Filius erat, si virtus erat, non poterat Spiritus ingredi; sicut nec regnum potest ingredi intra regnum. Cuius autem ei caelitus emissa vox testimonium detulit dicens: "Hic est Filius meus dilectus, in quo bene complacui"?'

divine personality, and because he regarded Jesus as a man fore-ordained by God, who, by his superior moral growth and development, won divine dignity. Harnack (*Dogmen-Gesch.* ii. p. 240) remarks: 'Hier liegt also der letzte, in sich consequente Versuch vor, den christlichen Monotheismus zu wahren, die philosophische Logos-lehre völlig abzuthun und das Göttliche in Christus als eine göttliche Wirkung aufzufassen. Allein dieser Versuch war nicht mehr zeitgemäss.' Photinus is said to have denied the miraculous birth. The teaching of Bonosus was similar in tendency.

[1] Thus at the close of the dialogue (p. 185) Archelaus writes: 'Appellati sumus ex Salvatoris desiderio Christiani, sicut universus orbis terrarum testimonium perhibet, atque apostoli edocent; sed et optimus architectus eius, fundamentum nostrum, id est ecclesiae, Paulus posuit, et legem tradidit, ordinatis Ministris et Presbyteris et Episcopis in ea; describens per loca singula, quomodo et qualiter oporteat ministros Dei, quales et qualiter fieri Presbyteros, qualesque esse debeant, qui episcopatum desiderant; quae omnia bene nobis, et recte disposita, usque in hodiernum, statum suum custodiunt.'

[2] It is noticeable that both Mani and Archelaus assume that if Jesus from birth had been *filius* and *virtus Dei, Christus*, God merely transformed into man (p. 181), then he must have been all along an apparitional and not a real man of flesh and blood. Archelaus asserts the Adoptionist view by way of denying the docetic view of Christ. He has never heard of a view which asserted the divine incarnation and which was *not* also docetic. Divine incarnation and docetism to his mind imply one another.

And just above, in the same speech, Archelaus, like the writer of the *Key*, identifies Jesus Christ with the least in the kingdom of heaven: 'Quando Iesus de Ioanne testimonium dat, et dicebat, quia maior in natis mulierum nullus surrexit Ioanne Baptista; qui autem minor est in regno caelorum maior est illo: Dic mihi qua ratione maior illo est in regno caelorum? Nunquid Iesus minor erat Ioanne in regno caelorum? Dico, absit .... sine dubio minor erat Ioanne Iesus inter natos mulierum; in regno autem caelorum maior illo erat.' Before election Jesus was mere man and less than John.

In his reply Mani says: 'Mihi enim pium videtur dicere, quod nihil eguerit Filius Dei, in eo quod adventus eius procuratur ad terras, neque opus habuerit columba, neque baptismate, neque matre, neque fratribus, fortasse neque patre, qui ei secundum te fuit Ioseph; sed totus ille ipse descendens, semetipsum in quocunque voluit transformavit in hominem, eo pacto, quo Paulus[1] dicit, habitu repertus est ut homo.' Athanasius, controverting an Adoptionist, would have used almost the same argument as that which Mani here addresses to Archelaus. If the pre-existing Divine Being merely assumed the form of man, then what significance attaches to the episode of the descent of the Divine Spirit upon Jesus in the Jordan? Mani believed that the one excludes the other, and makes it meaningless. Accordingly he ruled out the story of the baptism. And the orthodox Church also went some way in the same direction. For it left out of the creeds[2] all reference to the baptism of the Lord at the same time that it gave prominence to the rival and barely compatible incident of the miraculous conception; and it ejected from the text of Luke iii. 22 the alternative, and perhaps earlier, reading: 'Thou art my beloved Son: *this day have I begotten thee.*' As to the assertion of Mani that his antagonist believed in the natural paternity of Joseph, 'patre qui ei secundum te fuit Ioseph,' it

[1] Phil. ii. 7.

[2] This omission must strike every one who considers the great importance which the general perspective of all four Gospels gives to the baptism of Jesus. Harnack notices this point (*Dogmen-Gesch.* ed. 3, vol. i. p. 183), and remarks that Ignatius alone (*ad Smyrn.* 1; cf. *ad Eph.* xviii. 2) hints of a creed in which the baptism was mentioned. The stress laid by Archelaus on the baptism implies that his creed gave it prominence; and it is noteworthy that in the form of creed propounded by Nerses (see p. 159) for acceptance by Armenian Manicheans the baptism is insisted on. The Manicheans denied it. The great Church kept it in the background and tried (see cliii foll.) to minimize its significance. The Armenian baptismal creed still retains it.

is not clear from these *Acts* that Archelaus denied the miraculous birth. But Mani was perhaps aware that Archelaus read in his Gospel the form of text in Matthew i. 16, which survives in the Lewis Syriac Codex. For this is likely to have been the form of text used by the Syriac-speaking bishop of Karkhar. But whether or no Archelaus had such a form of text, there is little doubt that he accepted the teaching of the miraculous birth [1].

Continuing his reply, Mani sets before us in the plainest way the position of Archelaus, who yet accounted himself to be an orthodox opponent of the new heresy: 'Si enim hominem eum tantummodo ex Maria esse dicis, et in baptismate Spiritum percepisse, ergo per profectum Filius videbitur, et non per naturam.' Here the words *per profectum* answer to the Greek κατὰ προκοπήν, the watchword of the Adoptionists.

Moreover, in the sequel Archelaus enunciates that same doctrine of a parallel descent of the Spirit on Christ-like men, whereby they became themselves Christs or Paracletes, which, as we saw, is hinted at in *The Shepherd* of Hermas, and was regularly recognized among the Montanists, the Paulicians, and the Manicheans themselves; he is speaking with reference to the descent of the Spirit on Jesus at the baptism, and adds: 'Spiritus enim secundum rectam rationem habitat in homine, et descendit, et permanet, et competenter hoc et factum est, et fit semper [2], sicut tu te ipsum ante hoc tempus profitebaris esse paracletum Dei.... Spiritum enim venisse super te dixisti, quem promiserat Iesus esse missurum; et unde nisi de caelo descendat? Et si descendit Spiritus super hominem dignum se [2], super te autem veras columbas descendisse sentiendum est?' It is clear that Archelaus believed that the Spirit descends under proper conditions and often on the elect, who, through its immanence in them, become Paracletes. He only objected to *Mani's* laying claim to such inspiration. But it is not to combat that claim that the passage is written, but in answer to Mani's contention that, if Jesus was a real man of flesh and blood, then a real dove must have descended upon him—a contention based on Paul's phrase *sicut homo* in

---

[1] He calls Jesus indeed (p. 180) 'hominem naturaliter factum ex Maria habentem carnem et sanguinem.' But here *naturaliter* does not exclude miraculous birth. It is, however, only Mani who (p. 170) speaks of *incontaminata virgo*.

[2] It is difficult to reconcile this with the passage, 'Sicut enim paracleti pondus,' &c., on p. c, below. The explanation is that Christ and his disciples were inspired in a higher degree, but not by a Spirit different in kind.

Phil. ii. 7, which Mani argued had the same sense as *sicut columba* in Matt. iii. 16.

Then Archelaus proceeds to declare that the Son of Mary was a mere man until the voice in Jordan, in recognition of his brave championship of righteousness, proclaimed him the Christ of God: 'Non ita est quoniam exinanivit semetipsum, formam servi accipiens. Dico autem de eo qui ex Maria factus est homo.' That is to say, the Son of Mary was not the being who, in Paul's phrase, 'emptied himself, and took the form of a servant.' This self-emptying being was the Christ who descended on the Son of Mary at baptism. This is clear from what follows, for he continues: 'Quid enim? Non poteramus et nos multo facilius et lautius ista narrare? Sed absit ut a veritate declinamus iota unum. Est enim qui de Maria natus est Filius, qui totum hoc quod magnum est voluit perferre certamen, Iesus. Hic est Christus Dei, qui descendit super eum, qui de Maria est.' This means that the Christhood was bestowed on the merely human Son of Mary at the baptism as a reward for his fortitude in the struggle. After a few words Archelaus continues thus: ' Statim (i. e. after the baptism) enim in desertum a Spiritu ductus est Iesus ut tentaretur a diabolo. Quem cum diabolus ignoraret, dicebat ei, " Si Filius es Dei . . ." Ignorabat autem propter quid genuisset (sc. Spiritus) Filium Dei, qui praedicabat regnum caelorum, quod erat habitaculum magnum, nec ab ullo alio parari potuisset; unde et affixus cruci, cum resurrexisset ab inferis assumptus est illuc, ubi Christus Filius Dei regnabat. . . ' Then he asks why the disciples only fell on their faces 'in una hora illa, quando sicut sol resplenduit vultus eius? Nonne propter habitaculum illud, quod ex Maria fuerat effectum? Sicut enim Paracleti pondus nullus alius valuit sustinere, nisi soli discipuli, et Paulus beatus; ita etiam Spiritum qui de caelis descenderat, per quem vox paterna testatur dicens, " Hic est Filius meus dilectus," nullus alius portare praevaluit, nisi qui ex Maria natus est, super omnes sanctos Iesus.' And he finally insists that Jesus was tempted as a mere man. 'Dominus vero meus Iesus, si tentus est, ut homo ab hominibus tentus est. Si non est homo, nec tentus est. Si non est tentus, nec passus est, nec baptizatus est. Si ille non est baptizatus, neque quisquam nostrum baptizatus est.'

The above passages are remarkable for their resemblance, not only to the extract we have given from *The Shepherd* of Hermas, but also to a very early Adoptionist book, the pseudo-Cyprianic *De Montibus Sina et Sion*, in ch. 4 of which we read: 'Caro dominica a Deo Patre Iesu vocata est; Spiritus Sanctus, qui de caelo descendit, Christus, id est unctus Dei vivi a Deo vocatus est; Spiritus carne mixtus Iesus Christus.' Here we have almost the words of Archelaus: 'It was the Christ of God that descended upon the Son of Mary.' And in ch. 13, the same tract, like Hermas, identifies the Holy Spirit with the Son of God, 'Sanctus Spiritus, *Dei Filius*, geminatum se videt, Pater in Filio et Filius in Patre utrosque se in se vident.'

So far we have traced the history of Adoptionist opinion from its earliest cradle in Rome and Judaea to the confines of Armenia. And here, where it figures in dramatic form as the orthodox antithesis to the heresy of Mani, it also begins to approach most closely to the form in which *The Key of Truth* presents it to us, though without forfeiting any of the characteristic features which it already bore in *The Shepherd* of Hermas. For Archelaus was ἐπίσκοπος Καρχάρων or Κασχάρων; Zacagni[1], the editor of the *Acts* or *Disputatio* prefers the former, Lequien (*Or. Chr.* tom. ii. pp. 1002 and 1163) the latter reading[2]. In the *Acts*, p. 36, Karkhar or Kashkar is called an 'urbs Mesopotamiae,' which is somewhat vague. Wherever it was, it was three days' hard riding from 'Castellum Arabion,' a fort on the river Stranga; and this river formed the boundary between the Roman dominions and the Persian at the time of the disputation, which took place during the reign of Probus, about 275–277. Mommsen shows (*Rom. Prov.* ii. 115) that from the year 282 the Roman frontier against Persia left the Tigris in the neighbourhood of Gaugamela and trended north-east nearly along the upper course of the great Zab, so as to include the whole of the upper basin of the Tigris in the Roman dominion. This, 'the earlier order' (as Mommsen calls it l.c.), temporarily lost during the rebellion of Zenobia, was, however, really re-established by Probus, as Von Gutschmid shows in his article on Agathangelus in the *Zeitschr. d. Deutsch. Morgenl. Gesell.* xxxi. 50. The persistent tradition of the Armenians that it was Probus who restored against the Persians the old frontier along the upper Zab and the Araxes, cannot otherwise be explained; and the *Disputation* of Archelaus indicates that a successful Roman expedition along the frontier of Media was just concluded, and

---

[1] See Routh's *Reliquiae*, vol. v. p. 8, to the pages of which I refer above.
[2] On p. 41 of the *Disputatio* we have 'Charra' written. This is the error of some scribe who knew Carrhae but not Karkhar. Carrhae was 300 miles from Arabion Castellum, and very remote from the Persian frontier of that day.

mentions Probus as the emperor then on the throne. Now that the native name for the upper Zab was Stranga we know from two sources. Firstly, Pseudo-Callisthenes, chs. 14, 15, says that Alexander, after crossing the upper Tigris, went on and crossed the frozen Stranga river, in order to fight the battle of Arbela. Secondly, Geo. Cedrenus relates that Asan (or Arslan) the Turk, marching (c. 1048) from Tabriz round the head of Lake Urmiah to invade Vaspurakan (east of Lake Van) pitched his camp κατὰ τὸν Στράγγα ποταμόν. The Arabion Castellum can also be fixed from Armenian sources. For Vardan the chronicler, a native of Pers-Armenia, writing about 1270, says that Sanatruk murdered St. Bartholomew at Arabion *qalaq* (i.e. Castellum). In the old Armenian Acts of Bartholomew the place is called *Urbianos qalaq*, i.e. Urbian city, a spelling which is natural enough in a translation from Syriac. Moses Chorenatzi, 21, writing not later than 700, calls it Arebanos *qalaq* in his Hist. 2. 36 [1]. The place of martyrdom of St. Bartholomew has always been venerated by Syrians and Armenians alike at a spot on the east side of the upper Zab, now called Deir. Here is the 'monastery and church of St. Bartholomew, erected on the traditional site of his martyrdom [2].' Since Vardan (who died in old age A.D. 1271) wrote, the old name *Arabion qalaq* has been lost, but it must have been opposite Deir, in a neighbourhood still strewn with ruins of the past.

Thus we have identified both the river Stranga and the Arabion Castellum. Karkhar or Kaskhar was, according to the Acts, p. 48, a city distant three days' ride from the Castellum. Marcellus, probably a Roman governor, lived there, and his fame had spread across the river Stranga, and so reached Persia. From the town of Karkhar to Arabion Castellum there ran a high road along which Marcellus had erected shelter-houses at intervals. Both places were in the Roman dominions. Mani came from some place in Persia two days' ride the other side of the Stranga, and was taking refuge on Roman territory in the Castellum, when the Roman authorities gave him up to the Persian king who wanted him. It must have been one of the fifteen castella in Roman Gordyene mentioned by Ammianus, xxv. 7, 9; and may even have been the 'castra Maurorum, munimentum perquam opportunum' of which he

---

[1] In this passage some MSS. read 'Arebonos,' which is probably most correct. The name may have meant the camp of the 'Arabs,' as Kessler (Mani) supposes in a disquisition otherwise full of arbitrary surmises.

[2] See Murray's *Handbook to Asia Minor*, 1895, p. 238.

there speaks. Probably Mani came from Urmia, which is about fifty miles south-east of Deir, along a still existing road. The only highroads of any consequence leading from Arabion Castellum were the one to Van, which is some sixty miles nearly due west, and the one which now goes to Julamerk further down the Zab. There is no road leading north up the Zab from Deir; for you soon come on the hills in which the Zab rises. It is certain therefore that Karkhar or Kaskhar was somewhere in Vaspurakan, and not very far from Van, perhaps in the direction of Bitlis. There were several places called Karkhar in Armenia; e.g. a fort on the west bank of the Euphrates[1], fifty miles south-east of Melitene and north-east of Samosata, now called Gerger, and in the government of Malatiah. This is too far away. Another is mentioned by Kirakos, an Armenian chronicler of the thirteenth century (ed. Ven. 1865, p. 207); and this one was apparently in the province of Artzakh, not far from Nakhidjevan on the Araxes. If so, this was also too far away. But Kirakos does not define its position, and it may have been further south-west. If it was really in Artzakh, it would have been the Araxes and not the Stranga which flowed between it and Persia. In any case the Karkhar of the *Acts* lay in Mesopotamian Armenia, not far from Van, and in the heart of the region where we have seen good reason[2] to locate the earliest Christianity of Armenia. Archelaus the Adoptionist must therefore have been bishop of an Armenian see in the same region as, and soon after, the Bishop Meruzanes[3] mentioned in Eusebius' history. He was probably a Syrian, as were most of the early South Armenian ecclesiastics. The script of the Armenian clergy in the upper basin of the Tigris continued to be Syriac till about 400 A.D.; it is even said that near Mosul Armenian MSS. are still to be found, written in Syriac characters. There was, moreover, an early and persistent tradition among the Armenians themselves that the Christianity of Armenia along the Median border, especially in Siuniq, the region east of Ararat along the Araxes, and bordering Albania (the modern Daghestan), was older than that of Gregory the Illuminator, and went back to St. Bartholomew

---

[1] This was an important place and seat of a Syrian bishop. Lequien (*Or. Chr.* ii. 1165-7) gives the names of many of its bishops.

[2] The Albanian language itself was known as the tongue of the Gargars or Karkars; but Albania (now the Daghestan country) lay too far away, and Karkhar was clearly a city of some size and importance.

[3] See p. cix.

and St. Thaddeus, to whom its succession of bishops went back. And certainly the Armenian topography of the *Acts* of the former saint is very accurate. It is said that he preached the Gospel of Matthew in Golthn round about Nakhidjewan, in Her and Zarewand in Pers-Armenia and in the *Urbianos qualaq* or Arabion Castellum, of which we have been speaking. The tradition undoubtedly contained truth, and the *Acts* of Archelaus, even if we had no other evidence, would be enough to prove that the Christianity of this region was, in the age of Gregory the Illuminator, as rigorously Adoptionist as it was passionately opposed to the propaganda of Mani. It is noticeable that Archelaus has no inkling of any other Christology than his own. It was the orthodoxy of the land.

Prof. Harnack (*Dogm.-Gesch.* i. 692) infers from these *Acts of Archelaus*, that 'at the beginning of the fourth century the Logos-Christology had not spread beyond the limits of the confederated Christendom of the Roman Empire.' But he is wrong in supposing that, after the end of the third century, no Christianity was possible in the Church which did not recognize the personal pre-existence of Jesus Christ. On the contrary, disguised under the name Paulician, this form of the Catholic Faith survived for centuries among the mixed Greek and Armenian inhabitants of the Taurus range in its entire length. There the teaching fell on good ground, and bore fruit in hundreds of villages on hill or plain. There it maintained a steady war against images, Mariolatry, and much else that the degenerate Greek world had adopted from Paganism. It was a Church for which the seven councils had no significance; for were not these synods of men who, having abandoned the true baptism, had lost their sacraments, their priestly orders, the apostolic tradition, nay, the very character and essentials of Christian communion? It was the Church of hardy mountaineers, the rampart of Christianity and Roman civilization against the Arab and Tartar hordes. Nor was it without its martyrs, who were counted by hundreds of thousands, and whose slayers invariably took their orders from the persecuting clergy of old and new Rome. And when reasons of state or bigotry failed to exterminate this primitive Church among the ranges of the Taurus, its members were deported by hundreds of thousands to Thrace. There they throve for centuries, and the spread of their tenets into Bohemia, Poland, Germany, Italy, France, and even into our own England, must have helped not a little to prepare the ground for the Puritan Reformation.

We are now in a position to answer the question: Was Paulicianism a mere excrescence on the Christianity of the post-Nicene age, or was it the recrudescence of an ancient and primitive form of the religion which the great Church had outgrown, but which had lingered on in remote and mountainous districts. It is now evident to us that the name Paulician originally had reference not to St. Paul, but to the last great champion of Adoptionist Christianity in the Greek world, Paul of Samosata; and Gregory Magistros spoke from sound knowledge when, in summing up his indictment of the Thonraki, he wrote thus: 'Here then you see the Paulicians, who got their poison from Paul of Samosata.' In the nineteenth canon of the Council of Nice Paul's followers are called 'Pauliani,' and it is enjoined that they shall be re-baptized;—this, no doubt, because they, on principle, deferred baptism. Now the name *Pauliciani* is simply the Armenian form of *Pauliani*, and, as Karapet Ter-Mkrttchian points out (p. 63), could only have arisen on Armenian soil. The addition *ic* or *ik*, this writer remarks, is derisive, 'welches, wie auch in anderen Sprachen, im Sinne des Spottes gebraucht werden kann.' With the addition *ean* or *ian* the word would mean the 'follower or son of wretched little Paul.' In the same way, the derivative *Manichean* may have the same history, and mean one who follows wretched little Mani. The Escurial account of the sect which is the *Grundschrift* of Photius, Petrus Siculus, Zigabenus, and other Greek writers, equally refers the origin of the Paulicians to Paul of Samosata. 'The Paulicians,' we read, 'who are also Manicheans, were by a change of name called, instead of Manicheans, Paulicians, from a certain Paul of Samosata, the son of a Manichean woman called Kallinike.' That Paul's mother may have borne such a name as Kallinike is likely enough; that she could have been a Manichean is impossible on chronological grounds. And J. Friedrich, the editor of this Escurial fragment, justly remarks that the association with Mani is merely due to the religious schematism, which, in the seventh and succeeding centuries, set down every form of dissent from the dominant orthodoxy to Manichean influence. Manicheanism was in those ages the *bête noire* of the orthodox catholic, just as free-masonry is in the present day. The affiliation to St. Paul can never have been ventured on except by the Paulicians themselves. For it is absurd to suppose that their opponents would have given to the remnant of the old Adoptionist Church the name of Paulician, either because they actually were or because they considered themselves in some special way, to be the adherents of Paul the Apostle. That would rather have been a reason to their enemies for not calling them Paulicians. In Mesopotamia the followers of Paul of Samosata long continued to be known as Pauliani. Ephrem names them in his hymns[1], and he and other writers associate them with Nestorianism, which was the Syrian counterpart of Paulicianism, and rested on a basis of Adoptionist opinion. Asseman (*Bibl. Orient.* i. 347) adduces a passage in which Nestorian opinion is directly traced back to the influence of Paul of Samosata. It is from Simeon Episc. Beth.-Arsamensis, bishop in Persia, 510–525 A. D. In this writing, after accusing his Nestorian contemporaries of holding, like the Jews, that Christ was a mere man, Simeon continues thus: 'A Simone insanum illum errorem accepit Ebion: ab hoc Artemon: ab Artemone Paulus Samosatenus, qui olim Antiochiae Syriae episcopus fuit sub Ethnicis Romanorum imperatoribus .. Hic enim Paulus Samosatenus plus quam Simon Magus et Ebion et Artemon praeceptores sui, blasphemare ausus est, de beata Maria haec dicens: Nudum hominem genuit Maria, nec post partum virgo permansit. Christum autem appellavit creatum, factum, mortalem, et filium ex gratia. De seipso vero dicebat: Ego quoque si voluero, Christus ero, quum ego et Christus unius eiusdemque simus naturae.'

How comes it that the Greek world, after using the name *Pauliani* in the fourth century to denote the party of Paul of Samosata, dropped it in the following centuries, and in the ninth knew them only under the Armenian form of the name? The answer seems to be this. The steady aim of the Imperial Government, as exampled by the mission of Gregory Magistros as late as the eleventh century, was to drive the adherents of the Adoptionist Church outside the limits of the Empire. They consequently took refuge in Mesopotamia, and later in the Mohammedan dominions generally, where they were tolerated and where their own type of belief, as we see from the *Acts of Archelaus*, had never ceased to be accounted orthodox. They were thus lost sight of almost for centuries by the Greek theologians of Constantinople and other great centres. When at last they again made themselves felt as the extreme left wing of the iconoclasts—the great party of revolt against the revived Greek paganism of the eighth century—it was the orthodox or grecized Armenians that, as it were, introduced them afresh to the notice of the Greeks. Thus it was through the

---

[1] See Asseman, *Bibl. Orient.* i. 128.

mediation of the Armenians themselves, and primarily as an Armenian sect, that the Greeks knew them.

Armenia was the ground on which the west met the east. The half of it which was Roman, that is to say within the pale of the Byzantine Empire, took its first *Catholici* or patriarchs from the Greek diocese of Caesarea[1]; and even after the invention, about 450, of the legend of the descent of the Holy Spirit in Edjmiatzin, this portion continued to passively adopt the decrees of all the Greek councils, with the single exception of that of Chalcedon; whose decisions the bishops and patriarchs of the orthodox Armenians for centuries accepted and rejected by turns, according as they wanted or did not want a cause of quarrel with the Greeks. But in the south-east of Armenia, which was for the most part outside the Roman Empire and under the over-lordship first of Persia and then of the Eastern Khaliphs, the old Adoptionist Church seems to have steadily held its own against the pneumatic Christology which had been imported from Caesarea along with monkery and the cult of the virgin, of the saints and of images. From the first it must have been a thorn in the side of the grecizing Armenians. The antiquity conceded to it in the pages of *John the Philosopher* suggests that it was one with the sect of Borborei or muddy ones, who, according to the writers Goriun and Moses of Khoren[2], were fiercely persecuted by Sahak and Mesrop in Persian Armenia. Goriun relates how Mesrop in the provinces and towns of Armenia, subject to the Emperor Theodosius, set himself under royal orders to combat the rash and insolent Borborides. Those who would not receive the word of truth, that is to say the pneumatic or Logos-Christology, were given over to terrible punishments; they were imprisoned, chained, and tortured; and after that, when they were still recalcitrant, they were either burned alive, or penned in and hunted out of the Roman dominions, loaded with every sort of ignominy.

It is probable that the so-called Messalians of Armenia, of whom we hear in the fifth century, were Adoptionists. In the year 447 (following the date given by Tchamtchian) the adherents of the Greek Church in Armenia held a council at Shahapivan over which presided Joseph, a pupil of Mesrop, at which it was decreed (Canon xix) that priests, deacons, or monks convicted of *mtslénu-*

---

[1] In the fifth century there were constantly two Catholici in Armenia, one in the Armenian, the other in the Persian half.

[2] Bk. iii. ch. 58.

thiun, i.e. Messalianism, are to be branded on the forehead with the image of a fox. Long afterwards, in the tenth century, this was still the punishment of Paulicians. A relapse into the heresy was to be punished by ham-stringing. No definite tenets are mentioned in the acts of this council. The reasons for identifying the victims of this brutal persecution with those who later on were called Paulicians and Thonraki are the following :—

1. All the Armenian writers from John of Otzun on, who describe Paulicianism, call it *mtslĕnuthiun*. John specially identifies it with the heresy combated by Nerses (probably Nerses I), and alleges that it had flourished in Armenia long before the Arab invasion (*c.* 650 A.D.).

2. It was widespread in south-eastern Armenia before the middle of the fifth century. It not only attracted bishops, priests, deacons, and monks, but native satraps (*nakhararq*), princes, feudal lords, headmen of villages with their entire families. This proves that, previous to the introduction of orthodox Greek Logos-Christianity through Caesarea, it was the national faith of Armenia. It cannot have been any learned heresy or monkish overwrought asceticism which thus attracted the entire population.

3. Lazar of Pharp, the Armenian historian, in his letter to Vahan, written *c.* 480 A.D. (printed by Emin, Moscow, 1853), writes as follows : 'The heresy of our Armenian land is not named after any teacher; is not written down in words. Its adherents are ignorant, as in their faith so in their teaching; in their actions, however slow and infirm.' This description indicates only a population of old-believers, strangers to the new Christology imported from Caesarea. Lazar was himself accused of this heresy.

4. Lazar hints at baptist tenets when he applies to them the proverb : 'For the bride of the swine a bath of drain-water.'

5. It was distinctively the Syriac Christianity of Armenia. Karapet Ter Mkrttschian justly writes as follows (p. 47): 'Wir erfahren nicht, wie lange sie schon hier im Lande geherrscht hatte, und ob man früher gegen sie eingeschritten war. Bedenken wir aber, dass die Glieder dieser Synode (i.e. Shahapivan) wohl hauptsächlich Schüler des Sahak und des Mesrop gewesen sind, Männer also von neuer, griechischer Bildung, deren ganzes Bestreben darauf gerichtet war, ihre Kirche neu zu beleben und die alten Missbräuche zu beseitigen, so können wir annehmen, dass bei ihren Vorgängern, die meist Syrer waren, oder Eingeborene syrischer Bildung … die Messalianer noch geduldet gewesen waren.'

6. This persecution of Adoptionists was in the fifth century inspired from Constantinople, as in the fourth it had been from Caesarea; and Proclus, in his *Ep. ad Armenos* (Mansi, v. 428), A.D. 435, assails the view among them (τὸν τῶν ἐμπλήκτων λόγον) that Christ was ψιλὸς ἄνθρωπος.

7. Lazar particularly distinguishes 'the heresy of Armenia' from other heresies, e.g. from that of Arius, of Apollinarius of Laodicea, of Nestor of Antioch, of Eutyches of Constantinople, of Kumbricius the slave, who afterwards assumed the name of Mani, and of many other 'guides to perdition.' He enumerates all these and says of them this: 'These have lapsed into incurable errors in matters of faith, but have erred in word only and not in act. For as regards personal chastity there is no sort of self-mortification in which they are not conspicuous, and especially in matters of food and drink and abstinence from pollutions.' We may infer that 'the heresy of Armenia' was steadily hostile to monks and to the overstrained asceticism of the school of St. Basil, which was then spreading in Armenia, radiating from Caesarea as its focus.

8. There is evidence that Antioch was, in the fifth century, a centre from which heresy made its way to Armenia. Thus in an Armenian MS. recently acquired by the Bodleian Library is preserved an old notice that, about 470-480, when John Mandakuni was Catholicos of Pers-Armenia and Giut of the Greek portion, certain teachers came from Antioch to Armenia. They were clothed in sackcloth, barefooted, and ascetic in their lives, and preached against the worship of the cross, and denied the Virgin Mary to be *theotokos*. Their names were Constantine, Petrus, and Theodore, and they appeared in the village of Aushin. It is possible, however, that these men were Nestorian missionaries only.

Yet it was almost certainly to these Borborides or Borborei that the first introduction of Christianity in Armenia was due. Eusebius relates in his history (bk. 6, ch. 46), that Dionysius of Alexandria, about the years 248-265, addressed a letter about repentance to the Armenian communities presided over by the Bishop Meruzanes. This name, in Armenian Merujan, bespeaks a member of the great Artsruni house or clan which ruled in Vaspurakan in the extreme south-east of Armenia, in the region of the headwaters of the Tigris. Here we know, from the *Acts of Archelaus*, that Adoptionism was fifty years later still the orthodoxy of the land. There can be little doubt that Meruzanes, the immediate neighbour of Archelaus, was a Christian bishop of the same type of faith. That the earliest Christendom of their land was of this type explains the fact that the orthodox Armenian historians of Armenia of the late fourth and fifth century, Agathangelos and Faustus, are so silent about the earlier and pre-Gregorian Christianization of Vaspurakan. They wished to ignore it, for in Armenia Christianity, to their way of thinking, began with the introduction of the Greek pneumatic Christology of Caesarea. To the same Adoptionist Christians of Vaspurakan was probably due the first Armenian version of the New Testament and of the Psalms. For the Mesropic version of the New Testament is no more than a fifth-century recension, made from fourth-century Greek MSS. brought from Constantinople or Alexandria, of an earlier translation based on the oldest form of the Syriac, as we find it either in the newly-found Lewis Codex or in Cureton's MS.[1] This earliest Armenian translation came from Syria along with many of the oldest Armenian ecclesiological terms; and if it was originally in use in this corner of Armenia among Adoptionist believers, we can understand why the Armenian fathers of the fifth century make so much mystery about the earlier Armenian translation. As one reads their confused accounts of the origin of their version of the Scriptures, one feels that they had here something to conceal. They did not wish to acknowledge their indebtedness to this earliest form of the Armenian Church.

It is also in this connexion to be noticed that the earliest Christianity of Armenia, according to the evidence of the orthodox historians themselves, was centred in Taron, which was also the constant home and focus of Paulicianism. The mother church of Armenia was at Ashtishat, not far from Mush, in the south of Taron. For Valarshapat, north of Ararat, the Roman Neapolis, did not become the religious metropolis before the middle of the fifth century.

Gregory the Illuminator was a contemporary of Archelaus, the Adoptionist opponent of Mani. Ashtishat, the home of Gregory and of Armenian Christianity, was not remote from Chaschar or Karkhar, and it was in the heart of the Adoptionist district of Armenia. Is it possible then that the Christianity of Gregory himself was adoptionist? There can hardly be a doubt that it was so, for Aristaces of Lastivert, who tells us as little as he can, admits as much. 'These enemies of ours,' he writes, 'had they been

---

[1] For a detailed proof of this see my article on the subject in the *American Journal of Theology* for October, 1897.

foreigners speaking another tongue, could have been easily guarded against, but "they went forth from among us" ... They are of our own tongue and nation, and have issued from one and the same spring like sweet water and bitter.' And the context (see below, p. 66) proves that Gregory the Illuminator was himself the one wellhead from which the 'sweet water and the bitter,' i.e. the orthodox Armenian and the Thonraki ultimately derived. But if this be so, it follows that Gregory's teaching was at least not anti-adoptionist. The Armenian fathers have, however, taken good care that posterity should not be too nearly acquainted with that teaching, whatever it was, for the so-called 'teaching of St. Gregory' cannot have been composed in its present form before 400 A.D. Yet even in its existing form it here and there is stamped with Adoptionist ideas, as witness the following passage (*The Discourses of St. Gregory the Illuminator*, in Old Armenian, Venice, 1838, p. 16):—

'For as the Son of God became Son of man[1] and put on our nature and fulfilled all righteousness in soul and body, so let us too put on rectitude and fulfil all righteousness in Christ; that we may become sons of God, and Gods through love. For the Son of God was made flesh by the will of God and endured all affections of human nature, sin excepted. Even so may it be ours by help of the divine power to pass through all passions without transgression, that we may be able to arrive *in full age*[2] at the perfection (*or* maturity) of Christ; and thus, being changed into the true image of God, we shall inherit the kingdom of Christ.' There are stronger traces of Adoptionism in the teaching of Gregory preserved in the History of him by Agathangelus. For example we here read (Arm. ed. Ven. 1862, p. 314) that the Spirit came down at the baptism and *rested* on Jesus, according to the reading in Lord Crawford's *Armenian Gospels* of Luke iii. 22. The Spirit, it adds, then gave Jesus his glory. In the same we read that John the Baptist, son of the high priest Zachariah, was the depositary of all the divine favours conferred of old on Israel, of priesthood, prophetic calling, kingship, and authority. All these had been

---

[1] The passage would have more point if it ran: 'For as the Son of man became Son of God, having put on our nature,' &c. And perhaps it originally ran in some such way.

[2] i.e. at thirty years of age, the time for baptism. There is a similar passage in the 'Teaching' as Agathangelos gives it. Cp. the Prayers for the Service of Name-giving in *The Key of Truth*, p. 90.

handed down in succession to John the Baptist; and he it was who 'conferred on our Lord Jesus Christ priesthood, prophetic calling, and kingship' (ibid. p. 320). And again lower down (p. 344): 'So then John gave priesthood, and unction, and prophecy and kingship to our Saviour Christ, and Christ gave it to the Apostles, and the Apostles to the clergy of the Church.'

I have already alluded to the antagonism shown by the old Arsacide Kings of Armenia during the fourth century to the introduction by Nerses of Greek religious ideas and institutions from Caesarea of Cappadocia. Nerses was the friend and lieutenant of St. Basil, and the representative beyond the Euphrates of the somewhat narrow and aggressive orthodoxy which inspires so many of Basil's epistles. The quarrel between Nerses and the Armenian King Pap is said by Faustus the Armenian historian to have resulted in the poisoning of the former. Whether it was so or not, it is certain that the Bishop Faustus who was nominated his successor by Pap was refused consecration by Basil when he came to Caesarea for it, but obtained what he wanted from Anthimus of Tyana, the Arian rival of Basil. Two of Basil's letters bear on the subject, and more or less confirm the Armenian sources, viz., Epistle 58 to Meletius the bishop, wherein he mentions Pap by name, and complains that Anthimus by his action had filled Armenia with dissensions (ὥστε στάσεων ἐμπληρῶσαι τὴν Ἀρμενίαν); and Ep. 313 to Poemenius, Basil's own nominee for the bishopric of the Armenian see of Satala, and formerly presbyter of Sivas. In this Basil complains, not of the murder of Nerses, but of a breach of the παλαιὰ εὐταξία; and declares that in disgust he had ceased to send any more pastoral letters[1] to Armenians, even to Poemenius, and had excommunicated Faustus. In other letters (e.g. no. 187) to the Count Terentius, who was less solicitous that Armenia should be orthodox than that it should be loyal to the Empire, Basil makes it quite clear that it was in Armenia a question between the partisans of Nicene orthodoxy and the party whose opinions further west he was himself combating in the person of Eunomius. In that letter he describes a journey he had himself undertaken to Getasa, Nicopolis, and Satala, in order to combat the heresy

---

[1] In Ep. 75 to the Church of Neo-Caesarea, Basil mentions that he was in the habit of sending letters to and receiving them from 'The Pisidians, Lycaonians, the Phrygians, and so much of Armenia as abuts on you' ὑμῖν ἐστι πρόσοικον.

of Armenia. It would appear from this letter that some Armenian ecclesiastics were ready to subscribe to Basil's written creeds so long as they were in his territory, but returned to heresy so soon as their feet touched their native soil; and even Theodotus, one of those who had come to complain to Basil of the opinions of a colleague Eustathius, found it politic to forsake the great exponent of Greek orthodoxy, so soon as he had led him as far as Nicopolis. And Basil complains of this insult to Terentius: 'How could I give to the Armenians bishops, when I was so treated by one of my own opinions, one who should have shared my anxieties, and from whom I hoped to obtain suitable instruments? For there are in his parish ($παροικίᾳ$) religious and intelligent persons, who are versed in the language and understand the other peculiarities of the (Armenian) race. I know their names, but will not now disclose them, lest I should prejudice them as my instruments in Armenia at some future time.' The last sentence reveals the unpopularity in Armenia of the Nicene orthodoxy, and entirely accords with the notices of Faustus the Armenian who relates in his history (iv. 15) that Arshak, the predecessor of Pap, deposed Nerses Catholicos, and set up a rival pontiff in his place, who was consecrated by bishops (probably Adoptionists) from the cantons of Korduq and Aldsniq in Pers-Armenia. It was Arshak's successor Pap who effected a final rupture with Caesarea, and, though a heretic, established the autonomy of the Armenian Church. To the period of this conflict between King Arshak and Nerses seems to belong letter no. 69 in the collection of Basil's correspondence. It is a memorial addressed by the orthodox bishops of Asia Minor to their brethren in Italy and Gaul, appealing to them for aid in their combat with the heresy akin to Arianism, only worse, which, like a storm, had swept over all the populations from Illyria's borders as far as the Thebaid. The movement was in favour of a more popular method of electing the bishops, and in matters of faith was directly opposed to the Nicene faith. Among the bishops subscribing to this letter we find Nerses himself and four others who were Armenian ecclesiastics, namely, Iosakes (Yousik), successor of Nerses, Chosroês, Theodotus, and Eustathius. Barsumas and Maris, whose names are also appended, may have been Syrian bishops. The next letter, no. 70, of Basil himself, belongs to the same epoch, and is again addressed to the orthodox in Italy and Gaul, asking them for aid. It is important as showing that the opinion of which the triumphant spread filled Basil with such dismay was Adoptionism. 'The only-born,' he says, 'is blasphemed, the Holy Spirit dishonoured; ... there is among them a great God and a little one; for "the Son" is not a name connoting the nature (i.e. of Jesus), but is esteemed a title conveying some sort of honour[1]. The Holy Spirit is not to be complementary of the Holy Trinity, nor a sharer of the divine and blessed nature, but to belong to the realm of created things, tacked on, no matter how, to the Father and the Son.' At the same time Basil acknowledges the essentially Christian organization of the heretics. 'They have their baptisms,' he says, 'their funerals[2]; they visit the sick regularly, console the sorrowing, minister aid to those in distress. In every sort of way they succour each other, and have their communions of the mysteries. Nothing is neglected by them to knit together the laity in unity of faith with themselves. In a little while, even if we gain a respite, there will still remain no hope of recalling to a knowledge of the truth men so long ago caught in the meshes of error.' In Epistle 10 to Gregory Theologus, Basil also mentions one Fronto, who had, in spite of his heresy, procured his elevation to the Armenian bishopric of Nicopolis. 'He has become,' he adds, 'by God's grace, the public abomination of all Armenia'—a statement which we may take for what it is worth. In Epistle 65 to the Church in Sozopolis Basil evidently glances at the same heresy, which, cresting the wave of Arianism, spread tumult and trouble throughout the churches. It assailed the mystery of the Incarnation[3], i.e. the divinity of Jesus prior to his baptism, and alleged that the Lord came with a heavenly body, so that there was no use for the Virgin, since Christ did not take from her of the flesh of Adam[4]. These are exactly the errors which the Greek sources later on ascribe to the Paulicians; though the *Key*, as we have it, does not make it clear that they held the latter. In yet another letter, no. 72, to the Evaiseni, evidently treating of the same heresy, Basil declares that it made the Spirit older than the Son[5] at the same time that it alleged it to be a created being, both characteristic opinions of the Adoptionists, and of which the former inspires, as we saw, *The Shepherd* of Hermas.

---

[1] Οὐχὶ φύσεως ὄνομα, ἀλλὰ τιμῆς τινος προσηγορία. The sonship belonged, that is, to Jesus not through his birth, but was conferred on him when he was elected by God at the Baptism in Jordan.
[2] Προπομπαὶ τῶν ἐξοδευόντων.
[3] Τὴν σωτήριον οἰκονομίαν.
[4] Τοῦ φυράματος τοῦ Ἀδάμ.
[5] Πρεσβύτερον εἶναι τοῦ υἱοῦ τὸ πνεῦμα.

It would be rash to affirm that the heresy of Armenia in these stormy last decades of the fourth century was identical in all respects with the forms of opinion combated elsewhere by Basil. It was error of a more primitive cast, though no doubt it had this in common with the heresy of Eunomius, that it affirmed the Son to be a ποίημα or κτίσμα; and it probably laid the same stress on the reality of Jesus' human ignorance [1] as did the teacher we have just named, of whose work against Basil we would justly deplore the loss, since, even in the latter's dialogue against him, he figures as a profoundly earnest and comprehensive spirit, anxious to accept the plain sense of the Gospels without twisting it [2] and to include (and not exclude) as many good Christians as he can in the Church. For this end Eunomius framed a creed which would drive as few out as possible; and, instead of trying to manufacture heresy, was eager to conciliate by insisting only on essentials. 'We believe,' he says (Basil, *Adv. Eunomium*, lib. i. p. 7 of ed. Paris), 'in one God the Father Almighty, from whom are all things; and in one only-begotten Son of God, God-Word, our Lord Jesus Christ, by whom are all things; and in one Holy Spirit the Paraclete.' 'This faith of ours,' he adds, 'is fairly simple, and held alike by all who are anxious to appear or to be Christians.' How much misery might have been spared in east and west if his spirit of moderation had triumphed! Instead of that we have the spectacle of a series of councils, each more ingeniously designed than the last to drive outside the pale of the Church a large body of devout and earnest Christians.

But although the Armenian heresy of the fourth century had much in common with the Arians and with the school of Eunomius and Marcellus of Ancyra, it was probably more rigorously Adoptionist than were these teachers whose doctrine was for the most part an attempt to combine the pneumatic or Logos idea with the primitive Adoptionist view.

Apart from the few notices of Greek writers, our knowledge of early Armenian Church history has come down to us purely through writers of the Caesarean or grecizing school; and they are either reticent or content to ascribe to their opponents nameless vices instead of defining their heterodoxy. But we are probably justified in concluding from the imperfect evidence we have, and

[1] Cp. the Catechism, p. 122.
[2] As does Basil in explaining away the text of Mark xiii. 32, 'Neither the Son, but the Father.'

of which I have now given the gist, that the earliest Armenian Christianity was introduced by Syrian missionaries who were Adoptionists. The ultimate radiating centre from which they drew their illumination was the Antioch of Paul of Samosata, and not the Caesarea of Basil. There is little real evidence to prove that Gregory the Illuminator was brought up at Caesarea, or that he went to Caesarea for consecration, or that he himself accepted the Nicene Christology. His 'teaching' still bears traces of Adoptionist ideas, and had it been orthodox his successors need not have recast it in so unsparing a fashion. The transference in the fifth century of the centre and focus of Armenian Christianity from Ashtishat in Taron to Valarshapat was consequent on the obstinate opposition of the population of Taron and Vaspurakan to the newly-imported Greek Christology, an obstinacy which lasted for centuries after. The Greek influence over the Armenian Church, begun by Nerses under the example and precept of Basil, culminated in what is known as the school of translators, led by Saints Sahak and Mesrop. They made the revision of the older Armenian New Testament, translated from the Old Syriac, and used the latest Greek MSS. in making it. The greater activity and intelligence of the 'translators' gradually took effect; the Adoptionist bishops and priests were tortured and driven out of parts of Armenia subject to Byzantium; and, by the end of the fifth century, Lazar of Pharp describes the old Adoptionist faith of his countrymen as an obscure heresy. Still it lingered on and kept up relations with 'the old believers' of Antioch, ready to blossom out into activity when an opportunity should occur. It may have been the Iconoclastic movement and the accession to the throne of Constantinople of one of themselves in the person of Constantine, nicknamed Copronymus, which furnished the requisite stimulus and opportunity.

The evidence for believing that this emperor, derisively called Caballinus by John of Damascus, was a pure Paulician, is very strong. Theophanes, his contemporary, declares in set terms that he was; and Theostêriktos, who was the disciple of St. Nicetas, and wrote a life[1] of his master under the Empress Irene, asserts that Constantine not only threw down images, but would not even allow the martyrs to be publicly called saints, re-naming churches *ad apostolos, ad quadraginta, ad Theodorum*, and so forth, omitting the prefix ἅγιος. He despised their relics,

---

[1] See this life in the *Acta Sanctorum*, April, tom. i. p. 260.

and was only a Christian outwardly, and at heart a Jew. He tried to abolish the name of the Virgin, and would not hear of her intercession, nor call her holy and blessed. As long as she had Christ within her, she was indeed τιμία; but after his birth was just like any other woman, a purse emptied of the gold it held. The monks, whom he named ἀμνημονεύτους, were objects of detestation to him as to the Paulicians. His rejection of infant baptism was, as we said above, artistically conveyed by the orthodox Greeks in their story that he fouled the font[1] in St. Sophia, when Germanus the patriarch was baptizing him as a child.

When then we read in Gregory of Narek and Gregory Magistros that Smbat was the *founder* of the Thonraki and gave them their laws, what are we to understand? Certainly not that he did more than commit to writing and formally draw up a system of ritual and observance which he and they had learned or inherited from others of an older time.

It is certain that Gregory Magistros did not regard Smbat as the author of the peculiar tenets and practices of the Thonraki. On the contrary, he twice refers his readers to John of Otzun, who lived a hundred years before Smbat, for an antidote to their poison, and he pointedly identifies them with the Paulicians and declares that they were followers of Paul of Samosata. Smbat himself, he says, was only a pupil of the Persian physician Mdjusik, of whom we know nothing.

The heresy was an old one in Armenia, but its adherents in Taron, before Smbat, were without organization, and had no church of their own. Until his advent they may have formed a conservative party within the Armenian Church, opposed to all grecizing elements and influences, perhaps upholding locally their own ideas and forms of priesthood, nurturing their own primitive creed, and retaining their institution of adult baptism with the less friction because, in the great Church itself, infant baptism was for centuries rather the exception than the rule. Even in the Greek and Latin Church adult baptism was still common in the fourth century. In the Armenian it probably continued much later[2] to be the rule. For the changes effected in

---

[1] Τὴν κολυμβήθραν ὅλην ἠχρείωσε ... ὥστε φωνῆσαι .. Γερμανόν. Οὗτος φανήσεται τῇ ἐκκλησίᾳ δυσωδία μεγάλη. John Damasc. in Migne, *P. G.* vol. xcv. col. 337. Theophanes, a contemporary, tells the same story.

[2] John of Otzun (718 A.D.) is the first to mention it, and he was well aware that in the days of Cyril of Jerusalem it was the exception and not the rule in the Church.

the great Church usually took effect in Armenia one or two hundred years later.

In the English Church we see what is called a Low Church party entertaining ideas of the priesthood, of the sacraments, of the use of lights, crosses, &c., quite opposed to the dominant party, which is named by them the Ritualist or Romanizing party. Now if this so-called Low Church party, after enduring much petty persecution, were driven out or seceded, and formed themselves into a separate Church, with a rival primate of their own, there would happen exactly what, so far as we can judge, took place in Southeastern Armenia early in the ninth century under Smbat. The Adoptionists were driven out or seceded and established themselves as a separate and organized[1] Church with a primate or patriarch of their own. Gregory Magistros implies as much when he says that Smbat gave them their laws and, quitting the path of illumination (i.e. the Church of Gregory the Illuminator), entered a blind alley. He gives twice over the list of their pontiffs from Smbat's age up to his own.

If it be asked, How could a party holding tenets so opposed to those of the great fifth century Armenian doctors, Nerses, Sahak, Mesrop, Elisaeus, have lurked so long within the fold, the answer is to be found in the political condition of Armenia. The population was broken up into great independent clans, separated from each other by huge mountains, and led by udal chieftains. A bishop in those days presided, not over a diocese, but over a clan. Inside a clan, therefore, a peculiar ecclesiastical use or faith could propagate itself unmolested for generations, and did so; for the religious unity of the clans must have been as weak and precarious as was their political unity. It was indeed the constant feuds between the clans, and the dislike of their chieftains to any political subordination under a king or under one another, that finally shattered the state of Armenia, or rather never allowed a state in the true sense of the word to be constituted.

Long before the ninth century, the grecizing party had got the upper hand in the Church of Armenia, and appropriated to itself the catholicate. But the Adoptionist type of Christianity, the

---

[1] It may be inferred from Gregory Magistros' mention (see p. 148) of the letters of the congregations of Khnus, Thulail, and Kaschê (in Pers-Armenia near old Djoulfa on the Araxes), that there was regular correspondence between the chief See of Thonrak and the other Paulician churches, scattered over Armenia from Albania beyond the Kur to the Western Euphrates.

Christianity of Archelaus of Karkhar, still held its own among some of the clans of South-eastern Armenia, notably among the Bagratuni. In the ninth century its adherents finally seceded or were driven out, and became a rival Church to that which, having established its headquarters at Valarshapat, had as early as A.D. 450 invented the legend of the descent of the Holy Spirit in Edjmiatzin. The now separated Adoptionist Church seems to have had its entire strength in Taron, where remained the mother-church of all Armenia, the shrine of St. Gregory at Ashtishat, a monumental protest against the fictitious claims of Edjmiatzin. It is evident that the first pontiff set up by the Adoptionists in opposition to the Catholicos of Edjmiatzin was named Smbat. He it was in all probability who committed to writing for the use of his clergy the ancient forms and prayers of his Church. The manual so composed he called *The Key of Truth*. The prayers and liturgical parts of this book, as I have noticed above, are older in style than the rest, and had probably been in immemorial use when they were thus written down and 'published,' as the exordium says. It is not improbable that Gregory the Illuminator originally composed them.

But the Adoptionists did not view themselves as seceders, but as the true and original and orthodox Church of Armenia. 'We are the apostolic men,' they argued. 'We the people who have not swerved in faith' (Greg. Nar. p. 61). 'We are of the tribe of Aram (i.e. true Armenians), and agree with them in faith.' So the modern Paulicians still answer (see above, p. xxiii): 'We are sons of the Illuminator.' They took their stand on the *regula fidei*, and perhaps used in good faith then as now the Apostles' Creed[1], anathematized in equally good faith the ancient heretics, especially Manes, and demanded of Peter the Catholicos in the eleventh century that he should recognize them for what they claimed to be. 'Will you persuade us to receive you into the Church with those principles of yours?' replies Gregory Magistros to the Thulaili who made the demand. But he, like Aristaces (see p. 66), hints that they were an offshoot of the Church of the Illuminator. 'You are not of us,' he says, 'yet one sees no other to whom you could attach yourselves. You are neither hot like us, nor cold like the ancient heretics you denounce, but lukewarm.' According to Nerses Shnorhali, the Paulicians of Mesopotamia in the twelfth century still claimed the *antiqui patres* of Armenia as their own teachers (p. 90).

[1] See above, p. xxv, the confession of Manuk, son of David.

Gregory Magistros further hints that the Paulicians derived their orders through and from the Armenian Church itself. Smbat, he says, assumed externally the position of a high priest, but did not openly ordain bishops or consecrate the holy oil. But he employed bishops secretly fallen away. In other words, a number of bishops, who had never been anything else but Adoptionists, seceded with Smbat, who perhaps headed the movement as a layman, or even as the prince of the Bagratuni, until his consecration as their first pontiff. In its first burst of vigour the newly constituted Church seems to have effected an ecclesiastical revolution in Armenia, and to have deposed John of Owaiq, setting upon the throne of the catholicate a nominee of its own. But this is not certain.

It is probable, however, that Smbat, when he formed his new Church of old believers and gave it an organization and a line of rival primates of its own, also began the practice of anathematizing the orthodox Armenians, and of denying them even to be Christians; not, however, because they had wrong creeds, but because they were paedo-baptists. It must have been over the issue of infant baptism that the long-ripening quarrel came to a head, and burst out in open schism and mutual anathemas. Though the Adoptionist tenets had long before been anathematized by the grecizing party, the Adoptionists had never till now retorted. This is why Gregory Magistros says that Smbat 'set himself to deny all priestly functions.' He first had the courage to declare that the other party, having lost true baptism, had lost priesthood and sacraments as well. And this is the declaration which so frequently occurs in *The Key of Truth*.

Aristaces of Lastivert freely owns that the Paulicians of the province of Harq enjoyed the favour and protection of several of the local princes, but he says nothing about Smbat. And it may be that the importance of Smbat is exaggerated by the two writers who mention him. If we had the lost work of Ananias of Narek, from whom these writers drew much of their information, we should be able to speak more definitely. Of one thing we may be quite sure, and that is that even if the Persian Mdjusik and Smbat do stand behind *The Key of Truth*, yet they were only links in the tradition of the peculiar tenets therein set before us, mere intermediaries as was Paul of Samosata himself, and not originators. The author of *The Key of Truth* himself indicates that he was not originating, but only handing on and restoring to those from whom it had been a long time hidden a tradition as old as the apostles. His tone throughout is τὰ ἀρχαῖα κρατείτω. And an examination of the contents of the book in the light of the knowledge which we possess from other sources of the Adoptionist Church, assures us that it contains next to nothing that is purely Armenian, and very little that is not primitive.

This is notably the case with the Paulician rite of baptism. From the *Key* itself, from Isaac Catholicos (see p. lxxvi), and from the further information furnished by the inquisition of 1837–1840, we infer that it was put off till a believer was thirty years of age. In the orthodox Church itself of the fourth century it was still usual to so postpone the rite. Still less was the rejection of infant baptism a mark of lateness. 'We are quite in the dark,' writes Prof. Harnack, 'as to the way in which infant baptism won admission into the Church. It may be that it owes its origin to the thought that baptism was indispensable to blessedness; but none the less it is proof that the superstitious view of baptism had forced its way to the front.' In the time of Irenaeus (2. 23. 4) and of Tertullian (*De Bapt.* 18) the practice of child-baptism, based on an appeal to Matt. xix. 14, was already existent; but for its existence in an earlier age we have no testimonies; Clement of Alexandria[1] does not presuppose it. Tertullian wrote a polemic against it, urging not only that conscious faith was a necessary pre-condition of baptism, but also—what in his eyes was even more important—that the importance of the rite (*pondus baptismi*) requires its postponement. The arguments of Tertullian deserve to be quoted, because they are in almost verbal agreement with those urged by the writer of the *Key*:—

'They whose office it is to baptize know that baptism is not rashly to be administered. "Give to every one who beggeth thee," has a reference of its own, and especially concerns almsgiving. [With regard to baptism] on the contrary, the following precept should be observed: "Give not the holy thing to the dogs, nor cast your pearls before swine[2]."'

So in the *Key*, chs. xviii and xix, the catechumens must humbly ask for baptism, but the boon is not to be granted without diligent testing in faith and repentance of those who ask for it.

Tertullian, after denying that Philip was too ready or off-hand in baptizing the eunuch, proceeds thus:—

---

[1] The argument of W. Wall (*Hist. of Infant Baptism*, Oxford ed., 1836, vol. i. p. 84), based on Clem. Alex. Paedag. lib. iii. c. 11, if it proved anything, would prove that the *Paedagogus* was addressed to infants and not to adults.

[2] Tertullian, *De Baptismo*, ch. 18 (Clark's Ante-Nicene Library).

'But Paul too, it will be objected, was baptized off-hand. Yes, for Simon, his host, recognized him off-hand to be "an appointed vessel of election." God's approbation sends sure premonitory tokens before it; every "petition" of man may both deceive and be deceived. And so, according to the circumstances and disposition, and even age, of each individual, the delay of baptism is preferable; principally, however, in the case of little children The Lord does indeed say, "Forbid them not to come unto me." Let them "come," then, when they are grown up; let them "come," when they learn; when they are taught, let them come; let them be made Christians, when they have become able to know Christ.'

Tertullian has already dwelt on the risk run by sponsors in infant baptism; now he goes on to ask why children, whom one would not trust with an earthly treasure, should have committed to their keeping the divine. 'Let them know how to "ask" for salvation, that you may seem [at least] to have given "to him that asketh." For no less cause must the unwedded also put off baptism, for in them temptation is ever ready.' For the same reason even widowers are not to be baptized till they re-marry or are confirmed in their continence. 'If any understand the weighty import (*pondus*) of baptism, they will fear its reception more than its delay.' Such is Tertullian's conclusion.

In ch. xx of the same tract Tertullian insists on the necessity that those about to be baptized should spend the preceding night in prayer, fasting, and genuflexions, and vigils, and they shall confess all their past sins according to the Scripture, 'They were baptized, confessing their own sins.' And the confession was to be a public one. He concludes his treatise by advising the newly baptized to imitate, by strict abstinence after baptism, the forty days' fast of the Saviour. The Paulician practice was in all respects similar as it is represented in ch. xix of the *Key*.

And, as with the Paulicians so with Tertullian, the water, and not a vessel or building enclosing it, was the essential in baptism. 'It makes no difference,' he writes, 'whether a man be washed in a sea or a pool, a stream or a fount, a lake or a trough' (ibid. ch. iv).

One could believe that Tertullian's tract was at some time or other in use among those from whom the author of the *Key* derived his teaching. Nor is it a far-fetched supposition that the Greek work, which Tertullian avows he had written on the same subject ('de isto plenius iam nobis in Graeco digestum est'), had a vogue among the Eastern Adoptionists. As in the *Key*, an elect one alone can confer baptism, so in Tertullian, ch. 17: 'Dandi quidem habet ius summus sacerdos, qui est episcopus. Dehinc presbyteri et diaconi; non tamen sine episcopi auctoritate.' This was a point about which—if we may rely on the letter of Macarius (c. 330)—the early Church of Armenia was lax; but much else that Macarius condemns in the Armenians of that age Tertullian had upheld, in particular the delaying of baptism and the view that fonts and baptisteries are unnecessary. The same letter reveals that prevalence in Armenia of Arian or Adoptionist tenets, which St. Basil proves to have existed fifty years later. Macarius' letter is preserved in old Armenian, and in my ninth appendix I translate it, adducing reasons for regarding it as authentic evidence in regard to the religious condition of Armenia in the age of the Nicene Council.

There seems to have been no monkery in the Paulician Church; and its tone is very hostile to the institution as it existed in the orthodox Churches; a fact very explicable, if we bear in mind that in those Churches the monks were everywhere the most fanatical upholders of image-worship. The author of the Escurial Fragment says that the Paulicians taught that it was the devil who had revealed to mankind the holy monastic garb, revealed and given from God though an angel to men. In contrast therefore with the practice of the Manicheans and of the great persecuting Churches, but in accordance with the precept of St. Paul, the Paulician bishop had to be married, and to be the father of a family.

Nor was there any higher or lower clergy. The elect one, the living representative and successor upon earth of Christ and his disciples, was the only authority in the Church; and he was apostle, teacher, bishop, or parish-priest, as the exigencies of religious ministration required. The elect were peculiarly the organs of the Holy Spirit, and as such not greater or less one than the other. For 'God giveth not the Spirit by measure.' They too carried the imitation of Christ a step further than the merely baptized. They took upon themselves the same work of prophecy and ministry, of preaching the word and of suffering for the faithful, of surrender of self to the Holy Spirit that had elected and inspired them, as Jesus Christ, after his baptism, had undertaken. As he, after the descent of the Spirit on him in the Jordan, had retired for forty days into the solitude of the mountain to commune with God, so the newly elected one was taken by the bishop, who had breathed into him the Holy Spirit, to his house for forty days, there to meditate in seclusion 'in the precincts of the Church, to learn his duties, and consider the solemnity of the order to which he is called[1].' The custom of the orthodox Armenian Church is somewhat similar. And this Church also resembles the Paulician in its order of *Vardapet*, equal in dignity to the bishop, and probably the true successor of the λαλοῦντες τὸν λόγον of the earliest Church.

The Greek sources merely tell us that the Paulicians called their priests *sunecdemi*, or travelling preachers, and *notarii*, that is to say, copyists of the sacred books. These priests, they tell us, were indistinguishable from the laity in their habits or dress, in their diet and in the general arrangement of their life. The Greek writer who reports these details was well acquainted with the Paulician priest in his missionary aspect, and merely repeats to his readers the external features which most impressed him. There is no contradiction between his meagre notice and the fuller information of the *Key*; at the same time it exactly agrees with the information of Isaac Catholicos (see p. lxxix).

Yet there are some minor points in the Church organization which the *Key* does not quite clear up. We would like to know, for example, if the rulers (*ishkhanq*) who, as well as the bishop, independently tested the candidate for election, and then presented him to the bishop for the laying-on of hands and reception of the Spirit, were themselves elect ones, and therefore the spiritual equals of the bishop; or were they only baptized members of the Church? Since the writer uses the word *ishkhanuthiun*, which means 'rule' or 'authority,' to denote the priestly power to bind and loose, the word *ishkhanq* should signify those who are possessed of such authority, that is to say, all the elect ones of the Church. Yet the context rather implies that they were not the same as the presbyters or elders; for it declares that presbyters and *ishkhanq* were present together, and, just as the writer speaks of arch-rulers, so he speaks of arch-presbyters as being present. If we were to be guided by the terminology of the orthodox Armenian Church, and in this matter there is no particular reason why we should not be, we must answer that these 'rulers' were elect ones, just those depositaries of the power to bind and loose from whose order were

---

[1] See *The Armenian Church*, by Dr. Issaverdians, in English. Venice, 1877, p. 463.

chosen the few who were to discharge the functions of shepherd, of bishop, of hegumen, of vardapet, of apostle. The usage of the orthodox Armenians is in favour of this view, for Nerses of Lambron, who died in 1198, thus writes in his exposition of the mass (p. 42 of the Armenian text): 'The priestly order and that of monk or ascete are widely separate from each other. For the priesthood is a position of pre-eminence, and is a presbyterate among the congregation; but monkhood is self-mortification in following Christ, an order of self-abasement and of silence, and *not of rule*' (*ishkhanuthean*). Here then the *rulers* are the *priests* (*qahana*, Hebrew *Cohen*) and *elders*. So on p. 35 of the same work, Nerses says of the girdle which, like the Brahmanical sacred thread, the priests wore from the patriarch downwards, that it is indicative of the 'rule' they exercise in the temple amidst the congregation.

We are therefore inclined to suppose that the rulers were presbyters; and these presbyters were elect ones, holding no particular office, and deputed to discharge no special function in the Church. They would be a fairly numerous class if, as is likely, every believer made it his ambition to be elected, and receive the crowning grace of the Holy Spirit before he died. Here, however, we enter a region of uncertainties. If we could suppose that the writer uses *ishkhan* in one sense and *ishkhanuthiun* in another, we might identify the 'rulers' with the magistrates, and the 'arch-rulers' with the lords of the clans, whose approval of the candidate for a bishopric would naturally be required. So in the canons of Hippolytus the approval of the 'people' is requisite, and all ordinals allow for the consent of the laity or of the civil government. It must not be forgotten that the Paulician ordinal provides for the consecration of a pastor, as well as of an elect one.

The writer of the *Key* often uses the terms 'original' and 'effective sin,' answering to the Latin *peccatum originale et actuale* or *effectivum*. We do not find these terms in use among the orthodox Armenians before the thirteenth or fourteenth centuries, after which they are often used in connexion with baptism, for example in the manual or *Summa* of Gregory of Dathev, written in 1407, and a generation earlier in John of Erzingan. But already in the tenth century Gregory of Narek[1] uses the same word (*skzbanakan*) as the *Key*, a word answering to *originale* in the

---

[1] *Meditations*, 28 (of Arm. edition).

following obscure sentence: 'Let him be freed from the evil bonds of deadly evils original, final, and of the middle time.' In the book entitled *Khrat*, ascribed to the same writer, but probably of later origin, and perhaps by Gregory of Skiurh in the thirteenth century, we have the exact phrase 'original sin,' used of Adam's transgression. In the *Haysmavourq* or *Synaxary* of Cilicia of the same date we read of 'the original transgression of Adam.' But in such a case as this we cannot be guided by the usage of the orthodox Armenians, to whom the use of a particular phrase among the Thonraki would be a reason for not employing it themselves.

We do not know who were the intermediaries, but we may be sure that the phrase came to the Paulicians of Armenia from the west, where it was in common use in Latin writers as early as the end of the fourth century. Augustine, Bishop of Hippo in Africa, the first witness to its use, does not seem to have invented it himself. Caesarius of Arles, in his *Sermones* (Migne, *P. L.* vol. xxxix, 1830; he died in 542), used the phrase: 'De originali vero vel actuali peccato liberare vel resuscitare.' And as early as 520 we meet with it in Constantinople in the profession of faith of the Scythian monks directed against the Pelagians (Migne, *P. L.* vol. xlv, 1772): 'Sicut Pelagii et Coelestii sive Theodori Mopsuestini discipuli, qui unum et idem naturale et originale peccatum esse affirmare conantur.' We therefore infer that Theodore used it. Fulgentius also used the phrase in his *Liber de Fide ad Petrum*, § 33, a work of the early sixth century. There were a hundred channels, hidden from us to-day, through which the phrase might reach the Paulicians of the eighth or ninth century. And in trying to account for its use in the *Key*, we must bear in mind that the Adoptionist Church remained one and undivided, and was unaffected by the scission of east and west, which as early as the fifth century revealed itself, and in the ages which followed parted Greek and Latin orthodoxy ever more and more widely asunder. Thenceforth the only real union of east and west was an union of heresy or heresies, and the only bond between the great persecuting Churches was their common hatred of the persecuted sects. There continued after the fourth century the same unrestricted intercourse between the Adoptionists of the west and those of the east as there had been up to that age. Eusebius, *H. E.* vii. 30, testifies to the Latin influences which were already in the third century at work in Syria, when he records, on the faith of the bishops who condemned and deposed Paul of Samosata, that the heresiarch's spiritual father was Artemas, the leader of the Roman Adoptionists in the middle of that century.

It is conceivable that the phrase 'original and actual sin' originated among the Latin Adoptionists, and was by them passed on to their oriental brethren. This is the more likely because Augustine, in whom we first meet with the phrase, himself as a young man held Adoptionist opinions, without, as he tells us, being conscious of their heterodoxy. For in his *Confessions*, 7. 19 (25), he writes thus: 'Quia itaque vera scripta sunt, totum hominem in Christo agnoscebam; non corpus tantum hominis, aut cum corpore sine mente animam; sed ipsum hominem, non persona Veritatis, sed magna quadam naturae humanae excellentia et perfectiore participatione sapientiae praeferri ceteris arbitrabar.' He clearly imbibed his Christianity in Adoptionist circles in North Africa, and his teachers, whoever they were, regarded their opinion as *Catholica veritas*, just as did Archelaus and the Paulicians in the east, and, as we shall presently see, those of Spain as well. Is it not possible that Augustine also took from these Adoptionist circles his phrase 'original and actual sin?' It would easily have travelled to the Taurus and South Armenia in the seventh and eighth centuries; for, like southern Spain, all the north of Africa, Egypt, and Syria were under Mohammedan rule, and intercourse along this line was comparatively safe and easy.

But although the Paulicians adopted the phrase, they interpreted it in a way less hostile to humanity and to our convictions of divine love than many circles in which it has found a home. Little children, they taught, are without sin either original or actual; and therefore do not need to be baptized on that score. Perhaps the Paulicians were the more ready to receive the phrase 'original sin' from the Latin west because their orthodox Greek neighbours rejected it, when it was proffered them early in the fifth century from that quarter. In any case Augustine is the Latin father who has most points of contact with the Paulicians, and whom we can most readily conceive of as having influenced their phraseology.

Although there is very little in the *Key* which can be set down to Armenian and racial influence, yet there is much in it peculiarly opposed to the practices of the orthodox Armenians, and even more calculated to give them offence than to hurt orthodox Greeks. For in the Armenian Church the principle of heredity counted for much. The old priestly families went on after the introduction of Christianity just as they went on before it. The catholicate itself was at first hereditary in the Arsacide priestly family of Gregory the Illuminator; and the old shrine of Vahagn, the family temple of Gregory at Ashtishat, became the mother church of Armenia, and belonged to the clan long after the vices or heterodoxy of Gregory's descendants made it necessary to choose the Catholicos from the rival and equally old priestly family of Albianos. For centuries the bishoprics of certain dioceses ran in certain families; and down to the thirteenth century these families kept all but their own sons out of the priesthood. Not but that the Greeks, according to Galanus (*Conciliat. Eccl. Arm.* pars i. ch. 17), at an early time pointed out the evils of this system; for it was already combated at the sixth general Synod in 680, when it was resolved that suitable candidates for the priesthood in Armenia should not be refused because they did not belong to priestly families. It was probably the example of the Paulicians which led to this canon being made. Such good advice, however, made no impression on a race so conservative as the Armenian; and in the thirteenth century Nerses of Lambron waxes bitter in his complaints of this hereditary system, which still prevailed. 'We see,' he writes (*op. cit.* p. 517), 'the Church of Christ among us enslaved carnally and made a carnal inheritance. Enslaved not to aliens or to heathen, but to our own senseless desires and barbárous intendants.' 'This relic of barbarism, along with simony,' he says elsewhere (p. 548), 'has been the ruin of the Armenian Church.' There can be no doubt that the Paulician principle of election was very inimical to this hereditary system, and was felt to be so by the Armenian historian Aristaces, who makes it a special cause of complaint against Jacob, the convert of the Thonraki, that he began to *elect* his priests for their spiritual merits alone and in disregard of family considerations.

The same historian notices the hostility of the Paulicians to the institution of blood-offerings for the expiation of the sins of the dead, which still exists even in Georgia. The Armenians have a special ritual for such offerings. The Paulicians, in their opposition to this interesting relic of the pre-Christian epoch, were the spokesmen of a higher conception of sin and repentance.

The third practice of the orthodox Armenians specially opposed by the Paulicians was that of consecrating holy crosses. It was the Christian analogue to the ancient practice of setting up Bethels or holy stones. When the power of Christ had, by suitable invocations, been got into the stone, it became an object of adoration and worship, and capable of working miracles. This, like the other two practices mentioned, did not escape the censure of the orthodox Greeks; but the Paulicians went so far as to destroy these crosses when they could. And in parts of Armenia the word cross-stealer is still synonymous with outlaw or brigand. The modern Armenian novelist, Raffi of Tiflis, lately deceased, wrote a novel entitled *The Cross-Stealers*, in which he describes one of their villages. They probably still exist in Siunik and other districts south-east of Tiflis, and must be descendants of Paulicians.

There was in the Adoptionist Christology nothing to lead its adherents to specially affiliate themselves to the Apostle Paul. It is possible, however, that, when they heard themselves called Pauliani or Paulicians, they, whether from ignorance or other reasons, ventured upon such an affiliation. According to Gregory Magistros they would say: 'We love Paul, and we execrate Peter.' We hear nothing about it in the Armenian sources, but it is certain from the Escurial document that they named their congregations in the Western Taurus after the communities to whom St. Paul addressed his epistles, and several of their great missionaries took from the same epistles what were probably baptismal names, received when they were baptized into the Church. Mananali is the most Eastern of the congregations in which we hear of this innocent *Schwärmerei*. Further east, in Mush and Thonrak, the Armenian sources give no hint of it. It may therefore have been an idiosyncrasy of those congregations in which Greeks were perhaps more numerous than Armenians.

For we must never forget that the Paulician Church was not the national Church of a particular race, but, an old form of the apostolic Church; and that it included within itself Syrians, Greeks, Armenians, Africans, Latins, and various other races. Lurking in South-eastern Armenia, when it was nearly extirpated in the Roman Empire, it there nursed its forces in comparative security under the protection of the Persians and Arabs, and prepared itself for that magnificent career of missionary enterprise in the Greek world, which the sources relate with so much bitterness. These sources make it plain that many of its apostles were Armenians; and so notorious was it to the Greeks that the centre of the new religious revolt was in Armenia, that in the tenth and eleventh century the very name 'Armenian' was synonymous to the mind of a Greek believer with 'Paulician.' I should therefore conjecture that the renaming of congregations was a propagandist device peculiar to the Western Taurus, and one which was barely in vogue in Taron and Vaspurakan, where the Church had always, so to speak, been at home. It was an attempt to give to the name of Paulicians or Pauliani, which for those who coined it meant 'followers of Paul of Samosata,' the significance of 'followers of St. Paul.'

The prejudice against St. Peter in the Paulician Church was also less real than their antagonists pretended. It could not, of course, go back to the apostolic age in which the relations of the two great apostles were notoriously strained; and the *Key* goes far to explain the genesis of this particular libel on the Paulician Church, when, on page 93[1], it adds at the end of the list of the apostles the remark: 'These are the twelve apostles on whom the Church rests, and not on Peter alone.' It was hostility to the papal pretensions, and to the secular prostitution of St. Peter's name and authority by the usurping Bishops of Rome, which inspired this remark. The first recorded case, as Prof. Harnack points out (*Dogmen-Gesch.* p. 666), of a Christian who, taking his stand on the rule of faith, was yet condemned and excommunicated as a heretic, is that of Theodotus, whom the Bishop Victor so excommunicated in the year 190. Nearly one hundred years later the same policy of usurpation and extirpation of old and respectable Christian opinion was exampled in the great triumph of the Roman bishop over Paul of Samosata. It was a triumph of the disputed see of St. Peter, namely Rome, over the true one, Antioch. It is not surprising therefore that the writer of the *Key*, who inherited the traditions of the old Roman Adoptionists, sees in the Pope of Rome the archenemy of the truth, and rebukes his pretensions accordingly.

We shall more conveniently discuss the ritual use of the name Peter in the ceremony of election when we come to treat of the relation of the Paulicians to the Albigenses. We will now pass on to the whole question of their relation to famous sects before and after them with whom they have, by various writers, been identified.

Of their being descended from, or even connected with, the Marcionite Church, as Dr. Mkrttschian and others have suggested, there is no proof whatever; any more than there is of their being Manicheans, as the Greeks pretended. The true descendants of

---

[1] In the Armenian MS. (see p. 28 of the printed Armenian text) the words: 'The head of all' ... as far as 'wiles of devils' are written on a new title-page as it were and surrounded by rude scroll-work. The writer felt that, in the rituals of baptism and election now to be described in detail, he was about to set forth the real constitution of the Church. The new title-page and its contents are therefore very appropriate.

Marcion were certainly the Manicheans, and Mani was anathematized by the Paulician Church along with other heretics of the old time. 'You have enumerated the heresies of old, and have anathematized them,' writes Gregory Magistros (p. 142) to the Paulicians of Thulail in Great Armenia. 'They want to teach us, and so enumerate the groups of heretics one after the other, and say: "We do not belong to these; for they have long ago broken off from the Church, and have been excluded"' (p. 147). The Greek sources attest the same. And the Paulicians no doubt anathematized exactly the same groups of heretics whom the Adoptionist Bishop Archelaus[1], when he is combating Mani, anathematizes. They are indeed the heretics of old, namely, Valentinus, Marcion, Tatian, and Sabellius. And the contents of *The Key of Truth* enable us to see why the Paulicians anathematized Mani. His system was no less remote from theirs than was orthodox Catholicism, under many aspects the western counterpart of Manicheism. The differences are so obvious that I shall be content only to notice the few points of resemblance.

The Manichean Church, then, was divided into the two orders of *Electi* and *Auditores*, of *perfecti* and *catechumeni*. There is thus the name *elect* in common. But whereas the Manichean elect one was an ascetic of an extreme and Hindoo type, celibate, and living only on herbs, which the 'auditores' must gather for him lest he should violate his holiness by taking the life even of a vegetable, the Paulician elect one on the contrary was married, lived and dressed like other men, and worked for his living. So we read that Sergius was a woodcutter and earned his livelihood by the work of his own hands. And since Manicheism differed from Paulicianism with all the differences which must arise out of the deification and dissipation of Jesus Christ into a phantom or mahatma as against the frank recognition of his humanity, we must conclude that the two Churches derived the title of *elect* one not one from the other, but both through a joint inheritance of some remote early type of Christian organization, so early and so remote that the memory of it is lost. Another point in common is the veneration, almost amounting to adoration, with which in both churches the elect ones were regarded. But it is not clear that this sort of thing was peculiar to the Manicheans and Paulicians. Ignatius, in language which somewhat grates on the ear of a modern layman, declares that the bishop is, in relation to his congregation, not

---

[1] *Acts of Archel.* c. 37.

merely Christ, but God. *The Teaching of the Twelve Apostles*[1] expressly assigns to the teacher of the word the dignity of the Lord, of whose spirit he is the inspired organ. And, in judging the Paulicians on this point, we must bear in mind, first, that their conception of priesthood, like the Montanist idea of prophecy, was easily distorted by their enemies and turned into an occasion of scoffing and ribaldry; and secondly, that in their view, Jesus was never God, never creator and sustainer of the universe, as he came to be regarded among the orthodox Catholics, when they superimposed on the man of Nazareth the schematism of the pre-existent divine logos of the Alexandrine Jews. It was therefore a lighter thing to regard the recipient of the spirit of Christ in the way in which the Paulicians regarded their elect ones, than it was for the other churches to regard a priest or bishop as the Christ or Lord of the laity.

But although the Paulicians had so little in common with the Manicheans, it does not follow that there were no Armenian Manicheans. There were; and Gregory Magistros, Nerses Claiensis, and Paul of Taron clearly distinguish them from the Thonraki or Paulicians. These Armenian Manicheans were the *Arevordiq* or children of the sun, of whom a description is given from the works of Nerses in Appendix V. To it I refer the reader, who, underneath the exaggerations and falsifications of the Armenian writer, will yet find their Manichean character clearly recognizable. It only remains to add that the sect was of ancient foundation in Armenia; for, according to the Fihrist's Arabic account of Mani, he addressed a letter to the Armenians; and Samuel of Ani, a chronicler of the eleventh century, records that in the year 588 the commentary of Mani on the Gospels was translated into the Armenian tongue. If it could be recovered, it would be a monument of extraordinary value and interest; but since the sect was anathematized alike by Paulicians and by orthodox Armenians, such a work is not likely to have survived[2]

---

[1] See below, p. clxxxi.

[2] Samuel, in the eleventh century, chronicles the bare fact, but Kirakus (died 1272) gives, probably from old sources, though in a confused way, further interesting details (*Op. Armenicae*, ed. Venice, p. 29): 'In the tenth year of the Lord Abraham, and thirty-seventh of the Armenian era (= 588) eloquent Syrians came into Armenia and wished to sow the heresy of Nestorius, but were anathematized and persecuted. However, some received them, and they it was who translated their false books, the *Gortosak*, the *Kirakosak*, "The Vision of Paul," "The Repentance of Adam," "The Diathêkê (Arm. *Tiadek*)

I have not deemed it necessary to detail the wide differences by which the Manicheans were parted from the Paulicians. Before the discovery of *The Key of Truth* it was necessary to do so; and J. Friedrich has done it with remarkable acumen and success. Few inquirers are rewarded with so speedy a verification of their views as he; nor indeed are many inquirers in this field possessed of a faculty of judgement so sober and cautious. But the difference of the Paulician canon of scripture from the Manichean was all along capable of proof, and should have saved students from falling into so radical an error. We know too little of the Manichean tenets to explain what they signified by calling their priests the *elect*. But one cannot read the authorities for the study of Manicheism without realizing that it was a system which, probably through the mediation of Marcion, cast back its roots into the earliest period of Christianity. They were moreover, through Marcion, the peculiar disciples of St. Paul, as were no teachers of any other school. And their relative Conservatism is proved by the way in which they adhered to the canon and kept alive the anti-Jewish rancour of Marcion, long after the assured triumph of Christianity over Judaizing influences made the one and the other anachronisms.

We have already made the remark that the *Key* does not call outright the elect ones Christs. It is certain, however, from the confession of the year 1837[1], and from the passage about the Eucharist at the end of the Catechism, that they did so. We cannot tell what the lost chapters of the *Key* contained, but the whole drift of what remains proves that they so regarded them. According to it, the entire life of the Christian should be a rehearsal of the life of Christ; and the body of believers, the Church, is in a mysterious manner the body of Christ. 'I have been crucified,' says Paul (Gal. ii. 20), 'with Christ; yet I live, and yet no longer I, but there liveth in me Christ: and that life which I now live in the flesh, I live through faith in the Son of God, who loved me and surrendered himself up for my sake.' So in John xiv. 3: 'That where I am, ye also may be'; and John xvii. 23: 'I am in them, and thou in me, that they may be perfected into one.' Paul

Childhood of the Lord," and "*Ebios* and the Grape-cluster of Blessing," and the not-to-be-hidden books, and " The Explanation of the Gospel of Mani." And he that believes in them is cursed by the orthodox.' Kirakos mixes up the Nestorians and Manicheans in one account; with the exception of the last, we can hardly say which book belonged to which sect.

[1] See above, p. xxvii.

classified his utterances according as it was Christ that spoke in him or as he, the mere man, spoke. So in Hermas, *Mand.* ii. 8, 9 ; so also the *Didaché*, so also Montanus, to all three of which references we shall recur later on.

It was a belief which lent itself to caricature; and behind the libels of the enemies of Paul of Samosata, reported in Eusebius, *Hist.* vii. 30, we may discern the truth that he was venerated by the faithful as a Lord, as one in whom God 'had made his spirit to dwell' (Jas. iv. 5), as the image and successor on earth of Christ. In some such way the Paulician elect were assuredly regarded, and the very idea of an *elect* one, as the name implies, was that of a vessel of election, of a man chosen by the spirit in the same way in which the man Jesus was chosen. The spirit had descended upon him and abode in him, rendering him a new man, one in soul and body with Christ. The idea of such an union of the believer made perfect by faith with Christ was very old in Christianity. Thus, in the ancient tract *De aleatoribus*, 3, we have the *logion*: 'Nolite contristare Spiritum Sanctum qui in uobis est, et nolite extinguere lumen, quod in uobis effulsit.' In the same spirit are addressed the words of the still older pseudo-Cyprianic tract, *De duobus mont.* c. 13, 'Ita me in uobis uidete, quomodo quis uestrum se uidet in aquam aut in speculum' —an illustration the more striking because, as Harnack[1] points out, this early Latin tract is a monument of the Adoptionist faith. We often meet with the idea in Tertullian, e. g. *De Poenit.* 10, ' Non potest corpus de unius membri vexatione laetum agere : condoleat universum, et ad remedium conlaboret, necesse est. In uno et altero ecclesia est, ecclesia vero Christus. Ergo cum te ad fratrum genua protendis, *Christum* contrectas, *Christum* exoras. Aeque illi cum super te lachrymas agunt, *Christus* patitur, *Christus* patrem deprecatur.' So also in his *De Oratione*, c. xx. 26, ' Fratrem domum tuam introgressum ne sine oratione dimiseris. Vidisti, inquit, fratrem ? *Vidisti Dominum tuum* : maxime advenam, ne angelus forte sit.'

In these noble words is revealed to us the fact, which in his letter against the Paulicians Gregory of Narek distorts, basing upon it a charge of anthropolatry[2]. The same adoration was, in the Middle Ages, paid by the believers of the Albigensian Church to

---

[1] *Dogmen-Gesch.* i. (ed. 3), p. 676.

[2] This charge also meant that they adored one, to wit Jesus, who was from their standpoint merely human.

their elect or perfect ones. Thus in the *Liber Sententiarum* (culpa 61) one Gulielmus confesses before the inquisitors that 'he once adored James Auterius, the heretic, with his hands joined, bowing himself three times upon a bench before him, and saying each time "benedicite."' So a female heretic Gulielma (*Lib. Sentent.* 33), after being 'received into the damnable sect of heresy' in her last illness, 'caused herself to be adored as a heretic in their damnable manner.'

There remain two more points in respect of which the Paulicians remind us of Tertullian. The one is their attitude towards the cult of the Virgin Mary. They denied her perpetual virginity, and taught that Christ expressly denied her to be blessed. So to Tertullian[1] the mother of Christ was the type of the unbelieving synagogue, 'Quale ergo erat, si docens non tanti facere matrem aut fratres, quanti Dei verbum, ipse Dei verbum nuntiata matre et fraternitate desereret? Negavit itaque parentes, quomodo docuit negandos pro Dei opere. Sed alias figura est synagogae in matre abiuncta (? abiurata) et Iudaeorum in fratribus incredulis. Foris erat in illis Israel: discipuli autem novi intus audientes, et credentes, et cohaerentes Christo, ecclesiam deliniabant: quam potiorem matrem[2], et digniorem fraternitatem, recusato carnali genere nuncupat.' The belief in the perpetual virginity is also alien to Tertullian, who here again confirms the antiquity of the Paulician teaching. In the fourth century Helvidius was able to plead his authority in favour of common sense exegesis: against such testimony Jerome, arguing for the later view, could find no better argument than to write of Tertullian 'ecclesiae homo non fuit'[3].

The other point concerns the Eucharist, about which the Paulician theory is not clear or consistent with itself. The Greek source, *Scor.* viii, says that the Paulicians blasphemed against the divine mysteries of the Holy Communion of the body and blood, and taught that it was his words which the Lord gave to his disciples, when he said 'Take, eat and drink,' and not bread and wine. 'Nor is it right,' he says, 'that (mere) bread and wine be offered.' In the same way Tertullian (*De Res. Carn.* c. 37) says that in John vi the flesh and blood signify simply Christ's life-

---

[1] *De Carne Christi*, ch. 7.

[2] So according to *Scor.* vii the Paulicians called the Virgin τὴν ἄνω Ἱερουσαλήμ, ἐν ᾗ πρόδρομος ὑπὲρ ἡμῶν εἰσῆλθε Χριστός. See p. xlvi.

[3] C. Helvidium: 'Et de Tertulliano quidem nihil amplius dico, quam Ecclesiae hominem non fuisse.'

giving words to be received in faith: 'Itaque sermonem constituens vivificatorem, quia spiritus et vita sermo, eundem etiam carnem suam dixit: quia et sermo caro erat factus, proinde in causam vitae appetendus et devorandus auditu et ruminandus intellectu et fide digerendus.' This is written as a comment on the text John vi. 63, and also on the following: 'Qui audit sermones meos, et credit in eum qui me misit, habet vitam eternam et in iudicium non veniet, sed transiet de morte ad vitam.' There is a passage in the Paulician Catechism of exactly similar import. At the same time that he thus attempted a spiritual interpretation of the rite, Tertullian also held the grosser view of an actual change or *metabolé* of the elements into the real body and blood of Christ. And similarly the Paulicians fell into the same materialistic language. But they cannot have entertained in its full extent the superstition of transubstantiation; for the body of Christ into which the loaf was changed, was (as we have seen above, p. lv) equally the body of the elect ministrant. And as the unity of the flesh of the elect with that of Christ was of a spiritual kind— the unity to wit of one that abode in Christ and Christ in him— so the change of the elements according to the Paulician view, though it is pronounced to be a real and true change, must ultimately have been conceived of as a spiritual, or as we should say, a figurative[1] kind. I think that what Canon Gore[2] has said about Tertullian is equally true of the Paulicians: 'It is perhaps safest to assume that Tertullian was uncertain in his own mind as to the exact meaning which he assigned to the eucharistic language of the Church and the exact nature which he attributed to the eucharistic gifts.' If we had the Paulician sacramentary we would know more about their view. All we can safely say is that in whatever sense the elect one was Christ (*not* Jesus), in the same sense the elements became the body of Christ. The Catechism declares that the blessing of the elements produced the change of them into the body of Christ, no doubt by introducing into them the same spirit which at baptism entered Christ. This idea of a spirit introduced by invocation into a material thing was common alike to Christianity and to the older cults which preceded it. The

---

[1] So in the *Canons of St. Sahak* (400-450) it is declared that the bread and wine are offered on the altar as a *type* of the vivifying body and blood of Christ (ed. Ven. 1853, p. 106, Old Arm.). The language of *The Key of Truth* is identical, and in it we must have the primitive view of the Armenian Church.

[2] *Dissertations*, ed. 1, p. 312.

Paulicians rejected it as applied to stone crosses and perhaps to the water of the baptismal font. But it was natural enough that they should turn to it for an explanation or working theory of the Eucharistic mystery.

Large bodies of Paulicians were transported to Thrace in the eighth century and again in the tenth. The first of these emigrations[1] was organized by Constantine Copronymus, himself in all probability a member of the Paulician Church. Cedrenus[2], following Theophanes, relates that in its new home the heresy spread and flourished. It was again an Armenian emperor, John Tzimiskes, who in 970 deported another body of 100,000 Paulicians to the line of the Danube. One hundred years before the latter date we learn from Peter of Sicily, who resided nine months in the Paulician stronghold Tephrik, that the Paulicians of the Taurus were sending missions to convert the young Bulgarian nation to their religion. It is certain that in a large measure they succeeded in their object, and the result was the movement of the Bogomiles. We only know this sect from its enemies, who, true to their habit of distorting facts, half wilfully, half in ignorance, portrayed its adherents as Manicheans. It is certainly true, if the fragmentary accounts of them which survive are to be trusted, that they had

---

[1] The Armenian historian, Sebeos (ch. 6), relates that at a much earlier date the Roman Emperor, Maurice, had a scheme for the wholesale deportation to Thrace of the Armenian population living in his dominions. He at the same time proposed to Chosrow that he should deport the Armenians under his rule, i. e. in Vaspurakan, to the far east. 'They are a crooked and rebellious race,' he wrote to Chosrow, 'interposed between us and for ever disturbing our relations. Come then, I will collect mine and deport them wholesale to Thrace. You do the same with yours, and have them led away to the East. Then if they die, it is our enemies who die. And if they kill others, it is our enemies they will kill. And we shall live in peace. For as long as any of them are left on earth, we will have no rest.' The Adoptionist Armenians were probably more refractory to the Byzantine rule than the orthodox ones, for in their case religion as well as race was antagonistic. Maurice's plan was not carried out, though Chosrow agreed, owing to the opposition of the Armenians themselves; but in his reign there were already Armenian forces of foot and horse defending the line of the Danube under Armenian officers, e. g. under Mushel Mamikonean. It is clear that the wholesale deportation of heterodox Armenians to Thrace had long been contemplated as a measure of high policy; and Copronymus was the first Emperor able to carry out the plan, because he had their confidence and sympathized with them. As late as 1603 Shah Abbas revived and carried out the plan of Chosrow, and deported the inhabitants of South-eastern Armenia *en masse* to Ispahan.

[2] Ed. Bonn, ii. p. 10 (p. 453).

taken up Manichean elements, from which the Paulician Church was free. But it is more probable that they were by their persecutors merely assumed to be Manicheans, and described accordingly. It was much easier to copy out one of the many accounts of the Manicheans which were still in circulation, than to inquire what their tenets really were. Thus Peter of Sicily, though he lived among the Paulicians for several months, was content to copy out the Escurial document into his history[1]. So was Photius, who claims to have been present at many inquisitions of Paulicians, and to have learned their opinions at first hand. Like Peter of Sicily, he was blind and deaf where heretical opinion was in question.

We must then be doubly cautious not to believe all we read about the Bogomiles. What has been written about them appears to me to be for the most part hopelessly confused and untrustworthy. To sift it at all would require a separate work. I shall therefore pass it by one side, only trusting that some scholar equipped with a knowledge of the old Slavonic dialects will some day make it his task to write scientifically about them. According to Mr. Arthur Evans, who has written more fruitfully about them than any other author whom I have consulted, there are still communities of them in existence in the Balkan peninsula. Surely a diligent search made in likely places by a sympathetic person would result in the finding of some of their ancient books. Their literature is indispensable as a connecting-link between the Paulicians and the mediaeval Cathars of Europe.

As to the Armenian Paulicians themselves, it is certain that they held their own for many centuries in and about Philippopolis. We hear of them in the chronicles of the Latin Crusaders; and then there is a long blank, just as there is in the native Armenian sources, reaching to the eighteenth century. Then a chance remark in one of Lady Mary Wortley Montague's charming letters from the east reveals to us that there was still in Philippopolis a fairly flourishing congregation of Paulicians. For she writes from Adrianople, April 1, 1717, thus: 'I found at Philippopolis a sect of Christians that call themselves Paulines. They show an old church where they say St. Paul preached, and he is their favourite saint, after the same manner that St. Peter is at Rome; neither do they forget to give him the preference over the rest of the Apostles.' We see that in 1717 they gave the same account

---

[1] Yet he pretended to have obtained in Tephrik a more accurate account of them (ἀκριβέστερον τὰ περὶ αὐτῶν μαθών). See Migne, *P. G.* vol. civ. col. 1241.

of themselves to this gifted English lady as they had given in Thonrak 700 years before to Gregory Magistros. Another hundred years elapses, and we again hear of them in Philippopolis in 1819, when according to the *Allgem. Encyclop.* of Meier u. Kämtz (Leipzig, 1840, art. Paulikiani), a priest of the Greek Church in Philippopolis, in his ἐγχειρίδιον περὶ τῆς ἐπαρχίας Φιλιππουπόλεως (Wien, 1819, p. 27), says that not only among the inhabitants of that city, but in five or six neighbouring villages there lived numerous Paulicians, who had long before given up all Manichean tenets and become complete Papists (καθ' ὅλον παππίσται). Not much renunciation was needed, however, to resign tenets which they had never held.

The Latin Crusaders also found them in Syria[1], always on the side of the Saracens. Thus Curburan the Turk brings to Antioch from the east an army of Saracens, Arabs, Persians, and certain other troops who novitiis censebantur vocabulis, Publicani scilicet, Curti, Azimitae et Agulani[2]. There was a *Castra Publicanorum*[3] held by Armenians in the valley of Antioch; and there was, in 1099, a fortress manned by them called *Archê*, near Tripolis[4]. We read of them also at Neapolis in Palestine, and near Ascalon as well late in the eleventh century.

It is nearly sixty years later that we have our first notices of them in Europe under the name Publicani, which was the Eastern way of pronouncing Pauliciani. Sometimes this name is misunderstood and rendered *Telonarii*, the Greek equivalent of tax-gatherers. Often, to complete a spiteful blunder, the name *Sadducaei* is added because in the Gospels Publicans and Sadducees are associated. And this seems to have been a cheap device for bringing them into contempt as early as the eleventh century, for Gregory Magistros (p. 142) warns the Syrian Catholicos against their *Sadducean* leaven. According to the chronicle of Gulielmus, A. D. 1197, several Paulicians were condemned at the Council of Oxford in the year 1160, because they detested Holy Baptism, the Eucharist, and marriage. This means no more than that they rejected the institution of infant baptism approved of by their persecutors. They were Germans, adds Gulielmus, who, 'having taken their rise in Gascony, from

---

[1] See the references in *Petri Tudebodi de Hierosol. itin.* iii. 3, p. 26, and iv. 5, p. 33.

[2] See *Guiberti, Abbatis Gesta*, 189 H, under year 1099.

[3] See *Baldricus, Episc. Dolensis*, B 39, var. 16, under date 1097.

[4] Ibid., B 91 D, B 105, var. 19.

some unknown author, had multiplied like the sand of the sea in France, Spain, Italy, and Germany.' A few years later, 1179, the Publicani were condemned by name in the third Council of the Lateran, Can. 27. In this they are identified with the Albigenses about Toulouse, and also with the Cathari and Patrini. In the year 1198 Robert of Auxerre, in his chronicle, tells us that about that time the *Haeresis* had already widely ramified; and that at Nismes the Abbot of St. Martin's and the Dean of the Greater Church had been infected with it and condemned at the Council of Sens. Lastly, in 1228, Ralf of Coggeshall, in his chronicle, writes that in the year 1174 the pernicious heresy of the Publicani arose in France. It was thus agreed on all hands that the centre of the diffusion of the heresy was in France and in Gascony. That the heresy mentioned by these writers was akin to Paulicianism is certain. That it was either identical with it, or a direct offshoot of it, is improbable.

But before we pass to the Albigenses, let us notice the heretics of Cöln and the neighbourhood described by Eckbert, Abbot of Schonauge in 1160. 'When I was a Canon at Bonn,' says this writer, 'I and my like-minded friend, Bertolphus, frequently disputed with such persons, and I paid great attention to their errors and defences.' We learn from him that these heretics were very numerous in all countries, and were called in Germany *Cathari*, in Flanders *Piphles*, in France *Tixerant*, because they were weavers. They were well equipped with sacred texts to defend their own errors and assail the Catholic faith; they taught that the true faith of Christ existed nowhere except in their own conventicles, which they held in cellars, in workshops, and such-like underground places. They said that they led the life of apostles: they alone had a genuine priesthood, which the Roman Church had lost. They rejected the belief in purgatory, and taught that baptism of infants availed nothing, because they could not seek baptism by themselves, nor make profession of faith. And in secret, but more generally, they declared that water baptism was not profitable to salvation at all, but that only a special baptism of their own by the Holy Ghost and fire could save men. Except for this last particular these heretics might be at once identified with Paulicians; but other details which Eckbert supplies about them imply, if he spoke the truth, that they were deeply tinged with Manichean beliefs. For they kept the festival of Bema, in which the death of Mani was commemorated; but his friend Bertolph said that they called it *Malilosa*, and kept it not in the spring but in the autumn. The perfect members of the sect eschewed flesh, and were celibate. They denied that Christ had true human flesh, or humanity at all; and said that he only had an appearance of human flesh, and made a mere pretence of death and resurrection.

When this writer adds that *his informant told him* that the annual great festival of these heretics was called among those with whom he was connected, not *Bema*, but *Malilosa*[1], our faith in the first-hand character of Eckbert's knowledge is shaken; and when he further on appeals to Augustine, we feel sure that he is retailing to us not the truth, but second-hand lucubrations of his own, based on that saint's works against the Manicheans. These were in the hands of every mediaeval monk; and, as it was an age in which men were incapable of describing anything accurately, it is useless to look for truth in the accounts of heresy. The persecutors simply copied out earlier fathers like Augustine, and attributed to the persecuted the opinions which they thought, from their own reading of these older authorities, they ought to hold. It is thus impossible to say whether these heretics of Cologne and Bonn were Paulicians or not. I suspect that they were a remnant of an older Adoptionist Christianity, and not in the least Manichean.

In regard to the Albigenses we are on safer ground, for here we have a genuine writing of the sect to build our conclusions upon. This is the so-called Cathar ritual, of which, because of its importance, I add an English translation in my Sixth Appendix. It is preserved in a MS. of the first half of the thirteenth century in the Library of Lyon. Composed in the old Provençal tongue, it is certainly older than the MS. in which alone it has survived to us. I have added it among the documents illustrative of *The Key of Truth*, for, so far as I know, it has never been translated into English, or received the attention it deserves. We are immediately struck by the resemblance there is between the rite of *Consolamentum* which it contains and the Paulician rite of election; and the resemblance is punctuated by the independent information of Evervinus, that a member of the sect who had been admitted to this grade of initiation in the sect was commonly called an elect one. It was a spiritual baptism by the imposition of hands, which communicated to him who received it the plenary inspiration of the Holy Spirit, along with the power to bind and loose. It was

---

[1] I have seen no attempt to explain this name. Could it be Syriac, and was the feast a feast of prophetic utterances, or of tongues?

not the baptism instituted by John with water, but the baptism with the Spirit and with fire. Jesus bestowed it on his disciples when he blew upon them and said, 'Receive the Holy Spirit.' And they had handed it down in unbroken tradition to the Christians or good men who formed the Church. It involved a higher degree of abstinence from all forms of moral evil, a higher degree of self-renunciation than was expected of a layman or mere believer. It was preceded by another rite, which the Lyon MS. also contains, that of giving the Lord's Prayer along with the Book of the Gospel to one who was already a believer. These two rites of the reception of the Lord's Prayer along with the Gospel and of the *Consolamentum*, taken together, seem to correspond to the single Paulician rite of election. Yet they by no means wholly coalesce in their import. For in the *Consolamentum* the believer receives into his heart the spirit which cries *Abba, Abba*; he is adopted a son of God and wins eternal life, and that is quite as much the import of the Paulician rite of baptism as of the Paulician rite of election.

The Paulician rites of name-giving and baptism with water do not find their analogue at all in the Lyon MS., though we cannot argue from their absence that they were without them. Probably a person became a simple member of the Church, a *credens*, as he is called in this document, by receiving water baptism. And perhaps this inferior rite is not given in the Lyon MS., because it was presupposed. That they rejected infant baptism may be believed from the reports of the Inquisition and of their orthodox enemies. Thus Peter Chrysogonus, A.D. 1178 (Maitland, p. 165), relates that the heretics of Toulouse taught that baptism did not profit children. Peter Auterius, the great heresiarch of those parts in the early thirteenth century, and probably one of the greatest religious teachers and reformers that France has ever seen, taught that the baptism of the Roman Church is of no avail to children (ibid. p. 237). Evervinus, A.D. 1147, testifies the same of the heretics of Cologne, as does Eckbert. The Waldenses, who must not be confused with the Albigeois, seem, from the testimony of Ebrardus, A.D. 1212, to have also rejected infant baptism (Maitland, p. 387). It is possible, however, that Ebrardus confused the Waldenses with the Albigeois.

The Cathar ritual is less a form of clerical ordination than of spiritual baptism necessary to salvation, and so was given to men and women alike. It is preceded by the simple service of absolution of sins for the whole body of believers. It so far answers rather to the Paulician baptism than to their election. Yet it is probable that the

Paulician ordinal and the Cathar form of *Consolamentum* are both descended from a common source. For in both the candidate for admission takes the ritual name of Peter. In the Cathar form the rationale of this ritual appellation seems to have been lost; for it runs thus (p. 163): 'And *if* the believer hath the name Peter, the elder shall say as follows: "Peter,"' &c. This is in the preliminary rite of the reception from the Church of the Lord's Prayer and the book; but in the rite of *Consolamentum* he is again similarly addressed. In the Paulician rite it is not clear from the text as it stands, whether the candidate, after he has given to the formal ritual question of the bishop, 'What is thy name?' the equally formal answer, 'Thy servant's name is Peter,' is to have this symbolic name confirmed to him by the bishop, or whether he has it taken away, and another name formally substituted for it. But we should surely adopt the former of the two alternatives. The bishop, after the manner of Christ in the Gospel, changes his name to that of Peter, in formal acknowledgement that he was now and henceforth one on whom the Church of Christ was built. This was at once an appropriate symbolic usage, and a defiance of the usurping claims of the Bishop of Rome. On the other hand I cannot conceal from myself that there is evidence for an opposite interpretation. For the Greek source[1] assures us that the Paulicians treated the name of Peter as something of ill omen to be averted. If the candidate formally assumed the name, in order that the bishop might take it away and substitute another than that of the apostle who had denied the Lord three times, it may have been a Pauline name, such as we know the Paulician leaders assumed, which was so substituted. It is possible even that the Greek writer of the Escurial document actually had before him the same text as the *Key* contains of the ritual of election, and fell into the misinterpretation to which it lends itself. For we too feel its ambiguity. If the name Peter was taken away instead of being conferred, then the Albigensian ritual has reached a still more fossilized stage than we need suppose it to be in, if we accept the counter alternative. Either interpretation is equally a defiance hurled at Rome; but it hardly accords with the respect with which St. Peter, in spite of his faults so candidly recorded in the Gospel, is elsewhere regarded in the *Key*, and the deference with which his epistle is quoted, to suppose that the Paulicians ostentatiously flouted his name in their service of election. Amid all these doubts, however, two certainties

---

[1] See above, 107, *n.* 2.

stand forth: the one that in this symbolism we have a point of contact between the Albigeois and the Paulicians; the other that this Paulician ritual was either in Latin or in Greek, either by report or otherwise, known to the eighth or early ninth century author of the Escurial fragment.

We have already dwelt on the curious identity there was between the European Cathars and the Paulicians in their theory of the Eucharist. A cursory perusal of the *Liber Sententiarum*, or of Moneta's work, or of Maitland's useful treatise, shows us many other points of resemblance. The Cathars, for example, rejected the adoration of the cross (Maitland, p. 240, note), and the doctrine of Purgatory was denied by the heretics of Cologne (ibid. p. 349), of Trèves (ibid. p. 354), and of Oxford (ibid. p. 366); and just as the Paulicians opposed the spiritual Church composed of believers to the edifices of stone, so did the Cathars. Thus we have Ebrardus naively upholding against them the proposition that 'a building of stone ought to be called a church' (ibid. p. 387); and Ermengard, A.D. 1200, argues for the same position (ibid. p. 380). Even the great St. Bernard, A.D. 1200, found it necessary to controvert the truth that the Most High dwelleth not in a temple made with hands, when he heard it affirmed by the persecuted Cathars (ibid. p. 376). The same charge was also made against the Albigeois as against the Paulicians that they repudiated marriage; the truth being this, that the heretics did not make a sacrament of it, as did the orthodox or persecuting Churches. It is also likely enough that the Cathars really taught celibacy to be the higher state. But did not their orthodox persecutors teach the same, following St. Paul[1]? The truth is that teaching which was correct and apostolic in the mouth of the persecutor was devilish when it fell from the lips of the persecuted. Whatever the sentiment of the European Cathars may have been on such points, we know from the *Key* that the Paulician bishop had to be a married man. They were therefore less morbidly ascetic than the Roman and Greek Churches. The inquisitors relate that the elect of the Albigeois had to be celibate. But this can hardly have been the case. For Peter Auterius, their leader in Toulouse, had a son James, of whom the records of the inquisition make frequent mention. As to the Paulicians, they simply followed in such matters the teaching of Paul in his pastoral letters; and it is likely that the Albigeois did the same. Any and every doctrine based on St. John or St. Paul could easily be misrepresented as

---

[1] See Hieronymus, *C. Helvidium, passim.*

Manichean; and, what is more, if we knew the Manicheans themselves as they really were, instead of having to trust to the reports of their enemies, we should probably find that they went no further in the direction of asceticism and monkery than did their persecutors, who indeed may be suspected, in this particular, of having copied them at the same time that they anathematized them.

It is clear for another reason that the Albigenses were no mere Manicheans. The characteristic note of Manicheanism was the brusque rejection of the Old Testament writings; but in the Lyon MS. the Book of Solomon is quoted with approval. There is also good evidence that in their fasts they eschewed milk, cheese, eggs, meat, butter, all things in short (as Evervinus says, speaking of the heretics called Apostolici of Cologne) *quae copulatione generantur*. But this was and still is the canon of fasting observed in the eastern orthodox Churches, as also among strict adherents of the Roman Church. There is nothing specially Manichean about it, and the Paulicians probably conducted their fasts along the same lines. It was a rule of abstinence long anterior to Christianity; for in Philo and in the Neo-Pythagorean Greek writers we have constant mention both of Jews and of Pagans who observed it. Of the characteristically Manichean precept to kill nothing, not even a plant, in order to eat it, we hear nothing in the reports of the Albigeois inquisition. It was probably a precept of Mani alone, and borrowed by him from the Jainas of India. Equally little does the Lyon MS. in any way confirm the charge of exaggerated dualism brought by the persecutors against the mediaeval Cathars, and we should probably attach little weight to it. With the same amount of ill-will, one could prove a similar charge against the orthodox Churches and against the New Testament itself ten times over.

Much has been made of the practice called *Endura*, even by sensible writers like Maitland. But since the discovery of the Cathar ritual of Lyon, it is no longer possible to make it a charge against the Albigeois that they forced a believer, who during illness was consoled or hereticated (as the persecutors termed it), to starve himself or herself to death. On the contrary the elder, in giving the Lord's Prayer to the sick person, exhorts her or him as follows · 'Never shall ye eat or drink anything without first saying this prayer.' Was this an exhortation to starve themselves to death? The real abstinence imposed on the person consoled was 'to keep himself or herself from lying and swearing, and from all else forbidden by God.' It is indeed clear from the *Liber Sententiarum*, or Report of the Toulouse inquisition itself, that many, after receiving the *Consolamentum*, hastened their death by self-starvation; but it is equally clear why they did so. It was from fear that the cruelty of the inquisitors—and it was an age of fierce persecution which this book represents—might oblige them to recant and forfeit the assurance of eternal life which they had received. Thus in the *Culpa*, 76, a sick woman, Gulielma, after being consoled, urgently besought another woman named Serdana and some other persons that her death might be hastened, *fearing to be taken by the inquisitors for heresy*. Yet Maitland (p. 235), who reports this very case of *Endura*, as it was called, speaks of 'the horrible suicide, not only recommended, but required, in this sect.' If there was any sin in such a practice, it was on the inhuman cruelty and fanaticism of the Latin Church that the guilt rested, not on the victims of clerical brutality. The *Consolamentum* or spiritual baptism of the Albigeois was vouchsafed, not only to men, but to women as well. But it does not appear that women could become elect ones in the Paulician Church. We are left in doubt, because the ordinal in the *Key* is not only a rite of election, but something more besides. It is also the rite of consecrating a minister or good shepherd of the Church. It therefore corresponds to the conferring of orders in the orthodox Churches. The *Consolamentum*, on the other hand, as given to sick persons, answers rather to last unction, and therefore was as much for women as for men.

Another important point of difference between the *Key* and the Cathar ritual is that the latter interprets the precepts, Matt. xxviii. 19, 20, and Mark xvi. 15, of the baptism with Spirit and fire alone; the *Key*, however, of a general baptism given to all adults, male and female, and expressly identified with the baptism of John, which was not by the Spirit and fire, but by water only. We need not dwell further on the discrepancies between the Paulician manual and the Albigensian. They are too profound for us to be able to suppose that either ritual is descended from the other. Yet there is a clear affinity between them; and the easiest way of accounting for the facts is to suppose that both are descended from a common source. But this common source must have lain far back in the most primitive age of the Church. It was beyond question a very early Christianity, which survived, perhaps variously modified, in the Albigensian Church[1]. The same primitive faith,

---

[1] The Albigeois reserved the Sacramental bread in the same way as did the Christians of Tertullian's age. Their women took it about with them in their

after going through another cycle of change of its own, has survived in the Paulician Church. How far back the common source lay we cannot tell; probably not later than the second century; and there can hardly have been any common development of the two systems later than the fourth. For similar reasons it is not possible to regard the Catharism of the Rhinelands in the early middle ages as a transplantation to the west of the Paulician Church of Asia Minor.

Why then, it will be asked, do writers of the twelfth century give the name of *Publicani* to the Cathars of the west? I should conjecture that the Crusaders had returned from Syria with the knowledge of the corresponding eastern sect, and gave the name which they learned in the far east to the kindred heretics of the west. The very form of the name *Publicani*, and still more its equation with *Telonarii* in the history of Hugo Pictavius (A.D. 1167), shows that the name had come westwards through Greek intermediaries, either from Antioch or Constantinople, in the neighbourhood of both of which places the Crusaders had come into contact, friendly or hostile, with Paulicians at a much earlier time, namely 1090 to 1100. It is not until fifty years after Hugo's identification and over a hundred years after the Crusades, namely in 1223, that, according to Matthew Paris, Conrad, the Pope's legate, complains of direct relations between the Albigenses of France and the heretics of the east; and then it is not Paulician Armenians, but Bogomile Bulgarians, with whom they were in relation. They had, he says, a heresiarch, whom they called their pope, dwelling in the confines of the Bulgarians, of Croatia and Dalmatia, to whom they resorted that he might give them advice. The story indicates that by the year 1223 the Bogomiles of the Balkans had entered into some sort of intercourse with the Cathars of Toulouse. But it would be rash to conclude that the latter, of whom we already get glimpses as early as 1017 or 1022, were offshoots of the Paulicians. But here again we grope among uncertainties. For we are not sure whether the Canons of Orleans, burned at the latter date, were the same people to whom the name Albigenses was afterwards given. They were said to be Manicheans indeed; but that does not prove that they were Cathars, though they probably were. We again hear of them

pockets just as did a Carthaginian Christian lady of the second century or an Alexandrian of the fourth (see *Liturgies*, vol. i, by F. E. Brightman. Oxford, 1896, p. 509, n. 27).

in 1028 or 1031, when they were condemned at the Council of Charroux. In 1049 they are mentioned at the Council of Rheims as the new heretics who had arisen in France. Such evidence all points to the conclusion that the Albigensian heresy was an old and native growth of Languedoc, and that its adherents did not join hands with Paulicians or Bogomiles until long after the epoch of the Crusades.

We have, it is true, a statement in Reinerius Saccho, that the two Churches of Bulgaria and Dugranicia were the parent congregations of the various Cathar Churches of Europe, of which he gives the list as follows: the Church of the Albanenses of Sansano, of Contorezo, of Bagnolo, of Vicenza, of Florence, of Spoleto, of France, of Toulouse, of Cahors, of Albi, of Sclavonia, of the Latins at Constantinople, of the Greeks in the same city. But this author lived as late as 1254, and by that date, perhaps owing to the increased intercourse between east and west brought about by the Crusades, the heretics of the Balkans seem to have joined hands more or less firmly with those of the south of France and of Lombardy. The possibility must also be admitted that the Manicheans, who, in the time of Augustine, had teachers in the north of Africa so pre-eminent in saintliness of life, in intelligence, in critical acumen and literary ability, as from the fragments preserved in Augustine we know Faustus to have been, may have advanced into Italy and France long before the tenth century; making converts wherever they went, and perhaps imparting to the opinions of certain congregations of old believers that Manichean tinge which, if any credit is to be given to the reports of the persecutors, they in many cases had. Reinerius, the Judas Iscariot of the Albigensian Church, himself testifies that the Cathars were divided among themselves into many shades of opinion, some being more dualistic or Manichean than others (Maitland, p. 429); he also attests that as early as the year 1223 the opinions and observances of some of them had undergone important changes. It is not even safe to assume that the Cathars of the Rhine were the same as those of Gascony.

If we had the eucharistic rituals of the Paulicians, and of the Cathars who used the Lyon MS., we should know much more fully the relation in which they stood to each other. As it is, we cannot even affirm as certain that the users of the Lyon book were Adoptionists at all. They probably were; but it is not an explicitly Adoptionist document. And the *Consolamentum*, as set out in it, unlike the Paulician ritual of election, is a form for conferring on the believer the grace or *charisma* not merely of preaching and of the diaconate, but of recovery from sickness as well. It is in fact a general form of laying on of hands in order to the reception of all graces of the spirit whatever; as such and as the sole earnest of immortal life it was extended to women as well as to men. And as a rite which, except in the case of those who desired the grace of the Holy Spirit in order to preach and serve the brethren, was commonly deferred until a time of mortal sickness, it nearly resembles the deferred baptism common in the orthodox Church of the fourth century, when a believer was often not baptized till he lay on his death-bed; or, if earlier, then only in order to be ordained a priest or a bishop. That the Cathar *Consolamentum*, as we have it in the MS. of Lyon, was to a great extent the analogue of the deferred baptism of the fourth century, is the more probable because the document itself shows that the *consoled* or spiritually baptized alone formed the Church proper, and that the *credentes* were simply the catechumens of an earlier age.

Thus these Cathars were the complete antithesis of the later Catholics. They deferred baptism and formal admission into the true Church until death impended, the chief exception to this rule being the persons who were to perform ecclesiastical functions; these put forward the rite of baptism and formal initiation into the true Church to birth. They ended, these began life with baptism. But if this view of the Lyon document be correct, then it follows that they had either given up baptism with water altogether, as some believers already had begun to do in the days of Tertullian (see *De Baptismo*, ch. i); or else they retained it as a rite inferior to the baptism with fire and water, as the equivalent only of the baptism of John, to be used as the initiatory rite of the *credentes*, or catechumens. These, as merely having received it, did not become full members of the spiritual Church of Christ, as did those members of the Paulician Church who had received the baptism with water.

These considerations all point to the fact that the common source, which after all we must surely posit for the Paulician book and for the Cathar ritual, must lie far back somewhere about the year 200, and shortly after, if not before, the excommunication of Theodotus. The common starting-point may have also been in Rome. Anyhow, between that common starting-point on the one hand, and the ninth and late twelfth centuries on the other, when we get our glimpses of these two primitive survivals, there had been time for the two systems, the Paulician and the Cathar, to drift widely apart, all the while however retaining those common traits in their ritual which oblige us to assume a common source.

In consequence of the invasion of Tamerlane thousands of Armenian refugees fled to the north of the Black Sea, to the Crimea, and subsequently deeper into the ancient realm of Poland. In Transylvania many communities of them still remain, and they still have a handsome Church and episcopal See at Lemberg. Those who remain are mostly Armenians of the Gregorian rite, or have become Latin Uniats. The orthodox or Gregorian Armenians of the Balkan Peninsula also are still sufficiently numerous to have their own bishop. Now it is not to be supposed that so many orthodox Armenians thus migrated up into the heart of Europe as traders, and that the Paulician Armenians, of whom there were settled over 200,000 in Thrace five centuries earlier, did not do the same. And as the Paulicians of Philippopolis retained their own Church as late as the eighteenth century, so it is likely that they carried their rites and beliefs into Poland and Bohemia, and even as far as the Rhinelands. The notices of Petrus Siculus and Cedrenus prove that in the ninth century they had begun on European soil the same zealous propaganda which in Asia Minor had drawn upon them the bitter hostility of Constantinople. It is generally agreed —and all the sources allow it—that the Bogomile Church was largely their creation, and if we had monuments we should probably see more clearly that this was the case.

It is therefore a promising field of research to inquire whether the Paulicians were not partially responsible for many sects which at the Reformation make their appearance and exhibit, some more, some less, an affinity to Paulician tenets as set out in the *Key*. This is not the place to embark on such an inquiry, which would require a separate work. Perhaps the data no longer exist which would enable one to trace the channels of communication. To do so would require in any case a vast amount of research; but it does seem probable that in at least two of the sects of the age of the Reformation we have a survival of the same ancient form of the Catholic Church which the pages of the *Key* reveal to us. These two sects are the Anabaptists and the Unitarians, afterwards called Socinians from their great teacher Socinus. From the former are derived the great Baptist Churches of England and America, and also the Mennonites of Germany. The arguments of the sixteenth-century Baptists against Paedo-baptism are the same as we have in the *Key*, and—what we might also expect—an Adoptionist view of Christ as a rule went with them in the past; though the modern Baptists, in accepting the current doctrine of the Incarnation, have both obscured their origin and stultified their distinctive observances. From the first ages Adoptionist tenets have as naturally and as indissolubly been associated with adult baptism, as has infant baptism with the pneumatic Christology, according to which Jesus was from his mother's womb and in his cradle filled with the Holy Spirit, a pre-existent Divine being, creator, and controller of the universe.

The early writings of the Unitarian Baptists, however, display a clear recognition on their part that they were the remnant of the Adoptionist Church of Paul of Samosata and of Photinus. And I will conclude this part of my subject, which I hope to be able to elaborate more fully in another work, with the following very clear and just statement from the pen of a learned Socinian of the seventeenth century, Benedict Wiszowaty. Its date is 1666. I copy the text as Dr. Otto Clemen communicates it to the *Zeitschr für Kirchengeschichte* (Bd. xviii, Heft i, p. 140) from a MS. in his possession:—

'Confessio fidei Christianae secundum Unitarios inter quatuor in Transylvania religiones receptas numerata. Unitarii quoque pro Christianis habendi; credunt enim ... vera esse quae deus, per Christum Dominum revelavit, voluntque secundum eandem revelationem vivere, et salutem per Christum Dominum expectare . coeperunt vero (scil. Unitarii) Albae Iuliae, tunc Carolinae, in Transylvania appellationem Unitariorum assumere ad differentiam eorum quibus Trinitatis nomen placet. Unitarii enim S. Scripturae symboli apostolici primaevaeque ecclesiae vestigiis insistentes noluerunt vel ab aliquo homine denominare (? -ri), vel in Deo divisionem quaerere; sed unum, ut essentia, ita persona deum summum, creatorem coeli et terrae, qui est pater, unicum tam persona quam natura; Dominum Iesum Christum in uno Spiritu Sancto profiteri. Unde etiam voluerunt in Polonia Christiani ad distinctionem ab aliis Christianis, qui a baptismo *Chrescianin* dicuntur appellare (? -ri). Hodie in diversis locis diversas habent denominationes. Dicuntur etiam in Belgio Collegiantes ob unitatem spiritualis quam intendunt unionis; appellati sunt a baptismo Anabaptistae, quod multi eorum sacri baptismatis ritu non infantes, sed adultos fidei capaces voluerunt initiari, eosque non aspergendo, perfundendo, sed secundum divinum mandatum primitivaeque ecclesiae praxim ad sepulturae typum exprimendum mergendo. Nuncupati sunt etiam Pingoviniani, Rakoviani a praecipuis commorationis suae locis. Samosateniani a Paulo Samosateno, episcopo circa annum Christi 260 Antiocheno; Photiniani a Photino episcopo circa annum Christi 350 Sermiensi; Sociniani a Laelio et Fausto, ex principis Italici familia oriundo, Socinis; quoniam idem in defendendo unitatis in divinitate dogmate inter alios multum operae praestiterunt. Arianorum quoque titulo traducuntur. '

The *Key* gives us little information as to the fasts and feasts kept by the Adoptionist Church of Armenia. A reference in the margin to the forty days of holiness implies that they kept a quadragesimal fast; and Isaac Catholicos shows that they kept it, not before Easter, but after the Feast of the Baptism. We also know from a notice preserved in Ananias of Shirak [1] that the *Pauliani*, who were the same people at an earlier date, were Quartodecumans, and kept Easter in the primitive manner at the Jewish date. John of Otzun's language perhaps implies that the old believers in Armenia during the seventh century were Quartodecumans [2], as we should expect them to be. Perhaps we may also conclude from the report of the Russian inquisition in 1837, already referred to, that they kept the Feast of the *Wardawarh* or Transfiguration; but the reference may equally lie to the Feast of the Orthodox Armenians. They are accused by their Armenian opponents of setting at naught all the feasts and fasts of the Church, especially Sunday. And this is probably true, since most of the orthodox feasts and fasts were invented later than the third century, when the Adoptionists had already been excluded from the main stream of Catholic development. They kept the Festival of a Birth of Christ, but identified it with the baptism. In the great Church the Festival of Christmas was not instituted till nearly the close of the fourth century; and

---

[1] Ananias (early seventh century), *op. Arm.* Petersburg, 1877, pp. 22 and 23, and in *Byzant. Zeitschr.* 1897: 'But the Pauliani also keep the feast of the Pascha on the same day (as the Jews), and whatever be the day of the full moon, they call it *Kuriakê*, as the Jews call it Sabbath, even though it be not a Sabbath.' So much is clear, that they kept it with the Jews. For the rest Ananias' account is barely intelligible.

[2] *Oratio Synod.* ch. 3: 'Ipsi quoque Apostoli suis temporibus una cum Iudaeis festum sanctae Paschae diem celebrarunt. *Si quis tamen nostrum audeat cum Iudaeis celebrare*, et ante vernale aequinoctium, et ante primi Sabbati diem solvere ieiunium, anathematis poena fit continuo obnoxius.' In the context he is refuting the plea of the old believers that they kept to the example of Christ and his apostles.

it was even then some time before it was distinguished from the earlier Feast of the Baptism. The reason is obvious. According to the Adoptionist Christology, which in many countries preceded the pneumatic doctrine, the baptism was the spiritual birth of Christ. It was then that the Holy Spirit, as Archelaus says, begat him the Son of God. 'This day have I begotten thee,' was the utterance of the heavenly voice heard in Jordan, according to the earlier form of the text in Luke iii. 22, preserved in Justin Martyr, in Clemens Alexandrinus, in Codex D, and in the old Latin Version. When the Feast of the earthly birth from the Virgin was instituted late in the fourth century, this old form of text was felt to be too favourable to the Adoptionists, already become a heretical sect; and accordingly it was changed[1] into what we read in our English Version: 'In thee am I well pleased.'

The symbolic representation of Jesus Christ as a fish, common in the earliest Christian art, argues an Adoptionist faith on the part of those who invented and used it. 'Sed nos pisciculi secundum ἰχθύν nostrum Iesum Christum in aqua nascimur,' says Tertullian (*De Bapt.* ch. 1). 'But we, little fishes after the example of our ἰχθύς Jesus Christ, are born in water.' And a little further on, ch. 3, he remarks: 'Water was the first to produce that which had life, that it might be no wonder in baptism if waters know how to give life.' And John of Otzun, in the same discourse to which we have so often referred, ch. iv, says; 'Lavacri unctio spiritualis nos regeneratione adoptat: quae autem post baptismum est, unctio in nos adoptionis Dei gratiam advocat. Praeterea altare nos alit, haud vero gignit: lavacrum gignit, non alit.' And even the grecizing Armenians never gave up the baptism as the birthday of Jesus Christ. It was kept on Jan. 6; and the lection for the day was not the gospel of the Nativity, but of the Baptism. John of Otzun accordingly writes thus: 'Verum quod ego dico, id antiqua erat consuetudo iam ab antiquis temporibus originem ducens, atque ad nos usque perveniens. Eo namque die super aquas decantando Psalmum xxviii praemissâ antiphona, *Vox Domini super aquas*, atque Matthaei de baptismo Evangelium legendo, aquam benedicebant, oleo in eam infuso.' It was the rivers and running streams, and not water in fonts, that were so blest, for John

---

[1] Or more probably the text originally stood as it survives in the Ebionite Gospel quoted by Epiphanius : ' Thou art my beloved Son, in whom I am well pleased. This day have I begotten thee.' Subsequently the dangerous words were merely dropped out.

adds that the oppressors (the Mohammedans) tried to prevent the practice, probably from a fear that it bewitched the rivers and made them unwholesome. That this benediction of the waters was as old as the second century, may be inferred from Tertullian, *De Baptismo*, c. iv. On the same day was commemorated the manifestation of Jesus as the Christ through the descent of the Spirit as a dove upon him, according to the idea conveyed in John i. 31–33.

There was in Armenia quite a literature of apology for the keeping of the Birth and Baptism on the same day. But the writers as a rule either had forgotten or ignored the real significance of the union of the two feasts. Yet some of them give us interesting information, such as we do not obtain from Greek writers. Thus Ananias of Shirak [1], in his homily on the Birth of Christ, declares that the Feast of the Birth as separate from the Baptism was first invented by the followers of Cerinthus the heretic. Collections were made of *Testimonia* from the Fathers in defence of the Armenian custom; and in the Bodl. MS. Arm. Marsh. 467, saecl. xvii, fol. 338 A, there is preserved such a collection, of which I append the most interesting. They bear this title: 'Testimonies relating to the Birth of Christ and his Baptism. That it is right to feast them on one day on Jan. 6.' They are as follows:—

'From Clemens, in the apostolically determined canons: The apostles of the Lord fixed the day of the Lord's birth on Jan. the sixth.'

'From Macarius, the Patriarch of Jerusalem. Our Fathers were minded to perform [2] the mystery of Baptism at three feasts, at Easter, at Pentecost, and at the Birth which with the Baptism we feast on one and the same day.'

'From ———[3] Patriarch of Jerusalem. Canons and rules of the Church. For eight days shall old people and young fast, including the Sabbath and the Lord's Day. But on whatever day it shall fall they shall celebrate the day of the Birth and Baptism of the Lord. For these are divine and salutary.'

This fast of eight days before the Baptism survives in the Armenian [4] Church as the seven days' Fast of the Birth.

---

[1] For a translation of this tract see the *Expositor* for Nov. 1896.
[2] Reading *arhnel* for *arhavel*.   [3] The name in the rubric is left blank.
[4] In the homilies of Ephrem (Old Armenian version) the fast called the *arhadjavor*, or 'preliminary,' is explained as 'the fast which precedes the Lord's fast,'

'From Nectarius, Patriarch of Rome. The rules of the orthodoxy of the Church, fixed by the Apostles, ordain that the clergy and penitents shall fast during forty days, and for eight days entire the congregation (*or* the entire congregation), including the Sabbath and the first day of the week. And the Feast of the Epiphany [follows], I mean of the Birth and of the Baptism. For these are divine and salutary; on whatsoever day it shall fall they shall celebrate it.'

This extract is mutilated. It imports that the Feast of the Birth and Baptism was to be kept on the sixth of January, no matter what day of the week it fell upon. The fast of eight days must be the fast preliminary to the Baptism. Did that of forty days follow the Baptism, or was it the Easter fast? If the latter, why connect it with the Baptism? The prescription to fast on Saturday and Sunday is the same as in the last extract. Nectarius, the predecessor of Chrysostom, seems rather late for such prescriptions, but there was no early Pope of the name.

'From Gregory Theologus. The bishop shall fix for his Church, on the sixth of January, the day of the Birth of the Lord and of his Baptism, and on the fourteenth of February his coming into the Temple.'

'From Hippolytus, Bishop. In the ninth month the Lord was born, and in the thirtieth year he was baptized, on the same day; according to Luke, who says, "And Jesus was thirty years of age."'

'And, after a few words, he speaks of the Baptism. For it was unlikely that he should be born on one day, and be baptized on another, as that would have engendered a want of faith, and they would say that it was one person that was born, and another that was baptized. For they confessed two natures and two sons. And consequently, as many as were disobedient have divided the two Feasts. But the Church of the Faithful celebrates on one day the Feast of the Birth and of the Baptism.'

Hippolytus, supposing the above to be really his, overlooks the primitive reason for conjoining the two feasts, namely that the baptism was the true birth of Christ. The idea that Jesus was

or which 'heralds the fast of the king.' It is not clear, however, that with Ephrem the fast of forty days immediately followed the Feast of the Baptism, and did not come later as a fast preliminary to Easter. Consequently the 'preliminary' fast cannot be identified with the 'eight days' of this excerpt. Zenob (*Hist. of Taron*, p. 23, *c.* 800) explains the *arhadjavor* as the 'first fast' imposed by St. Gregory for five ('fifty' according to two MSS.) days on Trdat before baptism. Some explained it as the fast of St. Sergius of Cappadocia, *ignotum per ignotius*.

born and baptized on the same day of the month, the sixth of January, was a device for explaining the custom, universal in the early Church, of conjoining the two feasts. Such an explanation was urgently needed, in order to counteract the Adoptionist view that Jesus was not filled with the Godhead, but was a mere man, until the Spirit begat him as the Christ and only Son at the baptism.

Who were the disobedient ones who divided the two feasts? On this point Paul of Taron (d. 1125), from whom I give some extracts in my eighth appendix, has some curious information which fits in with this extract of Hippolytus, and explains the statement of Ananias of Shirak (c. 600–650) that the disciples of Cerinthus invented the Feast of the Birth on December 25. 'Artemon,' says Paul (p. 222, *Against Theopistus*), 'said this: "The Holy Spirit has revealed to me the day of the Birth of Christ (i.e. Jesus)."' And the revelation was this : 'Jesus was twelve days short of thirty years old when he was baptized. Zachariah went away to his house on Tisri the tenth. From that day Artemon reckoned the six months of Elizabeth's pregnancy, and on this foundation he calculated the Annunciation of the Blessed Virgin to be on March 25. From this last day he reckoned nine months and five days for the Virgin's pregnancy; and accordingly they (i.e. the Artemonites) kept on Dec. 25 the birth, not, however, of the Divine Being, but only of the mere man. Then on Jan. 6 they kept the Feast of the Baptism, and divided one feast into three (? two).'

The same account is given in the Bodleian MS. from which we translate these excerpts. It is quite possible that Artemon, who is in this account recognized as an Adoptionist, may have invented the feast of the human Birth of Jesus by way of safeguarding and preserving in its true significance the older Feast of the Baptism, which in his day the pneumatic Christologists were already bent upon abolishing, as being a stumbling-block in the way of their doctrine. Paul's excerpts are very precise, and have all the appearance of being authentic.

'From Severian, Bishop. From the commentary on Luke·

'The ancients fasted on two days in the week, and omitted (*lit.* passed by) on those days currently the commemoration of the saints. But they feasted, on whatever day it befel, alone the Feast of the Divine Voice [1] and of the Divine Son. For he is God,

---

[1] ածածայնոյն in MS. must be a corruption of ածաձայնոյն, which I render.

and releaseth all. I mean that they kept the Feast of the Birth and of the Baptism on one day.'

The above means that the Baptism was the chief feast, so important as to supersede a fast-day, supposing it fell on one.

'From the letter of Meliton to the Bishop Eutr[1]:

'We feast, according to the annunciation of the angel, in the ninth month the Birth; on the eighth day the Circumcision; at thirty years old the Baptism. And we honour as follows: the Birth and the Baptism shall be feasted on one and the same day.'

The above passage exhibits the same chronological schematism, devised for the same reason, as we saw in the extract from Hippolytus. And it again occurs in the next excerpt. I doubt if the excerpt is really from Melito of Sardis.

'From Cyprian, Bishop. Christ in the flesh, having completed his thirtieth year, is baptized on the same day on which he was born of the Virgin Mary.'

'From Marutha, Bishop of Nphrkert (Martyropolis or Justinianopolis). And this I say, not because the Feast of the Birth is one, and that of the Baptism another, but on one and the same day we must feast them both. However the things are different which occurred on this day.'

Here the last sentence glances at the Adoptionists, by whom Marutha must have found himself surrounded at Nphrkert. They appealed to the joint celebration of Birth and Baptism in behalf of their dogmatic views.

'From the catechism (*lit.* inquiries-by-question) of the Syrian Doctors:

'Sahak answered Afrêm his teacher: "So then, as it was ordained many a time that on the sixth of January, on the last[2] of *Qanûn*, the Son of God was born of the Virgin; why, if so, do the Churches feast December 25, which is the first of *Qanûn*?"

'The teacher said: "The Roman world does so from idolatry, because of the worship of the Sun. And [it feasts] on the 25th of December, which is the first of *Qanûn*; when the day made a beginning out of the darkness (or the night), they feasted the Sun with great joy, and declared that day to be the nuptials of the Sun. However, when the Son of God was born of the Virgin, they

---

[1] The meaning of the word or name *Eutr* I cannot conjecture.
[2] We should read the twelfth.

celebrated the same feast, although they had turned from their idols to God. And when their bishops (*or* primates) saw this, they proceeded to take the Feast of the Birth of Christ, which was on the sixth of January, and placed it then (viz. on Dec. 25). And they abrogated the Feast of the Sun, because it (the Sun) was nothing, as we said before. But the Birth of Christ is truly on the sixth of January, which is the last of *Qanûn*; as the holy apostles wrote in their book of canons in the descent of the Spirit. This the blessed Luke learned and wrote in his Gospel: Jesus was thirty years of age, beginning the day on which he was baptized. For there is a great mystery in the celebration of the birth and the baptism on the same day. For as the two natures, to wit, of God and man, were united without confusion, so also the two feasts were united in one, so as to become the faith of the holy Church.'

The above is curiously candid as to the origin of the custom of keeping Christmas on December 25. But the Roman bishops had another reason, namely to get rid of what had an Adoptionist significance. For as long as the Birth and Baptism were celebrated on one day, the Adoptionists could appeal to the joint feast in support of their views. The Syrian Doctors had also heard of Hippolytus' explanation, viz. that Jesus was baptized on his thirtieth birthday.

The same MS. has a collection of testimonia in defence of the practice of eating the Paschal lamb immediately before the Eucharist. This was clearly the example which the Paulicians set before themselves when they on principle first ate their full of meats and then proceeded to celebrate the Eucharist. I select two only. 'From Marutha, Bishop of Nphrkert: As in the holy Pascha. For first he ate the lamb of the shadow[1], and then began to eat (*lit.* taste) the spiritual Pascha (*lit.* Zatik).' From the same, after a few words: 'And after partaking of the shadow lamb[1], then he blessed the bread and gave it to them; as also Paul testifies, that after the meal Jesus took the bread, blessed and gave it them.'

As early as John of Otzun the Eucharist was separated from the Agapê by an interval. The above testimonium, however, belongs to an age when they were still conjoined. In this respect the Paulicians kept up the practice of the earliest Armenian Church.

Some further information with regard to the feasts of the old believers of Armenia, and of the orthodox Church of that land so far as it was still in a transitional stage, is obtainable from a source

---

[1] i.e. the lamb emblematic of himself.

we have already used. This is Isaac Catholicos, who in his *Invectiva in Armenios*, c. ii, denies that the Armenians kept the Feast of the Annunciation (τοῦ εὐαγγελισμοῦ) at all[1]. On the contrary, he says, they fasted on that day, and denied that the Gospel testifies to the Annunciation having taken place in March. 'That is why,' so they said, 'we do not feast it.' Isaac, on the other hand, can adduce no earlier authority for keeping the feast on March 25th than Eusebius Pamphili, Athanasius, and Chrysostom. ' The Armenians,' he complains, 'keep this feast neither in March nor in any other month, nor do they celebrate it in accordance with the Gospel six months after the conception of Elizabeth; for they really reject the truth of the Annunciation along with the Birth and Incarnation of Christ[2]'

Isaac continues in his ch. iii as follows: ' Then again from the Annunciation, they ought to count nine months, and then feast the Birth of Christ. But as it is, though they commemorate the conception of Elizabeth, yet they do not keep six months after it the Feast of the Annunciation ; nor again, nine months after that, do they keep the festival (πανηγυριζόντων) of Christ's birth. . . . On the contrary, they are downcast in countenance and in tribulation on the very day of this holy and brilliant feast, just like the Jews. Then in the twinkling of an eye, on the fifth evening of the month of January, they—I won't say feast, not a bit of it—but in a fantastic and dim show commemorate[3] the Annunciation and the Birth and the Baptism all at once by way of deceiving the hearers (i. e. laity). Thus they are clearly convicted of proclaiming each festival in mere seeming and fantasy, instead of proclaiming that Christ really became flesh. Therefore they are manifestly detected as gainsayers of the Gospel and as hostile to the incarnation of God.'

The above is interesting for the light it throws on the history of the religion. Among the Adoptionists of Armenia—and in this context we may include the semi-grecized orthodox body,

---

[1] Οὗτοι τὴν τοιαύτην φαιδρὰν καὶ φρικτὴν ἑορτήν, καὶ πρώτην τοῦ κόσμου σωτηρίαν, καὶ τῆς θεοτόκου χαρὰν ἀρνοῦνται μᾶλλον ὥσπερ Ἰουδαῖοι, καθάπερ πένθος αὐτὴν δεχόμενοι, οὐδαμῶς οὐδ' ὅλως αὐτὴν ἑορτάζουσιν ἢ μνημονεύουσι.

[2] The earliest Armenian Church certainly rejected the Incarnation in the current sense of the term, and the only Birth of Christ they celebrated was his spiritual birth in the Jordan, his birth as the *Christ*. His natural or human birth as Jesus they did not care to feast, still less the Annunciation. That this was so appears from the canons of St. Sahak, which are quoted below.

[3] Φανταστικῶς καὶ ἀμυδρῶς μνημονεύοντες.

as well as the Paulicians—the birth of John the Baptist is already commemorated before there is any feasting of the birth of Jesus from the Virgin. Truly, as we go back in the history of the religion, the figure of the Baptist looms larger on the Christian horizon. The human birth of Jesus and the announcement of it did not interest the Armenians till they began to believe that it was a pre-existent divine being, the Christ, the Word, the Son of God that was so born, and not a mere man[1].

In the canons of Sahak accordingly we find (p. 110) the Feast of St. John the Baptist heads the list of feasts kept in a *wanq* or rest-house: 'St. Gregory the Apostle and Confessor of Christ and father of the renewal of the whole land of Armenia, *appointed it first of all*[2].' 'The same St. Gregory,' continues Sahak, 'appointed *Sabbaths*, and fasts, and abstinences in fulfilment of vows.'

In Sahak's list of feasts, which represents the orthodox Armenian Church as early perhaps as 425, there is no hint of the Annunciation and Birth (as opposed to Baptism) of Jesus Christ. The feasts which follow that of John the Baptist are the following:—

(1) Feast of All Martyrs, 'which we call *matrounq*,' i.e. shrines[3].

(2) *Wardawarh*, i.e. 'Splendour-of-Roses or Rose-resplendent.' This was an old Pagan feast of Anahit. On it, says Sahak, the congregations and married priests presented the firstfruits and best of the corn crop bushel by bushel. It was afterwards identified with the Feast of the Transfiguration.

(3) The Feast of the Holy Manifestation, and *its* forty days, and the coming forward (ὑπαπαντή) of the Lord, and the close (*or* ending) of the preliminary (*arhadjavor*) fast. The 'coming forward' was the event narrated in Luke ii. 27 or iv. 14; the 'manifestation,' that of the Holy Spirit in the Jordan. It was on Jan. 6, or rather began at six p.m. on Jan. 5, the day on which the pre-baptismal fast

---

[1] Cp. *Iren. ad Mat.* i. 18 (p. 204): 'Ceterum potuerat dicere Matthaeus: *Iesu uero generatio sic erat*, sed praeuidens Spiritus Sancti deprauatores et praemuniens contra fraudulentiam eorum per Mt. ait: *Christi autem gener. sic erat.*' In view of the fact that *Iesu Christi* is the best-witnessed reading, Irenaeus has the air of protesting too much, and arouses a suspicion that *Iesu* alone stood in the oldest codices he knew of.

[2] This feast, adds Sahak, is to be kept in a *wanq* (where the clergy were celibate) 'because it was fixt (*or* established) by a Nazarene fast, and all other vows whatever are to be kept (*or* fulfilled) in a *wanq*.'

[3] On this day the people of each locality visited the shrine of its own martyr-saint and celebrated in it an Eucharist, so Sahak assures us.

ended. The forty days' fast began, I believe, in the Paulician Church, on the next day, January 6, probably at six p.m.

(4) The feast of the middle [of the] forty days of Zatik; the day of Lazarus, of the great fifth of the week of Zatik, on which our quickener (*or* Vivifier) bequeathed to his disciples the mystery (*or* sacrament) of the new covenant.

(5) The second day of the week of Zatik, a day of offerings and of thanksgiving[1].

(6) The Feast of the Assumption of the Lord into heaven.

(7) The last day of the month *Hroditz* (originally a Pagan feast).

These feasts, says Sahak, are to be held and the firstfruits eaten in a *wanq* or in consecrated places, not only by the celibate, but by the married clergy and strangers; and they shall not lodge [in order to hold them] in hamlets, but only in the *wanq*; the only exception being in favour of places where there may be no *wanq*.

The reference to Sabbaths as ordained by St. Gregory can hardly imply that the earliest Armenian Church kept the Sabbath. Probably the reference is to the *hebdomadarii, id est qui faciunt septimanas*, of the *Peregrinatio* of St. Silvia; for the Armenian word *shabath* may mean 'a week' as well as a 'Saturday,' and the context implies that some form of fasting is to be understood. Nor can we infer anything from the statement of Gregory of Narek (see p. 126) that the Paulicians of Thonrak reckoned the Lord's Day to be just like any other day. That the earliest Christians kept the Sabbath may indeed be inferred from the persistence in the vernacular tongues of the races which first adopted the religion of the word *Sabbath*, namely in the Romance tongues, in Greek, in Armenian, Syrian, and Georgian. And the Armenians themselves have always spoken of Sunday simply as the first day of the week. The Greek word κυριακή hardly occurs before John of Otzun. It is also certain from the works of Philo and Josephus that to most Gentile proselytes the Sabbath observance was the most attractive feature in Judaism. In spite of such considerations, however, one hesitates to interpret the words of Gregory of Narek in the sense that the Paulicians observed the Sabbath and not the Sunday; not, however, because such a thing is in itself unlikely,

---

[1] Sahak's text is obscure. It literally means: 'The feast of the second day of week of Zatik with offerings and with gifts of gratitude of the conventional Zatik.' The word rendered conventional may represent the adj. θετός or θέσις. The reference seems to be to the later date fixed for Easter.

for they were probably the remnant of an old Judaeo-Christian Church, which had spread up through Edessa into Siuniq and Albania. The real ground for distrusting Gregory on this point, as on others, lies in his virulence.

The early Armenian Christians, as is clear from the above canons of Sahak, spoke of rest-houses, synagogues, of proseuchae, and of shrines (*matrounq*), but hardly at all of churches; and individuals, especially if they were elders, were prone 'from ignorance,' as Sahak puts it, to celebrate the Agapê and Eucharist in their own houses, also to consecrate the oil of chrism, as well as collect in them the firstfruits of the offerings. Sahak insists that these rites must be performed in church, or in a *wanq*; and the firstfruits are to be taken to the house of the *head-priest* (= summus sacerdos), while the chief bishop alone shall hallow the chrism.

We have already surmised that, when the significance of the baptism of Jesus was lost sight of in the Church, the Quadragesimal fast ceased to be associated with it, and was made preliminary to Easter. It is therefore probable that the latter feast gained in importance as the baptism lost. The *Key* attaches vast significance to the birth through baptism of the Christ and Son of God. Of Easter and of the Passion and Resurrection of Christ we have in it barely any hint. In the two baptismal creeds these great incidents are not mentioned, and they would seem to have been chiefly valued as the preliminary to the Christ's enthronement by the Father's side as our one Intercessor. We know that the Pauliani continued to keep the Passover on the fourteenth of Nisan with the Jews. Is it possible that the Adoptionists did not, so clearly as their rivals, see in the suffering and dying Jesus Christ a victim for the propitiation of human sins? May not the latter conception have gained ground as the *pondus baptismi* came to be felt more lightly? Certainly it was a conception which in a measure conflicted with Adoptionist baptism, since this solemn rite, deferred until the age of full manhood, was viewed as the final washing away of sins, as a new birth, ushering the saints into the kingdom of God[1]. We must indeed be careful, where the *Key* is silent, and where we therefore depend on the testimony of enemies. But the evidence of Paul of Taron on this point has certainly an air of verisimilitude; and he hints plainly that the Thonraki denied the sacrifice of

---

[1] Therefore the earliest Church, in order to liberate the dead, offered no sacrifices, but vicariously baptized the living in their behalf; and this practice survived in the Marcionite Church.

Christ as an atonement for human sin. Aristaces equally testifies that they rejected the great and terrible mystery of the sacrifice of Christ; and in the same spirit they refused to honour the cross. It would appear that, like the primitive believers, for whom the *Didaché* was written, they interpreted their sacrament less as a sacrifice offered for the sins of men than as a meal symbolic of the unity of all the faithful; as an indication that the Church is the one indivisible body of Christ, of which each believer is a limb. This explains why, in the account of the Eucharist given both at the end of the *Key* (p. 123) and in the report of the Inquisition of Arkhwêli (p. xlix), so much importance is attached to its being *a single* or *one* unleavened loaf that is laid on the table[1]. This one loaf was the symbol of the union of all believers. The same conception of the Eucharist inspired their abhorrence of altars of stone and their determination to eat it in an ordinary room, and off an ordinary table of wood. Having such a significance for them, it was naturally not dissociated—as it was in the Great Church— from the Agapê or common meal of Christian love, of which it was the solemn and fitting conclusion. Their Agapê moreover—though this point cannot be so clearly made out—seems to have been a continuance of the old Paschal meal of the Jews, and in the meats consumed at it the flesh of pigeons[2] and of sheep was preferred in the earliest Armenian Church. Yet it was not like the Jewish Pascha held but once a year. More probably, as their enemies intimate, every common meal had among the Paulicians a sacred character.

With their peculiar view of the Eucharist, which we also find in *The Teaching of the Twelve Apostles,* and with their belief in the efficacy of simple baptism coupled with the intercession of Jesus

---

[1] 1 Cor. x. 17 : εἷς ἄρτος, ἓν σῶμα οἱ πολλοί ἐσμεν.

[2] Thus in the Armenian canons of Basil cited in the Bodleian MS. already referred to we read the following prescriptions:—

'From animals caught in the chase let no one dare to sacrifice (*or* make) a *matal*, but only doves and other birds.'

From the same: 'A strangled animal killed by violence let no one dare to sacrifice as a *matal*.'

From the same: 'The animal which one consecrates to the Lord, the same let him offer. But if it fall unexpectedly into a snare, let him salt it and distribute it to the poor.'

Such prescriptions have a Jewish and early-Christian ring. In considering whether the Paulicians acted on them, we must not suppose that, because they rejected the idea of sin-offerings for the dead, they did not regard the flesh eaten in their love-feast as an offering or sacrifice to God.

Christ to take away sin, there cohered among the Armenian Paulicians a repudiation of the *mataḷ*[1] of their countrymen, in the sense of an animal sacrifice offered in expiation of the sins of the dead. And with this repudiation was connected in turn their rejection of the belief in a Purgatory. Their countrymen, as we see from the accounts of Aristaces and of Paul of Taron, particularly resented this double denial. The *matal* was, we read, Gregory the Illuminator's substitute for the ancient sacrificial system of pagan Armenia, and as such was condemned with much asperity by the Greeks. It was a love-feast upon meats, and the animals eaten at it were regarded as victims offered in expiation of the sins of the dead. The Paulicians evidently had the common meal of flesh preliminary to the sacred rite of the Eucharist, but denied to the animals killed and eaten the expiatory character attributed to them by their orthodox compatriots. In this respect the Paulicians appear in the guise rather of reformers than of old believers. They were, in fact, Adoptionist Christians first and Armenians afterwards. They were never the Church of a separate race and country, as was the orthodox Armenian Church; and this the author of *The Key of Truth* intimates at once by the objective manner in which he speaks of 'the Armenians,' when he condemns them along with Latins and Greeks; and by the vehemence with which he insists on it that he and his fellow-believers alone constituted the genuine Apostolic Church.

The sturdy refusal of the Paulicians to give any other meaning to the word 'Church' than that of the invisible union in one body of the faithful connects them with the earliest Christians and with the Albigeois; and it also helps us to understand the mystical use of the term by the early Gnostics who made an aeon out of the *ecclesia*. The earlier Armenian fathers, as we might expect, resembled the Paulicians in their reluctance to identify the Church with any building of wood and stone. 'The precept of God,' wrote St. Sahak in his canons (c. 425), 'sets forth unto us no Church merely built of stones and logs, but the races of mankind built by faith on the rock of foundation. Wherefore the true faith is the Church, which assembles and builds us into one accord of knowledge of the Son of God. For the giver of life himself taught us, saying: "Thou art the rock, and on this rock will I build my Church, and the gates of Hell shall not prevail against thee." What then shall we understand by his calling Peter the rock?

---

[1] For the meaning of this word see note on p. 134.

Surely not that he was one of the stones? God forbid! But he meant the rational man, head of the apostolic order; and because with inflexible faith he avowed Christ to be the Son of God, therefore he received blessedness and was named the rock. So then also those that are built upon him are not lifeless stones, but men who share the same faith.'

The Key of Truth is in strict accord with the above. The faith demanded (p. 97) of the candidate for baptism is the faith of Peter, and in the ordinal the elect one receives the ritual name of Peter in recognition of his holding the faith. In the Albigeois ritual of *Consolamentum*, a document so primitive that it has in itself the germ of the Paulician Baptismal Service and ordinal not yet differentiated one from the other, the ritual use of the name Peter has the same significance.

And just as in the *Key* (p. 93) this spiritual Church is compared to the Ark of Noe, so St. Sahak declares that 'the Church, to wit the holy and spotless faith, is a ship of which the captain is the incarnate Word of God, and the apostles and prophets and doctors are the mariners.'

'Dumb and lifeless created things,' says St. Sahak in the same context, 'cannot manifest the mystery of the worship of God, but only the rational (λογική) Church can do so.' And just below, in an instructive passage, he writes thus: 'In thus exhibiting the indivisible unity of the Church, we have made clear what is a Church. Not however that we teach you to despise the spots honoured by buildings, *which are called meeting-houses* (συναγωγαί)[1]. For in them are gathered priests and clergy and worshippers of God to make their prayers and petitions, wherefore *they are also called praying-places* (=προσευχαί) *and sanctuaries* (=σεμνεῖα). And there is fixed in them the Lord's table[2] on which we offer the bread and wine *as a type* of the life-giving body and blood of Christ, which is ever freely (*lit.* without payment) distributed among us for the expiation and remission of sin. And in them also is erected a font of baptism .... In these we assemble daily and listen to Psalms sung and to the precepts of the commands of God. And because we ever assemble there, and because they are a harbour of refuge to us, who celebrate all the said rites in them, it has become

---

[1] Arm. *selan* = τράπεζα. The only Armenian equivalents of 'altar' had a Pagan ring, and were on the whole eschewed in connexion with Christian worship.

[2] With the term 'Jolowrdanotz' = συναγωγή, Sahak elsewhere couples *matrounq* = shrines.

a custom to call them Church, identifying them in name but not in actual reality[1].' In the sequel he declares that the term 'church' in this narrower and conventional sense is equally applicable to the *wanq*, or rest-houses and hospitals, already at that time established in Armenia and managed by celibate priests. The word afterwards came to signify a monastery; but Sahak ascribes their foundation in Armenia to Gregory the Illuminator; and in the *Acts of Archelaus* (*c*. 275–300) we read that one Marcellus had erected similar hospices or rest-houses along the high road from the Persian frontier, and Mani's emissary Turbo was at first denied access to them by those who presided over them[2] because he had not the *tessera hospitalitatis*. Such refuges for the sick and the hungry were founded all over Armenia in the last half of the fourth century by Nerses Catholicos; and the Arsacide King Pap's objection to them seems to have lain less against the institution itself than against the celibacy imposed by Nerses on the clergy who presided over them. When Sahak proceeds to condemn those who took elders into their houses to celebrate the Agapê and Eucharist, on the pretence that their houses were *wanq*, or shelter-houses, he seems to glance at the Paulician custom of celebrating the Eucharist in a private house.

The primitive customs and uses recorded or condemned by St. Sahak evidently survived among the Paulicians. For the Greek source *Scor.*, in § xi, says that they called their conventicles by the name of *proseuchae*[3]; and John of Otzun (*c*. 700), Gregory Magistros (*c*. 1050), and Paul of Taron (*c*. 1170), dilate on their hostility to churches, and fixed altars, and fonts of stone. Nerses of Lambron (*c*. 1170) in fifty passages reveals that there was the same feeling among the Armenians of the Western Taurus; though he does not qualify as Paulicians or as Thonraki those who entertained such prejudices, any more than does his contemporary, Isaac Catholicos. Nerses of Lambron thus records the 'irregularities' of the Armenians of his age: 'We do not,' they argued, 'enter the Church to pray, because our ancestors did not.' 'What ancestors?' retorts Nerses. 'Do you mean St. Gregory, or Nerses, Sahak, or any other of his sons[4]?'

[1] — ὁμωνύμως καὶ οὐ φυσικῶς. These canons of Sahak have an air of being a translation from Greek.

[2] 'Qui per singula loca mansionibus atque hospitiis praeerant' in *Acta Archelai*, c. iv, where these refuges are also called *diversoria*.

[3] Συνέδρια . . . πρὸς ἑαυτοὺς γὰρ ἐκεῖνοι προσευχὰς αὐτὰ λέγουσι.

[4] Nerses Lambron. p. 25..

'But,' went on the objectors to Nerses of Lambron, 'your churches are anointed with myrrh and consecrated[1]. Why are we perverted, because we say our prayers at home? Do we not say the same prayers in the church and out of it? Did not Paul say: "In all places shall they raise pure hands without anger or double-mindedness[2]."'

Nerses then gives an interesting, but insufficient, account of the ingrained prejudice of his countrymen against churches. 'When for our sins we passed under the yoke of aliens, and the sword of Ishmael prevailed over the entire land of Armenia, the inhabitants of the land emigrated into the country where [3] we now are, which belongs to the Romans. And not being in communion with them, for reasons which I have examined elsewhere, the Romans did not permit them to pray in their own special churches which were in this country. But they, being wanderers, and confident of returning again to their fatherland, only built humble chapels (*matrounq*) for temporary purposes, as we see. And when they found no means of going back, and began to multiply here, the church became too small to hold them all, and they of necessity built houses contiguous. But this building of houses which was of necessity became at last, when times changed, a root of evil and of indolence; for they were shy of praying in church as in the house of God, and grew remiss outside it as being in a common house. Self-indulgence got the better of true religion, and they began everywhere to build these houses by way of giving rein to their shyness; and so perforce they withdrew themselves from all decorum.'

We cannot accept this account, for we know that the prejudice against churches went back to the beginnings of Christianity in Armenia; and we are tempted to connect the Armenian custom with that of the Celtic Christians, who built clusters of tiny oratories, but never one large church.

As the result of seeing priests conducting prayers anywhere, the common people, continues Nerses [4], had taken to praying on house-tops or on beds. This again was merely an oriental habit in vogue amongst the earliest Christians. The same people, Nerses declares, disapproved of monks and celibacy, and decried

---

[1] Nerses Lambron. p. 26.
[2] Ibid. p. 29.
[3] i.e. Cilicia.
[4] Nerses Lambron. p. 31.

all sorts of church vestments[1] and trampled them under foot as mere superfluities[2]. 'Is not purity of soul enough?' they asked. 'What do you want to dress up for?' And Nerses answers: 'If you deem purity of soul enough without sensible signs, then you had better teach us to baptize without water, to pray without church, to offer the mass without bread.'

Nor was this the worst. There were many, so Nerses relates[3], who not only never went to church, but abstained from the sacrament for a whole year, or even for several years; and these not mere men of the world, but monks and priests. And instead of being ashamed of their neglect, they boasted of it, as if it were a thing to be praised. They declared that it was pious fear which kept them away, a sense that they were unworthy to share in the mystery. It was evidently a form of self-imposed penance on the part of those who so abstained.

Yet Nerses does not give us to understand that the people he so severely blames were an heretical sect, as they had long before become further east in Taron. They seem to have been imbued with a primitive and unorganized Christianity, to have been without any hierarchy and addicted to presbyteral government[4], to have been opposed to churches, vestments, and gorgeous feasts. Nerses set himself to counteract these prejudices, to reform them, and bring them up in all these matters to the level of the great Latin and Greek Churches, the separation from which of the Armenian he so keenly regretted. He never, like his contemporary Isaac Catholicos, came to be at feud with them; never, so far as we know, publicly exchanged anathemas with them. And this was probably due to the fact that he was on friendly terms with the Vatican, which, taking up a more statesmanlike attitude, sent missionaries to the primitive Christians of the Taurus, and tried to bind up and heal the wounds inflicted by the ruthless ferocity of the Byzantine Church.

In the preceding pages we traced the history of Adoptionist opinion from its earliest extra-canonical expression in *The Shepherd* of Hermas as late as the *Acts of Archelaus and Mani*. It is indicative of the silent revolution in Christian opinion which completed itself in the fourth century, that in the next great disputation

---

[1] P. 81 foll. According to Greg. Mag. (p. 145) the Thonraki said the same thing: 'We reckon the cross and the church and the priestly robes and the sacrifice of the mass (*or* offering) all for nothing.'
[2] Nerses Lambron. p. 87.   [3] Ibid. p. 105.   [4] Ibid. p. 525.

between a representative of the Church and a Manichean, it is no longer an Adoptionist who confronts the heresy, but a pneumatic Catholic; and one so accustomed to the latter type of creed, as to ride lightly over the difficulties which had taxed the ingenuity of Justin Martyr. The Antagonists now are Faustus and Augustine, and the scene of their disputation is North Africa. In his exquisite Latin, and with his usual subtlety, the former lays bare the new Catholic position. He is criticizing the narrative of Matthew's first chapter and writes thus (*Augustine c. Faustum*, lib. xxiii, c. 2):—

'Ut ergo huic interim dicenti (sc. Matthaeo) credam, filius Dauid erit mihi de Maria natus; adhuc de dei filio in hoc omni generationis textu nulla fit mentio usque ad baptismum scilicet; frustraque calumniam uos ingeritis scriptori (sc. Matthaeo), tanquam dei ille filium in utero mulieris incluserit. At uero hic clamitat, ut uidetur, et inscriptione ipsa sua se prorsus ab hoc sacrilegio uindicat, Dauid filium perhibens ex illa stirpe oriundum se scripsisse, non filium dei. Nam Iesum quidem eum, qui sit filius dei, si scriptoris huius mentem propositumque consideres, non tam ille de Maria uirgine uult nos accipere procreatum quam factum aliquando per baptismum apud fluenta Iordanis. Illic enim dicit baptizatum a Iohanne eum, quem Dauid in exordio filium designauit, factum aliquando filium dei post annos, dumtaxat secundum Lucae fidem, ferme triginta; ubi et uox tunc audita est dicens ad eum: filius meus es tu; ego hodie genui te. Uides ergo id, quod ante annos triginta, ut huic uidetur, de Maria natum est, non esse ipsum filium dei, sed id, quod de baptismo postea factum est ad Iordanem, id est hominem nouum tanquam in nobis eum credimus, ad deum ex gentilitatis errore conuersi: quod ipsum tamen nescio utrum satis cum ea fide faciat, quam uos Catholicam nominatis; sed interim sic Matthaeo uidetur, si sunt ipsius haec. Neque enim usquam in parturitionibus Mariae dictum legitur illud: *filius meus es tu, ego hodie genui te*, aut: *hic est filius meus dilectissimus, in quo bene complacui*; sed in expiatione eius apud Iordanem.'

The Manicheans maintained a singularly objective attitude towards the Church, and were keenly alive to the differences which parted the orthodoxy of the Tigris towards the end of the third century from the orthodoxy of Carthage at the close of the fourth. Doctrine that was Catholic then was no longer Catholic now. Accordingly Faustus continuing drives home against Augustine the point just raised of the incompatibility between the new 'Catholic' doctrine and the narrative of Matthew :—

'Quod si et tu credas ita, ut scriptum est, eris iam quidem Matthaeanus—sic enim mihi dicendum est—Catholicus uero nequaquam. Nam Catholicam fidem nouimus; quae tanto longe abest ab hac professione Matthaei, quanto procul est et a uero, siquidem symbolum uestrum ita se habeat, ut credatis in Iesum Christum filium dei, qui sit natus ex uirgine Maria. Uestrum ergo est de Maria accipere filium dei, Matthaei ab Iordane, nostrum ex deo.'

It is to be regretted that we have so little left of a writer who could point the contrasts of doctrine so well and tersely.

Beyond certain unguarded utterances of Tertullian and a hint of Augustine's [1], we have no trace of the Adoptionist Church in North Africa. But in Spain, a country of which the evangelization was largely the work of African missionaries, we find this type of Christology rife as late as the end of the eighth century. At this date, if you probed Spanish orthodoxy, you found Adoptionist tenets lying immediately under the surface. And it was also in Spain that this type of doctrine came to be known by the name Adoptionism, which in the preceding pages I have used to indicate it. This was in the controversy between Elipandus (the Archbishop of Toledo at the end of the eighth century) and Alcuin or Albinus.

We have enough of the writings of Elipandus left to be able to understand his position, in upholding which he evinced a remarkable contempt for the Papal See. In a letter against a Spanish docete named Migetius, this antagonism to the usurpations of Rome is freely displayed. Migetius had broached the opinion, if we may believe Elipandus, that St. Paul was the Holy Spirit and Third Person of the Trinity, and had appealed to the Pope. Elipandus in answer reprehends the teaching that the words, 'Thou art Peter,' &c., applied to Rome alone, and as Migetius had evidently not appealed in vain from the authority of the Spanish Primate to that of the Bishop of Rome, writes thus: 'Nos vero e contrario non de sola Roma Dominum Petro dixisse credimus, "Tu es Petrus," scilicet firmitas fidei, "et super hanc petram aedificabo ecclesiam meam"; sed de universali Ecclesia Catholica per universam orbem terrarum in pace diffusa' (Migne, *P. L.* vol. xcvi. 867). In this repudiation of the usurped authority of Rome we have a striking parallel to the attitude of the Paulicians and of the early British Church.

---

[1] See above, p. cxxvii.

Elipandus, however, was not a pure Adoptionist, but mechanically superposed on a basis of Adoptionist tenets, the belief in the incarnation in the Virgin's womb of a pre-existent Divine Logos, along with a formal acceptance of the decrees of the Councils and of the post-Nicene Fathers. The result was a see-saw. But he plainly neither felt the difficulties nor saw, as did his antagonists, the inconsistencies of his transitional position. Moreover, he was able to appeal in favour of his views to the Muzarabic liturgy of Spain. Thus in a controversial letter addressed to Albinus (*Elipandus ad Albinum*, Migne, vol. xcvi. 874) he cites the rituals of the Spanish Church of the eighth century as follows:—

'In missa de tertia feria Paschae: "Respice, Domine, tuorum fidelium multitudinem, quam per adoptionis gratiam Filio tuo facere dignatus es cohaeredem."' This means that through the grace of adoption the faithful were co-heirs with the Son. Such a sentence might well be found in a Paulician Sacramentary. Another citation which he makes is the following: 'Item in missa de quinta feria Paschae: "Praecessit quidem in adoptione donum, sed adhuc restat in conversatione iudicium."' This might mean that the gift of the Sonship came first through adoption at the baptism; in the divine converse which followed on the mountain, Jesus, the adopted Son, received, and still retains, the prerogative of Judge of all men. Another passage from the same liturgy to which Elipandus appealed is the following: 'Item ibi, "Dignum et iustum est, salutare nobis atque conveniens, gratias agere, laudes impendere, intelligere munera, vota deferre tibi, Omnipotens Pater; et Iesu Christo filio tuo Domino nostro, qui pietati tuae per ·adoptivi hominis passionem quasi quasdem in praesentis populi acquisitione manubias, cum non exierit e coelo, exhibuerit e triumpho.' Here the proper sense of *cum non exierit de coelo* seems to be that the risen Christ, now sitting at the right hand, without quitting heaven where he now is, exhibits to the Father the congregation present on earth as the spoils which in his adoptive humanity he had won. The two last passages cited by Elipandus are these: 'Item in missa de Ascensione Domini, " Hodie Salvator noster per adoptionem carnis sedem repetiit deitatis; hodie hominem suum intulit Patri, quem obtulit passioni, hunc exaltans in coelis quem humiliaverat in infernis; is visurus gloriam, qui viderat sepulturam."' . . . . 'Item in missa sancti Sperati, "Ingeniti Patris unigenite, Filius Dei Spiritu Sancto coaeternus et consubstantialis, qui ab arce sedis aethereae huius mundi infima petens, adoptivi hominis non horruisti vestimentum sumere carnis. "

In these extracts the phrase *homo adoptivus* may just as well signify the humanity *assumed* in the womb by a pre-existent Divine Being, as the mere man chosen out as its tabernacle by the Holy Spirit, and so raised to the dignity of Son of God.

Elipandus, it is true, affirms (*Col.* 875) that by the 'beatae Virginis partu' there came into existence neither 'caro sine deitate' nor 'deitas sine carne'; whereas a genuine Adoptionist believed that it was *caro sine deitate* that was so born.

Yet it was inevitable that his views should be condemned as heretical. For, though his Adoptionism was qualified in an orthodox manner, the speculations of Felix of Urgel, his associate, were more open to criticism. He denied, for example, and challenged the orthodox to prove the position: 'Quod ex utero matris verus Deus sit conceptus et verus sit Filius Dei (*Alc. c. Fel.* vii. 857). In the same spirit he contended that Jesus was born twice, first as a mere fleshly man of his mother, next as Son of God in his baptism: 'Accepit has geminas generationes: primam videlicet, quae secundum carnem est, secundam vero spiritalem, quae per adoptionem fit. Idem redemptor noster secundum hominem complexus in semetipso continet, primam videlicet, quam suscepit ex Virgine nascendo; secundam vero quam initiavit in lavacro et consummavit a mortuis resurgendo[1].'

In that age in Spain this Adoptionism was confused with the Nestorian heresy, about which in the East there had been so much noise; and Felix gives an account of the latter which more properly fits the Paulician opinion. It is as follows: 'Haec est sententia Nestorii haeretici, qui purum hominem absque Deo Virginis utero genitum impie adstruebat. In quem hominem ex eadem sancta Virgine procreatum et genitum, post nativitatem eius, Verbum Dei, hoc est divinitatem Filii Dei, descendisse et habitasse prae caeteris sanctis impudenter praedicabat.'

It would also appear from the *Epistola Heterii et Sancti Beati ad Elipandum* (A.D. 785) that among the Spanish Adoptionists an idea survived which naturally accompanies such tenets, and which underlies the Paulician ordinal, namely that the elect ones are Christs. For in this *Epistola*, ch. ix (Migne, vol. xcvi. 899), we read thus: 'Sed non est de illis Christis (viz. the text: unus Dominus

---

[1] *Alc. c. Fel.* ii. f. 809. I follow Neander (*Church Hist.* Eng. ed. v. 225) in adding the words, ' et consummavit,' which are requisite to complete the sense.

Iesus Christus per quem omnia et nos per ipsum) de quibus dictum est: Nolite tangere Christos meos (Ps. civ. 15). Sed neque de illis de quibus haeretici dicunt: Et ille Christus, et nos Christi.'

Alcuin attributes to Felix this very opinion that the elect ones are Christs[1]: 'Qui non natura,' he writes, 'ut Deus, sed per Dei gratiam ab eo, qui verus est Deus, deificati, dii sunt sub illo vocati.' And the same thing is implied in the following: 'In hoc quippe ordine Dei Filius dominus et redemptor noster iuxta humanitatem, sicut in natura, ita et in nomine, quamvis excellentius cunctis electis, verissime tamen cum illis communicat, sicut et in caeteris omnibus, id est in praedestinatione, in electione, gratia, in susceptione in adsumptione nominis servi' (*Alc. c. Fel.* iv. 820).

In Heterius' letter (col. 901) the Paulician opinion and the sense of the Gospel narrative are in one and the same sentence repudiated. Take the following passage: 'Nec sane *tunc unctus est Christus Spiritu Sancto, quando super eum baptizatum ut columba descendit:* tunc enim corpus suum, id est ecclesiam suam praefigurare dignatus est, in quo praecipue baptizati accipimus Spiritum Sanctum; sed ista mystica et invisibili unctione tunc intelligendus est unctus, quando Verbum Dei caro factum est, id est, quando humana natura, *sine ullis praecedentibus bonorum operum* meritis, Deo Verbo est in utero Virginis copulata, ita ut cum illo fieret una persona. Ob hoc eum confitemur natum de Spiritu Sancto et Virgine Maria. Absurdissimum est enim, ut credamus eum, *cum iam triginta esset annorum aetatis et a Ioanne baptizatus est, accepisse Spiritum Sanctum.* Sed venit ad baptisma Ioannis sicut sine peccato; ita plenus Spiritu Sancto.' Here the words italicized reflect the doctrine of *The Key of Truth*, and prove that the Spanish Adoptionists held, if half-heartedly, the same belief as the Paulicians. Against no other belief can the arguments of Heterius and Beatus be directed. And the same conclusion results from the next ch. xiii: 'Hoc totum quare diximus, nisi ut Iesum Christum qui de Virgine natus est, verum Deum et verum Filium Dei esse proprium firmaremus: Et *deum inter deos, et adoptivum cum adoptivis, et parvulum cum parvulis, et servum cum servis, ut haeretici blasphemant,* aperta fronte negaremus? Ululant ipsi, Scripturam non tractant.'

---

[1] St. Adamnan (679-704) shared this belief, and writes in his *Life of St. Columba*, bk. i. chap. 44, thus: 'On hearing this discourse of the saint, the humble stranger, greatly astonished, *worshipped Christ in the holy man* (i.e. in Columba).' So chap. 37: 'the brethren, still kneeling with joy unspeakable, and with hands spread out to heaven, *venerate Christ in the holy and blessed man.*'

For the Spanish heretics, like the Paulicians, took their stand on the Scripture alone. And it was not a select few who held such opinions. On the contrary, the popular character and wide diffusion in Spain of their opinions is witnessed to by the two writers we have just cited, and in the same chapter, as follows: 'Non solum per Asturiam, sed per totam Hispaniam, et usque ad Franciam divulgatum est, quod duae quaestiones in Asturiensi Ecclesia ortae sunt. Et sicut duae quaestiones, ita duo populi et duae Ecclesiae, una pars cum altera pro uno Christo contendunt . . . . . Una pars Episcoporum dicit quod Iesus Christus adoptivus est humanitate, et nequaquam adoptivus divinitate,' &c. As in Armenia, so in Spain, the Adoptionist faith was a home growth, and a popular form of faith; and Neander (vol. v. 219)[1] is very wide of the mark when he suggests that Felix of Urgel was the author of this form of Spanish opinion, and that he had devised it by way of recommending Christianity to the Arabs. Certainly the Adoptionist faith approximated to the Mohammedan view of Jesus Christ, and accordingly we find that Greek writers applied to the Paulician Emperor Constantine Copronymus the epithet Σαρακηνόφρων. But that only proves that the Mohammedan view of Christ was drawn from Adoptionist circles of Christians. That an opinion so widely diffused in 790 in Spain and Gaul had been invented only just before as a missionary device, it is absurd to suppose.

In ch. xl of the same *Epistola* (cols. 916, 917) is given the *Symbolum Fidei Elipandiae*. In it the Archbishop of Toledo begins by reciting his faith in a Trinity of Father, Son, and Holy Spirit, who are 'unius glomeratio charitatis, unius ambitus dilectionis coaeterna substantia.' This view of the tie binding the Persons into one as a tie of love reminds us of Paul of Samosata. The *kenosis* of the pre-existent Son is then asserted, and the theophanies of the Old Testament enumerated and explained as appearances of the Son of God, 'emptying himself of his invisible Godhead' ('Deitatem invisibilem exinaniens'). Then the Pneumatic doctrine is formally enunciated thus: 'Verbum Dei

---

[1] Neander writes (v. 220) : ' But what he (Felix) had to prove was, the doctrine of the incarnation of God, and of the Deity of Christ, against which and the doctrine of the Trinity the fiercest attacks of the Mohammedans were directed ; and by his apologetic efforts in this direction, he may have been led to seek after some such way of presenting this doctrine, as to remove, wherever possible, that which proved the stone of stumbling to those of the Mohammedan persuasion. Thus we might explain the origin of the Adoption type of doctrine.'

deitate exinanita, hominem factum, circumcisum, baptizatum, flagellatum, crucifixum, mortuum, sepultum, servum, captivum, peregrinum, leprosum, despectum, et, quod est deterius, non solum ab angelis, sed etiam ab hominibus minoratum.'

Then follows the tenet of adoption as he framed it, thus: 'Non per illum qui natus est de Virgine visibilia condidit, sed per illum qui non est adoptione, sed genere; neque gratia, sed natura.'

After which follows a genuinely Adoptionist outburst:—

'Et per istum Dei simul et hominis filium, adoptivum humanitate, et nequaquam adoptivum divinitate, mundum redemit. Qui est *Deus inter Deos*: qui utrum comedisset, an bibisset, ei cognitum manet, cui nonnulla actionis suae mysteria nescire voluit. Quia *si conformes sunt omnes sancti huic Filio Dei secundum gratiam, profecto et cum adoptivo adoptivi, et cum advocato advocati, et cum Christo Christi, et cum parvulo parvuli, et cum servo servi.* Credo etiam inter ipsa Sancti Spiritus charismata gratiarum, Spiritum Sanctum esse adoptivum in quo clamamus, Abba pater: in quo Spiritu non nego hominem Christum esse adoptivum. . . .'

I have given these somewhat long extracts, in order to leave no doubt in a matter of importance. It is obvious that such phrases as, 'Et ille Christus, et nos Christi'; or as, 'Deum inter Deos, adoptivum inter adoptivos'; or as, 'Cum advocato advocati,' did not arise, and were not new, in the Spain of the eighth century. They transport us at once into the circle of ideas of which *The Key of Truth* is a monument. All the holy ones, all 'the saints,' as the Epistles of Paul term the baptized, who conform to the Son of God according to grace, at once become 'adopted with the adopted one, paracletes with the Paraclete, Christs with the Christ, little ones with the little one, servants with the servant.' Here are expressed the thoughts, perhaps the truths, which inspired the Paulicians. Elipandus did not invent either phrase or idea; but they must have been handed down to him from the same age, must have ultimately flowed from the same fountain-head, from which the Paulicians inherited them.

If there is any doubt on this point the *Epistola Heterii* removes it by its statement of the tenets of the *Heretici*, as the party of Elipandus are called. They are these: 'Christ was anointed by the Holy Spirit, i.e. became the Messiah, then and then only, when, after he had been baptized, the Spirit descended on him as a dove. He was then chosen the Christ, because he had earned the dignity by his previous good works.' They held also, says Heterius, that though he was without sin when he came to John to be baptized, still he was not as yet filled with the Holy Ghost.' Why this was so the Adoptionist *Acts of Archelaus* explain; for in them we had the following reason adduced against the tenet of Jesus' divinity: 'Si perfectus erat, si virtus erat, si Filius erat, non poterat Spiritus ingredi, sicut nec regnum potest ingredi intra regnum.' The doctrine implied in the words: κατὰ προκοπήν, κατ' ἐκλογὴν υἱὸς Θεοῦ, could not be better expressed than Heterius expressed it. And if we compare the *sententia Nestorii*, which Felix in his recantation attributes to the same party, we see it to be in almost verbal agreement with *The Acts of Archelaus*. Thus the words, 'prae ceteris sanctis,' recall those of Archelaus, 'super omnes sanctos Iesus.' And as in the *Sententia* the man of Nazareth is 'purus homo absque Deo Virginis utero genitus'; so Archelaus writes, 'Dico autem de eo qui ex Maria factus est homo,' followed by the words, 'Christus Dei ... descendit super eum, qui de Maria est.' In the same context he even reproaches Mani with believing that 'God has transformed himself into a man, using the very terms of the pneumatic Christology ('quia Deus transformaverit se in hominem'). Thus Heterius assails in Elipandus the very tenets which Archelaus urges against Mani, namely that Jesus was born a mere man, and was only at his baptism chosen Son of God and Messiah, as a reward for his human advances in goodness. It is instructive also to note how conscious Heterius is of the mutual incompatibility of the two rival Christologies. If Jesus was already God in His mother's womb, then what sense attaches to the descent of the Spirit in the baptism? Heterius is aware that this episode is not wanted; and accordingly he tries to explain it away by pretending that in the narrative of the baptism the body of Christ, on which the Spirit descended, was merely allegorical of the Church. Our own Bede[1], hard pressed by the necessity of uniting the two Christologies in a single scheme, had propounded this very device.

It is evident then that in the Church of Asturia there was a purely Adoptionist party behind Elipandus of Toledo; and by the light of their more extreme tenets we must interpret, not only the creed of the latter, thinly veneered as it is, with a show of the pneumatic doctrine; but also the use in the Spanish Liturgy of the terms *adoptivus homo, adoptio carnis*. These phrases arose in an age when they meant what they should mean, viz. that the fleshly man Jesus was chosen out and adopted to be the Son of God by the

---

[1] See below, p. clxxx.

descent of the Spirit, and not that a pre-existent Divine Being adopted or put on flesh in the Virgin's womb, as a screen or disguise of his omnipotent Deity [1]. This latter sense was indeed imported into the phrase by the Latin Fathers whom Elipandus cites, and perhaps by the compilers of the Spanish Liturgy as well; but in doing so they forced an alien meaning upon it. They found before them the obstinate language of another Christology, and had to make the best of it. And Elipandus tries hard to make the best of it, as when, in his letter to Migetius (Migne, vol. xcvi. 871), he almost pathetically asks: ' Quare non dicatur adoptivus, qui ita totus est in nostris, sicut totus est in suis, praeter delictum? Ecce Ioachim, cuius filia gloriosa Dei Virgo Maria esse dignoscitur, adoptiva esse creditur. Quare non dicatur adoptivus Dominus Iesus Christus de eadem generatus?' He does not see that he gives his case away, when he draws this parallel between the Virgin and Jesus. For she was not regarded as pre-existent or divine, but in the Annunciation was, because of her previous saintly life, only chosen out (*dignoscitur*) as the *Virgo Dei* to harbour the Holy Spirit. What else did the pure Adoptionists claim in regard to Jesus but this very thing?

As in the earliest Roman Church of which we know anything definitely, the rival views, that God became man by natural birth, and that Jesus became Son of God *per profectum* and by election, were in conflict, yet had each to tolerate the other as orthodox until the year 190; so they were still in conflict in the Church of Asturia as late as the eighth century. As Paul of Samosata and later the Nestorians tried to combine the genuine Adoptionist belief with the pneumatic doctrine, but really only overlaid the one with an appearance of the other, so Elipandus mechanically juxtaposed with the earlier and more primitive view the phraseology of the Councils. Lastly, as the Emperor Aurelian, from motives of high policy, suppressed the Adoptionist theology in the person of Paul of Samosata in Syria in the third century, so, early in the ninth, Charlemagne, probably from similar motives, tried to suppress it in Spain in the person of Elipandus, Archbishop of Toledo. It did not suit imperial policy that there should be one type of Christology in Rome, and another there. However much the provincial Church might value its independence, and lay claim to an equal share with Rome in the authority of St. Peter, it must conform from reasons of state alone.

[1] The early Fathers commonly speak of the Incarnation as a veil or disguise assumed by a divine and all-powerful Being, eager to lay an ambush against Satan.

We cannot expect that the Spanish ecclesiastic of to-day would own that his national Church in its infancy held a form of creed which was afterwards pronounced heretical; still less that this primitive opinion held its own even as late as the ninth century. The higher ecclesiastics, no doubt, like Elipandus and the bishops who sided with him, managed to give an appearance of orthodoxy to their professions, by introducing watchwords of the Greek Councils held far away at the other end of the Mediterranean. But these did not fit in with the main structure of their belief. And acute opponents like Heterius and Albinus knew well what was underneath the surface, and, with unsparing pens, laid the heresy bare. That they invented the form of creed which they charged the party of Elipandus with holding is out of the question. There was no source from which they could have derived their very accurate description of Adoptionist belief, save the Spaniards who held it.

And to prove how clearly and accurately they conceived of it, we venture to add to the extracts from Heterius already given, one more which clinches the point. It is this (ch. 56, Migne, *P. L.* vol. xcvi. 926): 'Sed multi heretici in Ecclesia prodierunt, qui mediatorem Dei et hominum, hominem Christum Iesum purum hominem creatum dicerent, sed ex gratia deificatum, tantumque ei sanctitatis tribuerint, quantum de sanctis caeteris, eius videlicet famulis, agnovissent . . . quidam haeresiarcha[1] dixit: "Christo Deo facto; si volo, et ipse possum fieri." Et ille (sc. Elipandus) se aequari voluit, qui simili sensu de eo dixit: "Et ille Christus, et nos Christi. Et ille adoptivus, et nos adoptivi" Qui Iesum Dominum nostrum, non per mysterium conceptionis, sed per profectum gratiae Deum putavit; perversa allegatione astruens eum purum hominem natum; sed ut Deus esset, per meritum profecisse, atque ab hoc existimans et se et quoslibet illos ei posse coaequari qui filii Dei per gratiam fiant. . . . Non sicut iste haereticus (sc. Elipandus) decipit, aliter in humanitate, aliter in deitate est. Non purus homo conceptus atque editus, post meritum, ut Deus esset, accepit: sed nuntiante angelo, et adveniente Spiritu, mox Verbum in utero, mox intra uterum Verbum caro.'

And the bishops of Spain themselves, in their letter to the bishops of Gaul, wrote thus (Migne, *P. L.* vol. ci. 1332): 'Confitemur et credimus eum factum ex muliere, factum sub lege,

---

[1] Viz., Paul of Samosata, see p. cvi.

non genere esse Filium Dei, sed adoptione; neque natura, sed gratia.'

The Jesuit Enhueber, in his *Dissertatio Dogmatica Historica contra Christianum Walchium* (in Migne, vol. ci. col. 337 foll.), points out that in the history of the Spanish Church there were already, before the age of Charlemagne, many traces of similar heresy. I believe that a careful search in the libraries of Spain, especially in those parts of the country which longest remained under Muslim domination, might reveal some monuments similar to *The Key of Truth*, purely Adoptionist in their tendency, and uncoloured by the pneumatic Christology. The Adoptionist clergy, driven out of the domains of Charlemagne, took refuge in the Moorish dominion of Spain, just as the Paulicians of the East found a refuge in the Empire of the Khalifs. And under Moorish protection they must have lingered on for centuries.

We have no documents of the early British Church, which have not come down through the hands of Catholics, and been subjected to recension. But it is natural to suppose that the heresy of which it was accused so vaguely by Bede and others was really Adoptionism. It is possible that this Church adhered to the Jewish custom of celebrating Easter on the fourteenth of Nisan [1]. But the leading error in which they were implicated concerned baptism, and it is here that we touch the very centre and origin of the chief heresies of Adoptionists. However, Bede and other writers are very vague and reticent, though sweeping enough in their charges [2]. It is almost natural to suppose that the reason why the British bishops refused even to eat with St. Augustine was this, that the Church of the latter, having adopted infant baptism, was no longer a Christian Church at all. In his commentary on the Gospel Bede may be supposed, in combating errors, to have combated those which he was familiar with in his own country, and from which he was most anxious to save those for whom he wrote. Now it is remarkable how often and vigorously he assails Adoptionist views, especially in

---

[1] This is disputed, however, by competent authorities, who urge that the Britons merely clung to a calendarial error; and did not differ in principle from the rest of the West.

[2] The charge that the British bishops refused to join with Augustine in preaching 'the Word of God,' probably signifies that they were not sound about the Incarnation. The charge against the Paulicians was sometimes put in the same way.

explaining the Gospel of the Baptism of Jesus. The point is one of such interest that we quote a few typical passages :—

Bedae in Marci Evang. Expos. lib. 1 : 'Manet autem in illo Spiritus, non ex eo tantum tempore quo baptizatus est in Iordane, sed ex illo potius quo in utero conceptus est virginali. Nam quod in baptizatum descendere visus est Spiritus signum erat conferendae nobis in baptismo gratiae spiritualis.'

In Ev. Luc. Expos. lib. 1 : 'Nemo enim putet Dominum post baptisma primum Spiritus Sancti gratia perunctum, aut aliquem divinae naturae per tempora gessisse profectum, sed noverit potius a primo conceptus humani tempore quem verum hominem, eundem et Deum existere verum.'

In the same context Bede implies that the Lenten fast, as commemorative of the fasts of Moses and Elias of old, and of Jesus under the new dispensation, was by some kept immediately after the Epiphany, for he asks: 'In qua autem parte anni congruentius observatio quadragesimae constitueretur, nisi confinis atque contigua dominicae passionis.' Here he glances at some who did not keep it as a fast preliminary to our Lord's passion.

In his eleventh Homily, 'In die festo Theophaniae,' Bede again combats the Adoptionists. He is explaining the descent of the Spirit. The aim of the Gospel narrative here is, he says, 'ut hinc nimirum fides nostra confirmetur, per mysterium sacri baptismatis aperiri nobis introitum patriae coelestis, et Sancti Spiritus gratia ministrari. Numquid enim credi decet Domino tunc primum coelestia patuisse secreta, cum recta fides habeat non minus tempore quo cum hominibus conversatus est, quam et post et antea in sinu Patris mansisse, et sedem tenuisse coelestem. Aut a tricesimo aetatis suae anno, quando baptizatus est, Spiritus Sancti dona percepit qui prima conceptione Spiritu Sancto plenus semper exstitit.'

In discussing also the age of Jesus at baptism, he goes out of his way to say that it was the right age for priestly ordination, and so forth, as if he knew of some who deemed it to be the right age for baptism. As he spent his entire life in Weremouth, and never went outside these islands, it is difficult to believe that in such passages as the above he is not assailing a form of error which he saw around him.

In Bavaria and in Burgundy we have better evidence that the earliest Christianity was Adoptionist; for, from the life of St. Salaberga (*Acta SS. Sept.* vi. p. 521, die xxii), written about

688, forty years after her death, we learn that the *Gens Boicariorum* or *Boii*, in furthest Germany, were infected with the heretical belief that Jesus Christ was a mere man, 'absque Deitate Patris.' In Burgundy the same *Acts* relate (p. 522) that the heresy of Bonosus and Photinus infected the Warasci who lived in the province of the Sequani on both sides of the river Doubs. It was already an old heresy, 'aevo iam senes tabescebant,' about the year 600, and St. Salaberga and her teacher St. Eustasius spent their lives in combating it there and in Bavaria. It is a question whether they were successful, for at a later period we find Gascony a hotbed of Cathar heresy.

Although the inspiring idea of the Paulician ordinal is this, that the elect one is a Christ, yet it is never so boldly affirmed in it as in the monuments of the Spanish Adoptionists. Perhaps the idea was made explicit in the lost chapters, but in the parts preserved we only have it implied and presupposed, as for example in the following passage of the baptismal service: 'The baptizer must have been elected in accordance with the words of the heavenly Father to his beloved Son, "This is my Son elect, hear ye him."' But here after all we have a sufficiently precise equation of the elect one with Christ. We may set beside it the parallel passage of the *Teaching of the Twelve Apostles*, ch. 4: 'My child, by night and by day bethink thee of him who speaketh unto thee the word of God, and thou shalt honour him as Lord. For out of whom the Lordship is spoken, in him is the Lord[1].'

It is regrettable that Tertullian's work upon *Ecstasis* has not come down to us, for it would have thrown much light on the office of the early Christian prophet and of the elect one who succeeded him. *The Shepherd* of Hermas, however, in some degree fills up the lacuna in a passage (Mand. xi) in which are laid down rules for the 'discernment of spirits,'—a very urgent problem in those days of inspiration. 'No spirit given from God,' we read, 'waits to be interrogated; but being possessed of the power of the Godhead, it speaks all things of itself, because it is from above, from the power of the Divine Spirit. But the spirit which submits to be asked questions[2], and which speaks to suit the desires of men, is one which moves along the ground and is full of levity,

---

[1] Διδαχὴ κυρίου διὰ τῶν δώδεκα ἀποστόλων τοῖς ἔθνεσιν. κεφ. δ': Τέκνον μου, τοῦ λαλοῦντός σοι τὸν λόγον τοῦ Θεοῦ μνησθήσῃ νυκτὸς καὶ ἡμέρας, τιμήσεις δὲ αὐτὸν ὡς Κύριον· ὅθεν γὰρ ἡ κυριότης λαλεῖται, ἐκεῖ Κύριός ἐστιν.

[2] Like the Delphic oracle.

because it has not the power; and it does not speak at all unless it is asked questions. How then, say I, O Lord, shall a man know which of them is a prophet and which a false-prophet? Hear, he said, about the two kinds of prophets ... You shall from the way in which he lives judge of the man who has the Divine Spirit. Firstly, one who has the Divine Spirit which is from above is gentle and quiet and of humble mind [1], and abstains from all wickedness and vain lust of this age; and he keeps himself in want above all men, and answers no man because he is asked questions; nor does he speak in secrecy. Nor does the Holy Spirit speak whenever any one wants it to do so; but then it speaks, whenever God desires it to speak.'

In the phase of Christian opinion represented by *The Shepherd* of Hermas and by the *Didachê*, the possession of Jesus by the Holy Spirit differed from its possession of prophets and other 'vessels of election' rather in degree than in kind. Into Jesus the Holy Spirit entered and permanently rested in him; of other men it only took possession fitfully and from time to time, like the wind which bloweth where it listeth. In them it suspended the natural soul and superseded it. In him it coalesced therewith, because he alone was sinless, and, by successive feats of self-conquest, had made himself perfect. Still, as Origen declares [2], it was the Christ, or Logos, or Son of God *in Jesus*, and not the natural man himself, that uttered such sayings as these: 'I am the way, the truth, and the life,' and 'I am the door,' and 'I am the living bread, which came down from heaven.' It was this 'second God,' as the same writer, adopting a Philonean phrase, elsewhere says [3], which 'was familiarly united with [4] the soul of Jesus as with no other soul, because he alone had become able to perfectly support (*lit.* contain) the supreme participation in the absolute reason, in the absolute wisdom, in the absolute justice.'

The Adoptionist standpoint could not be more neatly expressed than Origen here expresses it. The Montanists and the Paulicians and followers of Mani believed that their prophets and elect ones were similarly inspired with Jesus, though not in the same degree. Thus the author of *The Key of Truth*, in his exordium, declared that he was inspired by the Holy Spirit to write his teaching,

---

[1] In Bede the tests whereby the British bishops proposed to test Augustine on his arrival at our shores were the same. The Pope's envoy does not seem to have fulfilled them to their satisfaction.

[2] Origen, *C. Celsum*, lib. ii. ch. 9. [3] Ibid. v. ch. 39, δεύτερος θεός.

[4] ᾠκειοῦσθαι καὶ ἡνῶσθαι,

which was 'the way, the truth, and the life'; and, as we have already remarked, the fragments of Sergius' epistles indicate that he was equally persuaded that the Holy Spirit spoke through himself as its organ. From the lips of a really noble teacher, such as was St. Paul or Sergius, such self-confident utterances are sublime, and we bare our heads before them; but in the mouth of a self-indulgent hierophant they become merely ridiculous, if not blasphemous.

The same idea underlies the narrative of the modern Thonraki on p. xxvii above, as well as the charges preferred against the Paulicians by Gregory of Narek and by Photius. By the light of the Paulician belief, and of the express words of Elipandus, we are also able to realize what it was that underlay the charge made against Montanus, that he considered himself to be the paraclete. The Montanist Church held a conception of the priest as one filled with the Spirit, which in the Great Church had faded away; and in it not only men, but women also, were raised, if not to be members of an organized priesthood, at any rate to the dignity of the prophetic office. God made his spirit to dwell in women as well as in men; and Prisca, one of the Montanist prophetesses, claimed to be 'Christ assuming the outward form of a woman.' In the Paulician Church the prophetic office has already been replaced by an organized priesthood or order of elect ones, from which it would appear that women were excluded. They had more respect for St. Paul's opinion on such points than to admit them. Indeed, had it been their practice to ordain women, the virulence of their enemies would surely have fixed upon it[1]. There is, however, enough in common between the Montanist prophet and the Paulician elect one to account for the considerable resemblance there is between the recorded sayings of the Montanist prophets and the utterances of Sergius in his letters[2], of the author of the *Key*[3], and even of the Paulician elect one of Arkhwêli[4]. Montanus, it is true, went further than these, if it be that he said: 'I am the Lord God, the Almighty, present to you in man's form,' and 'I the Lord God the Father have come,' and 'I am the Father and the Son and the Paraclete[5].' The Paulicians were too mono-

---

[1] It is affirmed in the historian Asoḷik (see p. 176, *n.* 4), but in no other source.
[2] See p. li foll.   [3] See the *Key*, p. 71.
[4] Compare the worship of Christ in Columba, p. clxxiii *n.*
[5] It must not be forgotten that we only know the Montanists through their enemies, who were bent on exaggerating and making ridiculous the old-fashioned tenets which survived among them.

theistic to tolerate language such as this, though they might have passed the utterance of Maximilla, the Montanist prophetess, who exclaimed: 'I am hunted as a wolf from the fold; I am no wolf. I am the word and spirit and power.' A trace of the same feeling is observable in the *Acts of Paul and Thekla*, § 21, where Thekla sees the Lord Jesus sitting by her *in the likeness of Paul*. So the faithful of Lugdunum, as they gazed with their outward eyes on the crucified Blandina, *beheld Jesus* who had been crucified for them (Euseb. *H. E.* 5. 1. 206). And in the *Acts of Philip* (ed. M. R. James, p. 161, 16), Jesus appears to the faithful in the form of Philip.

The same conception of the Sacerdos as a Christ or as a Paraclete also colours the heretical sects. Mani believed that he was the Paraclete, and the hierophant Marcus in Irenaeus, 1. 13, just as as if he were Christ or the Advocate, addresses the woman who is being elected or is receiving the spiritual baptism, as follows: 'I would fain impart to thee of my grace, since the father of all things beholds thy angel standing before him. But the place[1] of the majesty is in us. It is meet that we should be one with each other. Take first from me and through me the grace. Prepare thyself as a bride welcoming her bridegroom. That thou mayest be what I am, and I be what thou art. Implant in thy bridal chamber the seed of light. Receive from me the bridegroom and contain him, and be contained in him. Behold grace hath descended upon thee; open thy mouth and prophesy.' Such was the ritual of ordaining a prophetess; which, since it recalls much that we find in the New Testament and in Philo, must have been very old. It is possible that the συνείσακτοι γυναῖκες, of whom we hear in connexion with Paul of Samosata (Euseb. 7. 30, 362) were akin to the Marcosian or Montanist prophetesses. St. Nouna, who converted the Iberians, and the early Armenian saints, Rhipsima and Gaiana, probably belonged to the same category.

That this conception of the elect one as a Christ should be equally diffused among Christian circles so widely parted from each other as those of Palestine and of Iona, as the Montanists, the Manicheans, the Paulicians, and the Adoptionists of Spain; and that among the last we should meet with its most striking and comprehensive formula: 'God among Gods, Christ among Christs, advocate among advocates, servant among servants, little one among little

---

[1] Cp. Hermas, cited on p. xc, *n.* 1, and *Acta Iohannis* (ed. M. R. James), chap. xi, *Christus loquitur*: οἶκον οὐκ ἔχω καὶ οἴκους ἔχω· τόπον οὐκ ἔχω καὶ τόπους ἔχω· ναὸν οὐκ ἔχω, καὶ ναοὺς ἔχω . . . . ἴδε σεαυτὸν ἐν ἐμοὶ λαλοῦντι.

ones'—all this is very remarkable for the proof it affords that the idea was very primitive in Christianity. And it is also an idea that brings us into touch with other religions older than Christianity. For example the Buddhists of Thibet believe that their high-priest or Llama is a re-incarnation of Buddha, and in ancient Phrygia, as well as in other parts of Asia Minor, the priest was often regarded as one with the god over whose cult he presided.

We have already indicated (see p. lxxiv) the probability of the Paulicians having been in communion with the Montanist Church. It is difficult to set any other interpretation upon the passage preserved of the epistle of Sergius to Leo the Montanist, which I have translated above on p. lii. 'Beware of thyself,' he writes, ' lest thou inwardly rend the unswerving faith.' And he exhorts him to receive the Paulician shepherds and teachers, even as he had received the Apostles and the four prophets. This at the least implies that Sergius recognized in the Montanists a genuine branch of the Catholic Church; and how could Leo rend inwardly the Faith, unless there was already communion between the bodies of believers to which they respectively belonged? Nor could Sergius use the words 'unswerving faith'[1] unless he regarded the Montanists as having retained a true baptism and a genuine priesthood. But that implies that these 'homines religionis antiquae'[2] rejected paedo-baptism, and that they were Adoptionists.

A ruthless persecution of the Montanists took place under Justinian, when, according to Procopius (*Hist. Arcan.* 11), they shut themselves up in their temples and burned themselves alive. But they by no means became extinct; and nearly 200 years later Theophanes (p. 617, ed. Bonn) relates that rather than submit to be baptized in the orthodox manner they brought their prophesyings to an end[3] and fixed a day on which they entered their appointed homes of error and burned themselves alive.

This date brings us within one hundred years of Sergius the Paulician, and, as there was a tendency for persecuted sects to coalesce against their persecutors, it is not unlikely that the remnants of the Montanist Church were absorbed into the ranks of the Paulician. And accordingly, in the epistle of the patriarchs to the

---

[1] Τὸ τέμνειν τὴν ἀκλινῆ πίστιν.

[2] Vide *Acta S. Achatii apud Ruinart*, c. iv. Tertullian, in speaking of Montanism as the 'New Prophecy,' meant that its content only, and not its form and mode of delivery, was new.

[3] Διεμαντεύσαντο ἑαυτοῖς καὶ ὡρίσαντο ἡμέραν καὶ εἰσελθόντες εἰς τοὺς ὡρισμένους οἴκους τῆς πλάνης αὐτῶν κατέκαυσαν ἑαυτούς. This was A.D. 722.

emperor Theophilus, published among the works of John of Damascus (in Migne, *Patr. Gr.* vol. xcv. col. 373 and 376), the Paulicians are identified with the Montanists. In it the Iconoclast patriarchs, set up by the emperors Leo and Constantine in place of Germanus and Nicephorus, are called first Paulicians and then Montanists. And of the Iconoclastic triumph the writers exclaim: 'Again the Jews are glad . . . again the Montanists have seized the land.'

Professor Harnack has remarked that those Adoptionists who admitted the miraculous birth of Jesus already had a foot in the rival camp. And under this aspect the Paulician faith cannot be regarded as being so pure an example of its kind as was the Ebionism of Justin's age, which held that Jesus was a man born of men. The belief that Jesus was by nature sinless[1], has resulted in two very different views of the Virgin Mary. According to the one, Jesus, being the new Adam, free from the sin of the old, did not take his flesh from her, but was a new creation, a fresh start in humanity; and the mother to whom he really owed nothing was merely the channel through which he came into the world. As has already been remarked (p. xlvi), it is probable that the Paulicians held this view. And if we accept the evidence of the deposition of Manuk Davthean of Giumri (see p. xxv) as supplementing the lacunae of the *Key*, it is certain that they held and still hold it. 'Christ,' so the deposition runs, . . . 'was born a man of Mary, she losing her virginity, as it were, by the *dust-engendered* annunciation of Gabriel.' It is true that here the word Հողեղէն, which means earthy or dust-engendered, and renders χοϊκός in St. Paul's Epistles, might be explained as a corruption of Հոգեղէն, which means 'spirit-engendered, spiritual.' But such is probably not the case, for in the ordinal of the orthodox Armenians the novice is required to anathematize, among other heresies, that of 'Anthroïdus qui dixit *de terra* assumpsisse Christum corpus suum, eumque transisse per virginem sicuti per canalem[2].' Perhaps *Anthroïdus* in the above is a corruption of *Anthropoeidēs*. The view that Jesus was, like the first Adam, freshly formed of dust, was already heretical as early as the days

---

[1] This admission did not, even to the orthodox Armenians, exclude a susceptibility to temptation; and accordingly in the exordium of their ordinal it is laid down that Jesus, after his baptism, fasted forty days in order to fortify himself against the assaults of Satan the tempter, which were to follow.

[2] Denzinger, ii. 303.

THE IDEA OF THE VIRGIN BIRTH clxxxvii

of Irenaeus, and Marcion taught that Jesus was born of his mother as it were water through a tube. The purport of the heresy was not to represent Jesus as a mere appearance, for his flesh, because it was newly created out of dust by God, was no more putative than that of the first Adam; still less to present him as God incarnate; but only to dig a ditch, as it were, between Jesus and all human progenitors by way of eliminating in him the *tradux peccati* of the old Adam. Such a view is compatible with,—nay, tends to,—the brusque rejection of the honours decreed by the unreformed churches to the Virgin Mary; since, according to it, Jesus owed nothing to her. The rival Christology has attained the same end, namely the elimination of hereditary sin in Jesus, by other means. He is admitted to have taken his flesh from his mother, but she in turn is regarded as having been immaculately conceived, i. e. without original sin. Thus the fence which the Paulicians drew round Jesus is put further back around his mother. And this view is as favourable to the worship of the Virgin as the former was inimical.

But after all we are here groping among shadows. From p. 74 of the *Key* it results that the writer viewed Jesus as a Saviour raised up by God from the seed of David (Acts xiii. 23); and this view properly excludes the idea of his being a special new creation no less than that of his mother's virginity. It also fits in with the statement on p. 75 of the *Key*, that it was in the Jordan only that Jesus put on the raiment of light which the old Adam lost. We might infer that he only then became the new man, when the Shekinah descended upon him and he was filled with the Godhead. The Catechism, on the other hand, p. 120, has the question: 'For how many reasons did the God of all send into the world the new Adam, his beloved?' and so implies that he was the new Adam from his birth and not from his baptism only. And the section of the *Key* (p. 114), 'on the Creation of Adam and of our Lord Jesus Christ,' begins in a way which suggests that the writer went on, in the leaf torn out, to describe Jesus as a creation out of the dust evoked by a single word of God as the old Adam had been evoked. But if the *Key* ended with the ordinal (p. xlix, *n.* 2), then these sections are additions of a later age; and we can suppose the *Key* itself to have reflected the purer Adoptionist view, that Jesus was ἄνθρωπος ἐξ ἀνθρώπων, and only became the new Adam through the Baptism in the Jordan. The Christian imagination early felt the need of some more detailed and explicit account of the generation of Jesus than the Gospels afford, and that which we find ascribed to the Paulicians was, as is clear from Marcion's adoption of it, the first in the field; and its difficulties only came to be felt at a later time, when it was found to conflict with the place of honour assigned in a later stage of Christian opinion to the Virgin.

If the hypothesis, urged in the preceding pages, that the Paulicians were old believers, be true, we should expect their rites to bear some resemblance to those of the orthodox Armenian Church. And this is the case. For example, in the orthodox baptismal service, which is the same for adults as for infants, save that in the case of the latter the God-parent makes the answers, prayers closely analogous to those of the Paulician rite of name-giving are worked into the document, and are offered at the Church door, where the procession halts before entering. Witness the following from the Prayer over the Catechumen before Baptism: 'Accept now, good Lord, *the eager good will* of thy creature, *who hath set his face* to draw nigh unto thy holy and only true Godhead, bearing in himself a Christian name. And give him strength and help both to be made worthy and to attain unto the purification of the holy font of spotless life and to the heritage of adoption into the kingdom of heaven, Christ Jesus our Lord.' Both these clauses should evidently not stand in the same prayer. The first belongs to the service of baptizing an adult who has already received a Christian name, as the Paulician child receives one on its eighth day. The second properly belongs to a service of name-giving, held long before the baptism itself. For where is the sense of praying that a person may have strength to grow up and come to baptism, when within the space of some five minutes he will anyhow be baptized? And to return to the first clause,—to say nothing of the entire inapplicability of its phrases to a new-born infant,—how can the Catechumen already bear a Christian name before he is baptized and has had one formally conferred on him? Again, compare with the Paulician prayers in the name-giving service on p. 90, the following from the orthodox Baptismal service. The procession is still halting at the Church door and the priest prays thus: 'Look, O Lord, in thy pity upon him. Remove and drive away from him, by the calling out over him of thy all-powerful name, the lurking thoughts and words and deeds of foul spirits. . . . Fill him with thy heavenly grace, and make him to rejoice by thy most excellent calling, naming him a Christian. And *let him become worthy, in the proper season of baptism, of the second birth;* and let him, receiving thy Holy Spirit, become body and limb of thy holy Church.' This prayer is obviously more suitable to a service of name-giving than to the service of baptism itself. Thus the genesis of the orthodox baptism is plain. It is the older service of name-giving and the adult baptismal service of the Paulicians rolled up into one.

And the same result follows from another consideration. The Paulicians insisted that the catechumen must himself ask for baptism. They did not go about seeking out infants, to privily baptize them, all unconscious, into their Church. The same stipulation, that the catechumens must of free-will ask for the boon, survives in the baptismal service of the orthodox Armenians, though it has no applicability to children-in-arms. Witness the following dialogue at the font:—

'The Priest says: What dost thou ask for?

'The Catechumen: I ask for baptism.

'The Priest: Dost thou sincerely ask for it?

'The Catechumen: With faith I ask to be baptized, and to be purified from sin, and liberated from devils, and to serve God.

'The Priest: Let it be unto thee according to thy faith.'

And forthwith the Priest continues thus:—

'N. or M., the servant of God, having come *of his own free-will unto the catechumenate, and from the catechumenate unto baptism*, is now baptized in my hands in the name of the Father (and here he pours one handful of water over the child's head), and of the Son (and he pours another handful), and of the Holy Spirit (and he pours a third handful. And this is the essence of baptism, which he shall perform with uplifting of spirit).' And then the priest immerses him in the water three times [1].

The whole ceremony as here detailed is obviously suitable to an adult only, and those who compiled it had no idea of baptizing infants, who cannot come *of their own free-will* and *ask* for baptism. It is not strange that orthodox Armenian clergy so often lapsed into Paulicianism, when their own baptismal service was so redolent of the heresy.

The Paulician baptism, being conferred at the age of thirty, after much testing of the catechumen in faith and repentance, had the same solemnity for the individual which in the later Church the conferring of priestly orders alone retained. It is no matter for surprise, therefore, if certain features of the older rite of baptism,

---

[1] I print the rubric between brackets.

which, as it were, made every man or woman into an organ and recipient of the Spirit, were transferred by the orthodox Armenians to their service of ordination.

As the Paulician elect one asked the candidate for baptism (p. 96), 'What fruit of absolution hast thou?' so the orthodox candidate for priestly orders was asked, 'Utrum habeat etiam opus iustitiae[1]?' And the Paulician reasons for deferring baptism to the age of thirty, became reasons for deferring priesthood to that age, as we see in the following passage[2]: 'Quarto si dignus fuerit presbyteratu, videat utrum pervenerit ad mensuram aetatis necne; nam si fuerit immaturus et imperfectus aetate, ne ordinetur, nam omnis iuvenis puritatis studens erit et gloriae amans. Non enim habet ullam cogitationem impudicitiae, sed quando pervenerit ad mensuram aetatis, deinde apparent passiones naturae in eo, et a natura devictus cadit in peccata et errans conteritur.' And with the first paragraph of ch. xxi of the *Key* (p. 96), compare the following from the direction which prefaces the orthodox Armenian ordinal[3]: 'Sed secundum canonem imponat ei episcopus usque ad mortem. Primum ut habeat in se typum Christi, qui est mitis, humilis, misericors, hominum amator, mali immemor, et benignus. Quapropter dicit Dominus: Tollite iugum meum,' &c.

Lastly, the triple prayer in the presence of the Father, of the Son, and of the Holy Spirit, which in the *Key* belongs to the baptismal service (see pp. 98–100), is in the orthodox rite appropriated to the ordinal. The three prayers are of course somewhat different in the two cases, and in the orthodox ordinal the two first of the prayers only distantly resemble the two prayers to God and before Christ with which the Paulician ordinal concludes. Still there are resemblances. It would take too long to detail them[4]; but they are sufficient to convince us that the orthodox ordinal is based partly on the Paulician rite of baptism, partly on the service of election. In the transmutation all phrases which savour of Adoptionism have been carefully eliminated.

We have now reached the term of our investigations. It only rests to point out that this Paulician book aids us somewhat to simplify the history of Christian opinion. Philo, whose writings

---

[1] Denzinger, *Ritus Orient.* ii. 292.   [2] Ibid.   [3] Ibid. p. 296.
[4] The student can compare the orthodox ordinal in Denzinger, p. 292 foll. We may remark that the Armenian Ordinal of a Priest, preserved in Brit. Mus., codex 19548, twelfth century, omits all the first part of the rite as given in Denzinger, and only begins it with the recitation of the Psalms given on his p. 307.

anticipate Christianity as the glow upon the eastern heavens anticipates the sunrise, inspired with the belief in the ancient theophanies, which he interpreted as apparitions in human form of the Word of God, in a striking passage declares his conviction that it is easier for God to become man than for man to become God. He here sums up the two great divergent lines which speculations about the nature of Jesus were to follow. Already in the apostolic age, according to Prof. Harnack (*Dogmen-Gesch.* i. 181 = 160), the two opposed views were abroad in men's minds: 'Entweder galt Jesus als der Mensch, den Gott sich erwählt, in dem die Gottheit oder der Geist Gottes gewohnt hat, und der nach seiner Bewährung von Gott adoptirt und in einer Herrscherstellung eingesetzt worden ist (Adoptianische Christologie), oder Jesus galt als ein himmlisches Geistwesen (resp. das höchste himmlische Geistwesen nach Gott), welches Fleisch angenommen hat und nach Vollendung seines Werkes auf Erden wieder in den Himmel zurückgekehrt ist (pneumatische Christologie): diese beiden Christologien die streng genommen einander ausschliessen: der Gott-gewordene Mensch und das in Menschengestalt erschienene göttliche Wesen, &c.'

In *The Key of Truth* we have an example of the former, and we learn exactly with what conceptions of baptism, of priesthood, and, in a measure, of sacraments, it was associated. As Jesus was a mere man, ψιλὸς ἄνθρωπος, sin apart, it was not really irreverent (as the opposed Christologists supposed it to be) to regard as a Christ the Christian priest, elected by the Spirit and endowed with grace, according to the primitive formula, 'I am thou, and thou art I' (ἐγὼ σὺ καὶ σὺ ἐγώ)[1]. This conception of priesthood certainly went less naturally with the opinion that Jesus Christ was God, eternal and pre-existing. Nevertheless, the Manicheans and the Montanists and the Adoptionists of Spain, all accepted, more or less definitely, the opinion that he was God, and yet retained this conception of the *sacerdos*. Adult baptism, apart from its greater antiquity as an institution, was also essential to Adoptionist Christianity, of which the inspiring idea was that the believer should model his life on that of Christ. A conception of the Christian priesthood, so peculiar and widespread as that which we have described, must obviously have profoundly influenced the doctrine of the sacramental meal; and we find in the case of the Paulicians, and of the possibly allied Cathar sects of

---

[1] *Epiphan. Haer.* 26, 3.

Europe, that the transformation was not so much of the elements as of the priest celebrating the rite. Because he was Christ, therefore the elements became the body and blood of Christ in the moment when he pronounced over them the words, 'This is my body and blood.' Like all else that the *sacerdos* was and did, the eucharistic offering was as it were a rehearsal, or rather reproduction of Christ, a *repraesentatio*, in the Tertullian sense of the word.

It was probably the Adoptionist missionaries who carried everywhere with them the Western text (so-called) of the New Testament[1], and *The Shepherd* of Hermas, at one time included in the canon. For in this text there were many readings which reflected Adoptionism in one or another of its phases. There was, for example, in Matt. i. 16, the reading, 'Joseph begat Jesus,' which accords with the earliest Adoptionism of the Ebionites. In the account of the baptism, as already noticed, the Bezan codex of Luke adds the words, 'This day have I begotten thee'; and in the same codex, in Matt. iii. 16 the Spirit enters *into* Jesus, and according to the Georgian text and Syr^{sin}, it came and *rested* on him. In Luke iii. 22 Lord Crawford's MS. testifies that the older Armenian text read: 'When the Holy Spirit came down *and rested* on him.' Archelaus had a similar reading. He asks of Mani: 'Quomodo poterit vera columba verum hominem *ingredi* atque in eo permanere, caro enim carnem *ingredi* non potest[2]?' Sedulous attempts were made in the texts used by the rival school of Christologists to make it appear that the Holy Spirit only alighted temporarily on Jesus in the Jordan, and neither entered him nor stayed with him. Similarly, the phrase 'elect *or* chosen' was taken out where possible. Thus the Arabic Tatian witnesses to it in Matthew's account of the Transfiguration (Matt. xvii. 5), 'dilectus quem elegi.' So in John i. 34, ὁ ἐκλεκτὸς τοῦ Θεοῦ seems to have been read, and subsequently expunged. The Adoptionists, no doubt, appealed to such texts in proof of their doctrine that Jesus κατ' ἐκλογὴν ἐχρίσθη (see p. xci, *n.*). We can trace the use of the Western text of Acts on p. 92 of the *Key* in the words, 'like Simon's wife's mother,' where the original text must have been, 'like Simon Magus,' for Codex D, in Acts viii. 24, adds, ὃς πολλὰ

---

[1] I owe this suggestion to Mr. Rendel Harris.
[2] Mani is arguing that the whole story is absurd, because a real dove could not enter a man. Archelaus replies that the spirit was real, but not the dove-like body it assumed. That was only an ὁμοίωμα.

κλαίων οὐ διελίμπανεν. Gregory of Narek refers to this passage of the *Key* when he asks (p. 128): 'What trace of good in Simon?' To avoid such attacks the users of the *Key* substituted the meaningless words, for Simon's wife's mother did not weep.

But it was especially in its fasts and feasts that the Adoptionist Christianity contrasted with the Great Church. The holy year began with the Feast of John the Baptist; then, perhaps, came the fast of those who repented at his teaching. This was followed on January 6 by the Feast of the Baptism and Spiritual Re-birth of Jesus as the Christ and Son of God. Then began the quadragesimal fast commemorating the forty days and nights on the mountain, during which he was fortifying himself against the tempter. Later on came the commemorations of his entrance on the work of his ministry, of the institution of the Lord's Supper, and of Zatik or Easter, which was kept on the fourteenth of Nisan. The Sabbath was perhaps kept, and there were no special Sunday observances. The Agapê and Eucharist were not separated, and the latter retained much of its primitive significance. Wednesday and Friday were not kept as fast-days. Of the modern Christmas and of the Annunciation, and of the other feasts connected with the life of Jesus prior to his thirtieth year, this phase of the Church knew nothing. The general impression which the study of it leaves on us is that in it we have before us a form of Church not very remote from the primitive Jewish Christianity of Palestine.

In complete contrast was the *pneumatic* theology, as Harnack calls it, which saw in Jesus not a man who, at a mature age, was filled or possessed with the Divine Spirit, but God himself, putting on flesh in the womb of woman. This teaching allied itself at once with the belief in the miraculous conception, and with the schematism which the philosophic Judaism had already elaborated, namely of a Divine Word or Reason (Θεὸς Λόγος), eternal and pre-existent, Creator and Sustainer of the universe, image of God after which Adam was made, Son of God, and Mediator between God and all creatures, High Priest of Humanity, the same being that in the Old Testament had in frequent theophanies appeared in human form on earth, first coming down from heaven, and then, when his mission was fulfilled, returning to the right hand of the Father. In the Garden of Eden to Adam and Eve, at Mambre to Abraham and Sarah, in the bush to Moses, in the lion's den to Daniel, this Divine *Logos* had appeared; becoming manifest to human senses, and assuming a human voice, as a man with hands and feet, mouth and voice, feelings of anger and wrath, even with weapons, going in and coming forth among men. Such was the Philonean teaching about the epiphanies of the Word in the past, and it deeply influenced Christian thought.

Yet it had its dangers. It might lead men into thinking that Jesus Christ was merely an angel; and since, according to Philo, the Word in its ancient epiphanies wore an ethereal body, and instead of eating and drinking, only caused in men's minds the phantasy or appearance of eating or drinking, it too easily led them to a Docetic apprehension of Jesus, that is, to the opinion that he had a phantasmal body, and not real flesh and blood. If an angelic apparition then, so also now. Here we have the argument of Marcion and Mani, an argument which Tertullian found so cogent that to escape from it he altered the major premiss, and argued that the angels which appeared to Abraham were of real flesh and blood, and did really eat and drink. Some of the Docetic sects went further than others, and not only rejected the real flesh and blood of Jesus, but his human birth as well; and Mani assailed, as flat blasphemy, the opinion that the Divine Being would submit to enter the womb and be born. The orthodox, herein at one with the Adoptionists, retorted—a little inconsequently, it is true—that if there was no birth, then there was no passion, no resurrection, and no judgement.

But they themselves did not wholly escape the all-pervading taint of Docetism. For, as Harnack truly remarks[1]: 'Der Profectus, durch den Jesus erst zum Gott-gleichen Herrscher geworden sein soll (damit im Zusammenhang das Werthlegen auf den wunderbaren Vorgang bei der Taufe Jesu), ist für die eine (the Adoptionist); ein naïver Doketismus für die andere, charakteristisch.' And such a naïve Docetism we everywhere meet with, clinging like a skirt to the pneumatic Christology, even against its better will. It reveals itself in such beliefs as the following: that the Divine Word, Jesus Christ, was conceived through the ear[2] of the Virgin; and was born through her head[3] or right breast[4]. The birth was not a real one;

---

[1] *Dogmen-Gesch.* i. p. 185.

[2] Tertullian, *De Carne Christi*, ch. 17, in a parallel of Mary and Eve, implies this belief. Also Origen, *C. Celsum*, vii. 4. St. Ephrem held it; also the orthodox Armenian fathers, and in mediaeval hymns to the Virgin, we often have the line, 'quae per aurem concepisti,' e. g. in Bodl. MS. Latin Liturg. 10, fol. 91 v°.

[3] See the *Saltair na Rann*, Oxford, 1883, ll. 7529, 7530.

[4] See Adrian and Rithens, *Kemble's Salomon and Saturnus*, p. 204. This was

she at once bore him and did not bear him[1], and was never in a true state of parturition at all. His flesh was a mere blind, a disguise of his Godhood. It also showed itself in the denial of natural human functions to the Saviour. For, according to many, Jesus Christ, though he ate and drank, did not digest his food; for all digestion is a process of corruption, and his body was incorruptible[2]. For the same reason he was not liable to evacuations, nor to secretions; and the text affirming that he sweated was effaced from copies of the New Testament at an early date, and is avoided by Athanasius. This writer also affirmed[3] that he was naturally immortal, and that if he had not met with a violent death on the cross, he would never have died at all; that he was incapable of bodily disease or weakness, and although he felt hunger, he could not have been starved to death.

All these traits affected his body. But the same tendency of the pneumatic Christology was observable in the psychology of the Saviour. His inner life, according to all the great orthodox writers, was a constant oscillation between the human and divine; and his human ignorance was not real, but only what in theological phrase is termed an economy[4], and in plain English a pretence.

With the pneumatic Christology there came also another way of looking at baptism. Jesus was a Divine Being and filled with the Spirit from his mother's womb. If so, why should not baptism be turned into an *opus operatum*, independent of the merits and conscious faith of the individual? Why should it not be effective for new-born children as well as for adults? If Jesus in the very womb was God, why should not infants harbour the Holy Spirit also? So the requirements of repentance of sin, and confession were allowed to drop out of sight, and infant baptism became the rule in the churches which had made this type of Christology their own.

an Anglo-Saxon tradition. So the Bodhi-sattva was born from Mâyâ's right side (Kern, *Der Buddhismus*, 30 *n*.). Also Indra through his mother's side, see *Rv.* iv. 18. 1. So Osiris, in *Plutarch de Iside et Osiride*, xii. See art. by Andrew Lang, in *Nineteenth Century* for Sept. 1886, p. 434, *n.* 39, and Liebrecht, *Volkskunde*, 490. I owe these two notes to Dr. Whitley Stokes.

[1] So Clem. Alex., also Greg. Nyss. *Testimonia*, and Maximus Taurin.

[2] So the orthodox Armenian fathers, who also held the belief next mentioned. Cp. Elipandus' creed, p. clxxv: ' qui utrum comedisset an bibisset,' &c.

[3] e.g. *De Incarn. Verbi*, c. 21: ὡς μὲν ζωὴ καὶ δύναμις ὢν συνίσχυεν ἐν αὐτῷ τὸ σῶμα ... μηδὲ νοσεῖν ἔδει τὸν Κύριον ... ἀλλ' οὐδὲ ἐξασθενῆσαι ἔδει πάλιν τὸ σῶμα ... οὐ λιμῷ διεφθάρη (sc. τὸ σῶμα) ... οὐκ εἶδε διαφθοράν κ.τ.λ.

[4] For a detailed working out of this point the reader may consult Canon Gore's *Studies on the Incarnation*.

At the same time the priest became merely one who offers the eucharistic sacrifice and ceased to be a Christ. His liturgical character tended to obscure the prophetical aspect of his office, and room was provided for measuring the gifts of the Spirit and for drawing real distinctions of hierarchical grade, such as could not emerge, so long as the priest was an elect one, and the bishop no more than a *summus sacerdos*, not essentially different from, or more authoritative than, any other presbyter.

We have already glanced at the fortunes of the early Adoptionist Church. Driven out of the Roman Empire, we find it at the beginning of the fourth century and later encamped along the borders of the Greek and Latin worlds, in Mesopotamia, in Armenia and in Spain, in Bavaria, perhaps in Britain. It would seem also to have lingered on in the ancient Church of Phrygia. Perhaps it was the pressure from behind of the advancing tide of Islam, both in Spain and in the Taurus, which, in the centuries immediately following, hurled it back into the Roman Empire, there to take a fresh start. In the east its recrudescence was favoured by the iconoclastic movement, one of those great bursts of anti-idolatrous enthusiasm which about once in every five hundred years seem to sweep across the face of Aryan civilization, starting from the Semitic races in contact with us and too often dealing out destruction to the fairest monuments of our ancient art and religion. But this recrudescence within the Roman Empire of Adoptionist teaching was shortlived, and it was not there that it really bore fruit. Yet it was not stamped out, but only driven under ground. It still lurked all over Europe, but especially in the Balkans, in Lombardy, in Gascony, and along the Rhine. In these hiding-places it seems to have gathered its forces together in secret, in order to emerge once more into daylight when an opportunity presented itself. That opportunity was the European reformation, in which, especially under the form of Anabaptist and Unitarian opinion, this leaven of the early Apostolic Church is found freely mingling with and modifying other forms of faith. In engendering this great religious movement, we feel sure that the Bogomiles of the Balkan States played a most important part. They were the chief purveyors to Europe of Adoptionist tenets, partly imbibed from Paulician missionaries. But they are still a missing link, and the discovery of some of their monuments can alone complete the investigation which, in the preceding pages, we have only begun.

I. THE ARMENIAN TEXT

ԳԻՐՔ[1]

որ կոչի

ԲԱՆԱԼԻ ՃՇՄԱՐՏՈՒԹԵԱՆ

Գրեցաւ ի Թուականիս Փրկչին 1782[2], իսկ ըստ Հայոց ո̅մ̅լ̅
Եւ ի Կաւառն Տարօնոյ։

Իմն առ սիրելի ընթերցողդ.

Թէպէտ բազմութիւնք ըսպաղանացս և փորձութիւնք այլ-
կոծմանց աշխարհի և յօգնադիմի պարաւանդութիւնք յոյժ
առ զանազան մրբկութիւնս անցաւոր կենցաղոյս կարի վերա-
կացեալք ի վերայ մեր, ո՛չ ներքին մեզ[3] բուռն արկանել
զայսմանէ Տարկաւոր գործոյ[4], սակայն ստիպումն ճշմարտութեան տեառն մերոյ Յիսուսի որդւոյն Հօրն երկնաւորի,
և Թախանձումն Հոգւոյն սրբոյ, նաեւ ըստ աղաչանաց
բազմաց Հաւատացելոց, և սանաւանդ վասն ծայրագոյն
Տարկաւորութեան՝ զամենայն գալիք անցաւոր կենցաղոյս
յետս արկի և ո՛չ խնայեցի տալ ձեզ նորածնեալ մանկանցդ
սրբոյ Ընդհանրականի և Առաքելականի եկեղեցւոյն տեառն
մերոյ Յիսուսի Քրիստոսի զկաթն սուրբ, որով զարգասջիք

---

[1] ի Ձեռագրին՝ Գիրգ. [2] Ձ. 1882.
[3] Ձ. զմեզ. [4] Ձ. Գործոց.

ի Հալատոս։ Սասն որպյ ճեռնամուխ արար զմեզ Հոգի ՍօրՖ երկնաւորի առ ի գրել զայս ճանապարճ և ճշմարտութիւն և կեանք։ Օր ի վաղուց Հետէ փակեալ էր զճշմարտութիւն Հոգի խաբէութեան, զոր տերՖ մեր ասէ. փուշք Հեղձու֊ ցեալ էին զնա։ Սա էս զտակալ ինչ և զդուղնաբեալ բանս ձեզ ընձայեցի ճամառտութեամբ և ոչ ճոխաբար։ Օր դուք խորին մտօք ընդերձջիք ի փառս Յիսուսի որդոյ Բարեխոսին և ի պատիւ ՍօրՖ իւրոյ¹ . . . ։

Օայս Համառտ բանս քննե ցեք,
Խորին մտօք որոնե ցեք,
Եթե Համձոյ լիցի ձեզ բանն,
Յայնժամ զարդիճեք ընդ որոտ մաննե։

Յաղագս սուրբ մկրտութեան Տեառն մերոյ Յիսուսի Քրիս֊ տոսի, որ վասն Հալատացելոց և ապաշխարողաց աշա֊ դեցաւ և ոչ երեխայից, անապաշխարողաց և թերե֊ Հալատից և ոչ անմաբրից², որպէս յայտ է ի սուրբ և ի պատուական վարս Յոճաննու Մկրտչին զոր մեծա֊ գոյշ ճայնիւն իւրով նախ քան զՔրիստոս տեր և բարե֊ խոսն մեր ագաղակեր առ (կատարեալոն)³ ասելով։

Ոճնեայ մեզ Յիսուս և միշնորդ լէր վասն ամենայն Հալատացելոց քոց սիրելեացդ, զոր սրբանուէր և լուսաճեմ բանիւդ քով աղաչեցեր առ Հայր քո ասելով. Ոչ վասն նոցա միայն աղաչեմ, այլ և վասն ամենայն Հալատա֊ ցելոց բանիւն նոցա յիս են։

II,
աբ

¹ Զ. ՍօրՖ իւրոյ . . . ։ երեքին կեաքն ցուցանեն բառ մի եղծեալ։
² Զ. անմաղբից.
³ Բառ այս եղծեալ է, բայց տեսանելի.

3

Գլուխ Լ.ռաջներորդ [1].

Ապաշխարեցէք, զի մերձեալ է արքայութիւն յերկնից, և այլն։ Մատթէոս գլուխ 4, համար 2.

Արդ բանք սրբոյ Աւետարանին ոչ են ծածկեալ առ մեզ, այլ վասն այնորիկ [2] ճշմարիտ հաւաքաբանութեամբ [3] յայտնեաց Հայր տեառն մերոյ Յիսուսի Քրիստոսի որդւոյ իւրում սիրելւոյ։ Ա,ասն այնորիկ և սուրբն Յովհաննէս, մեծ(ն) ի ծնունդս կանանց, գոչէր ասելով առ ի ծնունդս իմից, թէ ապաշխարեցէք, ով մոլորեալք ի մեղ մեղ դիզեալ բարդեալ չարեաց ձերոց և ծաներուք դուք զմեղս ձեր զսկսնական, զոր ի ՓՏ աւուրց պահեալ կան ի ձեզ մթերեալ։ Ա,ասնորյ և սուրբն Յովհաննէս զայս ասելով զարթուցանէր զմիտս նոցա առ ի գալ ի սուրբ հաւատս և ճանաչել զնորագոյն փոքրիկն արքայութեան՝ զտէր Յիսուս Քրիստոս, Որդն Աստուծոյ, բարձօղն մեղաց։ Որ և ինքն Յովհաննէս զմատ սուրբ ձգեալ ասելով. Ահաւասիկ Քրիստոս Որդն Աստուծոյ, որ բառնայ զմեղս աշխարհի։ Դարձեալ յարէ ասելով․ Ես ոչ եմ այն, այլ առաքեալ եմ առաջի նորա։ Այսպէս և սուրբն Յովհաննէս նախ՝ զնոսա քարոզէր, երկրորդ՝ ուսուցանէր [4], երրորդ՝ ի Յա յապաշխարանս մուծանէր, չորրորդ՝ ի հաւատս բերէր, և Հա յետ այնորիկ իմարինոյ յաղթից մաքրէր։ Եւ ապայ տեր և բարեխօսն մեր՝ Որդն Աստուծոյ զՀոգեկան փրկութիւն Յա շնորհէր նոցա. Որ ուսեալք ի տեառնէ մերմէ Յիսուսէ Հա ընդհանրական և Առաքելական եկեղեցւոյն՝ այնպէս առնելին, զոր յայտ է ի գործս իւրեանց և մանաւանդ ի յաւանդութիւնս փրկչին մերոյ Յիսուսի Քրիստոսի, զոր հրամայէ առ ընդհանրական և առաքելական եկեղեցին ասելով. Մրկ. գլ. 16, Հմր. 15․ Երթայք (յ)աշխարհ

---

[1] Ձ. առաջներորդ.   [2] Ձ. վասն.
[3] Ձ. Լստ և այլուբ բազում ուրեք՝ հաւագաբանութեամբ.
[4] Ձ. Լստ և այլուբ բազում ուրեք՝ յուսուցանէր, յուսեալք, յուսուցիչ.

ամենայն և քարոզեցէք զաւետարանն ամենայն արարածոց․ որ Հաւատասցէ, մկրտեսցի, կեցցէ, և որ ոչ Հաւատասցէ դատապարտեսցի։ Սա՛ ն որդյ և տէրն մեր նախ զՀալատոս խնդրէր և ապայ զեժշկութիւնս շնորՀէր և յետ այնորիկ գմկրտութիւն սուրբ պարգեէր Հաւատացելոց և ոչ անՀաւատ երեխայից։ Լյապէս և սուրբն Յոհաննէս և սուրբ եկեղեցին տաւ տէառն մերոյ Յիսուսի Քրիստոսի. այսպէս առնէին մինչև նք ցարձակումն սատանայի։ Արդ, յորժամ արձակեցաւ սա ծեալ տանայ ի կապից իւրոց, յայնժամ սկսաւ բանալ զշշմարտու թիւն տեառն մերոյ Յիսուսի Քրիստոսի և սրբազան առաքե ի ի լոցն և էմոյծ զխաբէական Հալաքարանութիւն իւր իմէք ցին)։ վարդապետաց, զորս ըստ կարողութեասբ Հօրն երկնաւորին զփակեալ դուռն ճշմարտութեան բացցուք Բանալեօքն ՋՀշմարտութեան։ Որպէս և սուրբն Յոհաննէս բացեալ զդուռն ճշմարտութեան նախ քան զտէրն մեր Յիսուս Քրիստոս Հրամայեր ասելով առ կատարեալ անձինս. Թէ Լպաշխարեցէք, զի մերձեալ է արքայութիւն երկնից [1] են։

Արդ՝ ապաշխարիլն նոցա էր դառնալ ի չար գործոց իւրեանց և Հաւատալ ի Քրիստոս Յիսուս, առնուլ զսուրբ մկրտութիւն Հոգլոյն Հօրն երկնաւորին, առ ճանաչել զմեղս սկսնական և ցաւիլ ի վերայ նորա և արձակիլ ի կապանաց դիւաց, զոր ի նախաՀարց սերեալ կայր, Ոստի զտսա տեսեալ մէծի մարգարէին Յոհաննու բարկութիամբ զարթուցանէ զնոսա ասելով՝ ի Ս կս, գլ․ 3, Համար․ 7․

Օձունդք իմից, ո՞ եցոյց ձեզ փախչել ի բարկութենէն, որ գալոցն է։ Լրաբէք այսուՀետև պտուղ արժանի ապա նախ շխարութեան և մի սկանիցիք ասել եթէ ունիմք Հայր զԼբրաՀամ։ Օայս ասեմ ձեզ եթէ կարող է ասսուած ի քարանցս յայսցանէ յարուցանել զորդիս ԼբրաՀամու։

Արդ՝ որովՀետև սոքա յապառած քարի(ն)ս եղեալ էին, վասն այսորիկ զնոսա ծնունդս իժի և քարբի արար և զՅիսուս ի նոցանէ յարուցանել ետ, զի նովաւ զփրկութիւն շնորՀել տայ նոցա։ վասն որոյ և մասն Բնդհանրական և Լրաբելական

---

[1] Ձ․ Լստ և այլ բազումութեք՝ յանձինս, յերկնից․

սուրբ եկեղեցւոյն սուրբն Ղուկաս ԳԼ. 13, ՀՄր. 23. ասէ. Ի սորա զաւակէ Աստուած ըստ աւետեացն յարոյց Իսրայէլի զփրկիչն Յիսուս։ Այսպէս և մեք պարտիմք զշանականն ի Հաւատս ածել և զանկատարս ի կատարելութիւնս բերել և զանբանս բանիւն Յիսուսի Քրիստոսի լյուցանել և զքարացեալ սիրտս նոցա կակղացուցանել և զմթերեալ մախսը դառնութեան, զոր ի Հին աւուրց պաՀեալ կան, զնոսա զզուանօք փսխել տամք մատամբն աստուծոյ, և ապայ տամք նոցա զղեղա մեղաց, թէ սկզբնականի և թէ ներգործականի։ Օի որպէս և սուրբն Յովհաննէս նախ զապաշխարանս, զՀալատս ուսուցանէր և յետոյ՝նորիկ զմկրտութիւն շնորՀէր և ապա զծանապարՀ, զճշմարտութիւն և զկեանքն նոցա ցուցանէր ասելով. ԱՀաւասիկ Քրիստոս Գառն Աստուծոյ, որ բառնայ զմեղս աշխարՀի։ Այսպէս և մեք պարտիմք Հետևիլ ըստ այսմ ճշմարտութեան և ոչ խաբէական Հաւաքաբանութեան աւանդութեան այլոց, որք զանՀաւատս, զանասունս և զանապաշխարս մկրտեն, որք են ամէնեին սուտ և խաբէութիւն դիւական և ոչ աստուածական, զորս ըստ կարողութեամբ (sic) սուրբ Հոգւոյն ասասցուք։

Գլուխ երկրորդ

Վասն սուրբ Մկրտութեան.

Յաղագս տեառն մերոյ Յիսուսի Քրիստոսի թէ որպէս կանոն և պատուէր ետ այնպէս առնեմք աստուծով։

Նախ տէր մեր Յիսուս Քրիստոս մկրտեցաւ Հրամանաւ Հօրն երկնաւորի երեսուն ամեա(յ), որպէս սուրբն զղուկաս յայտնեալ զամս նորա. ԳԼ. 3, ՀՄր. 23. Եւ ինքն Յիսուս էր ամաց իբրև երեսնից, սկսեալ որոց որպէս կարծիւր որդի Յովսէփայ։

Արդ՝ ի ժամանակի կատարելութեան էառ զմկրտութին, էառ անդ զեշխանութին, էառ զքաՀանայապետութին, էառ

[margin:] Եւ ո՛ ն՛հալ երել որբ անք

լ ատ յն (Հալ բեակ Հալ բանո թեա առնե զերի Հու աստ ածու որպէ յայ գործ նոցա

Մ՛տ ԳԼ. 3 ՀՄր. Մ՛տ ԳԼ. 3 ՀՄր.

---

[1] Ջ. բառս այս եղծեալ.

ռ զթագաւորութիւն և զՀուվապետութի ։ Պարձեալ անդ ըն-
, տրեցաւ, անդ պերձացաւ, անդ պայծառացաւ, անդ զօրացաւ,
օ. անդ յարգեցաւ, անդ պահմանադրեցաւ, անդ փառաւորեցաւ,
ս. անդ գովեցաւ, անդ Հրձևեցաւ, անդ փայլեցաւ, անդ բերկրեցաւ
8. և անդ ուրախացաւ ։ Իսկ արդ՝ անդ եղէ գլուխս երկնաւ
Լ. 1, որաց և երկրաւորաց, անդ եղէ լոյս աշխարհի, անդ եղէ
3. ձանապարհ և ձշմարտութիւն և կեանք, անդ եղէ դուռն
   երկնից, անդ եղէ վեմ անյաղթելի ի դրանց դժոխոց, անդ
   եղէ Հիմն մերոյ Հաւատոյ, անդ եղէ փրկիչ մեզ մեղաւորացս, անդ լցաւ աստուածութեամբ, անդ կնքեցաւ, անդ
I. օծեցաւ, անդ ձայնեցաւ, անդ եղէ սիրելի, անդ եղէ պարա-
, ւեալ ի Հրեշտակաց, անդ եղէ գառն անարատ։ Նաես
   անդ զգեցաւ զլուսեղէն պատմուձանն զառաջին զոր կորոյս
   Ադամն ի դրախտին։ Արդ՝ անդ Հրաւիրեցաւ Հոգովն աս
   տուծոյ խոսիլ ընդ Հօրն երկնաւորին։ Նաես անդ կարգեցաւ
   թագաւոր երկնաւորաց և երկրաւորաց1 և սանդարամետա
   կանաց։ Եւ զայս րստ կարգի զայս ամենայն ետ Հայրն իւր
   մխածնին որպէս ինքն մխնորդ և բարեխօսն մեր Հրամայեալ
Լ. 9, իւր սուրբը ընդՀանրական և առաքելական եկեղեցւոյն ասէ.
8. Մատթէոս գլ. 28, Համր. 18. Եւ մատուցեալ Յիսուս խօսեցաւ ընդ նոսա և ասէ. տուաւ ինձ ամ իշխանութին յերկինս
   Մր.1 և յերկրի։ Որպէս առաքեաց զիս Հայր և ես առաքեմ զձեզ
Լ. 11 և այլն։ Այսպէս և տերն ուսեալ2 ի Հօրէ և ապա մեզ
28 ուսոյց3 առնել զսուրբն մկրտութի և զայլ ամենայն պատուէրս
20. իւր ի կատարեալ ժամանակի և ոչ այլ ժամու։ Որպէս գառն
ԲԲ. Աստուծոյ կանոնէ զմեզ՝ յետ յարութեան։ Մարկ. գլ. 16,
   Համր. 15. ասելով՝ երթայք (յ)աշխարհ ամենայն լ-քարոզեցէք
   զաւետարանն ամենայն արարածոց. որ Հաւատասցէ՝ մկրտեսցի
   կեցցէ և որ ոչն Հաւատասցէ՝ դատապարտեսցի ։
այ Արդ լուարուք և ի միտ առէք զանքակտելի վձիռ տեառն
բա մերոյ Յիսուսի Քրիստոսի զոր ոմանք Հակառակեալ ընդդեմ
բ կանոնաց տեառն մերոյ Յիսուսի՝ քակեցին զսուրբը պատուական

---

1 Ձ. յերկնաւորաց և յերկրաւորաց.   2 Ձ. յուսեալ.
3 Ձ. յուսոյց.

կանոնս, զոր ի Հօրէ ամենակալէ աւանդեցաւ տեառն մերոյ Յիսուսի Քրիստոսի, և կոխան արարին դիւական վարդապետութեամբն իւրեանց. որք սոքա մինչև Հանապազ ընդ դիմանան ընդդէմ ճշմարտութեան տեառն մերոյ Յիսուսի Քրիստոսի ...¹ որք են անբան մկրտեն և զանհաստ հաղորդեն։ Արդ ամենեքեանս կան արգելեալ ի տեառնէ և ի սրբոց առաքելոցն, որպէս յայտ է ի կանոնս փրկչին մերոյ Յիսուսի, զոր ասէ սրբազան առաքելոցն իւրոց, թէ Մի՛ տայք զսրբութիւն շանց և մի՛ արկանէք զմարգարիտս ձեր առաջի խոզաց, զի մի՛ առ ոտս կոխեսցեն զնա և դարձեալ երգիծուցանիցեն զձեզ, և այլն։ Ուստի ո՛չ գիտեմք, թէ սոքա որով իշխանութիամբ առնեն զայսոսիկ և կամ ո՛վ է ուսուցիչ սոցա։ Յայտ է թէ Հոգովն Հակառակին Հօր աստուծոյ, գործեն զգործս նորա, որպէս ծանուցանէ մեզ փրկիչն ասելով, թէ զզշչ լերուք ի չար մշակաց անտի և այլն։ Զայս ասելով յայտնէ տէրն մեր, թէ սոքա են մշակք նենգաւորաց, այսինքն սատանայի, զոր և մասն եկեղեցւոյ՝ սուրբն² Յո-Հաննէս՝ տայ այսպիսեաց զմիրոս ասելով։ Կաթուղիկեայց Ա.ն Առաք. Գլ. 3, Համր. 10. Ասուցիկ յայտնին ի միմեանց խաբ որդիք աստուծոյ և որդիք սատանայի։ Նա ես տէրն մեր Հալ յայտնէ ասելով այսպիսեաց, թէ ի պողղ նոցա ծանիջիք բան զնոսա, և զայլս լուեցուք։ Որ և տէր և բարեխօսն մեր թեա Յիսուս այնպիսեաց զդարձ պարգևեսցէ և զայսպիսին ի առն սուտ վարժապետէն ազատեսցէ։ որդի տան

Գլուխ երրորդ.

Արդ խոնարհեցուք և մեք սրբոյ եկեղեցւոյ ընդհանրա- կանին և Հետևեսցուք գործոց նոցա, որք միախոհ և միակրօն առնէին և մեզ ուսուցին։ Այժմ առնումք ի Հարկաւոր ժամանակի զսուրբն և զպատուական խորՀուրդս տեառն մերոյ Յիսուսի Քրիստոսի և Հօրն երկնաւորի.ի ժամանակ ապաշխա- րութեան և Հաւատոյ, որպէս ի տեառնէ ընդՀանրական և Առաքելական եկեղեցւոյ ուսեալ՝ այնպէս առնեմք և կատա-

---
¹ Զ. Ստ բառ մի եղծեալ։ ² Զ. և սուրբն։

բեալ հաւատով հաստատեմք զայնոսիկ, որք ոչ ունին զսուրբ մկրտութիւն, նա եւ ոչ ճաշակեալ են զմարմին և արբեալ են զսուրբ Արիւն տեառն մերոյ Յիսուսի Քրիստոսի։ Արդ՝ ըստ բանին տեառն հարկ է մեզ զնոսա նախ ի հաւատս բերել¹ յապաշխարանս մուծանել և ապա² նոցա տալ։ Որպէս և մասն եկեղեցւոյն³ Սուրբն Ղուկաս ի Գործս եկեղեցւոյն ասէ. գլ. 8, համր. 12. Բայց յորժամ հաւատացին Փիլիպպոսի, որ աւետարանէր վասն արքայութեան Աստուծոյ. և անուանն Յիսուսի Քրիստոսի մկրտեին ամենեքեան՝ արք և կանայք։ Եւ դարձեալ ի նոյն գլ. 8, համր. 36. ասէ. իբրև երթային զճանապարհային եկին ի չուր ինչ և ասէ ներքինին՝ ահաւասիկ չուր, զի՞նչ արգելու զիս ի մկրտելոյ։ Եւ ասէ ցնա Փիլիպպոս. եթէ հաւատաս բոլորով սրտիւ՝ մարթ է։ Պատասխանի ետ ներքինին և ասէ. հաւատամ եթէ Յիսուս Քրիստոս է որդի Աստուծոյ։ Նախ այսպէս զհաւատս լսին ի նոցանէ և ապա զճայրագոյն մկրտութի շնորհէին. Քանզի այսպէս էին առեալ ի տեառնէ, և ճշմարտութեամբ այնպէս բաշխէին։ Իսկ ումանք, վիժեալք յաւետարանէն և յեկեղեցւոյ նորին՝ հակառակութեամբ հարցանեն ի յանհաւատ կնքաճօրէ, որ է սուտ վկայ անդ կացեալ իբրև զաւանակ, ասելով ցնա. թէ երեխայս զի՞նչ խնդրէ ով . . .⁴ վկայ։ Եւ նորա պատասխանի տուեալ ասէ. զհաւատ, զյոյս, զսէր և մկրտութիւն։ Արդ՝ ով . . .⁵ ընթերցող, զճարդ ոչ ամաչես, կամ զիմդ ոչ պատկառես և ամենեին զասացեալդ⁶ և զհարցմունսդ ոչ մտածես, թէ զինչ ելանէ իբերանդ քումդ, որ է ճշմարիտ . . .⁷ հաւաքաբանութ, եթէ պատասխանին . . .⁸ վկային և եթէ հարցումն քոյ վասն երեխային ցնկրաճարն։ Որք են ամենին . . .⁹, զորս ըստ կարողութեամբ

---
¹ Ձ. բառս այսեղծեալ։   ² Ձ. անխտիր ապա և ապայ։
³ Ձ. եկեղեցւոյ և՛ եկեղեցոյ, ճոգւոյ և ճոգոյ անխտիր։
⁴ Ձ. բառս այս եղծեալ թուի լինել 'սուտ,' կամայլ բառ ինչ անարգական։   ⁵ Նմանապէս ըստ վերնոյն։
⁶ Ձ. յօդդ դ հանապազ գրի տ.   ⁷ բառք երկու եղծեալ։
⁸ բառ մի եղծեալ։   ⁹ բառք քանի մի եղծեալք։

տեառն մերոյ բարեխօսին Յիսուսի բացցուք ինչ սակաւ զմիտս ձեր։ Եւ ցուցանել տամք աստուծով զվարդապետն եւ զուսուցիչն ձեր թէ ո՛վ է։

Գլուխ Զորրորդ.

Յաղագս յայտնութեան եւ ցուցման զչայր եւ զուսուցիչն այնց, որք Հաւատացեալ են եւ զգործս նորա մեծաւ սիրով կատարեն, եւ գիտեն թէ գործ աստուծոյ է։ Որք և . . .[1] լիցի այնպիսի գործող կամ կանոնագչալատալ և ի միոս մեր բերել։

Որ միշնորդ և բարեխօսն մեր Յիսուս Քրիստոս կանոնէ զմեզ ճշմարիտ այսպէս. Թէ զգոյշ լերուք ի չար մշակաց անտի և այլն։

Աճամ տեռն մեր Քրիստոս վճէածեալ ընդ Հրէայն և Հերձուածողան, ցայց տալով զչայրն նոսա ասէ ի Յօհ. Գլ. 8, Հմր. 44. Դուք ի Հօրէ սատանայէ էք[2] և ցանկութիւն Հօրն ձերոյ կամք առնել, զի նա մարդասպան էր ի սկզբանէ և ի ճշմարտութեան ո՛չ եկաց, զի ո՛չ գոյ ճշմարտութիւն ի նմա.— յորժամ խօսիցի սուտ՝ իւրոց անտի խօսի, զի սուտ է և Հայր նորա։ Արդ՝ աշակերտքն նորին՝ եկայք և դուք դատ արարէք ճշմարտապէս զարարեալ սուտ վարութիւն մեր, որք են ամենալին առասպել և արտաքոյ սրբոյ Աւետարանին ընդՀանրական և Առաքելական սրբոյ եկեղեցւոյ. որ ո՛չ գտանի բնաւ ի սուրբ և պատուական Գործս Առաքելոց և կամ ի սուրբ Աւետարանս տեառն մերոյ Յիսուսի Քրիստոսի բարեխօսին։

Այլ արդ՝ այժմ բարձալ կարծիք ճշմարտապէս ի մտաց մերոց թէ, Հայրն ձեր ուսուցեալ է ձեզ ի վազուց Հետև և կապեալ է զձեզ առ իւր Աւետարան . . .[3]։ Վասն այսօրիկ և տէրն մեր բաց ի բաց վկայեաց և ասէ. զի ընկզանիցէ Հայրն ձեր մարդասպան էր և այլն։ Իսկ արդ՝ ստոյգ և ճշմատիտ է բան տեառն մերոյ Յիսուսի Քրիստոսի, զոր

---

[1] բառ ինչ քերեալ թուի լինել 'քալ.' [2] Ձ. ստնչէք.
[3] Աստանօր բառ մի քերեալ թուի լինել 'սուտ.'

Հրամայէ շարին այնորիկ։ Ո՛ի նախ եղև ի կերպ օձի և խօսեցաւ ի Հայ բարբառս չե՞լաւ, թէ ընդէ՞ր ստախօրէն պատուիրեաց ձեզ աստուած չուտել ի պտղոյդ անտի և չմերձենալ ի նա, զի գիտէր աստուած, թէ յորժամ առնդյք և մերձենայք դուք ի նմա, իսկոյն բացցին աչք[1] ձեր և լինիցիք իբրև զաստուած, վասնայսորիկ խստագոյն պատուիրեաց ձեզ ո՛չ մերձենալ և ո՛չ Հուպ լինիլ։

Իսկ կինն եւայ անսաց վերոյ գրեալ հօրն և դարձեալ Համոզցոյց զմիտ Ադամայ։ Արդ՝ յորժամ երկոքեանն Հաւանեցան միմեանց, իսկոյն մերկացան ի փառաց և անկան ի դրախտէն և տեսին յայնժամ զմերկութիւն միմեանց և ո՛չ ամաչէին, որպէս Հ_ունչ Աստուածութեան վկայէ, և այլն։

Այլ արդ՝ ցելաւ վարագոյր կուսութեան նոցա խաբմամբ օձն շարին, փախեաւ կուսական արիւնս նոցին, ձմեցաւ ապահի մարմինս նոցին, լուեցան կապանք Աստուծոյ, զոր պատուիրեաց նոցա, Հերձաւ ամօթ երեսաց նոցա, կորեաւ ամենեկին պատկառանս նոցա, խորշեցաւ գոյն լուսոյ Աստուածութեան յերեսաց նոցա, բարձաւ թագ թագաւորութեան նոցա և կորեաւ շղթայաշար[2] նորաստեղծ պալատն նոցա։ Նաևս զայլ ամենայն բարութիւնս նդին շարին էջան գլ. 8, ի նոցանէ և արար զնոսա իւր ծառայ։ Վասնայսորիկ Հրա- 4. մայեաց ասէր առՀբեայս անՀալատո՝ Որ առնէ զմեղս ծառայ է մեղաց և այլն։

Եւ այսպէս գիտելով տեառն մերոյ Յիսուսի Քրիստոսի ցյց ետ Հերձուածողաց, անՀաւատից, անբարշտոց, ստաց, իմո սուտ օրինաց, սուտ վարդապետաց և սուտ քաՀանայից, որք յամենայն ժամ ուսանին և երբէք ի գիտութիւն ճշմարտու- թեան ոչ Հասանեն և այլն։

մր.7. Ասելով տեառն մերոյ Յիսուսի թէ Հայրն և ուսուցիչն նոցա սատանայ է, և ես եկեցուք ի վերոյ գրեալ բանս մարդասպանին զոր եսպան զնախաՀայրն մեր Ադամ և արար

---

[1] Ձ. 'աչք.'

[2] Ձ Յետոյ սրբագրեալ՝ շղթայշխթայաշար.

զնոսա և զորդիս նոցա մինչև չիրկիչն մեր Քրիստոս իւր ծառայ և գերի, և պնդեաց զնոսա կապանօքն իւրովք, և այլն: Եւ այսպէս՝ մինչև ցնորաստեղծն Ադամ պաշէր զնոսա, այսինքն՝ զմարգարէս, զնահապետս, զայրս և զկանայս, զու֊ստերս և զդուստերս, զտալատացեալս և զանհալատս և զամենեսեան առ ինքն հալադէր։ Եւ այսպէս՝ գթալով Հօրն երկնաւորի՝ հածեցաւ ... ¹ զնոր Ադամ ի նդին խաբեա֊ ՂԿ կան յարբենէ։ Իսկ ... ² մարդն Յիսուս ծանեաւ զՀայրն Հմր. իւր և եկեալ աստմամբ սուրբ Հոգւոյն առ սուրբն Յոհաննէս, Հեզութեամբ և խոնարհութեամբ մկրտիլ ի նմանէ։ Եւ նդին ժամայն պասկեցաւ ի Հօրէ ամենակալէ թէ Դայ է որդի իմ սիրելի ընդ որ Հածեցայ, որպէս ի վերն գրեցաւ։ Արդ զնդին ճայն աստուածութեան լուեալ սատանայի իսկոյն աչ մեծ և երկիւղ անտանելի պատեաց զնա, լս սարսեալ դողայր անձու֊նաբար և զչարագոյն միտս իւր տարածէր այսր և անդր և ասէր։ Արդեօք զէ՞նչ լեցի ճայնս այս որ ի վերուստ Հնչեալ վասն սորա, զէ՞նչ լեցի Հոգւոյն սրբոյ գալուստն իվերայ սորա, զէ՞նչ լեցի այսքան մեծութիւն այսքան իշխանութիւն յերկինս և յերկրի, զէ՞նչ լենիցի այսքան փառք և պատիւ, զէ՞նչ լեցի արդեօք այսքան գնծութիւն և ուրախութիւն որ վասն սորա կատարեցաւ։ Զայս ամենայն տեսեալ սատանայի յյս նորա Հատաւ և սկսաւ յայնմ Հետէ զթակարդ իւր չարու֊թեան լարել պատրաստէր վասն տեառն մերոյ Յիսուսի Քրիստոսի, թէ որպիսի լարէ կամ թակարդէ զնա որսալ³, որպէս զԱդամ կամ որպէս զնահապետս և կամ որպէս զմարգարէս և զայլս ըստ կարգի։ Եւ այսպէս անկեալ մնայր ի տարակուսանաց և խոհութեան մէջ, մինչև ի ՑԵ ժամ փորձութեան։ Հմր.

---

¹ Ձ. բառ մի քերեալ թերևս ՝ստեղծել.՛

² Ձ. բառ մի քերեալ

³ Ձ. յորսալ, որպէս յուսեալ, յուսուցէչ յերկնից.

Գլուխ (Հինգ) երորդ.

Յաղագս քահանայօրեայ տեառն մերոյ Յի Քրիստոսի, որ եմուտ առ . . .¹ իւր և խօսեցաւ ընդ նմա խորհրդաբար և ընկալաւ զպատուիրանս Հօր իւրոյ, նա և յազթեաց զբելիարն գործըն իւրօք։

Որպէս Հրամայէ մեան ընդհանրական և առաքելական եկեղեցւոյն սուրբն Պօղոս առ եբրայեցիսն, ասէ ԳԼ. 3, Հմր. I. Ուստի եղբայրք սուրբք՝ երկնաւոր կոչմանն բաժանորդք, նայեցարուք ընդ Առաքեալն և ընդ Քահանայապետն խոստովանուեէ մերոյ ընդ Յիսուս Քրիստոս, որ Հաւատարիմ է արարչին իւրոյ, որպէս և Մովսէս յամենայնի տան նորա։ Ասնորոյ յոյժ Հաւատարիմ եղեալ . . .² մարդն Յիսուս առ Հօրն իւրոյ։ Ասն այսորիկ շնորհեաց նմա անուն գովելի որ ի վեր է քան զամենայն անուանս, այսինքն՝ եթէ երկնաւորաց և եթէ երկրաւորաց և եթէ սանդարամետականաց։ Նա և զամենայն ինչ Հնազանդ արար ի ներքոյ ոտից նորա, զոր սուրբն Պօղոս ասէ կայեն։ Մ'րդ ի հաճելն Հօրն, անեղէն իւրոյ սիրելւոյ՝ իսկույն Հոգին աճէ դնա ի լեառն փորձութեան և մուշանէ զայն ի խորհուրդ սուրբ Աստուածութեան։ Մ'ինչև գքառասուն տիւ և քառասուն գիշեր զմայլեցաւ տեսութեան, խոսակցութեան և պատուիրանաց Հօրն երկնաւորին, որպէս յայտէ մից աւետարանչացն սրբոց, և յորժամ գմայլումն և գլուսակցուէ եքարձ ինմանէ . . .³ իւր, յայնժամ.քաղցեալ։ Եւ տեսեալ նախանձին այնորիկ սկսաւ որսալ նախանձուեեամբ գոռողն այն զեիրկէն մեր ասելով․ եթէ որդի ես Աստուծոյ, ասա դե քարինքս այսոքիկ Հաց լինիցին, և այլն։ Մ'թեոս ԳԼ. 4, Հմր. 3։ Արդ պատասխանի (ետ) Յիսուս և ասէ գշարն այն. ով պատառող առիւծ, ով թշնամի, ով անձռոնի, ով լիրբ և ով մարդասպան դու, ընդ էր թեակալ խօսիս, ընդ թեակալ կամիս գթակարթն քո առ իս ձգել. ես ոչ եմ կարծիքդ քո դոր կարծես, ով լի ամենայն

---
¹ բառ մի քերեալ, թերևս 'արաբի՜ն.' ² բառ մի եղծեալ.
³ Նոյնպէս։ Թուի լինել 'ստեղծիչն.'

կեղծաւորութեամբ։ Պատասխանի ետ Յիսուս և ասէ. գրեալ է թէ ոչ Հացիւ կեցցէ մարդն միայն, այլ ամենայն բանիւ որ ելանէ իբերանոյ աստուծոյ։ Ահա յայտնեցաւ ճշմարտապէս միտ բանին, թէ տէրն մեր Յիսուս զմայլմամբ, խօսակցու֊ թեամբ և պատիւրանատութեամբ և փառք ամօւթեամբ ոչ քաղցեալ, մինչև ի լնանիլն ալուրցն¹ այնոցիկ։ Իսկ արդ՝ տեսեալ չարին այն, թէ ոչ խաբեցաւ որպէս չելաւ և զՂգամ միով բանիւ փրկիչն մեր Քրիստոս, դարձեալ առեալ ածէ զնա սատանայ ի քաղաքն սուրբ և կացուցանէ զնա ի վերայ աշտարակի տաճարին և ասէ ցնա. Արդ զքեզ աստի ի վայր, զի գրեալ է թէ Հրեշտակաց իւրոց պատուիրեալ է վասն քո և ի վերայ ձեռաց բարձցեն զքեզ, զի մի երբէք Հարցես զքարի զոտն քո։ Ասէ ցնա դարձեալ Յիսուս. գրեալ է թէ ոչ փորձեսցես զտէր աստուած քո։ Դարձեալ առեալ ածէ զնա սատանայ ի լեառն մի բարձր յոյժ, և եցույց նմա զամենայն թագաւորութիւնս աշխարհի և զփառս նոցա։ Եւ ասէ ցնա. զայս ամենայն քեզ տաց, եթէ անկեալ երկիր պագցես ինձ։ Յայնժամ ասէ ցնա Յիսուս. երթ յետս իմ սատանայ. զի գրեալ է տեառն աստուծոյ քում երկիր պա֊ գցես և զնա միայն պաշտեսցես։ Նա ես սուրբն Ղուկաս վասն չարին այն յար(ա)բերէ ասելով. գլ. 4, Հմր. 13. Վա֊ տարեալ զամենայն փորձութիւն սատանայի ի բաց եկաց ի նմանէ առ ժամանակ մի։

Գլուխ Վեցերորդ.

Յաղագս խաբելէ չարին այն, զոր յետ փորձութեան տեառն մերոյ Յիսուսի Քրիստոսի սկսեալ մինչև ցկրկնակի գա֊ լուստ տեառն մերոյ և փրկչին Յիսուսի Քրիստոսի առնէ։

Զոր ասէ մասն եկեղեցւյն սբ Ղուկաս գլ. 4, Հմր. 13. Եւ կատարեալ զամենայն փորձութիւնն սատանայի ի բաց եկաց ի նմանէ առ ժամանակ մի։

Արդ՝ յետ փորձութեան տեառն մերոյ Յիսուսի լցաւ մեծաւ բարկութեամբ ոստին² այն սատանայ և սկսաւ յայնմ օրէ

---

¹ Ձ. յալուրցն. ² Ձ. յոստին.

առնուլ զչնաբեալ գործիոն իւր չարութեան և Հետևիլ զկնի աշակերտացս տեառն մերոյ Յիսուսի Քրիստոսի և ամենայն Հալածացելոց նորա, որպէս յայտ է ի բանս սրբոյ Լեւտարա֊
նին, որ վասն Յուդայի մատնչին ասէ. Յոհնէս. ԳԼ. 13,
Հմր. 27. Եւ յետ պատառոյն ապա եմուտ ի նա սատանայ։
Արդ՝ յետ վճարելոյն նոյն սատանայի զգործս իւր չարութեան
ի Յուդայ,— և եառ դվկղձան նորին, և արագ զնա ծառայ
իւր, — իսկ և իսկ մտեալ ի քաՀանայս և ի քաՀանայապե֊
տոսն[1] Հրէից և զկնի նոցին չՀանդուրժեալ չարին այն եմուտ
ի սիրտ միոյ աղքան և տայր խոսել զՊետրոս կրկին անգամ
վասն գլորեցուցանելոյ և գաՀալէժ առնելոյ զնա։ Իսա և ս ի
յայլ ումանս։ Ի նոյն ժամոյն Հաստատեաց զնոսա, վասն
պետրոսի առ ինքն դրախել։ Իսկ միջնորդ և բարեխօսն մեր
Յիսուս Քրիստոս նախապէս իմացեալ[2] զվիորձութիւն չարին,
որ վասն պետրոսի պաՀեալ էր, ուստի տեր մեր սկսաւ զալ֊
եւոիս մեծ տալ Պետրոսի և ասէ. Ղուկաս ԳԼ. 22, Հմր. 31.
Եւ ասէ տէր. Սիմօն, Սիմօն, աՀա սատանայ խնդրեաց խար֊
բալել զձեզ իբրև զցորեան, այլ ես աղաչեցի վասն քո, զի մի
պակասեսցին Հալատք քո, զի դու երբեմն դարձցիս և Հաստա֊
տեսցես զեղբայրս քո։

Եւ մեք պարտեմք այժմ այս սուրբ և պատուական աղօթս
ասել յամենայն ժամ...[3] ընդդեմ տեառն մերոյ Յիսուսի Քր
իստոսի, զի քաղցրասցի ի մեզ և բարեխոս լիցի վասն մեր մեղաւ
որացս, առ ի աղատել զմեզ յամենայնից փորձանաց չարեաց
ամէն

Սուրբ Յիսուս, Սուրբ Տէր Քրիստոս, Սուրբ Որդի Ա֊
տուծոյ, վասն մեր բարեխոսեա։

Էր 1.   Եւ ապա ասա Հայր մեր և այլն։

Եւ ես տեսեալ սատանայի, թէ ոչինչ օգուտ գործք իւր
Լ. 8,   չարութեան, այլ ես քան վես խստացոյց զչարութիւն իւր
4.   ի վերայ Հալածացելոց և աշակերտաց տեառն մերոյ
Յիսուսի Քրիստոսի, որպէս յայտ է առաքեալը փրկչին
մերոյ. ի Յոհ. ԳԼ. 6, Հմր 67։

---

[1] Ձ. քաՀանայապետոսն.   [2] Ձ. յիմացեալ.
[3] բառ մի եղծեալ.

Գլուխ եօթներորդ.

Յաղագս Հակառակի Հօր Աստուծոյ
Ոա ես ասացուք.

Յայսմանէ բազումք յաշակերտաց նորա չոգան յետս և ոչ ևս շրջէին ընդ նմա։

Արդ՝ վերս գրեալ գազանն այն սպառնայր մեծաւ բարկութեամբ ի վերայ աշակերտացն տեառն մերոյ, վասն զի ասացեալն իւր ոչ անկաւ ի չարագոյն տրամախոյութեան իւրում, որպէս ի վերն վկայեաց սուրբն Ղուկաս նոյն չարին ասելով. Թէ ի բաց եկաց ի նմանէ առ ժամանակ մի։ Որգոն զի առ ժամանակս այս նոյն որդի կորստեան ի ժամ փորձութեան տեառն ի միտս իւր տրամադրեալ պաշտէր առ ինքն, զի զչարագոյն փափակն իւր ի սիրտս և ի լսելիս իւրոյ հածելեցին սերմանէ մինչև չկտարած աշխարհի։ Ասսասյորիկ միշ-նորդ և բարեխօսն մեր միշտ և հանապազ խրատէ զմեզ ասելով. Ղուկ. ԳԼ. 22, Համր. 40. Եւ իբրև էջաս ի տեղին ասէ ցնոսա. յաղօթս կացէք չմտանել ի փորձութիւն։ Այսպէս և տեր մեր գիտելով զխորհուրդս չարին այնորիկ, վասնորդյ պատու-իրելով պատուիրեաց մեզ արթուն կալ և աղօթս[1] առնել։ Եւ սուրբ ընդհանրականի և առաքելականի եկեղեցյս մայն՝ սուրբն Պետրոս, Առաջներորդ Կաթուղիկ. աս. ԳԼ. 5, Համր. 8, Արթուն լերուք և հսկեցէք, զի ոսոխն ձեր սատանայ իբրև գառիւծ գոչէ, շրջի և խնդրէ թէ զո՞ կլանից։ Ի ստ այսմ սարսի և մեզ պարտ է արթուն լինիլ և ո՛չ ի քուն մեղաց։ Որ ոմանք ծանրացեալք մեղօք հետևեցան նոյն հակառակին, որպէս յայտ է ի պատմութիւնս և ի չարաբողութիւնս իւրեանց, զոր յայտնեցուք ըստ կարողութեամբ սուրբ Հոգւոյն։

---

[1] Ձ. յարթուն, յաղօթս.

Գլուխ Ութերորդ.

Յաղագս սատանայի. Թէ որով կերպարանաւ երեւեցաւ նոցա, որք խաբեցան և եղեն նորա ծառայ, յայտնեցուցէք:

|ա- | 'Նախ' դրուՃք դժոխոցն այն կերպարանեցաւ ի կերպ օձի,
|լեց. | երկրորդ՝ ի կերպս ագռաւոյ, երրորդ՝ ի կերպ Հորդդյ,
|ևնչ, | չորրորդ՝ իկերպս գաղանաց, Հինգերորդ՝ ի կերպս լուսոյ,
| | վեցերորդ՝ ի կանանց, եօթներորդ՝ ի կերպս մարդկանց,
|ւոր | ութերորդ՝ ի կերպս կռօնաւորաց, իններորդ՝ ի կերպս վար-
|28 | ժապետաց, Ժերորդ՝ ի կերպս Հրաբեղոց, Ժաներորդ՝ եպիս-
|12. | կոպոսաց, Ժք երորդ[1] ի կերպս Ճգնաւորաց: Եւ այլ ամենայն

կերպս մտանէ և կերպարանի և նոյն կերպարանօք զփրկելին և զՃաձդյուն իւր կնքեալ Լդրոշմեալ պաՀէ առ ինքն մինչև ի կատարածի: Օ՜ի զէնքն և զլսւրսն զամենեսեանն չարաչար պատժէ, որ ասէ թէ որբ նոցա ո՛չ մեռանի և Հուրք նոցա ո՛չ շիջանի: Որ և տեր ած ամենակարող միշնորդութեամբ և բարեխոսութեամբ որդւոյն իւր սիրելւոյն փրկեալ ազատեսցէ զամենայն ուղղադաւանս ի նոյն փորձութևէ, ամէն.

Եւ աստ պարտեմք ասել զայս աղօթս
Ընդդէմ Քրիստոսի:

Ո՜վքաղցրագունեղ տէր իմ Յիսուս Քրիստոս, երկիր պագա- նեմք, աղերսեմք, Հայցեմք և խնդրեմք զքո ամենազօր տէ- րութիւնդ, որ կաս ընդ աջմէ Հօր քո ... [2], միշնորդեա և բարեխոսեա վասն մեր մեղաւորացս յայժմ և ի ժամու մա- Հուան մերում, ամէն:

---

[1] Ձ. Հանապազ 'երրորդ' փոխանակ 'երորդ' ի.
[2] բառ մի քերեալը թուի լինել 'արարչի.'

Գլուխ Թ.

Յաղագս կերպարանողին ասացուք։

Արդ ուսուցիչ և հայրն Հերձուածողաց և Հերետիկոսացս ի բազում կերպարանս կերպարանի. Բայց մեք միայն զերկոտասանն ասացաք. զի մի երկարութիւն լցցի ձեզ սիրելեացդ։ ուստի կերպարանելն շարին այս էր. զի նոյն կերպարանօքն զնոսա դիւրաւ առ ինքն ծառայեցուցանէ։ Առն այս պատճառի նախ լինի ի կերպ օձի, զի օձն էր խորագէտ, երկրորդ՝ ի կերպ ագռաւուց, զի ագռաւն սիրողդ զիշաց. երրորդ՝ ի կերպս հօրդուց. զի հօրդն էր սիրելէ Տէս և պիտանի մարդկանց, չորրորդ՝ ի կերպս գազանաց, զի լաք գազանք պատառողք են ամենայն պատկերաց։ Հինգերորդ՝ գրո ի կերպս լուսոյ. զի լոյսն մերժող է խաւարի, վեցերորդ՝ ի կերպս աղջկանց և կանանց. զի և նոքա զարդարօղք են ինքեանց վասն որսալոյ զմարդիկս. եօթերորդ՝ ի կերպս առանց զի նոքա փութով Հաւանին ասացելոց։ Ութերորդ՝ ի կերպս Տէս կրօնաւորաց. զի նոքա զկեղծաբարոյ վարս ունին, իններորդ՝ Առ ի կերպս վարժապետաց, զի նոքա են ուսուցիչք ամենեցուն։ Թա Ժներորդ ի կերպս առաքելոց, զի նոքա են բժիշկ Հոգւոց աց. և մարմնոց։ Մետասաներորդ՝ ի կերպս եպիսկոպոսաց և կաթու տու ղիկոսաց։ Երկոտասաներորդ Ի նոքա Հպարդ և բարձրամիտ են, և մանաւանդ աշ վախառօղք իշխանութեան տեառն մերոյ Յիսուսի Քրիստոսի, Վէ 2 նա լես են տնօրինօղք սուտ օրինաց, և լես են ագահ և սուտ Հմր. իրաց Հանձարօղք. իսկ արդ կերպարանին ի կերպս ճգնաւ֊ որաց, զի նոքա Հանապազ զբանջարս և զխոտեղէնս սիրեն, ի Հ֊ նաև զ․․․[1] և զծօմապաՀս պաՀեն, քանզի և կերակուրք վար նոցա Հանապաղ ի դիմային տեղիս բուսանի։ վասն այսորիկ և բնակութիւնք նոցա անդր լինի. քանզի յոյժ սիրեն զնա.

---

[1] և.

Գլուխ Ժեւրորդ.

Յաղագս վկայութեանց սրբոց Առաքելոց և արտադրյ եղեալ գրեանց թէ է ճշմարիտ կերպարանիւն¹ ... չարին։

Նախ սուրբն Պօղոս առ. երկրորդ կորնթացին յայտնէ զկերպս կերպարանիւն նոյն չարին ասելով. գլ. 11, Հմր. 12, Օր առնեմն և արարից, զի Հատից զպատճառս այնոցիկ, որք զպատճառումն կամիցին, զի որով պարծին և նոքա իբր և զմեզ գտանիցին։ Օր այնպիսիքն են սուտ առաքեալք, մշակք նենգաւորք, կերպարանին ի կերպարանս առաքելոցն Քրիստոսի, և չեն ինչ զարմանք, քանզի և ինքն Սատանայ կերպարանի ի Հրեշտակ լուսոյ և ոչինչ է մեծ, թէ և պաշտօնեայք նորա կերպարանին իբրև պաշտօնեայք արդարութեան, որոց կատարածն եղիցի ըստ գործոց իւրեանց։ Այլ . ²

որպէս և տէրն մեր Յիսուս Քրիստոս Հրամայեաց ընտրեալ աշակերտացն իւրոց. ասէ թէ երթայք յաշխարհ ամենայն և քարոզեցէք զաւետարանն արքայութեան ամենայն արարածոց, որ Հաւատասցէ մկրտեսցի կեցցէ, և որ ոչն Հաւատասցէ դատապարտեսցի, և այլն։ Տեսայք. ով կույք. թէ որպէս տէրն մեր զառնեէն ձեր սուտ և ունայն Հաւատք, և զձեզ ուրացող իսկ ասէ և որդի սատանայի կոչէ, որպէս ի վեր անդր գրեցաւ։ Արդ այժմ իմանայք դուք բարեպէս զսուտ Հայրն ձեր. իմանայք արդեօք զՀոգին ձեր, իմանայք ես դաստուածն ձեր, նա ես իմանայք զօսուցիչն ձեր, և ես իմացայք զվիային, զկաթուղիկոսն և դատաշնորդն ձեր, և իմացայք զդերայքրիստոն ձեր և այլն։ Օր միջնորդ և բարեխօսն մեր, կեանք և ապաւէն մեր ասէ յայտնապէս եւ

---
¹ բառ մի քերեալ.
² Ըստանոր պակասին երեք 30ԴԻ–53ԴԻ, այնէ թերթք 12 (երեք կամ էջ 24). Այս թուի ինձ լինել մասն ժԴ գլխոյ, պակասին ուրեմն մասն Ժ̄ գլխոյ, այլ և գլուխք ժա. ժբ և ժգ, նսև առաջին մասն ժդին.

որ սուտ խօսի յիւրոց անտի խօսի. և Հայրն նորա սատանայ
է։ Այսպէս տեսանելով տեառն մերոյ Յիսուսի և սրբոյ
ընդհանրական և առաքելական եկեղեցդյն ասեն, որպէս ի վերն
գրեցաք, և այժմ դարձեալ գրեմք ի Տիմոթէոս Կռաշնեբորդ
գլ. 4, Հմր. 1. Այլ յայտնապէս սուրբ Հոգին ասէ, թէ
ի ժամանակս յետինս քակտեսցին ումանք ի Հաւատոց և այլն։
Եւ դարձեալ ի միուս գիրս իւրեանց վասն ձեր կուրացելոցն
ասէ եւս եղեցին անձնասէրք, Հպարտք, ամբարտաւանք եւս
ամբարհաւաճք։ Նա եւս Հալանիք գործող ձերոց և ուրացեալ էք զսուրբ գործս տեառն մերոյ յիսուսի և սրբազան
առաքելոցն և էք Հեռւոյ Հօրն ձերոյ չարին, զոր եւ
ձեզ զօրէն իւր, այսինքն զանՀասատ մրտելլ զպատկերս
պաշտել, զարծաթ և գոսկի ի ձեռ պատկերի . . .¹ առնել
և երկիրպագանել, զմեդա արանց և կանանց քննել, իմանալ
և թողութիւն շնորՀել, զոր տէրն մեր Հրամայէ ասելով.
թէ, Ով կարէ թողուլ զմեդա, եթէ ոչ մի աստուած։ և
զայլ ամենայն քննեցէք զեանս սոցա և տայք զփառ Հօրն
երկնաւորի և որդւոյն միածնի։

Գլուխ ԺԵ երորդ

Յաղագս մկրտութեան տեառն մերոյ յիսուսի քրիստոսի և
ընտրեալ սրբազան աշակերտացն նորին, թէ որպէս
մկրտեին։

Իբրև գիտաց յիսուս եթէ լուան փարիսեցիքն եթէ յիսուս
բազում աշակերտս առնէ և մկրտէ քան զյոՀաննէս. քանզի
ոչ եթէ . . . . .²

[Գլուխ ԺԶ երորդ]

. . . ցս կրեցեն, ոչ ասեմ ձեզ, այլ եթէ ոչ ապաշխարեցէք,
նոյնպէս կորնչեցէք։

Արդ՝ տէրն մեր յիսուս քրիստոս երիս անձառելի խորՀրդոցս
այսցիկ այսպէս Հարկաւոր վճառաբանէ ասելով առ ունկնդ-

---

¹ Իառ մի կամ երկու քերեալ.
² Ստանօր թերթք անկեալ երկու (երես 56–59)։ պակասի
մեծագոյն մասն ԺԵ գլխոյն և տող ինչ ի ԺԶ-էն.

ռողս։ նախ՝ դապաշխարանս հարկիլ վճռէ, որպէս զսուրբն
ԳԼ. 3, յոհաննէս որ ի վերն ասացաւ. երկրորդ՝ զսուրբ մկրտութիւն
շնորհէ մեզ, որպէս նիկոդիմոսի ասէ. Պատասխանի ետ
յիսուս և ասէ ցնոսա Ամէն, ամէն, ասեմ քեզ, եթէ ոք ոչ
ծնցի վերստին, ոչ կարէ տեսանել զարքայութիւն աստուծոյ։
և երրորդ՝ վասն սուրբ պատուական մարմնոյ և արեանն
խըրոյ փրկիչն պատուիրէ յատուկ առնել, որպէս յայտ է ի
յոհան ԳԼ. 6, համր. 54. Ասէ ցնոսա յիսուս. Ամէն, ամէն
ասեմ ձեզ, եթէ ոչ կերիջէք զմարմին որդւոյ մարդոյ և
արբէք զարիւն նորա, ոչ ունիք կեանս յանձինս։ Սա ես
դարձեալ ի նոյն գլուխ ասէ բաժանաբար և ոչ միաւորեալ
ի համարն 56. Որ մարմին իմ ճշմարիտ կերակուր է և
արիւն իմ ճշմարիտ ըմպելի է։ Տեսէք բարեպէս և լաւ
քննեցէք զսուրբ գիրսն, որ վասն հալատացելոց հարկ շնորհէ
զապաշխարութիւն, զմկրտութիւն և սուրբ մարմին և արիւն
իւր, և դուռն փրկութեան ասէ վասն հալատացելոց և ոչ
անհալատից, որք[1] . . . . զի ամենին ոչ գիտեն զաստուած
և ոչ ճառայեն զյիսուս քրիստոս և զսուրբ եկեղեցին քրիստոսի, այսինքն զսուրբ առաքեալս։ Սա ես ոչ գիտեն
զութբախութիւն և զզորմութիւն, զշայրն և կամ զմայրն
իւրեանց, և են իբրև զգլինձ որք հնչեն և իբրև զձնձղայս
որք ղողանշեն, և այլն։ Արդեօք այսպիսեաց զինչ է մեզ
պարտ առնել ըստ օրինի։ Այլ յորժամ ծնանիցեն ի մարգն
իւրեանց, յայնժամ հարկ է ընտրելոցն յետ եօթն օրեալ
գնալ ի տուն ծնիցելոցն յալուր ութերորդի և յուսադրել
զծնօղս նոցա մեծալ սիրով և տալ նոցա զզարի ճոգևոր
խրատս, զի նոքա կրթեցեն զծնեալս իւրեանց ի յաստուած
պաշտութեն, ի հալատ, ի յոյս, ի սէր և այլ ամենայն բարեգործութիւնս, որպէս սուրբ պողոս առ տիմոթէոս առաջնորդ
գրէ, ԳԼ. 4, համր. 7 ասելով այսպէս. Այլ ի պեղծ բանից
[2] և յառասպելեաց պառաւանց հրաժարեցիր. բայց կրթեա՛
զանձն քո յաստուածպաշտութիւն. զի մարմնոյ կրթութիւն

---

[1] բառ մի կամ երկու քերեալ.
[2] բառք երկու կամ երեք քերեալ.

առ սակաւ ինչ օգտակար է, իսկ աստուածպաշտութիւն առ ամենայն ինչ օգտակարէ, և զաւետիս կենաց ունի զարդիս և զճանդերձելոցն։ Այսպէս ըստ կանոնաց սրբոց առաքելոցն ճարկէ նոցին ծնողաց միշտ և ճանապազ զալակունս իւրեանց յուսումն տալ տղայոց որպէս զկաթն, որք ոչ խնայեն ամենևին որպէս և սուրբն պօղոս առ առաջի կոր. ԳԼ 3, Հմր. 1, ասէ. Եւ ես, եղբայրք, ոչ կարացի խօսիլ ընդ ձեզ իբրև ընդ Հոգևորս, այլ իբրև ընդ մարմնաւորս, իբրև տղայոց ի քրիստոս զկաթն զամբեցի ձեզ և ոչ զկերակուր, զի ոչ ևս կարէիք, նա և արդ ոչ կարէք, քանզի դեռ մարմնաւոր էք։ Արդ՝ այսպէս և մեզ և ծնողաց նոցա պարդ է նախ զանուանադրութիւն առնել երեխային և ապայ յետ ժամանակի ինչ տամք զնոսա ի գործս բարիս յուսանիլ . . . .¹ յայնժամ արու իցէ, և եթէ էգ իցէ, զի աշա . . . .² մկրտեցի, ուսաք զի արուն յուշ ճանաչէ զվկզենական ցանկութիւն իւր, իսկ աղջիկն փութով զոր յայտէ խաբելն եւայի և ադամայ. զի նախ եւայ տարբացեալ և ապա զմինն ադամայ զարթոյց։ Այսպէս և պարտ է մեզ զնոսա ըստ ժամանակի նոցա. զանէծս նոցին որ ի Հօրէ ընկալան, իսկ այժմ յիսուսիւ քրիստոսիւ ի ծայրագոյն օրհնութիւնս վերընծայեմք։ Այսպէս այսօրիկ սուրբն յոճաննէս, մինորդ և բարեխօսն մեր յիսուս քրիստոս և սրբազան առաքեալքն իւր նախ զճալատս յուցանէին, յապաշխարանս բերէին և ապայ զմկրտութիւն շնորՀէին, որպէս յայտ է ի գործս վիրկէին մերոյ յիսուսի, զի նախ Հարցանէր կուրաց, կաղաց, գօսացելոց, դիւաՀարաց և մանաւանդ տերանց մեռելոց զճալատս և ասէր զնոսա, Հաւատա՞յք եթէ կարողեմ առնել ձեզ զայդ։ Իսկ նոցա ձայնքը մեծաւ աղաղակէին և ասէին՝ այո՛, տէր, կարող ես, և երկիրպագանէին նմա և բժշկեալ լինէին. Ես մեռեալք նոցա յարուցեալ լինէին։ Այսպէս և մեզ Հարկ է առնել զմկրտութիւն. ըստ տեառն մերոյ կատարել զի նոքա Հաւատով խնորեսցեն ի մէնջ և ապայ մէք տամք նոցա զմկրտութիւն

Նախ պար անու դրու առնէ որպ զկա

վն ՈՅՆ Հմր. ՈՅՆ Հմր. Մր ԳԼ. 2 Հմր.

---

¹ կէս տող բերեալ։
² բառք երկու եղծեալ (բերեալ)։

և զկատարեալ օրՀնութիւն։ Օոր օրինակ եթէ ոք կալեալ լիցի ի գողաց կամ յաւազակաց ի ծայր և ի ծերպս լերանց և կամ կապեալ են զձեռս և զոտս նորա պնդագոյն կապանօք և արկեալ են զնա ի ձորակ ինչ, արդեօք պա՞րտ է նմա աշխատել զի ինքն զինքն արձակեցէ, ապա թէ ո՞չ։ Իսկ նոցա պատասխանի տուեալ ասեն, թէ Հարկ է նմա ջանալ և աշխատել, մինչ զի զանձն իւր ապրեցուսցէ, զի մի գուցէ թէ գազանաց կերակուր լիցի։ Նյսպէս վճիռն տեառն, զոր Հրամայեաց ի բնաբանս մեր վասն ապաշխարութեան։ Օայս օրինակն Նախագուշակէ, եթէ որք ոչ Հաւատասցէ, ապաշխա- րեսցէ, ոչ կարէ մկրտիլ և արդարանալ, մաքրիլ ի մեղաց և ազատիլ ի կապանաց սատանայէ։ Որպէս միշնորդ և բարեխօսն մեր յիսուս քրիստոս Հրամայեաց զառակս զայս ասելով վասն ապաշխարողաց և անապաշխարողացն, Լուկաս ԳԼ. 14¹, Հմբ. 6. . . . .² Թզենի մի էր ուրումն տնկեալ յայգւոշ իւրում։ և եկն խնդրել զպտուղ ի թզենւոշդ. և ոչ եգիտ³։ Ա՛րդ կորեա՛մ զդա, ընդէ՞ր և զերկիրդ խաբանէ. Նա պատասխանի ետ և ասէ։ Տէ՛ր, թո՛ղ զդա յայս ամ ևս. մինչև շուրշ զդովաւ բրեցից և արկից աղբ. խերևս արասցէ զպտուղ ապաշխարութեան. Թէ ոչ՝ յամէ ևս Հատցես զդա։ Այլայժմ Հարկ է ձեզ ընթերցողացդ զի մեծաւ քննութեամբ իմանալ զառակս տեառն մերոյ յիսուսի քրիստոսի, որ նախ զապաշխարանս ասէ, իսկ միշապէս կամ անմիշապէս զառակն շնորՀէ լսողաց և առողաց։ Ուստի այժմ յայտնեցաւ ճանա- պարՀ և ճշմարտութիւն և կեանք մեր յիսուս քրիստոս որդի Հօրն երկնաւորի, եթէ որք ոչ ունիցեն զՀաւատս, զապա- շխարութիւնս, զյոյս և զսէր, ո՛չ կարեն մկրտիլ և ո՛չ կարեն մերձենալ ի սուրբ մարմին և արիւն որդւոյն աստուծոյ. Նա ևս ոչ կարեն մտանել յարքայութիւն աստուծոյ, որպէս ի վերև առ երիս խորՀուրդս ինքն իսկ անսղալ վկայեաց, թէ ո՛չ

---

¹ ընթերցչեր '13.'   ² տող մի եղծեալ.

³ 'ի բնաբանէ աւետարանաց առնեմք։ ասէցայդեղորձն. Ա՛Հա երեք ամք են՝ յորմէ Հետէ գամ խնդրել պտուղ 'ի թզենւոշդ՝ և ո՛. դտաննմ.

կարեն մռանել ի ծոց իւր սուրբ, նա եւ ոչ կարասցեն Հաղդ բղել ի փառս Հօրն իւրոյ երկնաւորի իւրոյ սիրելոյ[1]։

Գլուխ ԺԷ.

Յաղագս մկրտութեան.

Արդ՝ միշնորդ և բարեխօսն մեր յիսուս քրիստոս ասէ զառաքս չայս ի վերայ Հաւատացելոց և անՀաւատից։ քանզի նմանեցաւ արքայութիւն աստուծոյ տան կուսանաց, որոց փեսայ առեալ զլապտերս իւրեանց ելին ընդառաջ փեսային և Հարսին. Հինգն ի նոցանէ յիմարք էին և Հինգն իմաստունք։ Յիմարքն առին զլապտերս իւրեանց . . . .[2] Հարս տութեամբ ի կողմանս կողմանս, զոր տէր աստուած սուրբ միշնորդութեամբ և բարեխօսութեամբ որդւոյն իւր միածնին եկե պաՀեցէ զնոսա ի փորձութենէ Հօրն ձերոյ և ընդ սուրբ ընդՀ իմաստուն կուսանս դասեցէ։ Ուստի զի սորա ճանաչելով րակ մածին ի սուրբ և ի պատուական բանի քում և ամենեին ոչ Պղա. վրիպեցան ի քէն ամենասուրբ աւանդութենէ զոր շնորՀեցեր Հմր. անարատ որդւոյդ քո միածնիդ, որք ի ժամանակի կատարե-յեկ լութեան զպաշխարօղս և զՀաւատացեալս մկրտեն յանուն Սա յիսուսի քրիստոսի որդւոյդ քում սիրելոյ։ Նա եւ լեց ԳԷ.[2] զնոսա Հոգւովդ քով սրբով և զօրացո՛ զՀոգիս և զմարմինս Հմր. նոցա։ Ամեն զի որդեղ քո ճշմարիտ խոստացաւ մեզ ասելով. Որ Հաւատասցէ մկրտեսցի կեցցէ, և որ ոչն Հաւա տասցէ դատապարտեսցի։

Յաղագս անուանադրութեան երեխային.

Պարտեմք զկնի ծննդեան է օրեայ գնալ ի տուն ծնիցելոյն աշուլ ութերորդի. և սկսանիմք ասել զաղօթս սուրբ տեառն մերոյ յիսուսի զՏայր մեռն։

Եւ ապա զկնի Հայր մեռն ընտրեալն և ամենայն ժողո-

---

[1] տողս այս եղծեալ և վերստին գրեալ.
[2] Աստ թերթ մի անկեալ է (երես 66–67).

վուրդն միաբերան ասեն դաղօթս զայս ի վերայ երեխային Հաւատով՝ այսպէս.

Հայր տեառն մերոյ յիսուսի քրիստոսի աղաչեմք և խնդրեմք ի քէն պահեա՛ զերեխայս զայս ի չարէ և դէր զաչ քո սուրբ ի վերայ երեխային, և պահեա՛ զսա ամենայն փորձութենէ աշխարհի․

Ո՛չ տուր սմա կեանս ընդ կամաց քոց, զի անցուսցէ զժամանակս իւր տղայութեան և եղեցի քեզ որդյդ և սուրբ Հոգւոյդ Հաճելի. և Հասոյ զսա ի սուրբ մկրտութիւն. և կոչեա՛ զսա ընդ Հովհաննու թեւոց որդյդ քում սիրելւոյ։ Ես օրՀնեմ, տէր իմ և աստուած, զերեխայս միչնորդութեամբ յիսուսի, որդւոյդ քո սիրելւոյ. սրբեա՛յ զաղօս մարմնոյ սորա. և որ ըստ օրէ զարթացդ զսա շնորՀօքն քո, և ած զսա ի չափի ժամանակի սուրբ մկրտութեան, յայժմ և միշտ և յաւիտեանս յաւիտենից․ Ա՛մէն․

Եւ ապա ընթերձցէր զեանս սրբոյն Պօղոսի Կորն. առաչի ԳԼ 13, Հմր. 11.

Ի՛նչ տղայն եէ իբրե զաղայ խօսէի, իբրե զաղայ խորՀէի, իբրե զաղայ Համարեի, այլ յորժամ եղէ այր կատարեալ՝ զտղայութեանն ’ի բաց խափանեցի։ Ա՛յժմ տեսանեմք իբրե ընդ Հայելի օրինակաւ, այլ յայնժամ դեմ յանդիման. այժմ խելամուտ եմ փոքր ’ի շատէ, այլ յայնժամ գիտացից՝ որպէս և նայն ծանեաւ զիս։ Ի՛այց արդ՝ մեան Հաւատք՝ յոյս՝ սէր, որպէս երեքեան. և մեծ քան զսոսա սէր է։

Եւ յետ ընթեռնլյն պօղոսի պարտ է ընտրելյն Հարցանել զանուն երեխային. թէ զինչ կամիք կոչել զանուն երեխային այս ըստ օրինի և ո՛չ առասպել։

Եւ ապա ընթեռնու զսուրբ աւետարանն, Լուկոս ԳԼ 2, Հմր. 21.

Եւ իբրե լցան աւուրք ութն թլիատել զնա և կոչեցաւ անուն նորա յիսուս՝ որ կոչեցեան էր ’ի Հրեշտակէն մինչ և յղացեալ էր զնա յորովայնի

փառք քեզ փառաց թագաւոր, զի այժմի արարեր

զերեխայս այս անուանադրութեան։ Աղաչեմք զբոյ խնամա֊
կալ ծայրութիւնդ, պահեա զսա մինչ ի սուրբ ծնունդ
աւազանին, զի օրհնեսցուք զբեզդ զորդիդ եւ զսուրբ հոգիդ,
յայժմ եւ յաւէտ եւ յաւիտեանս, ամէն։

Ասա՛ զՀայր մեր եւ երբ ի տուն քո։
Աստուած շնորհաւոր պատուղ առնէ։

Խրատ վասն մկրտողաց, թէ զորպիսին պարտէ նոցա մկրտել։

Գլուխ Ժբ․

Արդ՝ որպէս տէրն Հրամայեաց ի կանոնս իւր սուրբ ձեզ
այնպէս պարտիք զեկեղցւն առ մեզ մկրտել. եւ սուրբն
Յոհաննէս զապաշխարանս ցուցանէր եկեղցւն առ ինքն,
եւ կամ որպէս սուրբ ընդհանրական եւ առաքելական
կաթուղիկէ եկեղեցին ուսեալ ի տեառնէ մերմէ յիսուսէ
քրիստոսէ առնէին։

Այսպէս եւ ձեզ սոցին նման առնել հարկ է, որպէս ի վեր
անդր խոսեցաք. Ո ի նախ ուսուցանէին, երկրորդ՝ զշատոս
խնդրէին, երրորդ՝ յապաշխարանս մուծանէին, եւ ապա զսուրբ
մկրտութիւն շնորհէին այնոցիկ, որք էին կատարեալ եւ մա֊
նաւանդ ճանաչէին զմեղս զսեփական։ Պարտեալ ձեզ
ընդրեյոցդ պարտ է զգուշանալ մեծաւ զգուշութեամբ
առնուլ նախ քան զմկրտութիւն զուսումն եւ զկրթութիւն,
եթէ զմարմնաւոր եւ եթէ զհոգեկան, զոր սուրբն պօղոս
ասէ. կրթեա՛մ զանձն քո յաստուածպաշտութիւն։ Այսպէս
եւ ձեզ հարկ է զեկեղցւն ի հաւատ, ի կույս, ի սեր եւ յապա֊
շխարութիւն տալ թարց դանդախանօք, կրթել ծայրագույն
փորձութեամբ, զի ով ոք իցէ, զի մի գուցէ թէ խաբեբայ
իցէ կամ կեղծաւոր եւ կամ կախարդ որպէս զսիմոն. տես
ի գործս, գլ. 8, համր. 13։

Այլ և ինքն սիմօն Հալատաց և մլրտեալ կանխեբ առ փիլիպպոս կեղծաւորութեամբ և խաբէութեամբ, որպէս զի առցէ զիշխանութիւն Հոգւոյն սրբոյ խաբէութեամբ. այնպէս և ձեզ սիրելեացդ, Հարկ է քննել զեկեալսդ, այսինքն զդոցին, զկեղծաւորս, որք զան առ ձեզ Հանդերձնիք ոչխարաց. որպէս տեսէն մեր յիսուս քրիստոս ասէ. ուստի զի այնպիսիք որպէս թէ կամիցեն զնքբեանս ձեզ սուրբ յուցանել վասն առնելոյ շաբբութիւն և զմարգարիտ ի ձեռն և կոխան արասցեն զնոսա. որպէս և սուրբն պօղոս առ Հռովմայեցին պատուիրէ ասելով, գլ. 16, Հմր. 18: .Օի այսպիսիք տեառն մերոյ յիսուսի քրիստոսի ոչ ծառայեն, այլ իւրեանց որովայնին. և քաղցրաբանութեամբ և օրՀնութեամբ պատրեն զիրաս անմեղաց. եթէ քաՀանայք, եթէ վարդապետք, եթէ սարկաւագունք, եթէ արք և եթէ կանայք, ոչ է պարտ զնոսա վաղվաղակի մլրտել և Հաղորդել մինչև զկատարեալ փորձութիւնս տալ:

Յաղագս մլրտելոցն, թէ որպէս պարտ է նոցա գալ ի սուրբ մլրտութիւն և թէ զինչ է նոցա Հարկ կամ զինչ է նոցա պատուղ յուցման, զի տեսցուք և Հալատասցուք նոցա, որպէս տէրն մեր կանօնէ զմեզ ասելով թէ ի պողոյ նոցա ծանիչիք զնոսա:

Գլուխ ԺԹ.

Մկրտելոցն պարտ և պատշաճէ ունիլ զղառն արտասուս որպէս զպետրոսն, որպէս զկոդոսն, որպէս զկրունիկ մարիամ և կամ որպէս զզքանչ սիմոնի և զայլս ստցին նման. զի սթք մեծալ զղշմամբ ընկալան զիստա և զպատիւս յիսուսէ քրիստոսէ վերկչէն մերմէ, որպէս յայտէ ի սուրբ աւետարանն և կամ ի գործս առաքելոցն սրբոց և այլն: Պարձեալ զինչ է պարտ ես այնոցիկ, որք կամենան առնուլ զսուրբը մլրտութիւն. զի նոցա պարտ է գալ Հեզութեամբ, խոնարՀութեամբ առ ընտրեալն, Հայցել ի նմանէ զարձակումն ի դիւաց և ծառայել տեառն մերոյ յիսուսի քրիստոսի և սրբազան եկեղեցւոյն: Իսկ արդ ընտրեալն Հրամայէ առ նոսա ասելով.

Թէ ո՛վ որդեակք իմ, զի դուք որք կամիք յայժմ, առնուլ
յինէն զարձակումն սուրբ՝ ձեզ պարտ է ասել . . . .
. . . . .¹
յուցանեն զձեզ և կամիցին շրջել զաւետարանն քրիստոսի։
Այլ թէ մեք կամ հրեշտակ յերկնից իջեալ աւետարանեսցէ
ձեզ աւելի քան զոր աւետարանեցաք լիցի նզովեալ։ Որպէս
յառաջագոյն ասացի և այժմ դարձեալ ասեմ, եթէ ոք
աւետարանեսցէ ձեզ աւելի քան զոր առիքն նզովեալ լիցի։
Դարձեալ զայս ես գրեմ ձեզ սիրելեաց՝ դուք բարեպէս
քննեցէք զսուրբ աւետարանն տեառն մերոյ յիսուսի քրիստոսի
և զսուրբ գործս առաքելոցն և ապայ դատապարտէք զմեզ,
զի մի՛ գուցէ թէ և դուք պատժեսջիք ըստ ժամանակի.

Եկա՛յք որդիք նոր սիօնի
Լուէ՛ք զպսակն տեառն յիսուսի
Պահէ՛ք ի ձեզ զոր ինչ խօսի,
Դասէ՛ք ի դասս յաջակողմի,
Եթէ լուէք եկեղեցւոյն
Փրկէ զձեզ աստուած անհուն։

___

¹ աստանօր թերթք երկու անկեալ (երեսք՝ 74-77)։

ա.   Գլուխ ամենեցուն է տեր յիսուս
      Որ դաւանի սուրբն պօղոս
9.   Եւ գլուխ քրիստոսի է աստուած և լյս

                Կործոց գլ. 1, համր. 13.

        պետրոս   և յակոբոս
        յովհաննէզ   և անդրեաս
        փիլիպպոս   և թումնաս
        բարդուղեմէոս   և մատթէոս
        յակոբոս   ալփեան
        և շմաւոն   նախանձայդդ
        և յուդայ   յակովբեան։
        Իսկ պօղոս անօթն ընտրութեան.
        Սոքա են եկեղեցի ընդհանրական,
        և ոչ պետրոս է մի միայն։

        Եկեղեցի ընդհանրական
        Որ վերձայնի նգյեա տապան,
        Սովաւ հոգիք յյժ փրկեցան.
        Եւ պատրանօք դիւաց կորբեան։

                Գլուխ քան։

    Յաղագս թէ զինչ է ևս պարտ ընտրելյն խօսիլ և կամ ասել
    տայ նոցա։ Այս ինչ դաւանութիւն ևս պարտ է
    ընտրելյն տալ ասել նոցա այսպէս։

    Խոստովանիմք և հաւատամք զաստուած մի ճշմարիտ գոլ
    զոր տերն մեր քրիստոս ասէ յոհան. գլ. 17, համր. 3. Այս

են յալիտենական կեանք, զի ծանիցեն զքեզ միայն ճշմարիտ աստուած եւ զոր առաքեցեր զյիսուս քրիստոս։ Պարձեալ խոստովանիմք եւ հաւատամք զյիսուս քրիստոս...¹ արաբիչ, որպէս սուրբն պօղոս առ եբրայեցիսն ասէ գլ. 3, Հմր. 2. Հաւատարիմ է արարչին իւրոյ, որպէս մովսէս յամենայնի տան նորա։ Պարձեալ հաւատա՛մք դուք զբարեխօսութիւն տեառն մերոյ յիսուսի քրիստոսի եւ ո՛չ այլոց։ Հաւատա՛մք դուք զսուրբ առաքեալսն եւ զամենեսեան, որք են ընդ– Հանրական կաթուղիկէ եկեղեցւի, եւ ո՛չ են լատինք, յօյնք կամ Հայք²։ Նա եւս Հաւատա՛մք դուք զյիսուս քրիստոս, զի Հօրն իւրոյ Հրամանաւ գալոց է դատել զկենդանիս եւ զմեռեալս։

Եւ յորժամ սոքա աւարտեն զՀաւատոց դաւանութիւնս առաջի ընտրելոյն եւ Համայն իշխանաց՝ յայնժամ պարտ է ընտրելոյն ասել զայս աղօթս ընդդէմ Հօրն երկնաւորի։

Աղօթք տեառն մերոյ յիսուսի քրիստոսի ընդդէմ Հօրն երկնաւորի։

Գոհանամ զքէն, Հա՛յր, տէր երկնի եւ երկրի, զի ծածկեցեր զայս իմաստնոց եւ գիտնոց եւ յայտնեցեր տղայոց։ Ա՛յո՛, Հա՛յր, զի այսպէս Հաճոյ եղեւ առաջի քոյ։ Ամենայն ինչ տուաւ ինձ 'ի Հօրէ իմմէ. եւ ոչ ոք ճանաչէ զՈրդի՛ եթէ ոչ Հայր, եւ ո՛չ զՀայր ոք ճանաչէ եթէ ոչ Որդի, եւ ում Որդին կամիցի յայտնել։ Եկա՛յք առ իս ամենայն վաստակեալք եւ բեռնաւորք, եւ ես Հանգուցից զձեզ։ Առէք զլուծ իմ 'ի ձեզ, եւ ուսարո՛ւք յինէն զի Հեզ եմ եւ խոնարհ սրտիւ. եւ գտջէք Հանգիստ անձանց ձերոց։ Օ՛ի լուծ իմ քաղցր է. եւ բեռն իմ փոքրոգի։

---

¹ բառս այս եղծեալ թուին լինել. 'Նոր արարած եւ ո՛չ արաբիչ...'
² բառս այս եղծեալ։

Եւ յետ աղբտման սրբոյ աղօթից տեառն մերոյ յիսուսի քրիստոսի :—

Արդ՝ այժմ եկեսցուք վասն մկրտողին թէ զի՞նչ պարտ է նմա եւ կամ ո՞րպէս պարտ է նորա կեալ եւ կամ որով կերպիւ բերէ առ ինքն զղշացեալն, եւ կամ որպիսի՞ ձեռով պաշտէ զնա. ուստի զայս ամենայն խոսիմք մկրտողին եւ մկրտելոյն աստուծով մի առ մի :

Այլ արդ՝ ՟ արկ է մկրտողին լինի ընտրեալ ըստ ասից ՟ օրն երկնաւորի առ որդին իւր սիրելի. Պ ուկ. ԴԼ 9, ՟ մր. 35. Դա է որդի իմ ընտրեալ, դմա լուարուք: Եւ երկրորդ՝ լինի ՟ եզ եւ խոնարհ ըստ հրամացելոյն տեառն մերոյ յիսուսի քրիստոսի, զոր բերանովն սրբազան աւետարանչացն՝ յո- ՟ աննէս ԴԼ 15, ՟ մր. 16, եւ ՟ մր. 19, եւ ԴԼ. 11, ՟ մր. 28, եւ մատթէոսի. Ուսարուք յինէն, զի ՟ եզ եմ եւ խոնարհ սրտիւ, եւ այլն :

Իսկ ուսուցիչ, խոհեմ, ՟ նազանդ, պարկեշտ, ողջախոհ, առաքինի, աստուածապաշտ, սիրելի ամենեցուն եւ ինքն սիրող ամենայն ՟ ալատացելոց: Այլ եւ մի լեցի առասպելլ շատա- խոս, ստաբան, գրգռող չարեաց: Նա եւ մի լեցի շռայլ եւ ժլատ, մի լեցի կեղծաւոր եւ խաբեբայ, մի լեցի ղօշակբաղ եւ ցանկասէր

Արդ՝ մի եղեցի կուսարար եւ բարկացող, եւ մի լեցի գինեմոլ եւ արբեցող, եւ մի լեցի փառասէր եւ շահընկալ. մի լեցի կաշառառու եւ ագահ, մի լեցի գող եւ աւազակ, մի լեցի մարդասպան եւ շղկող աղքատաց, մի լեցի դիւրահաւան եւ ՟ ակառակ, կագաւոր, մի լեցի պատռող արանց եւ կանանց, մի լեցի երդման, գրգռող ի չարիս, մի լեցի ղշպարտող այլոց, մի լեցի ՟ ապարտ եւ անննասէր, մի լեցի սիրող արծաթոյ եւ մի ամենայն ինչս աշխարհի, մի լեցի արատաւոր եւ խեղկատակ, մի լեցի շնացող եւ ծղլէ մի լեցի կոյր եւ կաղ մի լեցի խուլ եւ ՟ ամբ, մի լեցի առաւել երկայն քան զամենայն մարդիկս եւ մի կարճ եղեցի քան զամենայն մարդիկս: Եւ այսպէս ՟ րամայեն ՟ ոգւոյն սրբով ՚ի կանոնս իւրեանց. եւ մանաւանդ սուրբ առաքեայն պօղոս կանոնեաց զփորոսն ասելով, ԴԼ 1, ՟ մր. 7. Ո՝ ի պարտ է եպիսկոպոսին անարատ լինիլ՝ որպէս և Աստուծոյ տնտեսի. մի յանդուգն, մի բարկացող մի թշնամանող, մի հարկանող, մի գոշաքաղ. Այլ հիւրասէր, բարեսէր, ցած, արդար, սուրբ, ժուժկալ։ Սերակացու լինել հաւատարիմ բանին վարդապետութեան, զի կարող իցէ և մխիթարել ողջմտութեամբ վարդապետութեանն, և զհակառակորդսն կշտամբէլ։

Դարձեալ գրէ և սուրբ առաքեալն պօղոս առ տիմոթէոս այսպէս, գլ. 3, համր. 1. Հաւատարիմ է բանս. եթէ ոք եպիսկոպոսութեան ցանկայ բարւոյ գործոյ ցանկայ։ Պարտ է եպիսկոպոսին անարատ լինել, միոյ կնոջ այր, հեզ՝ ցած, պարկեշտ, հիւրասէր, ուսուցիչ. Մէ թշնամանող, մի հարկանող, այլ հանդարտ. մի կռուող, մի արծաթասէր. Ոչ իւրում տանն իսկ բարւոք վերակացու լեալ իցէ. որդեակս ունիցի, որ ՚ի հնազանդութեան կայցեն ամենայնիւ պարկեշտութեամբ։

Այսպէս և պարտ է ընտրելոյն զգուշանալ ամենայն չար խորհուրդոց ըստ առաքելոյն պօղոսին, զոր հրամայէ ասելով. Նմանողք ինձ եղերուք, որպէս և ես քրիստոսի. գովեմ զձեզ զի զամենայն ինչս իմ ունիցիք. Գլ. 11, համր. 10, առաջի կորնթա.

Ահա տեսա՛յք նագելիք մեր, թէ որպէս պատուիրէն զմեզ առաքեալքն տեառն մերոյ յիսուսի քրիստոսի. և թէ նոցա ոչ նմանիք, ոչ ոք ոչ կարեմք ընտրեալ և առաջնորդ լինել հաւատացելոց, և այլն։

Յաղագս մկրտելոցն, թէ որպէս պարտէ նոցա գալ առ ընտրեալն և մկրտիլ ի նմանէ։

Գլուխ քան և ա.

Արդ ասեմք առ այս, և դուք լերուք հեզորէն և ունկնդիր կանոնացս, թէ որպէս պարտ է գալ և դիմել առ ընտրեալն նորընծայն այն. քանդի հեզութեամբ և խոնարհութեամբ, որպէս տեռն մեր յիսուս քրիստոս հեզութեամբ և խոնարհութեամբ կացեալ առ սուրբն յոհաննէս մկրտիչն։ Այսպէս և նորաբոյս ծաղիկն այն այնպէս պարտ է գալ առ ընտրեալն։

Եւ իսկոյն ընտրեալն կանգնեալ ի յոտս ասելով. եկայք առ իս ամենայն աշխատեալք և բեռնաւորք լեա՛ Հանդուցից զձեզ. առէք զլուծն իմ ի ձեզ և ուսարուք յինէն զի Հեզ եմ և խոնարՀ սրտիւ, և գտջիք Հանգիստ անձանց ձերոց. զի լոյծ իմ քաղցր է և բեռն իմ փոքրոգի։ մտթ. գլ. 11, Համր. 28։ Եւ դշացեալն կարի փափականօք անկեալ ի յոտս ընտրելոյն, ադաչանօք և արտասուօք ասէ, ո՛վ ընտրեալդ յաստուծոյ և յիսուսէ քրիստոսէ, ադաչեմ և խնդրեմ զձեզ արձակեա՛ զիս զանարժանս ի կապից սատանայէ:

Ա՛ռ Հրապարակս ասել պարտ է:

Դարձեալ ընտրեալն քաղցր դիմօք և մեծաւ սիրով Հարցանէ զնա թէ Որդեա՛կ իմ, դու որ կամիս արձակիլ ի կապանաց դիւաց սատանայի զի՞նչ ունիս պտուղ արձակման, ասա մեզ առջի ժողովրդեանս։ Իսկ զշացեալն եթէ կատարեալ Հաւատս ուսեալ և առեալ է անկեղծ Հաւատով իսկոյն ի մեջ չորյն ի ծունկս եկեալ ասէ մեծաւ սիրով և արտասուօք առ ընտրեալն ասելով այսպէս. Դա՛խ Հաւա- տովս Հաւատամ զդերն մեր զյիսուս քրիստոս, որպէս սրբազան առաքեալքն Հաւատացին. ի մատթէ գլ. 16, Համր. 13, և որպէս ի գործս գլ. 8 մինչև ցՀամարն 18. Եւ ասէ ցնոսա. իսկ դուք զո՞ ասէք զինէն թէ իցեմ՛ պատասխանի ետ սիմօն պետրոս և ասէ ցնա. Դուես քրիստոս որդին աս- տուծոյ կենդանւոյ, և այլն: Յովհ. գլ. 6, Համր 70: Եւ մանաւանդ սուրբ առաքեալն պօղոս դաւանելով ասէ, Դլուխ ամենեցուն քրիստոս և գլուխս քրիստոսի աստուած. Առաջ. կորնթ. գլ. 11, Համր. 3. Որպէս յայտ է ի սուրբ աւետարանն ասելով յոՀ. գլ. 17, Համր. 3. Ա՛յս են յաւիտենական կեանք, զի ծանիցեն զքեզ միայն ճշմարիտ Աստուած՛ և զոր առա- քեցեր զՅիսուս Քրիստոս.

Ա՛յսպէս խոստովանիմ և Հաւատամ, պաշտեմ և երկիր պագանեմ զՅայն աստուած և զորդին միածին և բարեխոս և զսուրբ Հոգին բաշխող շնորՀաց մեզ Հաւատացելոցս:

Եւ արդ մինչ Հաւատացեալն վճարէ զսուրբ դաւանութին

իսկ և իսկ ընտրեալն առնու զջուրն ի ձեռս իւր և յերկինս հայելով ասէ, ես զխորհուրդն, զձևն և զդիտաւորութիւն առ ինքն պահելով միշապես կամ անմիջապէս զջուրն լցուցանէ ի վերայ գլխոյն ասելով․ յանուն Հօր և Որդւոյ և Հոգոյն սրբոյ մկրտեցաւ այս անուն այր կամ կին վկայութեամբ ժողովր֊ տեան զոր կան աստ։ Եւ ապա ընթեռնու զսուրբ աւետարանս տեառն մերոյ յիսուսի քրիստոսի․ մտթէ. գլ 3, Հմր. 13.

Յայնժամ գայ յիսուս ի գալիլէէ իյորդանան առ յոչաննէս մկրտիլ ի նմանէ։ Մրկս. գլ. 1, Հմր. 9. Եւ եղև յաւուրն յայնոսիկ եկ Յիսուս ՚ի Նազարեթէ Գալիլեացւոց և մկրտե֊ ցաւ ՚ի Յովհաննէ ՚ի Յորդանան։ Ղկս. գլ. 3, Հմր. 21. Եւ եղև ՚ի մկրտիլ ամենայն ժողովրդեանն, և ընդ Յիսուսի մկրտիլն` և կալ յաղօթս, բանալ երկնից, եւ այլն։ ՅՀն. գլ. 1, Հմր. 29. Ի վաղիւ անդր տեսանէ զյիսուս զի գայր առ նա և ասէ։ Եւ զայլն ընթերցջիր լիովին ի վերայ մկրտելոյն։

Դարձեալ առնու առաջի իւր ընտրեալն զնորընծայն․ իսկ նորընծայից պարտ է աչիւ և գողութեամբ ի ծունկս եկեալ մերկ և զգլուխս իւրեանց խոնարհեցուցեալ և Հաստատագոյն Հաւատով ի մտոս բերեալ զարձակումն ի սատանայէ․ իսկ ընտրեալն առնու զջուրն ի ձեռս իւր, խորՀրդով բանիւ զմին և գործով, լցուցէ զջուրն ի վերայ գագաթոյ միոյ և ասէ նախ յանուն Հօր և լցցէ զջուրն ի գլխոյն երեք անգամ յանուն զմին որդւոյ և յանուն Հոգւոյն սրբոյ.... [1] միալորաքար։

Ուստի Հայրն արձակող է ի կապանաց, որդին յուսադրող է մեղաւորաց և Հոգին սուրբ սէր է ի սիրտս լցողաց Հաւատա֊ ցեալ մկրտելոցն և այլն։

Կալարուք ձեզ զօրինակս զայս։—

Ով ի թագաւոր ոք արձակէ զիշխանս ումանս ի բանդէ մեղաց, իսկ որդին կոչէ զնոսա առ ինքն և յուսադրէ զնոսա մեծաւ բանիւք, և Հոգի սուրբ Թագաւորին իսկոյն եկեալ պսակէ զպյնոսիկ և ընդ նոսա բնակի ի յաւիտեանս յաւիտենից. ամէն։

զմին
դէմ
զմին
դէմ
դայ
լցցէ

---

[1] բառք երկու կամ երեք եղծեալ․

Ընթերցեր զսուրբ Լևետարանս.

Յայնժամ գայ Յիսուս 'ի Գալիլեէ 'ի Յորդանան առ Յովհաննէս՝ մկրտիլ 'ի նմանէ։ Եւ Յովհաննէս արգելուլ չնա և ասէ. Ինձ պիտոյ է 'ի քէն մկրտիլ, և դու առ իս գաս։ Պատասխանի ետ Յիսուս և ասէ ցնա. Թո՛յլ տուր այժմ. զի այսպէս վայելէ է մեզ լնուլ զամենայն արդարութիւն. և ապա թոյլ ետ նմա։ Եւ իբրև մկրտեցաւ Յիսուս, ել վաղվաղակի 'ի ջրոյ անտի. և աճա բացան նմա երկինք և ետես զՀոգին Աստուծոյ՝ զի իջանէր իբրև զաղաւնի, և գայր 'ի վերայ նորա։ Եւ աճա ձայն եղև յերկնից որ ասէր. Դա է Որդի իմ սիրելի, ընդ որ հաճեցայ։

Անդդէմ է Հօր.

Գոհանամք, մեծացուցանեմք և փառաւորեմք զքո ամենազօր Հայրութիւնդ, զի արժանի արարեր զծառայս քո 'ի ժամ մկրտութեան որբ մկրտեցան յանուն որդւոյ քո միածնիդ։ Եւ այժմ երկիր պագանեմք, հայցեմք և խնդրեմք 'ի քէն, հայր սուրբ, պահեա զոստս ի խաբէութենէ դիւաց և աղատեա ի փորձութենէ չարեաց։ Անքեամ հայր սուրբ զսիրաս, զշողիս և զմարմինս սոցա պատուական մարմնով և արեամբ որդւոյ քո միածնիդ, միշտ և հանապազ.

Պարձեալ ընթերցէք զգործս առաքելոց, գլ. 2, հմր. 1.

Եւ 'ի կատարել աւուրցն Պենտեկոստէից էին ամենեքեան միաբան 'ի միասին։ Եւ եղև յանկարծակի հնչիւն յերկնից՝ եկեալ իբրև սաստիկ հողմոյ. և ելից զամենայն տունն յորում նստէին։ Եւ երևեցան նոցա բաժանեալք լեզուք իբրև 'ի հրոյ. և նստաւ իւրաքանչիւր 'ի վերայ նոցա։ Եւ լցան ամենեքեան Հոգով սրբով և սկսան խօսել յայլ լեզուս որպէս և Հոգին տայր բարբառել նոցա.

Լևետարան մարկոս, գլ. 1, հմր. 9.

Եւ եղև յաւուրսն յայնոսիկ եկն Յիսուս 'ի Նազարեթէ Գալիլեացւոց, և մկրտեցաւ 'ի Յովհաննէ 'ի Յորդանան։ Եւ նոյնժամայն ընդ վերանալ 'ի ջրոցն, ետես յեղեալ զերկինս, և զ՟ոգին Լ՟ստուծոյ իբրև զաղաւնի՝ զի իջանէր ['ի վերայ նորա։ Զայն եղև] յերկնից և ասէ. Դու ես Որդի իմ սիրելէ, ընդ քեզ հաճեցայ.

Եւ ապա ասեմք դայս աղօթս ընդդէմ որդւոյն Հօրն երկնաւորի։

Երկիր պագանեմք, աղերսեմք և Հայցեմք 'ի քէն, քրիստոս որդի աստուծոյ, ընկալ զտսա 'ի թիւս աշակերտոց սրբոց քոց և առաքեա՛ զՀոգի Հօր քո 'ի սիրտս սոցա, զի դու խոստացար նոցա. եթէ ես ո՛չ երթայց Հոգի սուրբ ո՛չ եկեսցէ առ ձեզ։ Լ՟յլ այժմ ջերմ սիրով երեսս անկեալ խնդրեմք 'ի քէն վասն ծառայից քոց, որք այժմ մկրտեցան յանուն քո սուրբ և զպասետալ մեան անսուտ խոստման քոյդ տերութեան առ 'ի սիրտս սոցա. և ամենայն 'ի քեզ Հաւատացեալ ծառայից քոց

Եւ դարձեալ ընթերձվէք զգողոսին առ Դաղատացիսն, ԳԼ. 3, Հմր. 24.

Ապա օրէնքն դաստիարակ եղեն մեզ 'ի Ք՟րիստոս Յիսուս, զի 'ի Հաւատոցն արդարասցուք։ Լ՟յլ իբրև եկին Հաւատքն, ո՛չ ևս ընդ դաստիարակաւ եմք։ Ք՟անզի ամենեքին որդիք Լ՟ստուծոյ [էք՝] Հաւատովք ['ի Յիսուս Ք՟րիստոս]։ Որք մկանգամ 'ի Ք՟րիստոս մկրտեցայք, զՔ՟րիստոս զգեցեալ էք. չէք խտիր, Ո՛չ ՟րևի և ո՛չ ՟հեթանոս, ո՛չ ծառայի և ո՛չ ազատի, ո՛չ արուի և ո՛չ իգի. զի ամենեքեան դուք մի էք 'ի Ք՟րիստոս Յիսուս։ Ապա եթէ դուք Ք՟րիստոսի էք, ուրեմն Լ՟բրաՀամու զաւակ էք՝ ըստ աւետեացն՝ ժառանգք։

Ալբսյ աւետարանին յիսուսի քրիստոսի ըստ ղուկաս, ԳԼ. 3, Հմր. 21.

Եւ եղև 'ի մկրտիլ ամենայն ժողովրդեանն, և ընդ Յիսուսի մկրտիլն՝ և կալ յաղօթս, բանալ երկնից, Եւ իջանել ՟հոգւոյն Ալբսյ մարմնաւոր տեսլեամբ իբրև զաղաւնի 'ի վերայ նորա. և գալ ձայն յերկնից՝ որ ասէր. Դու ես Որդի իմ սիրելէ, ընդ քեզ Հաճեցայ։

'Նա ես ասա՛ զաղօթս զայս ընդդէմ Հոգւոյն սրբոյ․

Օրհնեալ ես Հոգի Հօրն երկնաւորի, որպէս եղեալ 'ի Հօրէ և եկեալ եւուր տեառն մերոյ յիսուսի քրիստոսի զեշխանու֊ թիւն 'ի վերայ ամենայն մարմնոյ և արարեր զնա թագաւոր և գլուխ երկնաւորաց և երկրաւորաց և սանդարամետականաց, զոր լցեալն 'ի քէն սուրբն պօղոս ասէ․ 'Նա ես զՀրեղէն լեզուս բաժանեցեր 'ի սուրբ առաքեալն և միաբանեալ զնոսա 'ի մի բանն, և արարեր զնոսա կաթուղիկէ եկեղեցի որդւոյ Հօր աստուծոյ։ Եւ այժմ երկիրպագութեամբ աղեր֊ սեմք 'ի քէն էջ 'ի սոսա և լից զսիրտս մկրտեցելոցս, որք այժմ մկրտեցան 'ի քրիստոս յիսուս, զի մի գուցէ թէ պիղծ Հոգին մերձեսցի 'ի Հաւատացեալս միածնին որդի Հօրն երկնաւորի։ Արբեաւ զՀոգիս զմիտս սօտա և արա՛ տաճար և բնակարան Հօրն անեղին, օրդւոյն բարեխօսին յայժմէ և միշտ և յաւիտեանս յաւիտենից, Ա՛մէն։

Ընթերցուածն 'ի գործոց առաքելոց, գլ․ 8, Հմր․ 26-40 [1]․

Հրեշտակ Տեառն խօսեցաւ առ Փիլիպպոս և ասէ․ Արի և գնա՛ դու 'ի կողմն Հարաւոյ ընդ ճանապարհ որ իջանէ յԵրուսաղէմէ 'ի Գազայ․ այս է անապատ։ Եւ յարեաւ գնաց։ Եւ ահաւասիկ այր մի Եթէովպացի, ներքինի Հզօր՝ Կանդակայ տիկնոջ Եթէովպացւոց, որ էր 'ի վերայ ամենայն գանձուց նորա․ որ եկեալ էր երկիրպագանել յԵրուսաղէմ, Եւ էր անդրէն դարձեալ․ և նստեալ 'ի կառս իւրում․ ընթեռ֊ նոյր զմարգարէն զԵսայի։ Ասէ Հոգին ցՓիլիպպոս․ Մատի՛ր և յարեաց 'ի կառդ յայդոսիկ։ Եւ ընթացաւ փիլիպպոս՝ և լսէր զի ընթեռնոյր զԵսայի մարգարէ, և ասէ․ Գիտիցե՞ս արդեօք՝ զոր ընթեռնուցուդ։ Եւ նա ասէ․ Զիա՞րդ կարի֊ ցեմ՝ դիտել թէ ոք ոչ առաջնորդեսցէ ինձ․ և աղաչեաց զՓի֊ լիպպոս ելանել ընդ նմա։ Եւ գլուխ գրոցն՝ զոր ընթեռնոյր՝

---

[1] Ձ․ Հմր․ 30.

էր այս· Իբրև զոշխար ՛ի սպանդ վարեցաւ, և իբրև զորոջ առաջի կտրչի իւրոյ անմուղչ, և այնպէս ոչ բանայ զբերան իւր։ ՛Ի խոնարհութեան նորա դատաստան բարձաւ, զազգատոհմն նորա ո՞ պատմեսցէ. զի բառնան յերկրէ կեանք նորա։ Պատասխանի ետ ներբինին Փիլիպպոսի, և ասէ. Աղաչեմ զքեզ՝ վասն ո՞յր ասէ մարգարէն զայս, վասն իւր, եթէ վասն այլոյ ուրուք։ Երաց Փիլիպպոս զբերան իւր և սկսաւ ՛ի գրոցս յայսցանէ աւետարանեաց նմա զՅիսուս։ Իբրև երթային զճանապարհայն, եկին ՛ի ջուր ինչ, և ասէ ներքինին. Ահաւասիկ ջուր՝ զի՞նչ արգելու զիս ՛ի մկրտելոյ Ել ասէ Փիլիպպոս ցնա։ Եթէ հաւատաս բոլորով սրտիւ մարթ է։ Պատասխանի ետ և ասէ. Հաւատամ՝ եթէ է Յիսուս ՛Քրիստոս Որդի Աստուծոյ։ Եւ հրամայեաց կացուցանել զկառն. և իջին երկոքեան ՛ի ջուրն՝ Փիլիպպոս և ներքինին, և մկրտեաց զնա։ Եւ իբրև ելին ՛ի ջրոյ անտի՝ Հոգին Սուրբ եկն ՛ի վերայ ներքինւոյն. և Հրեշտակ Տեառն յափշտակեաց զՓիլիպպոս՝ և ոչ ևս ետես զնա ներքինին. և գնայր զճանապարհ իւր ուրախութեամբ։

Եւ ապայ ընթերձիր զաւրբ աւետարանն յոհան.
գլ. 20, հմր. 19.

Սրբոյ աւետարանիս տեառն մերոյ յիսուսի քրիստոսի ըստ յոհաննու.

Կամ այսպէս սկսիր ասէ. Սուրբ աւետարանն տեառն մերոյ յիսուսի քրիստոսի է, զոր յոհաննէս ասէ։

Եւ էր երեկոյ ՛ի միաշաբաթուց աւուրն. և դրօքն փակելովք՝ ուր էին աշակերտքն Յիսուսի ժողովեալ վասն ահին Հրէից, եկն Յիսուս՝ և եկաց ՛ի մէջն նոցա, և ասէ ցնոսա. Ողջոյն ընդ ձեզ։ Իբրև զայս ասաց՝ եցոյց նոցա զձեռսն և զկողս իւր. և խնդային աշակերտքն իբրև տեսին զՏէր։ Ասէ ցնոսա դարձեալ. Ողջոյն ընդ ձեզ, որպէս առաքեաց զիս Հայր իմ, և ես առաքեմ զձեզ։ Եւ զայս իբրև ասաց՝ փչեաց ՛ի նոսա՝ և ասէ. Առէք զՀոգի Սուրբ։ Եթէ ումեք

թողուցուք զմեղդ՝ թողեալ լիցի. և եթէ զղրուք ունիցիք՝
կալեալ լիցի։

Պարծեալ պարտ է նախ քան զամենայն աղօթս զՏայր մեր՝
ասել

Եւ ապայ տուր զխաղաղութիւն ասելով այսպէս. խաղաղութիւն Տօր, խաղաղութիւն օրզեսյ, և խաղաղութիւն
Տոգւոյն սրբոյ եկեսցէ ի ձեզ։ Ամէն։

Պաղձան որ է մկրտութեանն։

Եւ յաղագս խրատոյ ձեռնադրութեան.

Գլուխ [ԻԲ]։

Օխիսուս որդի Տօրն երկնաւորի օգնեա մեզ և բարեխօսեա
վասն մեր, և վասն ամենայն Տաւատացելոց, որ խոստացար անսուտ բանիւդ, յոՏան. գլ. 17, Տմր. 20։

Այլ ոչ վասն նոցա միայն աղաչեմ, այլ և վասն ամենայն
Տաւատացելոց բանիւն նոցա յիս.

Պարծեալ ասասցուք վասն առն այնորիկ թէ որպէս պարտ
է ձևա ընտրել և ապա ձեռնադրել զմարդն զայն, զի մի՛ զուցէ
թէ պարտական գտանիցիմք ըստ տեառն մերոյ յիսուսի քրիստոսի և սուրբ առաքելոյն պօղոսի զոր ասէ և կանոնէ առաջե-
րորդ տիմոթեոս, գլ. 5, Տմր. 22. Օձեռս վաղվաղակի ուրուք
վերայ մի՛ դնիցես և կցորդ լինիցիս մեղաց օտարաց և այլն։
Այլ ես բարեխօս և միջնորդ մեր յիսուս արգելեալ ասէ. մի՛
տայք զսրբութիւն շանց և մի՛ արկանէք զմարգարիտս ձեր
առաջի խոզաց։ Աշա այսպէս պարտ է ընտրելոյն և իշխանաց
չտալ զիշխանութիւնն առն այնորիկ. քանզի մեծ է աշ և
երկիւղ զձեռս դնել ՚ի վերայ այնպիսեաց և կցորդ լինել
մեղաց օտարացն և այլն. ապայ պարտ է նոցա մեծ զգու-
շութիւնս կալեալ մեղաց նորա ոչ Տաղորդիլ որդոն ոչ է

աստուածային Հրաման. ոչ քրիստոսի ընտրեցյուն և ոչ ընթան րական և առաքելական սուրբ եկեղեցւոյն։ Նա ես եկես ցուք 'ի բանս 'ի գործս և 'ի կանոնս փրկչին մերոյ. Նա և ընտրեալ առաքելոցն սրբոց, զոր ուսեալ էին քաշանայապետէն Յիսուսէ և մեզ աւանդեցին զոր սուրբն պօղոս. գաղատացւոց գլ. I, Համր. II ասէ։ Յուցանեմ ձեզ եղբարք զաւետարանն, որ աւետարանեցաւ յինէն. զի ոչ է ըստ մւոց մարդոյ. Հանգի և ոչ ես 'ի մարդոյ առի, և ոչ ուսայ յումեք. այլ 'ի յայտնութենէն Յիսուսի Քրիստոսի։ [Կորնթա. գլ. 15, Համր. I. Եփես. գլ. 3, Համր. 3.]

Օ.ի աՀա բստ այսմբանի երանեալքն այնոքիկ ընկալան 'ի քրիստոսէ, և քրիստոս փրկիչն մեր էառ 'ի Հօրէ ամենակալէ, որպէս ինքն Հրամայեաց ասելով 'ի մոթէոս։ Եւ մատուցեալ գլ. 2 Յիսուս խօսեցաւ ընդ նոսա՝ և ասէ. տուաւ ինձ [ամենայն] իշ- Համր. խանութիւն յերկինս և յերկրի. որպէս առաքեաց զիս Հայր, և Մտ ես առաքեմ զձեզ"։ Նա ես մարկոս գլ. 16, Համր. 15։ Ըյսպէս գլ. 3, նախ տեքին մեր.քրիստո ընտրեցաւ 'ի Հօրէ և էառ զշնորՀս Հօրն Համր. երկնաւորի, զոր ասէ մոթու. գլ. 12։ ԸՀա մանուկ իմ զոր Մրկ ընտրեցի, և սիրելի իմ ընդ որ Հաճեցաւ անձն իմ. եդից զՈգի գլ. I; իմ 'ի վերայ նորա, և իրաւունս Հեթանոսաց պատմեսցէ։ Համր. Եւ իբրև մկրտեցաւ Յիսուս ել վաղվաղակի 'ի ջրոյ անտի. և Դու աՀա բացան նմա երկինք և ետես զՈգին Աստուծոյ՝ զի Համր. իջանէր իբրև զաղաւնի, և գայր 'ի վերայ նորա։ Եւ աՀա Մտ ձայն յերկնից որ ասէր. Դա է Որդի իմ սիրելի, ընդ որ գլ. 3 Հաճեցայ։ մրկա. գլ. 10, Համր. 10, և ղուկաս գլ. 3, Համր. 22, Համր. յոՀան. գլ. I, Համր. 32։ Եւ զայլքն ընթերձցէք 'ի սուրբ գիրս որ նախ ընտրեցաւ յիսուս 'ի Հօրէ և առաքեալքն 'ի նմանէ։ Ուստի և առն այնորիկ պարտ է ընտրիլ իշխանաց և ապա եպիսկոպոսաց. Երդ պարտ է առաջնորդին նախ քննէ զնա Հեզութեամբ և խոնարՀութեամբ. թէ ունի նա գիմաստութիւն կատարեալ գսէր որ է գլուխ ամենեցուն, գխոՀեմութիւն, գՀեզութիւն, գխոնարՀութիւն, զարդարու թիւն, զարիութիւն, գողջախոՀութիւն և գհանաստեղծու- թիւն։

Նա և ունի արդեօք գժուժկալութիւն, գՀամբերութիւն,

զկատաղարութիւն, զՅովլապետութիւն, զախքատասիրութիւն, զզթութիւն և զքաղաքավարութիւնս և զայլ ամենայն բարե֊
գործութիւնս և զզղշումն Հանդերձ խղճմտանօք։ զայս պարտ
է ուսուցչին փորձելով իմանալ և ապայ իջև Հարկ նդյն
վարդապետին Համեել. իսկ եթէ ոչ ունիցի մարդև այն զկատարեալ քննութիւնս դայստիկ, ոչ է պարտ առաջնորդին կամ
իշխանաց զձեռս իւրեանց դնել 'ի գլուխ նորա, որպէս տէրն
մեր և ընթանրական առաքելական սուրբ եկեղեցին արգելէ
զմեզ չհնել զձեռս մեր 'ի վերայ այնպիսեացն և մի լինել
կցորդ և մասնակից մեղաց նորա. որպէս միջնորդ և բարեխօսն
մեր յիսուս զգուշացուցանէ զմեզ ասելով, թէ զգուշ լերուք
'ի չար մշակաց ամաի, որ գան առ ձեզ Հանդերձիւք ոչխարաց
և 'ի ներքոյ են գայլք յափշտակողք, և այլն։

Ահա տեսա՛ք սիրելիք մեր, թէ որպէս տէրն արգելէ
զայսպիսիս. զձեռս չհնել 'ի վերայ այնպիսեաց. այսինքն
սուտ մարգարէից, կեղծաւորաց, անՀաղանդից, չիմարաց և
այլն։ Դարձեալ ձեզ աստուածասէր իշխանացդ և իշխանա-
պետացդ ոչ է պարտ զձեռս ձեր վաղվաղակի դնել 'ի վերայ
այնպիսեացն, զոր սուրբն պօղոս 'ի կանոնս իւր պատուիրէ
I, այսպէս առ տիտոն ասելով, զի պարտ է եպիսկոպոսին
էջ 7. անարատ լինել և այլն. և այսպէս ընտրեան այն պարտ
է ամենայն կողմանց անարատ և սուրբ եղիցի. նա ևս խորագէտ
և միամիտ, զոր ընտրեան ի Հօրէ ամենակալէ ասէ. եղիցուք
խորագէտ իբրև զօձ և միամիտ որպէս զաղաւնի, և այլն։

Տեսէք և բարեպէս քննեցէք, զի մի գուցէ թէ Հակառակ
լիջիք այս սուրբ կանոնացս, նա և Հայէն ամենակարող տացէ
մեզ զչնորՀս իւր սուրբ բարեխօսութեամբն օրդույն իւր
սիրելւյ․ և բանայցէ զայս Հոգւոյ մերոյ առ ի ճանաչել
զայսպիսի խաբերայն. այսինքն զգող, զաւազակ, զմարդաս-
պան, զպոռնկորդիս, զՀնացող, զՀանպասող, զատախսս,
զևեղզատակ, զշարաբան, զՅայՀոյիչս, զկրառույս, զեղա-
ցեալս, զարուագէտս, զսողաբարդս, զկուասէրս, զանՀաշտս,
զանմեղ սպանօղս, զձրյս, կաղլերդս, զշռային, զժլատս, վա-
ևուսումն, զյիմարս, զյնորեալս, զառասպելս, զանՀալանս,
զևոքնասէրս, զանպարՀալաձն, զանքարտուածն, զեերկգէմն,

զազգս, զբիձալուրս, զանշնորՀս, զլերբս, պսուտվկայս, զիա֊
րասերս,զարձաթասերս,զկեղձալուրս, զզորսատույս, զիւրասերս,
զակնաույս, զցանկացողս չարեաց, զզաղտամիտս, զդիւրա֊
Հալանս սուտ մարգարէից, սուտ վարդապետաց, սուտ քարո֊
զողացս և սուտ գրեանցս, որք յամենայն ժամ ուսանին և երբեք
'ի գիտութիւն ճշմարտութեան ոչ Հասանին, որպէս ընդՀան֊
րական և առաքելական եկեղեցին պատուիրէ մեզ. զայնպիսին
մեծալ փորձութեամբ ընտրել. որպէս և գլուխն եկեղեցւոյն
Հրամայեաց 'ի վերն ասելով թէ զգուշ լերուք 'ի չար մշակաց
անտի և այլն:

Արդ զվերոյ գրեալն զայսոսիկ՝ պարտ է մեզ. զձեռս մեր
չհնել 'ի վերայ այնպիսեաց և չլինել մեղաց այնոցիկ կցորդ
և մասնակից։ Պարձեալ ասեմք ալ այս. արդեօք գտանի՞
այնպիսի ոք, որ զայս ամենայն արատութիւնս ոչ ունի. և
կամ եղեա՞լ է այսպիսի ոք, որք 'ի նոցանէ յետս կասեալ
և Հրաժարեալ է: Այո՛, գլյ ես որդեակք իմ, այսպիսի այր,
որ Հարիւրապատիկ առաւել քան զայսոսիկ եղեալ է, բայց
յորժամ եկեալ է ի ժամ ընտրութեան, յայնժամ յանձնատեալ
և լեակատար զղջացեալ է և առեալ է զշնորՀս Հօրն երկնա֊
ւորի. որպէս մասն ընդՀանրական և առաքելական սուրբ
եկեղեցւոյն սուրբ ղուկաս պատմէ մեզ ասելով գործոց ԳԼ 7,
Հմր. 59. Եւ սոցոս էր կամակից սպանման ստեփաննոսի:
Պարձեալ ԳԼ 9, Հմր. 1 զոր ասէ. Իսկ Սողոս տակաւին լցեալ
սպառնալեօք և սպանմամբ աշակերտացն Տեառն, մատուցեալ
առ քաշանայապետն՝ խնդրեցաց 'ի նմանէ թուլթս 'ի Դա֊
մասկոս առ ժողովուրդն. որպէս թէ զոք գլրցէ զայնր
ճանապարՀալ արս կամ կանայս, կապեալս ածցէ յԵրուսա֊
ղէմ և այլն: Ահա՛ տեսայք նազելիք իմ զդնալն սողոսի և ապայ
զղջալն նորին և զդառնալն ի քրիստոս տեր մեր և առնուլ
զՀոգին սուրբ և դասել 'ի դաս ընդՀանրականի և առաքելա֊
կանի սուրբ եկեղեցւոյն, և եղել անօթ ընտրութեան, Հաս֊
տատող ճշմարտութեան, պարձանք Հալատոյ և պարիսպ
առաքելոցն սրբոց, որ ընդՀանրական և առաքելական վեր
ճայնեալ եղեն քրիստոսիւ:

Բստ յայսմ բանին ասէ երանելին սուրբն պօղոս զի ուր

առաւելասցին մեղք, անդ առաւելասցին և շնորհք. Պարձեալ յարբերելով ասէ. զի մինչ տղայն էի իբրև զողպայ խօսէի, իբրև զողպայ համարէի, այլ յորժամ եղէ այր կատարեալ զողպայութեան 'ի բաց ընկեցի։ Ա՛յսպէս սիրելիք, թէպէտ ծես է մարդկանց գլորել, բայց ո՛չ է ծես յառնել և կանգնել։ Կալցուք և մեք զօրինակս զայս տեառն մերոյ, որ վասն մեր մեղաւորացս ասէ վասն անառակ որդւոյն զոր եկեալ առ Հայրն ասէ. Ա՛յր մեղայ յերկինս և առաջի քո, չեմ արժանի կոչիլ որդի քո, այլ արա իբրև զմի 'ի վարձկանաց քոց։ Եւ Հայրն նորա գթալով անկեալ զպարանոցաւն համբուրելով ասէ, զի այս որդին իմ մեռեալ էր և եկաց, կորուսեալ էր և գտաւ։ Եւ դարձեալ կրկնէ մեծաւ սիրով և ասէ. Հանէք զպատմուճան զորայ և տու՛ք զմատանին 'ի ձեռս նորա և արարէք զմա զեղն պարարակ, զի այս որդին իմ մեռեալ էր և եկաց, կորուսեալ էր և գտաւ։ Արդ այժմ յիմացաք դուք զկշիր տեառն մերոյ և սրբազան առաքելոյն, զոր անսուտ վճռանօքն վճռեցին մեզ և պատուիրանօքն պատուիրեցին ամենայն Հաւատացելոցս։ Պարձեալ եկեսցուք 'ի կարգս խրատոյն, զոր նախ ասացաք թէ պարտ է անարատ լինել առն այնորիկ յամենայն կողմանց, և ապա տալ նմա զեպիսկոպոսութիւն քահանայութեան, եպիսկոպոսութեան, վարդապետութեան, առաքելութեան, առաջնորդութեան և ընտրելութեան. որ սոքա ամենեքեան մի և նոյն գործ են և ո՛չ են սոքայ մեծ կամ փոքր 'ի վերայ միմեանց, այլ են Հարբթ Հաւասար, որպէս և բարենիօսն մեր յիսուս պատուիրեաց սրբազան ընտրելոցն, ասէ. ղուկ. գլ. 26, Հմր. 26. Այլ դուք ո՛չ այնպէս, այլ որ մեծն է 'ի ձեզդ, եղիցի իբրև զկրտսերն. և առաջնորդն իբրև զսպասաւորն, և այլն։ Այսպէս իշխանութիւն մի է, որպէս տէրն մեր Հրամայէ ասելով, մաթթոս գլ. 16, Հմր. 15, զոր խոստանայ տալոյ զիշխանութիւն ամենայն առաքելոցն իւրոց, այսպէս մաթս. գլ. 18, Հմր. 18, ասէ ես և տայ զկատարեալ զիշխանութիւնս ամենայն ընտրելոցն իւրոց. Ամէն ասեմ ձեզ, զոր կապիցէք յերկրի եղիցի կապեալ յերկինս և զոր արձակիցէք յերկրի եղիցի արձակեալ յերկինս։ Յա ես յոՀան. գլ. 20, Հմր. 23, եթէ ումէք թողուցուք զմեղս, թողեալ լեցի նոցա և եթէ զսւրուք ունիցիք՝ կալեալ լեցի։

Արդ այսպէս եթէ լատինք, եթէ յոյնք և եթէ Հայք ՚ի ժամ արձակմանս իւրեանց ասեն. եթէ կաթուղիկոսք և եթէ եպիսկոպոսք, եթէ վարդապետք և եթէ քահանայք նոցա ասեն. ըստ ժամանակի, և ես կարգիւս քահանայական իշխանութեամբ արձակեմ զքեզ յամենայն մահակցութենէ մեղաց, և այլն։

Տեսանք սիրելիք մեր, զի նոքա ևս վկայեն զմի լինելն իշխանութեան և ոչ մեծ կամ փոքր. ուստի Հոգին սուրբ մի եք որ էջ ՚ի վերայ ընդհանուր առաքելոցն և արար զնոսա ընդհանրական և առաքելական կաթուղիկէ սուրբ եկեղեցի. զոր հալածամք զքանս, զդաւանութիւնս, զխոստովանութիւնս և զգործս նոցա միշտ և յաւէտ և յաւիտեանս յաւիտենից. Ամէն։

Ալխճան խրատոյս։

Յաղագս ձեռնադրութեան ընտրելոյն և ՚ի կոչումն սույն աստիճանիս։

Արդ՝ զկնի ճշմարիտ համբելոյն Առաջնորդին իշխանաց և իշխանապետացն. ապայ պարտ է երիցանց ածել զայրն այն առաջի առաջնորդին մեծաւ զգուշմամբ և արտասւօք։

Եւ սկանիցեն իշխանք և իշխանապետք, բերմամբ ասելով զաղօթս զայս առ եպիսկոպոսն (ասելով) այսպէս։—

Հայր սուրբ երեսս անկեալ աղաչեմք, խնդրեմք և հայցեմք ՚ի քէն մեծաւ սիրով, զի ձեռնադրեա զարս զայս վասն կառավարութեան Հոգւոց մերոց. Ամէն.

Եւ դարձեալ եպիսկոպոսն ասէ իշխանացս այսպէս.

Արդ՝ զի դուք որք կամիք զսա ունել ձեզ Հովիւ, քաջ արդեօք բարեպէս փորձեցիք դուք զայս, որպէս և ես փորձեցի զսա մեծաւ քննութեամբ և սիրով։

Իսկ նոցա պատասխանի տուեալ ասեն առ առաքեալ
տեառն մերոյ յիսուսի քրիստոսի :—

Այո՛, Հայր պատուական մեր, զի զամենայն Հրամայեալդ
քոյդ տերութեանդ կատարեալ եմք աստուծով:

Եւ դարձեալ ընդրեալ ասէ իշխանաց և ամենայն լսողաց.
Թէ ես անպարտ եմ՝ ըստ այսմ մասի և դուք պարտական:

Եւ ապայ ընդրեալն սկսանի զբանս [1] տեառն մերոյ բարե
խօսին Հարցանել ընթերցօղն այսպէս: Մտթ. գլ. 20,
Հմր. 23.

Արդեօք կարէ՞ն ըմպել զբաժակն զոր ես ըմպելոց եմ
և կամ զմկրտութիւն իմ մկրտել զոր ես [2] մկրտելոց եմ: Եւ
նորա պատասխանի տուեալ յօժար կամաւ և սիրով ասէ
ցառաքնորդն. Այո, Հայր սուրբ զի ծառայն քոյ յանձն
առնում զգանս, զբանդս, զչարչարանս, զնախատինս, զխաչս,
զՀարուածս, զնեղութիւնս և զամենայն փորձութիւնս աշխա
րՀի, զոր տերն և բարեխօսն մեր և ընդՀանրական և առաքե
լական սուրբ եկեղեցին առին անձինս իւրեանց, և սիրով
ընկալայն զնոսա: Այսպէս և ես անարժան ծառայ յիսուսի
քրիստոսի մեծաւ սիրով և յօժար կամաւ զամենեսեանս զայսօսիկ
առնում յանձն իմ մինչև 'ի ժամ մաՀուան իմոյ. Ամէն:

Եւ ապա տէրն այն առնու առաջի իւր և ինքն բաձմեալ
'ի վերայ աթոռոյն և սկանիցի ասել նախ զանուն Հօր
և որդոյ և Հոգւոյն սրբոյ, Ամէն:

Եւ ապա ասացէ զաղօթս տեառն մերոյ յիսուսի քրիստոսի:
Եւ յետոյ սկսանիցէ ընթեռնուլ զսուրբ աւետարանն,
Մտթ. գլ. I, մինչև ցՀմր. 16:

Այլ ևս գործոց գլ. 6, մինչև ցՀմր. 8.

Եւ ապա ընթերցցեր գործոց գլ. I, մինչև ցՀմր. 5: ՟այր
մեր որ, և այլն.

---

[1] ? բունս.   [2] ձ. եմ.

Պարձեալ աւետարան Մ՝թս. գլ. 3, մինչև գՃմր. 17.

Նա հս գործոց գլ. 13, Հմր. մինչև գ 6.

Եւ յետ այսցիկ եպիսկոպոսն կոչէ զեշխանն առ ինքն, և իշխանացն եկեալ դնիցեն զձեռս իւրեանց ի վերայ ընթերցողին, իսկ եպիսկոպոսն առնու զսուրբ աւետարանն 'ի ձեռս իւր և տայ ի ձեռն ընթերցողին, և ապա Հարցանէ զանուն նորա Հեզութեամբ և խոնարՀութեամբ թէ ՕՀինչ է անուն քո որդեակ իմ սիրելի: Եւ նորա պատասխանի տուեալ ասէ, թէ է անուն ծառայիքո պետրոս։ Իսկ առաքեալն փոխեցէ զանուն նորին ըստ աւետարանին և յետ փախելոյ զանուն Մրկ խնդրողէն յայնժամ տայ զեշխանութիւն ասելով այսպէս։ Գլ. 3 Հմր. Ա՛ռ քեզ իշխանութիւն կապելոյ և արձակելոյ զորդիս Պ կա մարդկան 'ի յերկինս և 'ի յերկրի, մոթս. գլ. 18, Հմր. 18, Հմր. և յՀն. գլ. 23, Հմր. 23.

Ըստ տալով զեշխանութիւնս իսկ և իսկ պարտ է ընթեռնուլ զսուրբ աւետարանս։ Օկնի ընթերցմանն սոցին Հարկ է հս ընթեռնուլ զաւետարանն ծնդեան, ղուկ. գլ. 2, Հմր. 13, և մոթս. գլ. 2, Հմր. մինչև գ 13։

Իսկ յետ ընթերցման սրբոյ աւետարանին ղուկ. և գայ այն տեղին, զոր Հրեշտակք երգէին զերգս իւրեանց, պարտ է եպիսկոպոսին, նոր ընտրելոյն, իշխանաց, իշխանապետաց և ամենայն ժողովրդոցն երգեն զփառք 'ի բարձունս աստուծոյ, և երկիր խաղաղութիւն, 'իմարդիկ Հաճութիւն։

Օայսքանս պարտ է ասել և ոչ յաւելի։—

[Թ]ազգաւոր Թագաւորաց, տէր և արարող ամենայն եղանակացս, որ արարեր զնախաՀայրն մեր 'ի Հողոյ և զնախամայրն մեր 'ի կողէ նորա. իսկ նոցա ՀանդուրժեալքՈւ սուրբ պատուիրանիդ պատրեցան պատրանօքն բանսարկին։ Արդ գթութիւդ քոյ աստուածութեանդ արարեր զնոր մարդն վերուս, որպէս և սուրբն պօղոս ասէ. մարդով եղև մաՀ և մարդով վերկութիւն։ Այսպես և ......¹ քրիստոս յիսուս պաՀեալ

¹ բառք երկու քերեալ.

զանձառելէ պատուէրանէ քո և զաղչանեաց զգլուխ զշակառա֊
կոզին.քոյ, զոր ինքն միածին որդիդ քո սիրելին ասէ, յՅն. դլ. I5,
Հմր. IO, եթէ պաՀիցէք զպատուիրանս իմ, կացցէք 'ի սէր իմ;
որպէս և ես զպատուիրանս Հօր իմոյ պաՀեցի և կամ 'ի սէր
նորա ։ Ա՛սպէս և գլուխն մեր.քրիստոս պաՀեաց զՇմարիտ բա֊
նդ և զպատուիրանդ.քյս տէրութեանդ և ելից զպարոս մեր
և ընկալաւ 'ի քէն զորՀնութիւնս անվախճան։ Եւ այժմ երեսս
անկեալ աղաչեմք խնդրեմք և Հայցեմք 'ի քէն, ընկալ զաղա֊
չանս մեր բարեխոսութեամբ միածնիդ քո և միշնորդութեամբ
սուրբ մկրտութեան նորին և կենսատու պատուական մարմնոյ
և արեան նորին և սուրբ անտանելի շարշարանաց նորին.
տուր սմա զշնորՀս քյս սուրբ, զոր այժմ եկեալ է և խնդրէ
'ի քէն զշնորՀս քո սուրբ իշխանութեան և ընդ սիրելի
որդւոյդ քում դասիլ զոր ասէ. զի ուր ևան իցեմ՝ (անդ)
և պաշտօնեան իմ եղիցի:

Եւ ապա իշխանացն առնուն զձեռս իւրեանց յետ և 'ի վեր
բարձեալ զեազուկս Հանդերձ եպիսկոպոսին, ասեն դայս
աղօթս միաբան 'ի վերայ նոր ընտրելոյն այսպէս:—

Կեանք և ապաւէն, միշնորդ և բարեխոս. Ա՛րդ գլուխ
երկնաւորաց և երկրաւորաց և սանդարամետականաց, դուռն
երկնից. ՃանապարՀ ձշմարտութեան և կեանք 'ի քեզ ուղղա֊
պէս Հաւատացելոց, զի դու խոստացար անսուտ բանիւ.քով
թէ որ դայ առ իս 'ի խալար մի՝ մնասցէ և կամ՝ զեկեայն
առ իս ոչ Հանից արտաքս.

Ա՛րդ զի սա, որ մկրտեցյալ յանուն.քո սուրբ և ընտրեցյալ
Հօր Հոգով.քով սրբով, և այժմ սպասեալ մնայ անսուտ
խոստման.քյ. նստարուք 'ի քաղաքիդ յերուսաղէմ մինչև
զգենուցուք զօրութիւն 'ի բարձանց: Ա՛յլ այժմ երեսս
անկեալ առ ոտս.քյ ջերմ սիրով, դառն արտասուք աղերսեմք,
Հայցեմք և խնդրեմք 'ի քէն՝ առաքեա՛ 'ի սա զշնորՀս Հօր.քյ,
զի եկեալ յարդարեսցէ զՏողի, զմիտ և զմարմին սորայ և
պայծառացուսցէ զսա յամենայն շար խորՀրդոց և տուր 'ի
սմա զՏողի.քո զոր առեր 'ի Հօրէ 'ի գետն յորդանան, զորացո
զսա և բաց, տէր, զմիտս սորա առ 'ի յիմանալ զգիրս և

47

առնուլ զխաչս սիրով և եկեսցէ զկնի քո յայժմ և յաւէտ և յաւիտեանս յաւիտենից, Ամէն։

Եւ ապա եպիսկոպոսն երիս անգամ փչեսցէ 'ի դէմս նոր ընտրելոյն ասելով այսպէս. Ա՛ճ փչումն տեառն մերոյ յիսուսի քրիստոսի բացցէ զմիտս քո, ո՛վ սիրելի որդեակ իմ, և զօրացուսցէ զքեզ 'ի գործս քո. Ամէն

Եւ ապա ընթերձցէր զսուրբ խոստումն Հրեշտակապետին զոր խոստացաւ վասն յիսուսի.

Աւետն ղկ. գլ. I, համր. 26.

Եւ յամսեանն վեցերորդի՝ առաքեցաւ Գաբրիէլ Հրեշտակ Աստուծոյ 'ի քաղաք մի Գալիլեացւոց, որում անուն էր Նազարէթ, Առ կոյս խօսեցեալ առն, որում անուն էր Յովսէփ՝ 'ի տանէ Դաւթի. և անուն կուսին Մարիամ։ Եւ եկեալ առ նա՝ Հրեշտակն ասէ. Ուրախ լեր բերկրեալղ, Տէր ընդ քեզ։ Եւ նա ընդ բանն խռովեցաւ, և խորհէր ընդ միտ՝ թէ որպիսի ինչ իցէ ողջոյնս այս։ Եւ ասէ ցնա Հրեշտակն. Մի՛ երկնչեր Մարիամ, զի գտեր շնորհս յԱստուծոյ։ Եւ աՀա յղասջիր՝ և ծնցես որդի, և կոչեցես զանուն նորա Յիսուս։ Նա եղիցի մեծ, և Որդի Բարձրելոյն կոչեսցի. և տացէ նմա Տէր Աստուած զաթոռն Դաւթի Հօր նորա. և Թագաւորեսցէ 'ի տանն Յակովբայ 'ի յաւիտեանս. Եւ Թագաւորութեան նորա վախճան մի՛ լիցի։ Եւ ասէ Մա- րիամ ցՀրեշտակն. Օ՛իա՞րդ լինիցի ինձ այդ, քանզի զայր ո՛չ գիտեմ։ Պատասխանի ետ Հրեշտակն և ասէ ցնա. Հոգի Սուրբ եկեսցէ 'ի քեզ, և զօրութիւն Բարձրելոյն Հովանի լիցի 'ի վերայ քո. քանզի և որ ծնանելոցն է 'ի քէն՝ սուրբ է, և Որդի Աստուծոյ կոչեսցի։ Եւ աՀա Եղիսաբէթ ազգական քո՝ և նա յղի է 'ի ծերութեան իւրում. և այս նոր վեցերորդ ամիս է նորա՝ որ ամուլն կոչեցեալ է. Զի ո՛չ տկարասցի առ Աստուծոյ ամենայն բան։ Եւ ասէ Մարիամ. ԱՀաւասիկ կամաղախին Տեառն, եղիցի ինձ ըստ բանի քում։ և գնաց 'ի նմանէ Հրեշտակն։

ՅՀն Հմր.

եթ արբո թեա խ օր թեր զսու աւե րանն կտա նոր որբ տռնա զծող սուր

Եւ դարձեալ ի գործս առաքելոցն ընթերձչիր, գլ. 2, Հմր. 1 մինչև ցՀմր. 21։—

Եւ 'ի կատարել աւուրցն Պենտեկոստէից էին ամենեքեան միաբան 'ի միասին։ Եւ եղև յանկարծակի Հնչիւն յերկնից՝ եկեալ իբրև սաստիկ Հողմոյ. և ելից զամենայն տունն յորում նստէին։ Եւ երևեցան նոցա բաժանեալ լեզուք իբրև 'ի Հրոյ. և նստաւ իւրաքանչիւր 'ի վերայ նոցա։ Եւ լցան ամենեքեան Հոգւով Սրբով, և սկսան խոսել յայլ և յայլ լեզուս՝ որպէս և Հոգին տայր բարբառել նոցա։ Եւ էին յԵրուսաղէմ բնակեալ Հրեայք՝ արք երկիւղածք՝ յամենայն ազգաց՝ որ 'ի ներքոյ երկնից։ Եւ իբրև եղև բարբառս այս՝ եկն միաբան բազմութիւնն՝ և խռնեցաւ, զի լսէին իւրաքանչիւր լեզուս խոսել նոցա։ Զարհանային ամենեքեան, և զարմանային՝ և ասէին ընդ միմեանս. Ո՞չ աՀաւասիկ ամենեքին սոքա որք խոսինս՝ Գալիլեացիք են։ Եւ զիա՞րդ լսեմք մեք իւրաքանչիւր բարբառս մեր՝ յորում ծնեալ եմք։ Պարթևք և Մարք և Իլամացիք և որ բնակեալ են 'ի Միջագետս, 'ի Հրէաստանի և 'ի Գամիրս, 'ի Պոնտոս և Ասիա. 'ի Փռիւգիայ և 'ի Պամփիւլեայ՝ յԵգիպտոս և 'ի կողմանս Լիբէացւոց, որ ընդ Կիւրենացիս, և որ եկք Հռովմայեցիք. Հրեայք՝ և եկք նոցուն, Կրետացիք և Արաբացիք՝ լսեմք խոսից նոցա 'ի մեր լեզուս զմեծամեծս Աստուծոյ։ Զարհանային ամենեքեան զարմացեալք, և ասէին զմիմեանս. Ո՞րն կամիցի այս լինել։ Եւ կիսոցն ընդ խաղ արկեալ ասէին, թէ քաղցուալից իցեն։ Ցարուցեալ Պետրոս Հանդերձ մետասանիւքն՝ ամբարձ զձայն իւր՝ և խոսեցաւ ընդ նոսա. Ա՛րք Հրէաստանեայք և որ բնակեալ էք յԵրուսաղէմ ամենեքին, այս ձեզ յայտնի լիցն և ունկն դիք բանից իմոց։ Ո՛չ որպէս դուք կարծէք՝ թէ սոքա արբեալ իցեն. զի դեռ երեք ժամք են աւուրս։ Ա՛յլ այս է որ ասացաւ 'ի ձեռն մարգարէին Յովելեայ։ Եւ եղիցի յետ այսորիկ յաւուրս յետինս՝ ասէ Աստուած, Հեղից յՈգւոյ իմմէ 'ի վերայ ամենայն մարմնոյ. և մարգարէասցին ուստերք ձեր, և դստերք ձեր. և երիտասարդք ձեր տեսիլս տեսցեն, և ծերք ձեր երազովք երազեսցին։

Եւ 'ի վերայ ծառայից իմոց՝ և 'ի վերայ աղախնեայց իմոց՝ յաւուրս յայնոսիկ Հեղից յՈգւոյ իմմէ, և մարգարէասցին։ Եւ տաց նշանս յերկինս 'ի վեր՝ և նշանս յերկիր 'ի խոնարհ, արիւն և հուր և մրրիկ ծխոյ։ Արեգակն դարձցի 'ի խաւար, և լուսին յարիւն՝ մինչև եկեալ իցէ օր Տեառն մեծ և երևելի։ Եւ եղիցի ամենայն որ կարդասցէ զանուն Տեառն՝ կեցցէ։

Եւ ապա ասա զաղօթս զայս․

Գոհանամ և մեծացուցանեմ զքեզ Հայր երկնաւոր, Աստուած ճշմարիտ, որ զմիածին որդիդ քո սիրելի փառաւորեցեր հոգւով քով սրբով, ես զսուրբը զընդհանրական և առաքելական եկեղեցի որդւոյդ քո միածնիդ զարդարեցեր պէսպէս շնորհօք։ Եւ այժմ երկիր պագանելով աղաչեմք զքեզ Հայր բարեդույթ, առաքեա 'ի նոր ընտրեալս այս զքո անսպառելի շնորհդ, որ եկեալ լցուսցէ զսա և եղիցի սմա պարիսպ և զէն ամենայն[1] Հակառակողին քո, որ միշտ և Հանապազ յօրալ կամի զշատացեալքս քո միածնիդ. Արդ դիր զաշ քո սուրբ 'ի վերայ ծառայի քո ընտրելոյդ և պահեա զսա 'ի չարէ և 'ի փորձութենէ աշխարհի բարբ խոսութեամբք որդւոյդ քո ճշմարտի, յայժմ և միշտ և յաւիտեանս յաւիտենից ամէն.

Եւ ապա ընդերձցիր զսուրբը աւետարանս, ՅՆ. ԳԼ. 20, ՀՄր. 19 մինչ գՀՄր. 24 ։—

Եւ էր երեկոյ 'ի միաշաբաթոջ աւուրն. և դրօքն փակէ լովք՝ ուր էին աշակերտքն ժողովեալ վասն աՀին ՝րէից, եկն Յիսուս՝ և եկաց 'ի մէջի նոցա, և ասէ ցնոսա. Ողջոյն ընդ ձեզ։ Իբրև զայս ասաց՝ եցոյց նոցա զձեռսն և զկողս իւր. և խնդացին աշակերտքն իբրև տեսին զՏէր։ Ասէ ցնոսա դարձեալ. Ողջոյն ընդ ձեզ, որպէս առաքեաց զիս Հայր իմ, և ես առաքեմ զձեզ։ Եւ զայս իբրև ասաց՝ փչեաց 'ի նոսա և ասէ. Առէ՛ք զՀոգի Սուրբ։ Եթէ ումէք թողուցուք

---

[1] թերևս 'ընդդէմ.'

զմեղս՝ թողեալ լիցի նոցա. և թէ զուբուք ունիցէք՝ կալեալ լիցի։

Եւ զպատուէր սրբյն պօղոսի ընթերցջիր. եփրայեցիս գլ. 13 և Հմր. 17.

Ունկնդիր լերուք առաջնորդաց ձերոց, և Հպատակ կացէք նոցա. զի նոքա տքնին վասն ոգւոց ձերոց՝ որպէս թէ Համարս տալոց իցեն ընդ ձեր. զի խնդութեամբ արասցեն զայն՝ և մի յոգւոց Հանելով. զի այն ո՛չ յօգուտ ձեր է։ Աղօթս արարէք վասն մեր. զի Հաստատեալ գիտեմք եթէ բարւոք միտս ունիմք. յամենայնի կամիմք բարւոք զնացս ցուցանել։ Եւ առաւել աղաչեմ՝ զի զայն առնիցէք, զի վաղագոյն պատսպարեցայց ձեզ։ Եւ Աստուած խաղաղութեան՝ որ եՀան ՚ի մեռելոց զՀովիւն Հօտից զմեծն արեամբ յաւիտենական ուխտին զՏէրն մեր Յիսուս ՚Րբիստոս, Հաստատեսցէ զձեզ ՚ի գործս բարու- թեան՝ առնել զկամս նորա. և արասցէ ՚ի մեզ զՀաճոյսն առաջի իւր ՚ի ձեռն Յիսուսի ՚Րբիստոսի. որում փառք յաւիտեանս. ամէն

Եւ ապա ասա զաղօթս զայս ընդդէմ քրիստոսի:

Հաց Հրեշտակաց և Հալատացելոց, միշնորդ և բարեխօս մեզ մեղաւորացս, գառն աստուծոյ յիսուս, օգնեա՛ մեզ և մա- նաւանդ այս նոր ընաբեալ ծառային, զոր խանեցեր ՚ի թիւս աշակերտոց քոց սիրելեաց. Կացո՛ դա ՚ի վերայ շնորՀեալ աւետարանիդ ընդՀանրական և առաքելական եկեղեցւդ Հաստատ և վէմ անխախտելի ՚ի դրանց դժոխոց. և տուր սմա զբաջ Հօվւութիւն, որ արածիցէ մեծաւ սիրով զՏօտ քյ բանաւոր. զոր մասն ընդՀանրական և առաքելական սուրբ եկեղեցւոյն՝ սուրբն պետրոս ասէ. կթղկեց գլ. 5, Հմր. 2. Աբածեցէք որ ՚ի ձեզ Հօտ է աստուծոյ, որովՀետև կոչ- մամին քյ խանեցաւ սա ընդ սուրբն. քո. պաՀեա՛ զծառայս քո ընդ ընաբեալն քյ, զի մի յիշխեցէ մերձենալ ՚ի սմա պիղծ Հոգի դիւաց. ամրացո՛ զընորբեալդ քյ ՚ի գործող զոր աւանդեցեր ամենայն ընորելոցդ և Հաւատացելոցդ ՚ի քեզ. Ամէն։

Որդ զկնի աղօթիցս այսոցիկ տուր զխաղաղութիւն ամենայն ժողովրդեան. և ապա առցէ եպիսկոպոսն զնոր ընտրեալն առ ինքն և խրատէ զնա մեծաւ սիրով. ես ընթեռնուլ տա զսուրբ աւետարանն միշտ և Հանապազ. նա ես զսուրբ կտակարան ընդհանրական և առաքելական եկեղեցւոյն. զի սոքօք լիապէս առնու զշնորհս Հոգոյն սրբոյ մինչև զքառասուն օր։

Գլուխ (?).

Խուծմունք վասն Հարկաւոր բանից տեառն մերոյ յիսուսի քրիստոսի, զոր սուրբ աւետարանիչքն վկայեալ են. Մտթս. գլ. 1, Հմր. 25.

Եւ ո՛չ գիտաց զնա մինչև ծնաւ զորդին իւր զանդրանիկ . . . . . .[1] եւ յետ ութօրեայ կոչեցաւ անուն նորա յիսուս, զոր Հրեշտակն գաբրիէլ ասաց 'ի կուսութեան ժամանակի։ տե՛ս 'ի Ղկ. գլ. 1, Հմր. 26.

Վասն այսորիկ սուրբ աւետարանիչք և սրբազան առաքեալքն, նա ես տէրն մեր յիսուս քրիստոս նախ քան զծնունդն մարիամու կոյս ասեն և յետ ծննդեանն կին կոչեն, և զկուսութիւն նորա 'ի բաց բառնան, զոր յայտ է նախ ասացեալ որդոյն աստուծոյ։ Յհն. գլ. 2, Հմր. 4.

'Ի կանայ գալիլեացւոց ուր արար զշորն գինի. Օ՜ կայ իմ և քոյ, կին դու, զի չև է Հասեալ ժամանակ իմ։ Յհն. Հմր.

Կամ 'ի ժամ չարչարանաց 'ի վերայ փայտին բարձեալ կայր, ասէ ցմայրն իւր. Կին աՀա որդի քո. և ցսիրելի աշակերտն իւր յանձնեալ ասելով. աՀա մայր քո։ Յհն. գլ. 1 Հմր.

Ա՛յլ վկայութիւնք բազումք 'ի սուրբ աւետարան և կտակարան առաքելոցն. զսակաւս ասեմք վասն ճշմարտութեան օգտի և ո՛չ առ նախանձու։ Որպէս յայտ է 'ի ժամ չարչարանաց տեառն յիսուսի, զոր Հրամայեն աւետարանիչքն

---

[1] աստանօր բառք քանի մի քերեալ։

ա. ասելով. Ի՞ն և անդ կանայք յորս եկեալ էին մարիամ մագ-
բ. թաղենացի և մարիամ յակոբայ և յովսիայ մայր, զոր 'ի
 յայլում տեղւոջ՝ այսինքն 'ի գալառն յիսուսի ցյց տալով
 և զարմացմամբ ասեն. Ո՞չ սա է որդի Հուսան, ո՞չ մայր
ա. սորայ կոչի մարիամ և եղբայրք սորա յակոբոս, յօսէ, սիմոն
 և յուդաս. և քորք սորա առ մեզ են։ Գարձեալ սուրբն ղուկաս
բ. 'ի բաց բառնայ զերանութիւն և տայ այնոցիկ որք 'ի քրիստոս
 յիսուս Հալատացին։ Գլ. II, Համր. 27. Եւ մինչդեռ նա ընդ
 ժողովուրդս խօսէր կին մի ճայն եբարձ 'ի ժողովրդենէն անտի
 և ասէ. երանի յորովայնի որ կրեաց զքեզ և ստեանց որք
 դիեցուցին զքեզ։ Եւ յիսուս դարձեալ բանայր 'ի լուր
 ժողովրդեանն զերանութիւն 'ի մօրէ իւրմէ և տայ յայնց
7. որք զբանն իւր առնեն և պահեն։ Օր և յոՀաննէս
 աւետարանիչն բաց 'ի բաց յայտնէ զանՀալատս ասելով
 վասն եղբարց տեառն յիսուսի. Ել և գնայ աստի, զի և
 աշակերտքն քյ տեսցեն զգործս քո զոր գործես, քանզի
 և եղբայրք նորա զի չէ ես էին Հալատացեալ 'ի նա։ Եւ
 մանաւանդ անօշն ընտրութեան մատն ընթանրականի և
 առաքելականի սուրբ եկեղեցւոյն սուրբն պօղոս ասէ վասն
տ. տեառն մերոյ յիսուսի. Օի ծնաւ 'ի կնոջէ և եմուտ ընդ
 օրինօք։

Ասպէս՝ նախ քան զծնանիլն մարիամու զնորաստեղծն
ադամ՝ դարբիւել Հրեշտակապետն կոյս ասէ և ողջոյնէ
զնա, բայց յետ ծննդեան նոյն Հրեշտակն ո՞չ կոյս ասէ.
Որպէս յայտ է 'ի սուրբ աւետարանն, զոր 'ի տեսեան ասէ
յովսէփայ. արի առ զմանուկն և զմայր իւր և փախիր
յեգիպտոս։ Եւ դարձեալ յետ ժամանակի ինչ. երեցաւ
3. Հրեշտակն տեառն 'ի տեսեան և ասէ. արի առ զմանուկ
 և մայր իւր և գնայ յերկիրն քո.

Յաղագս ստեղծման Ադամայ և տեառն մերոյ յիսուսի
քրիստոսի։

Նախ Հայր յերկնաւոր, աստուած ճշմարիտ, բստեղծ զեր
կինս Հանդերձ իւրայնօք և զերկիր ամենայն սերմբք իւրովք,
զարդարեաց զնոսա։ Որպէս յայտ է 'ի շունչ աստու-

ծութեան։ Դարձեալ տեսեալ բարերարին աստուծոյ, թէ ամենայն ինչ բարի է, կամ եղև նմա առնուլ զթագաւոր ոմն 'ի վերայ ամենայն էակաց. և մանաւանդ վասն չարագդյն բանսարկուին որպէս յայտ է մից բանին զոր ասէ. արասցուք մարդ ըստ պատկերի մերում և ըստ նմանութեան։ Լյսպէս 'ի քթրոտել ական միով բանիւ ըստեղծ գերկինս և գերկիր։ Իսկ միով բանիւ ըստեղծ զչինն աղամ և արար զնա թա֊ գաւոր և իշխան ամենայն արարածոց։ Վասն որոյ տեսեալ սատանայի զգերազանց թագաւորութիւն աղամայ նախանձե֊ ցաւ, որպէս դիրք աստուածային վերբերէ առ նա ասելով. զի նախանձու բանսարկուին մահ եմուտ աշխարհ. նա ևս սուրբն պօղոս ասէ թէ մարդով եղև մահ և մարդով յարու թիւն։ Լյլ ևս կրկնէ զայս ասելով. Որպէս աղամաւ Լոշ ամենեքեան մեռան նոյնպէս և քրիստոսիւ կենդանասցին։ Կորն Արդ նախապէս ասացաք թէ Հայրն ամենակարող միով բանիւ Գէ 1 էստեղծ զաղամ 'ի Հողոյ և զելայ ի կողէ նորա, սմին նման Հմր. 'ի յա 1 . . . .

. . . ասէր Հայր 'ի ճեռս քոյ աւանդեմ զՀոգի իմ. նա ևս Ոււ աղաչէր վասն թշնամեաց թէ Հայր թող սոցա, զի ոչ գիտեն Գէ 2 զինչ գործեն։ Ել դարձեալ ասէ առ մարիամ մագդաղենացի Հմր. աշակերտին իւր յետ յարութեան, զի չէ ևս ելեալ եմ առ Հայրն իմ և առ Հայրն ձեր, և աստուած իմ և աստուածն ձեր։ Ել դարձեալ սուրբը ընդՀանրական եկեղեցին միաբերան Մտ ասեն թէ քրիստոս մեռաւ և աստուած յարոյց զնա 'ի մեռելոց. Գէ 2 գոն և այլ բազումք, որ ոչ գրեցաք. Հմր.

Ցաղագս բարեխոսութեան տեառն մերոյ յիսուսի քրիստոսի Ոււ և ոչ այլ սրբոց կամ մեռելոց և կամ քարից և փայտից Գէ 2 և պատկերաց. զոր ոմանք ուրացեալ են զգաատուական միջնոր֊ Հմր. դութիւն և բարեխոսութիւն սիրելէ որդւոյն աստուծոյ, և ՅՀն. Հետևեալ են մեռելոց և մանաւանդ պատկերաց, քարից, Գէ 1 փայտից, չրոց, ծառոց, աղբերաց և այլ ամենայն յուևայն Հմր. իրաց, որպէս ասեն և երկիր պագանեն, գիսունկա և գմոմս այլ Հմր.

---

[1] աստանօր թերթ մի 'ի բաց պատառեալ (երես բնագրին, 126-127)։

ընծայեն և զոհս մատուցանեն, որք սոքա ամենեքեան են Հակառակ աստուածութեան։ Օ՛ր տէրն մեր զայս ամենայն առ ոտս իւր սուրբ առեալ ասէ. Ես եմ դուռն. եթէ ոք ընդ իս մտցէ ելցէ, մտցէ և ճարակ գտցէ և այլն.

Եւ դարձեալ ասէ. թէ ես եմ ճանապարհ և ճշմարտու թիւն և կեանք։

Նա ես ասէ. ես իսկ եմ յարութիւն և կեանք։

Դարձեալ ասէ. ես եմ միջնորդ և բարեխօսն ձեր ·

5.
ա. Որպէս ասէ ցպետրոս, զուկաս. և ես աղաչեցի զՀայր իմ վասն քոյ։

3. Այլ ես ասէ առաքելոցն իւրոց. և ես աղաչեցից զՀայր, զի և այլ մխիթարիչ տացէ ձեզ։

Եւ ես առ մեզ Հաւատացելոցս ասէ. Ո՛չ վասն նոցա
I. աղաչեմ, այլ և վասն Հաւատացելոց բանիւ նոցա յիս։

Արկնէ ասելով, Հայր ո՛չ վասն նոցա աղաչեմ, զի բարեաս զսոսայ յաշխարհէ, այլ զի պաՀեսցես զնոսա ՚ի չարէ։

o.

Յաղագս վկայութեանց առաքելոց սրբոց։

5.
Նախ սուրբն ստեփաննոս եետես զաբեխսութիւն տեառն մերոյ յիսուսի քրիստոսի ՚ի ժամ քարկոծման, զոր պատմէ սուրբ ղուկաս ՚ի գործոց գլ. 7, Համր. 55. Եւ եետես զերկինս բացեալ և զյիսուս զի կայր ընդ աջմէ աստուծոյ։

գլ. 8, Եւ սուրբն պօղոս ասէ. Իսկ արդ ո՞վ է որ դատապարտ
4. առնիցէ, եթէ Յիսուս Քրիստոս որ մեռաւն, և մանաւանդ թէ յարուցեալ իսկ է. և է ընդ աջմէ Աստուծոյ, որ և
Է 2, բարեխօս իսկ է վասն մեր։

Դարձեալ ասէ. քանզի մի է Աստուած, և մի միջնորդ
՟հս Աստուծոյ և մարդկան՝ մարդն Յիսուս Քրիստոս. Օ՛ր սուրբ յօՀան ՚ի կաթուղկեաց ասէ. Որդեակք, զայս գրեմ ձեզ. մի մեղիցէք, և եթէ մեղցէ ոք, ունիմք առ աստուած
6. բարեխօս զյիսուս քրիստոս, զարդարն և զանարատն, և նա
գլ. 2, է քաւութիւն և թողութիւն մեղաց մերոց. և ո՛չ թէ մերոց,

այլ և ամենայն[1] որբք չհա ուղղապէս Հաւատան։ Նա և իւր սուրբ պատուական մարմին և սուրբ անարատ արիւնն է առ ինքն բարեխօս, և ո՛չ այլ ինչ։

Յաւելորդ բանից ասցելոց.

Դարձեալ Հարցանեմ ձեզ ուրացող փափիչդ և Հեռուողացդ ձերոց. Թէ դուք որք զերեխային որք 'ի յարգանդ մարցն իւրեանց պէս պէս Հնարիւք. որք ոչ իսկ են եկեալ յաշխարՀ. և կամ ծնեալ են մեռեալ. զոմանս 'ի յորովայնս մկրտէք և զոմանս 'ի մեռելութեան թեակալ մկրտէք. որք են սոքա ամենեին դիւական և ո՛չ աստուածական։

Օ՛ի աստուածն ամենից ո՛չ տայ զայսպիսի շնորՀս առ սիրելեան իւր, քանզի ինքն պարզ է և շնորՀեալ շնորՀն իւր է պարզ և ճշմարիտ։ Ոստի յայտ է 'ի ձերոց գործոց, զոր երբեմն բնադատէք 'ի ճշմարտութեեն զճշմարիտն իսուխ ասելով. մի ոք յերեխայից և մի ոք 'ի թերաՀաւատից և մի ոք յ(ան)ապաշխարողաց և յանմաքրից. չէ յարժան մերձենալ 'ի սուրբ աստուածային խորՀուրդս։

Արդ՝ եթէ դուք աստուծոյ, քրիստոսի և ընդՀանրականի և առաքելականի սրբոյ եկեղեցոյն ո՛չ լսէք, գոնեա սուտ վկայութեանց և խոստմանց ձերոց անսացէք. քանզի երեք են խորՀուրդք աստուածային, զոր ի վերուստ Հնչեալ որդյն իւր միածնին. և սրբոյ յօՀաննու մեծին մարգարէին։ Նախ՝ ապաշխարութիւն. երկրորդ՝ մկրտութիւն, և երրորդ սուրբ Հաղորդութիւն. զի զերեքեանքս այստրիկ կատարելոց են և ո՛չ երեխայից անապաշխարողաց և կամ անՀաւատից։

Եւ դարձեալ Հարցանեմ ձեզ կարգազուրկացդ, թէ յերեխայն այն որ կայ առ ձեզ յորումն ժամու խնդրեաց, կամ յորումն տեղի աղաչեաց 'ի սուտ վկայէ անտի. թէ ես 'ի քէն խնդրեմ զՀաւատ, զյոյս, զսէր և զայլ ամենայն բարեգործութիւնս, 'ի սուտ վկայէ անտի։

Օ՛ի եթէ երեխայն այն 'ի յաւանակէ[2] անտի խնդրէ Նպա

---
[1] ձ. 'ամ.' մարթ է ընթեռնուլ 'ամենեցուն.'
[2] ձ. յաւանակի.

ընդէր 'ի ձեռչ կարգադուրկացդ ոչ խնդրէ։ Արդ այսմանէ սուտ բանից ձերոց յայտնեցաւ ճշմարտութիւն տեառն մերոյ Յիսուսի քրիստոսի որպէս զաբեզական. և եղե ամենայն օրէնս ձեր սուտ և խաբէութիւն. զոր տերն մեր Յիսուս քրիստոս Նախապէս ասէ. եւ որ սուտ խօսի Յերբոց անտի խօսի և Հայր նորա սատանայ է։ Յօհան, Գլ.   , Հմր. ·

Խրատ Քրիստոնեականի.

Եթէ ոք կամի, որդեակք իմ, զուղղափառ դաւանութիւն ստանալ նախ նոցա պարտ է լեփկատար զՏարկաւոր Հարցմունս և զդաւանութիւնս ուսանիլ։ Եւ ապա գայ և խնդրէ զսուրբ մկրտութիւնն և զպատուական մարմին և արիւն տեառն մերոյ Յիսուսի քրիստոսի ուտէ և ըմպէ. ի Հալատացեալ ժամանակի և ոչ 'ի անսաւտ յերեխայութեան։

Յաղագս քրիստոնեականի վարդապետութեան.

Դլուխ (?).

Հարց. Դու քրիստոնեայ ես ·
Պատասխանի. Այո՛, ես քրիստոնեայ եմ։
Հ. Քրիստոնեայ ասելն զինչ ասել է։
Պ. Այն ասել է. որ դոեկրն մեր Յիսուս քրիստոս ճանաչէ թէ զինչ է և դպատուիրան նորա պաՀէ։
Հ. Ո՞րինչ է պատուիրան և Հրաման տեառն մերոյ Յիսուսի քրիստոսի զոր պաՀեմք։
Պ. Այն է զոր տերն մեր պատուիրեաց աշկերտաց և Հաւատացելոց իւրոց ասելով ,Ո՛ի եթէ սիրեցէք զիս, դպատուիրանս իմ պաՀեցէք։ Որպէս և ես դպատուիրանս Հօրն իմոյ պաՀեցի։
Հ. Քանի՞ են պատուիրանք տեառն մերոյ Յիսուսի քրիստոսի։
Պ. Ութ այսքան են. Նախ յուսումն, երկրորդ ապաշ-

խարութիւն, երրորդ Հաւատ, չորրորդ մկրտութիւն, Հինգե֊
րորդ Հաղորդութիւն, և վեցերորդ սէր որ է դլուխ ամենե
ցուն։

Հ. Թէ զի՞նչ է քրիստոս և կամ որպիսի պարտեմք չնա
ճանչել և Հաւատալ։

Պ. Պարտեմք զէ որպէս ընդհանրական և առաքելական
սուրբ եկեղեցին Հաւատաց և մեզ հարկ է այնպէս Հաւատալ։

Հ. Որպէ՞ս Հաւատացին երանելի առաքեալքն, ուսմ՛ մեզ։

Պ. Որպէս սուրբ յոՀաննէս աւետարանիչն յայտնէ ասելով
թէ մեք Հաւատացաք և ճանեաք թէ դու ես քրիստոս որդին
աստուծոյ որ աշխարհս գալոց էիր։

Հ. Արդ և նոքա որք զերեխայն մկրտեն մկրտութիւնն
նոցա ճշմարիտ է և թէ ունայն։

Պ. Թէ են ունայն և խաբէութիւն. քանզի երեխայքն ոչ
ունին զպապշխարութիւն, ոչ ունին գյուսումն և ոչ ունին
զՀաւատս սուրբ. վասն այնորիկ ո՛չ է ճշմարիտ մկրտութիւն
նոցա և ո՛չ փրկութիւն։ Պող
ԴԷ 5
Հմր.

Հ. Ապա որո՞վ է արժան սուրբ մկրտութիւն և Հաղոր֊
դութիւն։

Պ. Նոցա է յարժան սուրբ մկրտութիւն և Հաղորդութիւն,
որք ունին զեղղ ընկզենական և ներգործական։

Հ. Մի՞ թէ յերեխայք որք ծնանին ՛ի մարզն իւրեանց
արդեօք ոչ ունին զեղղ ընկզենական և ներգործական։

Պ. Այո որդեակք իմ, ճշմարտապէս ո՛չ ունին զայսպիսի
մեղս յերեխայք։

Հ. Արդեօք ունին զՀաստատութիւն ՛ի սուրբ գրոց
վասն յերեխայից։

Պ. Այո՛, Հայր պատուական, ունիմ զճշմարիտ վկայու֊
թիւն ՛ի սուրբ աւետարանէն զոր պատուիրեաց տէրն մեր
սուրբ եկեղեցւոյն յետ յարութեան ասելով. Թէ երթա՛յք
աշխարհս ամենայն և քարողեցէք զաւետարանն ամենայն
արաբածոց. որ Հաւատասցէ և մկրտեսցի կեցցէ և որ ո՛չ
Հաւատասցէ դատապարտեսցի։ Տեսմ՛ր, նազելի իմ, նախ
զՀաւատս, զպապշխարութիւնս պատուիրէր և ապա Հրաման
սուրբ մկրտութեան տայր։

58

Հ. Քանի՞ք էին, որդեակք իմ, որք պաՀեցին զքառասուն տիս եւ զքառասուն գիշերս, մինչեւ յքրիստոս որդի աստուծոյ։

Պ. Զորք են պաՀողք. այսինքն՝ ենովք եւ եղիայ, որք պաՀելով յերկինս վերացան, երկրորդ՝ աբրաՀամ, որ ընկալաւ զաւետիսն սաՀակայ 'ի ՀրեշտակացՆ աստուծոյ. եւ երրորդ՝ մեծն մովսէս պաՀելով էառ զտասնաբանեայ պատուիրանս։

Հ. Քրիստոս տէր եւ բարեխօսն մեր արդեօ՞ք պաՀեաց բզքառասուն տիւ եւ զքառասուն գիշեր իբրեւ զնոսա։

Պ. Այո՛ պաՀեաց եւ էառ 'ի ՀօրԷ ամենակալէ զԹագաւորութիւն յերկնաւորաց եւ յերկրաւորաց եւ սանդարամետականաց։

Հ. Արդեօ՞ք աստուած ամենակարող 'ի նախաՀարց անտի ընդէ՞ր ո՛չ արաբ Թագաւոր եւ գլուխ ամենեցուն։ Ո՞չ ապաքէն նոքա եւս պաՀեցին զօրան զայնոսիկ։

Պ. Թէպէտ նոքա պաՀեցին, բայց ո՛չ էին . . . . . .[1] որպէս զտէրն մեր յիսուս քրիստոս. Այլ նոքա յղացեալ եղեն ընկղշնական մեղօք, նոքա ունէին զմեղս բղկսբնական եւ ներգործական։ Բայց միՆորդն մեր քրիստոս ո՛չ յղացեալ եղեւ ընկղշնական մեղօք եւ ո՛չ ունէր զմեղս բղկսբնական եւ ներգործական որպէս զնոսա, զոր սուրբ յօՀաննէս աւետարանիչն յայտնէր ասելով. գլ. I, Հմր. 13. Ոյք ո՛չ յարենէ եւ ո՛չ 'ի կամաց մարմնոյ եւ ո՛չ 'ի կամաց առն, այլ յաստուծոյ ծնան։ Եւ բանիւն մարմին եղեւ եւ բնակեցաւ 'ի մեզ։

առ եց.
Հ. Արդեօ՞ք աստուած խօսեցաւ ընդ տեառն մերոյ յիսուսի քրիստոսի, ապա Թէ ո՛չ։

Պ. Թէ աստուած ամենակարող խօսէր ընդ որդոյ իւր միածնին միշտ եւ Հանապազ որպէս սուրբ յօՀաննէս աւետարանիչն վկայեաց ասելով, Թէ որոտումն լինի։ Իսկ կէսքն 'ի նոցանէ ասէին Թէ Հրեշտակք խօսեցան ընդ նմա, բայց ինքն միշնորդ եւ բարեխօսն մեր բատուղեաց զՀօրն խօսակ֊

8 եւ ս 29.
ցութիւն ասելով. Ո՛չ վասն իմ ինչ եկ բարբառս այս, զի դուք Հաւատասջիք յիս։ Եւ դարձեալ ես ասէ. ես յանձնէ

---

[1] ճ. բառ մի կամ երկու քերեալ։

իմմէ ոչ ինչ խօսիմ, այլ զոր լուայ 'ի Հօրէ իմմէ զայն ծանուցի ձեզ։

Հ. ՝Քանիք են բանք տեառն մերոյ յիսուսի քրիստոսի որ զմարդս փրկէ·

Պ. Չորք են որ զմարդս փրկեն. ՝Նախ՝ ապաշխարու֊ թիւն, երկրորդ՝ ուղիղ դաւանութիւն, երրորդ՝ սուրբ մկրտու֊ թիւն, և չորրորդ՝ սուրբ պատուական մարմին և արիւն տեառն մերոյ յիսուսի քրիստոսի.

Հ. Ըպա դրօշմ, կարդ քահանայութեան, վերջին օծում և պսակն ո՞չ են փրկութիւն Հոգւոց մերոց. այլ են անՀարկ և ոչ Հարկաւորք։ Որպէս սուրբ եկեղեցին քրիստոսի ասէ. եթէ ոք ամուսնացուցանէ զկոյսն իւր բարւոք առնէ, և եթէ ոք ոչ ամուսնացուցանէն լաւ ևս առնեն։ Ըյսպէս իմոյ զդրօշմն, զկարդ քահանայութեան և զվերջին օծումն, որք ո՞չ են Հարկաւորք և դուռն փրկութեան։

Հ. Ըստուածն ամենայնի զնոր ադամ սիրելին իւր քանի՞ բանի Համար աշխարհս առաքեաց։

Պ. Չորս Հարկաւոր իրաց. այսինքն նախ՝ վասն ըկզզեն֊ ական մեղաց պատճառի. երկրորդ՝ վասն ներգործական մեղաց. երրորդ՝ վասն միշնորդութեան, Հաշտութեան և բարեխօսու֊ թեան, զոր այժմ է. Չորրորդ՝ վասն կատարածի աշխարՀի առաքէ զմածին որդին իւր Հայրն ամենակալ և դատել տայ զկենդանիս և զմեռեալս։

Հ. Ո՛վ Հայր պատուական, յարժա՞ն է մեզ զբարեխօսու֊ թիւն սրբոց ունել, ապա թէ ոչ[1].

Պ. Թէ ո՞չ է արժան և Հարկ բարեխօսութիւնս նոցա ունիմք·՝քանզի նոքա կարօտ են վասն կենդանեաց բարեխօ֊ սութեան և ո՞չ կենդանիք նոցա, որպէս յայտ է 'ի խորՀրդա֊ բանս Հերետիկոսաց և Հերցուածողաց, զոր 'ի ժամ պատարագի ասեն անդ զոլղեղ թէ քահանայք թէ սարկաւագունք, եթէ դպիրքն, այսինքն՝ Ըրաքելոց, սրբոց[2], մարգարէից, վարդապե֊

---

[1] ի լուսան. գրեալ: ՝և յորժամ փառաւորեսցի տէրն մեր յիսուս, յայնժամ պսակէ զսուրբան իւր։ Պաղոս թեսա. երկրդ. գլ I, Համր. 10.՝   [2] ձ. ՝սբ.՝

տաց, մարտիրոսաց, հայրապետաց, ճգնաւորաց, կուսանաց, միանձանց և ամենայն սրբոց եղցէ յիշատակ ՚ի սուրբ պատարագս աղչեմք։ Նա ես քահանայք և դպիրքն միաբերան եղեալ ասեն մեծաւ ձայնիւ բարբառով։ Յիշեա՛յ տէր և ողորմեա՛յ. ես ժամարարն ասէ թէ. հանգո՛ զհոգիս սրբոց, և այլն։

Հ. Թէ զինչ է պատճառ ես, ոչ առնեմք բարեխօս զսուրբս.

Պ. Մեքետա նոքա վասն սիրոյն քրիստոսի չարչարեցան, բայց ոչ ունին զիխաւս և ոչ զհամարձակութիւն և ոչ զպսակս արքայութեան աստուծոյ, որպէս յայտնէ սուրբ եկեղեցին քրիստոսի ասելով թէ սուրբքն ընկալան զպետոխին կենաց յաւիտենականի. Հասին ալետեաց, խցին զբերանս առիւծոց, եցոց և այլն. Նա ես տէրն մեր յիսուս զպետոխս տալով ասէ առ սիրելեան իւր այսպէս. Թէ զի ուբ են իցեմ անդ և պաշտոնեայն իմ եղցէ։ Պարձեալ ես ասէ. Պուք յայժմ ոչ կարէք գալ զկնի իմ, բայց ապա եկեսցիք զկնի իմ։ Եւ ես ցյց տալով զտեղեն նոցա ասէ. Թէ Օղեանք բազումք են ՚ի տան հօր իմոյ։ Տեսմ՛էր, որդեակք իմ նազելի, թէ որպէս յայտնեցաւ մի սրբոյ ալետարանին և սրբոյ եկեղեցւոյն։ Որք յուսովք են լցեալք և ոչ փառօք և պսակօք սուրբքն ամենայն, զոր միջնորդ և բարեխօսն մեր յիսուս Հրամայէ ասելով անձամ դատաստանն իւրում։ Եկա՛յք օրհնեալք հօր իմոյ, ժառանգեցէք զանբապատ և զանվախճան ուբախութիւնս. Ասպէս և իմա՛յ զեղջալուրս, որք տանջին Հրոյն անշիջանելի։ Նա ես, որդեակ իմ սիրելի, կա՛նչ քեզ զեանս մեծին մարգարէին մովսեսի, զոր պատմէ թէ փարաւն բարկացեալ մեծալ բարկութեամբ ՚ի վերայ յովսեփայ և կալեալ զնա և եդ ՚ի բանդի, իսկ բանդարկելոց ումանց զտեսիլն ինչ տեսին և դարձուրեցան։ Արդ ՚ի մէջ բանդին այնմիկ զտեսիլն իւրեանց պատմեցին յովսեփայ. իսկ նախաՀայրն մեր յովսեփի պատմաց զտեսիլն նոցա Հոգովն աստուծոյ ասելով. Ո՛վ այր դու զի աճա՛ ՚ի վաղլեան աւուր փարաւն արբայն զբեզ մեծալ փառօք պսակէ. Իսկ ցմիւսն ասէ. քանդի և դու ՚ի վաղին պատժելոց ես թագալորէ։

Յեսեբր նազելէ որդեակ իմ, զի ոմն աւետեօքն յովսեփայ պսակեցաւ և ոմն ասացելովն պատմեցաւ. որպէս առաջ տեառն մերոյ յիսուսի քրիստոսի զոր ասէ վասն դաղարու և աբրահամու։

Նա ես սուրբ եկեղեցին քրիստոսի ասէ թէ որով և հոգոց որբ էին 'ի բանդին երբեալ քարոզեաց, ուստի քարոզէլն տեառն մերոյ յիսուսի քրիստոսի զայս նշանակէ. Այսինքն զաւետիս և զայս մեծ էու[1] նախապետաց և մարգարէից հոգոցն, թէ պսակելոց է զձեզ Հայրն իմ 'ի կատարածի աշխարհի և ցմեզղալորսն քարոզեաց ասելով, թէ պատմելոց է զձեզ Հայրն ամենակարող մեծաւ պատժօք։—

Յաղագս միոյ դատաստանի և ոչ երկու։

Գլուխ (?)։

Հարց. Քանիք են դատաստան աստուծոյ վասն մեռելոց և կենդանեաց։

Պատասխանի. Թէ է մի միայն դատաստան և ոչ երկու·

Հ. Ապա թէ մի է դատաստանն աստուծոյ զոր քրիստոսն առնէ, ապա ընդէ՞ր ոմանք ուրացողք ասեն թէ երկու թէտր են դատաստանք և ոչ մի. զմինն առանձնական ասեն և զմինն գբքո ընդհանրական։ տես։

Պ. Վասն այնորիկ ասեն և սուտ խօսին զի Հայրն նոցա Սու սատանայ է. որպէս և տէրն մեր ասէ, զի որ սուտ խօսի ի բբոց բաստ անտի խօսի և Հայր նորա սատանայ է։ գբեա

Հ. Աղաչեմ զքեզ Հայր պատուական զի յուսուսցես մեզ տեսէ զորբան լիննլն դատաստանի։

Պ. Ասեմքեզ զի ընդհանրական և առաքելական եկեղեցին զմի դաւանի ասելով թէ մարդոյս միանգամ մեռանիլ և յետ Եբր այնորիկ դատաստան. զայս կամի ասեի սուրբ եկեղեցին թէ ԳԼ 9, Հմր.

---

[1] ձ. եղ.

որպէս մարդոյս մի անգամ է մահ, այսպէս և յարութիւն և դատաստան նոցա է մի և ոչ երկու.

Հ. Որդ քրիստոս տէր և բարեխօսն մեր, դիտէ՞ր արդեօք ցշարութիւն մտաց նոցա որ դսուտ և զանձառնի յօրէնսն Հաստատէին, ապա թէ ոչ։

Պ. Էյմ՛ Հայր պատուական ճշմարտապէս դիտէր, վասն այնորիկ ասէ թէ ,Օգուշ լերուք ՚ի չար մշակաց անտի և կամ ՚ի պտղոյ նոցա ծանիջիք զնոսա, որք են սուտ և խաբեութեան աշակերտ են և ոչ իմոյ ճշմարտութեան. Որպէս և սուրբ եկեղեցին յայտնեաց ասելով.

Հ. Արդեօ՞ք տէրն մեր քրիստոս դիտէ՞ր զօրն դատաստանի, ապա թէ ոչ։

Պ. Ո՛ի Հայրն երկնաւոր, աստուած ճշմարիտ, ո՛չ յայտնեաց զօրն այն որդւոյն իւրում սիրելոյ. որպէս և ասէ վասն կատարածի աշխարհի թէ ո՛չ ոք գիտէ, ո՛չ Հրեշտակք յերկինս և ո՛չ որդի, բայց միայն Հայր. այլ եւ ասէ ես յանձնէ իմմէ ո՛չ խօսիմ, այլ զոր ինչ պատուէր ետ ինձ Հայր իմ զայն խօսիմ. Տեսէ՞ր նազելի իմ թէ քրիստոս որդին ասաութոյ յանձնէ իւրմէ ոչ ինչ կարէր ասել եթէ ոչ Հայր նորա յայտնէր նրմա։

Հ. Որդ որովՀետև տէրն մեր յիսուս քրիստոս ո՛չ կարաց առանց Հօրն պատուիրանի դիտել զօրն դատաստանի, ապա զիա՞րդ ոմանք ուրացողք ասեն և Հակառակին ընդդէմ ճշմարտութեան որդոյն ասաութոյ թէ գոյ առանձնական դատաստան և քաղարան վասն մեղաւորաց։

Պ. Ո՛ի նախ ասացի քեզ թէ նոքա են ժառանգ Հօրն խաբէութեան, զոր Հոգովն նոյն չարին միշտ և Հանապազ զսուտ օրէնս և զսուտ պատուիրանս կարգեն։ Տես սիրելի իմ զվարժապետն նոցա, որ կերպարանեցաւ ՚ի կերպ կրօնաւորի և քարոզէր նոցա զտանջանս դժոխոց, առ ՚ի որսալ ղՀոգիս նոցա.

Այսման որ է Հարցմանց

Յաղագս սրբագործութեան մարմնոյ եւ արեան տեառն
մերոյ յիսուսի քրիստոսի բարեխօսին.

Գլուխ (?).

Արդ կամեցաւ տէրն մեր յիսուս քրիստոս զիւր մարմին եւ արիւնն իւր սուրբ բաշխել աշակերտաց եւ Հաւատացելոց

Նախ ընկալաւ օրինակաւս այսոքիկ. եբաց զմիտս նոցա ասելով. զի մարմինն իմ ճշմարիտ կերակուր է եւ արիւնն իմ ճշմարիտ ըմպելի է. եւ դարձեալ ասէ. ես եմ Հացն կենաց իջեալ 'ի յերկնից, որ ուտէ զՀացս զայս կեցցէ յաւիտեան :

Այսպէս տէրն մեր յորժամ աւարտեաց զօրինակուն զայսոսիկ. բազում աշակերտաց անտի շրջան յետոս. յայնժամ դարձեալ ասէ ցայլ աշակերտսն իւր, թէ երթայք դուք պատրաստեցէք մեզ զսեղան սրբութեան. որ անդ առնելոց եմ զխորՀուրդ փրկութեան. վասն Հաւատացելոց իւրոց սիրելեաց. եւ յորժամ երեկոյ եղեւ կայր յիսուս բազմեալ եւ երկոտասանքն ընդ նմա : Ստառ զմի Հաց աևխմոր 'ի ձեռս իւր, օրՀնեաց, գոՀացաւ, եբեկ եւ ասէ. Առէք կերէք, այս է ՄԱՐՄԻՆ իմ, որ վասն ձեր բազմաց բաշխի 'ի քաւութիւն եւ 'ի թողութիւն մեղաց. (Այսպէս եւ 'ի բաժակին ասէ) :

Մեկնութիւն սրբոյ խորՀրդոյ տեառն մերոյ յիսուսի քրիստոսի :

Ով աՀա միշնորդ եւ բարեխօսն մեր յիսուս քրիստոս, գառն եւ ասաստուծոյ, ետառ զՀաց 'ի ձեռս իւր, օրՀնեաց զնա, ասեն սուրբ աւետարանիչքն

Այսինքն խնդրելով աղերսեաց զՀօրէ ամենակալէ զի փոխարկեսցէ զՀացն զայն ճշմարիտ մարմին իւր պատուական. վասն այնորիկ ասէ օրՀնեաց, այսինքն աղաչեաց զտէառնէ, զի փոխարկեսցի Հացն այն ճշմարտապէս մարմին իւր, որ եւ ինք փոխարկեցաւ Հոգին Հօրն երկնաւորի ստուգապէս. եւ յորժամ ետես թէ փոխարկեցաւ Հացն այն իւր մարմին, յայնժամ գոՀացաւ զՀօրէ ամենակալէ, որ փոխարկեցաւ մարմին եւ արիւնն իւր :

Արժմ իմացաւք, որդեակ իմ, օրհնութիւն մեկնութեան և գոհութեան.

Արդ, Հայր սուրբ, բարեպէս իմացայ զայն. երես անկեալ աղաչեմ զքեզ, Հայր պատուական, մեկնեա՛ մեզ զասացեալ իմ, թէ Այս է մարմին իմ որպէս և ասաց յետ յարութեան ցպետրոս, թէ Լրածեա՛մ զոչխարս իմ. զայս ասելով գիտեմք միշնորդ և բարեխօսն մեր յիսուս քրիստոս թէ գալոց են սուտ փափք և փոխարկելոց են ըստ կամաց իւրեանց. որք լոկ հացիւ խափեն զամենեսեան և առնեն զայն մարմին և արիւնն իւրեանց և ո՛չ թէ քրիստոսի. վասն այսորիկ և տէրն մեր յիսուս քրիստոս ասէ, թէ Այս է մարմին իմ։ Նա ես զայս կամի ասել թէ ով ոք զշուրջ ինչ, զլոկ հաց ինչ և կամ զթացեալ պատառ ինչ առնէ և բաշխէ խաբէութեամբ զմիամիտ ժողովուրդըն, նոցա է մարմին և արիւն և ո՛չ քրիստոսի։

Փառք յաւիտեանս յաւիտենից, Ամէն։

Գրեցաւ 'ի գաւառն Տարդնոյ յամի տեառն 1782, իսկ ըստ Հայոց ռմէ-ին.

(Յիշատակարան[1].)

. . ամենապայծառ յոհաննէս վահագունդն. քանզի սրբա մեծաւ ջերմեռանդութեամբ խնդրեցին 'ի մէնջ. Իսկ վասն խնդրելոյն նոցին յաճախեաց 'ի սիրտ իմ սերն ճշմարտութեան։ Վասն որոյ ո՛չ կարացի թագուցանել զշնորհ սուրբ Հոգւոյն. Այլ սկսայ կարգաւ գրել զսուրբ խորհր֊ դարան և զբանալի ճշմարտութեան վասն սիրոյն խնդրողաց և ընդունողաց։ Նա ես երեսս անկեալ ջերմ սիրով և հալածում խնդրեմ 'ի ձենջ, զի դուք զԹերութիւն, զպակա սութիւն և զղպամուսնա շարադրութեան կամ քերթողու թեան, այլ ես թէ զվանկից, թէ զդրոց, թէ զբառից և թէ բղեանից և եթէ զուվի մասանց արհեստին։ եթէ 'ի սրանէ

---

[1] ճ. ասատնոր թերթ մի կամ քանի մի անկեալ։

զսղալումն և զպակասութիւն ինչ գտանիցէք, ոչ եթէ 'ի մէնջ եղեալ է, այլ անվարժ գրչաց գոլով 'ի սմա մտեալ է։

Փառք Հօրն էականի և որդւոյն իւր միջնորդի և բարեխօսի. Այժմ և միշտ և յաւիտեանս յաւիտենից. Ամէն։

Ես Ֆրետերիկ Կոնիբիր տրուպս ուսուցչաց Աքսֆորդի, հայագէտ և հայասէր յետ գտանելոյ յաշխարհի մեծաց հայոց օրինակ մի մատենից այսորիկ որ կոչի բանալի ճշմարտութեանն, բազում աշխատութեամբ և ջանիւք 'ի լոյս ածի զսա, և 'ի լեզու մայրենի իմ անգղիական թարգմանեցի. Այլ տպագրեալ է մատեանս այս հոգեշահ, հրամանաւ և ծախիւք վարդապետացն և իմաստնոցն և մեծաւորացն համալսարանին Աքսֆորդի 'ի դպարանի իւրեանց, յամի տեառն մերոյ ռպղէ։ Եւ յոյժ տրտմեցայ ես զի անչափ թերթք բնագրին, անկեալ եղեն ոմանց չնեմողութեամբ. և մանաւանդ զի չկարացի գտանել, ևս վասն տպագրելոյ զխորհրդարանն եկեղեցւոյն այնորիկ ընդհանրականին իւրոյին, զորմէ գրիչն բնագրին զեկոյց 'ի յիշատակարանին. Վասն որոյ յընթեռնուլն ձեր զմատեանս, եթէ գտանիցի ոք օրինակ մի ամբողջ և լիակատար գրոցս այսոցիկ, ասեմ զբանալւոյն և զխորհրդարանին, խնդրեմ և յոյժ աղաչեմ զձեզ զի զսոսա առ իս յուղարկեսջիք. զի ևս տպագրիցին յաւելուածք այսոքիկ հարկաւորագոյնք մատենի մերոյ։

ERRATA IN THE ARMENIAN TEXT

In the preceding Armenian text occur the following Errata, of which many were detected by a collation of the printed text with the MS. in Edjmiatzin:—

P. 1, l. 15, for սանաւանդ read մանաւանդ — p. 17, l. 9, read ազրաւոյ։ 10, գիշացս 13, խաւարի։ 15, Եերորդ։ 21, Հպարտ — p. 18, l. 17, read Հաւատացէ։ ll. 21, 22, and 23, for իմանայք read իմացայք։ 23, for զաստուածն read չաստուածն։ 25, միշնորդ — p. 19, l. 17, for տայք read տўք — p. 20, l. 8, read ասէ։ 18, for Ճառայեն read Ճանաչեն։ 29, read առաշնեբորդ։ 31, Հրայար-եսչիր — p. 21, l. 11, read պարտ։ 13, իցէ։ 17, for և read եզև և։ 25, Հարցանէր։ 27, ճայնիւ։ 32, խնդրեսցեն — p. 22, l. 2, զողող։ 29, մտանել։ 33, յորմէ — p. 23, l. 14, զասեցէ։ 25, Ծնդեան։ 26, սկանեմք։ 28, մերին — p. 24, l. 7, for] ւ read Եւ, and for ընդ read ըստ։ 13, read զարգացո՛։ 33, արարեր — p. 25, l. 2, read Հայրութիւնդ, պաՀեա։ 25, սէր — p. 26, l. 10, omit յիսուսի։ 33, եկեղեցւոյն — p. 27, l. 1, որդիակք — p. 28, l. 6, յովՀաննէս։ 20, խոսել — p. 29, l. 4, պողոս։ 22, Որդին։ 24, բռնաւորք — p. 30, l. 11, Հրամայելոյն։ 12, զոր։ 14, սրտիւ — p. 31, l. 13, որք։ 30, տերն — p. 32, l. 5, փոքրոդի։ 8, քրիստուէ and զքեզ — p. 33, l. 3, միջապէս։ 5, ժողովորդեան։ 12, omit ընդ p. 36, l. 14, որդւոյն — p. 39, l. 12, Եառ — p. 40, l. 5, Հածիլ։ 8, after ընթան-րական add և։ 28, Ճանաչել — p. 41, l. 33, առաբելոց սրբոցն p. 42, l. 9, վարձկանաց։ 17, վՃուեցին։ 24, փոքր։ 33, ձեզ p. 43, ll. 1 and 14, նոցա — p. 44, l. 21, for տերն read պետն։ 22, Հոր —p. 46, l. 17, եպիսկոպոսաւն — p. 47, l. 18, Ծնցիս։ 31 mg., առնու — p. 48, l. 13, նոցա.

ENGLISH TRANSLATION

LIST OF SIGNS USED IN THE TRANSLATION

Square brackets [ ] round a word or words indicate additions which are either necessary to complete the sense, or which almost certainly stood in the text, but have been more or less successfully erased.

Round brackets ( ) indicate parallel or more literal English equivalents of an Armenian word.

Dots . . . . . . indicate total erasure in the MS. of words, because of their unorthodox tendency. Three dots are assigned to each word erased.

The rubrics as given in the MS. are printed in italics in the English translation.

Passages which the context shows to be interpolations are asterisked.

The text references are in the English text and notes merely those given in the margin of the Armenian MS. They are often wrong; but I leave them uncorrected, in order that the reader may have a faithful picture of the Armenian text as it stands. In some cases the Armenian New Testament, used by the hand which added these references, may have had another numeration, than ours, of the verses.

CONTENTS

	PAGE
Exordium of Author	71
On Baptism of Jesus Christ	72
Chap. I. On Repentance and Faith as Conditions of Baptism	72
Chap. II. On Baptism according to Canons of Jesus Christ	74
Chap. III. On Baptism. Criticism of Greek Rite	76
Chap. IV. Against the Orthodox who are inspired by Satan	78
Chap. V. On the Forty Days of our Lord and the Temptation	80
Chap. VI. On Satan's Activity against the Apostles	82
Chap. VII. On the Adversary of God the Father	83
Chap. VIII. On the Twelve Disguises of Satan	83
Chap. IX. On the Same	84
Chap. X. Against the Orthodox. Mostly lost	85
Chaps. XI, XII, XIII. All lost	
Chap. XIV. Against the Abuses of the Orthodox Churches	85
Chap. XV. On Baptism of Jesus Christ and of Apostles. Partly lost	86
Chap. XVI. On the Three Sacraments or Mysteries	87
Chap. XVII. On Baptism	89
The Ceremony of Namegiving on Eighth day after Birth	90
Chap. XVIII. Directions concerning Candidates for Baptism	91
Chap. XIX. Same continued. Partly lost	92
New Title-page and List of Apostles	93
Chap. XX. Confession of Faith, Baptismal Prayers, and the Qualifications of the Baptiser, who shall be an Elect	93
Chap. XXI. The Rite of Baptism	96
Chap. XXII, part i. Regulations concerning Candidates for Election	101
Chap. XXII, part ii. The Rite of Election	106
Chap. [?], part i. Solutions of New Testament. Sayings about the Virgin Mary	112
Chap. [?] cont., part ii. On Creation of Adam and of our Lord. Partly lost	114
Chap. [?] cont., part iii. On Intercession of Jesus Christ and against Saints, &c.	115
Chap. [?] cont., part. iv. Testimonies of Apostles to the above	116

	PAGE
Supplement against Papal Practices	116
A Catechism for Christians	117
Ch. [?]. Catechism continued. That there is but one Judgement and no Purgatory	121
On the Consecration of the Flesh and Blood	123
Exposition of the Holy Mystery of the Eucharist	123
Colophon of the Copyist of 1782	124

LIST OF ENGLISH EQUIVALENTS USED TO RENDER TECHNICAL ARMENIAN TERMS

վարդապետ = Vardapet or Doctor.

ընտրեալ = Elect. So in Arm. N. T., Acts ix. 15, Rom. ix. 11.

ընտրութիւն = Election.

ընդհանրական = 'Universal' (*lit.* general), epithet of the Church.

եպիսկոպոս = Bishop or Overseer.

դիտաւորութիւն = Intention (in the Sacrament of Baptism).

իշխան = ruler.

իշխանապետ = arch-ruler.

իշխանութիւն = authority.

մասն = 'part,' but is translated *member* in the phrase 'member of the Church.'

երեց = presbyter or elder.

առաջնորդ = president (= ἡγουμένοις in Heb. xiii. 17, which is read in Ordination Service in the Key, p. 106).

ընթերցող = reader.

կանոն = a canon (in tenth cent. Arm. = any direction or rule of religious observance).

կանոնեմ = direct or ordain, make ordinance.

խորհուրդ = mystery or sacrament (*lit.* thought).

ուսուցիչ = Teacher.

պետ = Chief (in the Ordinal).

THE ENGLISH TRANSLATION

THE Book called the Key of Truth. It was written[1] in the era of the Saviour 1782, but of the Armenians 1230; and in the province of Taron.

Address to my dear readers.

Although the throng of distractions, and the temptations and storms of the world, and the manifold hindrances, strong to disturb our transitory life in various ways,—although these have sorely beset us and suffered us not to undertake this necessary work; nevertheless the pressing needs of the Truth of our Lord Jesus the Son of the heavenly Father, and zeal of the Holy Spirit [urged us];—yea, and also to meet the prayers of many believers, and especially because of supreme necessity—I have cast behind me all the affairs[2] of this transitory life, and have spared nothing in order to give unto you, my new-born children of the universal and apostolic Church of our Lord Jesus Christ, the holy milk, whereby ye may be nourished in the faith.

Wherefore the Spirit of the Father in Heaven hath taken hold of us and inspired us to write this 'way and truth and life.' Forasmuch as for a long time past the spirit of deception had shut up the Truth, as our Lord saith: The tares had suffocated it. Furthermore it is a little and slender discourse that I have published to you, briefly and not opulently. The which ye shall read with deep attention, unto the glory of Jesus the Son, the Intercessor, and unto the honour of his Father ...[3]

---

[1] i.e. copied.

[2] The Arm. word here, *galiq*, is of uncertain sense: it may mean 'events.' In the writings of Ananias Catholicos (tenth century) it bears the sense which I here give it.

[3] After Father a word is erased in the MS. which may have been 'and Creator.'

This brief discourse shall ye search and deeply o'er it meditate. If it please you, then revere it, as it were a voice of thunder.

Concerning the holy baptism of our Lord Jesus Christ, which hath been handed down for the sake of those who believe and repent, and not of catechumens, or of the unrepentant and of those who lack faith, nor either of the impure; as is manifest in the holy and precious life of John the Baptist, who with his loudly calling voice, before Christ our Lord and intercessor, cried unto the adult[1], saying:

* Help us, Jesus, and become intercessor for all the faithful, thy beloved ones. For with thy sanctifying and illumining words thou didst pray to thy Father, saying: Father[2], not for these alone do I pray, but also for all who have believed in me through their word, &c.*[3]

CHAPTER I

'Repent ye, for the kingdom of heaven is at hand,' and the sequel (Matt. iv. 2).

So, then, the words of the holy gospel are not hidden unto us; but for this reason the Father of our Lord Jesus Christ revealed [them] in true argument to his loved Son. For this reason also the holy John, greatest among the children of women, called aloud saying to the generation of vipers: Repent, O ye that are gone astray in sin after sin, thronging thick together, of your evil [deeds]; and recognize your original sin, which from of old days lies in you stored up[4]. For this reason St. John in saying this woke up their minds to proceed unto the true faith and to know the new 'least one of the kingdom[5],' the Lord Jesus Christ, the lamb of God, who taketh away our sins. Even as John himself, stretching forth his holy finger, said: Behold Christ, the lamb of God, which taketh away the sins of the world. Again he continues by saying: I am not he, but am sent before him. Thus then St. John, firstly, preached unto them; secondly, taught; thirdly, induced them to

---

[1] *Or* 'completed,' 'fulfilled,' 'initiated.' An attempt has been made in the MS. to efface the word, which however is still clearly legible.

[2] In margin John xi. 20 (lege xvii. 20).

[3] The paragraph asterisked must be an interpolation.

[4] Paul, Hebr. ii. 9.   [5] Matt. xi. 11.

repent[1]; fourthly, brought them to the faith; and after that cleansed them in the flesh from stains. And then our Lord and Intercessor, the Lamb of God[2], bestowed on them spiritual salvation. Thus the universal and apostolic church learned from our Lord Jesus, and continued so to do, as is clear in their Acts and especially in the traditions of our Saviour Jesus Christ, which he imposes on the universal and apostolic church, saying, Mark xvi. 15: 'Go ye into all the world and preach the Gospel to all creatures. Whoever shall believe, shall be baptized, shall live; and he who shall not believe, shall be judged.'

Wherefore also our Lord first asked for faith, and then graciously gave healing; and after that bestowed holy baptism on believers; but not on unbelieving catechumens. So also St. John and the holy Church of our Lord Jesus Christ—so did they continue[3] to do until the assault of Satan. For when Satan was let loose from his bonds, then he began to steal away the truth of our Lord Jesus Christ and of the holy apostles; and he insinuated his deceitful arguments among teachers, [against] whom as the heavenly Father enables us, let us with the Keys of Truth[4] open the door of Truth close shut [by them]. Even as St. John opened the door of Truth prior to our Lord Jesus Christ, and uttered this command unto the adult (*or* perfected) souls: 'Repent, for the kingdom of heaven is at hand,' and the rest.

Now their repentance lay in turning from their evil works and believing in Christ Jesus; in receiving the holy baptism of the Spirit of the heavenly Father, and in recognizing their original sin, and in their being afflicted because of it, and in their release from the fetters of demons, which from their forefathers on had been drawn tight round them. Wherefore, when he beheld them, the great prophet John in anger roused them, saying, Luke iii. 7: 'Offspring of vipers, who showed unto you to escape from the wrath to come[5]? Do ye therefore bring forth fruits worthy of repentance; nor make beginning to say, We have for a father Abraham. This

---

[1] In margin, John i. 36.   [2] John iv. 2.

[3] Against this sentence some words were written in the margin, but have been wholly erased.

[4] This seems to be aimed at the pretension of the Popes as the successors of Peter to possession of the power of the Keys. There is also an echo of Luke xi. 52, but there it is the key of *gnôsis*, which the lawyers have taken away.

[5] In margin is written against this and what follows: 'He permitted not this Evil, that they should draw nigh. So also he permits not the Latins, the Greeks, and the Armenians.'

I say unto you, that God is able out of these stones to raise up children of Abraham.'

But, forasmuch as they had fallen among rugged stones, he called them offspring of vipers and asps. [God] also caused Jesus to arise from among them, for through him he graciously vouchsafes to them salvation. Wherefore also a member [1] of the universal and apostolic holy church, St. Luke, declares, xiii. 23 : Of this man's seed God according to his promises raised up unto Israel the Saviour Jesus. So also must we lead the reasonable [2] unto faith, and bring the imperfect unto perfection, and fill those who have not the word with the word of Jesus Christ, and soften their hearts of stone, and as for the gathered bile of bitterness, which from old days hath been stored up, this we cause them to vomit up with loathing by the finger of God, and then we give them a remedy for sin, whether original or operative in them. For as St. John taught first repentance and faith, and after that granted baptism and then showed them the way, the truth, and the life, saying: 'Behold Christ, the lamb of God, who taketh away the sins of the world'; so we also must follow in accordance with this truth, and not according [3] to the deceitful arguments of the tradition of others, who baptize the unbelieving, the reasonless, and the unrepentant. These are utterly false and [full of] the deceit of demons, and are not godly; whom we will declare as the Holy Spirit enables us.

CHAPTER II

Concerning holy baptism. About our Lord Jesus Christ, that as he laid down canons and precepts, so do we proceed with God's help.

First was our Lord Jesus Christ baptized by the command of the heavenly Father, when thirty years old, as St. Luke has declared his years [4], iii. 23: 'And Jesus himself was of years about thirty, beginning with which [5] as he was supposed son of Joseph.' So then it was in the season of his maturity that he received

---

[1] *Lit.* 'a part.'

[2] In margin a hand writes: 'And not the unbelieving catechumens who are without reason.'

[3] Against what follows is written in the margin of MS. the following: 'Latins and Greeks and Armenians perform the three mysteries of the Divine with deceitful arguments, as is clear in their works.'

[4] In margin Matt. iii. 16 and iii. 12.

[5] The Arm. Vulgate wrongly renders ὥν in this passage as ὤν.

ON BAPTISM

baptism; then it was that he received authority, received the high-priesthood[1], received the kingdom and the office of chief shepherd. Moreover, he was then chosen, then he won lordship[2], then he became resplendent, then he was strengthened, then he was revered, then he was appointed[3] to guard us[4], then he was glorified, then he was praised, then he was made glad[5], then he shone forth, then he was pleased, and then he rejoiced. Nay more. It was then he became chief of beings heavenly and earthly, then he became light of the world, then he became the way, the truth, and the life[6]. Then he became the door of heaven, then he became the rock impregnable at the gate of hell[7]; then he became the foundation of our faith; then he became Saviour of us sinners; then he was filled with the Godhead[8]; then he was sealed, then anointed[9]; then was he called by the voice, then he became the loved one, then he came to be guarded by angels, then to be the lamb without blemish. Furthermore he then put on that primal raiment of light, which Adam lost in the garden. Then[10] accordingly it was that he was invited by the Spirit of God to converse with the heavenly Father; yea, then also was he ordained king[11] of beings in heaven and on earth and under the earth; and all else [besides] all this in due order the Father gave[12] to his only born Son;—even as he himself, being appointed our mediator and intercessor, saith to his holy, universal, and apostolic church, Matt. xxviii. 18: And Jesus came and spake unto them and said: 'There hath been given unto me all authority in heaven and on earth. As the Father sent me, so do I send you,' and what follows. Thus also the Lord, having learned from the Father, proceeded to teach us to perform holy baptism and all his other commands at an age of full growth (*or lit.* in a completed or mature season), and at no other time. As the lamb of God directs us after his resurrection, Mark xvi. 15, saying: 'Go ye into all the world, and preach the gospel to all creatures. Whoever shall believe, shall be baptized, shall live; but he that shall not believe shall be judged.'

So, then, hearken unto and receive into your minds the irre-

---

[1] Paul, Hebr. v. 10.   [2] Matt. xi. 18.   [3] Luke i. 33.
[4] The Arm. word may also mean 'was covenanted.'   [5] John x. 11.
[6] Matt. xvii. 2.   [7] Mark ix. 1.
[8] Cp. Geo. Mon. p. 76, xx. εἶτα φής, ὡς ἐπὶ τοῦ 'Οκταβίου Καίσαρος, τοῦ ἀνεψιοῦ τοῦ 'Ιουλίου Καίσαρος τοῦ μοναρχήσαντος, γενέσθαι χάριτι ἢ ἀμοιβῇ τῶν πόρων καὶ τοῦ τελέσαι τὴν ἐντολὴν τὸν Χριστὸν υἱὸν τοῦ Θεου.
[9] Luke ix. 28.   [10] Matt. iv. 1.   [11] John xi. 28 and 20.   [12] Paul, Hebr. v. 8.

fragable decree of our Lord Jesus Christ. For some[1] in violation of the canons of our Lord Jesus Christ, have broken and destroyed the holy and precious canons, which by the Father Almighty were delivered to our Lord Jesus Christ; and have trodden them under foot with their devilish teaching. These are they who ever and always oppose the truth of our Lord Jesus Christ [2] baptizing those who are irrational (*or* without the word) and communicating the unbelieving. All these lie under the ban of the Lord and of the holy apostles, as is clear in the canons of our Saviour Jesus, since he saith to his holy apostles: 'Give not holiness to dogs, nor cast your pearls before swine, lest they forthwith trample it under foot, and then turn and rend you,' and the rest. Do we not then know by what authority they do these things, or who is their teacher? Manifestly, by the spirit of the adversary[3] of the Father, of God, do they their works; even as the Saviour warned us, saying: 'Beware of evil-doers,' and the rest. In saying this our Lord showeth us that they are workers of deceitful [agents], that is of Satan. Moreover, a member (*lit.* part) of the church, St. John passes sentence on such ones, saying[4] in his catholic first epistle, iii. 10: 'In this are manifest one from the other the children of God and the children of Satan.' Our Lord moreover manifests them when he says of such that 'by their fruits ye shall know them' and the rest we need not quote. Thus our Lord and intercessor Jesus will give to such as these their reward, but such as those he will liberate from the false teacher.

CHAPTER III

Let us then submit humbly to the Holy Church Universal, and follow their works who acted with one mind and one faith and taught us. Now still do we receive in the only proper (*lit.* necessary) season the holy and precious mystery of our Lord Jesus Christ and of the heavenly Father:—to wit, in the season of repentance and of faith. As we learned from the Lord of the universal and apostolic church, so do we proceed: and we estab-

---

[1] In the margin is written: 'See the haysmavours (i.e. the synaxaries) and in their evil councils that shed blood, and also in the false books of the Latins, called Clemens.'

[2] One word erased in MS.

[3] G. M. p. 71, vi. ἔχουσι δὲ πρώτην αἵρεσιν τὴν τῶν Μανιχαίων, δύο ἀρχὰς ὁμολογοῦντες ὡς κἀκεῖνοι.

[4] In margin is written: 'Those who proceed with deceitful argumentation are children of Satan.'

ON BAPTISM

lish in perfect faith those who [till then] have not[1] holy baptism; nay, nor have tasted of the body nor drunk the holy blood of our Lord Jesus Christ. Therefore according to the word of the Lord, we must first bring them unto the faith, induce them to repent, and then give it[2] unto them. As also a member of the church[3] St. Luke in the Acts of the Church saith, viii. 12: 'But when they believed Philip preaching good tidings about the kingdom of God and the name of Jesus Christ, they were all baptized, men and women.' And again in the same, viii. 36, he saith: 'As they went on their way, they came unto a certain water, and the eunuch said: Behold, here is water; what doth hinder me from being baptized? And Philip said unto him, If thou dost believe with all thy heart, it is possible. The eunuch answered and said: I believe that Jesus Christ is Son of God.' Thus then they first heard a declaration of faith from them and then bestowed supreme baptism. For so had they received it from the Lord, and so they truly did bestow it on others. But some aborted from the gospel and from His church, in opposition [thereto], ask of an unbelieving baptismal father, who is a false witness brought forward, as it were a profession of faith, saying to him: 'What doth the catechumen seek, O [false][4] witness?' And he makes answer and says: 'Faith, hope, love, and baptism.' How then, O [false][5] reader, art thou not ashamed[6]? or how dost thou not blush? so utterly dost thou fail to reflect as to thine utterances and thy questions that whatever proceedeth from thy mouth, is not[6] true [but false][7] argument, whether the answer of the [false] witness or thy question about the catechumen to the baptismal father? These are utterly . ·. . . . . . . , and as our Lord and intercessor Jesus enables us, we will a little open your minds, and with God's aid help to show who is your doctor and teacher.

---

[1] In margin, against this and what follows is written: 'That is to say, the Latins, Greeks, and Armenians, who are not baptized,' see in Mark xvi. 16.

[2] In margin thus: 'baptize, see in Mark xvi. 16.'

[3] In margin is written: 'About the flesh and blood, John vi. 56, who have not eaten and drunk.'

[4] In the MS. a word is half effaced which seems to have been *sout* = false.

[5] In margin of MS. is written: 'Bear not false witness. See in the holy commandments of God.'

[6] Correcting *որ* into *ոչ*.

[7] Each bracket represents a word or two erased from the MS. I have restored the sense of the entire passage.

CHAPTER IV

Doth make manifest and point out the father and teacher of them who have believed and with much love fulfil his works, and know that it is God's work. And God [forbid]¹ that we should believe or bear in our minds such works or canons.

Our mediator and intercessor Jesus Christ doth direct us truly as follows: 'Beware of evil workers,' and the rest.

Already our Lord Christ passed sentence on the Jews and schismatics, when he pointed out their father, saying, John viii. 44: 'Ye are from Satan your father, and ye wish to do the desire of your father. For he was a murderer from the beginning. But he abode not in the truth, because there is not truth in him. When he speaketh false he speaketh out of his own, for he is false and his father.' Now, then, ye his disciples, come hither and judge of yourselves truly of your falsified (*or* falsely performed) baptism, ye that are wholly mythical and contrary to the holy Gospel of the universal and apostolic holy church, that it is not at all to be found in the holy and precious Acts of the Apostles or in the holy Gospels of our Lord Jesus Christ our intercessor.

By this time, however, true opinion has been banished from your minds[2]; since your father has taught you from of old and has bound you to his [false][3] gospel. For this reason our Lord most explicitly bore testimony, saying: 'From the beginning your father was a murderer,' and the rest. But now is the word of our Lord Jesus Christ found accurate and true, which he directs against that evil one. For at the first he was in the form of a serpent and spake in the Armenian language unto Eve, saying: 'Wherefore hath God sternly commanded you not to eat of the fruit, and not to approach it?'[4] Because God knew that when ye take thereof and approach it, at once your eyes will be opened and ye will be as gods; therefore he strictly commanded you not to approach or touch the same.'

But the woman Eva obeyed the father of whom we have spoken[5]

---

[1] I restore conjecturally a word erased. The whole title is manifestly corrupt as it stands. Perhaps we should add 'not' before the words 'God's work.'

[2] Correcting *Մերոյ* to *Ձերոյ*.

[3] A word is erased in MS. which seems to have been = 'false.'

[4] The Armenians still believe that their language was spoken in the garden.

[5] i.e. Satan, father of lies.

and in turn satisfied the mind of Adam. So then, when each had persuaded the other, at once they were stript naked of glory and were driven from the garden; and then they beheld each the other's nakedness, and were not ashamed, as the Spirit of God beareth witness in the sequel.

Now, however, was rent the veil of their virginity through the deceit of the same evil one. Virgin blood escaped for them, their perishable flesh was afflicted; the ligaments of God were torn asunder, those which he imposed on them; the modesty of their countenances was torn away, their reverence was wholly lost; the colour of light of the Godhead faded from their faces; the crown of their kingship was taken away, and their newly-fashioned palace was lost, fastened about with chains. Nay more, all other blessings were lost to them through that same evil one, and he made them his slaves. This is why the precept was uttered to the Jews who believed not: 'He that worketh sin, is the slave of sin,' and the rest [1].

And out of such knowledge did our Lord Jesus Christ give proof unto schismatics, unbelievers, the impious, liars, the false to law (*or* false examples), false teachers [2] and false priests, 'who are ever learning, yet never are able to come to the knowledge of the truth,' and the rest.

Thus our Lord Jesus meant that their father and teacher is Satan. Let us next come to the dealings [3] already alluded to of the murderer, who slew our forefather Adam [and Eve], and made them and their children, until our Saviour Christ, his slaves and captives, and fastened them in his chains and so forth; and so in bonds until the advent of the newly-created Adam kept them; I mean the prophets, patriarchs, men and women, sons and daughters, believers and unbelievers, and all others whom he drew in a throng to himself. And so it was that it pleased [4] the heavenly Father in pity [to create] [5] the new Adam out of the same deceitful blood. But [the created] [5] man Jesus knew his Father, and by inspiration of the Holy Spirit came to St. John in all gentleness and humility to be baptised by him. And at the same time he was crowned by the almighty Father, who said: 'Yonder is my well-loved son in whom I am pleased,' as was written above.

---

[1] John viii. 34.   [2] 2 Tim. iii. 7.   [3] *Or* 'affairs' *or* 'words.'

[4] Luke x. 33 is the reference given in margin of MS.

[5] A word is erased in MS. in both places, which appears to have been as rendered.

Now, when Satan heard this same voice of the Godhead, he was at once seized with great fear and terror insupportable; and he quaked and trembled beyond measure, and he divided his evil mind this way and that, and said: Whatever can be that voice which resounded about him from above? What can be the coming upon him of the Holy Spirit? What can be all this greatness, all this authority in heaven and on earth? What can be all this glory and honour? What indeed all this rejoicing and gladness that has accrued because of him? When Satan beheld all this, he was in despair, and began thenceforth to make ready the snare of his wickedness against our Lord Jesus Christ; and he bethought him, by what snare or gin he might catch him, as he had caught Adam and the patriarchs and the prophets and all others in order. And so he abode in perplexity[1] and great trouble until the time of the temptation.

CHAPTER V

Concerning the forty days of our Lord Jesus Christ who entered in to his [maker][2] and conversed with him mysteriously and received commands of his Father, yea and overcame Beliar with his hosts (or strength).

As a member of the universal and apostolic church, St. Paul, directs, in writing, to the Hebrews, ch. iii. 1: Wherefore, holy brethren, partakers of a heavenly calling, contemplate the Apostle and High-priest of our Confession, Jesus Christ, who is faithful to his maker, as also was Moses in all his house. Forasmuch as the [created][3] man Jesus became very faithful to his Father, for this reason, the Father bestowed on him a name of praise which is above every name[4], that is, of beings whether in heaven or on earth or under the earth. He also put all things in subjection under his feet, as Saint Paul says elsewhere. When therefore he had pleased his increate and loved Father, at once the Spirit led him on to the mountain of temptation[5] and admitted him into the mystery[6] of holy Godship. For forty days and forty nights he feasted on contemplation, on fellow-converse, and on the com-

---

[1] John iii. 35 is the reference in margin of MS.

[2] A word is effaced in MS. It must have been = 'creator.'

[3] A word entirely obliterated in MS. It must have been արարած = 'made,' κτίσμα.

[4] Paul, ad Phil. ii. 9.   [5] Mark i. 12 and Hebr. vii. 22.

[6] Or render 'sacrament' or 'counsel.'

mandments of the heavenly Father, as is plain to us from the holy Gospels; and when his [maker][1] took away the feasting and the fellow-converse from him, then he hungered. And the envious tyrant, seeing that, began to try to ensnare our Saviour with envy [of glory], saying[2]: 'If thou art the Son of God, speak, that these stones may become bread,' and the rest, Matt. iv. 3. * But Jesus made answer and said to that evil one: 'O ravening lion[3], O enemy, O monster, O shameless slayer of men, wherefore dost thou thus address me with an "if[4]"; dost thou desire under cover of the doubt[4] to draw thy snare over me. I am not thy fancy which thou fanciest me, O full of all deceit.' * Jesus made answer and said: 'It is written that man shall not live by bread alone, but by every word which goeth forth from the mouth of God.' Now have we made clear the meaning of the text which says that our Lord Jesus, because of his feasting, his fellow-converse and receiving of commands and glory of Godship, hungered not until the completion of those days. So then the evil one saw that our Saviour Christ was not to be tricked like Eva and Adam with a single word; and Satan next took and led him into the holy city, and placed him on a pinnacle of the temple and said to him: 'Throw thyself down thence, for it is written that to his angels he has given charge concerning thee, and on their hands they shall bear thee up, lest thou ever dash thy foot against a stone.' Jesus again said unto him: 'It is written that thou shalt not tempt the Lord thy God.' Again Satan took him into a mountain exceeding high and showed him all the kingdoms of the world and the glory of them. And he said unto him, 'All this will I give thee, if thou wilt fall down and worship me.' Then said Jesus to him: 'Get thee behind me, Satan, for it is written, that thou shalt worship the Lord thy God, and him alone shalt thou serve. Yea, and St. Luke adds about the evil one, ch. iv. 13, that having completed every temptation Satan departed from him for a season.

---

[1] The word is half obliterated. It must have been as rendered.

[2] Matt. iv. 3.

[3] This apostrophe to the devil, as far as the words 'full of all deceit,' seems to be an interpolation.

[4] Թէական in MS. must be a corruption of Թէականաւ, which means 'by an hypothesis, a conjecture or doubt, by an "if."'

CHAPTER VI

Concerning the deceitfulness of the evil one, which he practises after the temptation of our Lord Jesus Christ continuously until the second coming of our Lord and Saviour Jesus Christ.

The same is set forth by a member of the church, St. Luke, ch. iv. 13: 'And having completed every temptation Satan departed from him for a season.'

So then, after the temptation of our Lord Jesus, the adversary Satan was filled with much wrath, and began from that day to take to himself astute instruments of his wickedness and to follow after the disciples of our Lord Jesus Christ and after all who believed on him, as is clear from the words of the holy Gospel, which says about Judas the traitor, John xiii. 27: 'And after the sop, then Satan entered into him.' Therefore Satan, after accomplishing his acts of wickedness in Judas—and he procured[1] his end and made him his servant, forthwith entered into the priests and high priests of the Jews. And after them, without waiting, the evil one entered into the heart of a damsel and caused her to address Peter twice over in order to subvert him and cast him over the precipice. Yea and into yet others he entered. At the same hour he also confirmed them, in order to secure Peter to himself. However, our intercessor and mediator Jesus Christ divined beforehand the temptation of the evil one which was in store for Peter; and that is why our Lord began by giving great warning to Peter, saying, Luke xxii. 31: 'Saith the Lord, Simon, Simon, behold Satan sought to sift thee as wheat, but I made supplication for thee, that thy faith may not be wanting, that thou mayest in time turn again and establish thy brethren.'

And we must now at every hour say this holy and precious prayer ... in the presence of our Lord Jesus Christ, that he may relent towards us and intercede for us sinners, to liberate us from all evil temptations. Amen.

> Holy Jesus, Holy Lord Christ
> Holy Son of God, for us make intercession [2].

And then say 'Our Father,' and the rest.

And then[3], Satan seeing that his works of wickedness availed nothing, hardened and whetted his wickedness still more than

---

[1] Arm. lit. = 'sustinens,' which makes no sense.
[2] John, *Cath. Ep.* ii. 1.   [3] Paul, Rom. viii. 34.

before, and more and more against the believers and disciples of our Lord Jesus Christ, and against the apostles of our Saviour, as is clear from John vi. 67.

CHAPTER VII

Concerning the adversary of God the Father let us also speak.

'From that time many of his disciples went back, and did not walk with him any more.'

Now, the wild beast, of whom I have written above, continued to threaten with great wrath the disciples of our Lord; because he that was said to be his did not fall a victim to his most evil plan, as St. Luke above testified, saying of this very evil one, that he left him and went away for a season. So firmly at this season this son of perdition, in the hour of the Lord's temptation, cherished in himself the determination to sow his evil longings in the hearts and ears of those who should please Him even until the end of the world. For this cause our mediator and intercessor never ceases to warn us, saying, Luke xxii. 40: 'And when he came unto the place he said unto them, Pray ye that ye enter not into temptation.' So well did our Lord also know the designs of the evil one, and therefore expressly enjoined us to watch and pray. And a member of the holy universal and apostolic church, St. Peter, in his first catholic Epistle saith, ch. v. 8 : 'Be sober, be watchful, for your adversary, Satan, like a lion roareth, walketh about and seeketh whom he may devour.' After this manner must we also be wakeful and not asleep in sin. For some, being weighed down with sin, have followed this adversary, as is clear in their histories and ceremonies, which same we shall expose with the help of the Holy Spirit.

CHAPTER VIII

Concerning Satan, in what form he has appeared to those who have been deceived and become his slaves, this we will set forth.

At the first this gate of hell took the form of a serpent[1]; secondly, of a raven; thirdly, of a calf[2]; fourthly, of wild beasts; fifthly, of light; sixthly, of women; seventhly, of men; eighthly, of clerics; ninthly, of teachers of the school; tenthly, of apostles;

---

[1] In margin against what follows this: Birth (or genesis) of Cain, of Exodus, in Bible 1 Kings (=Samuel) xxviii. 12.

[2] The word *hordoj* here used in MS. means either a 'seal,' or a 'calf,' or a 'monster.'

eleventhly, of bishops; twelfthly, of monks[1]. And all other forms he assumes as a disguise; and in these same forms he seals[2] and stamps those who love and please him, and guards them for himself until the end. For in evil wise doth he chastise himself and all his, according to the saying: Their worm dieth not, and their fire is not quenched. And may the Lord God Almighty, by the mediation and intercession of his loved Son, save and liberate all who make true confession of faith from such temptation. Amen.

And here must we say this prayer before Christ.

O sweet Lord of mine, Jesus Christ, we worship, we pray, we entreat and beseech thine all-powerful Lordship, who art at the right hand of thy Father [and maker][3], mediate and intercede for us sinners now and in the hour of our death. Amen.

CHAPTER IX

Concerning him that disguises himself let us speak.

Now the teacher and father of schismatics and heretics assumes many forms of disguise. But we have only mentioned twelve, in order not to be tedious to you, my loved ones. What is the reason why the evil one disguises himself? It is this, that by means of the disguise he may easily enslave them to himself. For this reason he first assumes the form of a serpent, because the serpent was full of guile. Secondly of a raven, because the raven is a lover of lewdness. Thirdly of a calf, because a calf is a friend of mankind and useful to us. Fourthly in the form of wild beasts[4]; because wild beasts are renders of all images. Fifthly of light, because light is disperser of darkness. Sixthly in form of maidens and of women, because they are too prone to adorn themselves because of their hunting after men. Seventhly in form of men, because they eagerly assent to things said. Eighthly of clerics, because they lead the lives of impostors. Ninthly of school teachers[5], because they are

---

[1] Geo. Monach. 73, x. τὸν διάβολον, μοναχικὰ ἐνδεδυμένον ἀμφία .... καὶ διδάσκουσιν ... παρὰ τοῦ διαβόλου ὑποδειχθῆναι τὸ παρὰ τοῦ θεοῦ δι' ἀγγέλου τοῖς ἀνθρώποις ὑποδειχθὲν καὶ δοθὲν ἅγιον σχῆμα, ὅπερ οἱ μοναχοὶ ἐνδεδύμεθα. See also the Key, p. 122.

[2] A reference to paedo-baptism.

[3] A word nearly effaced in MS. which was clearly as rendered.

[4] In margin of MS. this note: See in the book (*or* epistle) of expiation (*or* of purgatory). I do not understand the reference, which occurs again.

[5] In margin of MS. this note: See First of Kings (=Samuel) in the Bible, xxviii. 12.

teachers of all. Tenthly of apostles, because they are healers of soul and body. Eleventhly of bishops and catholici, because they are proud and overweening, and in particular traffickers in the authority of our Lord Jesus Christ; yea, and though dispensers of holy law, yet are also avaricious and excogitators of falsehoods. Lastly, they disguise themselves as monks[1], because they always love herbs and vegetables, yea and also ...[2] and they keep fasts, because their food grows always in damp places. Wherefore also their dwellings are there, for they like it much.

CHAPTER X

Concerning the testimonies of the holy apostles, and of writings which are external (i.e. gentile or pagan), *that it is true that the evil one takes the form of* .. [3]

First, St. Paul, in his second letter to the Corinthians, demonstrates the variety of forms assumed by this evil one, saying, ch. xi. 12: 'What I do, that will I do, that I may cut off occasions of them who desire occasions; that wherein they glory, they too may be found even as we. For such men are false apostles, deceitful workers, they fashion themselves into apostles of Christ. And no marvel, for even Satan fashioneth himself into an angel of light; and it is no great thing, if his ministers also fashion themselves as ministers of righteousness; whose end shall be according to their works. But . . . . [4]

[CHAPTER XIV]

. . . . as also our Lord Jesus Christ, having chosen his disciples, said: 'Go ye into all the world, and preach the gospel of the` kingdom to all creatures. Whoever believeth, shall be baptized, shall live; but whoever believeth not, shall be judged,' and the rest. Behold, O ye blind, how our Lord deems your procedure false and vain, and pronounces you to be deniers of him,

---

[1] In margin this note: 'In the lives of the fathers.'
[2] One word effaced in MS.
[3] Perhaps there stood here ' of a monk.'
[4] Here the folios 30r–53r, equal to twenty-four pages, are torn out of MS. These pages seem to have contained the last part of chap. x, all of chaps. xi–xiii, and the first part of chap. xiv. These chapters must have contained a free criticism of orthodox abuses.

and calls you children of Satan, as was written above. Lo, now do ye recognize right well your lying father; recognize of a truth your spirit; recognize even your false God. Nay, recognize also your teacher; yea, and furthermore do ye recognize the Pope, the Catholicos, and your president; and recognize your sham Messiah, and the rest. Of whom our mediator and intercessor, our life and refuge, doth manifestly speak, saying: 'And that which he speaketh false, he speaketh out of his own, and his father is Satan.' Thus our Lord Jesus and the holy universal and apostolic church saw and spoke as we wrote above. And now once more we write down from the First to Timothy, iv. 1: 'But expressly doth the Holy Spirit say, that in the last times some shall fall away from the faith,' and the rest. And again in another writing of his doth he speak of you that are blinded: 'And there shall be lovers of self, overweening, proud and insolent. Nay, more, ye have confidence in your works, but have denied the holy works of our Lord Jesus, and of his sanctified apostles; and are followers of your father, the evil one, who gave you his law, namely, to baptize unbelievers, to worship images, to make silver and gold into the form of an image . . . .[1] and to adore the same, to pry into the sins of men and women, to explore the same and grant remission, as to which our Lord ordained, saying: No one can remit sins, save only the one God. But do you investigate all their other words, and give praise to the heavenly Father, and to his only-born Son.

CHAPTER XV

Concerning the baptism of our Lord Jesus Christ and of his elected, hallowed, disciples, how they were baptized.

When Jesus learned that the Pharisees heard that Jesus is making many disciples and is baptizing [more] than John. For it was not that . . . .

[CHAPTER XVI][2]

. . . . suffered, I say not you; but if ye do not repent, ye shall likewise be destroyed.

Thus our Lord Jesus Christ decreed that these three ineffable mysteries (*or* sacraments) are essential when he spake to those

---

[1] One or two words effaced in MS. No doubt the words effaced were 'of Christ and of the Virgin,' or similar.

[2] Folios 56–59 of MS. are lost, including nearly all chap. xv and first lines of the title of chap. xvi.

ON THE THREE SACRAMENTS

who listened[1]. First he lays stress on and ordains repentance; like St. John, who was mentioned above. Secondly, he grants us holy baptism, as he said to Nicodemus[2]: 'Jesus made answer and said to them, Verily, verily I say unto you, except a man be born again, he cannot see the kingdom of God.' Thirdly, as regards his holy, precious body and blood, the Saviour commands us to make them (separately) from one another, as is clear from John vi. 54: 'Jesus said unto them, Verily, verily I say unto you, Except ye eat the flesh of the Son of man and drink his blood, ye have not life in yourselves.'

Moreover, in the same chapter, he again speaks of them separately and not as one numerically, v. 56: 'For my flesh is true food and my blood is true drink.' Look well at and thoroughly scan the holy writ; how that for the sake of the faithful it bestows and enforces repentance, baptism, and his holy body and blood. And the door of salvation speaks concerning believers and not unbelievers who ...[3] For in no wise at all do they know God, nor is their knowledge of Jesus Christ and of the holy church of Christ, that is of the holy Apostles. Moreover, they know not joy and sorrow, their father or their mother, and are like brass that sounds or cymbals that clash, and so forth.

In such matters then what is it right for us to do according to law[4]? Naught but this: when children are born of their mothers, then it is necessary for the elect after seven days to proceed to the house of the children born, on the eighth day; and he shall comfort the parents with great love and give to them good spiritual advice, that they shall train up their offspring in godliness, in faith, hope, love, and in all good works, as St. Paul writes in his first to Timothy, ch. iv. 7, saying[5] as follows: 'But from filthy words and old wives' fables hold aloof: but exercise thyself unto godliness, for exercise of the body is profitable for a little; but godliness is something profitable for all things, and hath the promise of life, of that which now is and of that which is to be.' Likewise, according to the canons[6] of the holy apostles it is necessary for the parents

---

[1] Or render: 'When he saith what is thus necessary.'
[2] John iii. 2.   [3] One or two words destroyed in MS.
[4] = κατὰ νόμον, i.e. according to true ecclesiastical rule.
[5] In margin was a note of four words, all erased save the first, which is 'baptism.'
[6] The writer uses the Greek word merely as = 'precepts,' and *canonem* the verb as = 'I direct.' The reference is not to the apostolical canons, elsewhere condemned in the Key as the Latin forgery of Clemens.

themselves ever and always to give for instruction and study to their infant offspring as it were milk; and they shall not be at all sparing [thereof]. As also St. Paul, in his first to Corinthians, ch. iii. 1, says: 'And I, brethren, could not speak unto you as unto spiritual, but as unto carnal[1], as unto babes in Christ. I fed you with milk, not with meat; for ye were not able. Nay, not even now are ye able. For ye are yet carnal.'

So then, for us also and for the parents it is right first of all to perform the name-giving of the catechumens, and then after some time we cause them to be instructed in good works........[2] at that time whether it be male or female; in order that he or she already ......may be baptized. Accordingly, if a male, the child will learn to be on its guard against its original desires; while, if a maiden, it will be discreet [and shun the sin][3] which was manifested in the deception of Eva and Adam. For first was Eve dishonoured, and then she woke up the mind of Adam. So also must we [awake] them in their due seasons, [and tell them] of the curse they inherit from their sire; albeit we now through Jesus Christ lead them unto the highest bliss. For this cause St. John, our mediator and intercessor Jesus Christ, and his holy disciples, first showed the faith, then brought to repentance, and last of all bestowed baptism; as is clear from the actions of our Saviour Jesus. For he first asked for Faith of the blind[4], the halt, the withered, the demoniacs, and especially of the lords dead[5], and said to them: 'Do ye believe that I am able to do this unto you?' But they in great fear cried out, saying, 'Yea, Lord, thou canst.' And they worshipped him and were healed. Also their dead were raised. So must we also perform baptism when they are of full age like our Lord; so that they may seek it in faith from us, and that then we may give them baptism and perfect blessing.

Suppose, for example, a man who is caught by thieves or robbers on a mountain-top or in a ravine, and they have bound his hands and feet fast with fetters and cast him into some gully, surely it is necessary for him to struggle to free himself, or is it not? But

---

[1] In margin is this note: 'First it is necessary to perform the name-giving, as milk.'

[2] Half a line erased in MS.

[3] Something seems lacking in the text, though the copy marks no lacuna.

[4] Concerning the blind, John ix. 40, Luke xi. 27, Mark ii. 5.

[5] The text might possibly = 'of lords (*or* masters) of the dead.' Perhaps it is a corruption of something. But a similar expression occurs in Priscillian's works of the patriarchs and prophets in hell.

they make answer and say that he must work hard and struggle, until he liberate himself; for fear lest he fall a prey to the wild beasts. Such also is the enactment of our Lord, which he laid down in our texts, with regard to repentance. In this very wise does he warn us that he who does not believe and repent cannot be baptized and be justified, be purified of sin and be freed from the fetters of Satan. To this effect our mediator and intercessor Jesus Christ delivered the parable which tells of the repentant and unrepentant, Luke xiii. 6 [1]. 'A certain man had a fig-tree planted in his vineyard; and he came seeking fruit from the fig-tree, and found none. [And he said to the vinedresser, Behold these three years I come seeking fruit thereon and found none.] So [2] cut it down; why doth it cumber the ground? He answered and said: Lord, let it alone this year, till I shall dig about and dung it. Perhaps it will bear fruit of repentance; if not, after another year thou shalt cut it down.'

But now it is needful for you, readers, to examine thoroughly and understand the parables of our Lord Jesus Christ, who primarily means repentance, but directly or indirectly graciously vouchsafes the parable to those that listen and receive it. Wherefore now hath our Lord Jesus Christ, Son of the heavenly Father, revealed the Way and the Truth and the Life, that those who have not faith, repentance, hope, and love cannot be baptized nor draw nigh unto the holy flesh and blood of the Son of God. Nay more, cannot enter the kingdom of God; as above in regard to the three mysteries, he himself bore sure witness, that they cannot enter his holy bosom; nay, nor participate in the glory of his heavenly Father well-loved.

CHAPTER XVII

Concerning Baptism.

Thus our mediator and intercessor Jesus Christ spake this parable as touching believers and unbelievers [3]. For the kingdom of God hath been likened unto ten virgins, who took their lamps and went forth to meet the bridegroom and bride. Five of them

---

[1] An entire line effaced in MS. Perhaps the orthodox churches were here identified with the unrepentant.

[2] The first part of Luke xiii. 7 has dropped out of MS. by homoioteleuton.

[3] In margin against what follows this note: 'The bridegroom who is Jesus, and the bride the holy church universal. Paul to Ephes. ch. v. 32.'

were foolish and five wise. The foolish took their lamps[1]
...... from place to place, whom shall the Lord God, through the mediation and intercession of his Son only born, preserve from the temptation of your father and rank them with the holy wise virgins. So that they knowing did abide in thy holy and precious word, and in no wise erred from thy all-holy tradition[2], which thou didst vouchsafe unto thy spotless Son, thine only-born. And they (*lit.* who) in the season of full growth baptize those that repent and believe in the name of Jesus Christ, thy loved Son . .[3] yea and replenish them also with thine holy spirit and strengthen their minds and bodies. Because thy Son did truly promise us, saying: 'He that believeth shall be baptized, shall live; but he that believeth not, shall be judged.'

Concerning the giving of a name to the Catechumen.

We must seven days after the birth proceed to the home of the newborn child on the eighth day, and we then begin by saying the holy prayer of our Lord Jesus, 'Our Father.'

And then, after saying 'Our Father,' the elect one and all the congregation with one accord repeat this prayer over the catechumen with faith, thus:

> Father of our Lord Jesus Christ, we beg and entreat thee, keep this catechumen from evil, and fix thy holy eye upon him, and keep him from all temptation of the world; and give him life according to thy good will, that he may pass through the season of his childhood and become acceptable to thee, to thy Son, and to thy Holy Spirit. And bring him through to reach holy baptism, and call him under the shelter of the wings of thy beloved Son. And also bless, O my Lord and God, the catechumen through the mediation of Jesus, thy beloved Son. Cleanse him from fleshly pollutions, and day by day prosper and increase him in thy grace, and bring him unto the full measure of the time of holy baptism, now and ever and to eternity of eternities. Amen.

And then read the words of St. Paul, 1 Cor. xiii. 11.

When I was a child, I spake as a child, I felt as a child, I thought as a child. But when I became a full man, I put away childish things. Now we see as if in a mirror by symbol, but

---

[1] A folio is lost here from MS. containing pp. 66, 67.
[2] Matt. xxviii. 18.   [3] I suspect a word has fallen out here.

then face to face. Now I understand in part, but then I shall know even as he knoweth me. But now abide Faith, Hope, Love, as it were three; and the greatest of these is Love.

And after the reading of Paul, 'tis meet for the elect one to ask the name of the catechumen: 'By what name do ye desire to call this catechumen according to law[1] and not with a fabulous name?'

And then he readeth the holy gospel, Luke ii. 21[2]

'And when eight days were fulfilled to circumcise him, his name was called Jesus, which was so called by the angel before he was conceived in the womb.'

Glory to thee, King of Glory, that thou hast made this catechumen worthy to be given a name. We beseech thy foreseeing majesty, guard him until he attain to the holy birth of the font, that we may praise thee, thy Son, and thy Holy Spirit, now and for ever and ever. Amen.

Repeat the 'Our Father,' and go to thy house.

God doth produce the fruits of grace.

Directions for those baptizing; of what sort shall they be who may be baptized.

CHAPTER XVIII

But as the Lord commanded in his holy canons, even so shall ye baptize those who come unto us. And St. John directed those who came to himself to repent. Or as the holy universal and apostolic Catholic Church having learned from our Lord Jesus Christ did proceed; so also must ye after them do, as we said above. For they first taught; secondly asked for faith; thirdly induced to repent; and after that granted holy baptism to those who were of full age, and in particular were cognizant of their original sin. Again ye, the elect ones, must observe the utmost care that they receive before baptism instruction and training, both of body and soul, as St. Paul saith: 'Practise thyself in godliness.' So must ye without delay bring those who come unto faith, hope, love, and repentance, and with extreme care and testing practise them, no matter who they be, lest peradventure any one should be an impostor, or deceitful, or a wizard, like Simon, in Acts viii. 13.

---

[1] 'Law,' so used in the fifth to the twelfth centuries, meant the Christian Religion as opposed to Paganism.

[2] In margin: 'Also Luke i. 63.'

But Simon himself believed and was baptized and rose up against Philip in trickery and charlatanry, in order to obtain the power of the holy spirit by deceit. So also ye, my loved ones, must examine those who come to you, that is thieves and counterfeit ones, who come to you clothed as sheep[1]. As our Lord Jesus Christ saith: Forasmuch as such as these would fain prove themselves holy to you in order to obtain[2] holiness and the pearl from you, and would then trample them under foot; as Saint Paul commandeth in his letter to the Romans, saying, ch. xvi. 18: 'For such as these serve not our Lord Jesus Christ, but their own belly; and by their smooth and fair speech they beguile the hearts of the sinless'—whether priests or doctors or deacons[3], whether men or women, you must not at once baptize them nor communicate them until they have been completely tested.

Concerning those who are being baptized, how they shall come unto holy baptism; and what is their duty and what is the fruit they shall display, that we should see it and confide in them; as our Lord directs us, saying: By their fruits shall ye know them.

CHAPTER XIX

It is right and fitting that those to be baptized should shed bitter tears, like Peter, like Paul, like the harlot Mary, or like Simon's wife's mother, and others resembling them. For they with great contrition received glory and honour from Jesus Christ our Saviour, as is clear in the holy gospel, and in the Acts of the holy Apostles, and elsewhere. Again, what is meet for those to do who wish to receive holy baptism? It is meet that they should approach in gentleness, in humility to the elect one, solicit from him release from demons, and that they may serve our Lord Jesus Christ and his holy church. But then shall the elect one advise them, saying: O my little children, forasmuch as ye now desire to receive from me holy release, ye must say . . . . . . [4] they trouble you and will desire to subvert the Gospel of Christ. But though we, or an angel come down from heaven, should preach unto you a gospel in excess of that which we preached, let him be anathema.

---

[1] Matt. vii. 10. [2] Reading *arnoul* for *arnel*.

[3] Geo. Mon. p. 74, xiv. καὶ τοὺς πρεσβυτέρους καὶ λοιποὺς ἱερεῖς τοὺς παρ' ἡμῖν ἀποβάλλονται.

[4] Two leaves lost in MS., viz. four pages, 74-77, torn out. They probably contained a recantation of orthodox errors.

As I said before, so say I now again, If any man preach unto you a gospel in excess of that which ye received, let him be anathema.'

Again I write this unto you, dearly beloved, that ye shall diligently search the holy gospel of our Lord Jesus Christ and the holy Acts of the Apostles, and then condemn us[1], lest perhaps ye also be punished in season.

> Come my children of the new Zion,
> Take on you the crown of the Lord Jesus.
> Cherish in yourselves each word spoken,
> Take your places in the ranks on the right hand.
> If ye listen unto the Church,
> The infinite God shall save you.

> The Head of all is the Lord Jesus,
> Whom the holy Paul[2] doth confess,
> And the head of Christ is God and Light.

> Acts, ch. i. vs. 13.

> Peter and Jacob,
> John and Andrew,
> Philip and Thomas,
> Bartholomew and Matthew,
> Jacobus of Alpheus,
> And Simon the Zealot,
> And Jude of Jacob;
> Also Paul, the vessel of Election.

> These are the Church Universal,
>   nor is it Peter alone.

> Church universal,
> Which was foreshadowed in the Ark of Noe.
> Through it have many souls been saved,
> Which were lost through the wiles of devils.

CHAPTER XX

Concerning what it is meet for the elect one to speak or what he giveth them to say. It is meet for the elect one to give them also this profession of faith to repeat, as follows:

We confess and believe that there is one true God, of whom our Lord Christ speaketh, John xvii. 3: This is life Eternal, that

---

[1] i.e., in case we have taught you anything contrary to the holy gospel.
[2] Ephes. v. 29.

they should know thee the only true God[1] and him whom thou didst send, Jesus Christ. Again we confess and believe in Jesus Christ, [a new creature and not][2] creator[3], as St. Paul saith to the Hebrews, ch. iii. 2: He is faithful to his creator, as was Moses in all his house. Again ye shall believe in the intercession of our Lord Jesus Christ and of no others. Ye shall believe in the holy apostles and in all who are the Universal Catholic Church, and are not Latins, Greeks, or [Armenians][4].

Furthermore ye shall believe in Jesus Christ, that by his father's command he is to come to judge the quick and the dead[5].

And when they shall have finished the confession of faith before the elect one, and at the same time before the rulers, then shall the elect one say this prayer before the face of the heavenly Father:

The Prayer of our Lord Jesus Christ in the presence of the Heavenly Father.

I thank thee, Father, Lord of heaven and earth, that thou hast hidden this from the wise and learned and hast revealed it to babes. Yea, Father, for so it was pleasing in thy sight. All things have been given unto me by my Father; and no one knoweth the Son, but only the Father; nor doth any one know the Father save the Son, and to whom the Son shall desire to reveal. Come unto me, all ye that are weary and heavy-laden, and I will give you rest. Take up my yoke on you and learn of me, for I am gentle and lowly in heart; and ye shall find rest for your souls. For my yoke is easy and my burden is light.

And when they have finished the holy prayer of our Lord Jesus Christ—

Now then, let us proceed to consider the baptizer, what he must [be], or how he must live, or in what manner he shall bring unto

---

[1] Perhaps the Paulicians interpreted these words to mean the God in heaven as opposed to the demiurge who ruled the visible world—'the god and lord of this world,' as Satan is elsewhere styled in the New Testament.

[2] There are words here effaced in the text which appear to be as translated. Mr. Alex. Eritzean of Tiflis, independently examining the MS., deciphered the words partly erased in the same manner.

[3] Geo. Mon. p. 76, xx. καὶ οὐ μόνον κτίσμα τοῦτον ἐπικαλεῖς κατὰ τὸν ματαιόφρονα Ἄρειον, ἀλλὰ καὶ τῶν ἀγγέλων καὶ τῶν ἀνθρώπων αὐτῶν μεταγενέστερον.

[4] The word is erased in the MS.

[5] Geo. Mon. p. 75, xx. ἐπίβαλε σὺ ὁ Χριστιανός. Καὶ γενήσεται δευτέρα παρουσία τοῦ Χριστοῦ καὶ Θεοῦ ἡμῶν καὶ κριθησόμεθα παρ' αὐτοῦ οἱ ἄνθρωποι; καὶ ὁμολογήσει τοῦτο ὁ βέβηλος.

himself the repentant, or in what form minister to him. Wherefore we declare all this unto the person baptizing and to the person being baptized with God's help, in detail.

Now therefore it is necessary for the baptizer to be elect according to the words of the heavenly Father to his beloved Son, Luke ix. 35: He is my Son Elect. Hear ye him. And secondly, he shall be gentle and lowly according to the command of our Lord Jesus Christ, which he gave by the mouth of his holy evangelists, John xv. 16 and 19, and xi. 28. Also in Matt.: 'Learn of me, for I am gentle and lowly in heart,' and the rest.

Now the teacher [shall be] wise, obedient, modest, sober, virtuous, god-fearing, loved by all, himself a lover of all the faithful. But let him not be superstitious, a babbler, a liar, an inciter of evil. Neither shall he be dissolute or vicious, nor shall he be deceitful and an impostor, nor shall he be fond of low gain nor a lover of pleasure.

Let him then not be contentious and choleric; nor let him be a wine-bibber and a drunkard. Neither shall he be fond of glory or a taker of profits. And he shall not be a taker of gifts and greedy, nor a thief and a robber; nor shall he be a murderer and a grinder of the poor. Let him also not be weak in faith, or perverse, litigious. Let him not be a deceiver of men and women. Let him not be double-tongued, an inciter unto evil; let him not be a calumniator of others. Let him not be proud and selfish, let him not be a lover of silver or of any of this world's riches. Let him not be scarred with impurity, or a buffoon. Let him not be an adulterer and effeminate. Let him not be blind or halt, let him not be deaf or mute. Let him not be tall to excess above all men, nor let him be shorter than all men. And thus the [apostles] ordain by the Holy Spirit in their canons. And in particular the holy Apostle Paul directed Titus, saying, ch. i. 7: 'For the bishop (*or* overseer) must be blameless, as God's steward; not self-willed, not soon angry, not quarrelsome, no striker, not greedy of filthy lucre. But hospitable, a lover of good, sober-minded, just, holy, temperate. To be a protector of the faithful word of the teaching, that he may be able both to exhort in soundness of doctrine and to convict the gainsayers.'

Again, St. Paul writes to Timothy thus, ch. iii. 1: 'Faithful is the saying, If a man seeketh the office of a bishop (*or* overseer), he seeketh a good work. The bishop (*or* overseer) must be without reproach, the husband of one wife, temperate, sober-minded, orderly, hospitable, apt to teach. No brawler, no striker; but gentle. Not contentious, no lover of money. For of his own house he shall be a good supervisor, and shall have children who are in subjection with all gravity.'

Thus then the elect one must beware of all evil thoughts according to the Apostle Paul, according to the command he gave, saying: Be ye imitators of me, as also am I of Christ. I praise you for that you have all my riches. Ch. xi. 10 of First to Corinthians.

Behold and see, my godly ones, how the Apostles of our Lord Jesus Christ enjoin us. And if ye resemble not them, then ye (MS. = we) cannot any more become elect and presidents of the faithful, and so forth.

Concerning them who are baptized, how they shall come unto the elect one and be baptized by him.

CHAPTER XXI

Now then we say on this matter: Do ye be submissive to the law and have an ear to the canons, which direct how the novices[1] shall go and present themselves to the elect one. For in gentleness and humility [shall they go], as our Lord Jesus Christ in gentleness[2] and humility stood before St. John the Baptist. So also this new-born shoot must come unto the elect one. And forthwith the elect one shall rise to his feet and say: 'Come unto me all ye that are troubled and heavy laden, and I will give you rest. Take my yoke upon you and learn of me, For I am gentle and lowly in heart; and ye shall find rest for your souls. For my yoke is easy and my burden is light.' Matt. xi. 28. And the penitent, with much eagerness throwing himself at the feet of the elect one, with supplications and tears, saith: O thou, elected by God and by Jesus Christ, I pray and beseech thee, set me, who am not worthy, free from the bonds of Satan.

This before the people he shall openly say.

Next the elect one, with benign glance and great love asketh him, saying:—

My little child, thou who wishest to be released from the bonds of the devils of Satan, What fruit of absolution hast thou? Tell it to us before the congregation. But the penitent, if he have learned and received the perfect faith, with unfeigned trust, shall at

---

[1] Or 'the newly presented.'   [2] Matt. iii. 14.

THE RITE OF BAPTISM

once come on his knees into the midst of the water and say with great love and tears to the elect one as follows:—

First do I faithfully believe in our Lord Jesus Christ, as the holy apostles believed, in Matt. xvi. 13, and as in Acts viii. to v. 18 'And he said unto them, But ye, whom do ye say that I am? Simon Peter made answer and said to him, Thou art Christ, the Son of the living God,' and the rest. John vi. 69. And in particular the apostle Paul, making profession saith: 'The head of all is Christ, and the head of Christ is God,' 1 Cor. xi. 3. As also is clear in the holy gospel saying, John xvii. 3, 'This is life eternal, that they should know thee, the only true God, and him whom thou didst send, Jesus Christ.' So do I make confession and believe, serve, and worship God the Father, and the Son, mediator and intercessor, and the Holy Spirit, the dispenser of grace to us who believe.

And then, as he that has believed completes his holy profession of faith, the elect one instantly takes the water into his hands, and looking up to heaven (saith),—also observing in (*or* toward) himself the mystery (*or* sacrament), the form (*or* figure) and the intention,—shall directly or indirectly empty out the water over the head saying: In the name of Father and Son and Holy Spirit is baptized this man or woman—mentioning the name—by the testimony of the congregation here present.

And then he reads the holy gospel of our Lord Jesus Christ:—

Matt. iii. 13: 'Then cometh Jesus from Galilee to the Jordan unto John to be baptized by him.' Mark i. 9: 'And it came to pass in those days that Jesus came from Nazareth of Galilee and was baptized by John in the Jordan.' Luke iii. 21: 'And it came to pass in the baptizing of all the people, that Jesus was baptized and was praying; and the heavens were opened,' and the rest. John 1. 29: 'On the morrow he seeth Jesus coming unto him and saith,' and read also the rest in full over the person baptized.

Next the elect one receives before him the novice; but the novices shall in fear and trembling on their knees draw nigh, naked, bending low their heads and with firmest faith, bearing in mind the release from Satan. But the elect one takes water in his hands, and with mystery[1] (*or* sacrament) with word and with act, shall fully empty out the water over one head (at a time) and say

---

[1] In margin of MS. the following note: 'One before the Father: one before the Son; one before the Holy Spirit he shall fill.'

first, In the name of the Father; and he shall empty out the water on the head three times [and after that] in the name of the Son and in the name of the Holy Spirit .. [1] in union,

Because the Father giveth release from the bonds, the Son giveth hope to sinners, and the Holy Spirit is love in the hearts of those who listen, believe, are baptized, and the rest.

Ye shall keep to this figure.

For a certain king releases certain rulers from the prison of sin, but the Son calls them to himself and comforts them (*lit.* gives hope) with lofty (*lit.* great) words, and the holy spirit of the king forthwith comes and crowns them, and dwells in (*or* with) them for ever and ever. Amen.

Read thou the holy gospels.

'Then cometh Jesus from Galilee to the Jordan unto John to be baptized by him. But John would have hindered him saying, I have need to be baptized by thee, and comest thou to me? Jesus made answer and said unto him: Suffer it now, for thus it becometh us to fulfil all righteousness. Then he suffereth him. And when he was baptized Jesus went up straightway from the water; and behold the heavens were opened unto him; and he saw the spirit of God, descending like a dove; and it came upon him. And behold there was a voice from heaven which said: He is my beloved Son, in whom I am well pleased.'

He is in the presence of the Father.

We thank, we magnify and glorify thine Almighty Fatherhood, that thou hast made worthy thy servants in the hour of baptism, who have been baptized in the name of thy Son, the only-born. And now we adore, we ask and beseech of thee, Holy Father, preserve them from the wiles of devils and free them from the temptation of evil ones. Seal, Holy Father, their hearts, their souls and bodies with the precious flesh and blood of thine only born Son, now and evermore.

---

[1] Two or three words are destroyed in MS. The lacuna should probably be filled up somewhat as follows: 'Of the Holy Spirit, *separately, and not* in union.' For the note in the margin proves that the three successive handfuls of water were regarded as symbolic of the distinctness of the three Persons. The erasure proves that the Paulicians anyhow gave another interpretation to the baptismal formula than do Trinitarians.

THE RITE OF BAPTISM

Next ye shall read the Acts of the Apostles, ii. 1.

'And when the days of Pentecost were completed, they were all with one accord together. And there was on a sudden a sound, coming from heaven, as of a mighty wind, and it filled all the house in which they sat. And there appeared unto them divided tongues, as of fire, and there sat one on each of them. And all were filled with the Holy Spirit, and began to speak with other tongues as the Spirit gave them utterance.'

Gospel of Mark, i. 9.

'And it came to pass in those days that Jesus came from Nazareth of Galilee, and was baptized by John in the Jordan. And forthwith, as he went up out of the waters, he saw the heavens rent asunder, and the Spirit of God, like a dove, descending from heaven, [and a voice came out of the heavens][1] and said, Thou art my beloved Son; In thee am I well pleased.'

And then we say this prayer before the Son of the Heavenly Father.

We adore, we entreat and beseech of thee, Christ, Son of God, receive these among the number of thy holy disciples, and send the Spirit of thy Father into their hearts, for thou didst promise them, saying: If I go not, the Holy Spirit will not come unto you. But now with ardent love, falling on our faces, we beseech thee in behalf of thy servants, who now have been baptized into thy holy name, and now anxiously await the faithful promise of thy Lordship, [made] unto their hearts, and unto all thy servants who have believed in thee.

And next thou shalt read Paul to the Galatians, iii. 24–29.

'So that the law hath been our tutor to bring us unto Christ, that we might be justified by faith. But now that faith is come, we are no longer under a tutor. For ye are all sons of God, through faith [in Christ Jesus]. For as many of you as were baptized into Christ did put on Christ. There can be neither Jew nor Greek, there can be neither bond nor free, there can be no male and female: for ye are all one in Christ Jesus. And if ye are Christ's, then are ye Abraham's seed, heirs according to promise.'

From the holy gospel of Jesus Christ according to Luke, iii. 21–22.

'Now it came to pass, when all the people were baptized, that, Jesus also having been baptized, and praying, the heaven was

---

[1] Omitted in MS. through homoioteleuton.

opened, and the Holy Ghost descended in a bodily form, as a dove, upon him, and a voice came out of heaven which said, Thou art my beloved Son; in thee I am well pleased.'

Also this further prayer in the presence of the Holy Spirit.

Blessed art thou, Spirit of the Heavenly Father, forasmuch as thou wast made by the Father, and coming, didst give unto our Lord Jesus Christ authority over all flesh; and didst make him king and head of beings in heaven and in earth and under the earth; even as St. Paul, filled with thee, declareth. Furthermore, thou didst divide the fiery tongues unto the holy Apostles and unite them unto the one word, and didst make them the Catholic Church of the Son of God the Father. And now with all reverence do we entreat thee, that thou come down into these, and fill the hearts of the baptized, who have now been baptized into Christ Jesus. Lest peradventure the unclean spirit approach them that have believed in the only born Son of the heavenly Father. Cleanse their spirits and minds, and make them a temple and dwelling-place of the Father increate, of the Son our intercessor, now and ever and unto eternity of eternities. Amen.

Lection from the Acts of the Apostles, viii. 26-40.

'But an angel of the Lord spake unto Philip, saying, Arise, and go toward the south along the way that goeth down from Jerusalem unto Gaza: the same is desert. And he arose and went: and behold, a man of Ethiopia, a eunuch of great authority under Candace, queen of the Ethiopians, who was over all her treasure, who had come to Jerusalem for to worship; and he was returning and sitting in his chariot, and was reading the prophet Isaiah. And the Spirit said unto Philip, Go near, and join thyself to this chariot. And Philip ran to him, and heard him reading Isaiah the prophet, and said, Understandest thou what thou readest? And he said, How can I, except some one shall guide me? And he besought Philip to come up and sit with him. Now the chapter of the scripture which he was reading was this: He was led as a sheep to the slaughter; and as a lamb before his shearer is dumb, so he openeth not his mouth: in his humiliation his judgement was taken away: his generation who shall declare? for his life is taken from the earth. And the eunuch answered Philip, and said, I pray thee, of whom speaketh the prophet this? of himself, or of some other? And Philip opened his mouth, and beginning from this scripture, preached unto him Jesus. And as they went on the way, they came unto a certain water; and the eunuch saith, Behold, here is water; what doth hinder me to be baptized? And Philip said, If thou believest with all thy heart, thou mayest. And he answered and said, I believe that Jesus Christ is the Son of God. And he commanded the chariot to stand still: and they both went down into the water, both Philip and the eunuch; and he baptized him. And when they came up out of the water, the Holy Spirit came upon the eunuch, and an angel of the Lord caught away Philip; and the eunuch saw him no more, and he went on his way rejoicing.

And then thou shalt read the holy gospel, John xx.

From the holy gospel of our Lord Jesus Christ, according to John.

Or thus begin by saying: The holy gospel of our Lord Jesus Christ is that which John saith:

'When therefore it was evening on that day, the first day of the week, and when the doors were shut where the disciples of Jesus were met together, for fear of the Jews, Jesus came and stood in their midst, and saith unto them, Peace be unto you. And when he had said this, he shewed unto them his hands and his side; and the disciples were glad, when they saw the Lord. He said to them again, Peace be unto you: as the Father hath sent me, even so send I you. And when he had said this, he breathed into them, and saith unto them, Receive ye the Holy Ghost: whose soever sins ye forgive, they are forgiven unto them; whose soever sins ye retain, they are retained.'

Once more it is meet before all prayers to say the 'Our Father.'

And then give the Peace in these words: May the Peace of the Father, the Peace of the Son, and the Peace of the Holy Ghost, come unto you. Amen.

HERE ENDETH THE FORM OF BAPTISM.

And concerning the order of laying on of hands.

CHAPTER [XXII].

Jesus, Son of the Heavenly Father, help us and intercede for us, and for all the faithful, for thou didst promise with thy faithful word: John xvii. 20, 'But not only for them do I pray, but also for all them that believe on me through their word.'

Again let us speak about that man, and say how it is right to elect him, and then to lay hands (i.e. ordain) on him; lest by chance we be found guilty according to our Lord Jesus Christ and the holy apostle Paul, who declares and directs in his First to Timothy, v. 22: 'Lay hands hastily on no man, nor become partaker of the sins of aliens,' and the rest. But also our intercessor and mediator Jesus Christ, hindering us, saith: 'Give not holiness to dogs, and cast not your pearls before swine.' Behold, it is thus incumbent on the elect one and the rulers not to give the authority to such a man[1]. For it is a fearful and awful thing to lay hands upon such as these, and to become partakers of the sins of aliens, and so forth. Therefore it is necessary for us to be greatly on our guard against them, and avoid participation in their sins; so far forth as it is no divine command, either of Christ the elect or of the universal and apostolic holy church (to do so). Let us further consider the words, the actions, and the canons of our Saviour, yea, and also of the elected holy apostles, who were taught by the high priest Jesus, and handed down unto us their tradition[2]. As St. Paul in his Epistle to the Galatians, i. 11, says: 'I make known to you, brethren, as touching the Gospel which was preached by me, that it is not according to the mind of man. For neither did I receive it from men, nor was I taught it by any one, but from the revelation of Jesus Christ.' 1 Cor. xv. 1: Eph. iii. 3.

Behold then, according to these words, these blessed ones received it from Christ; and Christ our Saviour received it from the Almighty Father, as he himself insisted, speaking in Matthew[3]: 'And Jesus came and spoke to them, and said: Unto me hath been given authority in heaven and on earth. As the Father sent me, so send I you.' Also Mark xvi. 15. Accordingly our Lord Christ was first elected by the Father[4] and received the grace of the heavenly Father, as saith Matthew, chap. xii.: 'Behold my servant, whom I elected, and my well-beloved in whom my soul was well-pleased. I have laid my spirit upon him, and he shall declare judgements unto the Gentiles.' 'And when Jesus was baptized[5], he went up straightway from the water, and lo! the heavens were opened to him, and he saw the Spirit of God

[1] i.e. to an untried man.
[2] Cp. the thirteenth-century Cathar ritual in the New Testament of Lyons, ed. Clédat, p. xvii.
[3] Ch. xxviii. 18.
[4] Matt. iii. 17; Mark i. 11; Luke iii. 22; 18.   [5] Matt. iii. 16.

descending like a dove and coming upon him. And lo, a voice from heaven which said, This is my beloved Son in whom I am well pleased.' Mark x. 10, Luke iii. 22, and John i. 32. And the rest ye shall read in holy writ, that first was Jesus elected by the Father, and the apostles by him. Accordingly it is right for this man to be elected by rulers and then by bishops. Now the President must first test him in gentleness and humility, and see if he has perfect wisdom, love which is chief of all, prudence, gentleness, humility, justice, courage, sobriety, and eloquence. He must also possess in very deed continence, patience, moderation, pastoral care, love of the poor, pity and good conduct of life and all other good works, and repentance along with quick conscience. All this the teacher must test and ascertain; and only then shall it be incumbent on the Vardapet to approve him. But unless a man has borne these thorough tests, it is not right for the President or rulers to lay their hands on his head. Since our Lord and the universal and apostolic holy church inhibit us from laying our hands upon such ones and from becoming sharers and partakers of their sin. Even as our mediator and intercessor, Jesus, warns us against it saying: 'Beware of evil workers, who come to you in sheep's clothing, but within are ravening wolves,' and so forth.

See and mark, my loved ones, how the Lord forbids us to lay hands on such as these, that is on false prophets, deceivers, disobedient, foolish, and so forth. Again, it is not meet for you, God-loving rulers and arch-rulers, to rashly lay your hands on such men; as St. Paul in his canons doth enjoin upon Titus, saying: 'For the bishop must be blameless,' and the rest. And accordingly the elect one must be on all sides spotless, and must be holy. Furthermore, he shall be shrewd and singleminded, as He that was elected by the Almighty Father saith: 'Ye shall be shrewd as the serpent and singleminded as the dove' and the rest.

Look ye and diligently examine, lest perchance ye violate these holy canons. Nay, more, may the Almighty Father give us his holy grace through the intercession of his beloved Son, and may he open the eyes of our souls unto the detection of such deceivers; that is to say, of thieves, robbers, murderers, sons of fornication, adulterers, detractors, evil speakers, scurrilous, foul-mouthed, blasphemers, quarrelsome, effeminate, paederasts, swinish in their lives, fond of strife, irreconcileable, slayers of the innocent, timid, sluggish, dissolute, niggardly, slow to learn, foolish, ecstatic, superstitious, without faith, lovers of self, overweening, supercilious, double-faced, greedy, spotted with evil, graceless, libidinous, false witnesses, lovers of glory, lovers of silver, counterfeits, undiscerning, lovers of self, respecters of persons, longers after evil, privily-minded, lightly believing in false prophets and false doctors, in false preachers and false books; who in every season and sundry trust not to the knowledge of truth, as the universal and apostolic church enjoins us to do. These must be elected with much testing, as also the Head of the Church enjoined above, saying: 'Beware of evil workers,' and the rest.

Therefore, upon such as the aforesaid it is incumbent on us not to lay our hands, nor become sharers and participators in their sins. Further, we may say on this matter: Is there really found such an one as is free from all these vices? or was there ever anyone who, having had these vices, has turned away from them and renounced them [1]? Yes, there is indeed such a man, my beloved, as has been a hundredfold worse than these, and who yet, when he reached the time of election, then recovered himself, and fully and completely repented and received the grace of the heavenly Father; as a member of the universal and apostolic holy church, St. Luke, declareth unto us, saying in Acts vii. 60, 'And Saul was consenting unto the slaying of Stephen.' Again, ch. ix. 1, we read: 'But Saul, yet filled with threatening and slaughter of the disciples of the Lord, went unto the high priest and asked of him letters to Damascus unto the synagogues, that if he found any who were of that way, whether men or women, he might bring them bound to Jerusalem,' and the rest.

Behold and mark, my godfearing ones, how Saul goes forth, and then how he repents, and turns to Christ our Lord, and receives the Holy Spirit and is ranked in the ranks of the universal and apostolic holy church; and becomes a vessel of election, establisher of the truth, pride of the faith and rampart of the holy apostles who were proclaimed by Christ the universal and apostolic church.

And this is the meaning of the blessed St. Paul when he said that where sin aboundeth there shall also abound grace. Again, he elsewhere saith, alluding thereto: 'While I was a child I spoke as a child, I thought as a child; but when I became a man full-grown, I put away the things of childhood.'

---

[1] The Armenian of this sentence is ambiguous. I render as I think the sense must be.

Thus, my beloved, although it is natural for men to fall, is it not also natural for them to rise again and stand up straight? Let us also hold to this figure of our Lord, in which, dealing with us sinners, he compares us to the prodigal Son, who came to his father and said: Father, I have sinned unto heaven and before thee, and am no more worthy to be called thy son, but make me one of thy hired servants. But his father, in compassion, fell on his neck and kissed him and said, This is my son who was dead and is alive again, was lost and is found. And again he repeated in his great love and said, 'Bring forth his robe and put a ring on his hand and kill for him the fatted calf, for he is my son who was dead and is alive again, was lost and is found.' So now do ye understand the decree of our Lord and of the holy apostles, which with true award they decreed for us and explicitly enjoined on all the faithful.

Let us return to the sequence of our direction, already expressed, that it is necessary for that man to be on all sides free from blemish, before we give him authority (*or* rule) of priesthood, of episcopate (*or* overseership), of doctorate, of apostleship, of presidency, and of election. For all these are one and the same thing; nor are they one greater or lesser than another. But they are on an entire level, as our intercessor Jesus enjoined on his holy elect ones, saying, Luke xxvi. 26: 'But be ye not so, but he that is great among you shall be as the least, and the master (*lit.* leader) as the servant,' and the rest. In this wise is authority one, as our Lord enjoins saying, Matt. xvi. 15, where he promises to give authority to all his apostles. Likewise Matt. xviii. 18, he says the same, and also gives complete authority to all his elect ones 'Verily I say unto you, whatsoever ye shall bind on earth, shall be bound in heaven, and whatsoever ye shall release on earth, shall be released in heaven.' Furthermore, John xx. 23, 'Unto whom ye shall remit sins, it shall be remitted unto them; but whosesoever ye shall retain, it shall be retained.'

Accordingly it is thus that Latins, Greeks, and Armenians alike speak in the hour of their releasing (? = absolution). Whether catholici or bishops (*or* overseers) or vardapets (i. e. doctors) or their priests, they all alike, as suits the occasion, say: 'I also in due order, with priestly authority, release thee from all participation in sin,' and the rest.

Behold, my beloved ones, how they also bear witness that authority is one, and is not greater or less. For one was the Holy

Spirit which came down upon the universal apostles and made them the universal and apostolic Catholic Holy Church. And we believe in their words, profession of faith, confession and works, for ever and ever unto eternity of eternities. Amen.

HERE ENDETH THE DIRECTION.

Concerning the laying of hands on the elect one and of their calling unto this grade.

Now after he hath been truly approved by the President, by the rulers and arch-rulers, then shall the elders lead that man before the President in great repentance and in tears.

And the rulers and arch-rulers shall begin by saying, as they bring him, this prayer unto the bishop (*or* overseer), saying as follows: Holy Father, we humbly[1] pray thee, entreat and beseech thee out of thy great love, to lay hands on this man for the true guidance of our spirits. Amen.

And the Bishop[2]*, in turn, saith unto the Rulers as follows:*

Ye then, who desire to have him as your good shepherd, have ye indeed diligently tested him, as also I have tested him with great humility and love?

But they make answer and say to the Apostle of our Lord Jesus Christ:—

Yes, our venerable father; for we have fulfilled all the commands of your Lordship with the help of God.

And again the elect one saith to the rulers and to all that listen: 'I am without responsibility (*or* innocent) in this particular, and ye are responsible.'

And then the elect one begins in the very words of our Lord and Intercessor by asking of the reader as follows, Matt. xx. 23:—

'Art thou then able to drink the cup which I am about to drink, or to be baptized with the baptism with which I am about to be baptized?'

And he gives answer with ready will and love, saying to the President: Yes, holy father, for I, thy servant, take on myself scourgings, imprisonment, tortures, reproaches, crosses, blows,

---

[1] *Lit.* falling on our faces.   [2] *Or* overseer, *as usual.*

tribulation, and all temptations of the world, which our Lord and intercessor and the universal and apostolic holy Church took upon themselves, and lovingly accepted them. So even do I, an unworthy servant of Jesus Christ, with great love and ready will, take upon myself all these until the hour of my death. Amen.

And then the Chief receiveth him before him, and, himself sitting down on the throne, shall begin by first saying: 'In the name[1] of the Father and of the Son and of the Holy Ghost. Amen.'

And then he shall repeat the prayer of our Lord Jesus Christ.

And after that he shall begin to read the holy Gospel, Matt. i. to verse 16; and also Acts vi. to verse 8.

And then do thou read Acts i. to verse 5, 'Our Father, which art,' and the rest.

Next again the Gospel of Matt. iii. to verse 17: also Acts xiii. to verse 6.

And after this the bishop calls the rulers unto himself, and the rulers having come shall place their hands upon the reader; but the bishop takes the holy Gospel into his hands, and gives it into the hands of the reader, and then asks his name, gently and humbly, saying:

'What is thy name, my little son beloved?'

And he makes answer and says:—

'The name of thy servant is Peter[2].'

But the apostle shall change his name in accordance with the Gospel[3], and after changing the name of the supplicant[4], he then gives him authority, saying as follows: Take to thyself authority of

---

[1] I read, 'In the name.' The Armenian omits 'in.'

[2] Geo. Mon. 72, x. ἔτι δὲ καὶ τὸν ἅγιον Πέτρον; τὸν μέγαν πρωταπόστολον πλέον πάντων καὶ δυσφημοῦσι καὶ ἀποστρέφονται, ἀρνητὴν ἀποκαλοῦντες αὐτόν. Ibid., p. 78, xx. ὁ σοὶ τῷ μιαρῷ ἀποτρόπαιος ὁ κορυφαῖος τῶν ἄλλων Πέτρος. And cp. Rituel Provençal (at end of the Provençal New Testament of Lyons, edition L. Clédat, Paris, 1887, p. xii, French translation): 'Et puis que le croyant fasse son *melioramentum* (i.e. acte de contrition) et prenne le livre de la main de l'ancien. Et l'ancien doit l'admonester et le prêcher avec témoignages convenables. Et si le croyant a nom PIERRE, qu'il lui dise ainsi : "PIERRE, vous devez comprendre que, quand vous êtes devant l'église de Dieu, vous êtes devant le Père et le Fils et le Saint Esprit. Car l'église signifie réunion, et là où sont les vrais Chrétiens, là est le Père et le Fils et le Saint Esprit, comme les divines écritures le démontrent. Car Christ a dit dans l'évangile de Saint Matthieu (xviii. 20)."' Cp. also p. xvi of the same: 'PIERRE, vous voulez recevoir le baptême spirituel, par lequel est donné le Saint Esprit dans l'église de Dieu, avec la sainte oraison, avec l'imposition des mains des " bons hommes."'

[3] Mark iii. 11 (*sic*); Luke vi. 14. [4] Or 'of the one asking or seeking.'

binding and loosing the sons of men in heaven and on earth, Matt. xviii. 18, and John xx. 23.

Here, in giving authority, there shall instantly be read the holy Gospels. After the reading of them it is incumbent also to read the Gospel of the birth, Luke ii. 13, and Matt. ii. as far as verse 13.

But after the reading of the holy Gospel of Luke, and the passage is that in which the angels sang their songs, it is meet that the bishop, the newly elected one, the rulers, arch-rulers, and all the congregation should sing: 'Glory in the highest to God, and on earth peace, to men good-will.'

This much and no more shall they say·

King of kings, Lord and Creator of all beings, who didst create our first father out of clay and our first mother out of his rib; but they did not patiently endure thy holy commandment, but were deceived by the deceits of the Devil (*lit.* slanderer). Yet nevertheless out of thy divine compassion thou didst create the new man Jesus, as the holy Paul saith: By man came death and by man salvation. Thus also the ......[1] Christ Jesus kept thy ineffable commandments and bruised the head of thine adversary; as saith thine only-born Son himself, thy well-beloved, John xv. 10: 'If ye keep my commandments, ye shall abide in my love; even as I have kept my Father's commandments, and abide in his love.'

Thus did our head Christ keep thy true words and the commandments of thy Lordship, and paid in full our debts and received from thee blessedness unending. And now we humbly[2] supplicate, entreat, and beseech thee, accept our prayers through the intercession of thine only-begotten, and through the mediation of his holy baptism and of his life-giving precious body and blood, and of his holy insupportable sufferings. Bestow thy holy grace on this one, who now is come and asks of thee the grace of thy holy authority, and that he may be ranked along with thy holy Son, according to that which is said, that 'wherever I shall be, there also shall be my worshipper.'

And after that the rulers shall take their hands back and, lifting up their arms along with the bishop, shall say this prayer all together over the newly elected one, as follows:

Our life and refuge, our mediator and intercessor. Now head of beings heavenly and earthly and of those under the earth, door of

---

[1] Two words are effaced in MS. They were probably 'the new created man.'

[2] See note 2 on p. 94.

heaven, way of truth, and life of those who rightly believe in thee. Since thou didst promise with thy faithful word, saying: 'He that cometh unto me shall not remain in darkness; and him that is come unto me I will not cast out.' Now therefore, forasmuch as this man, who hath been baptized in thy holy name, and hath been elected by the Holy Spirit of thy Father, doth now earnestly await thy faithful promise [which said]: 'Ye shall abide in the city of Jerusalem, until ye be clothed with power from on high.' Now therefore, falling on our faces at thy feet with ardent love, with bitter tears, we beseech, entreat, and beg of thee, send into him the grace of thy Father, that it may come and adorn his spirit, mind, and body, and make him resplendently pure from all evil thoughts. And bestow on him thy Spirit, which thou didst receive from the Father in the river Jordan. Strengthen him and open his mind to understand the scriptures and to take up the cross in love; that he may follow after thee now and ever and unto eternity of eternities. Amen.

And then the bishop shall blow three times in the face of the newly-elected, saying: Now may the breath of our Lord Jesus Christ open thy mind, O beloved little son of mine, and strengthen thee in thy works. Amen.

And then ye shall read the holy promise of the archangel which was made concerning Jesus. Luke i. 26–38:—

'Now in the sixth month the angel Gabriel was sent from God unto a city of Galilee, named Nazareth, to a virgin betrothed to a man whose name was Joseph, of the house of David; and the virgin's name was Mary. And he came in unto her, and said, Hail, thou that art highly favoured, the Lord is with thee. But she was greatly troubled at the saying, and cast in her mind what manner of salutation this might be. And the angel said unto her, Fear not, Mary: for thou hast found favour with God. And behold, thou shalt conceive in thy womb, and bring forth a son, and shalt call his name Jesus. He shall be great, and shall be called the Son of the most high: and the Lord God shall give unto him the throne of his father David: and he shall reign over the house of Jacob for ever; and of his kingdom there shall be no end. And Mary said unto the angel, How shall this be, seeing I know not a man? And the angel answered and said unto her, the Holy Ghost shall come upon thee, and the power of the Most High shall overshadow thee: wherefore also that which is to be born of thee is holy, and shall be called the Son of God[1]. And behold, Elisabeth thy kinswoman, she also hath conceived a son in her old age: and this is the sixth month with her that was called barren. For no word from God shall be void of power. And Mary said, Behold, the handmaid of the Lord; be it unto me according to thy word.'

And next read thou in the Acts of the Apostles, ii. 1 as far as verse 21 inclusive:

'And when the days of Pentecost were now complete, they were all together in one place. And suddenly there came from heaven a sound as of the rushing of a mighty wind, and it filled all the house where they were sitting. And there appeared unto them tongues parting asunder, like as of fire; and it sat upon each one of them. And they were all filled with the Holy Spirit, and began to speak with divers tongues, as the Spirit gave them utterance. Now there were dwelling at Jerusalem Jews, devout men, from every nation under heaven. And when this voice was heard the multitude came together, and were confounded, because that every man heard them speaking in his own language. And they were all amazed and marvelled, saying, Behold, are not all these which speak Galilaeans? And how hear we every man in our own language, wherein we were born? Parthians and Medes and Elamites, and the dwellers in Mesopotamia, in Judaea and Cappadocia, in Pontus and Asia, in Phrygia and Pamphylia, in Egypt and the parts of Libya about Cyrene, and sojourners from Rome, both Jews and proselytes, Cretans and Arabians, we do hear them speaking in our tongues the mighty works of God. And they were all amazed, and were perplexed, saying one to another, What meaneth this? But others mocking said, they are filled with new wine. But Peter, standing up with the eleven, lifted up his voice and spake forth unto them, saying, Ye men of Judaea, and all ye that dwell at Jerusalem, be this known unto you, and give ear unto my words. For these are not drunken, as ye suppose; seeing it is but the third hour of the day; but this is that which hath been spoken by the prophet Joel; And it shall be in the last days, saith God, I will pour forth of my spirit upon all flesh: and your sons and your daughters shall prophesy, and your young men shall see visions, and your old men shall dream dreams: yea and

---

[1] On verse 35 the following note in margin: 'If it be the forty days of holiness, the newly-elected one reads the holy gospel and testament, and at once he receives the Holy Spirit.'

on my servants and on my handmaidens in those days will I pour forth of my Spirit; and they shall prophesy. And I will shew wonders in the heaven above, and signs on the earth beneath; blood, and fire, and vapour of smoke: the sun shall be turned into darkness, and the moon into blood, before the day of the Lord come, that great and notable day. And it shall be that whosoever shall call on the name of the Lord shall be saved.'

And then say this prayer.

I thank thee and magnify thee, Heavenly Father, true God, who didst glorify thine only-born beloved Son with thy holy spirit. Also the holy universal and apostolic church of thine only-born Son didst thou adorn with divers graces. And now adoring, we pray thee, merciful Father, send on this thy newly-elected one thine infinite grace; that coming it may fill him and be to him a rampart and armour against thine adversary, who for ever and continually desires to ensnare those who have believed on thine only-born. Now therefore, lay thy holy right hand upon thy servant here elected, and keep him from evil and from temptation of the world by the intercession of thy true Son, now and ever and to eternity of eternities. Amen.

And then thou shalt read the holy Gospel, John xx. 19, *as far as verse* 24:

'When therefore it was evening, on that day, the first day of the week, and when the doors were shut where the disciples were met together, for fear of the Jews, Jesus came and stood in their midst, and saith unto them, Peace be unto you. And when he had said this, he shewed unto them his hands and his side. The disciples therefore were glad when they saw the Lord. Jesus therefore said to them again, Peace be unto you: as the Father hath sent me, even so send I you. And when he had said this, he breathed into them, and saith, Receive ye the Holy Ghost: whosesoever sins ye forgive, they are forgiven unto them; whosesoever sins ye retain, they are retained.'

And also the precept of St. Paul shalt thou read, Heb. xiii. 17-21.

'Obey them that have the rule over you, and submit to them: for they watch in behalf of your souls, as they that shall give account to you; that they may do this with joy, and not with grief: for this were unprofitable for you. Pray for us: for we are persuaded that we have a good conscience, desiring to live honestly in all things. And I exhort you the more exceedingly to do this, that I may be restored to you the sooner. Now the God of peace, who brought again from the dead the great shepherd of the sheep with the blood of the eternal covenant, even our Lord Jesus Christ, establish you in every good work to do his will, working in us that which is well-pleasing in his sight, through Jesus Christ; to whom be the glory for ever and ever. Amen.'

And then say this prayer before Christ.

Bread of angels and of the faithful, mediator and intercessor of us sinners, Lamb of God, Jesus, help us and especially this thy newly-elected servant, whom thou hast joined unto the number of thy loved disciples. Establish him on thy Gospel vouchsafed to thine universal and apostolic Church, the sure and immovable rock at the gate of hell. And bestow on him a goodly pastorship, to tend with great love thy reasonable flock; even as St. Peter, a member of the universal and apostolic holy Church, saith in his catholic Epistle, ch. v. 2 : 'Tend the flock of God which is among you.' Forasmuch as through thy calling he hath been joined with thy saints, keep this thy servant with thine elect; that no unclean spirit of devils may dare to approach him. Fortify thine elected one in the work which thou didst commit unto all who are thine elect and who have believed in thee. Amen.

Then after this prayer do thou give the peace to all the people; and then the bishop shall take the newly-elected one to himself, and instruct him with great love, and give him to read the holy Evangel[1] ever and always. Yea and also the holy testament of the universal and apostolic Church; in order that thereby he may in fullness receive the grace of the Holy Spirit, during a space of forty days.

CHAPTER [?].

Explanations of important sayings of our Lord Jesus Christ, to which the holy evangelists bear witness. Matt. i. 25.

'And knew her not until she brought forth her firstborn Son . . . . .[2] And after eight days his name was called Jesus, which

---

[1] Geo. Mon. p. 74, xvi. Προσκυνοῦσι δὲ τὸ παρ' ἡμῖν εὐαγγέλιον. Ibid. p. 70, ii. ἔσχον διδάσκαλον Κωνσταντῖνον ... οὗτος γὰρ παρέδωκε τὰς αἱρέσεις αὐτοῦ . τὸ εὐαγγέλιον δὲ καὶ τὸν ἀπόστολον ἐγγράφως, ἀπαράλλακτα μὲν τῇ γραφῇ ... νομοθετήσας αὐτοῖς καὶ τοῦτο· μὴ δεῖν ἑτέραν βίβλον τὴν οἱανοῦν ἀναγινώσκειν, εἰ μὴ τὸ εὐαγγέλιον καὶ τὸν ἀπόστολον.

[2] A few words effaced here in MS.

name the angel Gabriel revealed in the time of her virginity.' See Luke i. 26.

For this reason the holy evangelists and the sanctified apostles, yea, and our Lord Jesus Christ, declare Mary, prior to the birth, to be a virgin, but after the birth call her a wife and utterly deny her virginity, as in the aforesaid the Son of God asserts in John ii. 4.

In Cana of Galilee, where he made the water wine: 'What have I to do with thee, thou woman, for not yet is my hour come?'

When in the hour of the passion he was raised on the cross, he said to his mother: 'Woman, behold thy son.' And to his loved disciple he committed her, saying: 'Behold thy mother.'

There are many other testimonies in the holy gospel and testament of the apostles; and we state but a few in order to help the truth, and not out of grudging. For example, that is clear which in the hour of the passion of the Lord Jesus the Evangelists insist upon, saying[1]: 'There were also there women, to whom were come Mary Magdalene, and Mary, mother of Jacob and Josia.' And in another place, namely in the country of Jesus, they give proof by saying in astonishment: 'Is not he the son of the carpenter? is not his mother called Mary[2]? and his brethren are John, and José, Simon and Judas, and his sisters are with us.'

Again, St. Luke[3] expressly denies blessedness to her, and assigns it to those who have believed in Jesus Christ, ch. xi. 27: 'And whilst he was discoursing[4] to the multitude, a certain woman raised her voice out of the multitude, and said: Blessed is the womb that bore thee, and the paps that gave thee suck.' But Jesus in return took away, in the hearing of the multitude, blessedness from his mother, and gave it to those who do and keep his word.

And also John the Evangelist most openly shows their unbelief, when he relates of the brethren of the Lord Jesus (that they said to him), Get thee hence, that thy disciples also may see the works

---

[1] Matt. xxvii. 56.   [2] Matt. xiii. 55 and Mark vi. 3.

[3] Geo. Mon. seems to glance at this very passage as well as what precedes, p. 78, xxi. τὰς δὲ εἰς τὴν ἀειπαρθένον καὶ κυρίως καὶ ἀληθῶς Θεοτόκον Μαρίαν βλασφημίας ὑμῶν ... οὐδὲ ἡ γλῶσσα ἡμῶν ἐκφῆναι δύναται ... ἐπιτιθέναι ἀπὸ τοῦ ἐν τῷ εὐαγγελίῳ ῥητοῦ τοῦ φάσκοντος· ἀπηγγέλη τῷ Ἰησοῦ· ἡ μήτηρ σου καὶ οἱ ἀδελφοὶ [σου] ἑστήκασιν ἔξω ἰδεῖν σε θέλοντες· ὁ δὲ ἀποκριθεὶς εἶπεν πρὸς αὐτούς· μήτηρ μου καὶ ἀδελφοί μου οὗτοί εἰσιν οἱ τὸν λόγον τοῦ Θεοῦ ἀκούοντες καὶ ποιοῦντες αὐτόν. Cp. Tertul. adv. Marc. iv. 26, and August. c. Faustum, xii. 8.

[4] Luke xi. 27.

which thou doest, for his brethren also did not yet believe on him[1]. And in particular the vessel of election and member of the universal and apostolic holy church, St. Paul saith of our Lord Jesus: 'He was born of a woman, and came in under the law[2].'

Thus, previously to Mary's bearing the new-created Adam, Gabriel the archangel pronounces her a virgin and greets her; but after the birth the same angel does not call her a virgin. As is clear in the holy Gospel[3], from what he says in the dream to Joseph: 'Arise, take the child and his mother, and flee into Egypt'; and again, after some time, the angel of the Lord appeared in a dream, and said: 'Arise, take the child and his mother, and depart into thy land.'

Concerning the Creation of Adam and of our Lord Jesus Christ.

First, the heavenly Father, the true God, fashioned (*or* created) the heavens with all that belongs thereto, and the earth with all its kinds; he equipped them. As is clear in the inspiration of God (i.e. in the inspired Scriptures). Again, the benevolent God, seeing that all things were good, was pleased to make a king over all beings; and especially because of the most evil slanderer (i.e. the Devil), as is proved by the sense of the word which says: 'Let us make man in our image and likeness.' Thus in the twinkle of an eye he, by a single word, fashioned heaven and earth. But also by a single word he fashioned (*or* created) the old Adam, made him king and ruler of all creatures. Wherefore Satan, beholding the paramount kingship of Adam, was envious, as divine writ says in reference to him: 'By the envy of the slanderer death came into the world.' Moreover, St. Paul says[4] that by man came death and by man resurrection. And he also repeats this, when he says: 'As by Adam all men died, so also by Christ shall they be made alive.' Now at the first we said that the Almighty Father with a single word fashioned (*or* created) Adam out of clay, and Eva out of his rib, like unto him in . . . .[5] said, Father, into thy hands I commit my spirit[6]. Also he prayed for his enemies: Father, forgive them, for they know not what they do. And again he says[7] to Mary

[1] John vii. 3.   [2] Gal. iv. 4.
[3] Matt. ii. 13. [4] 1 Cor. xv. 21.
[5] One folio is here torn out of MS., pp. 126-7. It is just the passage so lost which must have contained the Paulician account of the body and generation of Christ.
[6] Luke xxiii. 46.   [7] John xx. 17.

Magdalen, his disciple, after his resurrection, I am not yet ascended unto my Father and unto your Father, and to my God and to your God. And again the holy universal Church with one mouth declareth: that Christ died and God raised him from the dead. There are also many other [testimonies], which we have not cited.

Concerning the mediation[1] of our Lord Jesus Christ, and not of any other holy ones, either of the dead, or of stones, or of crosses[2] and images. In this matter some have denied the precious mediation and intercession[3] of the beloved Son of God, and have followed after dead [things] and in especial after images, stones, crosses[2], waters, trees, fountains, and all other vain things; as they admit, and worship them, so they offer incense and candles, and present victims[4], all of which are contrary to the Godhead. All these things our Lord put under his feet when he said[5]: 'I am the door. If any one shall enter with me, he shall go out and shall go in, and shall find pasture,' and the rest.

And again, he saith[6], I am the way, and the truth, and the life.

And he doth furthermore say[7]: I indeed am the resurrection and the life.

Again he saith[8]: I am your mediator and intercessor.

As he saith to Peter in Luke[9]: And I have prayed to the Father in thy behalf.

But he also said to his apostles: And I will pray to the Father, that he may give to you another Comforter.

And also to us who believe he saith[10]: Not for them do I pray, but for them also who believe on me through their word.

He repeats, saying[11]: Father, not for them do I pray, because thou hast taken them out of the world, but that thou mayest guard them from the evil.

---

[1] Luke xxii. 31.
[2] Geo. Mon. p. 72, ix. βλασφημοῦσι δὲ καὶ εἰς τὸν ἅγιον σταυρόν.
[3] John xvii. 5, 17, 20.
[4] The custom of offering victims in church and eating their flesh continues in Armenia and Georgia until to-day. Thus Gregory of Dathev, c. 1375 (see Bodl. MS. Arm. e. 11, fol. 13 verso), in his manual condemns the Mahometans because they refused to eat of the Armenian victims.
[5] John x. 9.   [6] John xiv. 6.   [7] John xi. 25.
[8] Matt. xxvi. 53.   [9] Luke xxii. 31.   [10] John xvii. 20.
[11] John xi. 15 (sic).

Concerning the testimonies of the Holy Apostles.

First did St. Stephen behold the intercession of our Lord Jesus Christ at the time of his stoning, as St. Luke relates in Acts vii. 55: And he saw the heavens opened, and Jesus standing on the right hand of God.

And St. Paul saith[1]: So now who is he that shall condemn? Surely Jesus Christ, who died, yea rather, was raised indeed, and is on the right hand of God, who also is intercessor for us.

Again he saith[2]: For there is one God and one mediator also of God and men, the man Jesus Christ. Of whom St. John, in his catholic epistle, speaks[3]: Little children, this I write unto you. Sin not; and if any one sin, we have with God an intercessor Jesus Christ, the righteous and the spotless. And he is the expiation and remission of our sins; and not of ours only, but also for all those who rightly believe in him. Yea, and the Intercessor himself took his holy precious body and his holy unblemished blood, He and no other.

Supplement to the foregoing words.

Again I ask you, gainsaying Popes and your followers—you who baptize them that are catechumens still in their mother's wombs by all sorts of means, though they have not yet come into the world, or are born dead; some of them in the womb and some in death, ye baptize conditionally[4]. All these things are devilish, and not divine.

For the God of all who bestows such gifts of grace on his loved ones, since he is himself sincere, has also bestowed gifts of grace which are sincere and true. Hence it is clear from your deeds, how ye sometimes are convicted by the truth, and are forced to speak the truth, as when ye say: Let no catechumen, nor any that is wanting in faith, nor any one that is unrepentant or impure. It is not meet that he should draw nigh to the holy divine mysteries.

Now if ye do not hearken unto God, Christ, and the universal and apostolic holy Church; ye should anyhow obey your own false testimonies and promises. For there are three divine mysteries, which he proclaimed from above to his only-born Son and to St. John the great prophet. First, repentance. Second, baptism.

---

[1] Rom. viii. 34.
[2] 1 Tim. ii. 5.
[3] Hebr. vii. 26; 1 John ii. 1.
[4] The same word thêakav is used here as in ch. v. p. 15. The reference is not to the practice of baptism for the dead, but to that of baptizing corpses.

Third, holy communion. For these three he gave to the adult, and not to catechumens who have not repented, or are unbelieving.

And again I ask you, violator of ordinances, about this catechumen of yours, when did he ask or where did he petition the false witness, saying: I ask from thee faith, hope, love, and all other good works, from a false witness?

For if your catechumen asks from his tenderest age, then why does he not ask it direct from you, violators of the ordinances? So then your very falsehoods serve to show forth like the sun the truth of our Lord Jesus Christ. And your whole custom is found to be false and mere deceit; of which our Lord Jesus Christ primarily saith: 'And what he speaketh false, he speaketh out of his own, and his father is Satan,' John [1].

Instruction of a Christian.

If any one desire, my little children, to acquire the orthodox faith, it is first necessary for him to learn fully the necessary questions and the confession. And then he shall go and ask for holy baptism; and the precious body and blood of our Lord Jesus Christ shall he eat and drink, at a time when he hath believed, and not during his unbelieving time as a catechumen.

Concerning the Christian Doctrine.

CHAPTER [?][1]

Question. Art thou a Christian?

Answer. Yes, I am a Christian by the grace of Christ.

Q. How are we to define a Christian?

A. Thus—one who knows our Lord Jesus Christ, what he is, and keeps his commandments.

Q. What is the command and precept of our Lord Jesus Christ, which we keep?

A. That which our Lord prescribed to his disciples and his faithful, saying: 'If ye love me, ye will keep my commandments. As I also have kept the commandments of my Father.'

Q. How many are the commandments of our Lord Jesus Christ?

A. These. First, Hope. Second, Repentance. Third, Faith. Fourth, Baptism. Fifth, Communion. Sixth, Love, which is chief of all.

[1] The chapter and verse are not filled in.

Q. What is Christ, and as what must we know him and believe him to be?

A. Even as the universal and apostolic holy Church believed, so must we also believe.

Q. How did the blessed apostles believe? Teach us.

A. As St. John the Evangelist showeth, saying: 'We have believed and know that thou art Christ, the Son of God, who wast to come into the world.'

Q. So then, as touching those who baptize catechumens, is their baptism true or vain?

A. It is vain and a fraud. For catechumens have not repentance, have not hope, neither have they the holy faith. Wherefore their baptism is not true and is not salvation.

Q. Then whose baptism and communion is valid?

A. Their holy baptism and communion only is valid who have original and operative sin.

Q. Surely catechumens who are [newly] born of their mothers have not original and operative sin?

A. Yea, my children, they truly have not such sin, these catechumens.

Q. Hast thou then firm ground in holy scripture as touching catechumens?

A. Yes, venerable father, I have true witness from the holy Gospel, which our Lord enjoined on the holy Church, saying after his resurrection: 'Go ye into all the world, and preach the Gospel to all creatures. He that shall believe and be baptized shall live; and he that believeth not shall be judged.' Behold, my reverent one, first did he enjoin faith, repentance, and then he gave the command of holy baptism.

Q. How many, my little children, were there who fasted the forty days and forty nights, until came Christ, the Son of God?

A. Four[1] are those who so fasted. Enoch and Elias who, fasting, were raised to Heaven. Secondly, Abraham, who received the promise of Isaac from the angels of God. And thirdly, Moses[2], fasting, received the ten commandments.

---

[1] Petrus Sic. col. 1297, quotes a letter of Sergius to Leo, a Montanist, in which reference is perhaps made to these four prophets as follows: ἀλλὰ παρακαλοῦμαι (so read for παρακαλέσαι), ὥσπερ ἐδέξω ἀποστόλους καὶ προφήτας οἵ τινές εἰσι τέσσαρες, δέξαι καὶ ποιμένας καὶ διδασκάλους, ἵνα μὴ θηριάλωτος γίνῃ.

[2] Even the Manicheans respected the ten commandments, but not as specifically Moses' revelation, but as 'olim promulgata per Enoch et Seth et caeteros eorum similes iustos.' See August. c. Faust. man. xix. ch. 3.

Q. Christ our Lord and Intercessor, did he really fast forty days and forty nights like them?

A. Yes, he fasted, and from his Almighty Father received the kingship over things in heaven and on earth and under the earth.

Q. Wherefore then did not God Almighty make one of the patriarchs king and head of all? Did they not also fast those days?

A. Although they fasted, yet they were not . . . .[1] as was our Lord Jesus Christ. But they were conceived in original sin, they had original sin and operative. But our mediator Christ was not conceived in original sin, and had not original sin or operative like them, as St. John the Evangelist made clear saying, ch. i. 13: 'Which were born, not of blood, nor of the will of the flesh, nor of the will of man, but of God. And the word[2] became flesh, and dwelt among us.'

Q. Did then God converse with our Lord Jesus Christ, or not?

A. Almighty God conversed with his only-born Son ever and always, as St. John the Evangelist bore witness, saying, It thundereth[3]. But some of them said, An angel hath spoken unto him. But our mediator and intercessor himself confirmed it, that the Father conversed with him, saying: Not for my sake came this voice; but that ye may believe in me. And again he saith: I from myself speak nothing; but what I have heard from my Father, that will I make known unto you.

Q. How many are the words of our Lord Jesus Christ which save man?

A. Four are they which save man. First, Repentance. Second, Right Faith. Third, Holy Baptism. And fourth, the holy precious body and blood of our Lord Jesus Christ.

Q. (*and A.*) So then confirmation, the order of priesthood, last unction, and marriage, are not salvation of our souls. But are unnecessary and not obligatory. Even as the holy Church saith: 'If he giveth his virgin in marriage, he doeth well. And if they give her not in marriage, they do still better.' Thus shalt thou regard confirmation, order of priesthood, and last unction, which are not obligatory nor the door of salvation.

---

[1] One or two words effaced in MS. The words so effaced may have implied that Christ did not take his flesh from the Virgin. They were anyhow heretical.

[2] MS. reads '*by* the word.' I have corrected.

[3] John xii. 28, 29.

Q. For how many reasons did the God of all send into the world the new Adam his beloved?

A. For four necessary things. That is: First, because of original sin. Second, on account of operative sin. Third, for sake of mediation, reconcilement, and intercession, which now is [1]. Fourthly, because of the end of the world, the Father Almighty sent his only-born Son, and appointed him to judge the quick and the dead.

Q. O venerable father, is it right [2] for us to have the intercession of saints, or is it not?

A. We hold that their intercession is not right or essential. For they need the intercession of the living, not the living theirs [3]. As is clear from the sacramentaries of the heretics and schismatics, who at the hour of mass (*lit.* oblation) rightly here say [4]: 'Of all whether priests, or deacons, or scribes, that is apostles, saints, prophets, doctors, martyrs, patriarchs, monks, virgins, recluses, and of all saints, let there be, we pray, commemoration in the holy oblations.' Yea, and priests and scribes with one voice say out loud: 'Remember, O Lord, and pity.' Also he that offereth saith: 'Give rest to the souls of the saints,' and the rest.

Q. What further reason is there why they cannot make intercession?

A. Although they suffered for the love of Christ, still they have not glory, nor release, nor the crown of the kingdom of God [5]. As the holy Church of Christ makes clear when it says: 'The saints received the promise of life eternal, they obtained promises, stopped the mouths of lions [6],' and the rest. Furthermore our Lord Jesus, in giving his promise, spake to his loved ones thus: 'Wheresoever I shall be, there shall also be my worshipper.' Again he also says: 'Ye cannot now come after me; but then ye shall have come after me.' And also he points out the place to them, saying: 'There are many mansions in my Father's house.'

See, my reverent children, how hath been made clear the mind

---

[1] Or perhaps trans.: 'in the present.'

[2] In the margin is written: 'And when our Lord Jesus shall be glorified, then shall he crown his saints.' Paul, 2 Thess. i. 10.

[3] Geo. Mon. p. 72, x. τοὺς προφήτας καὶ τοὺς λοιποὺς ἁγίους ἀποβάλλονται, ἐξ αὐτῶν μηδένα τινὰ ἐν μέρει τῶν σωζομένων εἶναι λέγοντες.

[4] Cp. Brightman, *Liturgies (in the Liturgy of the Armenians)*, pp. 440-443. There the prayer 'Remember, O Lord, and have pity,' is said by the priest privately, and not by the deacons as well.

[5] Paul, 1 Thess. iv. 16.   [6] Heb. xi. 35.

of the holy Gospel and of the holy church. Those who are filled with hope, and not with glory and crowns, are all saints [1], as our mediator and intercessor Jesus directs, saying in his ineffable judgement: 'Come ye blessed ones of my Father, be ye heritors of joy without term or end.' In the same way [2] shalt thou regard the sinners who are tormented in fire unquenchable.

Furthermore, my beloved little son, take to thee the word of the great prophet Moses, which tells how Pharaoh was very wrath with Joseph, and took him and put him in prison; and some of the imprisoned saw a dream and were afraid. So then in the middle of the prison they told their dreams to Joseph. But our forefather Joseph by the spirit of God told them their dreams, saying to the one: My good man, behold on the morrow Pharaoh the king crowneth thee with great glory. But to the other he said: Thou also on the morrow shalt be punished by the king. See, my reverent child, that one with the promise of Joseph was crowned, and the other with his words was punished. Of like purport is the parable of our Lord Jesus Christ which tells about Lazarus and Abraham.

Furthermore the holy church of Christ tells how he went and preached to the spirits which were in prison, for the preaching of our Lord Jesus Christ signifies this, namely that he gave promises and great hope to the spirits of patriarchs and prophets, saying, My Father will crown you in the end of the world. But to the sinners he preached, saying: The Father Almighty will chastise you with heavy chastisement.

Concerning the judgement that is one and not two.

CHAPTER [?]

Question. How many judgements of God are there as touching the dead and the living?

Answer. There is but one judgement and not two.

Q. Then, if there [3] is one judgement of God which he holdeth through Christ; why do some gainsayers say that there are two judgements and not one—the one, they say, private and apart, and the other universal.

---

[1] This sentence may also be rendered: 'The saints are all filled with hope and not,' &c.

[2] In marg. of MS. this note: 'Mark the parable of the Lord Jesus, Luke xvi. 19, where he speaks of the living.'

[3] This note in marg. of MS.: 'See in the book of Theophilus.'

A. They thus speak lies merely because their father is Satan. Even as our Lord says, that which he speaketh false he speaketh out of his own, and his father is Satan [1].

Q. I pray thee, venerable father, to give us instruction as touching how many judgements there be.

A. I tell thee that the universal and apostolic church confesses one only, saying that man dies once and after that is judgement. This is the meaning of the holy church, that as for man death comes once, so also will his resurrection and judgement be one and not two.

Q. Then did Christ, our Lord and intercessor, truly know the wickedness of their minds, who have established false and monstrous laws, or did he not?

A. Yes, venerable father, he truly knew, and therefore said: 'Beware of evil workers,' and 'by their fruits ye shall know them' who are disciples of lies and deceit, and not of my truth. As the holy church expressly declareth.

Q. Did our Lord Jesus Christ really know the day of judgement or no?

A. Since the heavenly Father, true God, did not reveal that day to his beloved Son; as he saith concerning the end of the world: 'No man knoweth it, not the angels in heaven, nor the Son; but the Father alone.' Further he saith: 'Out of my own self I speak nothing; but whatsoever command my Father gave me, that I speak.' Behold, my reverent one, how Christ, the Son of God, of his own self could not say aught, unless his Father revealed it to him.

Q. But forasmuch as our Lord Jesus Christ could not by himself without the ordinance of God know the day of judgement, how do some gainsayers declare, in opposition to the truth of the Son of God, that there is a separate judgement and place of expiation for sinners?

A. Because, as I at the first told thee, they are the heritors of their father's deceit; and through the spirit of that same evil one they ever and always ordain false laws and false precepts. Behold, my loved one, their teacher, who has disguised himself [2] in the form of a monk [3] and preached unto them the torments of hell, in order to ensnare their souls.

HERE END THE QUESTIONS.

[1] Note in marg. 'See the false books of Sebastia' (Sivas).

[2] This note in marg. of MS.: 'See in the book of the Place of Expiation' (*or* Purgatory). Presumably it was the work of Theophilus referred to above.

[3] See note 1, on p. 84.

CONSECRATION OF THE FLESH AND BLOOD 123

Concerning the Consecration of the Flesh and Blood of our Lord Jesus Christ, the Intercessor.

CHAPTER [?]

Now our Lord Jesus Christ willed to distribute his holy flesh and blood unto disciples and believers.

First he began with the following figure[1]. He opened their minds, saying: 'My flesh is the true food and my blood is the true drink.' And again he said[2]: 'I am the bread of life which came down from heaven. He that eateth this bread shall live for ever.'

When our Lord had thus ended these figures, many of the disciples forthwith turned back. Then he again said to his remaining disciples: Do ye go and get ready for us the table of holiness, where I shall presently perform the mystery of salvation, for my[3] own believers and beloved ones. And when it was eventide Jesus went and sat down, and the twelve with him. He took one loaf[4] unleavened in his hands, blessed it, gave thanks, broke it and said: 'Take ye, eat. This is my BODY which for you many is distributed unto the expiation and remission of sins.' [So also saith he in regard to the cup[5].]

Exposition of the Holy Mystery of our Lord Jesus Christ.

That our mediator and intercessor Jesus Christ, the Lamb of God, took the bread[6] in his hands and blessed it, this the holy Evangelists declare.

That is to say he earnestly besought the almighty Father that he would change the bread into his true precious body. This is why it says: 'He blessed,' that is, he prayed the Lord that he would change the bread truly into his body. And so it was assuredly changed by the spirit of the heavenly Father. And when he saw that the bread was changed into his body, then he thanked the almighty Father for having changed it into his body and blood.

Now dost thou understand, my little child, the interpretation of the blessing and thanksgiving?

Yes, holy father, I have right well understood it. Humbly I pray

---

[1] The words might also be rendered ' in this manner.'

[2] In margin is this note: 'John vi. 51, and as far as verse 59 he speaks in a figure (*or* in a manner).'

[3] MS. has 'his' for ' my.'   [4] *lit.* = ' one bread.'

[5] The brackets are in the MS.

[6] Here is written in marg. this note: 'And here he truly doth distribute.'

thee, venerable father, interpret to us this his use of the word
'mine,' namely: 'This is *my* body,' as he also said after the
resurrection to Peter: 'Feed *my* sheep.' When he said this, did
our mediator and intercessor Jesus Christ know that there would
come false popes who would change [it] according to their good
pleasure? Who with bread[1] alone cajole all men and make that
their own flesh and blood, and not Christ's. For this cause also
doth our Lord Jesus Christ say: 'This is my body.' Yea more,
this doth he imply: that whosoever shall make any water, any
mere bread, or any moistened morsel, and distribute (the same)
deceitfully to the simple people, it is their own flesh and blood
and not Christ's [2]

To whom glory for ever and ever. Amen.

This was written[3] *in the province of Taron in the year of the
Lord* 1782; *but according to the Armenian Era* 1230.

(COLOPHON[4].)

.... of the all glorious John Vahaguni. For they with
great fervour were elected by us. But because of their being elected
the love of truth abounded in my heart. Wherefore I could not
hide the grace of the Holy Spirit. But I began to write out in
order the holy Sacramentary and the Key of Truth for love of
those who ask and receive. Moreover, I humbly entreat you with
warm love and faith to forgive the shortcomings, the insufficiencies,
and the faults of composition or of grammar. And also as touching
the syllables, or writing, or verbs or nouns (*lit.* words) or eight
parts of the art, if in regard to them ye find any errors or shortcomings, they are not due to ourselves, but have found their way
into it as being (the faults) of unpractised copyists.

Glory to the Father truly existent, and to his Son our mediator
and intercessor. Now and ever and unto eternity of eternities.
Amen.

[1] Geo. Mon. p. 72, οὐ χρή, φησι, προσάγεσθαι ἄρτον καὶ οἶνον.

[2] I add a literal Latin rendering of this important passage : Hoc dicens
cognouit mediator et intercessor noster Iesus Christus quia uenturi sunt falsi
papae, et mutaturi sunt secundum uoluntatem sui? Qui mero pane decipiunt
omnes et faciunt illum corpus et sanguinem sui sed nequaquam Christi. Propterea et dominus noster Iesus Christus dicit quia Hoc est corpus meum.
Immo hoc uult dicere quia quicunque aquam aliquam (*or* aliquid), merum
panem aliquem (*or* aliquid) siue tinctum frustum aliquid faciat et distribuat
dolo ad simplices congregationes, illorum est corpus et sanguis, sed non Christi.

[3] That is to say 'copied'; for *grem* is constantly so used.

[4] One or more pages of MS. are here lost.

ERRATUM.

P. 124, l. 18, *for the words* 'were elected by us. But because of their being elected' *substitute the following:* 'besought us. But because of their beseeching'

Key of Truth

APPENDIX I.

THE original of the copy from which the following letter is printed by Father Basil Sarkisean[1] in his volume on the 'Manichean Paulician Heresy' (Venice, 1893, in Modern Armenian), is preserved in a codex called the *Book of Letters*, which used to be in the library of the Fathers of Antony at Constantinople. This codex was written out in 748 of the Armenian Era = A.D. 1300, in Hromkla by Thomas the Vardapet, on charta bombycina, from an older copy which belonged to Gregory Vkayasêr in the year 527 = A.D. 1079. The convent of Kdjav, to the Abbot of which the letter was written, was very ancient, and was situated in the province of Mokatz.

About the year 987 accusations were made against many Armenian monks and priests of being secret or open members of the Thonraki sect. Among those accused was Gregory of Narek, the famous saint and author of a book of devotions which is still in the hands of every Armenian priest. A council was held at Ani before which he was acquitted, and, to fully exculpate himself, he was forced to write the following letter to the Abbot of Kdjav, who notoriously leaned to the side of the heretics.

LETTER

Of the gracious Doctor Gregory of Narek, which he wrote to the celebrated convent of Kdjav, concerning the tenets of the cursed Thonraki, Ianês and Iamrês, who came in the guise of sheep, but within is a ravening wolf; who moreover by his fruits was made known to all. Him the holy doctor having heard of, wrote in order to liberate others from the evil tenets:—

Lord Father[2], I write this because an untrustworthy rumour of evil tendency,—although those who heard it considered it trustworthy, nor was there any ill-will to prejudice them—admits of no other means of contradiction.

For I heard that the unmentionable and obscene lechery of the heresy of the cursed Thonraki sect is mentioned among your pious ones. And I was lost in astonishment at a statement so improper on

---

[1] Many of Father Sarkisean's valuable notes I translate, adding his initials B. S.

[2] Nothing more is known of this Abbot, nor do we know at all if any steps were taken in consequence of this letter to purge his convent of heresy (B. S.).

the part of the enemies of God, who declare that you furthermore reported to Mushel[1], a learned man by repute, that you had been satisfied by a bearer of letters whom you had sent that they (i.e. the Thonraki) are not alien to the apostolical tradition[2]; and that you are keenly desirous to share in their lot and associate yourself closely with those who have been cut off by the sword of the avenging heathen Amir[3] Apl-Vard, who is in fact a rod of wrath in the hand of the Lord Jesus.

We learn from the same source that you ask, What writing directs any one to be anathematized? asserting the marvellously composed letter of contradiction of our blessed Lord Ananias[4], to be nonsensical or absurd, or spoken against God. Now if all this has been inspired by you,—I omit to say agreed to by you and (I spare so to write) relished by you—then you have summed up in yourself the aforewritten [opinion] that 'their chosen food became loathing.'

There is much that is divine and everything that is apostolical that is yet denied by them and abolished. Of divine ordinances, there is the laying on of hands[5], as the apostles received it from Christ. There is the communion in his body[6], as the Apostle defined it, saying: In eating the bread of communion, we receive and eat God himself, who was united with flesh. This communion-bread, before which we tremble, Smbat[7] taught to be ordinary bread. And as for the birth through spiritual throes, I mean by water and Spirit, of which it was declared that it makes us sons of God, concerning this, he taught others that it consisted of mere bath water.

And as to the exalted day of the Lord[8], on which [the word of God] created the first light and perfected thereon the light of his rising, and prefigured by an economy the quickening light of his Advent,—this day, adorable for all it doth image, he has explained to them is to be counted just like any other days.

---

[1] B. S. conjectures that Mushel was i.q. Mushel Bagratuni Abasean, mentioned by the historian Asolik as a governor of Kars in 984. But, as he was a Vardapet, I doubt this identification. In any case it was an honoured name in Armenia from the earliest times. It is written with a strong *l* answering to Greek λ. Or translate: 'that you (and) specially Mushel ... reported that.'

[2] This testimony that the Abbot and Mushel had satisfied themselves after examination that the claim of the Thonraki sect to be an apostolical church and to possess the apostolical tradition was a valid one, is both important and interesting. It is the claim which is made on almost every page of the Key.

[3] This Amir cannot be identified with certainty. The reference proves that the Paulicians took the field against the Mahometan invaders, and were not spared by them.

[4] This letter, written under compulsion of the Armenian Catholicos by Ananias of Narek, Gregory of Narek's uncle, is preserved but does not merit translation, being mere invective. Ananias was, like his nephew, accused of being a Thonraki or Paulician.

[5] But we saw above that prominent Armenian churchmen of the tenth century admitted that their heretical rivals had the true apostolical tradition.

[6] The account preserved in the Key of the Paulician Eucharist is so fragmentary that it is not easy to say against what aspects of it Gregory of Narek directs his remarks. The grain of truth in them must be that the Paulicians rejected the orthodox sacraments in favour of their own.

[7] Smbat (the same name as Sinbad) is stated below to have been the founder of the Thonraki Church.

[8] The Key gives us no information as to how the Paulicians regarded the Lord's day.

APPENDIX I 127

Then among the observances which we know to have been repudiated by them as neither apostolic nor divine, [we know to be] the mysterious prayers of genuflexion [1], though the Creator of all, Jesus Christ, bowing bent the knee. We know that the Font is denied by them, in which Christ himself was baptized; that the communion of immortality, which the Lord himself gave to taste unto all, is denied. We know their filthy habit of lecherous promiscuity [2], where the Lord reproved and suppressed even a glance. We know that they deny the adored sign [3] (i.e. the Cross), which God, made man, raised and carried on his shoulder as his own glory and authority. We know of their anthropolatrous apostasy, more abominable and cursed than idolatry; of their self-conferred [4] contemptible priesthood, which is a likening of themselves to Satan [5]; of their depreciation of the sacrament (*lit.* crown) of marriage [6], which our Lord, by his own miracles, and through his own God-bearing mother, prized and honoured. This sacrament (*lit.* crown) they contemn, and reckon the mere fact of union in love with one another to be perfect love, and from God and pleasing to Christ; saying that God is love and desires the love union alone, and not the sacrament of marriage (*lit.* crown). I know, too, of their railing and cavilling at the first-fruits [7], which Abel and Noe and Abraham and David and Solomon and Elias appointed to conciliate the Divine wrath. We know how they dare to call the head of their abominable sect a Christ [8]; of whom Christ testified beforehand, saying, There shall arise false prophets. And this is the meaning of the prophet's saying: The fool said in his heart, there is no God.

Such, then, are the apostolic [9] men of your Mushel who examines and finds them to be people of unswerving faith. These, then, are they whom my father's brother, a Vardapet of great acumen, closely investigated, as being himself an apologist of God. And he, like a learned champion, radically demolished the fabulous blasphemies of the lawless Thonraki sect; and had he not done so we should hardly

---

[1] We gather that the Paulicians prayed standing erect in the primitive Christian manner. The continuity of observance in their Church is strikingly illustrated by the fact that its modern adherents still forbid genuflexions, as we learn from the confession adduced in pp. xxv, xxvi of the Prolegomena.

[2] Here the malice of the writer must be discounted. It was the regular and stereotyped charge against all heretics, even the purest in their lives. It, of course, refers to their denial that marriage was a sacrament.

[3] See the Key, p. 115.

[4] The Armenian word is a compound and $= α\mathring{υ}τόχειρ$, 'with one's own hand.'

[5] See note 8, below.

[6] See the Key, p. 119.

[7] Perhaps the Key, p. 115, should be compared, where offerings of incense, candles, and victims are prohibited.

[8] The elect one, according to the Key, was the image of Jesus Christ on earth, his office was to reproduce on earth the life and calling of Christ himself. See the Key, pp. 95 and 106. The same charge of pretending that he was Christ or the Holy Spirit was advanced against Sergius the Paulician, who is identified by Dr. Mkerttschian and the historian Tchamitch with Smbat. See also the Prolegomena, pp. lxi foll.

[9] The claim of those who used the Key and of him who wrote it was that the Paulician was the only true apostolic church. See above, note 2, p. 126, and Prolegomena, pp. xxxiii and xli.

have known[1] from report even the name of the foul creatures, so insignificant is their fame. What gifts then of election[2] have they seen in the abominable Kumbricus[3], what trace of good in Simon[4], or what hope to look forward to in the antichrist, of all of whom they are the disciples? For, forgetful of the ineffable favours and kindness bestowed on them through the Passion, they call these their refuge[5], though they have lied about the same. For they are packs of dogs and bands of thieves, troops of wolves and arrays of devils; tribes of brigands and masses of weevils, hordes of savages and legions of crucifiers, congregations of evil ones and men of blood, swarms of poisonous snakes and herds of wild beasts, enemies of mankind, societies of wizards and heretics, the scorn not only of churchmen, but of heathen as well.

For I must relate what a certain valiant man said, who destroyed and put to an infamous death their cursed ancestors. This is what he said to the second Iamrês[6]: 'If Christ rose on the third day, then since you call yourself Christ[7], I will slay you and bury you; and if you shall come to life again after thirty days, then I will know that you are Christ, even though you take so many days over your resurrection. Now he was in close contact with them as a neighbour, and he had learned the story of the bitter phrensy of these offenders from many who had told it him, and he certainly believed[8] in the true resurrection of Christ, and was making mock of them as proper objects of ridicule, when he left behind him the memory of this laudable saying. For it was God and no earthly being who raised up this idea in him, and it was providence which enjoined him to reprove or destroy the wicked according to their wickedness; just as providence gave for food the terrible serpent of Ind, and chastised the Jews through the Chaldeans, and in judgement overwhelmed those who crucified Jesus by the hand of Titus and Vespasian and Adrian, and reprimanded the Egyptian nation with a twofold destruction by the hand of Cyrus. And he is said to have hung up in the dread oracular temple of Beliar himself the lance with which he smote them. Now the very devils knew God the only-born and confessed him to be judge of all; but the foul Smbat, a second Simon, allowed himself to be worshipped by his disciples, men rooted in bitterness and sowers of tares; just like that wizard of Samaria, and Montanus and Pythagoras the illiterate and heathen philosopher.

I have set down a few points out of many, and I await your answer.

---

[1] Why was Gregory so anxious to disclaim all knowledge of the sect? Because he was accused of belonging to it. Was the accusation true? Probably he had, at least in secret, once belonged to it, for his enemies nicknamed him 'Apostate.'

[2] Gregory glances at the 'Election' and 'Elect ones' of the Paulicians.

[3] i.e. Mani called Κύβρικον. Gregory perhaps draws upon Photius or the Archelaus acts.

[4] In the Key Simon Magus is mentioned on pp 91, 92.

[5] See the prayer in the Ordination Service in the Key, p. 108.

[6] A sobriquet for Smbat.   [7] See above, note 8, p. 127.

[8] Yet Gregory adduces this story by way of illustrating how the Thonraki were the scorn of *heathen* as well as of churchmen. He was not ashamed to gloat over Mahometan mockery and murder of his own countrymen, and this although—as is clear from the context—the Paulicians had given their lives in order to repel the Mahometan invaders of Armenia. See the Prolegomena, pp. lxiii foll.

For it is a leading principle of our Lord's canon, which says: And by thy words shalt thou be justified, and out of thy works shalt thou be judged. But if you admire their writings[1], we know that Satan too recited a psalm on the day of the temptation of the Saviour of all. But unless you place on record a double curse and manifold anathema against their founder Smbat and their dead and wizard-like cults and their profession of faith[2]; and unless you in writing declare that what they represent as good is mere ordure over and over, and find the same to be excess of apostasy, and intimate the same in your letter to me, which is the way in which it beseems you to clear your character and to get rid of the scandal and prejudice: anyhow, know for certain that I have written entirely out of consideration for your good and peace and love. For if your citadel of refuge[3] be betrayed by you, its own guardian, then of yourself will you become a traitor to your high office. And since this Mushel writes that he is a Vardapet[4], you must arm a champion against the enemy and repair the breach that has been effected, and defend exposed places, and be light and salt and mentor to him that is in the dark, according to the divine canon. But if your light be to his thinking darkness, he is beyond doubt a viperous sorcerer and senseless giver of poison. For his science is not holpen by the finger of God, his voice is ill-starred and inspired by evil, and his report is deceitful—a destroyer of peace.

And now with what conscience can he repeat the words: 'Out of what writings can I anathematize any one?' Paul anathematized even an angel that should think things alien to his gospel, and he did not scruple to repeat the anathema twice. And David cursed his transgressions and subscribed to the reprimand. And the Lord saith of those who have deserted from the ranks and are altogether on his left hand: Depart from me ye cursed ones. And we received from the Council of Nice[5], and learned an anathema on the vainglory of heretics, which is formally directed to be used twice over in the hymn of the confession of faith which follows after the reading of the gospel. An answer to the letters of Petros from Sahak prescribed forms of anathema against those excommunicated at Chalcedon. And there are the heads of Cyril of Alexandria's anathemas against Nestorius, and the Henoticon letter of the Emperor Zeno, which curses by name the utterly heretical sects.

Now if we are by ordinance obliged to curse those whose shortcomings are but in part, how much more[6] must we curse the manifoldly heretical ranks of this congregation, which is cut off from Christ and united by bonds to Satan. And now, Lord Abbot, take no offence at the terms of my letter, nor take unfeigned love as if it were hatred. For the love of Christ compels me to this, and we only desire you to

---

[1] Or more probably գրաբանութիւն should be rendered 'quoting of the Scriptures.'

[2] See the Key, pp. 93, 94 and 97.

[3] i.e. the convent to the Abbot of which this letter is addressed.

[4] Therefore Mushel was probably a doctor of the Armenian Gregorian Church.

[5] This anathema is still repeated by Armenians at the end of the Nicene Symbol.

[6] This passage proves at least that the Thonraki had nothing to do with the Nestorians and other heretical sects enumerated in the Henoticon. See the Prolegomena.

be spotless. And do you order to be copied the volumes[1] full of learning which the father Ananias, with great care, wrote against these schismatics.

[1] This work of Ananias is unfortunately lost. If it could be discovered, it might give valuable information. Nerses Schnorhali quotes it in his Epistola I (see *Sancti Nersetis Clajensis Opera*, vol. i. pp. 58–64, Venice, 1832), but his citations, though valuable, hardly make up for the loss. Gregory Magistros, early in the eleventh century, also quotes this lost work of Ananias in his letter to the Patriarch of Edessa, which, along with the letter of Nerses Schnorhali, will be given in English below.

APPENDIX II.

ARISTACES of Lastivert, whose two chapters on the Thonraki sect are here translated, was an eyewitness of most of the events described in his history, which opens with the year 989 and ends with 1071; particularly of the siege and sack of the royal city of Ani by Alp-Arslan the Second, king of Persia, in the year 1064. It is evident, however, that he could not have taken part in the proceedings with respect to the Thonraki here set forth; for they took place within the first decade of the eleventh century. We must, therefore, use due caution in regard to the narrative.

I translate from the Venice edition of 1844, which contains a good text, though based on late MSS. I have omitted some superfluous matter, especially citations of scripture, marking the omissions with dots. Aristace's history was rendered into French, and published in 1864 at Paris by M. Ev. Prud'homme.

HISTORY OF ARISTACES, VARDAPET OF LASTIVERT.

CHAPTER XXII.

Concerning the evil heresy of the Thonraki which appeared in the province of Harq[1]*, and convulsed the people.*

Jacobus was a bishop who had the charge of the church of the family of Harq; and at the beginning of his term of authority he exampled all the virtues. He dressed in sack-cloth, fasted, went

James bishop c Harq; l virtues

---

[1] A description of this region is given in Indshidshian, *Descriptio Armeniae* (Mod. Armenian), Venice, 1806. Harq is a region lying south-east of Erzeroum (Karin), on the eastern slopes and valleys of the volcanic mountain Pinkeôl. This tract is separated from Karin by two watersheds, between which runs the upper stream of the river called Mourtz, or Pinkeôl Sou. The more northern of these ranges is called Mardali-Thêqman, just south of Karin. Khnus or Khnz is a naturally fortified village town in the centre of this region, at the meeting point of several considerable streams, which have risen on the north-east slopes of Pinkeôl, and flow first eastwards and then south to join the south-east branch of the Euphrates.

bare-footed; and he chose for his priests who always accompanied him, men coarsely clad and simple, who avoided a life of pleasure, and constantly occupied themselves in the singing of psalms.

By such a mien he stirred others far and near to admiration, and every one was anxious to see him; while those who had been very haughty and overweening because of their authority, submitted themselves so entirely to his influence, that, had he bid them draw their last breath, there was not one of them who would have opposed him, or, have ventured to open his mouth and murmur.

Yet all this was hypocrisy and not sincere; for it is the fruit which makes known the tree, as we heard from our Lord. Moreover, the Apostle writes to the same effect, and says: 'Satan himself doth take the form of an angel of light.' How much more do his worshippers transform themselves into apostles of Christ. For just as men mix deadly drugs in honest food that others may take it, and, swallowing as if it were food, may be caught by the deadly drug; and just as fishermen conceal their hooks with bait, that the fish may be deceived by the food and be taken on the hook; so also do the workers of wickedness. For they dare not openly show their pit of destruction to any one; because then no one would be induced by them—however much out of his senses he might be—to fall of his own will into an abyss, out of which he could not get up again. This is why they disguise themselves under cover of our godly religion in order to deceive the simple-minded, and by their soft words take captive the minds of the innocent. For their words eat into such, like a cancerous growth; and just as this is difficult to heal, so those who are taken by them can with difficulty keep themselves safe.

And because of them doth our Lord warn us in his saving gospel: 'Beware of false prophets who come to you in lambs' clothing, but within are ravening wolves.' Also the Apostle teaches the Philippians in the same way, being instructed by the Lord's commands: 'Beware ye of dogs, beware of evil workers.' For it is easy to be on one's guard against outside enemies, but it is hard to shelter oneself from the assaults of one's own kinsmen, as happened to Abel and Joseph. Now these enemies of ours, had they been of foreign-speaking races, no matter what, could have easily been guarded against; but as the blessed John writes: 'They went out from among us, but they were not all of us,' and therefore it is difficult to know them. They are of our own tongue and nation, and have issued from one and the same spring, like sweet water and bitter. Although St. Jacob declared it impossible, yet among us this has happened. From the sweet spring which our glorious leader struck, going down into the depths of the earth for fifteen years of sweat and toil—struck and made to flow in a copious stream from the depths of the hole—[this has come forth]; yea, from the limpid and pure well which the seer Ezekiel saw, and into which no poisonous rivulets of heresy could penetrate. For the bulwark of truth was firmly set on the rock of faith until these last times¹, though our Illuminator himself with prophetic spirit saw what should come, that the sheep should become wolves and shed our blood. And this happened when the lawless men multiplied upon the earth, and the good master of the house slept who had sown the seed. Then the enemy found his field, and sowed the tares amid the wheat according to the parable of the Gospel. The dregs of bitterness were mingled with the living water which, like a fountain, issued from the master's house. But of old it was revealed to the doctors of the church², who plucked out the tares by the root from the field of our faith; and pressed out and strained off the dregs of bitterness, and made wholesome the waters with the salt of truth, according to the old and just policy of St. Elisha. But enough of this. It is time to return to the main subject of my discourse, in order to confirm what we have said.

The first-born satellite, then, of the father of all evils, his earliest conspirator, so soon as his deceptive reputation for goodness was bruited abroad by senseless persons, began at once to make our faith his target at which to sling his arrows, even as the shafts of the lightning are driven into an ancient oak. For the fellow was very fluent of speech, and by his eloquence bewitched the ears of many. Then he planned in this way to subvert the holy church from its foundations. And he forgot the Lord's command and infallible promise to Peter: 'Thou art the Rock, and on this rock I will build my church, and the gates of hell shall not prevail against it.' He trusted not in this, but listened to the private advice, as it were, of any man; and so entered into controversy, and thought to shear off the glory of the church; just as of old the harlot did with the locks of Samson. Just as she betrayed his unconquerable person to the gentile, so he, to renders of the truth, that holy church, which our Lord Jesus Christ had bought with his precious blood, and crowned and glorified with the all-victorious cross; establishing therein a sacramental table after the fashion of the tree of life in Eden. Whose fruit making us immortal we know to be the true body of the Saviour, according to his faithful precept: 'Whoever shall eat my flesh shall not see death for ever.' Consider, then, his low cunning, how like a snake he contrived by his corruptions to pour the destructive poison into those who were sound in the faith.

C. 1002.

In the first place he began by establishing election among priests according to worth, and told the unworthy to keep silence. And as this seemed to please the many, he proceeded to add other innovations. For he ordered the worthy ones only to present offerings (*or* masses) three times in the year. And, although in the Nicene canons it is written that, 'Even though a man be very sinful, yet you must receive his confession, and communicate to him the Lord's body and blood,

Appoint election priests.

---

¹ But from the other sources we know that, as early as 1000, Paulicianism was on the decline in Taron as elsewhere, and was no new thing.

² See pp. lvii foll. of the Prolegomena.

and hold him worthy of all masses (*lit.* offerings) and all Christian orders'; yet he utterly declined to accept auricular confessions. But he taught as follows, that if a man has not in his own soul himself repented of his sins, then commemorations help him not, neither offerings. And along with his instruments he would scoff and jeer, for they would bring an animal and set it before them, and say as follows: 'Alas, thou unhappy animal. Leave alone the fact that yonder man in his time committed sins and died, still what sins hast thou committed, that thou shouldst die with him[1].'

And beside this, the congregations were divided into two parties, because some accepted this teaching, but others not. And all were disturbed and perplexed, and were asking what was to be the outcome of the matter. Moreover, those who at the time were in the desert and in grottos, for ever doing the pleasure of God in their solitary and ascetic lives, were deeply afflicted, and with tears besought the benevolent Lord to visit them. And there was also held twice over a council of many fathers and pontiffs and priests, and of numbers of other people of all sorts, not to be counted. Yet since the governors of the province were all as it were spell-bound by his hypocritical demeanour, they declared that they would all die as it were by war, before they would give him into the hands of the council. So he, like Nestorius, sat in his house and reaped great encouragement, and by means of a message made his defence to the council, relying on the help of the governors rather than of God. For he did not bear in mind the psalm of David: 'It is better to trust in God, than to

---

[1] The following passage from Nerses Shnorhali, born c. 1100, and Armenian Catholicos 1165, is a defence of the custom of sacrificing animals in church in expiation of the sins of the dead. It is from his first epistle, chap. 2, and I cite the Latin translation, published at Venice 1833, vol. i. p. 51 : 'Porro immolatio, si quis illam agere uelit in memoriam dormientium in Christo, ita fiat. Ad ecclesiae iannam congregentur una cum oblationis domino sacerdotes; siue multi fuerint siue pauci, siue unus tantum, ponantque salem coram sancta cruce, et scriptos Psalmos ac officia concinnent, lectionesque et orationes magno timore perlegant, ac deuoto corde dormientis nomen commemorent, atque a domino ueniam peccatorum illius deposcant, ac salem benedictum porrigant, immolentque bestiam et statutas eorum partes dent sacerdotibus. Ex residuo autem prius esurientes alant et indigentes, ac postea, si quid supererit, charos et amicos. Atque, primo die excepto, ne quid servent ex eo in cibum domus suae pro aliis futuris diebus, propterea quod deo oblatum est.' This sacrifice was called a *mataḷ* and was 'ad animarum requiem.' The canon *De Sacerdotibus* of St. Isaac, Armenian patriarch in the fourth century, relates the origin of these sacrifices. At the time of the conversion of Armenia, the pagan priests who had lived ' ex profanis idololatriae uictimis ' asked how they and their families were now to live. Whereon St. Gregory the Illuminator ' praecepit populo, ut loco oblationum quas immundis idolis antea offerebant, unico Deo immolatas animalium oblationes benedicto sale commixtas, in Paschate resurrectionis Domini, et in quacunque dominica festiuitate, nec non illustrium sanctorum, et in commemoratione defunctorum in Christo .... Iussitque dare conversis ex idolatria sacerdotibus illarum immolationum partem ; non solum, sicuti modo largiuntur, ex pelle et coxendice, sed et amplius adhuc.' Thus a premium was held out to priestly families which should be converted to the new religion.

trust in governors'; and the miscreant thought he would with the help of men triumph over the truth. But God, who permits not the rod of sinners to prevail in the lot of the just, lest the just should reach out their hands unto wickedness, who doeth the will of them that fear him and heareth their prayers, who stilleth the raging of the storm, and bringeth rain in the drought—and that at the prayer of a single just man, he visited us and brought salvation to his people. For he knows in his profound wisdom how to lay from afar the foundation of mighty events. So in this case, in his providence he did what was really best for us, and it happened thus.

There was a religious man in the province of Karin[1] by name Esaiah, of a pious family, who, because of Jacob's good report, had gone and joined him, when the disquiet and inquiries I have described were stirred up about him. His suspicions were aroused, and he scanned him narrowly; for he was a very sage man and had gained his entire intimacy, being regarded as one of his most trusty followers. He accordingly looked into and informed himself about the filthy cult of Jacob, and at once when he had done so went and related the same to the holy patriarch Sargis[2], who, on hearing thereof and ascertaining the fact, summoned to himself with gentle words the miscreant and rewarded him according to his deserts. For he deprived him of his priest's orders, and branded his forehead with the likeness of a fox, and at the same time issued a proclamation to this effect: Any one of the faith of the holy Illuminator who shall enter and join the fold of the law-breaking Thonraki, who are wild beasts arrayed against mankind, shall suffer this just sentence and penalty. And he bade the miscreant be kept in prison, for he hoped that he might perhaps repent and promise to keep away from the filthy sect. For he was full of pity for the lost soul.

But since, according to the words of Jeremiah, the fire cannot forget to burn, nor the Indian lose his black colour, nor the leopard his spots, so could this wicked man not lose his wickedness. For one night he broke out of prison and took to flight, and passed into the land of the Greeks, till he came to the royal city of Constantinople, where he maligned our faith, and sought to be baptized according to their rites. But they in their wisdom, being informed of the facts, would not receive him; but answered: One whom the Armenians disdain and reject in a matter of faith, we too refuse to accept. So when he did not succeed in this, he went away and came into the province of Apahuni into the dwelling-place of Satan, the congregation of apostates from God and den of wild beasts which is called Thondrakis. However, they aver that even they would not receive him because of his exceeding filthiness; wherefore he departed into the mountain of Klath[3]. There he was found by his own people in the hamlets and in remote spots, and with them he remained quiet. And after spending

---
[1] i. e. Erzeroum.   [2] This Sargis became Patriarch, c. 1002.
[3] Akhlath, or Khelath, is on Lake Van.

his days there, he went and died miserably in the city called Muharkin. As he had not conformed to the canonical writings nor had been in union with Christians, he was cast out and abandoned. Wherefore he died like an ass and was buried like an ass, leaving an ill memory behind him; in order that all who hear this story may imprecate curses upon him.

CHAPTER XXIII.

How in the borders of Mananali there burst out a conflagration of folly.

<small>itzik,
nk,</small>

Kountzik was an incestuous monk who lived hard by the fortified city called Shiri, where to the present day they call a hamlet by his name. He was far advanced in years and had in himself the leaven of filthiness. For he had imbibed it from the teaching of a libidinous monk, who reported about himself that he was of the Albanians. However, he was a scion of Satan and a storehouse of Satanic counsels, so that the smoke of the oven of hell[1] was continually bursting into flame from his lips; whereby many took the poison and were lost.

<small>iverted
ian</small>

<small>onverts
tain</small>

Well, this Kountzik, being a busy worker of Satan, ensnared a certain woman, named Hranoysh[2], who was of a leading and distinguished family, and was mistress of a leading and distinguished family, and was mistress of a hamlet conterminous with his. When she was filled with the deadly breath of his venom, she was not satisfied with her own destruction, but provided many to help on their deceits. And she first of all corrupted two women who were related to her family, and whose names were respectively Akni and Kamaray,—and indeed she was a genuine doer of Satan's will[3]. But they were both true sisters, and having caught the wild instinct of fornication, as is usual in their fold, they proceeded with the cleverness of witches to make themselves teachers of Satan   . And they smote and cruelly wounded many innocent hearts. For having in their patrimony two villages, they made them ready as dens and lairs in which the dragon of the crafty serpent might nestle and pour out the flood of his spleen. And they made themselves cup-bearers and gave those who lived round them to drink of the draught of destruction. Wherefore Moses wrote: 'Their wine is the rage of dragons, the rage of vipers impossible to heal.'

<small>converts
e Vrvĕr.</small>

A certain prince, Vrvĕṛ by name, made himself the brother and instrument of these witches. Aforetime he had been sound in the faith and foremost in all zeal for piety; so much so that he had built a convent on his own estate and gathered in it ascetic brethren. And he supplied from his wide marches (*or* 'on liberal terms') all the

---

[1] From this metaphor, with which compare *Greg. Mag.*, p. 146, we are to understand the doctrines of the Thonraki, or Thondraki as Aristaces spells it.

[2] Hranoysh was a common female name in the royal house of the Bagratuni.

[3] The Armenian word Kamarar = 'doer of the will,' and is used as a pun on the name Kamaray.

wants of their lives, and their abbot was known by the name of Andrew, and was very famous for his zeal in all works of religion. To them repaired the prince year by year for the fast of the forty days, and remained engaged with them in pious exercises until the days of the great Pasek[1]. And he performed many other good works in the way of ministering to them, and took the lead of all in feeding the poor and in obedience to the priests. Him the evil one inveigled through these women; for they with the abandonment of passion fornicated promiscuously with him, without taking any account of their nearness of blood to him . . . .

The poor wretch Vrvēr was thus ensnared by them and made naked his shame, and fell from the faith and became an enemy of God and of his saints. He forsook the Lord, who through the holy font begat him; forgot God, who with his own flesh and blood fed him. He went forth from his house fallen from honour, and forgot his divine vows, and severed himself from participation in the monkish orders; and where aforetime was a meeting-place of religious men, which he had built at great expense and with trouble, where the lines of psalmodists and choirs of ministrants had joined the hosts above in hymning God in sweet-voiced songs, there to-day the voices were silenced and their place was tenantless and waste.

And after this what? The unhappy wretch allied himself with the devilish women, and going round the hamlets which were their native places, and which we mentioned a little above, and of which the names were respectively Kashē and Aḷinsoy[2], they converted all the inhabitants to themselves. And then they turned into a wilderness,—so mad were they in their devilish phrensy,—the churches, which in their snakes' haunts had been aforetime built. And in the villages, whenever an opportunity presented itself, they shamelessly tore down the symbol of our salvation and the armour of our Lord's victory . . . . Vrvēr preache Paulicia tenets.

But since I have mentioned the cross, I will bring into my narrative another tale of miracle, which will make all my readers tremble.

In the ravines of the mountain Pakhr, which is now-a-days called the hill of Emery (Gaylakhazut) there was a village of our first fathers called Many-Springs; where the divine cross had been set up with much splendour and pomp; so that the vulgar name of the spot was changed and it is called Cross to this day. On the day of the great Pentecost, on the night which is called the new Lord's day, the workers of the will of Satan came with a hammer and, smiting the crown of the sign which received God upon itself, ground it to powder and cast it on the ground. Then they themselves secretly crept back into their snakes' holes . . . . His con destroy crosses i Pakhr.

Now after his wont at cockcrow the elder rose and came before the cross, to perform the service of the great Lord's Day. And when he

---

[1] i. e. Easter.
[2] I cannot fix these localities, which must, however, have been somewhere south of Erzeroum in the province of Taron.

saw so marvellous a sight he began to rend his garments; and the inhabitants of the place, roused by his loud cries, came bounding up and crowded together to see it. And when their chiefs beheld the wonder, they raised shrill lamentation and beat their breasts and were about to return; and at the time there was general weeping and wailing of men and women, old and young, all at once. And while they were thus distraught, on a sudden an idea flashed upon them inspired by the ineffable wisdom of God. During the night on which the evil deed was done, snow had suddenly fallen and whitened the face of the earth; so that they got on the tracks of the lawbreakers and, following them up, soon reached their lair. And tidings were sent instantly to the blessed patriarch Samuel, who on hearing of the matter hastened to the spot with a large concourse of followers. And he mustered to himself the bishops and elders and fathers of the region, and going with them he burned and destroyed the lairs of the lawless ones, cursing their goods and possessions, as Jesus aforetime did Jericho, that no one might dare to take aught. But six of them, who were said to be doctors (*lit.* Vardapets)[1] of their evil and filthy religion, he placed under arrest, and a council having met at the city-village called Djermay[2], he directed that they should be branded on the forehead with the image of a fox; so that this might be a sign of them for ever, clear and palpable to all. Lest any one without knowing it should communicate with them; and in order that, like wild beasts, they might be persecuted by all mankind. Thereafter he blessed the congregation which had assisted him in his labours and dismissed them in peace.

But when in the course of the summer a judge was sent from the Emperor to hold an assize in the region called Elia[3], he on reaching the neighbourhood of the churches was met by the infamous Vrvēr. The latter preferred an indictment against the venerable patriarch Samuel and the other bishops who were with him, saying: 'They have laid waste my house and have sacked and burned my village.' And he laid a claim against him for many treasures and chattels. And when the judge heard this he was mad with anger, and sent his soldiers to bring in all haste before him the blessed bishop.

However, when the soldiers came, the head of the bishops wrote dispatches to the incumbents of the church, to the elders and the eremites to muster unto him without any delay. And when the tidings reached them, as if divine providence had given them all warning, a multitude of persons without delay met in one place; not only of

---

[1] The use of the word Vardapet points to the recognition by Aristaces of a regular order of doctors or teachers among the Paulicians, such as we read of in the Key, pp. 95, 103.

[2] Consul Brant notes a village Chevermer, perhaps identical, due west by a few miles of Mûsh, in the western part of the plain of Mûsh, a few miles south of the Murad Chai (*Journal of the Royal Geographical Society*, July, 1838). Here it was that the *Key of Truth* was copied in 1782.

[3] For the position of Elia see the Prolegomena, p. lxix.

priests, but still more of laymen, in numbers so great that I cannot write them down, and the multitude of them flocked as far as the shore of the river Euphrates, where Mananali[1] approaches thereunto.

Samuel musters faction a Manana

And there was at that season a downfall of rain, so torrential that the Euphrates had risen and flowed full of surging billows. But the soldiers had brought a ship, and proceeded to hurry across the aged bishop Samuel and his brother's son Theodore to the borough called Kothēr, for it was there that the judge was. But the crowd caught hold of the bishops and would not let the soldiers take them. The latter, however, said: 'We will first ferry them over and then the crowd.' And by so saying they persuaded them, and having got the bishops along with the ship, they crossed to the other side. And then they made fast the ship, and he put the bishops in prison. But when the multitude perceived their stratagem, how that the ship did not return to them as had been promised, they encouraged one another with loud cries of exhortation to perish in crossing the water, rather than stay quiet while the leaders of their faith were insulted.

The jud court at Kothēr.

And now the hour of night was nigh, and the sun having gathered up his scattered rays was returning to the mother[2], giving free space to the heavenly company of the ether. Then the ranks of priests dashed forward, and without indeed parting the waters with the mystery of the cross, they yet held in their hands that same symbol of the Lord's victory, and, raising it on their shoulders, they fortified themselves with faith and began to stem the high-surging throng of waters. And these gave way and let the multitude pass, as a hard-mouthed horse yields when bruised by the bit. And no one was injured of all that multitude, no not one. And when they had passed over they sang all the night a hymn of thanksgiving to God, having for the leader of their choir the spotless Mary, who is the holy Church[3], bearing in her hand the cymbal, that is the truth of the faith .... and they sang for all to hear: 'Bless the Lord, for he hath wrought marvels,' along with the words which follow. And with such lofty strains they brought the night to an end in prayer to God.

---

[1] Mananali, now Theqman, lies due south-east of Erzeroum, twelve hours or more by the public road, and six or seven by mountain path. Mananali was rather the name of a region than of a town. It is the high valley or group of valleys in which run the head streams of the Pinkeôl Sou, which joins the Eraskh river on the north confines of the region due east of Erzeroum. Both streams flow out of the north side of the Pinkeôl mountain. Kurds and Armenians inhabit these valleys, which are full of wild sheep, and, in spite of the severe winter, the pastures are good. Moses of Chorene mentions a cave here, bk. 3, 45.

[2] Cp. Sirach xl. 1.

[3] This was a Manichean and probably Marcionite tenet, e. g. *Acta Archelai*, ch. 47, 'Nupserit Ioseph uirgo, castissima et immaculata ecclesia.' Routh regards 'ecclesia' here as an interpolation, but wrongly, for Manes intends, parenthetically, to insist on his own conception of the Virgin Mary. The Albigeois had the same teaching, Maitland, p. 273; and it constantly meets us in orthodox fathers.

But the judge, on hearing of the providential act and of the miracles, knew that God watches over our nation . . . . . And at the dawn of day, for it was the first of the week, he went to the bishop's palace, which is called Frrisn, and gave a just verdict and upheld in their rights the chiefs of the people. And they ordered the unworthy and guilty Vrvēr to prove his case. Now there is an animal called a cuttle-fish, which they say is able to turn all colours in order to escape its pursuers. So he saw that he could not face the might of truth, since the darkness is ended when the light beams forth, and falsehood is destroyed when truth is revealed. So what did he do, or to what device did he resort? He confessed to being a Greek (*lit.* Roman), and made himself an adopted son of the bishop whose name and title was Episarat, having bribed him to consent. And the latter came before the court and humbly begged him as a favour to himself, and the judge consented. For the brother of the malefactor was of royal rank, and, because of his spirit and valour, was one of the chosen friends and acquaintances of the emperor; for which reason the judge was very respectful. Accordingly he gave him to the bishop in trust, as the latter requested him to do. But all the rest of his companions whom they found they beat severely, and scourged and banished them and burned their houses. And the multitude praised the judge and departed in peace. But the judgement of God soon overtook him, although he then escaped punishment. For . . . . . his body was destroyed by leprosy. However, he did not come to repentance, nor ever remember his early piety. But he adhered to the same devilish heresy, until he was removed from this life; and the torments of his flesh continually warned and reminded him of the hell in which he was to be tormented.

But as for their filthy observances, we deemed it indecent to commit them to writing, for they are too loathsome; and since it is not everyone that is proof against what he hears, a recital of many sins might draw listeners into lust, or even lead them to commit such things themselves. For this reason I have avoided them. But what is manifest about them and fit to be repeated is as follows. Church and church ordinances they utterly reject—its baptism; the great and terrible mystery of the mass (*lit.* offering); the cross and the ordinance of fasts. But let us, truly believing in the holy Trinity, keep the sure confession of unshaken hope, which we learned from the holy fathers. And from their apostate congregation let us turn away our faces and send out curses upon them.

APPENDIX III.

GREGORY MAGISTROS, whose letters, after the accounts of Gregory of Narek and Aristaces, form our chief Armenian source of information about the Paulicians of Armenia, died A.D. 1058, having probably been born late in the tenth century. He resided much in Constantinople and was a good Greek scholar, who translated into Armenian Plato's Laws, Timaeus, Phaedo, and other dialogues. He was in favour with the Greek emperors, who in assailing Ani destroyed the last vestige of Armenian independence. Constantine Monomachus made him Duke of Mesopotamia, and commissioned him to carry on in the newly-annexed south-east regions of Armenia the persecutions of the Paulicians, begun more than 200 years before in the Western Taurus. In the letters here given he recites his exploits in his usual bombastic manner. Their date is between 1054 and 1058. The Armenian text is not published in full, and accordingly I base my translation mainly on Karapet Ter-Mkherttschian's German rendering of the original, as given in a good but late codex of Gregory's letters preserved in the Munich library. Where I could, I have controlled his version from extracts made by myself from that codex in 1891, and from excerpts printed in Chamich's *History of Armenia*, and in Father Karekin's *History of Armenian Literature*.

Answer of Gregory Magistros to the letter of the Thulaili, who were a remnant of the new Manicheans, and who had come to the Catholicos of the Syrians and wished to cajole him:—

You who have been stolen away by the wolf Smbat and his lying followers, who laid everything waste and pulled down the hedges,—to the gallows with you, unhappy wights, lost in the mazes of your shifty and bootless speculations. Be ye the withered and mutilated limbs, unfruitful branches in the vineyard, trees which, hewn up by the roots and cast out of the well-hedged garden, have become rotten wood; even as the evil spirit which led you to utter destruction, has chosen for your brood a dwelling-place of the name Thonrak. For this name signifies that it is made to be burned, and it is truly fitting that the rotten timbers and the lopt off branches should be burned. But the holy Spirit extinguished with his holy baptism the flames of this insufferable fire, and so the spot came to be called after the name of St. George.

The name, however, of your present abode signifies, if you regard the etymology of it, 'weakened,' or 'weak in the limbs'; just as Khnus recalls a hole stopped up in which the deepest darkness reigns.

I have received and read the letter addressed by you in your childish vulgar impertinence to the Illuminator of our souls, who sits on the throne of the holy apostle Thaddaeus and of his spiritual son Gregory. What a laughable surge with a hubbub of deceit! Is it possible that you should think you can persuade him, who now occupies the patriarch's throne, to accept that for which more than fifteen pontiffs have anathematized you and your pack of dogs that have fallen victims to your beast of prey? Tell me foolhardy one, that by thy wilfulness hast torn thyself from the breast, how wilt thou induce him to approve of thy perverse and darkened intellect. How will the Saviour tolerate your having stolen those whom with his blood he bought? I know well he will not tolerate it, any more than he allowed Peter in Alexandria to come to terms with Arius. For the only-born revealed to him in a dream Arius with cassock torn aside, and so let him see what the dragon housed within him held concealed. No more can you persuade with your filthy and corrupted morals. Come now, thou abortion, if thou canst hear; though thou seemest to be not only blind, but also deaf and dumb. What! wilt thou persuade us to receive you into the Church with these principles of yours? We fear to; for (the law) forbids the leper to be admitted into the tent, because the leper carries death in himself. But if a little spot makes all the members unclean, how else can it be with him that is wholly dead in leprosy? And if we expel from the Church those who have sinned and enjoin penitence on them before we re-admit them into communion—for the priest prays that they may be made worthy (of communion) with the words: 'May these who have become spiritually whole become members of thy Church'—surely all this is ridiculous in your case, who adhere to your lusts and have been baptized with the venom of the deadly serpent.

You had enumerated the heresies of old and anathematized them. We laugh at such an idea. We know, you wretches, that you respect neither anathema nor blessing. We know that you recognize neither him nor another. You are not of us; yet one sees no other to whom you could have attached yourselves. It were much better had you listened to those who have cursed you, so that we, freed from your deadly poisons and secret shafts and Sadducee leaven, and from you, wolves in sheep's clothing, might sleep in peace. I find that you resemble not only the sectaries, but that you add Judaism and circumcision, and are much worse than they. We only ask you either to be warm like us, or cold like the wholly perverse, but not just lukewarm, for that is loathsome and tempts one to spit.

Do ye then ask for medicine for your wounds, or show yourselves quite without blemish? I will give you a piece of advice, you guides of the evil one, you madmen. Hold yourselves far aloof from these innocent children, who are scattered here and there among Christians, and let them come and receive baptism, since they execrate Smbat and his followers down to Esu, no less than the light-haired hound Lazar[1] and his partisans, whom may the Lord Jesus smite with the breath of his mouth . . . . . During 170 years have thirteen patriarchs of Great Armenia, as many of Albania, a myriad of bishops, and priests and deacons innumerable admonished you, and ye have not

---

[1] For a fuller list of the heresiarchs see p. 145.

APPENDIX III

harkened. They have spoken and confuted you, and ye have not been ashamed. They have anathematized and proscribed you, and you have not repented, until at last the Holy Ghost and the prayer of my ancestor and progenitor, St. Gregory, led me forth. And I came to Mesopotamia and encountered the deadly, stormy, muddy flood which, flowing forth from the cursed Thonraki Smbat, rolled death along in its waves. After I had purified it I set forth and went up to the wellhead, in which the viper and scorpion and dragon of wickedness had nestled. I demolished it, as my ancestors did Aschtischat. Then I named the village after the chapel of St. George, which had been taken possession of by the hound Smbat. I hope too in the Lord God, in him that sits enthroned on the cherubin, that he may by my hand shed the pity of his loving-kindness upon you; that you may forget your wicked disease and all your bad habits, you who have been filled with poison by your godless and bad leaders and hatched out a brood of the evil one. But if not, then if so help me the strong right arm of my God, you shall be delivered into my hand. And if you do not repent, then will he awaken other watchers and renewers of the hedge in order to remove you out of the world.

I admonish you, however. Leave us and our land in Mesopotamia, and all who are under the supremacy of the holy kingdom of the Romans, in peace and quiet; teach and confirm your evil heresy neither by writing nor by speech. And now may their blood and your own be on your head. Down with your name and your words and your deed, to the ground with it all. Otherwise shall the might of God find you out, and in his wrath and zeal shall he vex you.

Gregory campaign.

destroy Thonraki and re-named it after St. George.

The heretics to quit the Roman Empire.

The Answer (of Magistros) to the letter of the Catholicos of the Syrians, at the time when he was duke in Vaspurakan[1] and Taron[2]. After the Manicheans had been rooted out of the territory of the Greeks and from Thonrak, the remnant of this condemned race went to the Catholicos of the Syrians, to try and win him over by their deceit. He wrote a letter to Gregory Magistros Arschakuni ... to which the following was in answer:

. We have read the letter of those thieves and outcasts from the entire Catholic Church, which they had written to the holy Patriarch Petrus (1019–1058), and which thou hast communicated to us in thy wisdom. . . . . . It appears to me to be an inspiration of God that nothing might be hidden from thy pure and exalted majesty. For God has made thee worthy of the struggle and campaign, in order that thou, like the other fathers, thy predecessors, mightest take the field against the God-resisting sword of heretical wizardry and against the mischievous gabble of this obscure race. In such wise are these wolves in sheep's clothing wont to steal children; against whom the Saviour announcing his divine promises warned us: 'Beware of those who are in sheep's clothing, but within are ravening wolves.' The Apostle also warns us against these evil workers.

But do thou, holy Pontiff and successor of Jesus, in manly truth, read, if thou canst find it in thy District, the writing of the holy and thrice-blessed Vardapet Anania, which he wrote at the instance of the Lord Catholicos of Armenia Anania, and also the writing of the

Gregory recommends the book of Ananias and John against Smbat.

---

[1] Now province of Van. [2] Now Mûsh.

Lord John, the overseer of Armenia, whose names we have written in this letter. From these thou wilt see the truth about this evil beast of prey, this bloodthirsty, sodomitic, whoring, lustful, phrensied, loathsome Smbat. This accursed one appeared in the days of the Lord John and of the Smbat Bagratuni: and he had learned his evil erroneous teaching from a Persian physician and astrologer, whom they called Mdjusik. Can I say or write too much to you, a man who loves Christ? I will only put it in brief, in order to inform you of the whole plague of doubt in its monstrous transformations; of their sly craft and childish want of education and godless doctrine; of their outlandish choice by consent [1], of their nightly making of holy oil, of their grotesque declamations; of their nightly crimes and of their strange and horrible and loathsome bearing of sufferings [2]; of their priest-makings without high priest, of their obscure ordination [3] and graceless baptism; of their unilluminated gloom and hopeless confession of faith; their irreverent reverence, their darkness-loving illumination, their angel-like race of demons; these wolves in sheep's clothing, these men turned into black he-goats, these wretches who are alienated from the Spirit and have put on Satan, who are become scholars of Smbat the false-cleric, that has shaken the foundation of the apostles and prophets—that Smbat, who (just as dogs and wolves according to him [4] appeared in the form of a priest but without priestly worth) came forth out of the district Tsalkotn [5] from the village of Zarehavan, and lived in Thonrak. There he began to teach all the sum of evil that can possibly in this life come into a man's head, omissions and neglect of every act as well as of all belief. He preached that one ought to annihilate or rather reckon as in vain all priestly functions. He himself assumed externally the position of a high priest, but did not venture to openly ordain for himself bishops or deacons, or to consecrate the oil, but said instead: All this is nonsense. However, in order to cajole the people, they employ bishops secretly fallen away and excluded from the Church to perform by night their worthless ordinations with nothing at all, while they disdain and make mock of the holy oil which is distributed by the Leader [6]. Therefore they are full of vices and indulge their sensual lusts, without finding anything to hinder them; but in so far as they transmit all this, they hide their evil heresy like Pythagoras. For this θέων would not only not eat beans, but, to prevent himself from divulging the marvellous character of his creation, he bit off his tongue with his own teeth and died forthwith. So too these thieves never reveal by any sign their nest of destruction, but to any one who asks they point out another place and lead him astray. They stick fast in error, and reckon it a bad tradition, that we should profess openly instead of believing in spirit only. And when Christians get hold of them they deny the accursed Smbat and those who succeeded him:

---

[1] Perhaps the agreement in regard to candidates for election is glanced at.

[2] This seems to refer to the pledge of the candidate for election, to take on himself all sufferings and pain. See p. 106.

[3] *Lit.* 'laying on of hands.'

[4] See the Key, ch. viii. p. 83.

[5] South of Ararat. Zarehavan, according to Indshidshian, p. 180, is a village in the Tchrgan province, which lies south of Bitlis (բարիշոյ). It is, according to Indshidshian, inhabited by Persian Armenians. But Ճախկուն province lies north of Ala Dagh, south-east of Alashgert, according to Alishian.

[6] i.e. Hegumenos, or orthodox patriarch of Armenia.

Thodros, Anane, Sargis, Cyrill, Joseph, Jesu. These are they who lived in his sect, and who now already for more than 170 years have been anathematized by all Patriarchs of Armenia and Albania. The latter have warned us against approaching them, eating with them, speaking to them, entering their houses. For their wine is a bitter wine, and by the bitterness of their tongues you may know their grapes. From the garden of Sodom is their vine, and their shoot from Gomorrha. Never by their sweet and enticing words must they cajole your pure reason and clean hearing, for they begin with sweet words and end with wicked ones. Their words are soft as oil, and they themselves like arrows. With lures they hide their deadly hooks, and so catch the innocent.

Thou hast written in thy divine letter that thou hast asked the people who lived near them, and that they had not allowed that they knew anything about them repugnant to Christian morals. I will explain the matter to thee, O divine Head[1]..... These (heretics) have written that they are being persecuted for a grudge. O lie, wonderful and astounding! If they be of us and of our creed, what is there to grudge them? What academy or doctrine? What famous men, bishops and fathers, what great cross-bearing brotherhoods? What monks withdrawn together in any narrower order, and bearing the cross? What hermits that have put on Christ, or honest people living on hill, or in dale or glen? What musical songs or melodies? What splendid well-ordered festivals and diverse fragrances (düffte)? What priestly robes with all the festive gatherings of the priesthood, when with all the array of shining clergy and deacons they surround the divine and holy altar? What power of holy oil for the divine call or for ordination? What most pure and bloodless victim to slay, or what others of the same kind appropriate to a gnosis consecrated like ours to Christ? What worldly rule or worldly prerogatives? What products of talent or industry? What nobility inherited from ancestors? Are they rich in treasures, or do they form a separate people with language, king, and high priests? They are cut off from us, as the Georgians are from us and some from yourselves, for example the Nestorians and others. Ask with your own holy lips whether they can answer these charges. I know well that they will be dumb, and, though they are rational beings, will bay like dogs, or like brass will ring with an unmeaning and empty sound.

But if thou wilt know the dark ground of their apostasy and malicious temper, learn that for long they have waited in their hopeless hope that the son of perdition will appear as their leader—he whom Jesus Christ will subdue with the breath of his mouth. These people, all the while that they confess openly and send envoys to our pontiffs, enjoy themselves hugely over it. For we have seen with our own eyes and heard with our own ears—at times when they had no suspicion that we were acquainted with holy writ—how before bishops and congregations blasphemy would issue from many of their mouths, which we have not read in any divine books nor have heard from other slanderous tongues. They would say: 'We are no worshippers of matter, but of God; we reckon the cross and the Church and the priestly robes and the sacrifice of mass all for nothing, and only lay stress on their inner sense,' and so forth. But in such language

---

[1] Here Gregory gives examples of famous liars from ancient history, which may be left out.

they deem worthless not mere details in our traditions received from Christ, but the whole of it is to them a fairy-tale and mere prattle. This is how one of them, openly a false priest, in controversy with one of our Church, spoke before the whole congregation: 'Ho, for your empty hope! What hope of Christians then have you got?' And the others answered and said: 'Such hope as is meet and befitting.' But he went on with his godless utterances; for he took the paste, formed it in his hand, dipped it in the wine, and threw it away: 'This is the fraud of you Christians.' And that was Cyril, the cursed leader (or primate) of the Thonraki. But they indulge in many other blasphemies against the holy virgin, the mother of God, and against all our mysteries (*lit.* economies).

But we know that if thou shouldst refer to all this before these monsters, they will begin to condemn and to swear with all their might, and curse; for they have taken a vow to do so; and these Samaritan dogs, bloodthirsty brutes, are accustomed to such chicanery as this, for they know no law, and own no allegiance to the faith of Christ.

As for this Lazar, who, blind himself, has undertaken to lead the blind, he has for many a year been dead in spirit. Christ could not awake him had he lain four days, but only the forerunner of the Antichrist, so that he may be extirpated from our Pērastnoz and Theme, and suffer a double expulsion. Send, I pray thee, people to our district, to the holy monks and to the laity, to the Christian communities of God, (and ascertain) what a plague and calamity he has brought upon the Church. Now I will inform thee, for I know thou hast heard how, when I reached Mesopotamia, I rooted out of the land the tares sown by them[1]. But then, seeing how the fouling of the water increased, I followed the stream to the source, and came to the fire-altar of Thonrak, where the leaven of the Sadducees was buried, and the hidden embers of wickedness blazed. There by the might of God, and at the prayer of our holy pontiff and illuminator and ancestor, at the behest of the Lord in the days of our holy emperor Constantine Monomachus, crowned by Christ, and sole ruler, I cleaned out the noxious growth of weeds. They came and confessed their guilt and errors and the wickedness of their godless leader to the extent of repudiating the gall of bitterness and the doubts of despair. Our holy bishops, one of whom was Ephrem, Archbishop of Bētjni, and others, advised that we should erect in their midst a font[2], and bestow on them the participation in the Holy Spirit. Accordingly we confirmed them with the holy oil, in order that, by virtue of the hallowing voice of confession of the Trinity, the old men might be excluded and the young men attracted. And we enjoined them not to be subservient to that sect any more. We set up the symbol of the Lord in their midst, and communicated them in the divine and bloodless offering of the divine sacrament. Those, however, who were

---

[1] The Abbot Henry of Clairvaux, in his letter (A. D. 1178), gives a very similar account of his expedition to Albi 'to admonish the prince of the country—namely, Roger of Beders, and to cleanse his whole country by driving out the heretics.' Just as the Paulicians of Armenia were called Thonraki because Thonrak was their centre and the burial-place of their founder, so the heretics of Languedoc were known as Albigeois. See Maitland's *Facts and Documents*, p. 159.

[2] This was needed for the baptism of Paulician children who would not receive baptism till they reached adult age.

APPENDIX III

baptized were over a thousand in number, nor did they cease to come and bap
to us for enlightenment, when they realized their guilt and understood a thousa of the
the wicked heresy of those who misled their innocence. heretics.

But prior to the events narrated, two of their sham priests had led
up to this emancipation by acknowledging all their wizardry and their
wicked heresy. For they knew their wicked and monstrous leaders Two
accurately, and had been their attendants in their beastly dirty hovels renegade
in this burrow of foxes. They recounted to us word by word of their
heresy, as it at present stands; for their wickedness was for ever
on the increase, and is represented in three separate forms. To those The 'per
who are more matured (*or* perfected)[1] in wickedness, and are able to fect' in t heresy.
receive the deadly poison, they preach a sort of utter despair and
godlessness, such as we find among Epicureans. But others (are
taught) after the manner of Manichees, whom they anathematize, at
the same time that they pursue the same practices. To others they The her
make a show of teaching in conformity with Christian tradition; yet cursed Manes.
they themselves make no confession at all except of what is repugnant
to all Christian ordinances and beliefs[2]. And lastly, it is notorious
that they are separated[3], and wander about without bishops and
without priests; yet they make pretence, saying: 'We are of the tribe
of Aram, and agree with them in faith.' But they in no way agree
with us, but are much rather in opposition to us, and only resemble us
in mere name as one dog does another[4]. What comparison can there
be where natures are so wholly different? So I lay before your
holiness our letter, written about these people. It has been enjoined
not to approach these people, not to speak with them, not to admit
them to confession or to baptism; and these decisions are confirmed.
I however, trusting in the forgiveness of God and the precept of our
holy illuminator, have opened to them a door of mercy and humanity.
For the common people are not responsible for the deadly venom of
wrath which (their leaders) have made ready. But now these monstrous zealots, at the same time that they keep their poison-fangs
hidden, write to us in a learned way, as if we did not know what is
the laughing-stock of children, let alone of our wise men and publicists.
They want to teach us, and so enumerate the groups of heretics one Paulicia
after the other, and say: 'We do not belong to these; those have long claimed belong t
ago broken connexion with the Church, and have been excluded.' As the Chu
withered limbs or hair fallen out or weeds uprooted or chaff winnowed and not be hereti
out, these indeed are gone, some before the time of S. Epiphanius, at all.
who mentions them in his holy book called the *Panarium*, and after
him by S. Cyril; others again later who have been described by others
of our fathers. But as those fathers stigmatized the heretics of their
times, so have our pontiff, the holy John[5] and the Vardapet Anania, How the
stigmatized these of to-day, and have described their wicked, horrible were denounced
heresies. For these sin not merely in one or two points, but in their John an
whole legislation stand altogether outside of the new and old law. . Ananias.
This sect drew not from two or three sources only, but embraced all that

---

[1] կատարելագոյնք. In the Key, the same word expresses mature or adult age, and that is probably the sense here.

[2] A reference to the Paulician creed, see p. 94.   [3] i.e. excommunicated.

[4] *Lit.* 'and are only indicated by a common-sounding name as dog and dog and dog.'

[5] John of Otsun called them Paulicians, whence it is clear that Gregory Magistros identified the Paulicians and Thonraki.

was ever heretical—soothsaying, palmistry, incantations and magic arts, infidelities, wicked poisons—all in the single brew of their heresy, when they consented to that enemy of God, that hedgebreaker, diabolical madman, Smbat, giving them their laws, and, quitting the path of illumination, entered a blind alley........ These are the crimes of these malefactors. No fasts are theirs, except out of fear; no differences do they observe between men and women, not even as regards the family, though they do not venture openly on this. They respect nothing, either of things divine or of things created; but laugh all to scorn, the old law as well as the new. When, however, you ask them openly, they anathematize and swear vehemently and deny; though we know well enough what a pretence all this is.

Here then you see the Paulicians, who got their poison from Paul of Samosata. When we take on ourselves to question them, they say: 'We are Christians.' They are for ever sing-songing[1], quoting the Gospel and the Apostolon; and when we ask: 'Why do you not allow yourselves to be baptized, as Christ and the apostles enjoined?' they answer: 'You do not know the mystery of baptism; we are in no hurry to be baptized, for baptism is death[2]; and Jesus in the evening meal spoke not of an offering of the mass, but of every table.' They say: 'We love Paul, and execrate Peter; also Moses saw not God, but the devil.' That is to say, they hold Satan to be the creator of heaven and earth, as well as of the whole human race and of all creation; yet they call themselves Christians.

Look now at some others, at Persian magi of (the stock of) Zoroaster the Magus; nay, rather at the Sun-worshippers envenomed by these, whom they call the Arevordi. In your district are many of them, and they also openly proclaim themselves to be Christians. Yet we know that you are aware what error and lewdness they practise. And some there are of this accursed tribe of Thonraki, who call themselves Kaschetzi[3]; they also are a root of wickedness. The Thonraki in Khnun[4] find in Christ an occasion for blasphemy; that is, they write that Christ was circumcised, but the Thulaili reject that, and say: 'We confess no circumcised God.' But I would have you know that at heart they do not own him God, whether circumcised or not; but they only make of it a pretext for calumniating us.

In this connexion I will inform thy holiness. Those priests, who came forward and made known their heresies, and who were first baptized, and took the names of Polycarp and Nicanor, informed us that the letters which had come from various districts to the godless leader Jesu, were to be found in those hovels of lewdness. 'Make haste,' they said, 'seize and read them, and you will find in them the perversities of these devilishly minded men.' Well, we looked for them, found and read them; and they were full of wicked magic and lewdness; and this among other things has been made a ground of complaint against us.

In that dog-kennel[5], however, there lived men clad as monks, and a multitude of whorish women. So we ordered their roof-trees to be thrown down and burned, and the tenants of them to be hunted out of

---

[1] Or, 'chanting like psalms.'
[2] The Paulicians of course meant 'death to sin,' following St. Paul.
[3] կաշեցիք, i.e. dwellers in Kashê.   [4] խնունք.
[5] Dr. Mkrttschian suggests that this is the Κυνὸς χώρα of the Greek sources; but this is very doubtful. Gregory merely wants a term of abuse to apply to Thonrak.

our marches. To none of them, however, did we do any bodily harm, although the law prescribes that they should suffer the extreme of punishment. And, prior to ourselves, many generals and magistrates have given them over to the sword, and, without pity, have spared neither old men nor children; and quite rightly. What is more, our patriarchs have branded their foreheads, and burned into them the image of a fox[1]; for they resemble the thievish foxes which rob the vineyard, as the sage remarked. Others again have put their eyes out. 'You are blind,' they said, 'to spiritual things; therefore you shall not look on sensible things.' But for all that they have not been able to check the growth of their lust, nor to direct back into the bounds of legality their imbecile undisciplined mode of living according to their phrensied temper. On the contrary, with idle hypocrisy, they have appropriated to themselves the language and false signs of priesthood; by way of constructing a sort of bridge to lead wayfarers to destruction, or a gin, a bird-net, or snare, in order that the innocent may fall into a pit. Past persecutions the sect.

So we warn thy holiness to be on thy guard against their Sadducean leaven and their nasty meats and words. Deign not to set the cross on their heads. Likewise let not the bishops and priests in thy diocese (do so), lest they unwittingly fall under the anathema of the Fathers. But send to us with thy recommendation those who confess to their evil deeds and wizardry, and have broken away from their evil workers and presbyters; so that they may come to us and receive baptism. In any other case thou shalt not have mercy on them, or have any communication with them, or deign to look on them; but, like thy fathers and brothers like-minded with thee, curse them whenever they come into thy mind. So much for them. Paulicia Presbyte

Magistros also wrote the following in regard to the Manicheans in another of his letters:—

Gone astray through their vain imaginings, they sophisticate many in the whirligig of their fanciful notions, and patch up the doubts which suggest themselves to them into an idle web of tittle-tattle; so far forth as they represent our worship of God as a worship of idols. As if we, who honour the sign of the cross and the holy pictures, were still engaged in worshipping devils. And some of them teach this in open preachings, others hatch it up in their thoughts as a leaven of unbelief and wickedness. And many of them spare not to lay hands on the church, on all priestly functions, on our awful exalted sacrament of the divine body and blood. But all this derives from those scholars of the Manicheans, who, having been utterly cut off from God, and having no hope of resurrection, are named Thonraki. But thou who art a Christian, having been made worthy[2] of the calling and of being glorified through the holy font, hast in thyself the hope of resurrection, and dost pray to the Holy Trinity—when thou seest the sign of the cross thou shalt pray, because it reminds thee that Jesus Christ was crucified for thee; and thou must regard thyself as crucified along with him[3]. In its presence thou shalt lay aside all earthly thoughts, and Paulicia iconocla· How to regard crosses

---

[1] See p. 138, above.
[2] Magistros is addressing a renegade from the Paulician Church, who had recanted and been baptized by the orthodox Armenians.
[3] This was the Paulician doctrine.

greet it with pure lips, and say: 'Christ, thou Son of God, be thou merciful to me through this holy symbol in spirit and in body, and bethink thee that we are bought by thy blood, for thou didst ransom us through thy cross.' But thou shalt honour the pictures of the saints, and in thy prayers shalt meditate upon their sufferings and martyrs' deaths, submitting thyself to them as thy teachers. They are related to thee, and have become witnesses of the truth. So shalt thou invoke them as thine intercessors before the true God; in order that he who sleeps not may, according to thy trust in his servant the martyr, pity thee who lovest the martyrs.

Now will I in a few words lead into the right path and purify thine evil thoughts and hidden magical beliefs. And as thou art inclined to reckon this confession as something artificial and wrong, I will begin at the beginning, and set before thee the truth concisely: In the beginning the tree of life was honoured in Paradise . . . .[1] like all signs and wonders which were wrought by Joshua and the ark of the covenant. Examine them profoundly, that you may understand that you believe neither in the Old nor in the New Testament, and are not worthy to be a God-seeing Israelite, a son of Abraham, who believed in God, and it was reckoned to him for righteousness; nor one of us either who were heathen and for whom the light is risen. Recognize rather that thou art still in darkness, blind and without guide, at the same time that thou regardest all of us who are obedient to God and venerate his laws, and are subject to his bidding, as blind, privately abusing and calumniating us. Although then thou venturest not to meet us openly, yet in thy secret and darkling mind thou art sick, led astray, and reeling in unbelief. Hear me now, and lighten the eyes of thy spirit; walk in the path of our founder, and of the patriarchs, of the prophets and apostles, of the martyrs and holy church-teachers, and hear Moses (who saith): 'There shall be found in thy house no weight too great or too little; rather shall all be in the open before us and our children, and in secret before God the Father.'

We will then adhere to our confession of hope, and, illuminated with the light of his countenance, will walk in light; that the mercy of his loving-kindness may fall on us, and we fall asleep and wake in the hope that we may with resplendent mien walk before the Lord on the clouds in the ether, and praise Christ, who is God and our hope of resurrection, along with Father and Holy Spirit, to whom be honour and glory, power and dominion, for ever and ever. Amen.

Magistros returns to the subject in a letter 'To a deacon of the Lord Peter [2],' in the following words:—

I am fain to write to thee somewhat about the distressing breaking-up of our heavenly and sanctifying religion. For in consequence of the wicked insurrection excited by the evil wizardry of the Manicheans and of many other sects, this land is sunk in barbarism and darkness, and overhung with thick clouds.

---

[1] Gregory then enumerates, from his own point of view, all the objects mentioned in the Old Testament in order, deducing from them the propriety of image worship.

[2] Cod. Arm. 4 of the Munich Library, pp. 170-172.

APPENDIX III

Also in another letter 'About a monk named Schapuli[1], who held himself to be wise' (and was not), he writes as follows:—

As if you alone knew of the Church that it signifies combats and assemblies! Who is ignorant of that? But this same Church is also place and cause of redemption, and instrument of all works of healing for all of us. ... I know well that most of this is, as you write, calumny and lies; but a little deviation from the right path may lead far astray.

Signific of the v 'Churc

These two letters prove, as Dr. Mkherttschian remarks, in what a ferment men's minds then were. They have not, he continues, been noticed, because the name Thonraki does not occur in them. But we meet with this in another letter of Gregory 'To the Vardapet Sargis[2],' in which he enumerates his own merits, and exclaims:—

Tell me, my friend, how by the grace of God and the prayers of our illuminator and ancestor, the column raised by the Manicheans, i.e. the Thonraki, has been overthrown by my humble agency, and the light of God spread abroad; and that after these people had for more than 200 years infested the whole land, and raised up the fire-altar of their lust and lewdness, and all the time Christ's flock was neglected by pastors and heads of pastors, by kings and princes, and well nigh by all men.

Gregory destruct of the Thonra

Supplementary Note to Page 142.

M. Eritzean of Tiflis, in his article on the Thonraki in the Journal *Phords* (see Proleg. § 1), cites a somewhat different text of Gregory Magistros' letter to the Thulaili, which on p. 142 supplements the copy used by Dr. Mkherttschian. In the third paragraph of that page after the words: 'We laugh at such an idea,' add the following: 'We must not admit you, since you have deceitfully made your way into the Church in order to ensnare the innocent. Although you have written that you have cursed and curse Smbat, still your anathemas are worth nothing like your blessings. We know well that you respect neither Smbat nor any one else.'

---

[1] Cod. Arm. 4 of the Munich Library, pp. 172–174.
[2] Ibid., pp. 184–186.

APPENDIX IV

JOHN OF OTZUN

JOHN of Otzun was born about 688 in the town of Otzun, in the province of Tascir, in Great Armenia. He became Catholicos of Armenia in 718. In the following year a synod was held at Twin in Ararat, then the seat of the Armenian patriarchate, before which he delivered an *Oratio Synodalis*. In a part of this oration, ch. xii, which is unfortunately lost, he condemned the Paulicians. The title of this chapter is alone preserved in the preface of the MS., and runs as follows: 'Reprehensio in eos qui crucem benedicere, easque oleo, quod *myron* vocatur, linire vetant.'

At the same synod he published thirty-two canons, of which the last is directed against the Paulicians, and is as follows, according to the Latin translation which confronts the Armenian text in the Venice (San Lazaro) edition of 1834:

Neminem decet in pessimae obscaenorum hominum sectae locis, qui vocantur Pauliciani, diversari, illisve adhaerere, aut eos alloqui, aut ad invicem visitari; sed ab illis omnino recedere, eos execrari, et odio prosequi; quoniam filii Satanae sunt, aeternique ignis fomites, atque abalienati ab amore voluntatis Creatoris. Quod si quis illis adhaeserit, et dilectionem atque amicitiam cum iisdem fecerit, iste omnino puniendus est, gravique poena est plectendus, donec resipuerit, atque in fide convaluerit. Sin autem recidivus in id fuerit deprehensus, hunc praecipimus penitus excommunicari, et foras, ceu pestem, ex Ecclesiae Christi membris eiici, ne *radix amaritudinis sursum germinans impediat, et per illam inquinentur multi*.

About the same time he wrote a tract against the Paulicians, of which I give only the relevant portions:—

Ecce enim repertus est, tamquam aucupii rete, laqueus extensus inter suae ipsius gentis populum ad decipiendos rudes simplicesque ex hominibus, qui ex malo ad peius assurgentes ascenderunt, ex insectandis nimirum Imaginibus ad insectandam Crucem, et ad odio prosequendum Christum, atque exinde ad atheismum et ad daemonis cultum. Praeterea insidiantes invenerunt malitiae suae arma ad iugulandas Christi amatorum animas, inito cum tyrannis circumcisis pacto, docent tyronum suorum coetum illorum libros obscuritatum fabularumque refertos. Qui enim per suam ipsorum perversitatem gavisi sunt cum diabolo amicitiam inire, haud mirum est, illos cum eius quoque satellitibus unanimiter familiaritatem contrahere.

Huiusmodi porro homines ob rectae et a Deo nobis traditae religionis claritatem mussitantes foedissimis labiis suis conviciari nos audent, nos idololatras nuncupantes ob cultum, quem dominico Crucis signo exhibemus. Celeberrimum namque illud signum indiscriminatim ex quibusvis materiis firmo consilio extruimus: estque sane signum Cherubim quoque terribile atque venerabile, medela spiritalibus aeque ac corporalibus nostris infirmitatibus; daemones autem terrore ac tremore afficiens. Praeterea nos audacter ob depictam Incarnati Verbi Dei imaginem audent vituperare; insanientes ac furentes ex malo infidelitatis spiritu nobis obiiciunt sanctorum prophetarum verba ad refutandam gentilium idololatriam prolata; atque intellectu sane obcaecati nequeunt perspicere quaenam sit cultus nostri similitudo cum gentium polytheismo. Nos enim solius Unigeniti Filii Dei imaginem, Signumque victoriae colimus: ethnicos autem per infinitos, innumerosque cultus seduxit diabolus.

Postquam igitur luculentissime idololatrarum stultitiam denudavimus, non amplius opus est, ut alio novo nomine eos, de quibus iste sermo loquitur, designemus; eiusdem rei namque cooperatio ante oculos posita novae nuncupationis non indiget. Solem enim adorantes cum iis, qui illum colunt, consociantur: murium captoribus cultum praebentes, in eorum foveam, qui equum et canem sibi deos elegerunt, impulsi ruunt, aut in Aegyptiorum fluvium bestiarum nutritium immerguntur. In tenebris tenebricosas perpetrantes turpitudines, provoluti in Persicum materni stupri coenum sese impingunt; aut procidentes ipsa execrabilia Chamos et Astarthae idola deprecantur. Laudibus efferentes irruptiones ignis gehennae a diabolo prunarum excitatore accensae cum Ianne, et Mambre in Olympio monte humi prostrati, atque ore spumantes inclinati daemonem adorant. Infantium sanguini similam commiscentes illegitimam communionem deglutiunt; quo pacto porcorum suos foetus immaniter vescentium exsuperant edacitatem.

Quique illorum cadavera super tecti culmen celantes, ac sursum oculis in caelum defixis respicientes, iurant alieno verbo ac sensu: *Altissimus novit.* Solem vero deprecare volentes, aiunt: *Solicule, Lucicule*; atque aereos, vagosque daemones clam invocant, iuxta Manichaeorum Simonisque incantatoris errores. Similiter et primum parientis faeminae puerum de manu in manum inter eos invicem proiectum, quum pessima morte occiderint, illum, in cuius manu exspiraverit puer, ad primam sectae dignitatem provectum venerantur; atque per utriusque nomen audent insane iurare: *Iuro*, dicunt, *per unigenitum filium*: et iterum: *Testem habeo tibi gloriam eius, in cuius manum unigenitus filius spiritum suum tradidit.*

In primis, incestuosae Paulicianorum gregis sordescentes reliquiae, obiurgationem sane sustinuerunt a Nersete Catholico, sed minime resipiscentes, post illius obitum aufugientes, alicubi in quibusdam regionis nostrae finibus latitarunt. Ad quos iconomachi quidam ab Alvanorum Catholicis repraehensi advenientes adhaeserunt; aberrans siquidem a veritate consimiles sibi attigere cupit. Antequam autem subsidium hi penes antichristi praecursores invenissent, trepidantes pertimescebant rectam eximiamque Christianorum religionem: quin immo seipsum condemnat impius a cogitationibus suis exagitatus. Quum autem istud ceu magnum quoddam ac novum, quod iam vetus erat atque obsoletum, consequutos fuisse arbitrati sunt; tunc ex insidiarum suarum cubilibus obrepti in medio regionis atque per loca populis referta irruere ausi sunt; atque haec suffocantium diluvii aquarum portio confluit ad locum *Djirga* nuncupatum; ibique accurrentes undequaque congregati sunt, tamquam regionis vultures super corruptum quoddam cadaver. Sui autem nominis sordes inferre ausi sunt iis, qui caelestia bona per spem arripiunt, electis ex hominibus, atque divina habitatione dignis inventis, qui super terram caelestium vitam agere aggrediuntur. Contra hos audacter evomere praesumunt impietatis suae bilem, atque insanientes, ex mali spiritus blasphemia, *Sculpticolas* (*eos*) vocant.

Nullum sustineo dedecus ob illud, quo me contemnere censent, nomen recte perceptum: revera siquidem exculpimus, caelamus, cudimus, dolamus ea, quibus religionis nostrae sacra perficiuntur, Ecclesias, altaria, cruces, imagines; nec tamen per ista participes fimus Ethnicorum cultibus. Nam eorum delubra in idolorum receptacula condebantur; Ecclesiae vero sunt piorum orationis ac supplicationis aedes et loca congregationis eorum, qui ad Deum accedere volunt. Quamobrem valde differunt inter se templum Dei, et fanum idolorum; sicut et Paulus dicit. Praeterea eorum manufacta a vitio quodam originem, ut iam dixi, sumentia exculpta fuere; et cujuscumque facinoris daemon ingressus, habitationem suam efficiebat idoli fanum. . . . .

Num quando video lapideam aut auream Crucem elaboratam vel imaginem, in lapide forsitan aut in auro ponam spem meam? Id illorum est, qui *cum lapide et ligno moechabantur*, sicut Propheta ait; de quibus et David dixit: *Simulacra Gentium argentum, et aurum.* Nos autem illas dumtaxat, super quas expressimus similitudinem imaginis Christi Crucisque eius, a quibusvis materiis secretas honoramus. Etenim nomen, et similitudo nobis utrumque suadet, Christum nempe in iis habitare, atque nos illas sine haesitatione venerari. Neque id tantummodo, verum et Sacerdotis manus, ac verba sanctissimam Trinitatem super eas invocantia eius habitare faciunt virtutem. . . . .

Quare ecce nos per Apostolorum praedicationem credentes in sanctissimam Trinitatem consideramus per olei unctionem instrumenta salutis, Ecclesias, altaria, cruces, imagines; et credimus una simul cum eo divinam virtutem introire.

The following is from the *Oratio Synodalis* referred to above:—

Praeter haec istud quoque apud nonnullos vidimus malum opus a consuetudine roboratum. Ad matrimonium accessuri non adducuntur iuxta Christianorum legem in Ecclesias, ut universorum rituum religiosarumque Christifidelium disciplinarum participes effecti, ibidem in locis decentibus coronentur; sed sine missa, et sine oratione, et absque benedictione, communioneque foris manent, ubicumque voluerint. Sacerdos autem per cuiusvis illuc pergentis manum deferri iubet coronam, contemnens tum coronam tum coronatos, quodque hisce gravius est, Sacramentum ipsum ignominia afficiens. Et sane sanctus Apostolus dicit: *Sacramentum hoc magnum est, ego autem dico in Christo, et in Ecclesia*: ille vero arrogantia sua parvipendere conatur magnum nobilis connubii mysterium, seque ipsum a Dei ministratione depositum iugo subiicit; qui enim populi Dei servitium abiicit, Deo non servit.

APPENDIX V

NERSES SHNORHALI

NERSES SHNORHALI (the Graceful) was born about 1100, and was elected Catholicos of Armenia 1165; died 1173. Because he made Rom. Claj, Ρωμαίων Κοῖλα, the seat of his patriarchal church, he is also known as Nerses Clajensis. The letter in which he refers to the Paulicians was written before 1165, but after he was already a bishop, to Ariuz, prince of the town of Thelkuran. It is devoted to the errors then current among the Armenian clergy and congregations in the province of Hamaj in Syrian Mesopotamia. I cite from Capelletti's Version, Venice, 1833.

Nersetis Claiensis Epistola I. :—

Praeterea audivimus, quod nonnulli ex fallentibus Sacerdotibus iterum excitant faetidam maledicti Sembatis Tontraghensis celatam immunditiam, in audientium ruinam, dicentes : 'Ecclesia non est illa, quae ab hominibus aedificata est, sed nos tantum: atque liber Rituale, et Canones, qui in eo continentur, Crucis et Ecclesiae benedictio, et alia, non sunt admittenda.'

Adversus eos sane, qui hoc similiaque dicunt, laboraverunt illius temporis Doctores, sapienterque scripserunt, eorumque falsitatem satis diluerunt : et qui Beati Ananiae Nareghensis doctoris librum adversus maledictum Sembatem legit, integram habet hisce blasphemiis responsionem. Breviter tamen ac celeriter nos quoque pauca dicemus, ne ab erroneis eorum dictis rudes e populo decipiantur. (c. iv.)

De crucis autem benedictione istud intelligite. Sancti Apostoli, et Patres Apostolorum successores eumdem Spiritum habentes sic agebant : Quadrialatam Crucem ex quavis materia effectam coram locabant, atque impositis super eam manibus offerebant preces, prout Spiritus dabat eloqui illis iuxta temporis necessitatem; ut sensibilis illa materia spiritualem Dei virtutem exciperet ; et post haec ad Orientem illam erigebant, ac fidelibus, ut eam adorarent, praecipiebant. Atque ex hisce Crucibus perquam maxima prodibant signa et virtutes ; sicut in libris narratur.

Quum autem fidelibus imminutae sunt visibiles Spiritus gratiae, ob accipientium infirmam fidem ; id pulcherrime ab eodem Spiritu moti excogitarunt, ut super extructam Crucem legant Sacerdotes spiritualium Prophetarum, et Apostolorum, et Evangelistarum verba ex ipsorum parte ; atque offerant Sacerdotes scriptas postulationis preces, quasi per os illorum dicerentur; lavent (*Crucem*) aqua et vino ad similitudinem fontium, qui de latere in prima Cruce manarunt; atque Chrismate liniant in unctionem Spiritus sanctitatis: ut per Spiritus Sancti gratiam, et per intercessionem illorum, quorum verba super (*eam*) legunt, nominaque commemorant, eamdem divinam virtutem in illius Crucis figura inhabitet, sicuti prius in efformatis a Sanctis. Quo facto, Christus deinceps adorandus est in illa; non materia, sed Verbi Dei virtus, quam ab eo inseparabilem nos adorantes credimus. Qui eam vero absque huiusmodi benedictionibus adorant; materiam tantummodo, non Dei virtutem adorant. Etenim plures sunt figurae in Crucis formam effectae in coelo, et in terra, in insipientibus quoque animantibus, et super textile, et super variegatas picturas, quas adorandi mandatum non accepimus. Haud enim in ipsis divinae adsunt virtutes; et eum, qui creaturae adorationem tribuit, Sacri libri sub anathemate, paganorum instar, condemnarunt.

Si quis autem ex opponentibus contradixerit ob Chrismatis unctionem, utpote quae est superflua, et inconveniens: de hoc etiam dicamus, quod Chrisma prae se fert symbolum ac virtutem Spiritus Sancti. (c. v.)

Itaque, o tu Christifidelis, quotiescumque Crucem aspexeris, agnosce et crede, Christum super eam intueri sedentem; at quum oraveris ante illam, crede, Christum te alloqui, non autem, quae loqui nequit, materiam. Christus enim est, qui tuam excipit adorationem Cruci exhibitam; ipseque est, qui audit orationem oris tui, et implet petitionem cordis tui, quam postulas in fide. Et qui Crucem inhonorat vel blasphemat, Christum blasphemasse et inhonorasse, credat, minime vero visibilem materiam; atque ab eo expectet vel hic, vel in altero suo adventu cum illis, qui eum crucifixerunt, et cum infidelibus vindictae retributionem suscipere. (c. vi.)

Circa autem Ecclesiae benedictionem, de qua sicut ab oppositioribus audivimus, non esse opus dicitur, utpote quae a primis Patribus statuta non est, sed a novissimis, et penes tantum Armenios; quidquid de Crucis mysterio diximus et de Ecclesia intelligite. (c. vii.)

Quod autem dicunt: Index non est acceptabilis; quippe non ab antiquis Patribus, sed ultimis temporibus a quodam Mastotz scriptus ac statutus fuit; falsum est, haudquaquam verum. Quidquid enim in eo praecipitur, a priscis Patribus statutum est; nonnihil a nostris Illuminatoribus, nonnihil ab aliarum gentium Patriarchis; quorum cuiuslibet nomina initio uniuscuiusque Canonis sunt inscripta. Beatus autem Mastotz in unum librum Canones inter se divisos collegit; ideoque eius nomine ipsemet liber vocatur. Verum etiamsi ab eodem Sancto Mastotz fuissent universi dictati, quare non sunt acceptabiles? ... Vel damnum quod exinde est, ostendant; vel seipsos adversarios Christi eiusque legis declarent, a quibus omnis divina gratia, quae in Indice conscribitur, baptismi lavacrum, et sancta consecratio, et communio sancti Sacramenti vivifici, et Christiana sepultura auferatur.

Vos autem, o Dei populi, Nosterque in Christo rationalis Grex, recedite ab hisce lupis ovina pelle contectis; atque huiusmodi homines, qui divinis adversantur Sanctorum Patrum legibus, a Provincia vestra expellite; ne vos a vera traditione, atque ab Iesu Christi fide deficere faciant; neve diaboli zizania in divino veritatis verbi frumento seminent. (c. viii.)

Perhaps also the following passage from his Pastoral Epistle to the Armenian nation is aimed at the Paulicians. It is from ch. ix of that

APPENDIX V

epistle, and addressed 'To the country-folk and poor people,' among whom Paulician propaganda was most active. For note that it regards some sectaries who, without being Mahomedans (here called *Infideles*), spurned the faith, especially baptism and the priest who baptized. These false teachers evidently taught those who had been baptized as infants that their baptism was null and void. It is as follows:—

Item ne faciatis linguas vestras instrumentum Satanae improbis amarisque blasphemiis, maxime quae animam potius, fontisque lavacrum ac baptizantem Sacerdotem, et vultum, et os contaminant; quia plus quam abnegationem et circumcisionem magnum est hoc peccatum. Infideles enim, qui fidem abnegare cogunt Christianum, non instigant, ut Deus contemnatur; qui vero fidem spernit, non spernit hominem sed Deum, quia fides cuiuscumque Deum adorantis est Deus ipse, et qui spernit baptisma ac Sacerdotem baptizantem, huiusmodi contemptus fit Spiritui Sancto, in ipso enim per fontem nascuntur baptizati; et qui hominis animam ac vultum contemnit, haec blasphemia ad Deum refertur, quia anima est a Deo afflata, et vultus est Dei imago, quemadmodum et os pariter Corpus excipit ac Sanguinem Christi. *Nolite* igitur *contristare Spiritum Sanctum Dei*, hisce foedis obscoenisque verbis, ne Spiritus Dei, qui in vobis per fontem habitavit, elongetur a vobis, et intret loco ipsius habitetque in cordibus vestris spiritus Satanae.

Nerses also glances at the Paulicians in his *Libellus Confessionis fidei Ecclesiae Armenae*, written, 1165, at the request of Alexius, the chief Duke of the Imperial Army, and son-in-law of the Emperor Manuel. The passage is this:—

Dictum erat in epistola etiam circa Sanctorum imagines, quasi Armenii eas omnino non admittant; atque in hac parte, quae sit veritas, manifeste exponamus. Ex repugnantia, quae est inter utramque nationem plura mala Diabolus seminavit; sicut etiam apud nonnullos, e rudi nostro populo, aversionem a Sanctis imaginibus. Huiusmodi tamen homines vituperantur a Nobis; immo eos, qui blasphemare praesumunt, anathemate percutimus. Nos enim, qui regendi gradum tenemus, accipimus et adoramus imagines Salvatoris nostri incarnati; honore prosequimur et Sanctorum imagines; juxta uniuscuiusque ordinem; eas quoque in Ecclesiis nostris et super Sacrificii vestes pingimus; ignorantes autem et insipientes e nostris, qui easdem non excipiunt, reprehendimus et castigamus.

And in his *Responsio ad Epistolam Manuelis*, § vii, p. 226, he again glances at the Paulicians, who are the *ignorantes quidam e nostris*. The passage is as follows: —

Item et quoad Salvatoris eiusque Sanctorum imaginem ab ignorantibus quibusdam e nostris aversio ostenditur; Vosque inde scandalizamini, ceu legem universae Genti a Nobis impositam arbitrantes. Verum Nos, quique iuxta Nos sunt, ita habemus et praedicamus, quemadmodum videntes Crucem, quae Deum sustinuit, haud materiae visibili, sed invisibili Deo in ipsa posito adorationem exhibemus; ita de Salvatoris imagine, haud materiam et colores, sed Christum, qui invisibilis Dei Patris imago est, per ipsam adoramus. Imagines vero Sanctorum colimus et glorificamus, eos habendo advocatos mediatoresque coram Deo.

The same Nerses has preserved to us our only account of the Manichean Armenians. It is in his twentieth letter. It is worth noticing that the Manichean baptism, where it had been conferred, is recognized by Nerses as valid: 'qui ex illis baptizati non fuerint, inter catechumenos collocate.' It would appear, however, that these Manicheans deferred baptism to an adult age, as the children and infants were not yet baptized. In the case of the adult but still unbaptized members of the sect, baptism was to be put off till they had repented and believed. Not so in the case of the very young. Alcuin's advice in respect of the reception of the northern barbarians into the Church was similar. I print the relevant parts of the Letter of Nerses:—

Epistola XX.

Eiusdem Domini Nersetis Catholici epistola ad urbem Samosatam ob Solis-Filiorum *conversionem.*

Scitote, quod ad Nos olim pervenit epistola ex vobis circa *Solis-Filios* in urbe vestra degentes, qui volunt et postulant, ut ad Christi fidem admittantur: quippe qui, sicut gente et lingua Armenii sunt, ita iisdem et fide et anima in eadem concordia similes esse cupiunt. Venerunt etiam ex illis quidam coram Nobis, eademque supplicationis verba nobiscum locuti sunt. Nos vero illis ostendimus quidquid de eorum secta daemoniorum cultrice ex libris perlegeramus, et quidquid de ipsis ex eorum fautorum fama audiveramus, pluraque verbo et opere mala. Nam sicut inter Graecos Polomelitae obcaecati remanserunt inter gloriosam lucem Evangelii Christi, et absconditam in corde habentes Satanae sectam minime obtemperarunt Apostolorum praedicationibus; ita pariter et in Gente nostra *Solis-Filii* in diabolicarum tenebrarum parte manentes noluerunt a divina luce illuminari per sanctum Illuminatorem nostrum Gregorium; sed *dilexerunt magis tenebras, quam lucem* usque in hodiernam diem.

Porro si nostris temporibus in bono deficientibus misertus est illorum Deus, et obscuratum animae eorum oculum aperuit, ut daemoni abrenuntiarent, atque ad Deum non dolo sed veritate confugerent; Dei benignitatem laudemus. Ita quidem et isti, qui ad Nos venerunt, solemni iureiurando improbam respuerunt Sectam, atque ore suo quemlibet anathematizarunt, qui penes se absconditum huiusmodi atheismum servaverit. Et quidquid eis praecepimus, omnino exceperunt implendum.

Itaque divino iussu id faciendum illis, arbitrati sumus. Veniant omnes Sacerdotes una cum honorabilibus discipulis nostris in maiori Ecclesia, quae est in civitate, et congregentur huiusmodi *Solis-Filii*, omnes, viri et mulieres et pueri ad Ecclesiae ianuam; atque primum eos interrogate: Vultis ex toto corde, et ex tota anima, et ex totis viribus vestris recedere a primo vestrorum patrum errore, atque ad veram Dei cognitionem, ad Christianitatem redire?— Et quum id susceperint, et dixerint: Libenter et ultro disiungimur a diabolicis patrum nostrorum fraudibus, atque ad Christum confugimus:—tunc rursus illos ter interrogate, sicut Catechumeni in hora baptismi: Abrenuntiatis Satanae?... et omnibus cogitationibus et verbis et operibus eius?— Et quum assenserint, et dixerint: Abrenuntiamus: vertite eorum facies ad Occidentem, et dicite: Ter expuite in faciem diaboli, eumque contemnite, ceu immundum et falsum et iniustum. — Quum autem id fecerint, docete eos postea, nihil aliud existimare solem, nisi luminare mundi, quod Deus Creator creavit, et posuit in coelo ad illuminandam terram. Item et luna et stellae. Populum autem ne colatis plus quam salicem aut fagum aut aliam ex arboribus, et ne credatis populeum fuisse Crucis Christi lignum.

Neque tantum populeam arborem plus quam alias ne colatis; quin immo eam plus quam alias arbores contemnendam existimate: unde Satanas ipse contemnetur. Et si quis vestrum nosceret apud eos diabolicum quodpiam amuletum, id quoque palam facite, ac respuendum abiiciendumque eis indicate.

Deinde facies eorum ad Orientem vertite, eosque interrogate: Creditis Sanctissimam Trinitatem, Patrem et Filium et Spiritum Sanctum, qui sunt tres personae et una divinitas, una natura, una virtus, una potestas, unaque vis creatrix; cuius verbo omnes creaturae visibiles et invisibiles ex nihilo fuerunt; coelum et terra et quidquid est in coelo et quidquid in terra est, Angeli et homines ratione praediti, atque sol et luna et stellae orbis illuminatrices, atque animalia terrestria et aërea et aquatilia, omneque vegetabile, et plantae, et ea, quae non moventur, et ea, quae moventur; ita ut nulla reperiatur subsistens creatura incorporea vel corporea, quae non sit veri Dei creatura? — Creditis incarnationem Christi, qui, una e tribus personis, filius Dei, voluit, Patris ac Spiritus Sancti consensione, filius hominis fieri, nascens ex Maria semper Virgine propter hominum salutem; qui et baptizatus fuit a Iohanne in Iordane, atque a Patre et Spiritu fuit testatus; tentatus fuit a diabolo ac tentatorem vicit; insectatus est daemones.

Et quum susceperint, atque confessi fuerint verae Christianorum fidei professionem, quam scripsimus, perducite illos in Ecclesiam; et qui ex illis baptizati non fuerint, inter catechumenos collocate; adultos quidem confiteri facite, eisque parum quid poenitentiae imponite, et post aliquod temporis baptizate; infantes autem et pueros illico baptizate. Ab iis vero, qui prius fuerint baptizati, Confessionem sacramentalem excipite, eisque poenitentiam imponite, atque sancto Chrismate eorum frontem omnesque sensus signate dicentes: In nomine Patris et Filii et Spiritus Sancti; ac tandem inter Christi gregem eos commiscete.

Atque insuper nomen etiam, quod a suis maioribus obtinuerunt, ut *Solis-Filii* vocarentur, ex hoc nunc mutent, atque in nomine Christi magno et mirifico *Christiani* nuncupentur: quod sane nomen Antiochiae sancti quoque Apostoli Christifidelibus imposuerunt.

APPENDIX VI

The Provençal Ritual of the Albigeois translated from the Codex of Lyon, as printed in facsimile by Cledat, with annotations.

IN the Lyon Codex the following Latin prayers precede the ritual:—

Benedicite parcite nobis. Amen. Fiat nobis secundum verbum tuum[1]. Pater et filius et espiritus sanctus parcat vobis omnia peccata vestra. Adhoremus patrem et filium et espiritum sanctum. iii vegadas (i.e. three times).

There follows the Pater noster with panem supersubstancialem substituted for panem quotidianum.

Then, Quoniam tuum est regnum et virtus et gloria in secula. Amen.

Adhoremus patrem et filium et spiritum sanctum. iii vegadas.
Gratia domini nostri Ihesu Christi sit cum omnibus vobis.
Benedicite parcite nobis. Amen. Fiat nobis secundum verbum tuum. Pater et filius et spiritus sanctus parcat vobis omnia peccata vestra[2]

There follows in Latin St. John i. 1-17.

[SERVITIUM][3]

We are come before God and before you, and before the ordinance of the holy church[4], to receive service and pardon and penitence for all our sins, which we have done, or said, or thought, or worked from our birth until now; and we ask mercy of God and of you[5], that you should pray for us to the holy Father of mercy that he pardon us.

---

[1] Probably the whole congregation of *credentes* and *perfecti* repeated as far as *tuum*; then the elder responded with the blessing: *Pater, &c.*

[2] In the course of ritual, these Latin prayers are indicated under the titles *parcias, gratia, adoremus*.

[3] I add the title in brackets, because this part of the ritual is so called just below in the text.

[4] Cp. *Ebr.* 70: 'Dicunt quod bonus homo aut bona foemina aut congregatio utriusque Ecclesia est.' *Lib. Sent.* 348: 'Quod ecclesia Dei non erat in lignis et lapidibus, sed in bonis hominibus et Sanctis quales dicebant se ipsos; item quod ipsi solum modo et non alii poterant absolvere a peccatis et solvere animos.' *Disput. inter Cathol. et Patarinum* (in Martene, *Thes. Nov. Anecd.* v.) 1752: 'Nostra est Ecclesia ubi sunt homines iusti et casti, non mentientes, non fraudantes.' This note, with most which follow, is from Cunitz, *Beitr. z. Theol. Wiss.*, Jena, 1851.

[5] i.e. of the *perfecti*, who, being pure, were mediators between God on the one hand and sinners, or *credentes*, on the other.

Let us adore God and declare all our sins and our many grave offences in the eye of the Father, and of the Son, and of the revered Holy Spirit, and of the revered holy Gospels[1] and of the revered holy apostles, by prayer and by faith, and by the salvation of all loyal, glorious Christians, and of blessed ancestors fallen asleep, and of the brethren here present, and before you, holy lord (*or* sir), unto the end that you pardon all our sins. Benedicite parcite nobis.

For many are our sins in which we offend every day, by night and day, in word and deed, and in the way of thought, voluntarily and involuntarily[2], and mostly through our will, which the malign spirits bring up before us in the flesh which is our vesture. Benedicite parcite nobis.

But although the holy word of God teaches us, and also the holy apostles, and though our spiritual brethren warn us to put away all desires of the flesh and all impurity, and to do the will of God, the perfect good and complete; yet we, neglectful servants, not only do not do the will of God accordingly as it were meet, but we more often fulfil the desires of the flesh and worldly cares[3], so that we do harm to our spirits. Benedicite parcite nobis.

We walk with the worldly, with them we are familiar and talk and eat[4]; and in many things we offend, so that we do harm to our brethren and to our spirits. Benedicite parcite nobis.

With our tongues we fall into idle words, into vain parleyings, into laughter, mockery, and malice, into detraction[5] of our brothers and sisters, whom we are not worthy to judge, as neither to condemn the offences of the brothers and sisters. Among Christians we are sinners. Benedicite parcite nobis.

The service which we have received we have not kept it as we ought, neither the fast nor the prayer; we have transgressed our days[6], our hours we prevaricate. The while we are at holy prayer our senses stray after carnal desires, after cares of the world, so that at this hour we hardly know what thing to offer to the Father of the just. Benedicite parcite nobis.

---

[1] During this general confession, the elder presiding held the Codex of the Gospels and of the whole N.T. *ante pectus* and open, because the sins had been committed against them. *Reiner*, 1764. Notice what stress is laid on confession of sins being publicly made before the church and entire congregation of Christians, instead of to a single priest.

[2] Involuntary sin was due to the corruption of the will by evil spirits, and corresponds to the 'original sin' dwelt on in the *Key of Truth*.

[3] Notice the insistence on the flesh and on the world as the two great causes of sin; and compare the exordium of the *Key*.

[4] The *credentes* looked forward to washing away the stain of contact with non-believers in their final *consolamentum*. The *perfecti*, or already consoled, could only mix with non-believers in order to convert them, and for no other reason.

[5] So in *The Shepherd* of Hermas, καταλαλιά is the typical sin.

[6] Therefore the observance of certain days and hours was part of the 'customs' of the Cathar Church, as it was of the Paulicians. Cp. the *Key*, ch. vi.

O thou, holy and good lord (*or* sir), all those things which happen unto us, to our senses and our thought, to thee we declare them, holy Lord, and all the multitude of our sins do we lay at the mercy of God, and in holy prayer, and in the holy Gospel. For many are our sins. Benedicite parcite nobis.

O Lord, judge and condemn the vices of the flesh; have no mercy on the flesh born of corruption[1]; but have mercy on the spirit placed in prison[2], and arrange for us days and hours and *veniae*[3], and fasts and prayings and preachings, as is the custom of good Christians; that we be not judged or condemned at the day of judgement with the felons. Benedicite parcite nobis.

[CEREMONY OF THE RECEPTION, BY A BELIEVER, OF THE LORD'S PRAYER.]

If a believer is in abstinence[4] and the Christians are agreed to deliver unto him the prayer[5], they shall wash their hands, and the believers[6], if there be any present, shall do likewise. And then the one[7] of the good men[8], he that is next after the elder[9], shall make three

---

[1] The view of the flesh here implied is that which we find in Paul and in the early Church generally, though the Cathars were specially blamed by the orthodox for holding it. Among the Cathars, as in the orthodox Church, it seems to have led to abstention from wedlock, at least on the part of some.

[2] 'Adae spiritum, qui erat caelestis angelus, Lucifer apprehendit et in corpore carnes velut in carcere reclusit.' *Moneta*, 110. *Idem*, 288: 'Deus infundit animas corrupto vasi.'

[3] *Venias* is, in Ducange, explained as 'inclinationes vel genuflexiones religiosorum quae Graecis μετάνοιαι uocantur, quod ut plurimum in poenitentiam iniungi solerent.' The Middle Ages attached much importance to such prostrations, and so still do Oriental Christians. In the *Key* there is frequent express reference to the use of such prostrations during divine offices.

[4] The use of flesh was forbidden to the *perfecti*. They might only eat fish and vegetables. *Reiner*, 1761: 'Credunt quod comedere carnes et ova vel caseum etiam in urgenti necessitate sit peccatum mortale et hoc ideo quia nascuntur ex coitu.' The *credentes*, of course, were less strict. There seem to have been two classes of *credentes*, those who had conformed to the necessary *abstinentia* and were ripe for reception through the *consolamentum* into the *ordo* of *perfecti*, and those who merely believed and had received instruction in the faith, i.e. pure catechumens. The latter, according to Cunitz, had already received the 'prayer' in the manner here set forth, and are defined as 'believers to whom has been delivered the prayer.' The lower grade of *credentes* are called by Evervinus 'hearers,' *auditores*, i.e. catechumens.

[5] Similarly, in the early Church, the use of the prayer 'Our Father' was only conceded at baptism, and catechumens might not repeat it.

[6] The believer has been instructed in the faith, but is not yet a Christian. The abstinence is the trial of him preliminary to his reception.

[7] The MS. has *la. I*. Cunitz tr. 'the first.'

[8] The Cathari called themselves the *boni homines*, 'bos homes,' in MS.: *boni Christiani* and *amici dei* were other appellations which they assumed. See *Lib. Sent.* 128.

[9] The Elder was one of the Perfect appointed to pray and preach. Early inquisitional reports of the first half of the thirteenth century (e.g. *Vaissette*, 437; *Reiner*, 1766; *Moneta*, 275) state that the Cathari had a hierarchy of Bishop, Elder, and Deacon, but also that the lowest grade of Deacon could replace the Bishop in all functions. *Vaissette*, 437, speaks of a *maior ecclesiae*,

APPENDIX VI 163

reverences to the elder ; and then he shall get ready a table ; and then three other [reverences], and then let him lay on the table a napkin ; and then three more reverences, and let him place the book upon the table. And then let him say : 'Benedicite parcite nobis.' And then shall the believer perform his *melioramentum*[1], and take the book from the hand of the elder. And the elder shall admonish him and exhort him, using the proper testimonies[2]. And if the believer hath the name Peter, he shall say as follows :—

Peter, you should understand that when you are before the Church of God, you are before the Father, the Son, and the Holy Spirit. For the Church signifies reunion ; and wherever are the true Christians there are the Father and the Son and the Holy Spirit, as the divine scriptures declare. For Christ hath said in the Gospel of St. Matthew : 'Wheresover two or three persons shall be met together in my name, I am there in the midst of them.' And in the Gospel of St. John he saith : 'If any one love me, he will keep my word, and my Father will love him, and we will come unto him and we will dwell with him.' And St. Paul saith in the second Epistle to the Corinthians : 'Ye are the temple of the living God, even as God said through Isaiah, For I will dwell in them, and I will go and I will be their God, and they shall be my people. For the which cause ye shall go out from the midst of them and shall depart, saith the Lord. And ye shall not touch unclean things, and I will receive you. And I will be to you as a father, and ye shall be to me for sons and daughters, saith the Lord Almighty.' And in another place he saith : 'Examine ye the proof of Christ which speaketh in me.' And in the first Epistle to Timothy he says : 'These things I have written to thee, hoping to come unto thee soon. But if I am late, thou shalt know how thou shalt converse in the house of God, the which is the church of the living God, column and stay of truth.' And the same says to the Hebrews : 'But Christ is like a son in his house, which house we are.' For that the spirit of God may be with the faithful of Jesus Christ, as Christ showeth in the Gospel of St. John : 'If ye love me, keep my commandments ; and I will pray the Father, and he will give you another comforter, who shall be with you for everlasting, the spirit of truth which the world cannot receive ; for it neither seeth nor knoweth him, but ye will know him ; for he will dwell with you and shall be with you. I will not leave you orphans, I will come to you.' And in the Gospel of Matthew he says : 'Behold I am with you always (*lit.* every day) unto the end of the world.' And St. Paul says in the first Epistle to the Corinthians : 'Know ye not that ye are the temple of the living God and that the spirit of God is in you ? But if any one shall corrupt the temple of God, God will destroy him. For the temple

Matt. x 20.

John xi

2 Cor. vi 18.

2 Cor. xi

1 Tim. ii 15.

Heb. iii.

John xiv 18.

Matt. x: 20.

1 Cor. iii 17.

---

and in the *Lib. Sent.* we hear of a *maior hereticus* (13), and of a *Diaconus maior* (14). In the fourteenth century reports of the inquisition, we only hear of an *ancia* or *senior*. Cunitz supposes that stress of persecution had then simplified the hierarchy.

[1] Clédat understands by *melioramentum*, 'an act of contrition.' It was probably recited kneeling.

[2] The preaching and use of the New Testament in exhortation and in controversy was a special feature of the Cathars. Cp. *Lib. Sent.* 193 : 'Pluries audivit verba et admonitiones et praedicationem dicti heretici de nocte et audivit eum loquentem de evangeliis et epistolis.'

of God is holy, the which ye are.' Even so doth Christ show in the Gospel of St. Matthew: 'For it is not ye that speak, but the spirit of your Father that speaketh in you.' And St. John says in his epistle: 'Thereby we know that we live in him and he in us, for of his spirit he hath given unto us.' And St. Paul says to the Galatians: 'Because ye are sons of God, God hath sent the spirit of his son into your heart, crying: Father, Father.' By which you are to understand that your presentation which ye make before the sons of Jesus Christ confirms the faith and the preaching of the Church of God, according as the divine scriptures give us to understand. For the people of God parted itself of old time from its Lord God; and it parted itself from the counsel and will of its holy Father through deception by and submission to the malign spirits. And for these reasons and for many others it is given us to understand that the holy Father desires to have mercy on his people and to receive them into peace and into his concord, by the advent of his son Jesus Christ, of which this is[1] the occasion. For ye are here in presence of the disciples of Jesus Christ, in a place where there dwelleth in spirit the Father, the Son, and the Holy Spirit, as here below is shown; that you may receive that holy prayer, which the Lord Jesus Christ gave unto his disciples, to the end that your prayers and oraisons may be hearkened unto by our Holy Father. For which cause ye must understand if ye would receive that holy prayer, that ye must repent of all your sins and pardon all men. For our Lord Jesus Christ said: 'If ye pardon not men their sins, neither will your heavenly Father pardon your sins.' Furthermore it behoves you to purpose in your hearts to keep that holy prayer all through your lifetime, if God shall give you grace to receive it, according to the custom of the Church of God, with chastity and with truth, and with all the other goodly virtues which God shall vouchsafe unto you.

For which cause we pray the good Lord, who gave to the disciples of Jesus Christ virtue to receive that holy prayer in strength, to give you also grace to receive it, with strength and with reverence for him and for your salvation. Farcite nobis.

And then shall the elder repeat the prayer, and the believer shall follow it. And then shall the elder say:

This holy prayer we deliver unto you, that you may receive it from God, and from us, and from the Church; and that ye may have power to say it all the time of your life, by day and by night, alone and in company, and that you may never eat or drink without first saying this prayer. And if ye omit to do so, then it shall be incumbent on you to bear penance for the same. And he must say: 'I receive it from God, and from you, and from the Church.'

And after that he shall make his *melioramentum* and give thanks; and then the Christians shall perform a 'double' with *veniae*, and the believer after them.

---

[1] Perhaps the meaning is 'of which advent this (i.e. mercy and peace) was the aim and reason.'

APPENDIX VI

[RITUAL OF CONSOLAMENTUM.]

And[1] if he needeth to be consoled without delay, let him perform his *melioramentum*, and take the book from the hand of the elder. And the elder shall admonish him and exhort him with suitable testimonies, and with such words as befit a *consolamentum*. And he shall say as follows :—

Peter, ye would fain receive the spiritual baptism, by which is given the Holy Spirit in the Church of God, with the holy prayer, with the imposition of the hands of the 'good men.' Of this baptism our Lord Jesus Christ saith in the Gospel of St. Matthew to his disciples : 'Go ye and teach all nations, and baptize them in the name of the Father, and of the Son, and of the Holy Spirit. And teach them to keep all things which I have commanded you. And behold, I am with you always even unto the end of the world.' And in the Gospel of St. Mark he saith : ' Go ye into all the world, preach the Gospel to every creature. And whoever shall believe and shall be baptized shall be saved, but whoever shall not believe shall be condemned.' And in the Gospel of St. John he saith to Nicodemus : 'Verily, verily, I say to thee that no one shall enter the kingdom of God unless he be reborn of water and of the Holy Spirit.' And John the Baptist spoke of this baptism when he said : ' Of a truth I baptize with water, but he that cometh after me is mightier than I, whose shoe-string I am not worthy to tie. He will baptize you with the Holy Spirit and with fire.' And Jesus Christ saith, in the Acts of the Apostles : ' For of a truth John baptized with water, but ye shall be baptized with the Holy Spirit.' This holy baptism by the imposition of hands was instituted by Jesus Christ, according to that which St. Luke relates ; and he saith that his friends wrought it even as St. Mark relates : ' On the sick they shall lay their hands, and they shall be well.' And Ananias performed this baptism on St. Paul when he was converted, and afterwards Paul and Barnabas performed it in many places. And St. Peter and St. John performed it on the Samaritans. For so does St. Luke say, in the Acts of the Apostles : ' When the Apostles who were in Jerusalem heard this, that Samaria received the word of God, they sent to them Peter and John. And they, when they were come, prayed for them that they might receive the Holy Spirit, for as yet it was not come upon any one of them. Then they laid their hands upon them and they received the Holy Spirit.' This holy baptism by which the Holy Spirit is given, the Church of God hath kept[2] it from the Apostles until now, and it hath passed from ' good men' to ' good men ' until the present, and will continue to do so until the end of the world.

Matt. 19-20.
Mark x
John iii
John i.
Matt. ii
Acts i.
Mark x
Acts ix. 18.
Acts vii 17.

[1] The Ritual here given is of the *consolamentum*, which the believer could, if he liked, receive immediately after the last step, i.e. Reception of the Prayer. The ritual given is for such a *consolamentum* immediately following, and the book is still supposed to be lying on the white cloth, for its production afresh is not prescribed ; therefore it was already there.

[2] *Evervini Epist. ad Bernardum* (in Mabillon, *Analecta*, iii. p. 454) : 'Dicunt apud se tantum Ecclesiam esse, et quod ipsi soli vestigiis Christi inhaereant et apostolicae vitae veri sectatores permaneant.' And in explanation of the word ' baptism ' here used in the text, cp. ibid. p. 455 : ' quemlibet sic (per impositionem mannum) baptizatum dicunt *Electum*, et habere potestatem alios, qui

And ye must understand that power is given to the Church of God
to loose and bind, and to pardon sins and to retain them, as Christ
saith in the Gospel of St. John: 'As the Father hath sent me, even so
send I you. When he had said these things he blew and said to
them: Receive the Holy Spirit. Those whose sins ye forgive, they
are pardoned them; and those of whom ye shall retain them, they are
retained.' And in the Gospel of St. Matthew, he said to Simon Peter:
'I say unto thee that thou art Simon Peter, and on this rock I will
build my Church, and the gates of hell shall not have strength against
it. And to thee I will give the keys of the kingdom of heaven. And
whatsoever thou shalt bind upon earth shall be bound in heaven, and
whatsoever thou shalt unbind on earth shall be unbound in heaven.'
And in another place he said to his disciples: 'Verily I say unto you,
that whatsoever ye bind on earth shall be bound in heaven, and whatsoever ye shall loose on earth shall be loosed in heaven. And again,
truly I say unto you: If two of you agree upon earth, everything
which they ask shall be done for them by my Father, who is in
heaven. For where there are two or three persons gathered together
in my name, I am there in the midst of them.' And in another place
he said: 'Heal the sick, raise the dead, cleanse the lepers, cast out
devils.' And in the Gospel of St. John he says: 'He that believeth
in me will do the works which I do.' And in the Gospel of St. Mark
he says: 'But those who shall believe, these signs shall follow them.
In my name they shall cast out demons, and shall speak with new
tongues, and shall take away serpents; and if they drink anything
mortal it shall not hurt them. On the sick they shall lay their
hands and they shall be well.' And in the Gospel of St. Luke he
says: 'Behold I have given you power to tread under foot serpents
and scorpions and all the power of the enemy, and nothing shall
harm you.'

And if ye would receive this power or this potency, ye must needs
keep all the commandments of Christ and of the New Testament
according as ye can. And know that he has commanded that a man
should not commit adultery nor homicide, nor lie, nor swear any oath,
nor pick nor steal, nor do unto another that which he would not have
done unto himself; and that a man should pardon him that doeth him
wrong, and that a man love his enemies, and that a man pray for and
bless his calumniators and accusers, and that to him who smites him on
one cheek he shall offer the other, and to him who takes away his tunic
he shall also leave his mantle; and that one judge not nor condemn,
along with many other commandments which are laid by the Lord
upon his Church. And equally must you hate this world and its works
and the things which are of it. For St. John says in his Epistle: 'O
much loved ones, will not to love the world nor any things which are in
the world. If any one love the world, the charity of the Father is not
in him. For whatsoever is in the world is coveted of the flesh and

---

digni fuerint baptizandi, et in mensa sua corpus Christi et sanguinem conse-
crandi. Prius enim per manus impositionem de numero eorum, quos *auditores*
vocant, recipiunt inter *credentes*, et sic licebit eum interesse orationibus eorum,
usque dum satis probatum eum faciunt *Electum*.' Cp. also Epistola Eccles.
Leodiensis ad Lucium Papam II (Martene et Dur. *ampliss. collect.* i. 776):
'Haeresis haec diversis distincta est gradibus; habet enim *auditores*, qui ad
errores initiantur, habet *credentes*, qui iam decepti sunt, habet *Christianos* suos,
habet *sacerdotes*, habet et caeteros *praelatos*, sicut et nos.'

coveted of the eyes, and is pride of life, the which is not of the Father, but is of the world. The world will pass away, and the coveting of it, but he that doth the will of God shall be everlasting.' And Christ said to the Gentiles: 'The world cannot hate you, but myself it hates, John vii because I bear witness of it that its works are evil.' And in the book of Solomon it is written: 'I have seen all things that are done under Eccl. i. 1 the sun, and behold all are vanity and tormenting of spirit.' And Judas James said, instructing us in his epistle: 'Hate ye this soiled Jude 23. garment which is the flesh.' And by these testimonies and by many others it behoves you to keep the commandment of God and to hate this world. And if ye do it well unto the end, we have hope that your soul will have eternal life.

And he shall likewise say: 'I have this will and determination. Pray God for me that he give me his strength.' And then let the one of the 'good men' make his *melioramentum* with the believer unto the elder, and say: 'Parcite nobis. Good Christians, we pray you for the love of God that ye give of that good which God has given you to this our friend.' And then let the believer perform his *melioramentum* and say: 'Farcite nobis. For all the sins which I have done, in word or thought or deed, I come for pardon to God, and to the Church, and to you all.' And the Christians shall say: 'By God and by us and by the Church may they be pardoned thee; and we pray God that he pardon you them.' And then shall they console him, and the elder shall take the book[1] and place it on his head, and the other good men each [place] their right hand [on his head]; and they shall say the *parcias* and three *adoremus*, and then 'Pater Sancte, suscipe servum tuum in tua iustitia et mitte gratiam tuam et Spiritum Sanctum tuum super eum.' And let them pray to God with the prayer, and he that guides the ministration must say in low tone the 'sixtene'; and when the 'sixtene' has been repeated, he must say three *adoremus*, and the prayer once out loud, and then the Gospel[2]. And when the Gospel has been said they must say three *adoremus*, and the 'gratia' and the 'parcias.' And then they must perform 'the peace[3]' one with the other and with the book. And if there be believers present they shall also perform 'the peace'; and let the believers, if there be any, perform 'the peace' with the book and with one another. And then let them pray to God with 'a double' and with *veniae*, and they will have delivered [unto him the prayer].

The commission to hold a 'double' and to say the prayer shall not be held by a secular person.

If the Christians enter a place of danger, they shall pray God with a 'gratia.' If any one goes on horseback, let him hold a 'double.' And he shall say the prayer in entering a ship or a town, or in passing over a plank or over a hazardous bridge. And if they find any one with whom they must speak the while they pray to God, and if they

---

[1] *Moneta*, 278: 'Praelatus maior textum Evangelii super caput eius imponit, et alii fratres qui ibi sunt manum dextram capiti vel humeris eius imponunt.'
[2] Ibid.: 'Praelatus vero, qui librum tenet ... ait, In nomine Patris et Filii et Spiritus Sancti, et septies dicta oratione Dominica, tandem Evangelium Iohannis, quod in die natalis Domini cantatur, dicit: In principio erat Verbum. His ita celebratis credunt illi omnia peccata dimitti et gratiam Spiritus Sancti ei infundi.'
[3] i.e. kiss.

have [? said] eight prayers these can be taken for a 'simple.' And if they have sixteen prayers, they can be taken for a 'double.' And if they find any property on the road, they shall not touch it unless they know that they can return it. And if they see at once that people have passed in front of them to whom it might be returned, they shall take and return it if they can. And if they cannot, they shall put it back where they found it. And if they find beast or bird taken they shall not trouble themselves. And if a Christian would drink during the day time, let him have prayed to God twice or more times after eating. And if after the 'double' of the night they drink, let them do another 'double.' And if there are believers, let them stand upright when they say the prayer before drink. And if a Christian pray to God with Christian women, let him always guide the prayer. And if a believer to whom the prayer had been delivered was with the Christian women, let him go apart and go through it by himself.

If the Christians to whom the service of the Church is entrusted receive a message from a believer who is sick, they must go to him and must ask him privily how he has behaved towards the Church since he received the faith, and whether he is in aught indebted to the Church or has harmed it. And if he owes aught, and can pay it, he shall do so. And if he will not do so, he is not to be received. For if one prays God for a man who is unjust or disloyal, such prayer cannot avail. At the same time, if he cannot pray, he is not to be rejected.

And the Christians must show him the abstinence and the customs of the Church. And then they must ask him, in case he be received, if he has the mind to keep them. And he must not promise, if he be not firmly resolved to do so. For St. John says that the part of liars will be in a lake of fire and sulphur. And if he says that he feels himself strong enough to suffer all this abstinence, and if the Christians are agreed to receive him, they shall lay upon him abstinence in such wise as to ask him if he is minded to keep himself from lying and swearing, and from all else forbidden by God, and to keep the customs of the Church and commandments of God, and to keep his heart and his property, such as he has them now or shall have in the future, at the beck and call of God and of the Church, and at the service of Christian men and women, for ever henceforth so far as he can. And if he answer 'Yes,' they shall reply: 'This abstinence do we lay upon you for you to receive it from God and from us and from the Church. and to keep it so long as you live; for if you keep it well, along with the others which you have to discharge, we have hope that your soul will have life.' And he shall answer: 'I receive it of God, and of you, and of the Church.'

And then shall they ask him if he wishes to receive the prayer, and if he says 'Yes,' they shall dress him in a shirt and breeches, if it can

APPENDIX VI

be done, and they shall arrange to hold him sitting up, if he can raise his hands. And they shall lay a napkin or another cloth before him on the bed. And on this cloth they shall set the book, and shall say once *Benedicite*, and three times 'Adoremus Patrem et Filium et Spiritum Sanctum.' And he must take the book from the hand of the elder. And then, if he can wait, he that conducts the service shall admonish him and preach to him from suitable testimonies. And then he shall ask him with regard to the covenant, if he has it in his heart to guard and keep it according as he has covenanted. And if he says 'Yes,' they shall make him confirm the same. And then they must pass unto him the prayer, and he shall follow it. And then let the elder say to him : ' This is the prayer which Jesus Christ brought into this world, and he taught it to the " good men." And never shall ye eat or drink anything without first saying this prayer. And if ye are remiss therein, then ye must need do penitence for the same.' He shall say : ' I receive it from God, and from you, and from the Church.' And then let them salute him like a woman. And then they must pray God with a 'double' and with *veniae*, and then they must relay the book before him. And then he must say three times, 'Adoremus Patrem et Filium et Spiritum Sanctum.' And then let him take the book from the hand of the elder, and the elder must admonish him with testimonies and with such words as befit the *consolamentum*. And then the elder must ask him if he has it in his heart to keep and guard the covenant as he has covenanted to, and he shall cause him to confirm it.

And then the elder must take the book, and the sick man must bow his head and say : ' Parcite nobis. For all my sins of deed or word or thought, I ask pardon of God, and of the Church, and of you all.' And the Christians must say : ' By God and by us and by the Church may they be pardoned thee, and we pray God to pardon thee.' And then they must console him by laying their hands and the book on his head, and say : ' Benedicite, parcite nobis. Amen. Fiat nobis secundum verbum tuum. Pater et Filius et Spiritus Sanctus parcat vobis omnia peccata vestra. Adoremus Patrem et Filium et Spiritum Sanctum.' three times, and then, ' Pater Sancte, suscipe servum tuum in tua iustitia, et mitte gratiam tuam et Spiritum Sanctum tuum super eum.'

And if it be a woman, they shall say : ' Pater sancte, suscipe ancillam tuam in tua iustitia, et mitte gratiam tuam et Spiritum Sanctum tuum super eam.'

And then let them pray to God with the prayer, and they must say in low voice the 'sixtene.' And when the 'sixtene' has been said, they must say three times : ' Adoremus Patrem et Filium et Spiritum Sanctum,' and the prayer once out loud, and then the Gospel. And when the Gospel is said they must say three times : ' Adoremus Patrem et Filium et Spiritum Sanctum,' and the prayer once out loud. And then let them salute her like a man. And then they must perform the peace among themselves and with the book. And if there be believers, male or female, present, let them perform the peace. And then the Christians must ask for salvation, and depart.

And if the sick person die and leave them or give them anything, they must not keep it for themselves nor go off with it, but they must put it at the disposition of the order. However, if the sick person lives, the Christians must present him to the order and pray that he console himself afresh as early as he can; and let him do so of his own free will.

FORM OF RECEPTION OF AN ALBIGEOIS CONVERT.

From *Notices et Extraits des MSS. de la Bibliothèque Nationale*, Paris, 1890, 'Notice sur deux Anciens Manuscrits Français,' par M. P. Meyer, p. 76. In a French version made about 1250 of Pierre de Vaux-de-Cernai, *Histoire de la Guerre des Albigeois*, the MS. La Clayette, p. 616 b, has the following:

Quant aucuns se rendoit en la foi des hereges, cil qui le recevoit li disoit : 'Amis, se tu veus estre des miens, il covient que tu renoies toute la foi de Rome'; et il disoit : 'Je la renoi.' Lors li disoit li hereges : 'Reçoi le Saint Esperit des bons homes,' et puis li soffloit par deux foiz en la bouche ; puis li disoit : 'Or renoies a la croiz qui li prestres te fist el baptesme el piz et es espaules et el chief de l'oie et du creime ?' Et il disoit : 'Je le renoi.—Croiz tu que cele iave te puisse sauver ou tu fus baptisiez ?' Et il disoit : 'Je ne croi pas.—Or renoie au cresmel que li prestres te mist en la teste'; et il disoit : 'Je le renoi.' En itel maniere retienent li herege li un les autres, et renoient tot le sacrement du baptesme : lors li metent tuit la main sur la teste, et le baisent et le vestent de robe noire ; et dès lors en avant il est ausi com uns des autres.

The corresponding Latin text is as follows :

Quando aliquis se reddit haereticis, ille dicit qui recipit eum : 'Amice, si vis esse de nostris, oportet ut renunties toti fidei quam tenet Romana ecclesia. Respondet : 'Abrenuntio.—Ergo accipe Spiritum Sanctum a bonis hominibus,' et tunc aspirat ei septies in ore (*Bouquet*, xix, 6 E).

APPENDIX VII

Τοῦ ὁσίου πατρὸς ἡμῶν Ἰσαὰκ τοῦ καθολικοῦ τῆς μεγάλης Ἀρμενίας λόγος στηλιτευτικὸς κατὰ Ἀρμενίων. Κεφαλ. Η΄.

Ὁ Χριστὸς τριακονταετὴς ἐβαπτίσθη· οὐκ οὖν αὐτοὶ ἕως τριάκοντα ἐτῶν μηδένα βαπτίσωσιν. ὁ Χριστὸς βαπτισθεὶς μύρον οὐκ ἐχρίσθη, οὔτε ἡγιασμένον ἔλαιον. οὐκοῦν μηδ᾽ αὐτοὶ χρισθῶσι μύρῳ ἢ ἁγίῳ ἐλαίῳ. ὁ Χριστὸς ἐν κολυμβήθρᾳ οὐκ ἐβαπτίσθη, ἀλλ᾽ ἐν ποταμῷ· μηδ᾽ αὐτοὶ ἐν κολυμβήθρᾳ βαπτίσωσιν. ὁ Χριστὸς τὸ σύμβολον τῆς πίστεως τῶν τιη΄ ἁγίων πατέρων οὐκ εἶπε μέλλων βαπτισθῆναι· μηδ᾽ αὐτοὶ ὁμολογήσωσιν. ὁ Χριστὸς μέλλων βαπτισθῆναι πρὸς δυσμὰς οὐκ ἀπεστράφη καὶ ἀπετάξατο τῷ διαβόλῳ, καὶ ἐνεφύσησεν αὐτόν· οὔτε πάλιν πρὸς ἀνατολὰς ἐστράφη καὶ συνετάξατο τῷ θεῷ· αὐτὸς γὰρ ἦν ὁ ἀληθινὸς θεός· οὐκοῦν μηδ᾽ αὐτοὶ ταὐτὸ τοὺς ὑπ᾽ αὐτῶν βαπτιζομένους ποιήσωσιν. ὁ Χριστὸς βαπτισθεὶς τοῦ ἑαυτοῦ σώματος οὐ μετέλαβε· μηδ᾽ αὐτοὶ μεταλάβωσιν. ὁ Χριστὸς μετὰ τὸ βαπτισθῆναι ἐνήστευσεν ἡμέρας τεσσαράκοντα καὶ μόνον· καὶ μέχρις ρκ΄ ἐτῶν ἡ τοιαύτη παράδοσις κεκράτηκεν. . . .[1] ἀλλ᾽ ἡμεῖς ἐγγὺς τοῦ πάσχα, ἡμέρας ν΄. ὁ Χριστὸς τὸ μυστήριον τῆς θυσίας τοῦ ἄρτου ἐν ἐκκλησίᾳ οὐ παρέδωκεν· ἀλλ᾽ ἐν οἴκῳ κοινῷ, καὶ τραπέζῃ κοινῇ καθεζόμενος· οὐκοῦν μηδ᾽ αὐτοὶ ἐν ἐκκλησίαις ἱερουργήσωσι τὴν θυσίαν τοῦ ἄρτου. ὁ Χριστὸς μετὰ τὸ δειπνῆσαι καὶ χορτασθῆναι τοὺς μαθητὰς αὐτοῦ, τότε τοῦ ἰδίου ⟨μετέδωκεν⟩ σώματος· οὐκοῦν καὶ αὐτοὶ πρῶτον φαγέτωσαν κρέα, καὶ χορτασθήτωσαν, καὶ τότε κοινωνήτωσαν τῶν μυστηρίων. ὁ Χριστός, εἰ καὶ ὑπὲρ ἡμῶν ἐσταυρώθη· ἀλλὰ σταυρὸν προσκυνεῖσθαι οὐ διετάξατο, ὡς μαρτυρεῖ τὸ εὐαγγέλιον· οὐκοῦν μηδ᾽ αὐτοὶ σταυρὸν προσκυνήτωσαν. ὁ σταυρὸς ξύλον ἦν· οὐκοῦν μήτε χρυσοῦν, μήτε ἀργυροῦν, μήτε σιδηροῦν, ἢ χαλκοῦν, ἢ λίθινον σταυρὸν προσκυνήτωσαν. ὁ Χριστὸς ὠμοφόριον, καὶ ἐπιτραχήλιον, καὶ στιχάριον, καὶ φελώνιον καὶ μανδίον, οὐ περιεβάλετο· μηδ᾽ αὐτοὶ ταῦτα περιβαλλέσθωσαν. ὁ Χριστὸς τὰς εὐχὰς

---

[1] A clause has dropped out, which must have run somehow thus: οὐκοῦν καὶ αὐτοὶ μετὰ τὸν βαπτισμὸν τοῦ Χριστοῦ ἡμέρας τεσσαράκοντα νηστεύσωσιν. Perhaps it stood not here, but just before, after καὶ μόνον. The ἡμεῖς of course refers to Isaac, for the Paulicians are throughout expressed by αὐτοί. Isaac's reference to Lent shows that it was a church fast, and not a private one following individual baptism, that was inculcated by the Paulicians.

της λειτουργίας και των αγίων Θεοφανίων[1] και τας λοιπάς πάσας ευχάς, παντός πράγματος και απάσης ώρας ουκ είρηκε· μηδ' αυτοί ταύτας λεγέτωσαν, ή υπό των αγίων ευχών αγιωσθήτωσαν. ο Χριστός πατριάρχας, και μητροπολίτας, και επισκόπους και πρεσβυτέρους, και διακόνους, και μοναχούς, ουκ εχειροτόνησεν, ούτε τας ευχάς αυτών είρηκε· μηδέ αυτοί χειροτονείσθωσαν, ή υπό των ευχών ευλογηθήτωσαν. ο Χριστός εκκλησίας οικοδομείσθαι, και αγίας τραπέζας κατασκευάσαι, και μύρω χρισθήναι, και μυρίαις ευχαίς αγιάζεσθαι ου διετάξατο, ουδέ πεποίηκε· μηδ' αυτοί τούτο ποιησάτωσαν. ο Χριστός τετράδα και παρασκευήν ου νενήστευκε· μηδ' αυτοί νηστεύσωσαν. ο Χριστός κατά τας ανατολάς προσεύχεσθαι ου διετάξατο, μηδ' αυτοί κατά τας ανατολάς προσευχέσθωσαν. ταύτα γαρ πάντα και πλείονα τούτων Χριστιανών μυστηρίων όντα, δι' ων ημείς[2] αγιαζόμεθα, και πιστοί γινόμεθα, ο Χριστός δι' εαυτού ου παρέδωκεν, άπερ ο αρνούμενος και αθετών και μη παραδεχόμενος, Χριστιανός καλείσθαι ου δύναται. αλλ' ημείς, άπερ εκ των αυτού αποστόλων και παναγίων πατέρων παρελάβομεν ⟨ταύτα κρατούμεν⟩[3], εξ ων υπάρχει και η του τελείου άρτου παράδοσις, και η διά της λόγχης αποκαθαίρεσις, και η των αγίων εικόνων ποίησίς τε και προσκύνησις. ου γαρ εναντιούμενοι τω Χριστώ και αυτώ μαχόμενοι, και τα εκείνου ελαττούντες και σμικρύνοντες, ταύτα πάντα οι απόστολοι, και οι πατέρες εν εκκλησία παρέδωκαν· αλλά μάλλον τα εκείνου αυξάνοντες, και μεγαλύνοντες, και υψούντες, και τιμώντες, και δοξάζοντες μυστήρια ... ουκούν οι του τελείου άρτου την παράδοσιν αθετούσι, και ου παραδέχονται, και άζυμον άρτον εις θυσίαν προσφέρειν βούλονται, αθετήτωσαν και αρνήτωσαν ταύτα πάντα, άπερ ειρήκαμεν, άτινα ο Χριστός μεν δι' εαυτού ου παρέδωκεν· αλλ' οι απόστολοι και οι άγιοι πατέρες. ει γαρ αυτοί μεν εις την εαυτών διατροφήν εσθίειν άζυμον ου καταδέχονται, πως τούτο το βδελυκτόν, σώμα θεού κατασκευάσαι ουκ αισχύνονται. ουδέν γαρ έτερον οι ασεβείς, ή το τέλειον της Χριστού ενανθρωπήσεως[4] αρνείσθαι βουλόμενοι, ταύτα πάντα φλυαρούσι και προφασίζονται, αλλοτρίους και ξένους του Χριστού και των αγίων αυτούς δεικνύοντες.

Λόγος στηλιτευτικός του οσίου Ισαάκ, περί των κακοδόξων Αρμενίων και αιρετικών (p. 395 B).

Εγενήθην γαρ και ανετράφην εν μέσω των αιρετικών και αθέων, και διδαχθείς εν πάσαις ταις διδασκαλίαις αυτών, και σφόδρα υβριστής και αντι-

---

[1] Notice that it is particularly this feast of which they deprecated the celebration. The context forbids us to suppose that it was the old Feast of the Baptism of Christ that was objected to. It must rather be the new Christmas festival that had supplanted it on the sixth of January, to which the Paulicians of the twelfth century objected.
[2] By 'we' Isaac signifies himself and his party.
[3] Words so bracketed are those supplied by Combefisius.
[4] This touch plainly reveals that the 'Protestants,' whose confession Isaac has just given above, were Adoptionists.

τασσόμενος, καὶ λοιδορῶν τὴν τῶν Χριστιανῶν καὶ ὀρθοδόξων θρησκείαν. Ἀλλ' ἡ τοῦ θεοῦ φιλανθρωπία, διὰ πρεσβειῶν τῶν ἁγίων, μέχρι τοῦ παρόντος πολυτρόπως ἀνήλκυσε τοὺς Χριστιανοὺς ἐκ τῆς τῶν ἀθέων πλάνης καὶ πρὸς τὸ φῶς τῆς γνώσεως τῆς ἀληθείας προσέφερε. σπλαγχνισθεὶς δὲ καὶ ἐπὶ τὴν ἐμὴν ταπείνωσιν, καὶ οὐχὶ διὰ τὸ εἶναί με ἄξιον, ἀλλὰ διὰ τὴν αὐτοῦ εὐσπλαγχνίαν, καὶ διανοίξας τὰ τοῦ νοός μου ὄμματα καὶ τὴν διάνοιαν. . . . καὶ ἠρξάμην κηρύττειν, καὶ διαλαλεῖν ἐκ τῶν θεοπνεύστων γραφῶν, τὰ παρὰ τῶν αἱρετικῶν κεκαλυμμένα καὶ ἀγνοούμενα δόγματα. ὥστε διελαλήθη τὰ περὶ ἐμοῦ ἐπὶ πᾶσι· καὶ ἡ πρώην ἀγάπη καὶ συμφιλία, ἣν εἶχον πρὸς αὐτούς, μετετράπη εἰς ἔχθραν καὶ μῖσος, καὶ εἰς τελείαν μάχην. ὥστε συνεδριάσαντες, καὶ ἅπαξ, καὶ δίς, καὶ τρίς, καὶ συμβουλευσάμενοι μετὰ τῶν Ἀρμενίων ἐπισκόπων καὶ πρεσβυτέρων, καὶ τοῦ λοιποῦ λαοῦ, τοῦ θανατῶσαί με. ἔλεγον γάρ, ὅτι ὁ ἐγχειρίσας αὐτὸν καὶ θανατώσας, συγχωρηθήσονται αὐτῷ αἱ ἁμαρτίαι αὐτοῦ· καὶ τὸ αἷμα αὐτοῦ ἐφ' ἡμᾶς, καὶ ἐπὶ τὰ τέκνα ἡμῶν. μετὰ δὲ ταῦτα γραφὰς ἐπιτιμίων καὶ ὀργῆς μεγάλης ἔστειλαν πρὸς ἡμᾶς, ὅτι οὐκ ἔχεις ἐξουσίαν ὅλως ἱερουργῆσαι, ἐπεὶ ἀπέσχισας σεαυτὸν τῆς Ἀρμενίων θρησκείας. Ἐγὼ δὲ μετὰ χαρᾶς μεγάλης ἀντέγραψα αὐτοῖς· ὅτι οὐ μόνον τὴν ἱερωσύνην ἣν οὐκ εἶχα παραιτοῦμαι· ἀλλὰ καὶ τοὺς ἐπισκόπους καὶ τὴν θρησκείαν ὑμῶν βδελύττομαι καὶ ἀναθεματίζω. διὰ τοῦτο προσέφυγα τῇ ἀμωμήτῳ καὶ ἀληθινῇ πίστει, καὶ πρὸς τὴν ἁγιωτάτην μητρόπολιν ἐνέδραμον. καὶ ἔκτοτε τέρπομαι καὶ πάνυ ποθῶ τοῦ στηλιτεῦσαι καὶ κατάδηλα ποιῆσαι ἐπὶ πᾶσι, τὰς βδελυρὰς καὶ πολλὰς ὑμῶν αἱρέσεις.

APPENDIX VIII

PAUL OF TARON

THE following extracts are from the Epistle of Paul of Taron written against Theopistus, the Roman philosopher. The text used is the edition of Constantinople printed in the year of the Armenians 1201 = A. D. 1752-3.

Paul died A. D. 1123 in the cloister of St. Lazar in Taron, where he had lived. An ardent assailant of the doctrine of two natures in Christ, he is held in honour among the Gregorian Armenians; but was condemned in a counter synod convoked by the Catholicos Mekhitar, A. D. 1341-1355.

Theopistus was a Greek who accepted the council of Chalkedon and had written a book against the orthodox Armenians, in which he accused them of not keeping the festival of the Birth of Christ in the right way, of entertaining the heresy of Eutyches, and so forth. The following are the passages in which Paul, his antagonist, attacks the Paulicians:—

p. 259. And this (viz. the text Isa. vi. 3-4), if fully explained, has in it a mystery concerning the holy church. Now the ranks of the heretics are scandalized at the intimation that the holy church of God can be built of stones and clay[1]. Yet God himself of clay fashioned man along with his skin, which has many impurities and evil matters fraught with suffering.

Now, behold, when a man is ill and dies, and after the fourth day you raise the tombstone, you will behold the church of the Manicheans filled with deadly rottenness. But the stone and the clay is pure, and has not in it a corruptible nature. And for this reason God established his church of stones and clay; and named it the house of God, and it is indivisible and indissoluble unto eternity.

Wherefore all the ranks of the holy prophets declared this to be before creation (saying, 'The Lord was pleased with Sion and chose to dwell therein')[2].

p. 260. The Manicheans[3] read all the Divine Scriptures, yet run headlong into gainsaying. So it is that because of their want of faith the Prophet said (They have defiled thy holy temple), 'whom shall the holy indivisible Trinity curse.'

---

[1] The reference is to the Thonraki tenet thus given by Nerses (see p. 155): 'Ecclesia non illa est, quae ab hominibus aedificata est, sed nos tantum.'

[2] The Armenian text thus gives citations of the Bible in brackets.

[3] Paul means the Paulicians, and not the true Manicheans whom he describes lower down.

And it was not right for us to write at length, nor mention the Thondraketzi. Inasmuch as a kind which has not the witness to the faith, nor its foundation, nor God, hath no need of cross or of church.

But unto us who have faith was given the mystery of the holy cross and of the God-receiving temple of God; and we have raised aloft the saving tree of the cross of Christ. And as the Godhead is inseparable from the flesh, so is the power of Christ inseparable from the holy cross. For where the cross is, there is the crucified one So then he was raised aloft [on it] in the flesh, but in his power was united with it.

It is not right at all to converse with them or to share with them in the bread[1]; according to the Lord's word which says (beware of the leaven of the Sadducees and Pharisees). And (He shall hate the impious and love Thy laws).

And again they deny the sacrifice of Christ, and do not allow it to be offered for those who believed in Christ and have fallen asleep[2]. They say that for the sinner no sacrifice avails, but only for the just.

But if this be so, then the suffering of the cross was nothing unto us. Consequently by his death we have not been freed from the bonds of death, and Satan has not been destroyed, nor hell despoiled. Nor has Christ become king over us. We are still the heritage and portion of devils . . . .

p. 262. The Thondraketzi then in their evil gainsaying declare that the sacrifice or *matal* is of no avail to the dead. And so we have found them to be on a level with these heretics, who oppose the sacrifice of Christ which is fulfilled because of sin.

A certain Apellas[3], a filthy man and grown old in the flesh, soured by length of days and puffed up by devils, said concerning the Prophets, that they were opposed to the Holy Spirit; and he laid down this in writing, that the sacrifice which they offer for the dead is of no avail, whom shall God curse. The filthy Celestinus, who does not admit the birth and sufferings of God, but of the mere man alone.

p. 263. The Marcionites who do not admit the resurrection of the dead, and deny the holy sacrifice to be aught, and say that the God-receiving holy cross is mere wood, and have been blinded by the power hidden therein, just like these Thondraketzi. Proteron despised and insulted the holy cross of Christ, and said that he was in his own person the church; and like the Thondraketzi declared cross and church to be alien to the Godhead, nor permitted the sacrifice to be offered for those who slept in Christ. And when they baptize, he said 'There is no Holy Spirit.' And he himself was uxorious and obscene in his life. A certain Eranios, who consorted with the Arians. For no one ordained him a bishop[4], yet he organized much opposition to the holy church; and said 'It is not right to offer sacrifices for those who sleep.' Nor did he permit fasting on the fourth of the week and

---

[1] That is, the Sacrament.

[2] Compare the account of Aristaces above, p. 134. The Early British Church agreed with the Paulicians, for in the *De Synodo Patricii*, A.D. 450 (Hardouin, l. 1, 1794), we read: 'Qui enim in uita sua non merebitur sacrificium accipere, quomodo post mortem illi poterit adiuuare?'

[3] Perhaps Apelles, the successor of Marcion, is referred to.

[4] Paul glances at Smbat the heresiarch. Perhaps in this Eranius we should recognize the Iron or Irion who, in the days of Justinian, invented a calendar for which he was anathematized. See the Homily of Ananias of Shirak on Easter in *Byz. Zeitschr.*, vol. vi, August, 1897, pp. 579 foll.

on Friday[1], and he prevented the observance of Easter[2]. And he said that the bishop has no more honour than the priest[3]. And he ordered women to perform baptism and to mount the Bema[4]. Elkeson said that 'The dead are not helped by sacrifices nor by the compassion and prayers of the living tendered in their behalf.' And such is the vile heresy, with which they have filled the holy church of God, blaspheming the increatedness[5] and opposing the mystery of the economy of the Son of God [ordained] according to the goodly pity of Christ our God, which he wrought unto his faithful ones by his blood.

Such as these are those who agree with and witness to the Thondraketzi, and not to the orthodox. The Manicheans and Sadducees, having a single heresy, the former deny the resurrection of the dead[6], the latter the salutary holy sacrifice. They[7] have been taught the lore and have lost what cannot be found. And the Sadducees[8] have lost it without lore and letters, they who now are called worshippers of the Sun. These do not admit the resurrection of the dead, and are true worshippers of Satan. They believe not in the Holy Scriptures, nor accept them; and they say that He who died, underwent corruption and perished.

They liken this life to herbs and to trees, and say that [it is] as the herb, which when destroyed does not come to life again, whereas its root does so come to life.

There is no end to their discourses, but we eschew length.

By the will of the merciful God, we speak not thus, but as we learned from the holy commands of God, as the Prophet called aloud saying (The dead shall arise and all shall be quickened who have been laid in the tomb. They shall all awake and rejoice who rest in the earth)....

p. 265. Therefore it is right and meet to offer sacrifice for all who have believed in Christ . . . . . It is a true saying, brethren, that where Christ is, there are all the heavenly hosts. So then this rite is great and wonderful for the dead and for the living. For thus doth the church of God believe; that when a man's spirit is held fast in the hopeless Tartarus, and is sealed with ten seals, even a single person is able to give a reminder of it before God in order to its salvation. But those who perform this rite in purity and prayer, are

---

[1] This confirms the statement of Isaac Catholicos on p. lxxx.

[2] This probably means that the Eranios or Irenaeus in question was a quartodecuman.

[3] So in the *Key*, p. 105. But orthodox writers were equally blunt, e.g. Nerses of Lambron, in his work on the Orders of the Church, Venice, 1847, p. 81 : 'These three orders of Archbishop, Bishop, and Priest, though they differ in name one from the other, are none the less a single class, and have the same authority and honour, namely of standing immediately around God.'

[4] The Patriarch Chatschik (end of tenth century), in the *History of Asolik*, bk. 3, ch. 21, makes the same charge against the Paulicians, probably confusing them with Montanists.

[5] Because the Paulicians regarded Jesus as a creature.

[6] The Manicheans denied the resurrection of the body only.

[7] He seems here to mean the Thonraki, whom, like Aristaces, he regards as an offshoot, though heretical, of the orthodox Armenian Church.

[8] i.e. the true Manicheans, whose elect ones would not cut a salad for themselves from dread of taking life. See Augustine, *c. Manichaeum Faustum*, passim.

able to save those who are held in durance, and can dash to pieces the ten bolts of bottommost hell by the divine power, and enable the spirits to fly upwards into heaven; if only the deceased has died in true faith and in repentance, and not in atheism and blasphemy[1].

And if any one receives these rites from the living, and if the latter perform for them the sacrifice, it is truly potent. However, one must keep oneself pure and just, and all one's days not separate oneself from the door of the holy Church, ever regarding oneself as one dead; and one must eat of the dominical flesh, nor venture to eat any other flesh until one dies.

The following is from p. 229 of the letter of Paul of Taron:—

'Again another also of the Greeks wrote to the Armenians about Love to Vahan the Catholicos. It was he that did expound the lessons of James, for he was versed in the divine testaments, whose name was Theodorus, the Metropolitan of the city of Melitene.

'And he confirmed the canons of the holy apostles, and ramparted us round with immovable testimonies. And he wrote to the Armenians thus and said:—

'"But we with faith accept the decisions of St. Cyril of Jerusalem, in which he confirmed the keeping of the manifestation of the Lord on Jan. 6, and rejected their[2] view with scorn. And on Dec. 25 he appointed the feast of David the Prophet and the Commemoration of James the Apostle[3], and ordered us to celebrate them together."

'Likewise in the canon of the holy apostles we find it appointed on Jan. 6[4]. Wherefore also the blessed Macarius, Patriarch of Jerusalem, wrote to the Armenians to the effect that: "We of Jerusalem feast on one and the same day the Birth and the Baptism," as the holy Patriarch Cyril of Jerusalem handed down to us. So, then, you will find this so in the writing of Theodorus, Patriarch of the city of Melitene[5].'

[1] Here we have, perhaps, a summary of the teaching contained in the *Book of Purgatory* referred to in the margin of the Catechism (see p. 122).

[2] i.e. of those who celebrated the birth on December 25.

[3] Anania of Shirak (see his homily on Christmas translated in *Expositor*, Nov., 1896) attests that in the 'Lections' of Cyril, on the 25th of December, was kept the festival of these two, David and James.

[4] These canons are known as the Syriac teaching of the Apostles, and under the name of the 'false writing of the Latins, called Clemens,' are rightly denounced in the margin of p. 76 of the *Key* as a forgery. They were perhaps forged in Rome as a weapon for use against the Adoptionists in the third century; thence they passed into Syria, and thence into Armenia at the end of the fourth or early in the fifth century. The Armenian text is made from the Syriac, and has been edited by Dr. Dashean, Vienna, 1896 (*Modern Armenian*). Ananias of Shirak, early in the seventh century, used them in a text slightly different from that which is preserved. Cureton edited the Syriac text.

[5] Lequien, *Oriens Christ.*, tom. i. 440 foll., treating of the See of Melitene, mentions two bishops named Theodore. The first, who presided over the sixth Synod (680 A.D.), can hardly be the one alluded to by Paul, for in his day there was no Catholicos named Wahan. The second of the name was living in 998, and was present at the Synod of Sisinnius, held at Constantinople in that year. At an earlier time he might have written to Wahan, who became Catholicos 965, and died, after being deposed, in 977. Paul of Taron, however, only survived this Wahan by a few years, and was opposed to his Chalcedonist leanings. And the date of both seems too late for the persons referred to, especially for Theodorus.

APPENDIX IX

MACARIUS' EPISTLE TO THE ARMENIANS

THE following is translated from the Old Armenian text, of which the Rev. P. J. Kalemkiar, one of the Mechitarist fathers of Vienna, sent me a text, based on the following four MSS. preserved in the library of his Convent, viz. :

(a) Cod. Arm. No. 100 (old Catal. 58), Canon-book, on paper, xvii–xviii cent.

(b) Cod. Arm. 256 (old Catal. 44), Canon-book, on parchment, xvi–xvii cent.

(c) Cod. Arm. 58 (old Catal. 15), Canon-book, on paper, xvii–xviii cent.

(d) Cod. Arm. 297 (old Catal. 62 A), Canon-book, on paper, xvii–xviii cent.

The differences between these four MSS. rarely affect the sense; and they all descend, as we shall see, from an original which was mutilated in an important passage.

Macarius I became Patriarch of Jerusalem in 311 or 312. He attended the Council of Nice in 325 (Soz. i. 17; Theod. *H. E.* i. 15). Sozomen (*H. E.* ii. 20) places his death between 331 and 335. The Epistle to the Armenians must therefore have been written between 325 and 335, and is the earliest document we possess bearing on the history of the Armenian Church.

The authenticity of this letter has been questioned, but, as seems to me, on insufficient grounds,—

Firstly, the synchronisms are correct. Macarius in the last years of his tenure would have been the contemporary of Wrthanês, the successor of Aristaces, who was also one of the Nicene fathers. It is true that the Armenian tradition, based on Moses of Chorene, puts the date of Wrthanês' accession as late as 339; but, as Gelzer has pointed out, it is quite worthless. It is impossible that St. Gregory the Illuminator can have died as late as 332, which the same tradition makes him do. Wrthanês was his younger, Aristaces his elder son.

Secondly, the self-portraiture of Macarius is entirely just. Wrthanês was anxious to bring the Christianity of Armenia into line with that of the Nicene fathers, and probably sent his priests to the bishop of Jerusalem, because his advice was more likely than that of other pontiffs to carry weight with his fellow-countrymen, many of whom held opinions almost Ebionite in character. Macarius, on the other hand, shrinks from intervening, because, according to the constitution of the Church, he lacked authority. Now the Bishop of Jerusalem became a patriarch by a canon of the Council of Chalcedon, 451 A.D. It follows that the letter was written before that date. For a forger of a later date would not have put into the mouth of Macarius words depreciatory of his authority.

Thirdly, a forger would not have ascribed his spurious letter to Macarius, but to some more noted prelate, probably to Athanasius; or, if he confined himself to Jerusalem, to St. Cyril, whose *catecheses* were translated at an early time (fifth century) into Armenian.

Fourthly, no Armenian forger of a later date would have admitted that a bishop of Basen and Bagrevand was an Arian, nor after 450 A.D. have combined these two Cantons under a single bishop [1]. It is clear from the words of Macarius that Tourges claimed an independent jurisdiction, as a bishop; and refused to be subordinate to Wrthanês, the nominee of Caesarea. Thus he was not only a heretic, but a schismatic.

Fifthly, no forger would have written in so Adoptionist a tone. The baptism of the Lord was 'his illumining birth.' And after citing the saying, 'Except a man be born again of water and of spirit, he cannot enter the kingdom of God,' Macarius continues thus: 'in order that we may come to be after the same type (*or* manner) *born with him* and baptized with him.' Now the Armenian fathers of the fifth and later centuries, though they insisted on keeping Christmas along with the Baptism on January the sixth, were careful not to represent the Baptism as the re-birth of Jesus Christ, as Macarius here does. So far as I know no orthodox writer later than Tertullian ventured to do so, though of course it was the original significance of the feast. Such phrases, then, as the above cannot have been written later than about 330, after which date they would hardly have been palatable even to orthodox Armenians. And, indeed, they were so little to their taste that the entire passage in which they occur has been cut out of the copies of the letter, as it stands in the Armenian Canon-books. We should know nothing about it, save for the accident of Ananias citing it soon after the year 600 in his 'Homily on Christmas.'

By this time the letter had already been translated into Armenian, for the style throughout betokens an original written in the florid and verbose Greek of the fourth century. That it was originally written in Greek is in itself, under the circumstances, good proof of its authenticity.

---

[1] See note 7 on page 184, below.

Turning to the contents of the letter, it is interesting to note that several characteristic doctrines of the *Key* were already being keenly upheld in Armenia. Baptism was deferred, evidently on principle, and not for mere want of fonts. The scarcity of the latter is itself explicable from the aversion felt for them by the conservative party in the Armenian Church (see pp. lxxvii, lxxviii).

To the same party is referable the dislike of Episcopal government; and it is evident that the prerogatives of the bishop as against the body of presbyters were hardly established in Armenia at that time. The cantons of Basen and Bagrevand are in the province of Ararat; they lie to the west of the Mount Masis or Ararat, and reach southwards as far as Mount Niphates, on the north of Lake Van. They border Tsalkotn and were at a later time, as we have seen [1], the heart of the Paulician country; and when we read that their bishop Tourges [2] was an Arian, we may assume that he was an Adoptionist. The letter of Macarius is, therefore, important testimony to the strength and diffusion of the more primitive Christianity in the south-east of Armenia in the early part of the fourth century, almost during the lifetime of Gregory the Illuminator himself.

OF the blessed Macarius, Patriarch of the holy city Jerusalem: Canonical Letter to the Armenians concerning the regulation [3] of the Ordinances [4] of the Catholic Church, which it is not right by definition or by command to transgress. Chapters X.

Lo, through awe and fear of God, and loving solicitude for true religion among you, I have hastened to awake your pious and simple minds to seek for the right religion and just regulation [5] of the Catholic Church; and for the weighty ordinances of God [6], which it is necessary should be acquired with much circumspection and observed with unswerving faith by all who fear God. Among whom you also must not procrastinate and remain idle through any supine delay [7]; but must make haste through the grace of the Holy Spirit, through the fervour and longings of the divine love, which not only among those who are near us inclines to the quest for spiritual aid, but also in a far land urges [men] to hurry to the goal with vast longings and keen desire, for the sake of the quest that pleases God and of the salvation of souls. Bearing in mind the saying that thou shalt not hesitate to go a long way, if there be the promise of learning something service-

---

[1] See p. lix foll.

[2] The name is hardly an Armenian one, and seems rather to be Iberian, or perhaps Albanian. Tchamtchean, vol. i. 423, writes 'Sourgay.'

[3] *Lit.* 'the laying down of canons.'

[4] *a, d* omit 'of the ordinances.'   [5] and just regulation] *b* omits.

[6] *a, d* omit 'of God.'

[7] Supineness, that is the anxiety to defer baptism was, as we have seen (p. cviii), the leading characteristic of the immemorial heresy of Armenia, as Lazar of Pharp describes it about 480 A.D. And the same writer, in citing the proverb, 'For the bride of the swine a bath of drain water,' glances at the Paulician baptism in rivers, or 'in any vessel which comes handy.' So Gregory of Narek, p. 126: 'it (i.e. baptismal font) consisted of mere bath water.'

APPENDIX IX

able; yea, and having manifested in your souls that longing for spiritual toil for the sake of the divine gain of spiritual treasures, ye have sent a letter[1] from a far off land, from your regions of the east, unto the holy city Jerusalem; and this letter by the hand of reverent priests hath been laid before the multitude of bishops, who were gathered together from their several cities. Before whom appearing with humble entreaty, they have asked for an answer to this letter. Now although we were not willing, being weighed down by a sense of the slender authority we hold under the weighty usages of the Church; nevertheless, the earnest spiritual entreaty and the pious solicitude of these priests, has compelled us to write and impart to your spontaneous piety the essential heads of the ordinances of the Church, the firmness of the faith without any wavering, the entire regulations of the holy council[2], which has been held because of the heretics. These it is needful that all religious persons should accept, since it was held for the purpose of laying down the ordinances of the Church.

Furthermore, the spectacle of the very careful ordering of the life-giving baptism in the holy city has caused surprise and wonder, that the regions of the east are wanting in care in many particulars, such as the following. To wit, in sundry places they have no regular fonts, but baptize in any vessel which comes handy. And in some cases the deacons perform baptism[3]. And bishops and priests apart and of themselves hallow the oil of anointing; and as they have not in abundance the oil of confirmation, which is from the apostles and is kept here, they do not anoint the entire organs of sense of the child. And there are cases in which the priests in the time of baptism never observe the ordinances of the Council at all.

And in virtue of laying on of hands (ordination), the clergy are regarded as all of one rank, and do not subordinate themselves to superiors; and other irregularities due to pride and supineness have been introduced into the ordinances of the Church by the carnal ones, with the which those who have come hither have acquainted us.

Whereat we are surprised and wonder greatly, and from fear of God we have not shrunk from writing promptly, I Macarius, Archbishop of Jerusalem, and all the number of bishops who are under me; sending to the regions of the east unto your Christ-loving and reverent chief Bishop Wrthanês, and to the whole body of the bishops[4] and priests of Armenia; to the end that with much care and reverence they may fulfil the regular order [of administration] of the great sacrament of God, as it is fulfilled in the Catholic Church; whereby is bestowed out of the grace of the Spirit remission of sins and salvation

---

[1] The letter seems to have been sent by the Bishop Wrthanês, and the Presbyters of that northern section of the Armenian Church which, owing to the political *rapprochement* of the Arsacides to Constantine, was already going to Caesarea in Cappadocia for ordination and assimilating itself to Roman orthodoxy.

[2] The Council of Nice is referred to.

[3] In the *Key* the elect one can alone baptize. And the custom of deacons baptizing is the only one of the irregularities noticed by Macarius which was not insisted upon by the Paulicians of a later age as correct and primitive. The *Key*, however, never alludes to deacons.

[4] Most of these bishops would belong to Roman Armenia, where each city of any size would probably have had its own bishop.

of souls, being baptized in the holy font. And the Holy Spirit doth not despise those who are desirous of true religion, but, bending low, doth come down and make us holy through right faith by means of the water of the holy font.

And in all this, it is not right for the bishops and elders to be supine and to postpone the baptism of those who wish to draw nigh devoutly unto the religion of God. For it is rather the concern of priests and the weighty task of the leaders of the Church to instruct the willing in true religion, and teach them by word and doctrine to renounce Satan and dedicate themselves to God through the illumination of the holy font; and not to become the cause to any of perdition by want of submission and by any imperfection in the administration of baptism, by reason of their deferring it, in order not to confer the entire rite [1] upon those who offer themselves for baptism in the holy font. For this rite the universal Church of God fulfils without delaying it, with great care and anxious trepidation.

So then we have made careful investigation under the aforesaid heads, and now let us begin in writing to give the decisions which ye require.

(1) Whether it be right for deacons to perform baptism, and whether [in such cases] the sacrament is fully performed?

Be it known unto your Christ-loving fraternity, that to bishops and priests alone belongs this authority; and that it is not right for deacons to do it, because they are servants; and this [rite] is nullified by them. And it is superfluous to ask whether, in case of persons baptized by them, the rite has been fulfilled. However, it is proper to first inquire whether it is the usage of a particular region for deacons to baptize; and if one be found to have done so, he is innocent because, in ignorance of the ordinances of the Church, he merely followed the custom of the land. But if he was cognizant of the ordinances of the Church and transgressed them, let punishment be inflicted on him according to the scale of his transgression.

(2) If they have no hallowed font, and baptize in any vessel which comes handy, because there was not near a church built unto the glory of God and [accessible] for the entrance of the congregation, then truly there was nothing to blame. But if we have churches, we must also make baptisteries and a font, in which to baptize those who come in the right faith of true religion. However, if any one should chance to be in a place where there is not a church and regular font, it is not right to prevent any one from being baptized who desires to be; but we must perform his baptism without a regular font, because the circumstances compel us to; lest we be found a debtor for the salvation [of the man] by hindering his baptism. For the Holy Spirit gives grace according to our prayers and entreaties, and is not hindered by want of a font; and on every occasion it is the wish and desire that is enough for the grace of the Spirit. Nor is the rite fulfilled only in chief feasts; for the apostles did not baptize according to a choice of feasts; but according to the sufficiency of those who came to them, they were used to illuminate .... being born [2]

---

[1] *Lit.* 'ordering.'

[2] The Arm. verb may also have an active sense: 'Engendering them again.' But there is no need to try to make sense and connect with what precedes, for it is just here that the MSS. have been mutilated; and the excerpt of Ananias of Shirak should be read after the words 'used to illuminate.'

APPENDIX IX 183

again out of the waters, and with triple immersion burying in the water of the holy font, we signify the three days' burial of the Lord in the persons of those baptized, a thing which the divine apostle clearly shows when he says, 'Being buried with him in the baptism, let us become imitators of the likeness of his death, to the end that by the renewal of resurrection we may become participators with him in the life eternal.' And thus with right faith laying on our hands, the Holy Spirit is bestowed unto our salvation, illuminating those who are called to adoption. And in faith we are anointed with the oil of holiness; and thus in the several parts prescribed the ordinances of the holy Church are duly carried out, without any transgression of the prescribed rules; and we are made pre-eminent in the heavenly ranks [1], as we learned from the spiritual fathers, the disciples of the holy apostles.

(3) And how are the orders [2] of the holy Church disposed? *Function of the*
Let overseers be established in regular abodes, with authority to *Bishop.* administer rightly the goods [3], to the supervision of which they have been called. And in receiving from them let not [others] be puffed *Their hi* up with pride, holding themselves in their foolishness to be wise, nor *grade.* let them lapse into wickedness. For although grace is bestowed in a single way on the faithful, yet all are not alike in honour. And although the Infinite made himself little, yet he lost not the glory of the Godhead thereby [4]; and to all the apostles after his resurrection he was manifested as the giver of life; but some he ranks above the rest, and from the very first established the same over us. And accordingly Paul forbids us to go beyond one another, saying: 'Let each one unto whatever calling he hath been called, abide in the same.' And as I have prescribed let them be content with the positions severally appointed unto them.

(4) Accordingly with the unanimous approval of the clergy and *Duties* bishops and priests and deacons, I, Macarius, Archbishop of the holy *Bishop and of* city of Jerusalem, hand on to you this canon law, having learned it *Presbyt* from the histories of the apostles, and on the tradition of the fathers it is firmly based among us, that, as we said above, it belongs to bishops and priests alone to perform baptism and laying on of hands, and the chief bishop shall alone bless the oil of purification (*or* of *Bishop* holiness). But by reason of great distance and stress of circum- *to make* stances, at the command of the archbishop, two or three bishops met *Chrism.* together and deacons, administrants of holiness, ... [5] and the oil of anointing for the dead and the sick and the baptized, the priests shall by themselves alone bless, and the bishops. This our holy fathers prescribed, and let no one venture to change the rule rightly prescribed, lest the chain of their anathema engage them and cut them off from God.

(5) And how shall we draw nigh to the holy table and quickening *How th* sacrament? *Euchari*
Let no one venture to approach this portion of immortality *shall be received* in double-mindedness, or with want of faith, or in unworthiness

---

[1] *c* has 'ranks of the angels.'
[2] *or* 'ordinances,' by which I render this word elsewhere.
[3] This was the function of the earliest bishop, and accordingly in the canon of Sahak the offerings of the faithful are to be stored in his house.
[4] *d* has 'the glory of the holiness,' which is the *potior lectio*.
[5] There is clearly a lacuna here in the text, to the detriment of the meaning.

of works. For he will move the will of God unto wrath on all the earth, and will himself hear the saying: 'Wherefore at all dost thou recount my righteousness, since thou hast hated my precept?' But with correct walking and just faith let him approach and be illumined, and work out himself salvation for others also.

(6) And how is it right to celebrate the Sacrament, the salutary Sacrament of the body and blood of the Lord?

It is meet to celebrate it in fear and with care, and to make a right confession of faith, separate and apart from the sacraments of heretical tempters; lest, through the proximity of Arians[1], the name and truth of God be blasphemed according to the apostle.

(7) And in what way shall the offering of holiness be disposed?

Hot bread is to be laid on the holy[2] table, according to the tradition of the apostles, and incorruptible without any admixture[3]: for we are not saved by aught corruptible, but by the incorruptible body[4] of the spotless and unblemished lamb. And this table only shall the deacons adjust, but that which is fulfilled upon it the priests shall fulfil.

(8) And how shall the table of the Sacrament be arranged, and what other ordinances are there?

The table of expiation is under a veil, on which the Holy Spirit descends. And the font is behind in the same house, and out of honour set up on the right hand[5]. And the clergy in their several grades shall do the service, and the congregation outside the veil, and the catechumens at the door, listening; lest by outstripping one another their ranks be effaced; but let each set remain in his own position irreproachable.

(9) These principles of the faith and order of the Church I hand on to you in accordance with your supplications, and we pronounce an anathema on those who are otherwise minded. For having received from one another through laying on of hands the grace, we do not tolerate shortcomings; and we do not esteem as being all of the same honour the degrees of dignity[6] rightly ordained for the Church; and we reprimand persons mad for glory, that hold the opposite opinion, as hath been related to us of Tourges, the Bishop of Basen and Bagrevand[7], who for a little time was united with the Arians, and then felt scruples, and now again is insolently minded, [being] a bishop only with a throne (*or* seat), and arrogating to himself the same honour as an archbishop has, which he is not worthy to receive. For the fathers have not handed down the teaching that we

---

[1] This passage proves the prevalence in Armenia at that time of Arian, i.e. Adoptionist, opinion. The very Eucharist is to be used by the faithful as an engine for excluding them.

[2] *b, c* omit 'holy.'

[3] According ... admixture] *c* has: 'and the cup incorruptible and unmixt without aught according to the apostolic traditions'; *b* has: 'of the apostle,' in singular, for 'of the apostles.'

[4] *b, c* add 'and blood.'

[5] Or perhaps, punctuating differently, we should take this passage to mean that the clergy were to be on the right hand of the table.

[6] (?) ἀξιώματα.

[7] In Elisaeus Vardapet, *History of Wrthan*, 450 A.D. (ed. Venice, 1859, p. 22), we have a list of bishops preserved, according to which each of these cantons has its own bishop. Macarius plainly refers to an earlier time when one bishop was enough for both, and he an Arian or Adoptionist.

APPENDIX IX 185

should introduce into the Church any such antagonisms, and it is inexpedient to regard him as equal [to the archbishop], until by being called he succeeds to the honour of the throne.

Therefore you must gently summon such an one to obedience, but if he is obstinate, then shun him as an alien.

All the Churches greet you. Fare you well in the Lord, being firm and right in faith. Amen.

The lacuna on p. 182 admits of being filled in from the following passage of Ananias of Shirak (c. 600), who, it may be noticed, puts in the sixth chapter of the letter of Macarius what the modern MSS. put in the second. His text was, therefore, differently divided.

OF Ananias of Shirak, called the arithmetician, on the manifestation of our Lord and Saviour.

. . . But many years after they[1] laid down their canons, as some say, by the disciples of the heretic Cerinthus was this festival (sc. of the Birth on Dec. 25th) invented, and came to be received by the Greeks, as being a people fond of feasts and ardent in religion, and from them it spread over the entire world. But in the days of the holy Constantine, this feast had not been received in the holy Council of Nicea by the holy fathers; but they decided to keep the feast according to the aforesaid canon of the holy apostles. And the same is clear from the letter of the blessed Macarius, Patriarch of Jerusalem, which he wrote to the land of Armenia concerning the direction of the Holy Baptism. For he was one of the 318 fathers of Nicea. And it is written as follows in the sixth chapter of the directions laid down by him :—

'However, there are three feasts on which our fathers[2] in particular celebrated the rite of Baptism in the holy font with zeal and enthusiasm, being desirous on them more than on other days to urge unto baptism those who have given themselves up to God, and to fulfil [in them] the type of the great saving mystery, which on those holy and famous days was fulfilled. And men are full of longing to fulfil it in the holy places of Christ; and verily it is meet for all Christians who reverence Christ to fulfil on these days the calling of Baptism, namely, on the holy manifestation (*or* Epiphany) of the Lord's birth, on the saving Zatik of the life-giving passion of Christ, and on Pentecost full of grace, the day on which the divine descent of the quickening Spirit was diffused among us.

Wherefore it is proper to acquaint you with the particular import of each of these feasts, of the Birth and of the Baptism, to the end that ye may diligently fulfil the same. For our expiatory birth in the holy font is (*or* was) fulfilled on the same saving day with the illumining birth of Christ, because on that very day he took on himself to be baptized out of condescension to us[3]. For it was not because he was himself in any need of baptism; but he wished to cleanse us from the stain of sin. Accordingly he cries out loud, saying: 'Unless a man

[Marginal notes: Baptism the three great fe[asts]; Birth an[d] Baptism Christ o[ne] feast.]

---

[1] i.e. the Apostles. See note 4 on p. 177.

[2] The printed text (Petersburg, 1877) of Ananias is corrupt here. I restore the words 'our fathers' from the Marsh MS. 467 of the Bodley, so often referred to in my prolegomena.

[3] *or* 'in order to come down to us.'

be born of water and of Spirit, he cannot enter the kingdom of God.' To the end that we may come to be born along with him after the same type (*or* way) and baptized along with him on the day of the birth of Christ. But in the life-bringing resurrection of Zatik, by putting to death our sins in the waters of the font, we become imitators of the death with which our Lord Jesus Christ was put to death; and being buried with triple immersion in the water of the holy font, we shadow forth in the persons of the baptized the three days' burial of our Lord, according to the clear intimation of the divine apostle, who said[1]: 'Being buried with him in baptism, let us become like him in the likeness of his death, to the end that with the renewal of his resurrection we may become sharers with him in life eternal.' But on the day ᵃcost. of the grace-bestowing, hallowing Pentecost [we celebrate] the inspiration flashing with light of the quickening Spirit, which in the form of fiery tongues descended on the Apostles, that they might by laying hands on the baptized bestow on them the gifts of grace they had received from the Spirit. After the same type do we also on the same day lay hands on the baptized, and thereby the same Spirit is bestowed on them. And the type of it we carefully observe, and fulfil it without ceasing, to the end that we may become perfect.

So far Macarius.

[1] What follows seems to be a paraphrase rather than a citation of Rom. vi. 4, 5.

EXCURSUS ON THE ARMENIAN STYLE OF *THE KEY OF TRUTH*

In the following list I give post-classical and rare words occurring in the twenty-two chapters of the *Key*, followed by the names and dates of Armenian authors who use them. Most of my references are taken from the *Great Armenian Lexicon* (containing 6,600 closely-printed columns), Venice, 1836:—

p. 1. գայլք, 'events.' Anania Catholicos, tenth cent.

p. 2. սրբանուէր, 'sanctifying.' Common in Gregory of Narek, tenth cent. The prayer in which this word comes is interpolated in the text of the *Key*, but must be as old as the tenth century.

p. 2. լուսածեմ, 'illumining'; in the same prayer. Anania of Narek, *c.* 950. Theodore Qrhthenavor, seventh cent.

p. 3. մեղ մեղ դիզեալ բարդեալ, 'sin on sin, thronging thick together.' The characteristic combination դիզի, բարդեցի in Gregory of Narek, tenth cent. The entire phrase, դիզան մեղք 'ի մեղաց վերայ, in the middle Armenian version of Chrysostom on Genesis, a post-classical work of uncertain date.

p. 6. հովուապետութի, 'office of chief shepherd.' In Thomas Artsruni, ninth cent. But the word հովուապետ, 'chief shepherd,' is classical.

p. 6. հրճեցաւ, 'was made glad.' Chosrow, bishop, and father of Gregory of Narek, *c.* 950 A.D., and Moses Choren Paraphrase of Aphthonius; seventh cent.

p. 11. նորաստեղծ, 'new created,' epithet of Adam. Moses Choren, in Paraphrase of Aphthonius.

p. 11. շղթայաշար, 'fastened about with chains.' Gregory of Narek alone uses this word, and he only in the compound form շրթնաշղ֊թայաշար, i.e. 'with lips fastened together with chains.' The διορθωτής has actually restored the latter reading in the MS.; and շրթաշղթայաշար is the original reading according to Ter Galoust's copy. If we adopt this reading, we must render thus: 'their newly-fashioned palace (i.e. body) was lost, being bound about the lips with chains.' Thus the better evidenced reading is a very rare and artificially compounded word peculiar to Gregory of Narek.

p. 14. զահաւէժ, 'over the precipice.' In Gregory Magistros, eleventh cent., and in hymns of earlier date.'

p. 15. յարարողութիւն, 'ceremonies.' John Catholicos, ninth cent., and Wrdan, thirteenth cent., in a commentary on Psalms compiled from old sources.

p. 18. զնեռայքրիստոսն, 'anti-christ.' John Philosopher, tract against Paulicians, *c.* 718 ; Gregory of Narek, tenth cent., and Photius' letter to Ashot, ninth or tenth cent. The earlier word was Ներոն, i. e. Neron.

p. 19. վճռականէ, 'decrees.' Not in the great Armenian dictionary.

p. 25. զանգալսանօր, 'delay.' Gregory of Narek, and Chrysostom on St. John ; fifth and eleventh cents.

p. 28. վերձայնի, 'was foreshadowed.' In Chosrow and Gregory of Narek ; both tenth cent. These four verses seem to be an early interpolation.

p. 30. շուլլ, 'dissolute.' Gregory of Narek in the tract called *Khrat*, a moral treatise which is by some ascribed to a later writer of the thirteenth century ; though the authors of the great dictionary incline to regard Gregory of Narek as the author on grounds of style. The phrase for 'original sin' occurs in this tract, of which I have spoken in the prolegomena, p. cxxvi. A careful study of the *Khrat* convinces me that it is at least as old as the tenth century, if not older. It may be the work of Chosrow, father of Gregory of Narek.

p. 30. շահընկալ, 'a taker of profits.' In the Mashdotz, of various dates prior to about 800.

p. 31. հեզորէն, 'submissive to law.' In the version of Hesychius, seventh cent. ; and Wrdan's *Catena on Pentateuch*, compiled from old sources.

p. 31. նորարդյս, 'new born' or 'newly sprouting.' Only in Moses Choren. Panegyric on St. Rhipsima, seventh cent., and Erznkatzi, *c.* 1300.

p. 33. յուսադրող, 'giving hope.' Chosrow, tenth cent., and George, *Catena on Isaiah*, compiled in thirteenth century from classical fathers.

p. 39. բանաստեղծութիւն, 'eloquence.' Gregory of Narek, tenth cent.; Gregory Magistros, died *c.* 1058 ; and Gregory Mashkouori, died 1114.

p. 40. խեղկատակ, 'scurrilous.' Sarkis, *Catena on Catholic Epistles*, compiled from early fathers in twelfth cent., and Nerses Shnorhali, twelfth cent.

p. 40. շարաբան, 'foul-mouthed.' In the version of the *Lives of the Fathers of the Desert*, fifth to eighth cents.

p. 40. խոզաբարոյս, 'swinish in their lives.' In the *Tônakan* book, compiled from early sources, and in Wrdan's catena similarly compiled.

p. 42. ծէս, 'natural' or 'usual.' In *Oskiphorik*, Middle Armenian of uncertain date.

p. 42. հարթ հաւասար, 'on an entire level.' In John Catholicos, ninth cent.

p. 50. անխադելի or անխախտելի. In old versions of Basil and Cyril Alex., *Lives of the Fathers*, &c. A classical word.

In the above list are given only words which are very rare or unknown in the fifth century Armenian. The agreement with the vocabulary of Chosrow and of his son Gregory of Narek is very marked; and there are passages in the *Key* which the latter writer, when at his best, might well have penned, e.g. the first half of chap. ii.

In the liturgical parts of the *Key* there are no words or phrases which do not belong to the golden age of Armenian literature, i.e. to the fourth and fifth centuries.

I have already noticed the resemblances with Zenob's style in the use of որ or զոր at the beginning of a sentence. It is hardly necessary to give examples, which any Armenist can easily pick out for himself. He will find them in Zenob, pp. 9, 10, 12, 13, 14, 15, 17, 26, 56.

Two modern forms of verbs occur, and only two, in the *Key*, viz.: լսանիլ, p. 13, and կամենան, p. 26,—a very small allowance considering the history of the book.

The chief vulgarisms are either orthographic only, e.g. confusions of ղ and տ, of ք and խ, of խ and ղ, of փ and բ; or concern the use of prepositions. Thus թարգ, on p. 25, is used with the instrumental case, whereas in classical Armenian it governs a genitive. And after verbs signifying to give to, to speak to or address, to command, and so forth, the preposition առ or առ 'ի is sometimes wrongly used for the prefix ց. But even in these cases the right use predominates, proving that the exceptions are only modernisms which have crept into the text by reason of ignorant scribes. Such uses are even found in Zenob, e.g. p. 12: եւ 'ի զայեակն.

The use of the participle for a finite verb which is found in the Catechism is common in Zenob and in Gregory Magistros, and is frequent in Middle Armenian. The use of the indicative for the conjunctive mood after verbs of entreaty is also found in Zenob, e.g. p. 9, աղաչեմ զի մի ... մատուցանես. We also have in the *Key* the pronoun այն = 'ille,' added redundantly after nouns almost as a definite article, like ἐκεῖνος in the Gospels. This use can be paralleled from the works of Sebeos in the seventh century. It seems to be original in the *Key*, and not due to scribes. In default, however, of a grammar or dictionary, which takes account of such little points as those which I have noticed, it is not easy to say what could and what could not be written early in the ninth century. On the whole the difficulty lies in putting such very good Armenian as the *Key* is largely written in so late as 800; and it is remarkable that so late a copy contains so few vulgarisms.

NOTE ON THE TRANSLITERATION OF ARMENIAN NAMES.

The writer has not followed the scientific system invented by comparative philologists, such as Hübschmann and Brugmann; for most of their symbols are unintelligible except to students of philology. On the other hand it was necessary to avoid the usual mode of transliterating Armenian letters according to which Paulos, Petros, Karapet, Sahak, Pap, Taron, Turuperan, Mkherttschian, Alban, Grigor are disguised as Boghros, Bedros, Garabed, Sahag, Bab, Daron, Duruberan, Muggerditschian, Aghrouan, Krikor, and so forth. The following equivalents have therefore as a rule been used:

բ = b : գ = g : դ = d : ե = e : զ = z : է = ê or ē : ը = ĕ or ŭ : թ = th : ժ = j (as in jury) : լ = l : խ = kh : ծ = ts : կ = k : հ = h : ձ = ds : ղ = l or λ (which it always represented in Armenian transliterations of Greek names) : ճ = dsh : յ = h at the beginning a word, and y elsewhere : շ = sh : չ = tch : պ = p : ջ = dj (as in adjure) : ռ = rh or ṙ (a strong rolled r) : վ = w or v : տ = t : ր = r : ց = tz : ւ = v : փ = ph or f : ք = q : ու = ou or u.

INDEX

Abousa'ad, A.D. 847, invades Armenia and is slain, lxiv.
Adam, the Repentance of, translated into Armenian, cxxxii n.
— Jesus Christ the new Adam, clxxxvi.
Adoptionism of Paulicians, xxxv, xli, lxxxvii, 74, 75, 80, 100, 108, 114.
— of St. Augustine, cxxvii.
— the earliest faith of Armenia, ciii, cvii.
— contrasted with pneumatic Christology, cxci foll.
Adoptionist Church, its rites and beliefs, lxxxvii–ix, cxxix, cxciii.
in Spain, cxxvii, clxx foll.
in N. Africa, cxxvii, clxix.
its monuments, *The Shepherd* of Hermas, lxxxix, and *Acts of Archelaus*, xcvii.
— used Western Text of New Testament, cxcii.
— its leaders—Theodotus, xcii; Artemon, xc; Paul of Samosata, xcv; Photinus, xcvi n.
— its claim to apostolic origin, xci; see **Paulician.**
Adoptivus homo. Its meaning, clxxii, clxxvi foll.
Adoration of elect ones by the faithful, xxvii, lii.
— in early British Church, clxxiii n.
— among the Albigeois, lvi.
Adult Baptism, xxxiii, lxxvi, cxvii, clxii.
— insisted on by Tertullian, cxxi foll.
— among the Cathari of Cöln, cxl.
— among the Albigeois, cxlii.
— presupposed in orthodox Armenian form of baptism, clxxxviii foll.

Agapē before Eucharist continued by Paulicians, lxxix.
— in early Armenian Church, lxxxiv, clxiii.
— in Egypt in fourth cent., lxxxiii.
— pigeons eaten at, clxiii.
— separated from Eucharist in Armenia before 700 A.D., clviii.
Akhaltzik in Russian Armenia, Paulicians settle at, xxiii.
Albania of the Caucasus Paulician in faith, lvii, lviii, ciii, 136, 142, 153.
— its Catholici invested at Edjmiatzin, lviii.
Albigenses, their adoration of the Elect, lvi; see **Immanence.**
— Ritual of, 160 foll.; see **Consolamentum** and **Cathar.**
Alcuin on Adoptionists of Spain, clxxiii foll.
Alexius, Duke, son-in-law of Emperor Manuel, 157.
All Saints, Feast of, in Armenia, clx.
Alogi reject John's Gospel, xciii.
— were forerunners of Theodotus, xciii.
Altar of stone forbidden, lxxx, lxxxii, clxvi.
— the only Armenian equivalents have pagan associations, clxv n.
Anabaptists, a survival of the old Adoptionist Church, cl, cxcvi.
Ananias of Narek, his work on the Paulicians lost, lxii, 126, 130, 143, 155.
Ananias of Shirak on quartodecuman observance of Pauliani, clii.
— on invention of modern Christmas, clvi.

INDEX

Annunciation, Feast of, not kept in Armenia, clix.

Anthimus of Tyana consecrates Faustus, cxii.

Anthropolatry, why charged against the Paulicians, cxxxiv, 127 foll.

Antioch, Paulicians there during Crusades, cxxxix.

— Paulician missionaries go thence to Armenia, cix.

Aphtharto-docetism of the Armenians, cxcv.

Apl-Vard Amir murders Paulicians, 126.

Apostolic tradition of the Paulician Church, xxxiii, ciii, 73, 74, 76, 80, 86, 87, 91, 126, 127.

Arabion Castellum on the upper Zab, cii.

Arabs protect the Paulicians, lvii, lix.

Aradjavor, a Fast of the Armenian Church, lxxxv, clx.

Archelaus, Bishop of Karkhar, an Adoptionist, xcvii foll.

— his see lay in Pers.-Armenia, ci foll.

— resembled in faith the Spanish Adoptionists, clxxvi.

— mentions *wanq* or rest-houses in Pers.-Armenia, clxvi.

— his text of New Testament, cxcii.

Arevordiq, or Armenian Manicheans, cxxxii, 148, 157 foll., 176.

Argaous, Paulician centre, its topography, lxxiii.

Aristaces of Lastivert, his notice of Paulicians, lxix, cxx, cxxxviii, 131 foll.

Arkhwêli, Paulician settlement in Russian Armenia, xxiii.

Armenia, Christianity of, originally Adoptionist and of Syrian origin, ciii, civ, cix, cx, cxvi.

Armenian New Testament first translated from the old Syriac, cix, cx.

Armenians, orthodox, their baptismal service described, clxxxviii.

— their ordinal, cxc.

Arshak, Armenian king, deposes Nerses Catholicos, cxii, cxiii.

Artemas or Artemon of Rome, xc, cxxvi.

Artemas invented the modern Christmas, clvi.

Atonement, possibility that Paulicians rejected doctrine of, clxii.

Augustine, St., of Canterbury, clxxix, clxxxii.

— of Hippo, converted by Adoptionist Christians, cxxvii.

— influence of his work on Manicheans in Middle Ages, cxli.

— libels Priscillian, xlv.

Auterius, the Albigeois cxxxv.

Baptism, Paulician, xxvi, xxxv, xlix, cxxi, 77, 91, 92, 96.

— was adult only, xxxiii, l, lxxvi, cxvii, 181.

— followed rule of Tertullian, cxxi foll.

— conditional on repentance and faith, xxxiv, lxxxviii, 72-77, 117.

— without anointing, lxxvii.

— induces the Holy Spirit, xxxv, 100, 109, 111, 112.

— catechumen stripped in, xxxviii, 97.

— in running water, lxxvii, lxxxii, 180 *n.*; see Adult.

— on eighth day among orthodox Armenians, lxxxiii.

— deferred in fourth cent. to death-bed, cxlix.

— its analogue among Cathars, ibid.

Baptism of Jesus, its import among the Adoptionists, lxxxvii, lxxxix, xcvii, clxxiii foll., 185.

— Ancient lections on Feast of, cliii.

— was regarded as the real birth of Christ, xcviii, cliii foll.

— why omitted from orthodox creeds, xcviii.

— more important among Paulicians than His passion and resurrection, clxii.

Barsumas, Bishop, mentioned by Basil, cxiii.

Bartholomew, St., martyred at Arabion Castellum, cii.

Basen, Arian bishop of, 179, 184.

Basil of Cappadocia propagates Nicene faith in Armenia, cxii.

— goes to Nicopolis with Theodotus, cxiii.

INDEX 193

Basil on Armenian heresy, cxiii, cxiv.
— against Eunomius, cxv.
— Armenian canons of, about the Agapê, clxiii.
Basle, missionaries from, settle at Shusha, xxvii *n*.
— their printing-press, ibid.
Bavarian Christians, originally Adoptionists, clxxx.
Bede against Adoptionism, xv, clxxix.
Bezae Codex, its Adoptionist readings, cliii, cxcii.
Bodhi-Sattva, how born, cxciv *n*.
Bogomiles, converts of Paulician missionaries, cxxxvii, cl.
— were they Manicheans? ibid.
— their relations with the Cathars, cxlvii foll.
— their literature undiscovered, cxcvi.
Bouha, the Emir, A.D. 855, slays Smbat, lxv.
British Church, its buildings, clxvii.
— claimed authority of St. Peter, clxx.
— was it Adoptionist? xiv, clxxix foll.
— held doctrine of Immanence of Christ in the believer, clxxiii *n*.
Burgundy, Christians of, originally Adoptionist, clxxx.
Byzantine policy to eject Paulicians from the Empire, lxxi.

Caesarius of Arles on original sin, cxxvi.
Callisthenes (Pseudo-), on river Stranga, cii.
Canon of Paulicians, xxxvii, xliii, 148.
Canons, Syriac, of the Apostles, 76, 177 *n*. 4.
Cathar ritual of Lyon, cxli foll.
— its affinity to Paulician rites, cxlix.
Cathars of Trêves and Cöln, their view of the Eucharist resembles the Paulician, lv, cxl foll.
— of Toulouse, x, cxl.
— their rule of fasting, cxlv.
— their intercourse with the Paulicians of late date, cxlvii foll.
Cedrenus, Geo., on river Stranga, ix *n*., cii.

Charlemagne represses Spanish Adoptionists, clxxvii.
Chosroês, Armenian bishop in Basil's letters, cxiii.
Chosrow, King of Persia, convokes a council, lxvii.
— favours the Monophysites, lxviii.
Christ, His divinity denied by the Paulicians, vi, xxiv, xxvi, xli.
— Docetic view of, cxciv foll.
— our only Intercessor, xxvi.
— his passion little regarded by Paulicians, clxii.
Christhood of the Elect, xl, li foll., cxxxii foll.; see Immanence.
Christmas identical with Baptism of Christ, x, lxxviii.
— origin of modern feast, vii, clvi foll.; see Baptism of Christ and Artemon.
Church, Holy Apostolic and Universal, Paulicians claim to be it, xxxiii, xli, 73, 76, 80, 86, 87, 141, 142, 147, 148.
— regarded as union of the faithful, clxiv foll.
Churches of stone disliked by Paulicians, lxxviii, lxxx, lxxxv, clxvi foll.
Clédat's edition of Cathar New Testament and Ritual, 160 foll.
Clemen, Dr. Otto, on Socinians, cli.
Clemens, canons of, identify Birth with Baptism of Jesus Christ, cliv.
— their origin, 177 *n*. 4.
Clemens, Alex., does not recognize infant baptism, cxxi.
Clementine Homilies on Bishops, lv *n*.
Columba, St., Christ immanent in him, clxxiii.
Confession of sins to be made to God alone, and not auricularly to priests, xxvi, xxxvi, 96, 134.
Consolamentum of Albigeois, cxli, cxlv foll., 160 foll.
— compared with Paulician election, ibid.
— was a general form for conferring all gifts of the Spirit, cxlix.
Constantine Monomachus commissions Gregory Magistros to harry the Paulicians, 146.

Constantine V, emperor, a Paulician, xlii, cxvi.
— why called Copronymus, ibid.
— why called Σαρακηνόφρων, clxxiv.
Constantine, Paulician leader, born in Mananali, lxxiii.
Constantine Porphyrogenitus on Smbat, lxiii.
Councils, the Catholic, repudiated by Paulicians, xxv.
Cross, worship of, rejected by Paulicians, xxiii, xlii, lxxix, cxxviii.
Cross-stealers in modern Armenia, cxxix.
Crusades, their influence in bringing together Cathars of the West and Paulicians in the East, cxlvii.
Cunitz, first edits the Cathar ritual of Lyon, 160 foll.
Cyprian on Birth and Baptism of Jesus, clvii.
Cyril's *Catecheses* in Armenian, 179.

Dashian, Father, edits Syriac Canons, 177 *n.* 4.
De Montibus Sina et Sion, an early Adoptionist book, xiv *n.*, c.
— teaches the immanence of Christ in the faithful, cxxxiv.
Denzinger, Ritus Orientales, cited, cxc.
Development of doctrine in early Church, xcvi.
Diadin, the ancient Zarehavan, birthplace of Smbat the Paulician, lx.
Didachê of the Apostles contains usages of Paulician Church, lxxvii, lxxxiii.
— on immanence of Christ in the prophet, cxxxii, cxxxiv, clxxxi foll.
— its Eucharist compared with the Paulician, clxiii.
Djêwiurm, or Djaurm, or Tschaurm, or Djermay, a Paulician village in Turkey, xxiii, xxvii, 138.
— described, lxx.
Djrkay, early Paulician centre, lvii.
Docetism, absence of, in the *Key*, xxxix, 108.
— inherent in orthodox doctrine of the Incarnation, xcvii *n.*, cxciv foll.

Docetism of Mani, cxxxi, cxciv.
Dwin or Twin, early seat of Catholicos of Pers-Armenia, on Araxes, 152.
Dualists, Paulicians not, xxxvi, 79, 114; see Manicheans.

Ear, Virgin conceives through, cxciv *n.*
Eastward position forbidden, lxxx.
Ebionite Church Adoptionist, xci, xcii.
— their form of Gospel, lxxxix.
Ebios, heretical book translated into Armenian, cxxxii *n.*
Eckbert of Bonn (twelfth cent.) on Cathari, lv, cxl.
Edjmiatzin, Synod of, proceeds against Paulicians, xxiii, xxiv, xxvii, xxviii.
Elect ones can alone baptize, xxxiv.
— can alone bind and loose, xxxvii, cxxiv, 105, 108, 133, 149.
— regarded as Christs, xl, li foll., clxxiii, clxxxi, 40, 95, 102, 127, 144.
— among Manicheans, cxxxi.
Election of Jesus as Messiah in Justin M., xci.
— among Ebionites, xcii.
— in Theodotus of Rome, ibid.
— in Archelaus, c.
— among Adoptionists of Spain, clxxvi.
Elia, a Roman castellum, on the Murad Chai, lxix, 138.
Elipandus, Adoptionist archbishop of Toledo, clxx foll.
Endura among Cathars, cxlv foll.
Enhueber on Spanish Adoptionists, clxxix.
Epiphanius, his *Panarium*, 147.
Epiphany feast same as Baptism of Jesus, clx; see Christmas and Birth.
Eritzean, Mr., of Tiflis, on the Thonraki, xxiii foll.
Eucharist, Paulician, xxxvii, xlvii, cxxxv, cxci.
— as part of Agapê, lxxix, lxxxiii.
— single loaf in, xxxviii, xlix, clxiii, 123.
— resembled Eucharist of the Didachê, clxiii.

INDEX

Eucharist, heretical (i.e. orthodox), xxxvii, xliii, xlvii, 123, 124, 126.
— figurative character among Paulician, liii, liv.
— not to be celebrated in a church, lxxviii, clxii, clxvi.
Eucharistic elements the body and blood of the elect one, liii, cxxxvi, cxci, 123.
Eunomius, his errors and creed, cxv.
Eustathius, Armenian bishop in Basil's letters, cxiii.
Evans, Mr. Arthur, on the Bogomiles, cxxxviii.
Evervinus on Cathari, cxlii.
Exorcism, Paulician, xxxviii, 92, 97.

Fasting, ancient rule of, cxlv.
Fasts of Catholic Church rejected, xxv, xxvi.
— of early Armenian Church, clx foll.
Faustus, the Manichean, cxlviii.
— on Adoptionist faith, clxix.
Felix of Urgel, his Adoptionism, clxxii foll.
Fish as emblem of Christ of Adoptionist origin, vii, cliii.
Fonts, aversion to, of early Armenian Christians, lxxvii, lxxxii, 181; see Baptism.
Friedrich, J., on the Paulicians, xl n.
— on their Christology, xliv, cxxxiii.
Fronto, Armenian bishop of Nicopolis, a heretic, cxiv.
Frrisn, Armenian bishop's palace in Mananali, 140.
Fulgentius on original sin, cxxvi.

Gascony, Paulicians of, cxl.
Gelzer, Prof., on the Paulicians, lxxv.
Genesios cited, xli.
Genuflexions rejected, xxv, xxvi.
Georgian version of New Testament, lxxxix n.
Georgius Monachus, the *Codex Scorialensis* of, xl.
Giumri (Alexandrapol), Paulicians of, xxiv.
Gortosak, heretical book translated in Old Armenian, cxxxii n.

Gospel of the Infancy, translated into Armenian, cxxxii n.
Gregory the Illuminator, Paulicians claim descent from him, xxiii, lxxxii, cxix.
— carried about a wooden table for the Eucharist, lxxxii.
— was probably an Adoptionist, xiv, cx, cxi.
— his shrine at Ashtishat, cxix.
Gregory Magistros (eleventh cent.) commissioned by Constantine Monomachus to drive the Paulicians out of the Empire, lxxi.
— he failed to extirpate them, ibid.
— his literary activity, 141.
Gregory of Narek, his accusations of Smbat, li, lii.
Gregory Theologus on Baptism of Christ, clv.
Gutschmid, von, on Probus in Armenia, ci.

Harnack, Prof. Adolf, on *Acts of Archelaus*, civ.
— on infant baptism, cxxi.
— on omission from the creeds of Baptism of Jesus, xcviii n.
— on tract, *De Montibus*, cxxxiv.
— on Adoptionism, cxci, cxciv.
— on Methodius, vii.
Harq or Χάρκα, its topography, lxix.
— its Paulicians, cxx, 131 foll.
Hebdomadarii in early Armenian Church, clx.
Helvidius on Virgin Mary, cxxxv.
Heterii Epistola against Elipandus, clxxii foll., clxxviii.
Hierarchy absent in Paulician Church, xxxviii, lxxix, cxxiii, 105, 176.
— its genesis, cxcv.
— denied by Nerses of Lambron, 176 n. 3.
— aversion to, of early Armenians, 181.
Hippolytus on early Adoptionists, xcii foll.
— on Birth and Baptism of Jesus, clv.
Holy Spirit enters catechumen through Baptism, xxxv, 100, 109, 111, 112.

INDEX

Holy Spirit, possession by it, in *Shepherd* of Hermas, lxxxix.
— in *Acts of Archelaus*, xcix.
— among Spanish Adoptionists, clxxiii.
— a created being, xxxv, 100.

Iconoclasm, cxcvi; see Images.
Iconomachi in Albania of Caucasus, lvii, lviii.
Ignatius, his creed mentioned the Baptism, xcviii.
— calls the bishop Christ and God, cxxxii.
Images and Pictures repudiated as idolatrous, xxv, xxvi, xxxvi, 86, 115, 127, 137, 145.
Immanence of Christ in the elect, xl, li foll., cxxxii foll., clxxxi foll. expressed by Methodius, vii *n*. a tenet of the Spanish Adoptionists, clxxv foll. and of the early British Church, clxxiii.
Infallibility of Pope inimical to human intelligence, lvi.
Infant baptism rejected by Paulicians, xxxiv, lxxvi, lxxxiii, 73, 74, 76, 88, 92, 118, 126, 127, 140, 142, 146, 148.
Intercession of Virgin and saints rejected by Paulicians, xxxvi, 113, 114, 120.
Irenaeus on infant baptism, cxxi.
Isaac, Catholicos (twelfth cent.), an Armenian renegade, preserves a Paulician manifesto, lxxvi.
— on non-observance in Armenia of orthodox feasts, clix.
— Greek text of, 171 foll.

Jainas of India imitated by Mani, cxlv.
James, or Jacobus, Paulician bishop of Harq, 131.
Jesus Christ a creature, according to Eunomius, cxv.
John's Gospel not anti-Adoptionist, xciii.
— received by Theodotus, ibid.
— rejected by Alogi, ibid.
John the Baptist conferred on Jesus priesthood, prophecy, and kingship, cxii.
John the Baptist, his feast preceded those of all others, clx.
John of Damascus cited, cxvii.
John (Ohannes or Hovhannes) the priest, copyist of *The Key of Truth*, xxvii, lxxii.
— his propaganda in Khnus, xlix, lxxii.
John of Otzun, A.D. 718, on Paulicians, lvii foll., lxxxi, lxxxii, clii, 152 foll.
John of Owaiq, Catholicos, deposed, cxx.

Karapet Ter-Mkherttschian regards Paulicians as Marcionites, xlvii, lxxxvi *n*.
— on name Paulician, cv.
Karkhar, or Carchar, the See of Archelaus, ci.
— was in south-east Armenia, viii *n*., cii.
Kaschê, or Kashê (?), on Araxes, a Paulician canton, 148.
Kashē and Alinsoy, Paulician villages in Taron, 137.
Kdshav, monastery at, infected by Paulicianism, lxx, 125.
'Key of Truth,' copied in Khnus by John the Priest, xxvii.
— its form, xxix.
— its style, xxx, xxxi.
— its age, xxxi foll.
Khanus, village of, see Khnus.
Khelat, or Klath, on Lake Van, a Paulician centre, 135.
Khnus, or Khanus, Paulician canton in Turkey, xxiii, xxvii, lxix.
Kirakosak, heretical book translated in Old Armenian, cxxxii *n*.
Klath; see Khelat.
Kothēr, a walled village on the Murad Chai, 139.
Kountzik, an Albanian Paulician, 136.
Kunoskhora, a Paulician centre, where, lxxiii.

Lactantius, his Adoptionist leanings, xcvi.
Lazar of Pharp (fifth cent.) on Armenian heresy, lxxxv, cviii, 180 *n*. 7.

INDEX 197

Lenten fast, origin of, lxxviii.
Leo the Great on Priscillian, xlv.
Liber Sententiarum cited, lvi, cxliv, 160 foll.
Lizix, or Selix, a Paulician, xli.
Logos, Alexandrine doctrine of, cxxxii.
— its incarnations, cxciii.
— doctrine rejected, xl, 114, 147.
Lord's prayer, ceremony of giving to a Credens, cxlii.

Macarius of Jerusalem, A.D. 325-335, on abuses of Armenian Church, cxxiii.
— cited, cliv.
— his epistle to the Armenians genuine, 178 foll.
Malilosa, feast of Cathars of Cöln, cxli.
Mananali, the modern Karachoban on the Khinis Chai, not near Samosata, lxix, 139 foll.
— birthplace of Constantine the Paulician leader, lxxiii.
Mani, or Manes, condemned by Paulicians, xliv foll.
opposed by Archelaus, xcvii foll.
the true descendant of Marcion, cxxxi.
his commentary on Gospel translated into Armenian, cxxxii.
Manichean, a general term for heretics, cv.
— Paulicians not Manicheans, cxxxi.
— nor the Cathars, cxlv.
— elect ones in Manichean Church, cxxxi.
— the Armenian Manicheans, cxxxii, 148, 157 foll., 176.
— fasts of Manicheans, cxlv.
— excluded from Armenian rest-houses, clxvi.
Manuel, Emperor, 157.
Marcion's Church not a mystic or purely spiritual one, xlvii.
— on generation of Jesus Christ, clxxxvi.
— his phrase συνταλαίπωροι explained, liii.
— mentioned by Paul of Taron, 175.

Marcion, his text of Gal. vi. 17, liv.
— not connected with Paulicians, xlvii, cxxx foll.
Marcus, the heretic, his prophetesses, clxxxiv.
Mariolatry forbidden, lxxxi.
— by Tertullian and Helvidius, cxxxv; see Virgin Mary.
Maris, a Syrian, in Basil's letters, cxiii.
Marutha, Bishop of Nphkert, on Birth and Baptism of Jesus, clvii.
— on eating of Paschal lamb before Sacrament, clviii.
Matal, or animal sacrifice, among Armenians, cxxvii, clxiv, 134; see Sacrifice.
Matthew Paris on Cathar Pope, cxlvii.
Mechitar, or Mkhitar, of Airiwanq, A.D. 1300, cited, lxi.
Melitene, Theodore, Bishop of, 177.
Melito, half an Adoptionist, xciv.
— on Birth and Baptism of Jesus, clvii.
Meruzanes, Bishop of Armenia, c. 250 A.D., ciii, cix.
Messalians or Euchitae, lvii.
— Paulicians so-called, cvii, cviii.
Methodius on Immanence of Christ in the believer, vii n.
Millenarists, German, in Caucasus, xxvii n.
Mkherttschian, Dr. Karapet, 141, 151.
Mohammedan conception of Jesus, how far Adoptionist, clxxiv.
Mommsen, Prof. Theod., on Probus, ci.
Monkery condemned, xxxix, xliii, cxxiii, 83, 84, 122, 136, 137.
— ridiculed by Constantine Copronymus, cxvii.
Montague, Lady Mary, on Paulicians of Philippopolis, cxxxviii.
Montanist prophecy, cxxxii, cxxxiv, clxxxiii foll.
Montanists, were they in communion with Paulicians? clxxxv.
— identified with them, ibid.
Muharkin, or Nfrkert, lxx.
Mushel,* the Paulician prince, lxxiv, 126.

198 INDEX

Muzarabic Liturgy, its Adoptionism, clxxi.

Name-giving, Paulician rite of, on eighth day, xxxiv, 87 foll., 153.
Nana, author of Syriac commentary on John's Gospel, lxv.
— on Smbat, ibid.
Nectarius of Rome on Baptism of Christ, clv.
Nerses, Catholicos persecutes the Paulicians, lviii.
— the lieutenant of St. Basil, cxii.
— deposed by King Pap, cxii, cxiii.
— erected rest-houses in Armenia, clxvi.
Nerses of Lambron (twelfth cent.) on Paulician usages in Cilician kingdom, lxxxv, clxvi foll.
— on hereditary priesthood, cxxviii.
Nicene Creed rejected, lxxvii.
Nicopolis, Basil at, cxiii.
Nouna, Georgian saint, clxxxiv.

Ordinal, Paulician, compared with Cathar ritual, cxliii.
— and with ordinal of orthodox Armenians, clxxxix foll.
Origen on absence of Churches and altars among early Christians, lxxx.
— on nature of Incarnation, clxxxii.
Original sin, Christ without it, xxxv, 119.
— use of the term among Paulicians, cxxv foll.
— little children without it, xxxix, 118.

Pakhr, the hill of emery, a range near Erzeroum, 137.
Pap, King of Armenia, opposes Nicene faith, cxii.
— resorts to bishops of Pers-Armenia and rejects Caesarea, cxiii.
— opposed monkery, clxvi.
Paschal lamb eaten before Sacrament in Syria and Armenia, clviii.
Pasen, or Basen, and Bagrevand, Arian bishop of (c. 330), 179.
Passion of Jesus Christ, how regarded by Paulicians, clxii.

Paul Meherean on the Paulicians of eighteenth cent., lxxi foll.
Paul, St., the Paulicians affiliated themselves to him, cxxix foll.
— on immanence of Christ in the faithful, liv, cxxxiii.
Paul of Samosata, his view of Christ, xiii, xcv.
— why deposed by Aurelian, xciv.
— libelled by the orthodox, cxxxiv.
— Paulicians called after him, cv, cvi, cxvii, cxxix.
— Spanish Adoptionists followed his teaching, clxxiv.
Paul of Taron on Artemon, clvi.
— on Manicheans, 176.
— on purgatory, clxiv.
— excerpts from, 174 foll.
Pauli, Visio, when translated into Armenian, cxxxii n.
Pauliani, same as the Paulicians, xiii, cv, cvi.
— were quartodecumans, clii.
Paulicians, origin of the name, cv.
— means a follower of Paul of Samosata, cvi, 148.
— and not of St. Paul, cxxix.
Paulicians, Western, their geographical distribution, lxxiii.
— transportation of, to Thrace by Copronymus, lxxiii ; by Tzimiskes, civ, cxxxvii foll., cl.
— in Syria, cxxxix.
— in Oxford and Gascony, ibid.
Paulicians were old believers, xlviii, lxxxvi, cxix, clxiv.
— claimed to be Catholic Church, xxxiii, 73, 76, 80, 86, 87, 133, 147, 148.
— their place in general Church history, lxxxvi.
— their fasts and feasts, clii foll., cxciii.
— organic unity of their rites and belief, lxxvii.
Pers-Armenian Christianity Adoptionist, ciii, civ, cxiii, cxvi.
Peter, St., his epistles read by Paulicians, xxxix, xliii.

Peter, St., attitude of Paulicians to him not hostile, cxxx, 93.
 ritual use of his name in *Consolamentum* of the Cathari, cxliii, clxv and in Paulician ordinal, xlix. clxv, 107.
 his import according to St. Sahak, clxiv.
 according to Elipandus, clxx.
Peter of Sicily, or Petrus Siculus, on Paulicians, vi, xl foll., cxxxvii.
Philo on forty days' fast of Moses, lxxxvii.
— on fasting, cxlv.
— on Incarnations, cxc, cxciii.
Plato's Republic, analogy of, with Adoptionist Church, lxxxviii.
Pneumatic Christology defined and contrasted with Adoptionism, cxci, cxciii.
Pope of Rome excommunicates Theodotus, xc.
— triumphs over Paul of Samosata, xcv.
— his usurped authority repudiated by Paulicians, cxxx.
— and by Albigeois, 170.
Presbyters in Paulician Church, i.q. the elect ones, xxxviii, cxxiv, 106, 108.
Priesthood in orthodox Armenian Church hereditary, cxxvii foll.
Priscillian, no Manichean, xlv.
Probus, Emperor, recovers Armenia, ci, cii.
Procopius on the Montanists, clxxxv.
Prophetesses, Christian, clxxxiii foll.
Prophets in *The Shepherd* of Hermas, clxxxii.
— among Montanists, clxxxiii foll.
Proseuchae among early Armenians, clxii, clxv.
— among Paulicians, clxvi.
Provençal Ritual of Lyon, 160 foll.
Publicani, name for Pauliciani, cxxxix, cxlvii.
Purgatory denied, xxxvi, clxiv, 121, 122, 176.

Quadragesimal Fast after Epiphany, lxxviii, lxxxiv, clxii.

Quartodecuman observance among Pauliani, clii.

Raffi, modern Armenian novelist, cxxix.
Reader or Anagnostes in Paulician Church, xxxix, 106.
Rebaptism of orthodox Catholics by Paulicians, xxiv, xli.
Reinerius Saccho affiliates Cathar Churches of Europe to the Bogomiles, cxlviii.
Ritualism rejected, lxxix, lxxxii.
Rulers in Paulician Church, who were they, cxxiv.

Sabbath, probability that the Paulicians kept it, clxi.
Sacraments, Paulician, three only, xxxiii, 76, 77, 86, 87, 119, 154.
— orthodox sacraments denied, xlvii.
Sacrifices of animals for sins of the dead condemned, xxxix, cxxviii, clxii, 115, 127, 134, 176; see Mataḷ.
Sahak, Catholicos (fifth cent.), his canons on Agapê and Eucharist, lxxxiv, cxxxvi.
— on significance of 'Church,' clxiv *n*.
— on Quadragesimae of Epiphany, lxxxiv.
— his list of early Armenian feasts, clx foll.
— on functions of bishop, 183 *n*.
Saints, their intercession denied, xxv, xxxvi, xli, cxvi, 120.
Salaberga, St., combats Adoptionism, clxxxi.
Saracens, Paulicians side with them in crusades, cxxxix.
Σαρακηνόφρων, epithet applied to Paulicians, clxxiv.
Sargis or Sarkis Catholicos (*c.* 1002) persecutes the Paulicians, 135.
Sarkisean, Father Basil, 125.
Sasoun, its inhabitants in ninth cent. described, lxv.
Scriptures to be given to laity, xxxix, xliii.

INDEX

Scythian monks, A.D. 520, on original sin, cxxvi.
Sebeos, the historian, cited, lxvii, lxx.
— on deportation of Armenians, cxxxvii.
Sergius the Paulician not the author of the *Key*, xxxii.
  his epistles, xl, li foll.
  his date, lxxxvii.
  mentioned in Matthew of Edessa, lxviii.
Severian on Birth and Baptism of Jesus, clvi.
Shahapivan, Council of, in 447 condemns the Adoptionists of Armenia, cvii, cviii.
Shepherd of Hermas, an Adoptionist book, ix, xiv, lxxxix foll., cxcii.
  echoed by Archelaus, xcix.
  on inspiration, clxxxi foll., clxxxiv.
Simeon, Episc. Beth-Arsamensis, A.D. 510, on Paul of Samosata, cvi.
Simon Magus, how regarded among Paulicians, cxcii, 128.
Smbat, was he Chosrow's Shoum, lxvii.
— the Paulician, perhaps author of the *Key*, xxxii.
— organizes Adoptionists of Taron as a distinct Church, cxvii foll.
  called himself a Christ, li.
  born at Zarehavan, lxi.
  his age and personality, lxi–lxvii.
  his successors, lxvii.
  notices of, 126 foll., 142 foll.
Smbat Bagratuni, probability that he was Smbat the Paulician, lxi foll.
Socrates, Hist. on Agapê and Eucharist, lxxxiii.
Σωλῆνος, ὡς διά, import of, as applied to Virgin Mary, xlvi, clxxxvi foll.
Sozopolis, the Church at, cxiv.
Spain, early Christianity of, Adoptionist, cxxvii, clxx foll.
Sponsors in Baptism condemned, xxxviii, 88.
Stephanus of Siuniq on Smbat Bagratuni, lxiv.
Stoic influence in early Christianity, xci.
Stranga River, upper Zab, viii *n.*, cii.

Συνέκδημοι and νωτάριοι among the Paulicians, cxxiv.
Συνταλαίπωροι καὶ συμμισούμενοι, import of phrase, liii.
Sun-worship, origin of modern Christmas, clvii.
Synagogues and proseuchae, names used in early Armenian Church, clxii, clxv.
Syriac, use of, in earliest Armenian Church, ciii.
Syrian Catholicos, letter to, of Gregory Magistros, 143.
— doctors on invention of the Roman Christmas, clvii.

Table, only word for altar in Armenian Church, lxxxii, clxv.
Tamerlane's invasion of Armenia, cl.
Taron, early Christianization of, cx.
Tchamtchean's history of Armenia, lxvi.
Telonarii, name for Publicani, cxxxix, cxlvii.
Tephrike, Paulician fortress, fatal consequences of its fall, lxxvi.
Tertullian opposed to child-baptism, cxxi foll.
— his teaching resembled the *Key* in regard to Baptism, cxxii foll.
— in regard to Virgin Mary, cxxxv.
— and to Eucharist, *ibid.*
— on the immanence of Christ in the faithful, cxxxiv.
— on significance of symbolic representation of Jesus Christ as ἰχθύς, cliii.
— *de ecstasi*, clxxxi.
Thelkuran, or Telguran, near Amid, a Paulician district in twelfth cent.; lxxi, 155.
Theodora, Empress, her persecution of Paulicians and its fatal results, lxxiv foll.
Theodore, Bishop of Melitene, 177.
Theodotus, Armenian bishop, insults Basil, cxiii.
Theodotus of Rome, his belief, xcii foll.
— accepted fourth Gospel, xciii.

Theophanes on the Montanists, clxxxv.

Θεοτόκος. Term rejected by Paulicians, xl, xlii, cxvii, 114.

Thomas Artsruni (tenth cent.), his attack on Smbat Bagratuni explained, lxiii.

Thonrak, Paulician centre, its topography, lix, lx, 141 foll.

— in province of Apahunis, 135.

Thrace settled with Paulicians, civ, cxxxvii foll.

Thulail, a walled town in Taron, lxx.

— a centre of Paulicianism, lxx, 141 foll.

Tiflis, Governors of, relations with Paulicians, xxiv, xxviii.

Tixerant, a name for the Cathari, cxl.

Toulouse; see **Cathars** and **Albigeois.**

Trinity rejected by Paulicians, xxxv, 98.

Turges, or Tourges, Arian bishop in Armenia (c. 330), 179, 184.

Twin, modern spelling of Dwin, which see.

Unitarians, a survival of old Adoptionist Church, cl.

Unitarianism of Paulicians, xxxv, 79, 94, 108, 119, 148.

Unleavened loaf in Paulician Eucharist, xxxviii, xlix.

Vahan, Catholicos, 177.

Vestments, ecclesiastical, rejected by Paulicians, lxxix, clxviii.

Virgin Mary, her cult and intercession rejected, xxiv, xxv, xxxvi, xlii, cxvii, cxxxv, 113, 114, 146.

— in Helvidius and Tertullian, cxxxv.

— conceived through ear, cxciv.

— her flesh not in Jesus, xlvi, cxiv, clxxxvi foll.

Virgin birth, the, xcviii, clxxii foll.

Vrvēr, or Wrwēṟ, a Paulician prince in Taron, 136.

Waldenses rejected paedo-baptism, cxlii.

Wall, W., on infant baptism, cxxi n.

Wanq, or rest-houses, in Armenia, clxvi.

Wardawarh, or Armenian feast of the transfiguration, clii, clx.

Waters blessed on Jan 6, cliii.

Western text of New Testament disseminated by the Adoptionists, cxcii.

Wiszowaty, Benedict, on Unitarians and Anabaptists, cli.

Wrthanês, Catholicos, sends to Macarius of Jerusalem, 181.

Yousik (= Josakes, or Hesychius), Catholicos, subscribes to Basil's letter to Western Church, cxiii.

Zarehavan, Paulician centre, lx, 144.

Zeno's Henoticon, 129.

Zenob, his style, xxx, 189.

LIST OF WORKS CONSULTED.

Johannes Bornemann. *Die Taufe Christi durch Johannes.* Leipzig, 1896.

J. Friedrich. *Bericht über die Paulikianer, Sitzungsberichte der k. b. Akademie der Wissenschaften zu München.* 1896. Heft I.

Karapet Ter-Mkhrttschian. *Die Paulikianer.* Leipzig, 1893.

A Study of the Manicheo-Paulician Heresy of the Thonraki (modern Armenian). By Father Basil Sarkisean. Venice, San Lazar Press, 1893.

Die Armenische Kirche, von Aršak Ter Mikelian. Leipzig, 1892.

Prof. H. Gelzer. *Die Anfänge der Armenischen Kirche.* Berichte der k. Sächs. Gesellschaft d. Wiss. 1895.

Geschichte der Byzantinischen Literatur, von Karl Krumbacher (see especially the sketch of Byzantine history in this volume written by Prof. H. Gelzer). Zweite Auflage. München, 1897.

Alex. Eritzean. *The Armenian Thonraketzi.* In the New-Armenian Review *Phords*, Tiflis, 1880.

S. R. Maitland. *Albigenses and Waldenses.* 1832.

OXFORD
PRINTED AT THE CLARENDON PRESS
BY HORACE HART, M.A.
PRINTER TO THE UNIVERSITY

Lightning Source UK Ltd.
Milton Keynes UK
UKOW06f1845271015

261485UK00019B/547/P